John Francis Campbell

Popular Tales of the West Highlands Orally Collected

Vol. I

John Francis Campbell

Popular Tales of the West Highlands Orally Collected
Vol. I

ISBN/EAN: 9783337154950

Printed in Europe, USA, Canada, Australia, Japan

Cover: Foto ©Thomas Meinert / pixelio.de

More available books at **www.hansebooks.com**

POPULAR TALES

OF

THE WEST HIGHLANDS

ORALLY COLLECTED

𝔚𝔦𝔱𝔥 𝔞 𝔗𝔯𝔞𝔫𝔰𝔩𝔞𝔱𝔦𝔬𝔫

By J. F. CAMPBELL.

VOL. I.

EDINBURGH:

EDMONSTON AND DOUGLAS.

1860.

CONTENTS.

viii CONTENTS.

x

CONTENTS.

INTRODUCTION.

————◆————

THE FAIRY-EGG, AND WHAT CAME OUT OF IT.

ON the stormy coasts of the Hebrides, amongst sea-weed and shells, fishermen and kelp-burners often find certain hard light floating objects, somewhat like flat chesnuts, of various colours — grey, black, and brown, which they call sea-nuts, strand-nuts, and fairy-eggs. Where they are most common, they are used as snuff-boxes, but they are also worn and preserved as amulets, with a firm or sceptical belief in their mysterious virtues. Old Martin, who wrote of the Western Isles in 1703, calls them "Molluka beans," and tells how they were then found, and worn, and used as medicine; how they preserved men from the evil eye, and cured sick cattle by a process as incomprehensible as mesmerism. Practical Highlandmen of the present day call the nuts trash, and brand those who wear them, like their ancestors a hundred and fifty years ago, as ignorant and superstitious; but learned botanists, too wise to overlook trifles, set themselves to study even fairy-eggs; and believing them to be West Indian seeds,* stranded in Europe, they planted them, and some (from the Azores) grew. Philosophers, having

————
* *Mimosa scandens*, great pod-creeper. *Mucuna urens.*

a

discovered what they were, use them to demonstrate the existence of the Gulf Stream, and it is even said that they formed a part of one link in that chain of reasoning which led Columbus to the New World.

So within this century, men have gathered nursery tales. They set themselves earnestly to learn all that they could concerning them; they found similar tales common to many languages; they traced them back for centuries; they planted them in books, and at last the Brothers Grimm, their predecessors, and their followers, have raised up a pastime for children to be " a study fit for the energies of grown men and to all the dignity of a science."

So at least says the learned author of the translation of "Norse Tales," and there are many who agree with him.

Men have now collected stories from most parts of the world. They have taken them from the dictation of American Indians, South Sea Islanders, Lapps and Samoydes, Germans and Russians. Missionaries have published the fables of African savages; learned men have translated Arabic, Sanscrit, and Chinese manuscripts; even Egyptian papyri have been dug up, and forced to yield their meaning, and all alike have furnished tales, very similar to stories now told by word of mouth. But as some of these are common to races whose languages have been traced to a common origin, it is now held that nursery stories and popular tales have been handed down together with the languages in which they are told; and they are used in striving to trace out the origin of races, as philologists use words to trace language, as geologists class rocks by the shells and bones which they contain, and as natural philosophers used fairy-eggs in tracing the Gulf Stream.

The following collection is intended to be a contri-

bution to this new science of "Storyology." It is a
museum of curious rubbish about to perish, given as
it was gathered in the rough, for it seemed to me as
barbarous to "polish" a genuine popular tale, as it
would be to adorn the bones of a Megatherium with
tinsel, or gild a rare old copper coin. On this, however, opinions vary, but I hold my own that, stories
orally collected can only be valuable if given unaltered ;
besides, where is the model story to be found ?

Practical men may despise the tales, earnest men
condemn them as lies, some even consider them
wicked ; one refused to write any more for a whole
estate ; my best friend says they are all "blethers."
But one man's rubbish may be another's treasure, and
what is the standard of value in such a pursuit as this?

"And what are you going to do with them stories,
Mr. Camal ?" said a friend of mine, as he stood amongst
the brown sea-weed, at the end of a pier, on a fine
summer's evening, and watched my departure in a tiny
boat.

"Print them, man, to be sure."

My friend is famous for his good stories, though
they are of another kind, and he uses tobacco ; he
eyed me steadily for a moment, and then he disposed
of the whole matter monosyllabically, but forcibly,

"Huch ! !"

It seemed to come from his heart.

Said a Highland coachman to me one day, "The
luggage is very heavy. I will not believe but there is
stones in the portmanteaus ! They will be pickin' them
up off the rod, and takin' them away with them ; I
have seen them myself ;" and then, having disposed
of geology, he took a sapient pinch of snuff.

So a benighted Englishman, years ago in Australia,
took up his quarters in a settler's hut, as he told me.

Other travellers came in, and one had found a stone in a dry river-course which he maintained to be partly gold. The rest jeered at him till he threw away his prize in a pet ; and then they all devoured mutton chops and damper, and slept like sensible men.

So these tales may be gold or dross according to taste. Many will despise them, but some may take an interest in the pastime of their humble countrymen; some may be amused ; those who would learn Gaelic will find the language of the people who told the stories ; and those who would compare popular tales of different races, may rest assured that I have altered nothing ; that these really are what they purport to be—stories orally collected in the West Highlands since the beginning of 1859. I have but carried drift rubbish from the place where I found it to a place where it may be seen and studied by those who care to take the trouble.

The resemblance which the collection bears to others already made, is a strong argument for the common origin of the stories, and of the people who tell them. But, as a foundation for argument, I am bound to give the evidence on which I have formed my belief in their antiquity, for the stories would be rubbish indeed if they were not genuine traditions.

This is the account given by Mr. Hector MacLean, parish schoolmaster at Ballygrant in Islay, whom I have known from his boyhood, and who, at my request, collected stories last summer in the Long Island :—

" In the Islands of Barra, the recitation of tales during the long winter nights is still very common. The people gather in crowds to the houses of those whom they consider good reciters to listen to their stories. They appear to be fondest of those tales which describe exceedingly rapid changes of place in very short portions of time, and have evidently no respect for the

unities. During the recitation of these tales, the emotions of the
reciters are occasionally very strongly excited, and so also are
those of the listeners, almost shedding tears at one time, and
giving way to loud laughter at another. A good many of them
firmly believe in all the extravagance of these stories.

"They speak of the Ossianic heroes with as much feeling,
sympathy, and belief in their existence and reality as the readers
of the newspapers do of the exploits of the British army in the
Crimea or in India ; and whatever be the extravagance of the
legends they recite respecting them, it is exceedingly remarkable
that the same character is always ascribed to the same hero in
almost every story and by almost every reciter. Fingal, or rather
Fionn, is never called the king of any country or territory, but
the king of the Finn, a body of men, who were raised, according
to the traditions current in the Long Island and other parts of
the Highlands, in Ireland and in the Highlands, to defend both
countries against foreign invaders, more especially against the
Scandinavians. The origin these illiterate people assign to
them, according to the traditions handed down to them, is,
that the largest and strongest bodied young men and women
were selected and married together in order to produce a
brave and powerful race capable of withstanding and repelling
the incursions of foreign foes. Any hero that came west, east,
north, or south, and 'Cothrom na Finne' (the chance of the
Finne), is the term still used for fair-play in the Highlands.

"In no tale or tradition related to me regarding these heroes
have I heard the name, 'Rìgh Mhòr-bheinn,' (king of Morven)
ascribed to Fionn ; nor have I heard him described as the king
of any territory or country—always 'Rìgh na Finne or Fèinne.'
Fèinn or Finn is the plural of Fiann, which is probably derived from Fiadh dhuine ; either a wild man from his strength
and bravery, or else the man of deer, from their maintaining
themselves by hunting deer, extensive tracts of land being
allotted to them for that purpose. This last etymology I believe
myself to be the correct one.

"The most of the people in Barra and South Uist are Roman
Catholics, can neither read nor write, and hardly know any
English. From these circumstances it is extremely improbable
that they have borrowed much from the literature of other

nations. In North Uist and Harris these tales are nearly gone, and this, I believe, to be owing partly to reading, which in a manner supplies a substitute for them, partly to bigoted religious ideas, and partly to narrow utilitarian views."

This clear statement is accompanied by a description of each of the men who contributed, from which it appears in detail that the greater number speak Gaelic only, that many of them can neither read nor write, and that they are clever though uneducated; and this account I know to be correct in some cases, from my own personal knowledge of the men. Hector Urquhart, now gamekeeper at Ardkinglas, whom I have known for many years, agrees with MacLean in his account of the telling of these stories in other districts in former times.

This is his account—

"In my native place, Pool-Ewe, Ross-shire, when I was a boy, it was the custom for the young to assemble together on the long winter nights to hear the old people recite the tales or sgeulachd, which they had learned from their fathers before them. In these days tailors and shoemakers went from house to house, making our clothes and shoes. When one of them came to the village we were greatly delighted, whilst getting new kilts at the same time. I knew an old tailor who used to tell a new tale every night during his stay in the village: and another, an old shoemaker, who, with his large stock of stories about ghosts and fairies, used to frighten us so much that we scarcely dared pass the neighbouring churchyard on our way home. It was also the custom when an *aoidh*, or stranger, celebrated for his store of tales, came on a visit to the village, for us, young and old, to make a rush to the house where he passed the night, and choose our seats, some on beds, some on forms, and others on three-legged stools, etc., and listen in silence to the new tales; just as I have myself seen since, when a far-famed actor came to perform in the Glasgow theatre. The goodman of the house usually opened with the tale of *Famhair Mor* (great giant) or some other favourite tale, and then the stranger carried on after that. It was a common saying, 'The first tale by the goodman, and tales to daylight by the *aoidh*,' or guest. It was also the custom to put riddles, in the solving of which all in the house had to tax their ingenuity. If one of the party put a riddle which was not solved that night, he went home with the title of King of Riddles. Besides this, there was usually in such gatherings a discussion about the *Fein*, which comes from FIANTAIDH, giant; the Fiantaibh were a body of men who volunteered to defend their country from the invasions and inroads of the Danes and Norwegians, or *Lochlinnich*. FIUNN, who was always called King of the Fein, was the strongest man amongst them, and no person was admitted into the company who was less in height than he, however much taller. I remember the old black shoemaker telling us one night that FIUNN had a tooth which he consulted as an oracle upon all important occasions. He had but to touch this tooth, and whatever he wanted to know was at once revealed to him.

"The above is all I can at present readily call to mind of the way in which the evenings were spent in the Highlands thirty or forty years ago. The minister came to the village in 1830, and the schoolmaster soon followed, who put a stop in our village to such gatherings; and in their place we were supplied with heavier tasks than listening to the old shoemaker's fairy tales. From that period till I collected the few in this collection, I have not heard a tale recited. On going to visit my friends last summer I expected that I would get some old tales among them, but I found that the most of the old men who used to relate them in my young days had died, and the few who were then alive of them were so old that they had lost their memories, so that I only got but a trifle to what I expected.   HECTOR URQUHART.

March 1860.

John Dewar, a labourer, whom I never saw, but who has written and sent me many stories, agrees with the others. These men have never met, and have acted independently; and yet, in many cases, I have received versions of the same story from each and from other sources, and I have myself heard the same incidents repeated by their authorities, and by others whom they had never seen; sometimes even the very words.

The name of every narrator is given with his story, and I am satisfied on direct evidence that most of these were known in the Highlands at least forty years ago. Now, for the benefit of those who know as little of the subject as I did, let me give the theory of the distribution of popular tales, as I have gathered it from the able introduction to the Norse Tales and other sources, and then let me point out the bearing of this collection on that theory.

It is supposed that the races known as Indo-European came from Central Asia at some very early period, and passed over Europe, separating and settling down as nations; retaining words of their original language, and leaving the traces of their religion and history everywhere as popular tales; and that they found the land occupied. Each wave, it is said, "pushed onwards those who went before," but, as it seems to me, each in turn must have stopped as it arrived at the great sea, and there the waves of this stream of men must have mingled and stagnated.

As the flotson and jetsam of American rivers and of the Gulf Stream is constantly drifting northwards and eastwards, and finds a resting-place on some western shore, so the traces of the great human stream, which is supposed to have flowed westwards, should be found in greatest abundance stranded at the western sea. If this be correct, and if the plains of Asia sent migratory hordes eastwards as well as westwards, the tales and languages of the far East and West should most resemble each other, and should also resemble more than others the oldest forms of the myths and languages of those from whom they sprang. Brittany, Scandinavia, Ireland, and the west of Scotland, from their geographical position, should contain more of this light mental *debris* than Central Europe ; for the same reason that more of the floating rubbish of American rivers is found on the shores of Europe than anywhere on the great ocean ; and if mankind had a common origin, and started from the plains of Asia, and if popular tales really are old traditions, then the tales of Ceylon should resemble those of Barra, and those of Japan should resemble the others, because men travelling eastwards and arrived at Japan, could not easily advance farther. Mr. Oliphant tells us that both in China and in Japan groups are commonly seen listening to professional story-tellers in the streets, and it is to be hoped that some one will enable us to judge of their talents.

Be that as it may, fairy-eggs are not the only foreign products found on the shores of the Hebrides, and the people who dwell there know stories of larger growth than mere nursery tales. Great logs of drift-wood find their way to shore, and are turned to use. Such a log I once found, and used myself, long ago. It was half buried in the sand ; it had been long tossed by the sea, and battered against rocks, for it was heavy with water, splintered and ground. No tree like it grew anywhere near. There was no mark of a tool on it. The stumps of its roots and branches remained, and it seemed as if it had been torn up and wafted to its resting-place by winds and waves alone. I have now no doubt that it came from America. Had it been insignificant, and useless, like a fairy-egg, we might have left it, or preserved it as a curiosity ; but it was a useful log, and we were a party of chilled otter hunters, so, after a few speculations, we hoisted the prize on our shoulders, carried it to our dwelling, a neighbouring cave, and there we burned it.

I see it often, hissing and sputtering, and lighting up the bivouac with its red glare. Its ashes may be there still, but that tree is a tree no longer; its origin and wanderings cannot now be traced; it has shared the fate of many a popular tale. It was found and used up.

Such a log I lately saw in South Uist. No tool mark was on it; it had lost its own foliage, but it was covered with a brown and white marine foliage of seaweed and dead barnacles, and it was drilled in all directions by these curious sea-shells, which are supposed by the people to be embryo geese. It was sound, though battered, and a worthy Celtic smith was about to add it to the roof of a cottage, which he was making of boulders and turf. It was about to share the fate of many popular tales, and become a part of something else. It may be recognized as an American production hereafter, and its history is deeply marked on it, though it forms part of a house by this time. So a genuine popular tale may be recognized in a play or a romance.

Another such tree I saw in Benbecula, with bark still on the roots, and close to it lay a squared log, and near that a mast with white paint and iron bindings, blocks and crosstrees, still attached to it. A few miles off was a stranded ship, with her cargo and fittings, a wreck about to be sold, and turned to any use that the new owners might think fit. All these were about to be changed, and as it is with driftwood in the Highlands, so, as I imagine, it has been with popular tales everywhere. They are as old as the races who tell them, but the original ideas, like the trees from which logs, masts, and ships are made, have been broken up, cut, carved, and ornamented—lost and found—wrecked, destroyed, broken, and put together again ; and, though the original shape is hard to find, the fragments may be recognized in books, and wherever else they may now be found.

But as there are quiet spots in the world where drift-wood accumulates undisturbed, so there are quiet spots where popular tales flourish in peace, because no man has interfered with them. In Spitzbergen, according to the accounts given me by Norwegian bear hunters, and adventurous English nobles, trees, such as those occasionally found in Scotland, are piled in heaps. Trees, logs, broken spars, and wreck, gather and bleach and decay together, because there are no men on that wild shore to use them. So in the islands where the western "wanderers," "Albanich," settled down, and where they have remained for centuries, old men and women are still found who have hardly stirred from their native islands, who speak only Gaelic, and cannot read or write, and yet their minds are filled with a mass of popular lore, as various as the wreck piled on the shores of Spitzbergen. If such as these get hold of the contents of a story book, they seem unconsciously to extract the incidents, and reject all the rest,—to select the true wood, and throw away foreign ornament, just as they chip off the paint of a stranded mast, or scrape the sea-weed off a log when they build it into a roof. I have given one specimen of a story, which I believe to be derived from the "Arabian Nights," though it is quite impossible that the man who told it to Hector MacLean, and who told it to me also, in nearly the same words, can have got it directly from any book; for he cannot read at all, and he does not understand English.

I have found very little notice of these West Highland prose tales in books, but they are referred to. In 1703, Martin says that his countrymen then told long

tales about Fin MacCoul, but he adds that he will not
trouble the reader with them.

In 1780, Dr. Smith, in his book on Gaelic poetry,
says, that prosaic tales should be preserved in the same
manner may seem strange, but so it is.   He condemns
the "urskels" as "later tales," unworthy of notice,
probably because they were different from the poetry
of which he collected so much.

Gaelic dictionaries mention "legends" as sources
from which words have been taken.   Amongst the
Gaelic MSS. now in the Advocates' Library, there are
several which contain tales similar to those now told
in the Highlands.   One passage about the sailing of a
boat, which I have got, with variations, from a great
many people living in various parts of the Highlands,
I find in a MS. which was lent to me by the secretary
of the Celtic Society of London.   It is dated 23d
December 1808, signed Alexander Stewart, A.M., and
marked Poems of Ossian.   It contains 7721 lines of
Gaelic, mostly poetry, which by the references seem to
have been copied from something else.   The passage
to which I refer, occurs in a "Fragment of a Tale, p.
17," which occupies thirty-seven folio pages, and treats
of carrying off a lady from an island, and her recovery
by her husband.

Dr. MacLeod, the best of living Gaelic scholars,
printed one old tale, somewhat altered, with a moral
added, in his "Leabhar nan Cnoc," in 1834, but even
his efforts to preserve and use this old lore were un-
successful.

Those, then, who understood Gaelic, thought popular
tales unworthy of notice; those who did not understand Gaelic, could know nothing about them; and
there are many now living in the Highlands, who
speak Gaelic and yet believed, till they searched at my

request, that stories had become extinct in their districts. One good Highlander, who has helped me much, Mr. James Robertson, living at Inverary, so believed, till he heard his own nursemaid repeat No. 17, and a neighbouring fisherman tell No. 6. In the Highlands, as elsewhere, society is arranged in layers, like the climates of the world. The dweller on an Indian plain little dreams that there is a region of perpetual frost in the air above him; the Esquimaux does not suspect the slumbering volcano under his feet; and the dwellers in the upper and lower strata of society, everywhere, know as little of each other's ways of life, as the men of the plain know of the mountaineers in the snow.

Highland stories, then, have been despised by educated men, and they are as yet unchanged popular tales. It so happened that a piper was the instructor of my babyhood. He was a stalwart, kindly, gentle man, whose face is often before me, though he has long since gone to his rest. From him I first heard a few of the tales in this collection. They had almost faded from my memory, but I remembered their existence, and I knew where to search, so I began at the beginning of 1859 by writing to my Highland friends, of all degrees, for stories of all kinds, true stories excepted; and here let me thank them cordially for the trouble which they have taken, for they are too numerous to thank in detail.

I begged for the very words used by the people who told the stories, with nothing added, or omitted, or altered. Those who could wrote Gaelic, those who could not did their best in English,—translated, at first or second-hand, from Gaelic; and when I had so gathered many versions of a story, I thought I might safely conclude that it had been known in the country for many years, and was essentially a popular tale.

My next step was to go at Easter to a Highland district, near the lowlands, where a gamekeeper had marked down a lot of tale-tellers, and I was soon convinced that there was plenty of game, though hard to get.

This difficulty may be worth some explanation, for it exists elsewhere, and bears on the collection of tales everywhere. Highland peasants and fishermen, especially those dwelling near the lowlands, are shy and proud, and even more peculiarly sensitive to ridicule than peasants elsewhere. Many have a lurking belief in the truth of the stories which they tell, and a rooted conviction that any one with a better education will laugh at the belief, and the story, and the narrator and his language, if he should be weak enough to venture on English, and betray his knowledge of Sgeultachd and his creed. He cannot imagine that any one out of his own class can possibly be amused by his frivolous pastimes. No one ever has hitherto. He sees every year a summer flood of tourists of all nations pouring through his lochs and glens, but he knows as little of them as they know of him. The shoals of herrings that enter Loch Fyne know as much of the dun deer on the hill-side, as Londoners and Highland peasants know of each other. Each gets an occasional peep at the other as the deer may see the herrings capering on the loch— each affects the other slowly but surely, as the herrings do drive away the wild deer by attracting men to catch them ; but the want of a common language here as elsewhere, keeps Highlands and Lowlands, Celt and Saxon, as clearly separate as oil and water in the same glass.

The first step, then, towards the acquisition of a story is to establish confidence. It may be that the would-be-collector sees before him a strapping lad dressed in the garb of a west country fisherman—a rough blue bonnet, jacket, and trousers. He steps out and ranges up alongside. The Highlander glances from under his bushy eyebrows, and sees with his sharp grey eyes that the new comer is a stranger; he looks rather like a Saxon; Highland curiosity is strong, and he longs to ask whence he comes; but politeness is stronger, and it would be uncivil to begin questioning at once. So with a nervous kick of one foot, and a quick shy glance, the fisherman jerks out, "It's a fine day." "Tha n' latha briagh" (The day is fine) replies the stranger; and as he speaks, the whole face and manner of his companion change as if by magic; doubt and hesitation, suspicion and curiosity, become simple wonder; his eyes and his heart open wide at the sound of his native tongue, and he exclaims, " You have Gaelic !" " You will take my excuse by your leave, but what part of the Gaeldom are you from ?" And then having found out all that is to be discovered, the ice being broken, and confidence established, it oozes out gradually that the fisherman knows a story, and after much persuasion he tells it, while he rows the gentleman who can talk Gaelic across a Highland loch. At parting, he adds that he has only told it to please a " Gael," and that he would not have said one word to a Gall (stranger). But the man who is fluent in his boat, is shy and awkward when set down to repeat his story for transcribing, and it is only when set with one of his neighbours whom he knows, that his story is got on paper.

Or it may be an old dame in a tall white mutch with a broad black silk band, a red cloak, and clean white apron. She is 70, and can walk ten miles; she has known all the neighbouring families for generations. If you can claim cousinship with any, she is your friend ; but she *will* praise the ancestors and tell of the adventures of Rob Roy the Gregorach, the last of the freebooters. "But Mary can you say Murachag and Mionachag?" "Huch! my dear, that is an ursgeul that is nonsense. The Good Being bless you, I knew your grandmother," etc. etc. So one must rest contented with the fact, that old Mary knows one tale, and probably many more, which a week's persuasion might perhaps extract.

Or it may be a pretty lass, whose eye twinkles with intelligence at every catch-word, thrown out as a bait, but whom nothing will induce to confess that she knows the foolish tales which the minister has condemned.

Or it is an old wandering vagabond of a tinker, who has no roof but the tattered covering of his tent. He has pitched it in a quarry under a giant fir, the gnarled roots, half bare, hardly support the tree on the edge of a red clay bank, and form a kind of hollow, a " còs," in which the tinker and his tribe have nestled at odd times for years. A thin blue smoke is curling amongst the blackened roots, and winding itself about the noble tree. A stately mansion and a wide domain, and a blue highland loch, with a shoal of brown herring-boats, can be seen through the wood from the door of the tinker's tent ; and there he lies, an old man past eighty, who has been a soldier, and "has never seen a school ;" too proud to beg, too old to work ; surrounded by boxes and horn spoons, with shaggy hair and naked feet, as perfect a nomad as the wildest Lapp or Arab in the whole world. It is easy to make friends with such men. A kind word in their native language is all that is required, but to get their stories is another affair. "Donald, did you ever see the like of *this?*" Up

starts the old man on his elbow,—" Och ! och ! that's a
fairy arrow, I have seen that ; och! och ! no fairy arrow
will ever hit the man who has that—no fire will ever
burn the house where that is. That's lucky, well !
well !" and the old man sinks down on his bed of fern.
But the elf shot has hit the mark, and started a train of
thought, which leads at last to a wild weird story ; but
before that story can be written, the whole tribe decamp,
and are lost for a time.

The first difficulty, then, was the nature of the
people who knew the stories ; and the second, the want
of men able and willing to write Gaelic. It was easy
to write English versions of tales heard in Gaelic, but
I wanted the Gaelic as it was told, and I had neither
time nor ability to write it down myself. I therefore
sought out two men on whom I could rely, to collect
and write for me, and the largest share of this book
has been collected and written by them. One is Mr.
Hector Urquhart, gamekeeper at Ardkinglas on Loch
Fyne ; the other, Mr. Hector MacLean, schoolmaster
at Ballygrant in Islay, who has superintended the print-
ing of the Gaelic. They entered into the spirit of the
work at once, and they have executed their share of
it with the greatest fidelity. But while these are my
chief aids, I am largely indebted to many others for
written Gaelic ; for example, to one of my earliest
friends, Mrs. MacTavish ; to the Rev. Mr. MacLauchlan
of Edinburgh ; to Alexander Fraser, Esq. of Mauld,
near Beaulay ; to many of the schoolmasters on the
estate of Sir Kenneth MacKenzie ; to Mr. Donald
Torrie, Benbecula ; and to many others, including
John Dewar, a self-educated man of advanced age,
whose contribution does him the greatest credit.

The next step was to spend a summer holiday in
studying the actual condition of this popular lore,

b

where I had found that it existed in the greatest profusion. I landed at Ardmaddy in North Uist, and walked with a knapsack to the sound of Barra, and back to Stornoway ; crossing the sound of Harris in a fishing boat. I found a population differing from that of the main land, perhaps the least changed from their old ways of any people in the kingdom. Gaelic is their usual, often their only language. Every English word which has crept in has a Gaelic head and tail. Many, I know not how many, "have no English" at all, and have never been taught to read. In many islands the people are living undisturbed, where their ancestors have lived time out of mind. They are a small, active, intelligent race, with dark hair and eyelashes, and grey eyes ; quick, clever, and pugnacious. I had expected to find traces of Norwegian occupation in the people and their language. I watched carefully for Norwegian words and features ; and I found the people a complete contrast to Norwegian peasants, whom I know well, who are large, bony, light-haired fair men, sagacious rather than quick ; and generally slow to anger.

I could find nothing Scandinavian, except certain names of places, and certain ruins, which it is the fashion to attribute to the Lochliners. Even the houses and the old agricultural implements, where they are still used, are peculiar. For example, the old crooked spade still used in islands in the sound of Barra, and elsewhere, has no resemblance to any agricultural implement that I have ever seen anywhere out of the West Highlands. It is in fact a foot plough used without horses. It is remarkable that a steam plough should be at work at the same time, on the east coast of Cromarty at Tarbert. Every horse I met on the road stopped of his own accord. Every man asked my news, " whence I took the walking," where I lived, and why I came? Saddles were often sacks, stirrups a loop of twisted bent, bridles the same, and bits occasionally wood. Dresses were coarse, but good; but there was an air of kindly politeness over all, that is not to be found in homespun dresses in any other country that I know. When I was questioned, I answered, and told my errand, and prospered. "I was not a drover come to buy cattle at the fair;" "Neither was I a merchant though I carried a pack." "I was the gentleman who was after Sgialachdan." My collector had made my name known. I spoke Gaelic, and answered questions. I am one of themselves, so I got on famously.

Men and women of all ages could and did tell me stories, children of all sizes listened to them; and it was self-evident that people generally knew and enjoyed them. Elsewhere I had been told, that thirty or forty years ago, men used to congregate and tell stories; here, I was told, that they now spend whole winter nights about the fire listening to these old world tales. The clergy, in some places, had condemned the practice, and there it had fallen into disuse; stories seemed to be almost exterminated in some islands, though I believe they were only buried alive; but in other places this harmless amusement is not forbidden: and there, in every cluster of houses, is some one man famed as "good at sgialachdan," whose house is a winter evening's resort. I visited these, and listened, often with wonder, at the extraordinary power of memory shown by untaught old men.

It is perhaps beyond the province of a mere collector of old tales to be serious; but surely Gaelic books containing sound information would be a vast boon to such a people. The young would read them, and the old would understand them. All would take a warmer interest in Canada and Australia, where strong arms and bold spirits are wanted, if they knew what these countries really are. If they heard more of European battles, and knew what a ship of war is now, there would be more soldiers and sailors from the Isles in the service of their country. At all events, the old spirit of popular romance is surely not an evil spirit to be exorcised, but rather a good genius to be controlled and directed. Surely stories in which a mother's blessing, well earned, leads to success; in which the poor rise to be princes, and the weak and courageous overcome giants; in which wisdom excells brute force,—surely even such frivolities are better pastime than a solitary whisky bottle, or sleep, or grim silence; for that seems the choice of amusements if tales are forbidden, and Gaelic books are not provided for men who know no other language; and who, as men, must be amused now and then.

I have never heard a story, whose point was obscenity, publicly told in a Highland cottage; and I believe that such are rare. I *have* heard them where the rough polish of more modern ways has replaced the polished roughness of "wild" Highlanders; and that where even the bagpipes have been almost abolished as profane.

I have heard the music of the Cider Cellars in a parlour, even in polished England, when I had failed to extract anything else from a group of comfortably-dressed villagers. A half-polished human gem is but a spoiled crystal anywhere; and I prefer the rough diamond or the finished jewel.

But this is foreign to my work; my visits were to the tellers of old stories, and had nothing to do with political economy and public morals. I paid my visits, and heard the stories; and a goodly audience

often gathered to share the treat, and all seemed marvellously to enjoy it. If there was an occasional coarse
word spoken, it was not coarsely meant.

Let me describe one of these old story men as a
type of his kind. I trust he will not be offended, for
he was very polite to me. His name is MacPhie; he
lives at the north end of South Uist, where the road
ends at a sound, which has to be forded at the ebb to
get to Benbecula. The house is built of a double wall
of loose boulders, with a layer of peat three feet thick
between the walls. The ends are round, and the roof
rests on the inner wall, leaving room for a crop of yellow
gowans. A man might walk round the roof on the top
of the wall. There is but one room, with two low doors,
one on each side of the house. The fire is on the floor ;
the chimney is a hole above it ; and the rafters are
hung with pendants and festoons of shining black peat
reek. They are of birch from the mainland, American
drift wood, or broken wreck. They support a covering of turf and straw, and stones, and heather ropes,
which keep out the rain well enough.

The house stands on a green bank, with grey rocks
protruding through the turf ; and the whole neighbourhood is pervaded by cockle shells, which indicate
the food of the people and their fishing pursuits. In
a neighbouring kiln there were many cart-loads about
to be burned, to make that lime which is so durable in
the old castles. The owner of the house, whom I
visited twice, is seventy-nine. He told me nine
stories, and like all the others, declared that there
was no man in the islands who knew them so well.
"He could not say how many he knew ;" he seemed
to know versions of nearly everything I had got ; and
he told me plainly that my versions were good for
nothing. "Huch! Thou hast not got them right at

all." "They came into his mind," he said, "sometimes at night when he could not sleep,—old tales that he had not heard for threescore years."

He had the manner of a practised narrator, and it is quite evident that he is one; he chuckled at the interesting parts, and laid his withered finger on my knee as he gave out the terrible bits with due solemnity. A small boy in a kilt, with large round glittering eyes, was standing mute at his knee, gazing at his wrinkled face, and devouring every word. The boy's mother first boiled, and then mashed potatoes; and his father, a well grown man in tartan breeks, ate them. Ducks and ducklings, a cat and a kitten, some hens and a baby, all tumbled about on the clay floor together, and expressed their delight at the savoury prospect, each in his own fashion; and three wayfarers dropped in and listened for a spell, and passed their remarks till the ford was shallow. The light came streaming down the chimney, and through a single pane of glass, lighting up a track in the blue mist of the peat smoke; and fell on the white hair and brown withered face of the old man, as he sat on a low stool with his feet to the fire; and the rest of the dwelling, with all its plenishing of boxes and box-beds, dishes and dresser, and gear of all sorts, faded away through shades of deepening brown, to the black darkness of the smoked roof and the "peat corner." There we sat, and smoked and talked for hours, till the tide ebbed; and then I crossed the ford by wading up to the waist, and dried my clothes in the wind in Benbecula.

Another man of the same stamp, Patrick Smith, lives near the sound of Barra; and a third, "Donald MacDonald MacCharles MacIntyre," in Benbecula; and I heard of plenty more, whom I had not time to visit. I found them to be men with clear heads and wonderful memories, generally very poor and old, living in remote corners of remote islands, and speaking only Gaelic ; in short, those who have lived most at home, furthest from the world, and who have no source of mental relaxation beyond themselves and their neighbours.

At Gearrloch on the mainland, some old namesakes of mine are of the same stamp, but in these regions the schoolmaster has made himself at home. Tales have been forbidden, but other lore has been provided. There are many well attended English schools, so old men have access to books and newspapers through their children. Tradition is out of fashion and books are in.

Farther east stories are still rarer, and seem to be told rather by women than by men. The long romances of the west give place to stories about ghosts and fairies, apparitions, and dreams,—stories which would be told in a few words, if at all, in the islands. Fairy belief is becoming a fairy tale. In another generation it will grow into a romance, as it has in the hands of poets elsewhere, and then the whole will either be forgotten or carried from people who must work to gentles who can afford to be idle and read books. Railways, roads, newspapers, and tourists, are slowly but surely doing their accustomed work. They are driving out romance ; but they are not driving out the popular creed as to supernaturals. That creed will survive when the last remnant of romance has been banished, for superstition seems to belong to no one period in the history of civilization, but to all. It is as rife in towns as it is amongst the hills, and is not confined to the ignorant.

I have wandered amongst the peasantry of many countries, and this trip but confirmed my old impression. There are few peasants that I think so highly of, none that I like so well. Scotch Highlanders have faults in plenty, but they have the bearing of Nature's own gentlemen—the delicate, natural tact which discovers, and the good taste which avoids, all that would hurt or offend a guest. The poorest is ever the readiest to share the best he has with the stranger. A kind word kindly meant is never thrown away, and whatever may be the faults of this people, I have never found a boor or a churl in a Highland bothy.

Celts have played their part in history, and they have a part to play still in Canada and Australia, where their language and character will leave a trace if they do not influence the destiny of these new worlds. There are hundreds in those distant lands, whose language is still Gaelic, and to whom these stories are familiar, and if this book should ever remind any of them of the old country, I shall not have worked in vain in the land which they call "Tir nam Beann s' nan gleann s' nan ghaisgach."*

So much, then, for the manner of collecting the tales, and the people who told them. The popular lore which I found current in the west, and known all over the Highlands in a greater or less degree amongst the poorer classes, consists of :—

1st. That which is called Seanachas na Finne, or Feinne, or Fiann, that is, the tradition or old history of the Feene.

This is now the rarest of any, and is commonest, so far as I know, in Barra and South Uist. There are first fragments of poems which may have been taken from the printed book, which goes by the name of the History of the Finne in the Highlands, and the Poems of Ossian elsewhere. I never asked for these, but I

* The land of hills, and glens, and heroes.

was told that the words were "sharper and deeper" than those in the printed book.

There are, secondly, poetical fragments about the same persons, which, to the best of my knowledge, are not in any printed book. I heard some of these repeated by three different men.

Patrick Smith, in South Uist, *intoned* a long fragment; I should guess, about 200 lines. He recited it rapidly to a kind of chant. The subject was a fight with a Norway witch, and Fionn, Diarmaid, Oscar, and Conan, were named as Irish heroes. There were "ships fastened with silver chains, and kings holding them;" swords, spears, helmets, shields, and battles, were mentioned; in short, the fragment was the same in style and machinery as the famous Poems; and it was attributed to Ossian. The repetition began with a short prose account of what was to follow. Smith is sixty, and says that he cannot read. He does not understand English. He says that such poems used to be so chanted commonly when he was young. The same account of the manner of reciting similar poems was given me by a clergyman in Argyllshire, who said that, within his recollection, the "death of Cuchullin" used to be so recited by an old man at the head of Loch Awe.

Donald Macintyre, in Benbecula, recited a similar fragment, which has since been written and sent to me. The subject is a dialogue between a lady and a messenger returning from battle, with a number of heads on a withy; the lady asks their story, and the messenger tells whose heads they were, and how the heroes fell. It sounded better than it reads, but the transcriber had never written Gaelic before.

John Campbell, generally known as "Yellow John," living in Strath Gearrloch, about twelve miles west of

Flowerdale, repeated a similar fragment, which lasted for a quarter of an hour. He said he had known it for half a century. He is a very old man, and it is difficult to follow him, and the poetry was mingled with prose, and with " said he," " said she." It was the last remnant of something which the old man could only remember imperfectly, and which he gave in broken sentences; but here again the combat was with a Norway witch, and the scene, Ireland. Fionn Diarmaid and other such names appeared. Diarmaid had " his golden helm on his head ;" his " two spears on his shoulder ;" his " narrow-pointed shield on his left arm ;" his " small shield on his right ;" his sword was " leafy," (?) leaf-shaped. And the old man believed that Diarmaid, the Irish hero, was his ancestor, and his own real name O'duine. He spoke of "his chief MacCalain," and treated me with extra kindness, as a kinsman. " Will you not take some more" (milk and potatoes). " Perhaps we may never see each other again. Are we not both Campbells ?"

I heard of other men who could repeat such poems, and I have heard of such men all my life ; but as I did not set out to gather poems, I took no trouble to get them.

Two chiefs, I think one was MacLeod, sent their two fools to gather bait on the shore, and to settle a bet which fool was the best, they strewed gold on the path. One fool stopped to gather it, but the other said, " When we are at ' golding,' let us be ' golding,' and when we are at bait-making, let us be bait-making," and he stuck to his business. My business was prose, but it may not be out of place to state my own opinion about the Ossian controversy, for I have been asked more than once if I had found any trace of such poems.

I believe that there were poems of very old date, of which a few fragments still exist in Scotland as pure traditions. That these related to Celtic worthies who were popular heroes before the Celts came from Ireland, and answer to Arthur and his knights elsewhere. That the same personages have figured in poems composed, or altered, or improved, or spoilt by bards who lived in Scotland, and by Irish bards of all periods; and that these personages have been mythical heroes amongst Celts from the earliest of times. That "the poems" were orally collected by MacPherson, and by men before him, by Dr. Smith, by the committee of the Highland Society, and by others, and that the printed Gaelic is old poetry, mended and patched, and pieced together, and altered, but on the whole a genuine work. Manuscript evidence of the antiquity of similar Gaelic poems exists. Some were printed in 1807, under the authority of the Highland Society of London, with a Latin translation, notes, etc., and were reprinted in 1818. MacPherson's "translation" appeared between 1760 and 1762, and the controversy raged from the beginning, and is growling still; but the dispute now is, whether the poems were originally *Scotch* or *Irish*, and how much MacPherson altered them. It is like the quarrel about the chameleon, for the languages spoken in Islay and Rathlin are identical, and the language of the poems is difficult for me, though I have *spoken* Gaelic from my childhood. There is no doubt at all that Gaelic poems on such subjects existed long before Macpherson was born; and it is equally certain that there is no composition in the Gaelic language which bears the smallest resemblance in style to the peculiar kind of prose in which it pleased Mac-Pherson to translate. The poems have a peculiar rhythm, and a style of their own which is altogether lost in his English translation. But what concerns me is the popular belief, and it seems to be this—"Mac-Pherson must have been a very dishonest person when he allowed himself to pass as the author of Ossian's poems." So said a lady, one of my earliest friends, whose age has not impaired her memory, and so say those who are best informed, and understand the language.

The illiterate seem to have no opinion on the subject. So far as I could ascertain, few had heard of the controversy, but they had all heard scraps of poems and stories about the Finne, all their lives ; and they are content to believe that "Ossian, the last of the Finne," composed the poems, wrote them, and burned his book in a pet, when he was old and blind, because St. Patrick, or St. Paul, or some other saint, would not believe his wonderful stories."

Those who would study "the controversy," will find plenty of discussion ; but the report of the Highland Society appears to settle the question on evidence. I cannot do better than quote from Johnson's Poets the opinion of a great author, who was a great translator, who, in speaking of his own work, says :—

" What must the world think . . . After such a judgment passed by so great a critick, the world who decides so often, and who examines so seldom ; the world who, even in matters of litera-ture, is almost always the slave of authority ? Who will suspect that so much learning should mistake, that so much accuracy should be misled, or that so much candour should be biassed ? . . . . I think that no translation ought to be the ground of criticism, because no man ought to be condemned upon another man's explanation of his meaning. . . . ." (Postscript to the Odyssey, Pope's Homer, Johnson's Poets, pp. 279, 280).

And to that quotation let me add this manuscript

note, which I found in a copy of the report of the Highland Society, on the poems of Ossian ; which I purchased in December 1859 ; and which came from the library of Colonel Hamilton Smith, at Plymouth. ·

" The Reverend Dr. Campbell, of Halfway Tree, Lisuana, in Jamaica, often repeated to me in the year 1799, 1801, and 1802, parts of Ossian in Gaelic ; and assured me that he had possessed a manuscript, long the property of his family, in which Gaelic poems, and in particular, whole pieces of Ossian's compositions were contained. This he took out with him on his first voyage to the West Indies in 1780, when his ship was captured by a boat from the Santissima Trinidata flagship, of the whole Spanish fleet ; and he, together with all the other passengers, lost nearly the whole of their baggage, among which was the volume in question. In 1814, when I was on the staff of General Sir Thomas Graham, now Lord Lyndoch, I understood that Mr. Mac-Pherson had been at one time his tutor ; and, therefore, I asked his opinion respecting the authenticity of the Poems. His lord-ship replied that he never had any doubts on the subject, he hav-ing seen in Mr. MacPherson's possession several manuscripts in the Gaelic language, and heard him speak of them repeatedly ; he told me some stronger particulars, which I cannot now note down, for the conversation took place during the action of our winter campaign.

(Signed) " CHARLES HAM^ᵉ SMITH, Lt.-Col."

The Colonel had the reputation of being a great antiquary, and had a valuable library. James Mac-Pherson, a " modest young man, who was master of Greek and Latin," was " procured " to be a preceptor to " the boy Tommy," who was afterwards Lord Lyn-doch (according to a letter in a book printed for pri-vate circulation). As it appears to me, those who are ignorant of Gaelic, and now-a-days maintain that "MacPherson composed Ossian's Poems," are like critics who, being ignorant of Greek, should maintain that

Pope wrote the Odyssey, and was the father of Homer; or, being ignorant of English, should declare that Tennyson was the father of King Arthur and all his knights, because he has published one of many poems which treat of them. It was different when Highlanders were " rebels;" and it was petty treason to deny that they were savages.

A glance at " Johnson's Tour in the Hebrides," will show the feeling of the day. He heard Gaelic songs in plenty, but would not believe in Gaelic poems. He appreciated the kindness and hospitality with which he was treated ; he praised the politeness of all ranks, and yet maintained that their language was " the rude speech of a barbarous people, who had few thoughts to express, and were content, as they conceived grossly, to be grossly understood."

He could see no beauty in the mountains which men now flock to see. He saw no fish in fording northern rivers, and explains how the winter torrents sweep them away ; the stags were " perhaps not bigger than our fallow-deer ;" the waves were not larger than those on the coast of Sussex ; and yet, though the Doctor would not believe in Gaelic poems, he did believe that peat grew as it was cut, and that the vegetable part of it probably caused a glowing redness in the earth of which it is mainly composed ; and he came away willing to believe in the second sight, though not quite convinced.

That sturdy old Briton, the great lexicographer, who is an honour to his country, was not wholly free from national prejudice ; he erred in some things ; he may have erred in a matter of which he could not well judge ; he did not understand Gaelic ; he did not believe in traditions ; he would not believe in the translations ; and MacPherson seems to have ended by encouraging the public belief that he was the author of poems which had gained so wide a celebrity.

Matters have changed for the better since those days ; Celt and Saxon are no longer deadly foes. There still exists, as I am informed, an anti-Celtic society, whose president, on state occasions, wears three pairs of trousers ; but it is no longer penal to dispense with these garments ; and there are Southerns who discard them altogether, when they go north to pursue the little stags on the ugly hills, and catch fish in the torrents.

There are Celtic names in high places, in India, and at home ; and an English Duke is turning the Gaelic of Ossian's poems into English verse.

This, however, is foreign to my subject, though it bears somewhat on the rest of the traditions of the Finne. I have stated my own opinion because I hold it, not because I wish to influence those who differ from me. I have no wish to stir up the embers of an expiring controversy, which was besprinkled with peculiarly acrid ink, and obscured by acid fumes. I neither believe that MacPherson composed Ossian, nor that Ossian composed all the poems which bear his name. I am quite content to believe Ossian to have been an Irishman, or a Scotchman, or a myth, on sufficient evidence.

Besides these few remnants of poetry which still survive, I find a great many prose tales relating to the heroes of the poems ; and as these personages certainly were popular heroes in Ireland and in Scotland centuries ago, I give what I have gathered concerning them, with the conviction that it is purely Celtic tradition.*

* See page 256 of " Scotland in the Middle Ages," by Cosmo Innes, Edmonston and Douglas, 1860, for evidence taken from

The Scannachas of the Fine consists, then, of poetry already printed; fragments which are not in print, so far as I know, and which are now very rare; and prose tales which are tolerably common, but rapidly disappearing.

In all these, according to tradition, Fionn, Diarmaid, and the rest, are generally represented as Irish worthies. The scene is often laid in Ireland; but there are hundreds of places in Scotland in which some of the exploits are said to have been performed. I know not how many cairns are supposed to contain the bones of the wild boar, whose bristles wounded the feet of Diarmaid when he paced his length against the hair; Kyle Reay, in Skye, is named after a giant warrior who leaped the strait. There are endless mountains bearing Ossianic names in all parts of Scotland, and even in the Isle of Man the same names are to be found mixed up with legends. In April 1860, I met a peasant near Ramsay who knew the name of Fin MacCoul, though he would not say a word about him to me. In Train's history of the island, published by Mary Quiggin, 1845, at page 359, is this note :—

"In a letter, dated 20th September 1844, from a highly respected correspondent in the Isle of Man, he says—'Are you aware that the septennial appearance of the island, said to be submerged in the sea by enchantment near Port Soderick, is expected about the end of this month.' Though the spell by which this fancified island has been bound to the bottom of the ocean since the days of the great Fin M'Coul, and its inhabitants transformed into blocks of granite, might, according to popular belief, be broke by placing a bible on any part of the enchanted land when at its original altitude above the waters of the deep, where

"The fathers of our Scotch literature," and the report of the Highland Society it is permitted to remain only for the short space of thirty minutes. No person has yet had the hardihood to make the attempt, lest, in case of failure, the enchanter, in revenge, might cast his club over Mona also."

And in Cregeen's Manks dictionary, by the same publisher, 1835, is this Manks proverb—

"Ny three geayghyn s' feayrey dennec Fion M'Cooil
    Geay henneu, as geay huill,
    As geay fo ny shiauill."

Which I understand to mean—

The three coldest winds that came to Fion M'Cooil,
    Wind from a thaw, wind from a hole,
    And wind from under the sails.

In short, I believe that the heroes of Ossian belong to the race, not to any one set of poems, or to any single branch of the Celtic language.

2d. There are tales, not necessarily about the Fine, consisting partly of plain narrative and dialogue, which vary with every narrator, and probably more or less every time the story is told ; and partly of a kind of measured prose, which is unlike anything I know in any other language. I suspect that these have been compositions at some time, but at what time I cannot even guess.

These almost always relate to Ireland and Scandinavia ; to boats, knights, swords, and shields. There are adventures under ground, much battle, generally an island with fire about it (perhaps Iceland), and a lady to be carried off. There is often an old woman who has some mysterious vessel of balsam which brings the dead to life, and a despised character who turns out to be the real hero, sometimes a boaster who is held up to ridicule. I believe these to be bardic recitations fast disappearing and changing into prose ;

c

for the older the narrator is, the less educated, and
the farther removed from the rest of the world, the
more his stories are garnished with these passages.
"Fin MacCumhal goes to Graffee," published in 1857
from Mayo, is evidently a translation of a tale of this
kind. In all these, the scene is laid in Eirinn and Loch-
lan, now Ireland and Scandinavia, and these would
seem to have been border countries. Perhaps the
stories relate to the time when the Scandinavians
occupied part of the Western Isles.

3d. There is popular history of events which really
happened within the last few centuries : of this, I have
gathered none, but I heard a great deal in a very short
time, and I have heard it all my life. It is a history
devoid of dates, but with clear starting points. The
event happened at the time of Shamas (James) at the
battle of Shirra Muir ; at Inverlochy ; after Culloden.
The battle was between MacNeill and MacLeod.
MacLeod came from *that* castle. They met on *that*
strand. The dead are buried *there*. Their descendants
now live in such a place. He was the last man
hanged in Harris. *That* is called the slab of lamenta-
tion, from which the MacLeans embarked for Ireland
when the MacDonalds had conquered them, and taken
the land. MacLean exposed his wife on the Lady
Rock because she had made his servant blow up one of
the ships of the Spanish Armada, for jealousy of the
Spanish lady who was on board. The history is
minute and circumstantial, and might be very interesting if faithfully collected, but it is rather local than
national, and is not within the scope of my work. It
is by far the most abundant popular lore, and has still
a great hold on the people. The decision of a magis-
trate in a late case of " Sapaid" (broken heads) was very
effective, because he appealed to this feeling. It was

thus described to me : " Ah ! he gave it to them.   He leant back in his chair, and spoke grandly for half an hour.   He said you are as wild men fighting together in the days of King Shamas."

4th. There are tales which relate to men and women only, and to events that might have happened anywhere at any time.   They might possibly be true, and equally true, whether the incidents happened to an Eastern sage or a wise old Highlander.   Such tales as Nos. 19 and 20. These are plentiful, and their characteristic is sagacity and hidden meaning.

5th. There are children's tales, of which some are given.   They are in poetry and prose as elsewhere, and bear a general resemblance to such tales all over the world.   The cat and the mouse play parts in the nursery drama of the Western Isles, as well as in " Contes et Apologues Indiens inconnus jusqu' a ce jour," etc. ; a translation into French, by Mr. Stanislaus Julien, in 1860, of Chinese books, which were translated into that language from Sanscrit in 1565, by a Chinese doctor, and President of the Ministry of Justice, who composed " The Forest of Comparisons," in twenty-four volumes, divided into 20 classes, and subdivided into 508 sections, after twenty years of hard labour, during which he abstracted about 400 works. This is the name of one : Fo-choue-kiun-nieou-pi-king.

Let those who call Gaelic hard, try that ; or this : Tchong-king-siouen-tsi-pi-yu-king.

Let those who contemn nursery rhymes, think of the French savant, and the Chinese cabinet minister, and the learning which they have bestowed on the conversations of cats and mice.

6th. Riddles and puzzles, of which there are a very great number.   They are generally descriptive, such as,

"No bigger than a barley corn, it covers the king's board"—(the eye). I have given a few. If any despise riddles, let them bear in mind that the Queen of Sheba is believed to have propounded riddles to Solomon, and that Samson certainly proposed a riddle to the Philistines. I am told that riddles are common in India now.

7th. Proverbs, in prose and in verse, of which 1515 were printed in 1819, and many more are still to be got. Many are evidently very old from their construction, and some are explained by the stories, for example, "Blackberries in February" has no very evident meaning, but a long story explains that difficulties may be vanquished. A king's son was sent by a stepmother to get "that which grew, and is neither crooked nor straight"—(sawdust). "Blackberries in February," which he found growing in a charnel-house, and a third thing, equally easy to find when the way was known.

8th. There are songs, of which there are a vast number, published and unpublished, of all sorts and kinds, sung to wild and peculiar tunes. They are condemned and forbidden in some districts, and are vanishing rapidly from all. These used to be sung continually within my recollection, and many of them are wild, and, to my ear, beautiful. There are songs composed in a particular rhythm for rowing, for washing clothes by dancing on them; songs whose rhythm resembles a piobroch; love songs; war songs; songs which are nearly all chorus, and which are composed as they are sung. The composer gives out a single line applicable to anything then present, and the chorus fills up the time by singing and clapping hands, till the second line is prepared. I have known such lines fired at a sportsman by a bevy of girls who were

waulking blankets in a byre, and who made the gun
and the dog the theme of several stanzas. Reid's
Bibliotheca Scoto Celtica, 1832, gives a list of eighty-
one Gaelic books of poetry printed since 1785. There
are hymn books, song books, and poetry, composed by
known and unknown bards, male and female. Of the
former, Mackenzie, in his beauties of Gaelic poetry,
gives a list of thirty-two, with specimens of their works
and a short biography. Of the latter class, the unknown poets, there are many at the present day, and
who is to guess their number in times when men did
nothing but fight and sing about their battles. A very
few of these bards have become known to the world
by name, and, in all probability their merits never
will be known. Let any one translate Sir Patrick
Spens or Annie Laurie into French or Greek, or read
a French translation of Waverley, and the effect of
translation on such compositions will be evident.

9th. The romantic popular tales of which this
collection mainly consists.

I presume that I have said enough as to their collection, and that I may now point out what seems to
me to be their bearing on the scientific part of the subject; that I may take them as traditions, and argue
from them as from established facts. I have endeavoured to show how, when, and where I got the
stories; each has its own separate pedigree, and I have
given the original Gaelic, with the closest translation
which I was able to make.

Now, let me mention the works in which I have
found similar tales, and which are within the reach of
all who can read English. First—Tales from the Norse,
translated by G. W. Dasent, published 1859. Many of
the Gaelic tales collected in 1859 resemble these very
closely. The likeness is pointed out in the notes.

It is impossible that the book could have become
known to the people who told the stories within the
time, but if it were, a manuscript which has been lent
to me by the translator, proves that the stories were
known in Scotland before the translation from the
Norse was made public.

It is a verbatim copy made by a clergyman from a
collection of fourteen tales, gathered by " Peter
Buchan, editor of the Ancient Ballads and Songs of
the North of Scotland."   It is dated 1847, Glasgow ;
and signed, Alexander B. Grosart.   The tales are
written in English, and versions of all except three,
had previously come to me in Gaelic.   For example,
(No. 2), The Battle of the Birds closely resembles " The
Master Maid " from Norway, but it still more resembles Mr. Peter Buchan's " Greensleeves," found in
Scotland thirteen years before the Norse tales were
translated.   The manuscript was sent by Mr. Grosart,
after he had read the Norse tales, and it seems to be
clearly proved that these stories are common to Norway and to Scotland.

I have found very few stories of the kind amongst
the peasantry of the low country, though I have sought
them.   I find such names as Fingal in Mr. Buchan's
stories, and I know them to be common in the islands
where the scene is often laid.   The language is not
that of any peasantry, and I have come to the conclusion that this collection is mostly derived from
Gaelic, directly or indirectly, perhaps from the shoals
of West Highlanders and Irishmen who used to come
down as shearers every harvest, and who are now
scattered all over Scotland as farm-servants and drovers,
and settled in Edinburgh and Glasgow as porters.   I
know from one of these, a drover, who goes every year
to the south with cattle, that he has often entertained

lowland farm-servants by telling in English the stories which he learned as a child in South Uist. I know of men in Paisley, Greenock, and Edinburgh, who are noted for their knowledge of sgeulachd. But while I hold that this particular collection was not told in this form by lowland Scotch peasants, I know that they still do tell such stories occasionally, and I also know that Englishmen of the lower ranks do the same. I met two tinkers in St. James's Street in February, with black faces and a pan of burning coals each. They were followed by a wife, and preceded by a mangy terrier with a stiff tail. I joined the party, and one told me a version of " the man who travelled to learn what shivering meant," while we walked together through the park to Westminster. It was clearly the popular tale which exists in Norse, and German, and Gaelic, and it bore the stamp of the mind of the class, and of the man, who told it in his own peculiar dialect, and who dressed the actors in his own ideas. A cutler and a tinker travel together, and sleep in an empty haunted house for a reward. They are beset by ghosts and spirits of murdered ladies and gentlemen, and the inferior, the tinker, shows most courage, and is the hero. " He went into the cellar to draw beer, and there he found a little chap a-sittin' on a barrel with a red cap on 'is 'ed; and sez he, sez he, ' Buzz.' ' Wot's buzz?' sez the tinker. ' Never you mind wot's buzz,' sez he. ' That's mine; don't you go for to touch it,'" etc. etc. etc.

In a less degree many are like the German stories of the brothers Grimm. That collection has been translated, and a book so well known may possibly have found its way into the Highlands. It is impossible to speak with certainty; but when all the narrators agree in saying that they have known their stories all their lives, and when the variation is so marked, the resemblance is rather to be attributed to common origin than to books. I only once heard of such a book in the Highlands. It was given to a gamekeeper in Sutherland for his children, and was condemned, and put out of the way as trash.

The Gaelic stories resemble in some few cases the well-known tales of Hans Andersen, founded on popular tales told in Denmark.

And they resemble sundry other books which are avowedly founded on popular tales collected in various countries.

Some are like the French tales of the Countess D'Aulnoy, which have been translated. One is like part of Shakspeare, but it is still more like the Italian story in Boccaccio, from which part of Cymbeline is supposed to be taken. Perhaps Shakspeare may have founded Cymbeline on a popular tale then current in England as well as in Italy.

A few resemble the Arabian Nights, and in some cases I believe that the stories have been derived from early English translations of that well-known book. I used myself to read an edition of 1815 to my piper guardian, in return for his ursgeuls, but he seemed more inclined to blame the tyranny of the kings than to admire the Eastern stories.

MacLean has himself told the story of Aladdin in Gaelic as his share of a winter night's entertainment, and I have heard of several people of the poorer class who know the Arabian Nights well. But such stories are easily known after a little experience has been gained. The whole of a volume is run together, the incidents follow in their order, or in something like it. The difference in style is as marked as the contrast between a drift tree and a wrecked vessel, but as it is curious to trace the change from Eastern ways as seen through an English translation of a French view of the original Arabic, I give specimens. These contain the incidents embodied in stories in the Arabian Nights, but the whole machinery and decoration, manners and customs, are now as completely West Highland as if the tales had grown there. But for a camel which appears, I would almost give up my opinion, and adopt that of MacLean, who holds that even these are pure traditions.

In support of his view it may be said that there are hundreds of other books as well known in England as those mentioned above, of which neither I nor my collectors have ever found a trace. Jack and the Bean-stalk, and Jack the Giant-killer, Beauty and the Beast, and the Sleeping Beauty in the Wood, as known in England, are unknown in the Highlands. None of the adventures of Mr. Pickwick, or Sam Weller, or Jack Shepherd, or Gulliver, or Robinson Crusoe, are mixed up with the prose tales. No part of the story of Wallace, as told in the "Scottish chiefs," or of "Waverley," is to be found in popular history. There is nothing like "The Mysteries of London." There are none of the modern horrors of which ballads have been made, such as "Sad was the day when James Greenacre first got acquainted with Sarah Gale." There are no gorgeous palaces, and elegant fairies; there are no enchanters flying in chariots drawn by winged griffins; there are no gentle knights and noble dames; no spruce cavaliers and well-dressed ladies; no heroes and heroines of fashionable novels; but, on the contrary, everything is popular. Heroes are as wild, and unkempt, and savage as they probably were in fact, and kings are men as they appear in Lane's translations of the Arabian Nights.

Eastern tale tellers knew what Haroun al Raschid must have suffered when he put on the fisherman's clothes, and Mr. Lane has not scrupled to follow the original Arabic.

If the people of the West Highlands have added book stories to their traditions, they have selected those only which were taken from peasants like themselves in other countries, and they have stripped off all that was foreign to their own manners. The people have but taken back their own.

Besides books accessible to all English readers, I find similar stories in books beyond the reach of the people. I have pointed out in the notes all that were within my reach, and came under my notice ; but this part of the subject is a study, and requires time to acquire knowledge which I do not possess.

Such, then, is the evidence which bears on the immediate origin of the stories. I believe them to be pure traditions, very little affected by modern books, and, if at all, only by those which are avowedly taken from popular tales. A trip of five days in the Isle of Man in April 1860 has but confirmed this opinion.

That island, in spite of its numerous rulers, is still peculiarly Celtic. It has belonged to Norwegians. English, Scotch, Welsh, and Irish have fought for it. It has a Law Court with a Norwegian name held on a mound ; half the names in the island are Norse, such as Laxey (Salmon isthmus), Langness, Snafell ; but these names are not understood by the people who live at the places. Peel has a descriptive Gaelic name, which means island port ; a Salmon is Braddan, not Lax; and of the poorer classes living in the mountain farms, and on the points and distant corners of the island, there are still many who can hardly speak anything but Manks. Their hair is dark ; the sound of their voices,

even their houses, are Celtic. I know one turf dwelling
which might be a house in North Uist. There was the
fire on the floor, the children seated around it, the
black haired Celtic mother on a low stool in front,—
the hens quarrelling about a nest under the table, in
which several wanted to lay eggs at once.

"Get out, Polly! Drive her out, John!" And
then John, the son, drove out Polly, the hen, with a
stick; and the hen said, "Gurr-r-m;" and ran in under
the table again and said, "Cluck, cluck," and laid the
egg then and there. There was the same kindly, hospi-
table manner in the poorest cottage; and I soon found
that a Scotch Highlander could speak Manks as soon as
he could acquire the art of mispronouncing his own language to the right amount, and learn where to introduce
the proper English word. "La fine"—fine day—was
the salutation everywhere; and the reply, "Fine, fine."
But though nouns are almost the same, and the language is but a dialect of Gaelic, the foreigner was
incomprehensible, because he could not pronounce as
they did; and I was reduced to English. Now this
island is visited every summer by shoals of visitors
from the mainland; steam-boats bring them from
Liverpool, a thousand at a time, and they sweep over the
whole country. If visitors import stories, here, there
are plenty of strangers, and I was a stranger myself.
If stories are imported in books, here are the books also.
The first picture I saw on landing was a magnificent Bluebeard in a shop window. He was dressed as an Eastern
potentate, and about to slice off his wife's head with a
crooked scimitar, while the two brothers rode up to the
gate on prancing steeds, with horror on their faces and
swords in their hands. But there was not a trace of
any of that kind of story to be found amongst the
peasants with whom I spoke in the Isle of Man.

I found them willing to talk, eager to question, kindly, homely folk, with whom it was easy to begin an acquaintance. I heard everywhere that it *used* to be common to hear old men telling stories about the fire in Manks; but any attempt to extract a story, or search out a queer old custom, or a half-forgotten belief, seemed to act as a pinch of snuff does on a snail.

The Manksman would not trust the foreigner with his secrets; his eye twinkled suspiciously, and his hand seemed unconsciously to grasp his mouth, as if to keep all fast. After getting quite at ease with one old fellow over a pipe, and having learned that a neighbour's cow had born a calf to the " Taroo ustey," water bull, I thought I might fish for a story, and told one as a bait.

"That man, if he had two pints, would tell you stories by the hour," said a boy. " Oh, yes, they used to tell plenty of stories," said the old man, " Skyll as we call them."

Here was the very word mispronounced, " sgeul," so my hopes rose. " Will you tell me a story now ?" " Have you any churches in your country ?" " Yes, and chapels; but will you tell me a story ?" " What you got to sell in your bag ?" " What a shame now, for you, an old mananach, not to tell me a story when I have told you one, and filled your pipe and all." " What do you pay for the tobacco ?" " Oh, will you not tell the man a story !" said the boy. " I must go and saw now," said the old man; and so we parted.

But though this was the usual thing, it was not always so; and it soon became evident that the stories given in Train's history of the Isle of Man, are nearly all known to the people now; and these are of the same nature as some known in the Highlands of Scot-

land ; some are almost identical ; and nearly all the
Manks customs are common to the Western Isles.

Thus I heard of Fairies, "Ferish," who live in green
mounds, and are heard at times dressing mill-stones in
haunted mills ; of Taroo Ustey, the water bull ; of
Dinny Mara, the sea man, and of the Mermaid ; of
Caval Ustey, the water horse ; of Fion MacCooil ; of
a city under the waves ; of a magic island seen in the
far west.   I heard of giants.   No one would tell
about them ; but in a book I found how Goddard
Crovan threw a vast boulder at his scolding wife,
and how a Norman baron, named " Kitter " and
his cook ; " Faoch," and his magic sword, " Macubain,"
made by " Loan Maclibhuin, the dark smith of Drontheim ;" and " Hiallus-nan-urd, the one-legged hammer-
man"—are all woven into a story, and mixed up with
such Norwegian names as Olave and Emergaid, exactly
as a story is jumbled together in the Western Isles of
Scotland.

I got some stories which I have not found in the
Manks books, so I give them here, in the hope that
some Manksman may be induced to gather the popular lore of his own country.   This from a woman who
lives near the Calf of Man.

" Did you ever hear tell of the Glashan ? "

" No ; tell me about the Glashan."

" Well, you see, in the old times they used to be keeping the
sheep in the folds ; and one night an old man forgot to put them
in, and he sent out his son, and he came back and said the sheep
were all folded, but there was a year-old lamb, oasht playing the
mischief with them ; and that was the glashan.

" You see they were very strong, and when they wanted a
stack threshed, though it was a whole stack, the glashan would
have it threshed for them in one night.

" And they were running after the women.   There was one
of them once caught a girl, and had a hould of her by the dress,

and he sat down and he fell asleep; and then she cut away all
the dress, you see, round about, this way, and left it in his fist
and ran away; and when he awoke, he threw what he had over
his shoulder, this way; and he said (something in Manks which
I could not catch).

"Well, you see, one night the ould fellow sent all the women
to bed, and he put on a cap and a woman's dress, and he sat
down by the fire and he began to spin; and the young glashans,
they came in, and they began saying something in Manks that
means 'Are you turning the wheel? are you trying the reel?'
Well, the ould glashan, he was outside, and he knew better than
the young ones; he knew it was the ould fellow himself, and he
was telling them, but they did not mind him; and so the ould
man threw a lot of hot turf, you see, it was turf they burned then,
over them and burned them; and the ould one said (something
in Manks). 'You'll not understand that, now?' 'Yes, I do,
pretty nearly.' 'Ah, well.' And so the glashans went away and
never came back any more."

"Have you many stories like that, guidwife?" "Ah," said
she, "there were plenty of people that could tell these stories
once. When I was a little girl, I used to hear them telling them
in Manks over the fire at night; but people is so changed with
pride now that they care for nothing."

Now here is a story which is all over the Highlands in various shapes. Sometimes it is a Brollichan
son of the Fuath, or a young water horse transformed into
the likeness of a man, which attacks a lonely woman,
and gets burned or scalded, and goes away to his
friends outside. In the islands, the woman generally
says her name is myself; and the goblin answers,
when asked who burned him, "myself." This Manks
story is manifestly the same, though this incident is
left out. I have heard it in Lewes, and in many places
besides, and part of it is best omitted.

The Glashan, as I found out afterwards, frequented
neighbouring farms till within a very late period. He
wore no clothes, and was hairy; and, according to

Train's history, Phynoddepee, which means something hairy, was frightened away by a gift of clothes,— exactly as the Skipness long-haired Gruagach was frightened away by the offer of a coat and a cap. The Manks brownie and the Argyllshire one each repeated a rhyme over the clothes ; but the rhymes are not the same, though they amount to the same thing.

Here, then, is a Gaelic popular tale and belief in Man ; and close to it I found a story which has a counterpart in Grimm. I heard it from my landlady at Port Erin, and I met two Manksmen afterwards who knew it—

" The fish all gathered once to choose a king ; and the fluke, him that has the red spots on him, stayed at home to make himself pretty, putting on his red spots, to see if he would be king, and he was too late, for when he came the herring was king of the sea. So the fluke curled his mouth on one side, and said, ' A simple fish like the herring, king of the sea !' and his mouth has been to one side ever since."

It seems, too, that the Manks version of " Jack the Giant Killer " varies from the English ; for

" Jack the Giant Killer,"

" Varv a Vuehd in the river,"

killed a pig in the river; and the English hero did nothing of the sort. In short, the Isle of Man has its own legends, which have their own peculiarities; they resemble others, and do not seem to be taken from books. The same class of people tell them there as elsewhere ; the difficulty of getting at them is the same ; and the key to the secret is the native language. From what I gleaned in a five days' walk, I am sure that a good Manksman might yet gather a large harvest within a very narrow space. And now to return to my own subject.

I find that men of all ranks resemble each other; that each branch of popular lore has its own special votaries, as branches of literature have amongst the learned; that one man is the peasant historian and tells of the battles of the clans; another, a walking peerage, who knows the descent of most of the families in Scotland, and all about his neighbours and their origin; others are romancers, and tell about the giants; others are moralists, and prefer the sagacious prose tales, which have a meaning, and might have a moral; a few know the history of the Feni, and are antiquarians. Many despise the whole as frivolities; they are practical moderns, and answer to practical men in other ranks of society.

But though each prefers his own subject, the best Highland story-tellers know specimens of all kinds. Start them, and it seems as if they would never stop. I timed one, and he spoke for an hour without pause or hesitation, or verbal repetition. His story was Connall Gulban, and he said he could repeat fourscore. He recited a poem, but despised "Bardism;" and he followed me six miles in the dark to my inn, to tell me numbers 19 and 20, which I have condensed; for the very same thing can be shortly told when it is not a composition. For example.

In telling a story, narrative and dialogue are mixed; what the characters have told each other to do is repeated as narrative. The people in the story tell it to each other, and branch off into discussions about their horses and houses and crops, or anything that happens to turn up. One story grows out of another, and the tree is almost hidden by a foliage of the speaker's invention. Here and there comes a passage repeated by rote, and common to many stories, and to every good narrator. It seems to act as a rest for the memory. Now and then, an observation from the audience starts an argument. In short, one good story in the mouth of a good narrator, with a good audience, might easily go rambling on for a whole winter's night, as it is said to do.

The " Slim Swarthy Champion used to last for four hours." Connall Gulban " used to last for three evenings. Those that wanted to hear the end had to come back." One of my collectors said it would take him a month to write it down, but I am bound to add that he has since done it in a very much shorter time. I have heard of a man who fell asleep by the fire, and found a story going on when he awoke next morning. I have one fragment on which (as I am told) an old man in Ross-shire used to found twenty-four stories, all of which died with him.

. There are varieties in public speakers amongst the people as amongst their representatives, for some are eloquent, some terse, some prosy.

But though a tale may be spun out to any extent, the very same incidents can be, and often are, told in a few words, and those tales which have been written for me are fair representations of them as they are usually told. They are like a good condensed report of a rambling speech, with extraneous matter left out. One narrator said of the longest story which I had then got—" It is but the contents ;" but I have more than once asked a narrator to tell me the story which he had previously told to one of my collectors, and a collector to write down a story which I had previously heard, and I have always found the pith, often the very words. In no instance have I found anything added by those whom I employed, when their work was subjected to this severe test.

This is the account which one of my collectors gives of the old customs of his class—he is a workman employed by the Duke of Argyll ; he tells me that he

d

is self-educated ; and as he repeats some of the stories which he has written, from memory, his account of the way in which he acquired them is valuable.

I remember, upwards of fifty years ago, when I was a boy, my father lived in the farest north house, in the valley called Glen-na Callanach. I also used to be with my granfather; he lived near Terbert, Lochlomond side. I remember, in the winter nights, when a few old people would be togather, they would pass the time with telling each other stories, which they had by tradition. I used to listen attentively, and hear them telling about the ceatharnaich, or freebooters, which used to come to plunder the country, and take away cattle ; and how their ancestors would gather themselves togather to fight for their property, the battles they fought, and the kind of weapons they used to fight with ; the manners of their ancestors, the dress they used to wear, and different hardships they had to endure.

I was also sometimes amused, listening to some people telling Gaelic romances, which we called sgeulachds. It was customary for a few youngsters to gather into one house, and whither idle or at some work, such as kniting stockings or spinning, they would amuse each other with some innocent diversion, or telling sgeulachds. Us that was chieldren was very fond of listening to them, and the servant maid that was in my father's house would often tell us a sgeulachd to keep us queit.

In those days, when people killed their Marte cow they keept the hide, and tanned it for leather to themselves. In those days every house was furnished with a wheel and a reel ; the women spun, and got their webs woven by a neighbouring weaver ; also, the women was dyers for themselves, so that the working class had their leather, their linen, and their cloth of their own manufacturing ; and when they required the help of a shoemaker, or of a tailor, they would send for them. The tailors and shoemakers went from house to house, to work wherever they were required, and by travelling the country so much, got aquaint with a great maney of the traditionary tales, and divulged them through the country ; and as the country people made the telling of these tales, and listening to hear them, their winter night's amusement, scarcely aney part of them would be lost. Some of

these romances is supposed to be of great antiquity, on account
of some of the Gaelic words being out of use now. I remember,
about forty years ago, of being in company with a man that was
watching at night; he wished me to stop with him, and he told
me a (sgeulachd) romance; and last year I heard a man telling
the same story, about therty miles distante from where I had
heard it told forty years before that; and the man which told
me the tale could not tell me the meaning of some of the old
Gaelic words that was in it. At first I thought they were foreign
words, but at last I recollected to have heard some of them repeated in Ossian's poems, and it was by the words that was
before, and after them, that I understood the meaning of them.
The same man told me another story, which he said he learned
from his granfather, and Denmark, Swedden, and Noraway was
named in it in Gaelic, but he forgot the name of the two last-
named places.

It appears likely to me, that some of these tales was invented
by the Druids, and told to the people as sermons; and by these
tales the people was caused to believe that there was fairies which
lived in little conical hills, and that the fairies had the power of
being either visible or invisible, as they thought proper, and that
they had the power of enchanting people, and of taking them
away and make fairies of them; and that the Druids had charms
which would prevent that; and they would give these charms to the
people for payment; and maney stories would be told about people
being taken away by the fairies, and the charms which had to
be used to break the spell, and get them back again; and others,
on account of some neglidgeance, never got back aney more.

Also that there was witches; people which had communica-
tion with an evil spirit, from which they got the power of changing themselves into aney shape they pleased; that these witches
often put themselves in the shape of beasts, and when they were
in the shape of beasts, that they had some evil design in view,
and that it was dangerous to meet them. Also that they could,
and did, sometimes take away the produce of people's dairy, and
sometimes of the whole farm. The Druidical priests pretended
that they had charms that would prevent the witches from doing
aney harm, and they would give a charm for payment. When
the first day of summer came, the people was taught to put the

fire out of their houses, and to place it on some emince near the house for to keep away the witches, and that it was not safe for them to kindle a fire in their house aney more, until they bought it from beil' s druide. That fire was called beil-teine (beils-fire), and the first day of summer was called beil-fires day ; and also when the first night of winter came, the people would gather fuel and make blazing fire for to keep away the witches, or at least to deprive them of the power of taking away the produce of the farm, and then they would go to the Druid and buy a kindling of what was called the holy fire. The Druids also caused the people to believe that some families had been enchanted and changed into beasts, and as the proper means had not been used, the spell was never broken ; and that swans, seals, and mar-maids had been different beings, familys that had been enchanted.

Beil or Beul was the name which the Druids gave their god, and the Druids of Beil pretended to be the friends of the people ; they pretended to have charms to cure different kinds of diseases, and also charms to prevent fairies, ghosts, and witches, from annoying or harming people. It is a well-known fact, that the superstitions of the Druids has been handed down from genera-tion to generation for a great many ages, and is not wholy extinct yet ; and we have reason to believe that some of the tales, which was invented in those days for to fright the people, has been told and kept in rememberance in the selt and same manner. The priests of Beil was the men that was called Druids, the miracles which they pretended to perform was called meur-bheilcachd (beil-fingering), and their magic which they pretended to perform was called druichd (druidisem), and we have plenty of reason to believe superstitious tales as well as superstition, originated among the Druids.   John Dewar.

  " J. Campbell, Esq.
  " Sir—I hope you will corect aney errors that you may find on this piece which I wrote."

I have corrected only two or three errors in spelling, and the writing is remarkably clear, but I have left some words which express the Gaelic pronunciation of English.

The derivation of Miorbhuil, *a marvel*, from the finger of Bel, was suggested by Dr. Smith (see Armstrong's Dic.) J.F.C.

Now let me return to the cottage of old Macphie, where I heard a version of the Sea-Maiden, and let me suppose that one of the rafters is the drift log which I saw about to be added to a roof in the same island.

The whole roof is covered with peat soot, but that may be scraped away, and the rough wood appears. There are the holes of boring sea shells, filled with sand and marine products. It is evident that the log came by sea, that it did not come in a ship, and that it was long enough in warm salt water for the barnacles to live and die, and for their dwellings to be filled with sea rubbish; that it floated through latitudes where barnacles live. The fairy eggs, which are picked up on the same shore, point to the West Indies as a stage on the way. Maps of ocean currents shew the gulf-stream flowing from the Gulf of Mexico past the Hebrides, but the tree is a fir, for there is a bit of bark which proves the fact, and it appears that pines grow between 40° and 60° in America. It is therefore possible that the rafter was once an American fir tree, growing in the Rocky Mountains; that it was swept into the Mississippi, and carried to the Gulf of Mexico; drifted by the gulf-stream past the West India Islands to the Hebrides, and stranded by a western gale on its voyage to Spitzbergen. But all this must have happened long ago, for it is now a rafter covered with the soot of generations. That rafter is a strange fact, it is one of a series, and has to be accounted for. There it is, and a probable account of its journey is, that it came from East to West without the help of man, in obedience to laws which govern the world.

That smoked rafter certainly was once a seed in a fir-cone, somewhere abroad. It grew to be a pine tree; it must have been white with snow in winter, and green in summer, and glittering with rain drops and hoar-frost in bright sunshine at various times and seasons. The number of years it stood in the forest can be counted by the rings in the wood. It is certain that it was torn up by the roots, for the roots are there still. It may have formed a part of one of these wonderful natural rafts of the Mississippi, of which one in 1816 was "no less than ten miles in length, two hundred and twenty yards wide, and eight feet deep."* It has been to warm seas, and has worn a marine dress of green and brown since it lost its own natural dress of green branches. Birds must have sat on it in the forest,—crabs and shells have lived on it at sea, and fish must have swam about it ; and yet it is now a rafter, hung with black pendants of peat smoke. A tree that grew beside it may now be in Spitzbergen amongst walrusses. Another may be a snag in the Mississippi amongst alligators, destined to become a fossil tree in a coal field. Part of another may be a Yankee rocking chair, or it may be part of a ship in any part of the World, or the tram of a cart, or bit of a carriage, or a wheel-barrow, or a gate post, or anything that can be made of fir wood anywhere ; and the fate of stories may be as various as that of fir trees, but their course may be guessed at by running a back scent overland, as I have endeavoured to follow the voyage of a drift log over sea.

Macphie's story began thus :—" There was a poor old fisher in Skye, and his name was Duncan ; " and every version of the story which I have found in the Highlands, and I have found many, is as highland as the peat-reek on the rafters. The same story is known in many districts in Scotland, and it is evident, that it has been known there for many years. It is a curious fact. It is worth the trouble of looking under what is purely highland, to see if its origin can be discovered.

* Lyell's Principles of Geology, p. 267.

First, then, the incidents are generally strung together in a particular order in the Highlands, but, either separately or together, every incident in the story is to be found in some shape in other languages. Norse has it as "Shortshanks." Irish has it. German has it. It is in the Italian of Straparola as "Fortunio." In the French of le Cabinet des Feés, 1785. It is in every language in Europe as "St. George and the Dragon." It is in Mr. Peter Buchan's English of 1847 as part of "Greensleeves." It is in "Perseus and Andromeda." The scene of that story is placed in Syria, and it is connected with Persia. There is something in Sanscrit about Indra, a god who recovered the stolen cattle of the gods, but here the scent is very cold, and the hound at fault, though it seems that the Sanscrit hero was the sun personified, and that he had horses of many colours, including red and white, which were always feminine, as the horses in Gaelic stories are, and which had wings and flew through the air. These were "Svankas," with beautiful steps. "Rohitas," red or brown; Gaelic, horses are often described as "Seang," "Ruadh;" and here seems to be a clue which is worth the attention of Eastern scholars.

There is a mermaid in the story, and mermaids are mentioned in Irish, and in Arabic, and in Manks, and Italian: men even assert that they have seen mermaids in the sea within the last few years, amongst the Hebrides and off Plymouth.

There are creatures, Falcon, Wolf and Lion. Two of them were natives within historic times, one is still; but the third is a foreigner. There is an Otter, and a Sea Monster, and in other tales, there are Bears and Doves, and other animals; but every one of them, except the monster, is to be found on the road to the land where Sanscrit was spoken, and all these, and many more, play their part in popular tales elsewhere, while no real animal is ever mentioned which is peculiar to lands out of the road which leads overland to India.

Nearly all these have Gaelic names, and most of them are still living within a few days' journey of the Hebrides under other names. I saw a live wolf from a diligence one fine morning in Brittany, and I have seen bears in Scandinavia and in Germany. The only far-fetched animal is the Lion, and in another story a similar creature appears as " Cu Seang." Here is a fresh scent—for Sing is Lion in India—and *may* once have meant Lion in Gaelic; for though Leomhan is the word now used, Seang is applied to anything slender and active. Shune is a dog in Sanscrit, Siunnach a fox in Gaelic, and there are many other Gaelic words which point to the " eastern origin of Celtic nations." The story cannot have crossed the sea from the West. It is therefore probable that it came from the East, for it is not of home growth, and the question is, how did it get to Barra ?

It seems to have been known along a certain track for many ages. It is possible that it came from the far East with the people, and that it has survived ever since. It is hard to account for it otherwise. Those who have most studied the subject so account for popular tales elsewhere, and, therefore, John Macphie's story of the Sea-Maiden acquires an interest not all its own.

Much has been written, and said, and discovered about the popular migrations which have poured from East to West, and which are moving on still. Philology has mapped out the course of the human stream, and here, in the mind of an old fisherman, unable to

read, or to speak any language but his own, is the end
of a clue which seems to join Iran and Eirinn ; as a
rafter in his hut may link him with the Rocky Mountains.

Admit that this so-called fiction, and others like it,
may be traditions, which have existed from the earliest
of times, and every word and incident acquires an interest, for it may lead to something else.

The story certainly grew in the mind of man, as a
tree grows from a seed, but when or where ? It has certainly been told in many languages. It is worth inquiring how many races have told it.

The incidents, like drift trees, have been associated
with people and events, as various as birds, fish, alligators, walrusses, and men ; mountain ranges, and ocean
currents. They have passed through the minds of Ovid
and John Macphie. They have been adorned by
poets, painted by artists, consecrated by priests,—
for St. George is the patron saint of England ; and
now we find that which may have sprung from some
quarrel about a cow, and which has passed through
so many changes, dropping into forgetfulness in the
mind of an old fisherman, and surrounded with the
ideas which belong to his every-day life. Ideas differing from those of the people who first invented the
story, as the snow of the Rocky Mountains differs from
peat-reek.

Now, to look forwards, and follow in imagination
the shoals of emigrants from Germany, Scandinavia,
France, Ireland, and Scotland, who are settled in
clumps, or scattered over America and Australia ; to
think of the stories which have been gathered in
Europe from these people alone, and which they have
most certainly carried with them, and will tell their
children ; and then the route of popular tales here-

after, and their spread in former ages, can be traced and may be guessed.

I have inquired, and find that several Islanders, who used to tell the stories in Gaelic, are now settled in Australia and Canada. One of my relatives was nearly overwhelmed with hospitality in an Australian village, by a colony of Argyllshire Celts, who had found out that he was a countryman.

I was lately told of a party of men who landed in South America, and addressed a woman whom they found in a hut, in seven different languages; but in vain. At last, one of them spoke Gaelic, which he had not done for many years, and she answered, " Well, it is to thyself I would give the speech," for she was a native of Strathglas.

There is a Gaelic population in Upper Canada: there are Highland regiments in India: many of the Arctic explorers were Highlanders, and most of the servants of the Hudson's Bay Company still are : Dr. Livingstone is in South Africa ; and what is true of Highlanders is equally true of Germans and Scandinavians, they are spread over the world. In short, the "migration of races," and "the diffusion of popular tales," is still going on, the whole human race is mingling together, and it is fair to argue from such facts, and to try to discover that which is unknown from that which is proved.

What is true of one Gaelic story is true of nearly all ; they contain within themselves evidence that they have been domesticated in the country for a long time, and that they came from the East, but they belong to the people now, wherever they came from ; and they seem also to belong to the language.

Poems and compositions clearly do. In the prose tales, when animals speak, they talk in their natural

key, so long as they speak Gaelic, and for that reason,
among others, I believe them to be old traditions.
The little birds speak in the key of all little birds (ee) ;
they say, "beeg, beeg." The crow croaks his own
music when he says, " gawrag, gawrag." When driven
to say, " silly, silly," he no longer speaks the language
of nature. Grimm's German frog says, " warte, warte,"
he sings, " mach mir auf," and talks his own language.
So does his Gaelic relative, in No. 33, when he says,—

> " A chaomhag a chaomhag
> An cuimhne ach leat
> An gealladh beag
> A thug thu aig
> An tobar Dhomh
> A ghaoil a ghaoil."

He then imitates the quarking and gurgling of real
frogs in a pond in spring, in sounds which no Saxon
letters can express ; but when he sings,—

> " Open the door, my hinney, my heart,
> Open the door, my ain wee thing,
> And mind the words that you and I spak',
> Down in the meadow, at the well spring,"

he is speaking in a foreign tongue, though the story
has been domesticated in the Lowlands of Scotland for
many a long day, and is commonly told there still.
The Scotch story has probably been found and polished
by some one long ago, but when the frog comes
" loup, louping," he is at home in Low Country Scotch,
and these words are probably as old as the story and
the language.

If Motherwell's beautiful nursery songs were to
be collected from oral recitation anywhere, they would
prove themselves Scotch by this test : The watch-dog
says, " wouff, wouff ;" the hen is " chuckie ;" the

chickens, "wheetle, wheeties;" the cock is "cockie-leerie-law;" the pigeon, "croodle-doo;" the cow says, "moo." And so also the wood-pigeon who said, "take two sheep, Taffy take two," spoke English; but the blackcock, and cuckoo, and cock, in the Norse tales, who quarrelled about a cow, are easily known to be foreigners when they speak English, for the original Norse alone gives their true note. The Gaelic stories, tried by this test, certainly belong to the language as they do to the people; and now let us see if they can teach us anything about the people, their origin, and their habits, past and present.

First, the manners are generally those of the day. The tales are like the feasts of the pauper maniac, Emperor of the world, who confided to his doctor that all his rich food tasted of oatmeal brose. Kings live in cottages, and sit on low stools. When they have coaches, they open the door themselves. The queen saddles the king's horse. The king goes to his own stable when he hears a noise there. Sportsmen use guns. The fire is on the floor. Supernatural old women are found spinning "beyond" it, in the warm place of honour, in all primitive dwellings, even in a Lapland tent. The king's mother puts on the fire, and sleeps in the common room, as a peasant does. The cock sleeps on the rafters, the sheep on the floor, the bull behind the door. A ladder is a pole, with pegs stuck through it. Horses put their noses "into" bridles. When all Ireland passes in review before the princess, they go in at the front door and out at the back, as they would through a bothy; and even that unexplained personage, the daughter of the king of the skies, has maids who chatter to her as freely as maids do to Highland mistresses. When the prince is at death's door for love of the beautiful lady in the swan's down robe, and the queen mother is in despair, she goes to the kitchen to talk over the matter.

The tales represent the actual, every-day life of those who tell them, with great fidelity. They have done the same, in all likelihood, time out of mind, and that which is not true of the present is, in all probability, true of the past ; and therefore something may be learned of forgotten ways of life.

If much is of home growth, if the fight with the dragon takes place at the end of a dark, quiet Highland loch, where real whales actually blow and splash, there are landscapes which are not painted from nature, as she is seen in the Isles, and these may be real pictures seen long ago by our ancestors. Men ride for days through forests, though the men who tell of them live in small islands, where there are only drift trees and bog pine. There are traces of foreign or forgotten laws or customs. A man buys a wife as he would a cow, and acquires a right to shoot her, which is acknowledged as good law.

Cæsar tells of the Gauls, that " men have the power of life and death over their wives, as well as their children." It appears that an Icelandic betrothal was little more than the purchase of a wife ; and in this the story may be a true picture of the past.

Men are bound with the binding of the three smalls—waist, ankles, and wrists—tightened and tortured. The conqueror almost invariably asks the conquered what is his " eirig," an old law term for the price of men's blood, which varied with the rank of the injured man ; and when the vanquished has revealed his riches, the victor takes his life, and the spoil ; his arms, combs, basins, dresses, horses, gold and silver, and such deeds may have been done. The tales which treat of the wars of Eirinn and Lochlann,

and are full of metrical prose, describe arms and boats,
helmets, spears, shields, and other gear ; ships that are
drawn on shore, as Icelandic ships really were ; boats
and arms similar to those which are figured on old
stones in Iona and elsewhere, and are sometimes dug
out of old graves and peat mosses. I believe them to
be descriptions of real arms, and dresses, manners, and
events.

For example, the warriors always abuse each other
before they fight. So do the heroes of Ossian; so do
the heroes of Homer; so do soldiers now. In the *Times*
of the 29th of December 1859, in a letter from the
camp at Ceuta is this passage :—

"While fighting, even when only exchanging long shots, the
Moors keep up a most hideous howling and shrieking, vituperat-
ing their enemies in bad Spanish, and making the mountains re-
sound with the often-repeated epithet of "*perros*" (dogs.) To
this the Spaniards condescend not to reply, except with bullets,
although in the civil war it was no unusual thing to hear Carlist
and Christina skirmishers abusing each other, and especially in-
dulging in unhandsome reflections upon each others' Sovereign."

Again, the fights are single combats, in which individuals attack masses and conquer. So were the
Homeric combats. What will be the story told in
Africa by the grandson of the Moor here described,
when he sits on his flat roof or in his central court in
Tetuan, as I have done with one of the Jews now ruined ;
he will surely tell of his ancestor's deeds, repeat the
words in which Achmed abused the unbeliever, and
tell how he shot some mystical number of them with
a single ball.

"Upon the whole they stood their ground very stoutly, and
some of them gave proof of great courage, advancing singly along
the ridge until they caught sight of the first Spaniards posted
below it, when they discharged their *espingardas* and retreated."

"Stories" had begun in Morocco by the 9th of
January 1860, when the next letter appeared :—

"The Moors have been giving out fantastical histories of their
victories over the Spaniards, of their having taken redoubts,
which they might have held had they thought it worth while,
and in which they would have captured guns if the Christians
had not been so prudent as to remove them beforehand. These
are mere fables."

It may be so, but Moors seem to have fought as
wild, brave, undisciplined troops have always fought—
as Homer's Greeks fought, as Highlanders fought, and
as Fionn and his heroes fought, according to tradition.
Omit the magic of Maghach Colgar, forget that Moors
are dark men, and this might be an account of Diarmaid and Conan in the story, or of their descendants
as they were described in 1745 by those who were
opposed to them :—

"The Moors are generally tall powerful men, of ferocious
aspect and great agility, and their mode of coming on, like so
many howling savages, is not calculated to encourage and give
confidence to lads who for the first time find themselves in action.
It seems nearly impossible to make them prisoners. In one encounter (most of these little actions are made up of a number of
small fights between a few companies of Spaniards and detached
bodies of the Moors, who seem to have no idea of attacking in
battalion or otherwise than irregularly), in which a number of
Moors were killed, one of them was surrounded by four Caza-
dores, who came down upon him with fixed bayonets, shouting
and signing to him not to fire, and that they would give him
quarter. The Moor took no heed of their overtures, levelled his
long gun, and shot one of them, whereupon he was, of course, put
to death by the others."

So, looking to facts now occurring, and to history,
"traditional fictions" look very true, for battles are still
a succession of single combats, in which both sides

abuse each other, and after which they boast.   War is rapine and cruel bloodshed, as described by old fishermen in Barra, and by the *Times'* correspondent at Tetuan ; and it is not altogether the chivalrous pastime which poets have sung.

In another class of tales, told generally as plain narrative, and which seem to belong to savage times, a period appears to be shadowed out when iron weapons were scarce, and therefore magical ; perhaps before the wars of Eirinn and Lochlann began ; when combs were inventions sufficiently new and wonderful to be magical also ; when horses were sacred, birds sooth-sayers ; apples, oak trees, wells, and swine, sacred or magical.   In these the touch of the cold steel breaks all spells ; to relieve an enchanted prince it was but necessary to cut off his head ; the touch of the cold sword froze the marrow when the giant's heads leaped on again.   So Hercules finished the Hydra with iron, though it was hot.   The white sword of light which shone so that the giant's red-haired servant used it as a torch when he went to draw water by night, was surely once a rare bright steel sword, when most swords were of bronze, as they were in early times, unless it is still older, and a mythological flash of lightning.

This CLAIDHEAMH GEAL SOLUIS is almost always mentioned as the property of giants, or of other super-natural beings, and is one of the magic gifts for which men contend with them, and fight with each other ; and in this the Gaelic tradition agrees with other popular lore.

Fionn had a magic sword forged by a fairy smith, according to a story sent me from Islay, by Mr. Car-michael. King Arthur had a magic sword. The Manks hero, "Olave" of Norway, had a sword with a Celtic name, "Macabuin," made by a smith who was surely a Celt,—" Loan Maclibhuin," though he was " The dark Smith of Drontheim " in the story.* King Arthur and his sword belong to the Bretons and to many other languages, besides Welsh ; and the Bretons have a wild war song, " The wine of the Gauls, and the dance of the sword," which is given in Barzaz Breiz (1846).†

There is a magic sword in the Volsung tale, called " Gram," which was the gift of Odin ;‡ and a famous sword in the Niebelungen lied ; and there are famous swords in many popular tales ; but an iron sword was a god long ago amongst the Scythians.§ "An antique iron sword " was placed on a vast pile of brushwood as a temple in every district, at the seat of government, and served as the image of Mars. Sacrifices of cattle and of horses were made to it, and " more victims were offered thus than to all the rest of their gods." Even men were sacrificed ; and it is said that the weapons found in Scythian tombs are usually of bronze, " but the sword at the great tomb at Kertch was of iron."

* Train's History of the Isle of Man, vol. 2, p. 177.

† The Gaelic word for a sword proves that English, French, Breton, and Gaelic have much in common—(Eng.) glave, (Fr.) glaive, (Breton) korol ar c' hleze—dance of the sword, (Gaelic) claidheamh—pronounced, glaiv, the first letter being a soft " c," or hard " g," the word usually spelt, *clay*more. Languages said to be derived from Latin do not follow their model so closely as these words do one another—(Lat.) gladius, (Spanish) espada, (Italian) spada ; and the northern tongues seem to have preferred some original which resembles the English word, sword. If " spada" belongs to the language from which all these are supposed to have started, these seem to have used it for a more peaceful iron weapon, a spade.

‡ Norse Tales, Introduction, 62.

§ At page 53 of Rawlinson's Herodotus, vol. 3, is the trans- lation of the passage in which this worship is described.

e

It seems, then, that an iron sword really was once worshipped by a people with whom iron was rare. Iron is rare, while stone and bronze weapons are common in British tombs, and the sword of these stories is a personage. It shines, it cries out—the lives of men are bound up in it. In one story a fox changes himself into the sword of light, and the edge of the real sword being turned towards a wicked "muime," turned all her spells back upon herself, and she fell a withered fagot.

And so this mystic sword may, perhaps, have been a god amongst the Celts, or the god of the people with whom Celts contended somewhere on their long journey to the west. It is a fiction now, but it may be founded on fact, and that fact probably was the first use of iron.

Amongst the stories described in the index to the Gaelic MSS. in Edinburgh is one in which the hero goes to Scythia and to Greece, and ends his adventures in Ireland. And in the "Chronicles of the Eri," 1822, by O'Connor, chief of the prostrated people of his nation," Irish is usually called "the Phœnician dialect of the Scythian language." On such questions I will not venture. Celts may or may not be Scythians, but as a collector of curiosities, I may fairly compare my museum with other curious things ; and the worship of the Scimitar, 2200 years ago, by a people who are classed with the Indo-European races, appears to have some bearing on all magic swords from the time of Herodotus down to the White Sword of Light of the West Highlands.

If iron weapons, to which supernatural virtues are ascribed, acquired their virtue when iron was rare, and when its qualities were sufficiently new to excite wonder—then other things made of iron should have

like virtues ascribed to them, and the magic should be
transferred from the sword to other new inventions ;
and such is the case.

In all popular tales of which I know anything,
some mysterious virtue is attributed to iron ; and in
many of them a gun is the weapon which breaks the
spells. In the West it is the same.

A keeper told me that he was once called into a
house by an old woman to cure her cow, which was
"bewitched," and which was really sick. The ceremony was performed, according to the directions of the
old woman, with becoming gravity. The cow was led
out, and the gun loaded, and then it was solemnly fired
off over the cow's back, and the cure was supposed to
be complete.

In the story of the hunter, when the widow's son
aims at the enchanted deer, he sees through the spell,
only when he looks over the sight, and while the gun
is cocked, but when he has aimed three times, the spell
is broken and the lady is free.

So in a story (I think Irish) which I have read
somewhere, a man shoots from his hip at a deer, which
seems to be an old man whenever he looks over the
sight. He aims well, and when he comes up finds
only the body of a very old man, which crumbles into
dust, and is carried away by the wind, bit by bit, as
he looks at it. An iron weapon is one of the guards
which the man takes into the fairy hill in the story of
the Smith, No. 28. A sharpshooter fires off his gun
to frighten the troll in " the Old Dame and her Hen ;"
the boy throws the steel from his tinder box over the
magic horse, and tames him at once in the Princess on
the Glass Hill.* And so on throughout, iron is invested
with magic power in popular tales and mythology ; the

* Norse Tales, Nos. 3 and 13.

last iron weapon invented, and the first, the gun and the sword, are alike magical ; a "bit of a rusty reaping hook" does equally good service, and an old horse shoe is as potent a spell against the powers of evil as any known ; for one will be found on most stable doors in England.

Now comes the question, Who were these powers of evil who cannot resist iron ? These fairies who shoot *stone* arrows, and are of the foes to the human race? Is all this but a dim hazy, recollection of war between a people who had iron weapons and a race who had not ? the race whose remains are found all over Europe ?

If these were wandering tribes they had leaders, if they were warlike they had weapons. There is a smith in the pantheon of many nations. Vulcan was a smith ; Thor wielded a hammer ; even Fionn had a hammer, which was heard in Lochlann when struck in Eirinn, according to the story found midway in Barra. Fionn may have borrowed his hammer from Thor long ago, or both may have got theirs from Vulcan, or all three may have brought hammers with them from the land where some primeval smith wielded the first sledge hammer, but may not all these smith gods be the smiths who made iron weapons for those who fought with the skin-clad warriors who shot flint arrows, and who are now bogles, fairies, and demons ?

In any case, tales about smiths seem to belong to mythology, and to be common property. Thus the Norse smith, who cheated the evil one,* has an Irish equivalent in the Three Wishes,† and a Gaelic story, "The Soldier," is of the same class, and has a Norse equivalent in the Lad and the Deil. There are many of the same class in Grimm ; and the same ideas pervade them all. There is war between the smiths and

* Norse Tales, 16, 53.　　† Carleton. Dublin, 1846. P. 330.

soldiers, and the devil ; iron, and horses' hoofs, hammers, swords, and guns come into play ; the fiend is a fool, and he has got the worst of the fight ; according to the people, at all events, ever since St. Dunstan took him by the nose with a pair of tongs. In all probability the fiend of popular tales is own brother to the Gruagach and Glashan, and was once a skin-clad savage, or the god of a savage race.

If this theory be correct, if these are dim recollections of savage times and savage people, then other magic gear, the property of giants, fairies, and bogles, should resemble things which are precious now amongst savage or half civilized tribes, or which really have been prized amongst the old inhabitants of these islands, or of other parts of the world ; and such is often the case.

The work of art which is most sought after in Gaelic tales, next to the white glave of light, is a pair of combs.

Cir min oir agus cir garbh airgiod, a fine golden comb and a coarse comb of silver, are worth a deadly fight with the giants in many a story.

The enchanted prince, when he ceases to be a raven, is found as a yellow ringletted beautiful man, with a golden comb in the one hand and a silver comb in the other. Maol a Chliobain invades the giant's house to steal the same things for the king. When the coarse comb is forgotten the king's coach falls as a withered faggot. In another story which I have, it is said of a herd who had killed a giant and taken his castle, " He went in and he opened the first room and there was not a thing in it. He opened another, and it was full of gold and silver and the treasures of the world. Then he opened a drawer, and he took a comb out of it, and when he would give a sweep with it on the one side of his head, a shower of gold would fall out of that side ; and when he would give a sweep on the other side, a shower of silver would fall from that side. Then he opened another room, and it was full of every sort of food that a man might think there had ever been."

And so in many other instances the comb is a treasure for which men contend with giants. It is associated with gold, silver, dresses, arms, meat, and drink ; and it is magical.

It is not so precious in other collections of popular tales, but the same idea is to be traced in them all. There is a water-spirit in Grimm which catches two children, and when they escape they throw behind them a brush, a comb, and a mirror, which replace the stone, the twig, and the bladder of water, which the Gaelic prince finds in the ear of the filly, and throws behind him to arrest the giant who is in pursuit. In the nix of the mill pond an old woman gives a golden comb to a lady, and she combs her black hair by the light of the moon at the edge of a pond, and the water-spirit shews the husband's head. So also in Snow White the wicked queen combs the hair of the beautiful princess with a poisoned comb, and throws her into a deadly magic sleep. That princess is black, white, and red, like the giant in No. 2, and like the lady in Conal ; and like a lady in a Breton story ; and generally foreign stories in which combs are mentioned as magical, have equivalents in Gaelic. For example, the incidents in the French story of Prince Cherie, in which gifted children comb jewels from their hair, bear a general resemblance to many Gaelic and German stories. Now there is a reason for everything, though it is not always easy to find it out ; and the importance of the comb in these stories may have a reason also.

In the first place, though every civilized man and

INTRODUCTION.lxxix

woman now owns a comb, it is a work of art which
necessarily implies the use of tools, and considerable
mechanical skill. A man who had nothing but a knife
could hardly make a comb; and a savage with flint
weapons would have to do without. A man with a
comb, then, implies a man who has made some progress
in civilization; and a man without a comb, a savage,
who, if he had learned its use, might well covet such a
possession. If a black-haired savage, living in the cold
north, were to comb his hair on a frosty night, it is to
be presumed that the same thing would happen which
now takes place when fair ladies or civilized men comb
their hair. Crackling sparks of electricity were surely
produced when men first combed their hair with a bone
comb; and it seems to need but a little fancy and a
long time to change the bright sparks into brilliant
jewels, or glittering gold and silver and bright stars,
and to invest the rare and costly thing which produced
such marvels with magic power.

There is evidence throughout all popular tales that
combs were needed. Translations are vague, because
translators are bashful; but those who have travelled
amongst half civilized people, understand what is meant
when the knight lays his head on the lady's knee, and
she "dresses his hair." In German, Norse, Breton, and
Gaelic, it is the same.

From the mention of the magic comb, then, it
appears that these legends date from an early, rude
period, for the time when combs were so highly prized,
and so little used, is remote.

In Wilson's prehistoric "Annals of Scotland," page
424, is a drawing of an old bone comb of very rude
workmanship, found in a burgh in Orkney, together
with part of a deer's horn and a human skeleton;
another was found in a burgh in Caithness; a third is

mentioned; and I believe that such combs are commonly found in old British graves.

At page 554, another drawing is given of one of a pair of combs found in a grave in Orkney. The teeth of the comb were fastened between plates of bone, rivetted together with copper nails, and the comb was decorated with ornamental carvings. With these, brooches of a peculiar form were discovered. Similar brooches are commonly found in Denmark. I have seen many of them in museums at Bergen and Copenhagen; and I own a pair which were found in an old grave in Islay, together with an amber bead and some fragments of rusted iron.

A bronze comb is also mentioned at page 300, as having been found in Queen Mary's Mount, a great cairn near the battlefield of Langsyde, which was pulled to pieces to build stone dykes, and which was found to contain rude arms, bones, rings of bituminous shale, and other things which are referred to very early prehistoric ages.

At page 500 Mr. Wilson mentions a great number of monuments in Scotland on which combs are represented, together with two-handed mirrors and symbols, for which deep explanations and hidden meanings have been sought and found. Combs, mirrors, and shears are also represented on early Roman tombs, and hidden meanings have been assigned to them; but Mr. Wilson holds that these are but indications of the sex of the buried person. Joining all this together, and placing it beside the *magic* attributed to combs in these Highland stories, this view appears to be the most reasonable. The sword of the warrior is very commonly sculptured on the old gravestones in the Western Isles. It is often twisted into a cross, and woven with those endless knots which resemble certain eastern designs.

Strange nondescript animals are often figured about the sword, with tails which curl, and twist, and sprout into leaves, and weave themselves into patterns. Those again resemble illuminations in old Irish and Gaelic manuscripts, and when the most prized of the warrior's possessions is thus figured on his tomb, and is buried with him, it is but reasonable to suppose that the comb, which was so valued as to be buried with its owner, was figured on the monument for the same reason ; and that sword and comb were, in fact, very highly prized at some period by those who are buried in the tombs, as the stories now represent that they were by men and giants.

So here again the popular fictions seem to have a foundation of fact.

Another magical possession is the apple. It is mentioned more frequently in Gaelic tales than in any collection which I know, but the apple plays its part in Italian, German, and Norse also. When the hero wishes to pass from Islay to Ireland, he pulls sixteen apples and throws them into the sea, one by one, and he steps from one to the other. When the giant's daughter runs away with the king's son, she cuts an apple into a mystical number of small bits, and each bit talks. When she kills the giant she puts an apple under the hoof of the magic filly and he dies, for his life is in the apple, and it is crushed. When the byre is cleansed, it is so clean that a golden apple would run from end to end and never raise a stain. There is a gruagach who has a golden apple which is thrown at all comers, and unless they are able to catch it they die ; when it is caught and thrown back by the hero, Gruagach an Ubhail dies. There is a game called cluich an ubhail, the apple play, which seems to have been a deadly game, whatever it was. When the king's

daughter transports the soldier to the green island on
the magic tablecloth, he finds magic apples which trans-
form him, and others which cure him, and by which he
transforms the cruel princess and recovers his magic
treasures. In German a cabbage does the same
thing.

When the two eldest idle king's sons go out to
herd the giant's cattle, they find an apple tree whose
fruit moves up and down as they vainly strive to
pluck it.

And so on throughout, whenever an apple is mentioned in Gaelic stories, it has something marvellous
about it.

So in German, in the Man of Iron, a princess
throws a golden apple as a prize, which the hero
catches three times and carries off and wins.

In Snow White, where the poisoned comb occurs,
there is a poisoned magic apple also.

In the Old Griffin, the sick princess is cured by
rosy-cheeked apples.

In the Giant with the Three Golden Hairs, one of
the questions to be solved is, why a tree which used
to bear golden apples does not now bear leaves? and
the next question is about a well.

So in the White Snake, a servant who acquires the
knowledge of the speech of birds by tasting a white
snake, helps creatures in distress, gets their aid, and
procures a golden apple from three ravens, which "flew
over the sea even to the end of the world, where stands
the tree of life." When he had got the apple, he and
the princess ate it and married, and lived happily ever
after.

So in Wolf's collection, in the story of the Wonderful Hares, a golden apple is the gift for which the
finder is to gain a princess; and that apple grew on a

sort of tree of which there was but one in the whole world.

In Norse it is the same ; the princess on the Glass Hill held three golden apples in her lap, and he who could ride up the hill and carry off the apples was to win the prize ; and the princess rolled them down to the hero, and they rolled into his shoe.

The good girl plucked the apples from the tree which spoke to her when she went down the well to the underground world ; but the ill-tempered step-sister thrashed down the fruit ; and when the time of trial came, the apple tree played its part and protected the good girl.

So in French, a singing apple is one of the marvels which the Princess Belle Etoile, and her brothers and her cousin, bring from the end of the world, after all manner of adventures ; and in that story the comb, the stars and jewels in the hair, the talking sooth-saying bird, the magic water, the horse, the wicked step-mother, and the dragon, all appear ; and there is a Gaelic version of that story. In short, that French story agrees with Gaelic stories, and with a certain class of German tales ; and contains within itself much of the machinery and incident which is scattered else-where, in collections of tales gathered in modern times amongst the people of various countries.

So again in books of tales of older date, and in other languages, apples and marvels are associated.

In Straparola is an Italian story remarkably like the Gaelic Sea Maiden, and clearly the same in ground-work as Princess Belle Etoile. A lady, when she has lost her husband, goes off to the Atlantic Ocean with three golden apples ; and the mermaid who had swal-lowed the husband, shews first his head, then his body to the waist, and then to the knees ; each time for a golden apple ; and the incidents of that story are all to be found elsewhere, and most of them are in Gaelic.

So again, in the Arabian Nights, there is a long story, The Three Apples, which turns upon the stealing of one, which was a thing of great price, though it was not magical in the story.

So in classical times, an apple of discord was the prize of the fairest ; and the small beginning from which so much of all that is most famous in ancient lore takes its rise ; three golden apples were the prize of one of the labours of Hercules, and these grew in a garden which fable has placed far to the westwards, and learned commentators have placed in the Cape Verde Islands.

So then it appears that apples have been mysterious and magical from the earliest of times ; that they were sought for in the west, and valued in the east ; and now when the popular tales of the far west are examined, apples are the most important of natural productions, and invested with the magic which belongs to that which is old and rare, and which may once have been sacred.

It is curious that the forbidden fruit is almost always mentioned in English as an apple ; and this notion prevails in France to such a degree, that when that mad play, La propriete c'est le vol, was acted in Paris in 1848, the first scene represented the Garden of Eden with a tree, and a board on which was written " il est défendu de manger de ces pommes."

And it is stated in grave histories that the Celtic priests held apples sacred ; so here again popular tales hold their own.

Again, supposing tales to be old traditions, something may be gleaned from them of the past. Horses, for example, must once have been strange and rare, or sacred, amongst the Celts, as among other races.

The horses of the Vedas, which drew the chariot of the sun, appear to have been confused with the sun-god of Indian mythology. Horses decided the fate of kingdoms in Persia, according to Herodotus. They were sacred when Phaëton drove the chariot of the sun. The Scandinavian gods had horses, according to the Edda. They are generally supernatural in Grimm's German stories, in Norse tales, in French, and in many other collections. They are wonderful in Breton tales.

When the followers of Columbus first took horses to America, they struck terror into the Indians, and they and their riders were demigods; because strange and terrible.

Horses were surely feared, or worshipped, or prized, by Celts, for places are named after them. Penmarch in Brittany, means horse-head or hill. Ardincaple in Scotland means the mare's height, and there are many other places with similar names.

In Gaelic tales, horses are frequently mentioned, and more magic properties are attributed to them than elsewhere in popular lore.

In No. 1, horses play a very prominent part; and in some versions of that tale, the heroine is a lady transformed into a grey mare. It is to be hoped, for the hero's sake, that she did not prove herself the better horse when she resumed her human form.

In No. 3, there is a horse race. In No. 4, there are mythical horses; and in an Irish version of that story, told me in August 1860, by an Irish blind fiddler, on board the Lochgoilhead boat, horses again play their part, with hounds and hawks. In No. 14, there are horses; in one version there is a magic "powney." In 22, a horse again appears, and gives the foundation for the riddle on which the story turns. In 40, a horse is one of the prizes to be gained. In 41, the horse plays the part of bluebeard. In 48, a horse is to be hanged as a thief. In 51, the hero assumes the form of a horse. In many other tales which I have in manuscript, men appear as horses, and reappear as men ; and horses are marvellous. In one tale, a man's son is sent to a warlock and becomes a horse, and all sorts of creatures besides. In another, a man gets a wishing grey filly from the wind, in return for some meal which the wind had blown away ; and there is a whole series of tales which relate to water-horses, and which seem, more than all the rest, to shew the horse as a degraded god, and, as it would seem, a water-god, and a destroyer.

I had intended to group all these stories together, as an illustration of this part of the subject, but time and space are wanting. These shew that in the Isle of Man, and in the Highlands of Scotland, people still firmly believe in the existence of a water-horse. In Sutherland and elsewhere, many believe that they have seen these fancied animals. I have been told of English sportsmen who went in pursuit of them, so circumstantial were the accounts of those who believed that they had seen them. The witnesses are so numerous, and their testimony agrees so well, that there must be some old deeply-rooted Celtic belief which clothes every dark object with the dreaded form of the EACH UISGE. The legends of the doings of the water kelpie all point to some river god reduced to be a fuath or bogle. The bay or grey horse grazes at the lake-side, and when he is mounted, rushes into the loch and devours his rider. His back lengthens to suit any number ; men's hands stick to his skin ; he is harnessed to a plough, and drags the team and the plough into

the loch, and tears the horses to bits ; he is killed, and
nothing remains but a pool of water ; he falls in love
with a lady, and when he appears as a man and lays
his head on her knee to be dressed, the frightened lady
finds him out by the sand amongst his hair. " Tha
Gainmheach ann." There is sand in it, she says, and
when he sleeps she makes her escape. He appears as
an old woman, and is put to bed with a bevy of dam-
sels in a mountain shealing, and he sucks the blood of
all, save one, who escapes over a burn, which, water
horse as he is, he dare not cross. In short, these tales
and beliefs have led me to think that the old Celts
must have had a destroying water-god, to whom the
horse was sacred, or who had the form of a horse.

Unless there is some such foundation for the stories,
it is strange to find the romances of boatmen and
fishermen inhabiting small islands, filled with incidents
which seem rather to belong to a wandering, horse-
riding tribe. But the tales of Norwegian sailors are
similar in this respect ; and the Celtic character has
in fact much which savours of a tribe who are boatmen
by compulsion, and would be horsemen if they could.
Though the Western islanders are fearless boatmen,
and brave a terrible sea in very frail boats, very few of
them are in the royal navy, and there are not many
who are professed sailors. On the other hand, they
are bold huntsmen in the far north of America. I do
not think that they are successful farmers anywhere,
though they cling fondly to a spot of land, but they are
famous herdsmen at home and abroad. On the misty
hills of old Scotland or the dry plains of Australia, they
still retain the qualities which made a race of hunters,
and warriors, and herdsmen, such as are represented
in the poems of Ossian, and described in history, and
even within the small bounds which now contain the

Celtic race in Europe, their national tastes appear in strong relief. Every deerstalker will bear witness to the eagerness of Highlanders in pursuit of their old favourite game, the dun deer; the mountaineer shews what he is when his eye kindles and his nostril dilates at the sight of a noble stag; when the gillie forgets his master in his keenness, and the southern lags behind; when it is "bellows to mend," and London dinners are remembered with regret. Tyree is famous for its breed of ponies : it is a common bit of Highland "chaff" to neigh at a Tyree man, and other islands have famous breeds also It is said that men almost starving rode to ask for meal in a certain place, and would not sell their ponies; and though this is surely a fiction, it rests on the fact that the islanders are fond of horses. At fairs and markets all over the Highlands ponies abound. Nothing seems to amaze a Highlander more than to see any one walk who can afford to ride; and he will chase a pony over a hill, and sit in misery on a packsaddle when he catches the beast, and endure discomfort, that he may ride in state along a level road for a short distance.

Irish Celts, who have more room for locomotion, cultivate their national taste for horse flesh in a higher degree. An Irish hunter is valued by many an English Nimrod; all novels which purport to represent Irish character paint Irishmen as bold riders, and Irish peasants as men who take a keen interest in all that belongs to hunting and racing. There is not, so far as I know, a single novel founded on the adventures of an Irish or Highland sailor or farmer, though there are plenty of fictitious warriors and sportsmen in prose and in verse. There are endless novels about English sailors, and sportsmen, and farmers, and though novels are fictions, they too rest on facts. The

Celts, and Saxons, and Normans, and Danes, and
Romans, who help to form the English race, are at
home on shore and afloat, whether their steeds are of
flesh and blood, or, as the Gaelic poet says, of brine.
The Celtic race are most at home amongst their cattle
and on the hills, and I believe it to be strictly in
accordance with the Celtic character to find horses and
chariots playing a part in their national traditions and
poems of all ages.

I do not know enough of our Welsh cousins to be
able to speak of their tastes in this respect ; but I
know that horse racing excites a keen interest in Brittany, though the French navy is chiefly manned by
Breton and Norman sailors, and Breton ballads and
old Welsh romances are full of equestrian adventures.
And all this supports the theory that Celts came from
the east, and came overland ; for horses would be prized
by a wandering race.

So hounds would be prized by the race of hunters
who chased the Caledonian boars as well as the stags ;
and here again tradition is in accordance with probability, and supported by other testimony. In No. 4
there are mystical dogs ; a hound, GADHAR is one of the
links in No. 8 ; a dog appears in No. 11 ; a dog, who
is an enchanted man, in No. 12 ; there is a phantom
dog in No. 23 ; there was a " spectre hound in Man ;"
and there are similar ghostly dogs in England, and in
many European countries besides.

In 19, 20, 31, 38, and in a great many other tales
which I have in manuscript, the hound plays an important part. Sometimes he befriends his master, at
other times he appears to have something diabolical
about him ; it seems as if his real honest nature had
overcome a deeply-rooted prejudice, for there is much
which savours of detestation as well as of strong affec-

f

tion. Dog, or son of the dog, is a term of abuse in Gaelic as elsewhere, though cuilein is a term of endearment, and the hound is figured beside his master, or at his feet, on many a tombstone in the Western Isles. Hounds are mentioned in Gaelic poetry and in Gaelic tales, and in the earliest accounts of the Western Isles; and one breed still survives in these long-legged, rough, wiry-haired stag-hounds, which Landseer so loves to paint.

In one story, for which I have no room, but which is well worthy of preservation, a step-mother sends two step-children, a brother and sister, out into the world to seek their fortune. They live in a cottage with three bare yellow porkers, which belong to the sister. The brother sells one to a man for a dog with a green string, and so gets three dogs, whose names are Knowledge, Fios; Swift, Luath; Weighty, Trom. The sister is enraged, and allies herself with a giant who has a hot coal in his mouth. Knowledge tells his master the dangers which await him : how the giant and his sister had set a venomous dart over the door. Swiftness runs in first, and saves his master at the expense of his own tail, and then the three dogs upset a caldron of boiling water over the giant, who is hid in a hole in the floor, and so at the third time the giant is killed, and the only loss is a bit of the tail of Luath.

Then the king's son goes to dwell with a beautiful lady ; and after a time he goes back to visit his sister, armed with three magic apples. The sister sets three venomous porkers at him, and he, by throwing the apples behind him, hinders them with woods, and moors, and lakes, which grow up from the apples ; but they follow. The three dogs come out and beat the three pigs, and kill them, and then the king's son gets his sister to come with him, and she was as a servant-maid to the prince and the fine woman with whom he lived. Then the sister put GATH NIMH, a poisonous sting or thorn into the bed, and the prince was as though he were dead for three days, and he was buried. But Knowledge told the other two dogs what to do, and they scraped up the prince, and took out the thorn ; and he came alive again and went home, and set on a fire of grey oak, and burned his sister. And John Crawfurd, fisherman at Lochlong-head, told John Dewar "that he left the man, and the woman, and the dogs all happy and well pleased together." This curious story seems to shew the hog and the dog as foes. Perhaps they were but the emblems of rival tribes ; perhaps they were sacred amongst rival races ; at all events, they were both important personages at some time or other, for there is a great deal about them in Gaelic lore.

The boar was the animal which Diarmid slew, and which caused his death when he paced his length against the bristles,—the venomous bristles pierced a mole in his foot. It was a boar which was sent out to find the body of the thief in that curious story, an gillie carrach ; and in a great many other stories, boars appear as animals of the chase. The Fiantaichean or Feen, whomsoever they were, are always represented as hunting wild boars, as tearing a boar to bits by main force, or eating a whole boar. Cairns, said to have been raised over boars, are shewn in many parts of Scotland still. I myself once found a boar's tusk in a grave accidentally discovered, close to the bridge at Pool-Ewe. There were many other bones, and a rough flint, and a lot of charcoal, in what seemed to be a shallow human grave, a kind of stone coffin built up with loose slabs.

"Little pigs" play their part in the nursery lore

of England. Everybody who has been young and has toes, must know how

" This little pig went to market,
  And this little pig staid at home—
This little pig got roast beef,
  And this little pig got none ;
And this little pig went wee, wee, wee, all the way home."

There is a long and tragic story which has been current amongst at least three generations of my own family regarding a lot of little pigs who had a wise mother, who told them where they were to build their houses, and how, so as to avoid the fox. Some of the little pigs would not follow their mother's counsel, and built houses of leaves, and the fox got in and said, " I will gallop, and I'll trample, and I'll knock down your house," and he ate the foolish, little, proud pigs ; but the youngest was a wise little pig, and, after many adventures, she put an end to the wicked fox when she was almost vanquished, bidding him look into the caldron to see if the dinner was ready, and then tilting him in headforemost. In short, pigs are very important personages in the popular lore of Great Britain.

We are told by history that they were sacred amongst the Gauls, and fed on acorns in the sacred oak groves of the Druids, and there is a strong prejudice now amongst Highlanders against eating pig's flesh.

So oak trees are mythical. Whenever a man is to be burned for some evil deed, and men are always going to be roasted, fagots of " grey," probably green oak, are fetched. There is a curious story which the Rev. Mr. MacLauchlan took down from the recitation of an old man in Edinburgh, in which a mythical old man is shut up in an oak tree, which grows in the court of the king's palace ; and when the king's son lets his ball roll into a split in the tree by chance, the old man tells the boy to fetch an axe and he will give him the ball, and so he gets out, and endows the Prince with power and valour. He sets out on his journey with a red-headed cook, who personates him, and he goes to lodge with a swine-herd ; but by the help of the old man of the great tree, BODACH NA CROIBHE MOIRE, he overcomes a boar, a bull, and a stallion, and marries the king's daughter, and the red-headed cook is burnt.

So then, in these traditions, swine and oak trees are associated together with mythical old men and deeds of valour, such as a race of hunters might perform, and admire, and remember. Is it too much to suppose that these are dim recollections of pagan times ? DRUIDH is the name for a magician, DRAOCHD for magic. It is surely not too much to suppose that the magicians were the Druids, and the magic their mysteries ; that my peasant collectors are right, when they maintain that GRUAGACH, the long-haired one, was " a professor" or " master of arts," or " one that taught feats of arms :" that the learned Gruagach, who is so often mentioned, was a Druid in his glory, and the other, who in the days of Johnson, haunted the island of Troda as " Greogaca," who haunted the small island of Inch, near Easdale, in the girlhood of Mrs. Mactavish, who is remembered still, and is still supposed to haunt many a desolate island in the far west, is the phantom of the same Druid, fallen from his high estate, skulking from his pursuers, and really living on milk left for him by those whose priest he had once been.

" The small island of Inch, near Easdale, is inhabited by a brownie, which has followed the MacDougalls of Ardincaple for ages, and takes a great interest in them. He takes care of their cattle in that island night and day, unless the dairymaid, when there in summer with the milk cattle, neglects to leave warm milk for him at night in a knocking-stone in the cave, where she and the herd live during their stay in the island. Should this perquisite be for a night forgot, they will be sure in the morning to find one of the cattle fallen over the rocks with which the place abounds. It is a question whether the brownie has not a friend with whom he shares the contents of the stone, which will, I dare-say, hold from two to three Scotch pints."

Mrs. MacTavish, 1859, Islay.

If the manners and customs of druids are described as correctly as modern manners really are, then something may be gathered concerning druidical worship, but without knowledge, which I have no time to acquire, the full bearing of traditions on such a subject cannot be estimated.

The horse, and the boar, the oak tree, and the apple, then, are often referred to. Of mistletoe I have found no trace, unless it be the sour herb which brings men to life, but that might be the "soma," which plays such a part in the mythology of the Vedas, or the shamrock, which was sacred in Ireland.

Wells are indicated as mysterious in a great many tales—poison wells and healing wells—and some are still frequented with a half belief in their virtue; but such wells now often have the name of some saint affixed to them.

Birds are very often referred to as soothsayers—in No. 39 especially; the man catches a bird and says it is a diviner, and a gentleman buys it as such. It was a bird of prey, for it lit on a hide, and birds of prey are continually appearing as bringing aid to men, such as the raven, the hoodie, and the falcon. The little birds especially are frequently mentioned. I should therefore gather from the stories that the ancient Celts drew augury from birds as other nations did, and as it is as-serted by historians that the Gauls really did. I should be inclined to think that they possessed the domestic fowl before they became acquainted with the country of the wild grouse, and that the cock may have been sacred, for he is a foe and a terror to uncanny beings, and the hero of many a story; while the grouse and similar birds peculiar to this country are barely mentioned. The cat plays a considerable part, and appears as a transformed princess; and the cat also may have been sacred to some power, for cats are the companions of Highland witches, and of hags all the world over, and they were sacred to gods in other lands; they were made into mummies in Egypt, together with hawks and other creatures which appear in Highland tales. Ravens were Odin's messengers; they may have been pages to some Celtic divinity also. Foxes, and otters, and wolves, and bears all appear in mythical characters. Serpents were probably held in abhorrence, as they have been by other races, but the serpent gave wisdom, and is very mythical.

Old Macdonald, travelling tinker, told me a long story, of which one scene represented an incantation more vividly to me than anything I have ever read or heard. "There was a king and a knight, as there was and will be, and as grows the fir tree, some of it crooked and some of it straight, and he was a king of Eirinn," said the old tinker, and then came a wicked stepmother, who was incited to evil by a wicked hen-wife. The son of the first queen was at school with twelve comrades, and they used to play at shinny every day with silver shinnies and a golden ball. The henwife, for certain curious rewards, gave the stepdame a magic shirt, and she sent it to her step son, "Sheen Billy," and persuaded him to put it on; he refused at first, but complied at last, and the shirt was a BEITHIR (great snake) about his neck. Then he was enchanted and under spells, and all manner of adventures followed; but at last he came to the house of a wise woman who had a beautiful daughter, who fell in love with the enchanted prince, and said she must and would have him.

" It will cost thee much sorrow," said the mother.

" I care not," said the girl, " I must have him."

" It will cost thee thy hair."

" I care not."

" It will cost thee thy right breast."

" I care not if it should cost me my life," said the girl.

And the old woman agreed to help her to her will. A caldron was prepared and filled with plants; and the king's son was put into it stripped to the magic shirt, and the girl was stripped to the waist. And the mother stood by with a great knife, which she gave to her daughter.

Then the king's son was put down in the caldron, and the great serpent, which appeared to be a shirt about his neck, changed into its own form, and sprang on the girl and fastened on her; and she cut away the hold, and the king's son was freed from the spells. Then they were married, and a golden breast was made for the lady. And then they went through more adventures, which I do not well remember, and which the old tinker's son vainly strove to repeat in August 1860, for he is far behind his father in the telling of old Highland tales.

The serpent, then, would seem to be an emblem of evil and wisdom in Celtic popular mythology.

There is something mysterious about rushes. The fairies are found in a bush of rushes; the great caldron of the Feen is hid under a bush of rushes; and in a great many other instances TOM LUACHARACH appears.

I do not know that the plant is mentioned in foreign tales, but it occurs several times in border minstrelsy.

If the Druids worshipped the sun and moon, there is very little direct reference to such worship in highland stories now. There are many highland customs which point to solar worship, but these have been treated of by abler pens, and I have nothing to add on that head.

There is yet another animal which is mythical— the water-bull. He certainly belongs to Celtic mythology, as the water-horse does, for he is known in the Isle of Man and all over the islands.

There are numerous lakes where water-bulls are supposed to exist, and their progeny are supposed to be easily known by their short ears. When the water-bull appears in a story he is generally represented as friendly to man. I have a great many accounts of him, and his name in Skye is Tarbh Eithre.

There is a gigantic water bird, called the Boobrie, which is supposed to inhabit the fresh water and sea lochs of Argyllshire. I have heard of him nowhere else; but I have heard of him from several people.

He is ravenous and gigantic, gobbles up sheep and cows, has webbed feet, a very loud hoarse voice, and is somewhat like a cormorant. He is reported to have terrified a minister out of his propriety, and it is therefore to be assumed that he is of the powers of evil. And there are a vast number of other fancied inhabitants of earth, air, and water, enough to form a volume of supernatural history, and all or any of these may have figured in Celtic mythology; for it is hard to suppose that men living at opposite ends of Scotland, and peasants in the Isle of Man, should invent the same fancies unless their ideas had some common foundation.

Besides these animals, there is a whole supernatural world with superhuman gigantic inhabitants.

There are continual fights with these giants, which are often carried on without arms at all—mere wrestling matches, which seem to have had certain rules. It is somewhere told of the Germans that they in their forests fought with clubs, and the Celtic giants may once have been real men. Hercules fought with a club. Irishmen use shillelahs still, and my west country friends, when they fight now-a-days, use barrel staves instead of swords, and use them well, if not wisely ; but whether giants were men or myths, they are always represented as strange lubberly beings, whose dealings with men invariably end in their discomfiture. There are giants in Herodotus and, I believe, in every popular mythology known. There are giants in Holy Writ. They spoke an unknown tongue everywhere. They said " Fee fo fum" in Cornwall. They say "Fiaw fiaw foaghrich" in Argyll, and these sounds may possibly be corruptions of the language of real big burly savages, now magnified into giants.

The last word might be the vocative of the Gaelic for stranger, ill pronounced, and the intention may be to mimic the dialect of a foreigner speaking Gaelic.

An Italian organ-grinder once found his way to the west, and sang " Fideli, fidela, fidelin-lin-la." The boys caught the tune, and sang it to the words, "Deese creepe Signaveete ha," words with as much meaning as "Fee fo fum," but which retain a certain resemblance to the Italian sound.

If the giants were once real savages, they had the sense of smell peculiarly sharp, according to the Gaelic tales, as they had in all others which treat of them, and they ate their captives, as it is asserted that the early inhabitants of Scotland did, as Herodotus says that Scyths did in his time, and as the Feejee islanders did very lately, and still do. A relative of mine once offered me a tooth as a relic of such a feast; it had been presented to him in the Feejee Islands by a charming dark young lady, who had just left the banquet, but had not shared in it. The Highland giants were not so big but that their conquerors wore their clothes; they were not so strong that men could not beat them, even by wrestling. They were not quite savages; for though some lived in caves, others had houses and cattle, and hoards of spoil. They had slaves, as we are told that Scotch proprietors had within historic times. In "Scotland in the Middle Ages," p. 141, we learn that Earl Waldev of Dunbar made over a whole tribe to the Abbot of Kelso in 1170, and in the next page it is implied that these slaves were mostly Celts. Perhaps those Celts who were not enslaved had their own mountain view of the matter, and looked down on the Gall as intrusive, savage, uncultivated, slave-owning giants.

Perhaps the mountain mists in like manner impeded the view of the dwellers on the mountain and the plain, for Fin MacCoul was a "God in Ireland," as they say, and is a "rawhead and bloody bones" in the Scottish lowlands now.

Whatever the giants were they knew some magic arts, but they were always beaten in the end by men.

The combats with them are a Gaelic proverb in action :—

"Theid scoltachd thar spionnadh."

Skill goes over might, and probably, as it seems to me, giants are simply the nearest savage race at war with the race who tell the tales. If they performed impossible feats of strength, they did no more than Rob Roy, whose "putting stone" is now shewn to Saxon tourists by a Celtic coachman, near Bunawe, in the shape of a boulder of many tons, though Rob Ruadh lived only a hundred years ago, near Inverary, in a cottage which is now standing, and which was lately inhabited by a shepherd.

The Gaelic giants are very like those of Norse and German tales, but they are much nearer to real men than the giants of Germany and Scandinavia, and Greece and Rome, who are almost, if not quite, equal to the gods. Famhairan are little more than very strong men, but some have only one eye like the Cyclops.

Their world is generally, but not always, under ground; it has castles, and parks, and pasture, and all that is to be found above the earth. Gold, and silver, and copper, abound in the giant's land; jewels are seldom mentioned, but cattle, and horses, and spoil of dresses, and arms, and armour, combs, and basins, apples, shields, bows, spears, and horses, are all to be gained by a fight with the giants. Still, now and then a giant does some feat quite beyond the power of man; such as a giant in Barra, who fished up a hero, boat and all, with his fishing-rod, from a rock, and threw him over his head, as little boys do " cuddies" from a pier-end. So the giants may be degraded gods after all.

But besides "popular tales," there are fairy tales, which are not told as stories, but facts. At all events, the creed is too *recent* to be lightly spoken of.

Men do believe in fairies, though they will not readily confess the fact. And though I do not myself believe that fairies *are*, in spite of the strong evidence offered, I believe there once was a small race of people in these islands, who are remembered as fairies, for the fairy belief is not confined to the Highlanders of Scotland. I have given a few of the tales which have come to me as illustrations in No. 27.

" *They*" are always represented as living in green mounds. They pop up their heads when disturbed by people treading on their houses. They steal children. They seem to live on familiar terms with the people about them when they treat them well, to punish them when they ill treat them. If giants are magnified, these are but men seen through the other end of the telescope, and there are such people now. A Lapp is such a man—he is a little flesh-eating mortal—having control over the beasts, and living in a green mound— when he is not living in a tent, or sleeping out of doors, wrapped in his deer-skin shirt. I have lived amongst them and know them and their dwellings pretty well. I know one which would answer to the description of a fairy mound exactly. It is on the most northern peninsula in Europe, to the east of the North Cape, close to the sea, in a sandy hollow near a burn. It is round—say, twelve feet in diameter—and it is sunk three feet in the sand ; the roof is made of sticks and covered with turf. The whole structure, at a short distance, looks exactly like a conical green mound about four feet high. There was a famous crop of grass on it when I was there, and the children and dogs ran out at the door and up to the top when we approached, as ants run on an ant hill when disturbed. Their fire was in the middle of the floor, and the pot hung over it from the roof. I lately saw a house in south Uist found in the sand hills close to the sea. It was built of loose boulders, it was circular, and had recesses in the sides, it was covered when found, and it was full of sand ; when that was removed, stone querns and combs of bone were found, together with ashes, and near the level of the top there was a stratum of bones and teeth of large grass-eating animals. I know not what they were, but the bones were splintered and broken, and mingled with ashes and shells, oysters, cockles, and wilks (periwinkles), shewing clearly the original level of the ground, and proving that this was a dwelling almost the same as a Lapp " Gam" at Hopseidet.

Now, let us see what the people of the Hebrides say of the fairies. There was a woman benighted with a pair of calves, "and she went for shelter to a knoll, and she began driving the peg of the tether into it. The hill opened, and she heard as though there were a pot hook 'gleegashing,' on the side of the pot. A woman put up her head, and as much as was above her waist, and said, ' What business hast thou to disturb this tulman, in which I make my dwelling. ' " This might be a description of one of my Lapp friends, and probably is a description of such a dwelling as I saw in South Uist. If the people slept as Lapps sleep, with their feet to the fire, a woman outside might have driven a peg very near one of the sleepers, and she might have stood on a seat and poked her head out of the chimney.

The magic about the beasts is but the mist of antiquity ; and the fairy was probably a Pict. Who will say who the Pict may have been ? Probably the great Clibric hag was one, and of the same tribe.

" In the early morning she was busy milking the hinds ; they were standing all about the door of the hut, till one of them ate a hank of *blue* worsted hanging from a nail in it." So says the " fiction," which it is considered a sin to relate. Let me place some facts from my own journal beside it.

" Wednesday, August 22, 1850. Quickjok, Swedish Lapland.—In the evening the effect of the sunlight through the mist and showers was most beautiful. I was sketching, when a small man made his appearance

on the opposite side of the river and began to shout for
a boat. The priest exclaimed that the Lapps had come
down, and accordingly the diminutive human specimen
was fetched, and proved to be a Lapp who had established his camp about seven miles off, near Vallespik.
He was about twenty-five years old, and with his high
blue cap on could stand upright under my arm."

I had been wandering about Quickjok for a week,
out on Vallespik frequently, searching for the Lapps,
with the very glass which I had previously used to
find deer close to Clibric, which is but a small copy of
the Lapland mountain.

"Thursday, 23d.—Started to see the deer, with the
priest and the Clockar, and Marcus, and the Lapp.
The Lapp walked like a deer himself, aided by a very
long birch pole, which he took from its hiding place in
a fir tree. I had hard work to keep up with him.
Marcus and the priest were left behind. Once up
through the forest, it was cutting cold, and we walked
up to the 'cota' in two hours and a quarter. The
deer were seen in the distance, like a brown speck on
the shoulder of Vallespik; and with the glass I could
make out that a small mortal and two dogs were driving them home. The cota is a permanent one, made
in the shape of a sugar loaf, with birch sticks, and long
flat stones and turf. There are two exactly alike, and
each has a door, a mere narrow slit, opening to the
west, and a hole in the roof to let out the smoke. I
crept in, and found a girl of about fifteen, with very
pretty eyes, sitting crouched up in a corner, and looking as scared as one of her own fawns. The priest
said, that if we had come without our attendant genius,
the small Lapp, she would have fainted, or run away
to the hills. I began to sketch her, as she sat looking
modest in her dark corner, and was rejoicing in the

extreme stillness of my sitter, when, on looking up
from some careful touch, I found that she had vanished through the door-way. I had to bribe her with
bread and butter before she could be coaxed back.
A tremendous row of shouting and barking outside
now announced the arrival of the deer, so I let my
sitter go, and off she ran as fast as she could. I followed more leisurely to the spot where the deer were
gathered, on a stony hillside. There were only about
200 ; the rest had run off up wind on the way from the
mountains, and all the other Lapps were off after them,
leaving only my pretty sitter, the boy, and a small
woman with bleared eyes, as ugly as sin, his sister.

"How I wished for Landseer's pencil as I looked
at that scene ! Most of the deer were huddled close
together ; hinds and calves chewing the cud with the
greatest placidity, but here and there some grand old
fellows, with wide antlers, stood up against the sky line,
looking magnificent. I tried to draw, but it was hopeless ; so I sat down, and watched the proceedings of
my hosts.

"First, each of the girls took a coil of rope from
about her neck, and in a twinkling it was pitched over
the horns of a hind. The noose was then slipped round
the neck, and a couple of turns of rope round the
nose, and then the wild milkmaid set her foot on the
halter and proceeded TO MILK THE HIND, into a round
birch bowl, with a handle. Sometimes she sat, at
others she leant her head on the deer's dark side, and
knelt beside her. I never saw such a succession of
beautiful groups.

"Every now and then some half-dozen deer would
break out of the herd and set off to the mountain, and
then came a general skurry. The small Lapp man,
with his long birch pole, would rush screaming after

the stragglers; and his two gaunt, black, rough, half-starved dogs would scour off, yelping, in pursuit. It generally ended in the hasty return of the truants, with well-bitten houghs for their pains; but some fairly made off, at a determined long trot, and vanished over the hill. It was very curious to be thus in the midst of a whole herd of creatures so like our own wild deer, to have them treading on my feet and poking their horns against my sketch-book as I vainly tried to draw them, and to think that they who had the power to bid defiance to the fleetest hound in Sweden should be so perfectly tame as to let the small beings who herded them so thump, and bully, and tease them. The milking, in the meantime, had been progressing rapidly; and after about an hour the pretty girl, who had been dipping her fingers in the milk-pail and licking up the milk all the time, took her piece of bread and butter, and departed with her charge, munching as she went.

"The blear-eyed one, and the boy, and our party, went into the cota, and dined on cold roast reiper and reindeer milk. The boy poured the milk from a small keg, which contained the whole product of the flock; and having given us our share, he carefully licked up all that remained on the outside of the keg, and set it down in a corner. It was sweet and delicious, like thick cream. Dinner over, we desired the Lapp to be ready in the morning (to accompany me), and with the clocker's dog, 'Gueppe,' went reiper-shooting. The clocker himself, with a newly-slaughtered reindeer calf on his shoulders, followed; and so we went home."

A few days afterwards, I was at another camp, on another hill, where the same scene was going on. "In a tent I found a fine-looking Lapp woman sitting on a heap of skins, serving out coffee, and handing reindeer cream to the clocker with a silver spoon. She had silver bracelets, and a couple of silver rings; and altogether, with her black hair, and dark brown eyes glittering in the fire-light, she looked eastern and magnificent." Her husband had many trinkets, and they had, amongst other articles, a comb, which the rest seemed much to need.

Her dress was blue, so were most of the dresses, and one of her possessions was a bone contrivance for weaving the bands which all wore round their ankles. She must have had blue yarn somewhere, for her garters were partly blue.

I spent the whole of the next day in the camp, and watched the whole operations of the day.

"After dinner, the children cracked the bones with stones and a knife, after they had polished the outside, and sucked up the marrow; and then the dogs, which did not dare to steal, were called in their turn, and got the remains of the food in wooden bowls, set apart for their especial use."

The bones in the hut in South Uist might have been the remains of such a feast by their appearance.

"The cota was a pyramid of sods and birch sticks, about seven feet high, and twelve or fourteen in diameter. There were three children, five dogs, an old woman, Marcus, and myself, inside; and all day long the handsome lady from the tent next door, with her husband, and a couple of quaint-looking old fellows in deerskin shirts, kept popping in to see how I got on. It was impossible to sit upright for the slope of the walls, as I sat cross-legged on the ground."

This might be a description of the Uist hut itself, and its inhabitants, as I can fancy them.

"The three dogs (in the tent), at the smallest symptom of a disturbance, plunged out, barking, to add to the row; they popped in by the same way under the canvas, so they had no need of a door."

So did the dogs in the story of Seautraigh; they ran after the stranger, and stopped to eat the bones. And it is remarkable that all civilized dogs fall upon and worry the half-savage black Lapp dogs, and bark at their masters whenever they descend from their mountains, as the town dogs did at the fairy dogs. In short, these extracts might be a fair description of the people, and the dwellings, and the food, and the dogs described as fairies, and the hag, and the tulman, in stories which I have grouped together; told in Scotland within this year by persons who can have no knowledge of what is called the "Finn theory," and given in the very words in which they came to me, from various sources.

Lord Reay's forester must surely have passed the night in a Lapp cota on Ben Clibric, in Sutherland, when Lapps were Picts; but when was that? Perhaps in the youth of the fairy of whom the following story was told by a Sutherland gamekeeper of my acquaintance.

THE HERDS OF GLEN ODHAR.—A wild romantic glen in Strath Carron is called Glen Garaig, and it was through this that a woman was passing carrying an infant wrapped in her plaid. Below the path, overhung with weeping birches, and nearly opposite, run a very deep ravine, known as Glen Odhar, the dun glen. The child, not yet a year old, and which had not spoken or attempted speech, suddenly addressed his mother thus :—

S lionmhor bho mhaol Odhar,
Le laogh na ghobhl,
Chunnaic mise gam bleoghan
Anns a ghlean Odhar ud halla,
Gun chu gun duine,
Gun bhean gun ghille,

Many a dun hummel cow,
With a calf below her,
Have I seen milking
In that dun glen yonder,
Without dog, without man,
Without woman, without gillie,

Ach aon duine,	But one man,
S'e liath.	And he hoary.

The good woman flung down the child and plaid and ran home, where, to her great joy, her baby boy lay smiling in its cradle.

Fairies then milked deer, as Lapps do. They lived under ground, like them. They worked at trades, especially smith work and weaving. They had hammers and anvils, and excelled in their use, but though good weavers, they had to steal wool and borrow looms. Lapps do work in metal on their own account; they make their own skin dresses, but buy their summer clothes. A race of wanderers could not be weavers on a large scale, but they can and do weave small bands very neatly on hand-looms; and they alone make these. There are savages now in South Africa, who are smiths and miners, though they neither weave nor wear clothes. Fairies had hoards of treasure—so have Lapps. A man died shortly before one of my Tana trips, and the whole country side had been out searching for his buried wealth in vain. Some years ago the old silver shops of Bergen and Trondhjem overflowed with queer cups and spoons, and rings, silver plates for waist belts, old plate that had been hidden amongst the mountains, black old silver coins that had not seen the light for years. I saw the plate and bought some, and was told that, in consequence of a religious movement, the Lapps had dug up and sold their hoards. Fairies are supposed to shoot flint arrows, and arrows of other kinds, at people now. Men have told me several times that they had been shot at: one man had found the flint arrow in an ash tree; another had heard it whiz past his ear; a third had pulled a slender arrow from a friend's head. If that be so, my argument fails, and fairies are *not* of the past ; but Californian Indians now use arrow-heads which closely resemble those dug up in Scotland, in Denmark, and, I believe, all over Europe. Fairies are conquered by Christian symbols. They were probably Pagans, and, if so, they may have existed when Christianity was introduced. They steal men, women, and children, and keep them in their haunts. They are not the only slave owners in the world. They are supernatural, and objects of a sort of respect and wonder. So are gipsies where they are rare, as in Sweden and Norway ; so are the Lapps themselves, for they are professed wizards. I have known a terrified Swedish lassie whip her horse and gallop away in her cart from a band of gipsies, and I have had the advantage of living in the same house with a Lapp wizard at Quickjok, who had prophesied the arrival of many strangers, of whom I was one. Spaniards were gods amongst the Indians till they taught them to know better. Horses were supernatural when they came, and on the whole, as it appears, there is much more reason to believe that fairies were a real people, like the Lapps, who are still remembered, than that they are " creatures of imagination " or "spirits in prison," or "fallen angels ;" and the evidence of their actual existence is very much more direct and substantial than that which has driven, and seems still to be driving, people to the very verge of insanity, if not beyond it, in the matter of those palpable-impalpable, visible-invisible spirits who rap double knocks upon dancing deal boards.

I am inclined to believe in the former existence of fairies in this sense, and if for no other reason, because all the nations of Europe have had some such belief, and they cannot all have invented the same fancy. The habitations of Highland fairies are green mounds, they therefore, like the giants, resemble the " under

jordiske " of the north, and they too may be degraded
divinities.

It seems then, that Gaelic tales attribute supernatural qualities to things which are mentioned in
popular tales elsewhere, and that Gaelic superstitions
are common to other races ; and it seems worth inquiry
whether there was anything in the known customs of
Celtic tribes to make these things valuable, and whether
tradition is supported by history.

In the first place, then, who are Celts now ? Who
were their ancestors ? Who are their relations ? and
where have Gaelic tribes appeared in history ?

I believe that little is really known about the
Gael ; and in particular, the origin of the West Highlanders has been very keenly disputed. One thing
is clear, they speak a language which is almost identical with the Irish of the north of Ireland, and they
are the same people. The dialect of Irish, which varies
most from Scotch Gaelic, is clearly but another form of
the same tongue. Manks is another ; and these three
are closely related to Welsh and Breton, though the
difference is very much greater. Gaelic, Irish, and
Manks vary from each other about as much as Norse,
Swedish, and Danish. Welsh and Breton vary from
the rest about as much as German and Dutch do from
the Scandinavian languages. There are variations in
Gaelic, and I believe there are in all the five surviv-
ing Celtic dialects, as there are in the languages of
different counties in England, of every valley in Norway and Sweden, of every German district, and of every
part of France, Spain, and Italy. But one who knows
Gaelic well, can make himself understood throughout
the Highlands, as freely as an Englishman can in England, though he may speak with a Northumbrian burr,
or a west country twang, or like a true Cockney.

These, then, form the Celtic clan, the people of the west of Scotland, the Irish, the Manks, the Welsh, and the Breton. Who their relations are, and who their ancestors, are questions not easily answered, though much has been written on the subject. The following is a brief outline of what is given as Celtic history by modern writers whose works I have consulted lately:—

According to Henri Martin, the French historian,[*] the whole of Central Europe, France, and Spain, were once overrun by a race calling themselves Gael, and best known as Gauls. This people is generally admitted to have been of the same stock as Germans, Latins, Greeks, and Slavonians, and to have started from Central Asia at some unknown epoch. They are supposed to have been warlike, to have been tatooed like modern New Zealanders, and painted like North American Indians, to have been armed with stone weapons like the South Sea Islanders and Californian Indians ; but shepherds, as well as hunters, and acquainted with the use of wheat and rye, which they are supposed to have brought with them from Asia. One great confederation of tribes of this race was known to ancient historians, as Κελτοι. They were represented as fair and rosy-cheeked, large-chested, active, and brave, and they found the Euskes settled in the south of France, who were dark-complexioned, whose descendants are supposed to be the Euscualdonec or Basques of the Pyrennees, and who are classed with the Lapps of the north of Europe, and with tribes now dwelling in the far north of Asia. I have seen faces in Barra very like faces which I had seen shortly before at St. Sebastian in Spain. A tribe of Gauls made their way into Italy, and have left traces of their language there, in the names of mountain chains and great rivers. These

[*] Histoire de France, par Henri Martin ; 1855.

are named "Amhra," or "Ombres," and Amhra is
translated Valliant.   This invasion is calculated to
have taken place about 1500 B.C.

The Gael were followed by Kimri or Cimbri, a kindred people of a darker complexion, speaking a kindred
language, and their descendants are supposed to be the
Welsh and Bretons.   These in turn occupied the
interior of eastern Europe, and were followed by the
Scyths, and these, says the French historian, were
Teutons.

According to the learned author of the essay on
the Cimmerians, in the third volume of Rawlinson's
Herodotus, p. 184, it is almost beyond doubt that a
people known to their neighbours as Cimmerii, Gimiri,
or probably Gomerini, attained a considerable power
in Western Asia and Eastern Europe within the period
indicated by the dates B.C. 800, 600, or even earlier.

These people are traced to the inhabitants of Wales,
and Gael and Cymri are admitted by all to be Κελτοι;
and still keep up their old character for pugnacity by
quarrelling over their pedigrees.

Celts were undoubtedly the primitive inhabitants
of Gaul, Belgium, and the British Islands, possibly also
of Spain and Portugal ; but no word of the language
spoken by these ancient Cimbri has been preserved
by ancient authors, except the name, " and perhaps
the name Cimmerii may have included many Celtic
tribes not of the Cymric branch."   These Gauls appeared everywhere in Europe ; and, in particular, they
who had probably been driven out by the Scythians
invaded Scythia, intermixed with the people, and
formed the people known in history as Celto-Scythians;
who the Scyths were (according to the author) appears
to be uncertain.   All that remains of their language is
a list of words, picked out of the works of ancient

authors; and knowing what modern authors make of words which they pick up by ear, such a list is but a narrow foundation on which to build. Still on that list it has been decided that Scyths spoke a language which has affinity with Sanscrit, and in that list, as it seems to me, there are several words which resemble Gaelic more closely than the Sanscrit words given with them. And so, according to this theory, the Basques were found in Europe by the first Gael, and these were driven westwards by Kimri, and these again by Scythians, and these by Teutons, and all these still occupy their respective positions. The Basques and Lapps pushed aside; the Gael in Scotland and Ireland, driven far to the westwards; the Kimri driven westwards into Wales and Britanny; the Scyths lost or absorbed; and the Teutons occupying their old possessions, as Germans, Saxons, English, Scandinavians, and all their kindred tribes; and of all these the Basques and their relatives alone speak a language which cannot be traced to a common unknown origin, from which Sanscrit also came.

Whatever then throws light on the traditions of the first invaders of Europe is of interest to all the rest, for, according to this theory, they are all of the same clan. They are all branches of the same old stock which grew in Central Asia, and which has spread over great part of the world, and whatever is told of Gauls is of interest to all branches of Celts.

Rome was taken by Gauls about 390 B.C.; Greece was invaded by Gauls about 279 B.C., and they are then described as armed with great swords and lances, and wearing golden collars, and fighting savagely. At the end of the third century B.C., according to the French historian, Gaul might have been a common name for the greatest part of Europe, for Gauls were everywhere.

Now, what manner of men were these Gauls, when men saw them who could describe them?

All the Gauls kept their hair untouched by iron, and raised it like a mane towards the top of the head. As to the beard, some shaved it, others wore it of a moderate length. The chiefs and the nobles shaved the cheeks and the chin, and let their mustache grow to all their length. (Histoire de France, page 33.)

Their eyes were blue or sea-green, and shone under this thick mass of hair, of which the blond hue had been changed by lime-water to a flaming tint.

Their mustaches were "Rousses," which is the only word I know which will translate ruadh.

The warrior was armed with an enormous sabre on his left thigh; he held two darts in his hand, or a long lance; he carried a four-cornered shield, painted of various brilliant colours, with bosses representing birds or wild animals; and on his head was a helmet topped with eagles' wings, floating hair, or horns of wild animals; his clothes were particoloured, and he wore "brighis;" he was always fighting at home or abroad; he was a curious inquiring mortal, always asking questions; and truly he must have been a formidable savage that old French Gaul. Men's heads were nailed at the gates of his towns and his houses, beside trophies of the chase, much as modern Gael now hang up the trophies of their destructive skill, in the shape of pole-cats and crows.

The chiefs kept human heads embalmed and preserved, like archives of family prowess, as the Dyaks of Borneo and the New Zealanders still do, or did very lately. The father had the power of life and death over his wife and children, and exercised it too by burning the guilty wife; and, though some chiefs had several wives, and there are some scandalous stories of the manners and customs of the inhabitants of the islands; women were consulted together with men by the chiefs on matters of moment, and held a high place amongst the Gauls of France.

Now, this short description of the Gauls, rapidly gleaned from the pages of two modern books of high authority and great research, after my Gaelic stories were collected, agrees with the picture which the Gaelic tales give of their mythical heroes in many particulars. They have long beautiful yellow hair, Leadanach Buidh Boicheach. They are Ruadh Rousses. They have large swords, claidheamh, sometimes duileagach, leaf-shaped. They cast spears and darts, Sleadh. They are always asking questions, and their descendants have not lost the habit yet. Their dwellings are surrounded by heads stuck on staves, stob. They have larders of dead enemies. When a man is described as ragged and out of order, it is almost always added that his beard had grown over his face; and though beards are coming into fashion now, it is not a highland fashion to wear a beard; and many a stinging joke have I heard aimed at a bearded man by modern Highlanders. The shields of the warriors are Bucaideach, bossed; Balla Bhreachd, dotted and variegated; Bara chaol, with slender point; "with many a picture to be seen on it, a lion, a cremhinach, and a deadly snake;" and such shields are figured on the Iona tombs. The ancient Gauls wore helmets which represented beasts. The enchanted king's sons, when they came home to their dwellings, put off cochal, the husk, and become men; and when they go out, they resume the cochal and become animals of various kinds. May this not mean that they put on their armour. They marry a plurality of wives in many stories. In short, the enchanted warriors are, as I verily believe, nothing but real men, and their manners real manners, seen through a haze of centuries, and seen in the same light as they are seen in other popular tales, but, mayhap, a trifle clearer, because the men who tell of them are the descendants of the men described, and have mixed less with other men.

I do not mean that the tales date from any particular period, but that traces of all periods may be found in them—that various actors have played the same parts time out of mind, and that their manners and customs are all mixed together, and truly, though confusedly, represented—that giants and fairies, and enchanted princes were men; that Rob Roy may yet wear many heads in Australia, and be a god or an ogre, according to taste—that tales are but garbled popular history, of a long journey through forests and wilds, inhabited by savages and wild beasts; of events that occurred on the way from east to west, in the year of grace, once upon a time.

Tales certainly are historical in this sense when they treat of Eirinn and Lochlann, for the islands were the battlefield of the Celts and Scandinavians, and though they lack the precision of more modern popular history, they are very precise as to Irish names and geography. "They went to Cnoc Seannan in Ireland." Conall was called Gulbanach from Beinn Gulbain in Ireland. There is the "king of Newry," and many other places are named according to their Gaelic names, never as they are named in English. The same is true of the manuscript tales in the Advocates' Library. Places about Loch Awe are named, and the characters pass backwards and forwards between Ireland and Argyll, as we are told they really did when the Irish Celts invaded and possessed that part of the west of Scotland, and that invasion is clearly referred to in more than one popular tradition still current. When Lochlann is mentioned, it is further off, and all is uncertain. The king's son, not the king himself, is usually the hero. Breacan *MacRigh* Lochlainn is named, or the son of the king of Lochlann, without a name at all, but the Irish kings often have a whole pedigree; thus, Connall Gulbanach MacIulin MacArt Mac some one else, king of Ireland, and I lately heard a long story about "Magnus."

This again is like distorted, undated popular history of true events. They are clearly seen at home, the very spot where the action took place is pointed to; less clearly in Ireland, though people and places are named; they are dimly seen in Lochlann, and beyond that everything is enlarged, and magical, and mysterious, and grotesque. Real events are distorted into fables and magnified into supernatural occurrences, for the Gaelic proverbs truly say, "There are long horns on cattle in mist" or " in Ireland," and " Far away fowls have fine feathers."

But whether the stories are history or mythology, it is quite clear that they are very old, that they belong to a class which is very widely spread, and that they were not made by living men.

All story-tellers agree in saying that they learned them as traditions long ago; and if all those whose names are given had been inclined to tell "stories" in another sense, they could not have made and told the same stories at opposite ends of Scotland, almost simultaneously, to different people. James Wilson could not have told Conall Cra bhuidhe to Hector MacLean in Islay, about the same time that Neil Gillies was telling Conal Crobhi to me at Inverary, and a very short time before Hector Urquhart got No. 8 from Kenneth MacLennan in Gairloch. An old fisherman and an old porter could not have combined to tell a "story" which was in Straparola, in Italian, in 1567, to Hector MacLean in Barra, in 1859, and to the Rev. Mr. Mac-Lauchlan in Edinburgh, in 1860, unless these stories were popular facts, though despised as fictions; and they are curious facts too, for the frame of Conal is common to old German manuscripts, and some of the adventures are versions of those of Ulysses. There are many proverbs which are only explained when the story is known; for example, "blackberries in February" means nothing; but when explained by the story, the meaning is clearly the idea which an acquaintance of mine once embodied in a French toast, as "les impossibilités accomplies." The stories do not change rapidly, for I have gone back to a reciter after the lapse of a year, and I have heard him again repeat in Gaelic, what I had translated from his dictation, with hardly a change (vol. 1, p. 93).

I have now no doubt that the popular tales are very old; that they are old "Allabanaich," Highlanders and wanderers; that they have wandered, settled, and changed, with those who still tell them; and call themselves "Albannaich," men whose wandering spirit is not yet extinct, though they were settled in their present abodes "before the memory of man."

There was and is, a wandering spirit in the whole race, if Celts are Indo-Europeans. In the people who delighted in the adventures of Ulysses and Æneas, a longing spirit of western adventure, which was shewn in the fabled Atalantis, and the Island of the Seven Cities and St. Brandon—the spirit which drove the hordes of Asia to Europe, and urged Columbus to discover America, and which still survives in "the Green Isle of the great deep," "Eilan uaine an iomal torra domhain," of which so much is told, which Highland fancy still sees on the far western horizon, and which, as " FLATHINNIS," the Isle of Heroes, has now been raised from an earthly paradise to mean Heaven.

Much has been said about highland superstitions, and highlanders of the east and west, like their southern neighbours, have many, but they are at least respectable from their age; and because they are so widely spread over the world, I believe them to be nearly all fictions founded on facts.

Thirteen Highlanders would eat their potatoes together without fear, and one of them might spill the salt without a shudder. I never heard of a Celtic peasant consulting his table as an oracle, or going to a clairvoyant; but plenty of them dream dreams and see visions, and believe in them as men in Bible history did of old.

A man had been lost in crossing the dangerous ford, five or six miles of sand and rock, between Benbecula and North Uist, shortly before I was there in 1859. I was told the fact, and it was added incidentally, " And did he not come to his sister in a dream, and tell her where to find him? and she went to the place, and got him there, half buried in sand, after the whole country side had been looking for him in vain." Here is a similar story from Manchester :—

" FULFILMENT OF A DREAM.—An inquest was held last evening at Sheffield, before Mr. Thomas Badger, coroner, on the body of Mr. Charles Holmes, button manufacturer, Clough House Lane, who had been found drowned on Monday morning, in the Lead-mill dam in that town. The deceased left his home on Saturday night in company with his wife; they walked through the town together, and about nine o'clock, at which time they were at the top of Union Street, he said to her, ' I'm going to leave thee here, Fanny.' She said, ' Are you?' and he replied, ' Yes, I want to see an old friend who is going to Birmingham on Monday, and he is to be here.' She said to him, ' Well, Charlie, don't stop long, because I do feel queer about that dream,' and

he replied, ' Oh, don't say that ; I'll just have a glass, and then
come home. Go and get the supper ready, and I'll come directly.'
She then left him. When he got into the house he was invited
to drink with his friend, but he exhibited some reluctance, saying
that on the night before his wife had dreamed that she saw him
dead in a public-house, and that she had dreamed a similar dream
about a week before. Unfortunately, however, he yielded to the
temptation, got drunk, and did not leave the public-house till after
twelve. He was accompanied part of the way home by his friend,
and was never afterwards seen alive. Near his house are the
Lead-mill dams, and, in consequence of his not returning home,
his wife felt convinced that he had fallen in and got drowned. A
search was made, and on Monday morning his body was found
in the water, and was removed to the Royal Standard public-
house, where his wife saw the body, and identified it as that of
her husband. The jury returned a verdict of ' Found drowned,'
and recommended that an opening in the wall, near the dam,
through which it is supposed he had fallen, should be built up."—
Manchester Examiner.

There are plenty of lowlanders as well as "ignorant"
Highlanders who think that they are seers, without the
aid of a deal board through which to look into futurity,
by the help of a medium, and it is by no means uncom-
mon, as I am told, for the Astronomer-Royal to receive
English letters asking his advice, *ex officio*.

It may not be out of place to add a word as to the
spoken Gaelic of these tales ; the mode of writing it ;
and the English of the translation. First, then, it is
admitted by all that the Gaelic of the West Highlands
is a branch of the old Celtic stock, that is to say, the
language of some of the oldest invaders or inhabitants
of Europe of whom anything is known. Why it is I
know not, but from works on philology it appears that
the Highland dialect has been least studied, and for
that reason, if for no other, it is perhaps best worth
the trouble. I thought it best to ignore all that had
been said or written on the subject, to go direct to

those who now speak the language, especially to those who speak no other tongue ; to men who use words as they use their feet and hands, utterly unconscious of design ; who talk as nature and their parents taught them ; and who are as innocent of philology as their own babies when they first learn to say " Abbi."

I requested those who wrote for me to take down the words as they were spoken, and to write as they would speak themselves ; and the Gaelic of the tales is the result of such a process. The names of the writers are given, and I am satisfied that they have done their work faithfully and well. The Gaelic then is *not* what is called " classical Gaelic." It is generally the Gaelic of the people—pure from the source.

Next, as to orthography. I chose one man, Mr Hector MacLean, whom I knew to be free from prejudice, and who knows the rules of Gaelic spelling, to correct the press, and I asked him to spell the sounds which he heard, according to the principles of Gaelic orthography, whenever he wrote anything down himself ; and in correcting the press for the work of others, to correct nothing but manifest mistakes, and this he has done, as it appears to me, very well.

In Gaelic there are certain vowels, and combinations of them, which represent certain sounds ; and they are all sounded, and always in the same manner, *according to theory*, but in practice it is a very different matter. In speaking Gaelic, as is the case in other languages, various modes of pronouncing the same vowels exist in various districts. The consonants meet and contend and extinguish each other, and change the sound of the vowels in Gaelic more than in any other language which I know ; but they fight by rule, and the conquered and the slain encumber the words which are their battlefields, as dead or dying consonants stand-

h

ing beside the silent *h* which kills or controls them. One difficulty in writing Gaelic from dictation is to ascertain, in words of doubtful meaning, whether the sound *v* is to be expressed by *bh* or *mh*. The first letter was once at the head of a small regiment of letters, and sounded his own note *m* or *b*, and so he regulated the meaning of the rest, but having fallen in with an *h* in an oblique case, and being changed thereby to *v*, the whole history of the word must be known before it can be settled whether it should begin with *mh* or *bh*, and it is much more difficult in other cases, where the letter is silenced altogether. My mother, if Gaelic, might become *vy vother*—father, *ather*, but the sounds would be spelt *mhother*, *fhather*. The meaning in a book depends on the spelling, but in speaking, it is a different matter. There are shades of sound which an ear used to a language can detect, but which letters are wholly unfitted to express.

Gaelic scholars, then, who have a standard for Gaelic writing, and who adhere to it strictly, will probably find much which will appear to them erroneous spelling.

An English scholar reading Sir Walter Scott's novels will find plenty of words which are not in Johnson's Dictionary, and a student of Pickwick will find much in Sam Weller's conversation which he will not discover in that form in Shakspeare.

Had I found stories in the Isle of Wight I should have spelt good morning good marnin, because it is so pronounced ; falbh is spelt folbh when a story comes from some of the Western Islands, because it is so pronounced there ; and for the same reason iad is spelt cud. I have no doubt there are errors. I can only vouch for having chosen men who did their best in a very difficult matter ; for I do not believe that there are ten men now living who would write a hundred lines of Gaelic off hand and spell them in the same way. I very much doubt if ten men ever did live at the same time who would have agreed as to Gaelic spelling; and I know that I find forms of words in books which I have very rarely heard in conversation. For example, the plural in IIBII (*iv*) is very rare, the common form is AN.

The spelling of the first book printed in the Gaelic language, Bishop Carswell's Prayer-book, 1567, is not the same as the spelling of the Gaelic Bible. The Gaelic names in old charters are not spelt according to modern rule. The old Gaelic manuscripts in the Advocates' Library are spelt in various ways. Every man who has written Gaelic for me, spells words variously. Manks spelling is phonetic. Irish spelling is different; and where there is so little authority, I hope to be forgiven if I have ventured to ask men to follow their own road. I hope they will be forgiven if they have taken a short cut to gain a particular object, and if they have left the beaten path.

For the translation I am responsible, and I feel that the English needs excuse. It has been the fashion so far to translate Gaelic freely; that is, to give the sense of the passage without caring much for the sense of words. One result is, that dictionaries give so many meanings that they are almost useless to any one ignorant of Gaelic. There are many words in these tales which were new to me, and I have repeatedly been driven to gather their meaning from the context, or to ask for it at the source, because of the multitude of contradictory explanations given in dictionaries. Let me take one word as an example. In the first tale the hero meets CU SEANG NA COILL UAINE, and the meaning turned on the word SEANG. To that word the following meanings are attached :—Slender,

slender-waisted, hungry, hungry-looking, lank, lean,
active, handsome, strong; (applied to a shirt-front),
fine; "Sad am I this day arising the breast of my
shirt is not *seang;*" (applied to food in a proverb), meat
makes men "seang;" (applied to hinds in an ode), neat;
(applied to a horse), spirited; also slim, small, small-
bellied, gaunt, nimble, agile; (applied to lady), slender-
waisted. On looking further it appears that SEANGAN
is an ant; that SHUNKA is the Dakotah for all animals
of the dog species, and that the word came to be applied
to a horse, as spirit dog, when horses came first to
that country; and it further appears that there is a
word in broad Scotch which nearly fits the Gaelic,
SWANK; that SING means a lion in India; and that the
horses of the sun were swankas with beautiful steps
in Sanscrit. It seemed to me that the phrase might be
thus freely translated " The Forest Lion."

But though it seemed to me possible I might be
entirely wrong, so I gave the meaning of the words,
about which there could be no mistake :—

> CU SEANG NA COILL' UAINE.
> Dog slim of the wood green.

My belief is, that the word was an adjective, descriptive of the qualities of a lion wherever their likeness is to be found—as strength, activity, high courage,
bold bearing, slender form, hunger, satiety; but I did
not venture to translate CU SEANG by "*lion,*" nor by
"*greyhound,*" as I was advised to do. I translated it by
those words which seem to give the present meaning
of the Gaelic. CU, a dog; SEANG, slim; and the phrase
stands, " The slim dog of the green wood."

And so throughout I have aimed at giving the present real meaning of every separate word, but so as to
give its true meaning in the passage in which it occurs.

Where I have not been able to do both, I have tried
to keep as close as I could to the original idea involved.
For example, "In the mouth of night" is new to English, but it is comprehensible, and it is the exact meaning of the phrase commonly used to express the first
coming on of darkness. The expression is poetical. It
seems to refer to some old mythical notion that the
sun went into a cave or a tent to sleep, for "Take thy
sleep in thy cave" is a line in Ossian's "Address to
the Sun," and though it was suggested to me to alter
this translation, and make it "good English," I thought
it best to adhere to my original plan. Generally where
the phrase occurs it is translated "in the mouth of
night," though I was advised to write, "in the dusk,"
"in the evening," "at nightfall," "in the mantle of
night," "at twilight," "in the grey of the evening."

I admit that all these phrases express ideas which
might be attached to the words ; but what could an
unfortunate student make of a passage in which a word
meaning *mouth* according to all dictionaries, should
seem to mean *mantle*, or *fall*, or *grey*. It is very much
easier to write naturally and translate freely ; and as
I have tried hard to make my translation a close one, I
hope the bad English will be forgiven.

Those only who have tried to turn Gaelic into English can understand the difficulty. There are in fact
many Gaelic phrases which will not go into English at
all. For example, THA SO AGAM (I have this), *is this
at me*, or *with me*, or *by me*, is a phrase which cannot
be rendered for want of a word equivalent to AG or AIG,
which expresses position and possession, and is combined with *am, ad, e, inn, ibh*, and changed to *aca* to
express the persons. Gaelic will not bear literal translation into English, but I have tried to give the real
meaning of every word as nearly as I could, and to

give it by using the English word which most resembled
the Gaelic ; and thus I have unexpectedly fallen in
with a number of English words which seem to have the
same origin as Gaelic, if they are not survivors of the
language of the ancient Britons. I have translated CLAIDH-
EAMH, pronounced Claiv, by glave, TRAILL by thrall,
and so throughout wherever I have thought of an English word that resembled a word admitted to be Gaelic.

It is my own opinion, and it is that of Mr. Mac-
Lean, that the Gaelic language is the same from Cape
Clear in Ireland to Cape Wrath in Scotland, though
there are many dialects, and there is much variety.
The language was taught to me by a native of Lorn,
and he was chosen by the advice of men well able to
judge, as a native of the district where the best Gaelic
was then supposed to be spoken. Speaking from my own
experience, I can converse freely in Lorn Gaelic with
Scotch Highlanders in every district of Scotland, and
with natives of Rathlin. I can make my way with
natives of the North of Ireland, but I cannot converse
with the natives of some Irish districts. I could
not make the Manksmen understand me, but I can
readily understand most of the words in Manks and in
Irish, when pronounced separately.

There are a very great many words in Welsh and
in Breton which I can understand, or trace when they
are separately spoken, but the difference in these is
much wider. Peasants come from Connaught to Islay,
and in a very short time converse freely, though their
accent betrays them ; but an Argyllshire Highlander
is known in the north by his accent, just as a York-
shireman would be found out in Somersetshire. An
Islay man is detected in Mull, and a native of one
parish in Islay is detected when he speaks in another
but though there are such shades of difference, a High-

lander used to hear languages variously spoken should
have no difficulty in understanding any dialect of
Gaelic spoken in Scotland, and most of the Irish dialects.
But which of all these is the best who is to decide?
The author of a very good dictionary says, under the
word coig, that "in the islands of Argyllshire every word
is pronounced just as Adam spoke it." Dr. Johnson pronounced the whole to be the rude speech of a barbarous
people; and the Saxon knew as much of Gaelic as the
Celt did of Adam. One Gaelic scholar wished to change
the island words; a good Highlander told me that Dalmally was the best place for Gaelic, another was all for
Western Ross. Nobody has a good word for Sutherland Gaelic, but it is very pure nevertheless in some
districts; north country men are all for Inverness. I
have heard excellent Gaelic in the Long Island. On
the whole, I am inclined to think that dialect the best
which resembles the largest number of others, and
that is the dialect spoken by the most illiterate in the
islands, and on the promontories farthest to the west.
I will not venture to name any district, because I have
no wish to contend with the natives of all the others.

The spirit of nationality is one which has a large
development amongst my countrymen, and the subject of
language brings it out in strong relief. It is but a
phase of human nature, a result of the quality which
phrenologists describe as combativeness, and it seems
to be common to all the races classed as Indo-European.

It is a common opinion in England that one Englishman can thrash three Frenchmen; and I have no
doubt that a similar opinion prevails in France, though
I do not know the fact. Highlanders believe that
lowlanders generally are soft and effeminate; lowlanders think that mountaineers are savages. An Irish
Celt detests his brother Celt over the water. A Scotch

Celt calls another Eireannach when he abuses him, but let a common foe appear and they will all combine.

England, Ireland, and Scotland are up in arms, with rifles on their shoulders, at a hint of the approach of a Frenchman; but they joined France with heart and hand to fight the Russian and the Chinese; and as soon as the battle was over, they came back and fought at home.

The English lion stirred up the Scotch lion in the English press, and the northern lion growled over his wrongs. Ireland began to tell of the tyrant Saxon, and a stranger might think that the Union was about to fall to pieces. It is not so; it is but a manifestation of superfluous energy which breaks out in the other "union" over the water, and makes as much noise there as steam blowing off elsewhere.

I maintain that there is chronic war in every part of her Majesty's dominions. Not long ago a dispute arose about a manner of catching herrings. One set of men caught them with drift-nets, another with drag-nets, and one party declared that the other violated the law; blood got up, and at last a whole fleet of fishing-boats left their ground and sailed twenty miles down to attack the rival fleet in form. A gun-boat joined the party, and peace was preserved; but it was more the result of a calm, which enabled the light row-boats to escape from the heavier sailing fleet. Both parties spoke the same language, and on any subject but herrings, they would have backed each other through the world.

The purchase of an orange, and a box on the ear, grew into a serious riot in a northern town last year. The fight spread as from a centre, and lasted three days; but here it developed itself into a fight between Celt and Saxon. Both sides must have been in the wrong, and I am quite sure they were both ignominiously defeated, although they may hold the contrary.

Every election in the three kingdoms is a shameful riot, according to some public organ, whose party get the worst of it.

There is a regular stand-up fight in Paris periodically, the rest of Europe goes to war in earnest at every opportunity, and when there are no national or class wars, men fight as individuals all over the world. I was once at Christmas at a hurling match in Ireland. The game was played on ice on a lake, and after some hours the owner of the lake sent down a Scotch butler with bread and cheese and whisky for the players. They gathered about the cart in perfect good humour, when suddenly, without cause, an excited banker's clerk shouted, "Hurroo for——" (the nearest post town), and performed a kind of war dance on the outside edge of his skates, flourishing a stick wildly, and chanting his war song, "I'll bet ere a man in England, Ireland, or SCOTLAND." A knobby stick rose up in the crowd, and the Scotch butler was down; but an Irish boy who had not opened his mouth was the next. He went head-foremost into a willow bush amongst the snow, and three men in frieze great-coats kicked him with nailed shoes. In ten minutes the storm was over, the butler was up again in his cart dispensing the refreshments, the man in the bush was consoling himself with a dram, and all was peace. But that night the country party took up a position behind a stone wall, and when the others came, they sallied forth, and there was a battle-royal.

So I have seen a parish shinny match in the Highlands become so hot and furious, that the leaders were forced to get two pipers and march their troops out of the field in opposite directions, to prevent a civil war of parishes.

And so, a part of her Majesty's guards having gone

out to exercise at Clewer, and being stationed as " the enemy" at some point, obstinately refused to "retreat in disorder;" but stood their ground with such determination, that the officers had to sound the retreat on both sides to prevent a serious battle.

So at Eton, shins were broken in my tutor's football match against my dame's ; and boys injured themselves in rowing frantically for the honour of upper or lower sixes.

Two twins, who were so like, that one used to skip round a pillar and answer to his brother's name, and who probably would have died for each other, still fought in private so earnestly, that one carried the mark of a shovel on his forehead for many a long day ; and so boys fight, and men fight, individually and collectively, as parties, races, and nations, all over Europe, if not all over the world.

I decline to state my opinion as to which Gaelic is the best, for that is a peculiarly delicate subject, my countrymen having ceased to use their dirks, are apt to fight with pens, and I would rather see the children of the Gael, in this as in other matters, fighting shoulder to shoulder against foes, and working side by side with their friends.

The Gaelic language is essentially descriptive, rich in words, which by their sound alone express ideas. The thundering sound of the waves beating on the shore is well expressed by TONN, a wave ; LUNN, a heavy Atlantic swell.

The harsh rattling and crushing of thunder by TAIRNEANACH.

The plunge of a heavy body thrown into deep water by TUNN, plunge.

The noise of small stones and fine gravel streaming seawards from a beach in the undertow is heard in SGRITHEAN, gravel.

The tinkling of shells as they slip and slide on the sand at the edge of the sea is heard in SLIGEAN, shells.

The hard sharp knocking of stones in CLACH, a stone, and thence all manner of compound ideas follow as CLACHAN, a village ; CLACHAIR, a mason ; CLACHARAN, a stone chat.

The names of domestic animals usually resemble their notes. Bo, a cow ; gobhar, a goat ; caora, a sheep ; laogh, a calf. Words such as barking, growling, squealing, coughing, sneezing, suggest the idea by the sound, as they do in English. Many names of beasts and birds, which are not of this class, are descriptive in another sense. The grouse are the reddish brown cock and hen ; the fox, the reddish brown dog ; the wolf, the fierce dog ; the sandpiper, the little driolichan of the strand. The crow is the flayer, the falcon, the darter ; the otter the brown or black beast.

It is a language full of metaphorical and descriptive expressions. " He went to the beginning of fortune ;" " he put the world under his head ;" " he took his own body home ;" " he went away"—that is, he went home sick, and he died. " There were great masses of rain, and there was night and there was darkness." " Ye must not be out amidst the night, she is dark."

It is rich in words expressive of war, by no means rich in words belonging to the arts. CRANN, a tree, means a mast, the bar of a door, a plough, and many other things made of wood. BEAIRT means a loom, a block and tackling, and engines of various kinds.

It seems to contain words to express the great features of nature, which can be traced in the names of rivers and mountains in a great part of Europe, such as EAS, a rapid (pr. ace) ; ATH (pr. A. and AV.), a ford ; AMHAINN, OBHAINN, ABHAINN, a river, variously pronounced, *avain, a-wen, ovain, o-in, o-un, o-n.* Calais

I take to be CALA, a harbour; the word has no meaning in French. Boulogne might be BEUL OBHAINN, river's mouth; Donau, the Danube, might mean the brown river. Tana might mean the shallow, and both are descriptive.

Rhine might mean the division, and there is a district in Islay whose name is pronounced exactly as the name of the great German river. Balaclava is exceedingly like the name of an Islay farm, and might mean kite's town, BAILE CHLAMHAIN; but though such resemblances can hardly fail to occur to any one who knows the Gaelic language, it requires time and careful study to follow out such a subject, and it is foreign to my purpose. There are plenty of Gaelic words which closely resemble words in other European languages. Amongst the few Sanscrit words which I have been able to glean from books, I find several which resemble Gaelic words of similar meaning—JWALA, light flame, has many Gaelic relations in words which mean shining, fire, lightning, the moon, white, swan.

DYU, day, is like an diugh, to-day; MIRAH, the ocean, like muir mara, the sea; but this again is foreign to my purpose.

My wish has been simply to gather some specimens of the wreck so plentifully strewn on the coasts of old Scotland, and to carry it where others may examine it; rather to point out where curious objects worth some attention may be found, than to gather a great heap. I have not sought for stranded forests. I have not polished the rough sticks which I found; I have but cut off a very few offending splinters, and I trust that some may be found who will not utterly despise such rubbish, or scorn the magic which peasants attribute to a fairy egg.

POSTSCRIPT.

September 1860.

THE stories which follow page 266 of the first volume were intended for the second, but it has been found more convenient to place them in Vol. I. Those which were to have been given as specimens of tales probably derived from the "Arabian Nights," have been left out to make room for others.

In August and September 1860 I again visited the Western Highlands, carrying with me nearly the whole of these two volumes in print. I have repeatedly made the men who told the stories to my collectors repeat them to me, while I compared their words with the book. In two instances I have made men repeat stories which I had myself written down in English from their Gaelic, and I have found no important variation in any instance. I find that the story is generally much longer as told, but that it is lengthened by dialogue, which has often little to do with the incidents, though sometimes worth preservation. I have now seen most of the men whose names are mentioned, and I have myself heard versions of nearly every story in the book repeated, either by those from whom they were got, or by people who live far from them,—for instance, John Mackinnon, stableman at Broadford, in Skye, told me in September a version of No. 18, which contains nearly all the incidents which I had before got from Islay, and several which were new to me.

Including those which are printed, I have more than two hundred stories written down in Gaelic. I have about an equal number written in English from Gaelic, and I have heard a great many more, while Mr. Hector MacLean, Mr. Dewar, Mr. Carmichael, Mr. Torrie, Mr. Fraser, and others, are still writing down for me, in the Long Island, in Argyllshire, and elsewhere.

If I have time and opportunity, I hope hereafter to arrange these materials; to place the incidents in *each* story according to the majority of versions, and so strive to get the old form of the legends; for I am convinced that much is to be learned from this despised old rubbish, though it must be sifted before it can be turned to proper use.

In conclusion, I would tender my thanks once more to all those who have given me their assistance. In particular, I wish to express my sense of obligation to the Rev. Thomas Maclauchlan, Free Church Gaelic minister in Edinburgh, who has contributed many stories, written down by himself from the dictation of one of his parishioners, and who has himself published a volume of Celtic gleanings.

I am also much indebted to the Rev. Mr. Beatson, minister of Barra, who aided Mr. MacLean in his search for legends, and who shewed much kindness to myself; and I have received assistance from other clergymen of various persuasions, including the Rev. Thomas Pattison in Islay. I am happy to have it in my power to mention such names; for the strange idea possesses the people in many districts, that to repeat the most harmless sgeulachd is a grievous sin, and that fables, and poems, and novels of every sort ought to be put down and exterminated, because they are fictions. That spirit, if strong enough and put in action, would sweep away much of the literature of ancient and modern times ; and it seems strange to have to remonstrate against it now-a-days. Still, strange as it may seem, the spirit exists, and I am grateful for the support of enlightened liberal men. Surely the best treatment for "Super-stition," if this be superstition, is to drag it into light, the very worst to dignify it by persecution, and strive to hide it.

POPULAR TALES

OF

THE WEST HIGHLANDS.

———◆———

I.

THE YOUNG KING OF EASAIDH RUADH.

From James Wilson, blind fiddler, Islay.

THE young king of Easaidh Ruadh, after he got the
heirship to himself, was at much merry making,
looking out what would suit him, and what would
come into his humour. There was a GRUAGACH near his
dwelling, who was called Gruagach carsalach donn—
(The brown curly long-haired one.)

He thought to himself that he would go to play a
game with him. He went to the Seanagal (soothsayer)
and he said to him—"I am made up that I will go to
game with the Gruagach carsalach donn." "Aha!"
said the Seanagal, "art thou such a man? Art thou
so insolent that thou art going to play a game against
the Gruagach carsalach donn? 'T were my advice to
thee to change thy nature and not to go there." "I
wont do that," said he. "'T were my advice to thee, if
thou shouldst win of the Gruagach carsalach donn, to

B

get the cropped rough-skinned maid that is behind the
door for the worth of thy gaming, and many a turn will
he put off before thou gettest her." He lay down that
night, and if it was early that the day came, 't was earlier
than that that the king arose to hold gaming against
the Gruagach. He reached the Gruagach, he blessed
the Gruagach, and the Gruagach blessed him. Said the
Gruagach to him, "Oh young king of Easaidh Ruadh,
what brought thee to me to-day? Wilt thou game
with me?" They began and they played the game.
The king won. "Lift the stake of thy gaming so that
I may get (leave) to be moving." "The stake of my
gaming is to give me the cropped rough-skinned girl
thou hast behind the door." "Many a fair woman
have I within besides her," said the Gruagach. "I
will take none but that one." "Blessing to thee and
cursing to thy teacher of learning." They went to the
house of the Gruagach, and the Gruagach set in order
twenty young girls. "Lift now thy choice from
amongst these." One was coming out after another,
and every one that would come out she would say, " I
am she; art thou not silly that art not taking me with
thee?" But the Scanagal had asked him to take none
but the last one that would come out. When the last
one came out, he said, "This is mine." He went with
her, and when they were a bit from the house, her form
altered, and she is the loveliest woman that was on
earth. The king was going home full of joy at getting
such a charming woman.

He reached the house, and he went to rest. If it
was early that the day arose, it was earlier than that
that the king arose to go to game with the Gruagach.
"I must absolutely go to game against the Gruagach
to-day," said he to his wife. "Oh!" said she, "that's
my father, and if thou goest to game with him, take

nothing for the stake of thy play but the dun shaggy filly that has the stick saddle on her."

The king went to encounter the Gruagach, and surely the blessing of the two to each other was not beyond what it was before. "Yes!" said the Gruagach, "how did thy young bride please thee yesterday?" "She pleased fully." "Hast thou come to game with me to-day?" "I came." They began at the gaming, and the king won from the Gruagach on that day. "Lift the stake of thy gaming, and be sharp about it." "The stake of my gaming is the dun shaggy filly on which is the stick saddle."

They went away together. They reached the dun shaggy filly. He took her out from the stable, and the king put his leg over her and she was the swift heroine! He went home. His wife had her hands spread before him, and they were cheery together that night. "I would rather myself," said his wife, "that thou shouldest not go to game with the Gruagach any more, for if he wins he will put trouble on thy head." "I won't do that," said he, "I *will* go to play with him to-day."

He went to play with the Gruagach. When he arrived, he thought the Gruagach was seized with joy. "Hast thou come?" he said. "I came." They played the game, and, as a cursed victory for the king, the Gruagach won that day. "Lift the stake of thy game," said the young king of Easaidh Ruadh, "and be not heavy on me, for I cannot stand to it." The stake of my play is," said he, "that I lay it as crosses and as spells on thee, and as the defect of the year, that the cropped rough-skinned creature, more uncouth and unworthy than thou thyself, should take thy head, and thy neck, and thy life's look off, if thou dost not get for me the GLAIVE OF LIGHT of the king of the oak windows." The king went home, heavily, poorly, gloomily. The young queen came meeting him, and she said to him, " Moh-rooai ! my pity ! there is nothing with thee to-night." Her face and her splendour gave some pleasure to the king when he looked on her brow, but when he sat on a chair to draw her towards him, his heart was so heavy that the chair broke under him.

"What ails thee, or what should ail thee, that thou mightest not tell it to me ?" said the queen. The king told how it happened. "Ha !" said she, " what should'st thou mind, and that thou hast the best wife in Erin, and the second best horse in Erin. If thou takest my advice, thou wilt come (well) out of all these things yet."

If it was early that the day came, it was earlier than that that the queen arose, and she set order in everything, for the king was about to go on his journey. She set in order the dun shaggy filly, on which was the stick saddle, and though he saw it as wood, it was full of sparklings with gold and silver. He got on it ; the queen kissed him, and she wished him victory of battlefields. " I need not be telling thee anything. Take thou the advice of thine own she comrade, the filly, and she will tell thee what thou shouldest do." He set out on his journey, and it was not dreary to be on the dun steed.

She would catch the swift March wind that would be before, and the swift March wind would not catch her. They came at the mouth of dusk and lateness, to the court and castle of the king of the oak windows.

Said the dun shaggy filly to him, " We are at the end of the journey, and we have not to go any further ; take my advice, and I will take thee where the sword of light of the king of the oak windows is, and if it comes with thee without scrape or creak, it is a good mark on our journey. The king is now at his dinner, and the sword of light is in his own chamber. There is a knob on its end, and when thou catchest the sword, draw it softly out of the window 'case.'" He came to the window where the sword was. He caught the sword and it came with him softly till it was at its point, and then it gave a sort of a "sgread." "We will now be going," said the filly. "It is no stopping time for us. I know the king has felt us taking the sword out." He kept his sword in his hand, and they went away, and when they were a bit forward, the filly said, "We will stop now, and look thou whom thou seest behind thee." "I see," said he, "a swarm of brown horses coming madly." "We are swifter ourselves than these yet," said the filly. They went, and when they were a good distance forward, "Look now," said she ; "whom seest thou coming?" "I see a swarm of black horses, and one white-faced black horse, and he is coming and coming in madness, and a man on him." "That is the best horse in Erin ; it is my brother, and he got three months more nursing than I, and he will come past me with a whirr, and try if thou wilt be so ready, that when he comes past me, thou wilt take the head off the man who is on him ; for in the time of passing he will look at thee, and there is no sword in his court will take off his head but the very sword that is in thy hand." When this man was going past, he gave his head a turn to look at him, he drew the sword and he took his head off, and the shaggy dun filly caught it in her mouth.

This was the king of the oak windows. "Leap on the black horse," said she, "and leave the carcass there, and be going home as fast as he will take thee home, and I will be coming as best I may after thee." He leaped on the black horse, and, "moire!" he was the

swift hero, and they reached the house long before day.
The queen was without rest till he arrived. They
raised music, and they laid down woe. On the morrow,
he said, "I am obliged to go to see the Gruagach
to-day, to try if my spells will be loose." "Mind that
it is not as usual the Gruagach will meet thee. He
will meet thee furiously, wildly, and he will say to thee,
didst thou get the sword? and say thou that thou hast
got it; he will say, how didst thou get it? and thou
shalt say, if it were not the knob that was on its end
I had not got it. He will ask thee again, how didst
thou get the sword? and thou wilt say, if it were not
the knob that was on its end, I had not got it. Then
he will give himself a lift to look what knob is on the
sword, and thou wilt see a mole on the right side of
his neck, and stab the point of the sword in the mole;
and if thou dost not hit the mole, thou and I are done.
His brother was the king of the oak windows, and he
knows that till the other had lost his life, he would
not part with the sword. The death of the two is in
the sword, but there is no other sword that will touch
them but it." The queen kissed him, and she called
on victory of battlefields (to be) with him, and he went
away.

The Gruagach met him in the very same place
where he was before. "Didst thou get the sword?"
"I got the sword." "How didst thou get the sword?"
"If it were not the knob that was on its end I had not
got it," said he. "Let me see the sword." "It was
not laid on me to let thee see it." "How didst thou
get the sword?" "If it were not the knob that was
on its end, I got it not." The Gruagach gave his head
a lift to look at the sword; he saw the mole; he was
sharp and quick, and he thrust the sword into the
mole, and the Gruagach fell down dead.

He returned home, and when he returned home, he found his set of keepers and watchers tied there back to back, without wife, or horse, or sweetheart of his, but was taken away.

When he loosed them, they said to him, " A great giant came and he took away thy wife and thy two horses." " Sleep will not come on mine eyes nor rest on my head till I get my wife and my two horses back." In saying this, he went on his journey. He took the side that the track of the horses was, and he followed them diligently. The dusk and lateness were coming on him, and no stop did he make till he reached the side of the green wood. He saw where there was the forming of the site of a fire, and he thought that he would put fire upon it, and thus he would put the night past there.

He was not long here at the fire, when " Cu Seang " of the green wood came on him.

He blessed the dog, and the dog blessed him.

" Oov ! oov !" said the dog. " Bad was the plight of thy wife and thy two horses here last night with the big giant." " It is that which has set me so pained and pitiful on their track to-night ; but there is no help for it." " Oh ! king," said the dog, " thou must not be without meat." The dog went into the wood. He brought out creatures, and they made them meat contentedly. " I rather think myself," said the king, " that I may turn home ; that I cannot go near that giant." " Don't do that," said the dog. " There's no fear of thee, king. Thy matter will grow with thee. Thou must not be here without sleeping." " Fear will not let me sleep without a warranty." " Sleep thou," said the dog, " and I will warrant thee." The king let himself down, stretched out at the side of the fire, and he slept. When the watch broke, the dog said to him,

"Rise up, king, till thou gettest a morsel of meat that
will strengthen thee, till thou wilt be going on thy
journey. Now," said the dog, "if hardship or difficulty
comes on thee, ask my aid, and I will be with thee in
an instant." They left a blessing with each other, and
he went away. In the time of dusk and lateness, he
came to a great precipice of rock, and there was the
forming of the site of a fire.

He thought he would gather dry fuel, and that he
would set on fire. He began to warm himself, and he
was not long thus when the hoary hawk of the grey
rock came on him. "Oov! oov!" said she. "Bad
was the plight of thy wife and thy two horses last night
with the big giant." "There is no help for it," said
he. "I have got much of their trouble and little of
their benefit myself." "Catch courage," said she.
"Thou wilt get something of their benefit yet. Thou
must not be without meat here," said she. "There is
no contrivance for getting meat," said he. "We will
not be long getting meat," said the falcon. She went,
and she was not long when she came with three ducks
and eight blackcocks in her mouth. They set their
meat in order, and they took it. "Thou must not be
without sleep," said the falcon. "How shall I sleep
without a warranty over me, to keep me from any one
evil that is here." "Sleep thou, king, and I will
warrant thee." He let himself down, stretched out,
and he slept.

In the morning, the falcon set him on foot. "Hardship or difficulty that comes on thee, mind, at any
time, that thou wilt get my help." He went swiftly,
sturdily. The night was coming, and the little birds of
the forest of Branching bushy trees, were taking about
the briar roots and the twig tops; and if they were, it
was stillness, not peace for him, till he came to the side of

a great river that was there, and at the bank of the river there was the forming of the site of a fire. The king blew a heavy, little spark of fire. He was not long here when there came as company for him the brown otter of the river. . " Och! och!" said the otter. " Bad was the plight of thy wife and thy two horses last night with the giant." "There is no help for it. I got much of their trouble and little of their benefit." " Catch courage, before mid-day to-morrow thou wilt see thy wife. Oh! king, thou must not be without meat," said the otter. "How is meat to be got here?" said the king. The otter went through the river, and she came and three salmon with her, that were splendid. They made meat, and they took it. Said the otter to the king, "Thou must sleep." "How can I sleep without any warranty over me?" "Sleep thou, and I will warrant thee." The king slept. In the morning, the otter said to him, "Thou wilt be this night in presence of thy wife." He left blessing with the otter. "Now," said the otter, "if difficulty be on thee, ask my aid, and thou shalt get it." The king went till he reached a rock, and he looked down into a chasm that was in the rock, and at the bottom he saw his wife and his two horses, and he did not know how he should get where they were. He went round till he came to the foot of the rock, and there was a fine road for going in. He went in, and if he went it was then she began crying. "Ud! ud!" said he, "this is bad! If thou art crying now when I myself have got so much trouble coming about thee." "Oo!" said the horses, " set him in front of us, and there is no fear for him, till we leave this." She made meat for him, and she set him to rights, and when they were a while together, she put him in front of the horses. When the giant came, he said, "The smell of the stranger is within." Says she, "My treasure! My joy and my cattle! there is nothing but the smell of the litter of the horses." At the end of a while he went to give meat to the horses, and the horses began at him, and they all but killed him, and he hardly crawled from them. "Dear thing," said she, "they are like to kill thee." "If I myself had my soul to keep, it's long since they had killed me," said he. "Where, dear, is thy soul? by the books I will take care of it." "It is," said he, "in the Bonnach stone." When he went on the morrow, she set the Bonnach stone in order exceedingly. In the time of dusk and lateness, the giant came home. She set her man in front of the horses. The giant went to give the horses meat and they mangled him more and more. "What made thee set the Bonnach stone in order like that?" said he. "Because thy soul is in it." "I perceive that if thou didst know where my soul is, thou wouldst give it much respect." "I would give (that)," said she. "It is not there," said he, "my soul is; it is in the threshold." She set in order the threshold finely on the morrow. When the giant returned, he went to give meat to the horses, and the horses mangled him more and more. "What brought thee to set the threshold in order like that?" "Because thy soul is in it." "I perceive if thou knewest where my soul is, that thou wouldst take care of it." "I would take that," said she. "It is not there that my soul is," said he. "There is a great flagstone under the threshold. There is a wether under the flag. There is a duck in the wether's belly, and an egg in the belly of the duck, and it is in the egg that my soul is." When the giant went away on the morrow's day, they raised the flagstone and out went the wether. "If I had the slim dog of the green-wood, he would not be long bringing the wether to me." The slim dog of the greenwood came with the wether in his mouth. When they opened the wether, out was the duck on the wing with the other ducks. "If I had the Hoary Hawk of the grey rock, she would not be long bringing the duck to me." The Hoary Hawk of the grey rock came with the duck in her mouth; when they split the duck to take the egg from her belly, out went the egg into the depth of the ocean. "If I had the brown otter of the river, he would not be long bringing the egg to me." The brown otter came and the egg in her mouth, and the queen caught the egg, and she crushed it between her two hands. The giant was coming in the lateness, and when she crushed the egg, he fell down dead, and he has never yet moved out of that. They took with them a great deal of his gold and silver. They passed a cheery night with the brown otter of the river, a night with the hoary falcon of the grey rock, and a night with the slim dog of the greenwood. They came home and they set in order "a CUIRM CURAIDH CRIDHEIL," a hearty hero's feast, and they were lucky and well pleased after that.

Received June 9, 1859.

An old man, of the name of Angus MacQueen, who lived at Ballochroy, near Portaskaig, in Islay, " who could recite Ossian's Poems," taught this more than forty years ago (say 1820) to James Wilson, blind fiddler in Islay, who recited it to Hector MacLean, schoolmaster, Islay.

The Gaelic is dictated and written by Islay men.

RIGH OG EASAIDH RUAGH.

Bha rìgh òg Easaidh Ruagh an dèigh dha'n oighreachd f haotainn da fèin ri mòran àbhachd, ag amharc a mach dè a chordadh ris, 's dè thigeadh r 'a nadur. Bha gruagach fagus d'a chomhnuidh ris an abradh iad a ghruagach charsalach dhonn. Smaointich e ris fèin gun rachadh e a dh' iomairt cluiche ris. Dh' fhalbh e thun an t-seanagh-ail, 's thubhairt e ris, " tha mi air a dheanadh suas gun d'thèid mi dh' iomairt cluiche ris a' ghruagach charsalach dhonn." " Aha," arsa 'n seanagheal, " an duine mar so thu? am bheil thu cho uaibh-reach 's gu bheil thu a' dol a dh' iomairt cluiche ris a a' ghruagach charsalach dhonn? B'e mo chomhairle dhuit do nadur atharrachadh 's gun dol ann." " Cha dean mi sin." " B'e mo chomhairle dhuit ma bhùidhneas thu air a' ghruagach charsalach dhonn, an nighean mhaol charrach a tha cùl an doruis fhaotainn air son brìgh do chluiche, 's cuiridh e ioma car dheth mu'm faigh thu i." Chaidh e laidhe 'n oidhche sin, 's ma 's moch a thainig an latha 's moiche na sin a dh' èirich an rìgh a chumail cluiche ris a'ghruagaich. Ràinig e a ghruagach. Bheannaich e do'n ghruagaich 's bheannaich a ghruagach dà. Thuirt a ghruagach ris, " A righ òg Easaidh Ruagh, dè thug a' m'ionnsuidh an diugh thu? an iomair thu cluiche rium?" Thòisich iad 's dh' iomair iad an cluiche. Bhùidhinn an rìgh. " Tog brìgh do chluiche 's gu'm faighinn a bhi 'g imeachd." " 'S e brìgh mo chluiche thu thoirt domh na nighin maoil carraich a th' agad air cùl an doruis." " 'S iomad boireannach maiseach a th'agamsa stigh a bharrachd urra." " Cha ghabh mi gin ach i siod." " Beannachd dhuitse 's mollachd do d' oid-ionnsachaidh." Chàidh iad gu tigh na gruagaich 's chuir a' ghruagach an òrdugh fichead nighean òg. " Tog a nis do roghainn asda sin." Bha tè 'tighinn a mach an dèigh tè, 's a h-uile tè 'thigeadh a mach, theireadh i, " is mis' i, 's amaideach thu nach 'eil 'g am thobhairtse leat;" ach dh'iarr an seanaghal air gun gin a ghabhail ach an tè mu dheireadh a thigeadh a mach. 'N uair a thainig an tè mu dheireadh a mach thuirt e " so mo thè-sa." Dh' fholbh e leatha 's 'nuair a bha iad stàtuinn o'n tigh dh'atharraich a cruth, agus 's i boireannach a b'àille 'bha air thalamh. Bha'n rìgh 'dol dachaidh làn toil-inntinn leithid de bhoireannach maiseach fhaotainn. Ràinig e'n tigh. Chaidh e laidhe. Ma 's moch a thainig an latha, is moiche na sin a dh'èirich an rìgh, 'dhol a dh'iomairt cluiche ris a ghruagaich. " Is èigin domh dol a dh'iomairt cluiche ris a ghruagaich an diugh," ars' e r'a bhean. " O," ars' ise, " sin m'athair 's ma thèid thu dh'iomairt cluiche ris, na gabh ni sam bith airson brìgh do chluiche ach an loth pheallagach odhar

a tha 'n diollaid mhaid' urra. Dh' fholbh an rìgh, 's choinnich a
ghruagach e, 's gu cinnteach cha robh 'm beannachadh na bu tàire
na bha e roimhe aig an dithis ri chéile. "Seadh," ars' a ghruagach
"demur a chòrd do bhean òg riut an dé?" "Chord gu h-iomlan."
"An d' thàinig thu dh'iomairt cluiche rium an diugh?" "Thàinig."
Thòisich iad air a' chluiche, 's bhuidhinn an rìgh air a' ghruagaich an
latha sin. "Tog brìgh do chluiche 's bi ealamh leis." "'S e brìgh mo
chluiche gum faigh mi an loth pheallagach odhar air a' bheil an
dìollaid mhaide." Dh' fholbh iad, còmhla. Ràinig iad an loth
pheallagach odhar, thug e mach as an stàbull i, 's chuir an rìgh a
chas thairte, 's b'e 'n curaidh i. Chaidh e dhachaidh; bha làmhan
sgaoilt' aig a' bhean roimhe; 's bha iad gu sùnndach còmhla
an oidhche sin. "B' fheàrr leam féin," ursa 'bhean, "nach rachadh
thu 'dh'iomairt cluiche ris a' ghruagach tuillidh, chionn ma bhuidh-
neas e cuiridh e dragh ann ad cheann." "Cha dean mi sin;
thèid mi dh'iomairt cluiche ris an diugh." Chaidh e dh'iomairt
cluiche ris a' ghruagaich. 'N uair a ràinig e, thar leis gun do ghabh a
ghruagach boch. "An d' thàinig thu?" "Thàinig." Dh'iomair iad
an cluiche, 's mar bhuaidh mhollachd do'n rìgh bhuidhinn a' ghruagach
an latha sin. "Tog brìgh do chluiche," arsa rìgh òg Eas ruagh, "'s na
bi trom orm, chionn cha-n urrainn mi seasamh ris." "S' e brìgh mo
chluiche-sa," urs' esan, "gu bheil mi 'cur mar chroisean, 'us mar
gheasan ort, 'us mar *sheisean* na bliadhna, am beathach maol carrach
is mithreubhaiche 's is mi-threònaiche na thu féin, a thoirt do chinn 's
do mhuineil 's do choimhead-beatha dhiot, mar am faigh thu dhomhsa
claidheamh soluis rìgh nan uinneagan daraich." Chaidh an rìgh
dachaidh gu trom, bochd, duibhthiamhasach. Thàinig a bhànrighinn
òg na chomhdhail 's thubhairt i ris, "Mo thruaighe! cha 'n eil ni 'sam
bith leat a nochd." Thug a h-aoidh agus a h-ailleachd rudeigin do
thoilinntinn do'n rìgh nur a dh' amhairc e air a gnùis; ach nur a
shuidh e air cathair a tharruinn e d' a ionnsuidh thug e osann as, is
sgoilt a chathair fodha. "Dè th' ort, na bhiodh ort, nach fhaodadh
thu innseadh dhomhsa?" ars' a bhanrigh. Dh' innis an rìgh
demur a thachair. "Ud," ars' ise, "de amhail a chuireas thu air, 's
gur ann agad a tha 'bhean is fheàrr 'an Eirinn, 's an darra each is
fheàrr 'an Eirinn. Ma ghabhas thu mo chomhairle-sa thig thu as gach
ni dhiubh sin fhathast." Ma 's moch a thàinig an latha 's moiche na
sin a dh' éirich a bhànrighinn, 's a chuir i uidheam air gach ni chum
gum bitheadh an rìgh 'dol air a thurus. Chuir i 'n òrdugh an loth
pheallagach, odhar, air an robh 'n dìollaid mhaide; 's ged a chitheadh
esan 'n a maid' i, bha i làn dhealrach le òr is airgeid. Chaidh e air a
muin. Phòg a' bhanrigh e, 's ghuidh i buaidh làrach leis. Cha ruig

mise leas a bhi 'g innseadh ni sam bith dhuit, gabh thusa comhairle
do bhanachompanaich féin, an loth, 's innsidh i duit dé 's còir
dhuit a dheanamh.   Ghabh e mach air a thurus ; 's cha bu chianalach a
bhi air muin na steud odhar.   Bheireadh i air a' ghaoth luath Mhàirt
a bhitheadh roimpe, 's cha bheireadh a' ghaoth luath Mhàirt urra.
Thàinig iad am beul an athaidh 's an anamoich gu cùirt agus cathair
rìgh nan uinneagan daraich.   Urs' an loth pheallagach odhar ris, " Tha
sinn aig ceann ar turuis, 's cha-n' eil againn ri dol na 's fhaide, gabh
thusa mo chomhairle-sa 's bheir mi thu far am bheil claidheamh soluis
rìgh nan uinneagan daraich, 's ma thig e leat gun sgread gun sgrioch,
's comharradh maith air ar turus e.   Tha 'n rìgh nis aig a dhinneir, 's
tha 'n claidheamh soluis 'n a sheòmbar fèin ; tha cnap air a cheann, 's
nur a bheireas thu air a chlaidheamh tarruinn gu réidh mach a
" CASE " na h-uinneig e."   Thàinig e gus an uinneig far an robh an
claidheamh.   Rug e air a chlaidheamh 's thàinig e leis gu réidh gus
an robh e aig a bhàrr, 's thug e seòrsa sgread as an sin.   " Bithidh
sinn a nis, arsa 'n loth, aig imeachd, cha-n àm stad duinn e, tha fios
agam gun do mhothaich an rìgh dhuinn a toirt a chlaidheimh a mach.
Ghléidh esan an claidheamh 'n a laimh 's dh' fholbh iad, 's 'n uair a
bha iad treis air an aghaidh, thuirt an loth, " Stadaidh sinn a nis 's
amhaircidh thu co 'chi thu 'd dheigh."   " Chi mi, ars' esan, sgaoth
dh' eachaibh donna 'tighinn air bhàinidh."   " 'S luaithe sinn féin
na iad sin fathasd."   Dh' fhalbh iad 's 'n uair a bha iad astar
maith air an aghaidh, "amhairc a nis ars' ise co 'chi thu teachd."
" Chi mi sgaoth dh' eacha dubha, agus aon each blàr dubh, 's e a
tighinn air a chuthach, 's duin' air a mhuin."   " 'S e sin an t-each
is fheàrr an Eiriun, 's e mo bhràthair a th' ann, 's fhuair e ràidhe
banaltrachd a bharrachd ormsa, agus thig e seachad ormsa le
sreann, 's feuch am bi thu cho tapaidh 's 'nur a thig e seachad
ormsa an d' thoir thu 'n ceann de 'n fhear a th' air a mhuin ;
chionn an àm dol seachad amhaircidh e ortsa, 's cha-n 'eil claidheamh 'n a chùirt a bheir an ceann deth, ach a 'cheart chlaidheamh
a tha'd laimh."   'N uair a bha 'm fear so 'dol seachad thug e amh-
adh air a cheann a dh' amharc air ; tharruinn esan an claidheamh
'us thug e 'n ceann deth, 's cheap an loth pheallagach 'n a beul e.   B' e
so rìgh nan uinneagan daraich.   " Leum air muin an eich dhuibh,"
urs' ise, " 's fàg a chlosach an siod, 's bi 'dol dachaidh cho luath 's a
bheir e dachaidh thu, 's bithidh mise 'tighinn mar is fheàrr a db'
fhaodas mi 'n ur déigh."   Leum e air muin an eich dhuibh, 's am
Moire b' e 'n curaidh e, 's ràinig iad an tigh fada roimh latha.   Bha
'bhan-rìgh gun laidhe gus an d' ràinig e.   Thog iad ceòl 's leag iad
bròn.   An la'r na mhàireach thuirt esan, " 's éigin dòmhsa dol a dh'-

amharc na gruagaich an diugh, feuch am bi mo gheasan ma sgaoil."
"Cuimhnich nach ann mar a b-àbhaist a dh' amaiseas a ghruagach
ort. Coinnichidh e thu gu feargach fiadhaich 's their e riut, 'an
d'fhuair thu 'n claidheamh?' 's abair thusa gun d'fhuair. Their e riut
ciod e mar a fhuair thu e'? 'us their thusa, 'mar b'e an cnap a bh' air a
cheann cha d'fhuair mi e.' Foighnichidh e rithisd diot, 'demur a
fhuair thu 'n claidheamh,' 's their thusa, 'mar b'e an cnap a bh'
air a cheann cha d' fhuair mi e.' Bheir e 'n so togail air a dh'
amharc ciod e 'n cnap a th' air a chlaidheamh 's chì thu ball dorain
taobh deas a mhuineil, agus stob bàrr a chlaidheimh anns a bhall
dorain 's mar amais thu air a bhall dorain, tha thusa 's mise réidh.
B' e 'bhràthair rìgh nan uinneagan daraich e, 's tha fhios aige gus an
cailleadh am fear eile 'bheatha nach dealaicheadh e ris a chlaidheamh.
Tha bàs an dithis 's a chlaidheamh; ach cha-n 'eil claidheamh eile
dheargas orr' ach e." Phòg a bhanrigh e, 's ghuidh i buaidh làrach
leis, 's dh' fholbh e. Thachair a ghruagach air anns cheart àit' an
robh e roimhid. "An d' fhuair thu 'n claidheamh?" "Fhuair mi 'n
claidheamh." "Dèmur a fhuair thu 'n claidheamh?" "Mur b'e an
cnap a bh' air a cheann cha n' fhaighinn e." "Leig fhaicinn domh an
claidheamh." "Cha robh e mar fhiachaibh orm a leigeil fhaicinn
duit." "Demur a fhuair thu 'u claidheamh?" "Mur b'e an cnap a
bh' air a cheann cha d' fhuair mi e." Thug a ghruagach togail air a
cheann a dh' amharc air a chlaidheamh. Chunnaic esan am ball
dorain. Bha e urrant' ealamh; shàth e 'n claidheamh anns a bhall
dorain, 's thuit a ghruagach sìos marbh. Thill e dhachaidh, 's 'n uair
a thill e dhachaidh, fhuair e luchd gleidhidh agus coimhead ceangailt'
au sin cùl ri cùl; 's gun bhean, no each, no leannan aige, gun a bhi air
an toirt air folbh. 'N uair a dh' fhuasgail e iad, thubhairt iad ris,
"Thàinig famhair mòr, agus thug e air folbh do bhean agus do dhà
each." "Cha d' théid cadal air mo shùil no fois air mo cheum, gus am
faigh mi mo bhean agus mo dhà each air an ais. Le so a ràdh dh'
fholbh e air a thurus; ghabh e 'n taobh a bha lorg nan each, 's lean e
gu dian iad. Bha 'n t-athadh 's an t-anamoch a tighinn air, 's cha d'
rinneadh stad leis gus an d' ràinig e taobh na coill' uaine. Chunnaic
e far an robh làrach cruthachadh gealbhain, 's smaointich e gun cuireadh e tein' air, 's gun cuireadh e seachad an oidhch' ann. Cha b'
fhad 'a bha e 'n so aig a ghealbhan gus an d' thàinig cu seang na
coill' uain' air. Bheannaich e do 'n chù, 's bheannaich an cù dà. "Ubh!
ùbh!" ars' an cù, "b' olc diol do mhnatha 's do dhà each an so an raoir
aig an fhamhair mhòr." "'S e sin a chuir mise cho peanasach truagh
air an tòir a nochd, ach cha-n 'eil arach' air." "A rìgh," ars' an
cù," cha-n fhaod thu bhi gun bhiadh." Chaidh an cù stigh do 'u

choille, thug e mach beathaichean, 's rinn iad am biadh gu tlachdmhor.
" Tha dùil agam féin," ars' an rìgh, " gum faod mi tilleadh dhachaidh,
nach urrainn mi dol a chòir an fhamhair sin." " Na dean sin," ars'
an cù ; "cha-n' eagal duit a rìgh, cinn'idh do ghnothuch leat. Cha-n
'fhaod thu bhi so gun chadal." " Cha leig an t-eagal domh cadal 's
gun bharantas orm." " Caidil thus'," ars' an cù, " 's barantachaidh
mis' thu." Leig an rìgh e féin na shìneadh taobh an teine 's chaidil e.
Nur a bhrisd an fhàire thubhairt an cù ris, " Eirich," a rìgh, " 'us
gun gabhadh thu greim bìdh a neartaicheas thu, 's gum bitheadh thu
dol air do thurus. Nis," ars' an cù, " ma thig cruadhchas no càs ort,
iarr mo chuideachadh, 's bithidh mi agad a thiotadh." Dh' fhàg iad
beannachd aig a chéile 's dh' fholbh e. An àm an athaidh 's an
anmoich, thàinig e gu h-ailbhinn mhòr creige, agus bha cruthachadh
làrach gealbhain ann. Smaointich e gun cruinneachadh e connadh,
's gun cuireadh e air teine. Thòisich e air a gharadh, 's cha b' fhada
bha e mar so 'n uair a thàinig seobhag liath na creige glais' air.
" Ubh! ùbh!" ars' ise, " b' olc diol do mhnatha 's do dhà each an
rair aig an fhamhair mhòr." " Cha-n' eil arach' air," ars'
esan, " fhuair mi féin mòran d' an dragh is beagan d' an àbhachd.
" Glac misneach," ars' ise, " gheobh thu rudeigin d' an àbhachd
fhathasd. Cha n' fhaod thu bhi gun bhiadh an so," ars' ise.
" Cha-n' eil seòl air biadh fhaotainn ars' esan." " Cha-n fhada
bhitheas sinn a faotainn bìdh." Dh' fholbh i 's cha b-fhada bha i
n' uair a thàinig i 's tri lachan 's ochd coilich dhubha 'n a beul. Chuir
iad an ordugh am biadh 's ghabh iad e. " Cha-n fhaod thu bhi gun
chadal, ars' an t-seobhag." " Demur a chaidleas mi gun bharantas
'sam bith orm gu mo dhìon o aon olc a tha 'n so?" " Caidil thusa
rìgh, 's barantachaidh mis' thu." Leig e e féin 'n a shìneadh, 's
chaidil e. Anns a mhaidinn chuir an t-seobhag air a chois e.
Cruadhchas no càs a thig ort, cuimhnich aig àm sam bith gum faigh
thu mo chuideachadhsa. Dh' fholbh e gu dian, foghainteach luath,
laidir. Bha 'n latha folbh 's an oidhche tighinn, 's eunlaith bheaga
na coille craobhaich, dosraiche, dualaich, a' gabhail ma bhun nam
preas 's ma bhàrr nan dos; 's mu bha, cha bu tàmh 's cha bu chlos
dàsan e, gus an d' thàinig e gu taobh aimhne mhòr a bha sin, agus
aig bruach na h-aimhne bha cruthachadh làrach gealbhain. Shéid
an rìgh srachdanach trom teine. Cha b'-fhada bha e 'n so 'n uair a
thàinig ann an companas ris doran donn na h-aimhne. " Och," ars'
an doran, " b'-olc dìol do mhnatha 'n so an rair aig an fhamhair."
" Cha-n 'eil arach' air, fhuair mise mòran d' an dragh is beagan
d' an àbhachd." " Glac misneach, fo mheadhon latha màireach chì
thu do bhean. A rìgh, cha 'n fhaod thu bhi gun bhiadh," ars' an

doran. "Demur a gheibhear biadh an so," ars' an rìgh. Dh
fholbh an doran feadh na h-abhann, 's thainig e 's tri bradain leis
a bha ciatach. Rinn iad biadh is ghabh iad e. Thuirt an doran
ris an rìgh, "feumaidh tu cadal." "Demur a chaidleas mi 's gun
bharantachadh sam bith orm?" "Caidil thusa 's barantachaidh mis'
thu an nochd." Chaidil an rìgh. Anns a mhaduinn, thuirt an
doran ris, bithidh thu an nochd an làthair do mhnatha. Dh' fhàg
e beannachd aig an doran. "Nis," ars' an doran, "ma bhitheas
càs ort, iarr mo chuideachadh-sa, 's gheobh thu e." Dh' fholbh an rìgh
gus an d' ràinig e creag, 's dh' amhairc e sìos ann an glombas a bha
's a chreig, 's aig a ghrunnd chunnaic e a bhean agus a dhà each, 's cha
robh fios aige demur a gheobheadh e far an robh iad. Ghabh e mu
'n cuairt gus an d' thàinig e gu bun na creige, 's bha rathad ciatach
a dhol a stigh. Chaidh e stigh, 's ma chaidh, 's ann a thòisich is' air
caoineadh. "Ud! ud!" ars' esan, "'s olc so, mi fèin adh' fhaotainn
na h-uibhir de dhragh a tighinn ma d' thuaiream, ma 's ann a caoineadh a tha thu nis." "U," arsa na h-eich, "cuir thus' air' ur beul-
thaobh-ne e, 's cha-n eagal da gus am fàg sinne so." Rinn i biadh dà,
's chuir i air dòigh e, 's 'n uair a bha iad treis comhla chuir i air
beulthaobh nan each e. 'N uair a thàinig am famhair thubhairt e,
"THA BOLADH AN FHARBHALAICH A STIGH. Ars' ise, "M' ullaidh, is
m'aighear, is m' fheudail, cha-n' eil ann ach boladh a bhalaidh bhreuna
de na h-eachaibh." An ceann treis chaidh e 'thoirt bìdh do na h-eich,
's thòisich na h-eich air, 's cha mhòr nach do mharbh iad e, 's cha
d' rinn e ach snàgan air éigin natha. "Ghràidh," ars' ise, "tha
iad a brath do mharbhadh." "Na'm b' ann agam fèin a bhitheadh
m' anam g'a ghleidheadh 's fhad' o'n a mharbh iad mi," ars' esan.
"C' ait' a ghràidh am bheil d' anam an leòbhra, gabhaidh mise cùram
deth." "Tha e," ars' esan, "ann an clach nam bonnach." Nur
a dh' fholbh esan an la'r na mhàireach, chuir ise an òrdugh clach
nam bonnach gu fuathasach. An am an athaidh 's an anmoich
thàinig am famhair a stigh. Chuir ise a fear air beulthaobh nan
each. Chaidh am famhair a thoirt bìdh do na h-eich, 's leadair iad e
na bu mhotha 's na bu mhotha. "Ciod e 'thug ort clach nam bonnach a chur an òrdugh mur sin?" ars' esan. "Chionn gu bheil d'
anam innte." "Tha mi 'g aithneachadh nam bitheadh fios agad c'
aite 'bheil m' anam, gun d' thugadh thu tàire mhaith dhà." "Bheireadh." "Cha-n ann an sin a tha m'anam 's ann a tha e 'sa starsaich." Chuir ise an ordugh an starsach gu gasd' an la 'r na mhàireach. Nur a thill am famhair chaidh e thoirt bìdh do na h-eich, 's
leadair na h-eich e na bu mho:ha 's na bu mhotha. "Dé 'thug ort
an starsach a chuir an ordugh mar sud?" "Chionn gu bheil d' anam

c

innte." "Tha mi 'g aithneachadh na 'm bitheadh fios agad far am bheil m' anam gun gabhadh thu cùram dheth." "Ghabhadh," ars' ise. "Cha-n' ann an sin a tha m' anam, ars' 'esan. Tha leac mhòr fo 'n starsaich, tha molt fo 'n leachd, tha lach 'am broinn a mhuilt, agus tha ubh am broinn na lacha, agus 's ann anns an ubh a tha m' anam. 'N uair a dh' fholbh am famhair an la'r na mhàireach thog iad an leac, 's a mach a thug am molt. Na 'm bitheadh agamsa cù seang na coill' uaine, cha b' fhad 'a bhitheadh e 'toirt a' mhuilt a m' ionnsuidh. Thainig cù seang na coill' uaine ugus am molt 'n a bheul. 'N uair a dh'fhosgail iad am molt, a mach a bha 'n lach air iteagach leis na lachan eile. Na'm bitheadh agamsa seobhag liath na creige glaise, cha b' fhada' bhitheadh i 'toirt na lach a m' ionnsuidh. Thàinig seobhag liath na creige glaise 's an lach 'n a beul. 'N uair a sgoilt iad an lach a thoirt na uibhe a 'broinn, mach a ghabh an t-ubh ann an doimhneachd a chuain. Na'm bitheadh agamsa doran donn na h-amhann, cha b'fhada bhitheadh i 'toirt a m' ionn-suidh na uibhe. Thàinig an doran donn 's an t-ubh na beul, 's rug a bhanrigh air an ubh 's phronn i eadar a da laimh e. Bha 'm famhair a tighinn anns an athamanachd, 's 'n uair a phronn ise 'n t-ubh thuit e sìos marbh, 's cha do charaich e as a sin fhathasd. Thug iad mòran leo de dh' òr 's de dh' airgeid. Chuir iad oidhche shunndach seachad aig doran donn na h-abhann, oidhch' aig seobhag liath na creige glaise, agus oidhch' aig cù seang na coill' uaine. Thàinig iad dach-aidh 's chuir iad an òrdugh cuirm chridheil, 's bha iad gu sona, toilichte 'n a dhéigh sin.

2. I have another version of this tale, written by Hector Urquhart, told by John Campbell, living at Strath Gairloch, Ross-shire, received June 27, 1859. It is very well told. It varies a little from the Islay version, but the resemblance is so close, that to print it entire would be repetition. It contains many characteristic phrases which the other has not got, so I give this abstract. The Gaelic is as it came to me.

THE "SGEULACHD" OF THE WIDOW'S SON.—There was once a widow's son, and he was often stalking (SEALG). On a day of days and he stalking, he "sits" at the back of a knoll, before the sun and behind the wind (RI AGHAIDH GREINE 'S RI CUL NA GAOITHE), and there came the way a youth, like a picture (OGANACH DEALBHANACH), riding a blue filly (FAILORE GORM), and he sits beside him. They played at cards, and the widow's son won, and when evening came the youth said, "What is the stake of thy gaming?" (CE DHE BUIDH DO CHLUICHE?) and he said, "the blue filly under thee." He took her home, and she changed into the finest woman that man ever saw. Next day he went stalking, and on coming home in the mouth of night (AM BEUL NA OIDCHE), he learned that the big giant had taken away his sweetheart—CHA NEIL COMAS AIR AS EISE ACH NA BO MHISE BO TREASA CHA MHEALLADH EISE FAD I. "There is no help for it," said he, "but were I the stronger, he would not allure her far."

DH' ERICH MAC NA BANNTRICH. The widow's son arose, 's CHAIDH E NA CHRIOSIBH IALLA S' NA IALLA GAISGICH, and he went into his belts of thongs and his thongs of warrior, 's DH'FHALBH E LE CEUMANIBH GU TUISLEAG DOMH MHEANMNACH, and he went with leaping strides, cheerful to me (or? *Doimhainneachd*—of deepness) s' DHEANADH E MILE THORAN NA SLEIBH LEIS NA H UILLE CEUM A DHEANADH E, and he would make a thousand knolls of the hill with every step he made, s' B' FHEAR DHA NAMHAID A SHEACHANADH NA TACHAIRT AN LATHA SIN RIS, and his foe had better avoid him than meet that day with him. He saw a little hut "in the mouth of night," and though far away, not long to reach it, AIR A THUBHADH LE ITEAGAN GARBHA NAN EUN A MUIGH S LE ITEAGAN MINE NAN EUN A STEACH, thatched with coarse feathers of the birds without, and with fine feathers of the birds within, AGUS RUITHAG AN T UBHAL BHON DARNA CEAN DHON A CHIN EILE LE CHO COMHRAD S'A BHA E, and the apple would run from one end to the other end, so even it was. He went in and found no man, but two great fires on the fire-place (CHAGAILT) on the floor. SUIL DA DUG E, glance that he gave he saw a falcon coming in with a heath hen in her claws, and the next glance it was, GILLE BRIAGH BUIDH, a braw yellow lad, who spoke as in the Islay version, entertained him and told him in the morning to call on SEABHAG SUIL GHORM GHLENNA FEIST—the blue-eyed falcon of Glen Feist. Next day it was the same, and he came, AIR CIARADH DON FHEISGAR, at the turning-dun of the evening, to a second hut, thatched like the other, s' BHA SNATHNEAN BEAG SUARACH SIODA CUMAIL DION A DHROMA RIS, and there was a little sorry silken thread, keeping the thatch of its back on. DOBHRAN DONN, otter brown, came in with a salmon, and became a man, and spoke as the other, and told him in the morning to call on DOBH-RAN DONN SRUTH AN T' SHIUL—Brown otter of sail stream. The third day was the same, the hut was the same, but that there were two great fires on each fire-place, and there came in, MADADH MOR, big dog, with a hare by the throat, who became the finest man, AIR AN DUG E ROSK RIAMH, he ever turned face to; who said as the others did—"It was late when the big giant went past with thy sweetheart on his shoulder." At parting, he told him to call on MADADH GLAS DRIOM AN T-SHLEIBHE—grey dog of mountain back in time of need. That night he saw, TIGH MOR GEAL AN AN GLEANN FADA FAISICH, a big white house in a long desert glen, and saw his sweetheart with a golden comb in her hand, and she would take a while at combing her hair, and a while at weeping, and when she saw him she said—"My pity, what brought thee here? the giant will kill thee." "Two shares of fear on him, and the smallest share on me," said the widow's son.

She had laid it as crosses and as spells on the giant, not to come near her for a day and a year, and they were together in the giant's house till evening.

She hid him, and had a long talk with the giant when he came home, who was wheedled, as in the other story, into telling first that his life (BETHA) was in (CARN GLAS UD THALL) yonder grey cairn. The lady was addressed as NIGHINN RIGH CHOIGE MUGH— O daughter of king of COIGE MUGH, which kingdom is not within my geographical studies.

The giant came home, and found the grey cairn dressed out and ornamented, and after a deal of persuasion, gave out that his life was in SEANN STOC DARRICH—an old oak stump on the bank of yonder river. So the next day that was dressed out, and when he came home he said, "Do thou make the stock braw, BRIAGH, every day. On the third day they split the oak stump with an axe, and a hare leaped out. "There now is the giant's life away," said the king's daughter, "and he will come without delay and kill thee, and not spare me." Grey dog of mountain back was called, and brought the hare, and a salmon leaped out into the river. Brown otter of sail stream brought the salmon, and a heath hen sprang out. Blue-eyed falcon of Glen Feist brought the bird, and the giant came roaring—"King's daughter, let me have my life and thou shalt have the little chest of gold and the little chest of silver that is in yonder grey cairn." The widow's son answered, "I will have that, and I will have this;"

and he seized the axe, and the stock fell, and the giant was dead. And the widow's son and the daughter of King Coige Mugh, in Erin, staid in the house and the land of the giant, and their race were there when I was there last.

The warrior's dress of thongs is remarkable, and something like it is described in another tale. There is a curious picture at Taymouth of a man, supposed to be the Regent Murray, in a Highland dress, which may be the dress described. The upper part is composed of strips of some ornamented material, which might be stamped gilded leather; the rest of the dress is a linen shirt, with ruffles, and a plaid wrapped about the body in the form of a modern kilt, and belted plaid; he wears stockings and shoes of a peculiar pattern: the head-dress is a bonnet with an ostrich plume; the arms, a dirk and a long ornamented gun.

There is another picture at Dytchley, in Oxfordshire, which represents an ancestor of Lord Dillon in an Irish costume. The dress consists solely of a very short garment like a shirt, coloured, and very much ornamented with tags, which might be leather. The gentleman is armed with a spear, and the dress is probably a masquerade representation of a real Irish dress of some period.

I would here remark that the personages and places in all these tales are like the actors in a play and the scenes. The incidents vary but little, but the kings and their countries vary with every version, though there is a preference for Erin, Ireland; Lochlain, Scandinavia, or rather Denmark and Norway; and Greuge, the Greekdom, Greece.

3. I have a third version of this written by MacLean, told by John MacPhie, in South Uist. The old man was very proud of it, and said it was "the HARDEST" story that the transcriber had ever heard. He told me the same.

As often happens with aged reciters, when he repeated it a second time slowly for transcribing, nearly all the curious, "impassioned, and sentimental" language was left out. This is MacLean's account, and it entirely agrees with my own experience of this man, who is next thing to a professional reciter (see introduction). This version is the most curious of the three. I hope some day to get it better copied, so I do not abstract it now

It is nearer the Ross-shire version than the Islay story, and carries the scene to Greece from Ireland. The reciter is 79, and says he learned it in his youth from an old man of the name of John MacDonald, Aird a Mhachair.

The principle on which gaming is carried on in this and in other tales is peculiar. The stake is rather a ransom, for it is always settled after the game is decided.

The game played is TAILEASG, which Armstrong translates as, sport, game, mirth, chess, backgammon, draughts.

This story resembles in some particulars—

1. The Gaelic tale published by Dr. MacLeod, printed page 30, Leobhar Nan Cnoc. 1834.
2. The Sea Maiden, in present collection, and the stories referred to in the notes.
3. The Giant who had no Heart in his Body. Norse Tales. 1859.
4. The Seven Foals, where a horse advises his rider. Norse Tales.
5. Dapplegrim, where the same occurs, where there are two horses, and where the rider hides about the horses. Norse Tales.
6. Fortunio, where the horse also advises his rider.
7. This also resembles a part of the "Arabian Nights," where the Calender is changed into a monkey, and the princess fights a genius in various shapes.
8. "The Ball of Crystal," Grimm, where the power of an enchanter is in *a crystal ball*, in *an egg*, in *a fiery bird*, in *a wild ox*.
9. The Three Sisters, page 52, where a little key is found in *an egg*, in *a duck*, in *a bull*. This book is an English translation (1845) of Volks Märchen, by Musaeus, 1782. Said to have been published in English in 1790.
10. Another version of the Sea Maiden recited to me in South Uist. The soul of the Sea Maiden was in *an egg*, in *a goose*, in *a ram*, in *a wild bull*, and was got by the help of *an otter*, *a falcon*, *a wolf*, and *a lion*.

*Lempriere—Ægyptus—Kneph or Knouphis—*A God, represented as a *ram.* He was the soul of the world; his symbol a
circle, in the centre of which is a serpent with the head of a hawk,
or a globe with a serpent turned round it. Together with mind,
the primitive matter was given, both produced from the same great
principle, existing in it from all eternity, imperishable. The
primitive matter was rude and shapeless when the spirit imparted
to it the power of motion, and gave it the form of a sphere. This
became the sphere *or egg* of the world which *Kneph let fall from
his mouth* when he wished to form all things.

It is warmly contended by Irish writers that the religion of
the Celts, and the Celts themselves, came from Phœnicia and
Carthage.

If this story be mythological, here is something like it.

We have the *hawk, ram,* and a *bird;* and in the Inverary version we have a *fish* and the *egg,* with the life of bird, beast, fish,
and man in it.

There is in a place called *Lok Marien-ker,* in Morbihan, Brittany, a long, dark, underground passage, at the end of which are
certain rudely sculptured stones. On one of these is something
which bears some faint resemblance to the snake, who appears in
the next tale.

There is one word in this tale, "SEANG," which is not given
in dictionaries as a substantive. Sing, applied to an Indian
prince, means lion, and the beast here described might be one.
Seang, as an adjective, means thin, slim, slender, gaunt, and is
the root of *Seangan,* an ant.

In Prichard's "Celtic Nations," by Latham, 1856, a Dacota
word is quoted—"SUNGKA, which originally comprehended the
idea of Dog, Fox, and Wolf.

The word GRUAGACH, which here means some male personage, generally means a maiden. It also means "A female spectre
of the class of Brownies to which the Highland dairy-maids made
frequent libations of milk—*rarely* THE CHIEF OF A PLACE."—
Armstrong dic. This word, which has not its common meaning, may help to trace the language. The root is GRUAG, the
hair of the head.

A Gruagach used to haunt Skipness Castle, and is still remembered there as a supernatural female who did odd jobs about the house for the maids, and lived in the ruin.

"There was also a Gruagach in Kerrisdale, in Gairloch, in Ross-shire, once upon a time."

This may be the same word as *Groac'h* or *Grac'h*, a name given to the Druidesses, who had colleges in an island near the coasts of Brittany (p. 155, vol. i., Foyer Breton). The story given has many incidents common to the Gaelic stories.

The sword of light is common in Gaelic stories; and, stripped of supernatural qualities, the whole thing seems very like an account of some race contending with another, whose chief wore long hair, who had horses and bright (? steel) swords, to which extraordinary virtues were attributed, and who were at the same time beset by savages who lived in caves, and were assisted by other savages represented by creatures.

II.

THE BATTLE OF THE BIRDS.

From John Mackenzie, fisherman, near Inverary.

THERE was once a time when every creature and bird was gathering to battle. The son of the king of Tethertown* said, that he would go to see the battle, and that he would bring sure word home to his father the king, who would be king of the creatures this year. The battle was over before he arrived all but one (fight), between a great black raven and a snake, and it seemed as if the snake would get the victory over the raven. When the king's son saw this, he helped the raven, and with one blow takes the head off the snake. When the raven had taken breath, and saw that the snake was dead, he said, "For thy kindness to me this day, I will give thee a sight. Come up now on the root of my two wings." The king's son mounted upon the raven, and, before he stopped, he took him over seven Bens, and seven Glens, and seven Mountain Moors.

"Now," said the raven, "seest thou that house yonder? Go now to it. It is a sister of mine that makes her dwelling in it; and I will go bail that thou art welcome. And if she asks thee, Wert thou at the battle of the birds? say thou that thou wert. And if she asks, Didst thou see my likeness? say that thou

* Na cathair t'sheamain. Heather ropes are used for binding thatch on Highland cottages.

sawest it. But be sure that thou meetest me to-morrow morning here, in this place." The king's son got good and right good treatment this night. Meat of each meat, drink of each drink, warm water to his feet, and a soft bed for his limbs.

On the next day the raven gave him the same sight over seven Bens, and seven Glens, and seven Mountain moors. They saw a bothy far off, but, though far off, they were soon there. He got good treatment this night, as before—plenty of meat and drink, and warm water to his feet, and a soft bed to his limbs—and on the next day it was the same thing.

On the third morning, instead of seeing the raven as at the other times, who should meet him but the handsomest lad he ever saw, with a bundle in his hand. The king's son asked this lad if he had seen a big black raven. Said the lad to him, " Thou wilt never see the raven again, for I am that raven. I was put under spells ; it was meeting thee that loosed me, and for that thou art getting this bundle. Now," said the lad, " thou wilt turn back on the self-same steps, and thou wilt lie a night in each house, as thou wert before ; but thy lot is not to lose the bundle which I gave thee, till thou art in the place where thou wouldst most wish to dwell."

The king's son turned his back to the lad, and his face to his father's house ; and he got lodging from the raven's sisters, just as he got it when going forward. When he was nearing his father's house he was going through a close wood. It seemed to him that the bundle was growing heavy, and he thought he would look what was in it.

When he loosed the bundle, it was not without astonishing himself. In a twinkling he sees the very grandest place he ever saw. A great castle, and an orchard about the castle, in which was every kind of fruit and herb. He stood full of wonder and regret for having loosed the bundle—it was not in his power to put it back again—and he would have wished this pretty place to be in the pretty little green hollow that was opposite his father's house ; but, at one glance, he sees a great giant coming towards him.

"Bad's the place where thou hast built thy house, king's son," says the giant. "Yes, but it is not here I would wish it to be, though it happened to be here by mishap," says the king's son. "What's the reward thou wouldst give me for putting it back in the bundle as it was before?" "What's the reward thou wouldst ask?" says the king's son. "If thou wilt give me the first son thou hast when he is seven years of age," says the giant. "Thou wilt get that if I have a son," said the king's son.

In a twinkling the giant put each garden, and orchard, and castle in the bundle as they were before. "Now," says the giant, "take thou thine own road, and I will take my road ; but mind thy promise, and though thou shouldst forget, I will remember."

The king's son took to the road, and at the end of a few days he reached the place he was fondest of. He loosed the bundle, and the same place was just as it was before. And when he opened the castle-door he sees the handsomest maiden he ever cast eye upon. "Advance, king's son," said the pretty maid ; "everything is in order for thee, if thou wilt marry me this very night." "It's I am the man that is willing," said the king's son. And on that same night they married.

But at the end of a day and seven years, what great man is seen coming to the castle but the giant. The king's son minded his promise to the giant, and till now he had not told his promise to the queen.

" Leave thou (the matter) between me and the giant,"
says the queen.

"Turn out thy son," says the giant; "mind your
promise." "Thou wilt get that," says the king, "when
his mother puts him in order for his journey." The
queen arrayed the cook's son, and she gave him to the
giant by the hand. The giant went away with him;
but he had not gone far when he put a rod in the hand
of the little laddie. The giant asked him—"If thy
father had that rod what would he do with it?" "If
my father had that rod he would beat the dogs and the
cats, if they would be going near the king's meat," said
the little laddie. "Thou'rt the cook's son," said the
giant. He catches him by the two small ankles and
knocks him—" Sgleog "—against the stone that was
beside him. The giant turned back to the castle in rage
and madness, and he said that if they did not turn out
the king's son to him, the highest stone of the castle
would be the lowest. Said the queen to the king,
"we'll try it yet; the butler's son is of the same age
as our son." She arrayed the butler's son, and she
gives him to the giant by the hand. The giant had
not gone far when he put the rod in his hand. "If
thy father had that rod," says the giant, "what would
he would do with it?" "He would beat the dogs and
the cats when they would be coming near the king's
bottles and glasses." "Thou art the son of the butler,"
says the giant, and dashed his brains out too. The
giant returned in very great rage and anger. The
earth shook under the sole of his feet, and the castle
shook and all that was in it. "OUT HERE THY SON,"
says the giant, "or in a twinkling the stone that is
highest in the dwelling will be the lowest." So needs
must they had to give the king's son to the giant.

The giant took him to his own house, and he

reared him as his own son. On a day of days when the giant was from home, the lad heard the sweetest music he ever heard in a room at the top of the giant's house. At a glance he saw the finest face he had ever seen. She beckoned to him to come a bit nearer to her, and she told him to go this time, but to be sure to be at the same place about that dead midnight.

And as he promised he did. The giant's daughter was at his side in a twinkling, and she said, "To-morrow thou wilt get the choice of my two sisters to marry ; but say thou that thou wilt not take either, but me. My father wants me to marry the son of the king of the Green City, but I don't like him." On the morrow the giant took out his three daughters, and he said, "Now, son of the king of Tethertown, thou hast not lost by living with me so long. Thou wilt get to wife one of the two eldest of my daughters, and with her leave to go home with her the day after the wedding." "If thou wilt give me this pretty little one," says the king's son, "I will take thee at thy word."

The giant's wrath kindled, and he said, "Before thou gett'st her thou must do the three things that I ask thee to do." "Say on," says the king's son. The giant took him to the byre. "Now," says the giant, "the dung of the hundred cattle is here, and it has not been cleansed for seven years. I am going from home to-day, and if this byre is not cleaned before night comes, so clean that a golden apple will run from end to end of it, not only thou shalt not get my daughter, but 'tis a drink of thy blood that will quench my thirst this night." He begins cleaning the byre, but it was just as well to keep baling the great ocean. After mid-day, when sweat was blinding him, the giant's young daughter came where he was, and she said to him, "Thou art being punished, king's son."

"I am that," says the king's son. "Come over," says she, "and lay down thy weariness." "I will do that," says he, "there is but death awaiting me, at any rate." He sat down near her. He was so tired that he fell asleep beside her. When he awoke, the giant's daughter was not to be seen, but the byre was so well cleaned that a golden apple would run from end to end of it. In comes the giant, and he said, "Thou hast cleaned the byre, king's son?" "I have cleaned it," says he. "Somebody cleaned it," says the giant. "Thou didst not clean it, at all events," said the king's son. "Yes, yes!" says the giant, "since thou wert so active to-day, thou wilt get to this time to-morrow to thatch this byre with birds' down—birds with no two feathers of one colour." The king's son was on foot before the sun; he caught up his bow and his quiver of arrows to kill the birds. He took to the moors, but if he did, the birds were not so easy to take. He was running after them till the sweat was blinding him. About mid-day who should come but the giant's daughter. "Thou art exhausting thyself, king's son," says she. "I am," said he. "There fell but these two black-birds, and both of one colour." "Come over and lay down thy weariness on this pretty hillock," says the giant's daughter. "It 's I am willing," said he. He thought she would aid him this time, too, and he sat down near her, and he was not long there till he fell asleep.

When he awoke, the giant's daughter was gone. He thought he would go back to the house, and he sees the byre thatched with the feathers. When the giant came home, he said, "Thou hast thatched the byre, king's son?" "I thatched it," says he. "Somebody thatched it," says the giant. "Thou didst not thatch it," says the king's son. "Yes, yes!" says the giant.

" Now," says the giant, " there is a fir-tree beside that
loch down there, and there is a magpie's nest in its
top. The eggs thou wilt find in the nest. I must
have them for my first meal. Not one must be
burst or broken, and there are five in the nest." Early
in the morning the king's son went where the tree
was, and that tree was not hard to hit upon. Its
match was not in the whole wood. From the foot to
the first branch was five hundred feet. The king's
son was going all round the tree. She came who was
always bringing help to him. " Thou art losing the
skin of thy hands and feet." " Ach ! I am," says he.
" I am no sooner up than down." " This is no time
for stopping," says the giant's daughter. She thrust
finger after finger into the tree, till she made a ladder
for the king's son to go up to the magpie's nest.
When he was at the nest, she said, " Make haste now
with the eggs, for my father's breath is burning my
back." In his hurry she left her little finger in the top
of the tree. " Now," says she, " thou wilt go home with
the eggs quickly, and thou wilt get me to marry to-
night if thou canst know me. I and my two sisters
will be arrayed in the same garments, and made like
each other, but look at me when my father says, Go
to thy wife, king's son ; and thou wilt see a hand
without a little finger." He gave the eggs to the
giant. " Yes, yes !" says the giant, " be making ready
for thy marriage."

Then indeed there was a wedding, and it *was* a
wedding ! Giants and gentlemen, and the son of the
king of the Green City was in the midst of them.
They were married, and the dancing began, and that
was a dance ! The giant's house was shaking from
top to bottom. But bed time came, and the giant
said, " It is time for thee to go to rest, son of the

king of Tethertown; take thy bride with thee from amidst those."

She put out the hand off which the little finger was, and he caught her by the hand.

"Thou hast aimed well this time too; but there is no knowing but we may meet thee another way," said the giant.

But to rest they went. "Now," says she, "sleep not, or else thou diest. We must fly quick, quick, or for certain my father will kill thee."

Out they went, and on the blue gray filly in the stable they mounted. "Stop a while," says she, "and I will play a trick to the old hero." She jumped in, and cut an apple into nine shares, and she put two shares at the head of the bed, and two shares at the foot of the bed, and two shares at the door of the kitchen, and two shares at the big door, and one outside the house.

The giant awoke and called, "Are you asleep?" "We are not yet," said the apple that was at the head of the bed. At the end of a while he called again. "We are not yet," said the apple that was at the foot of the bed. A while after this he called again. "We are not yet," said the apple at the kitchen door. The giant called again. The apple that was at the big door answered. "You are now going far from me," says the giant. "We are not yet," says the apple that was outside the house. "You are flying," says the giant. The giant jumped on his feet, and to the bed he went, but it was cold—empty.

"My own daughter's tricks are trying me," said the giant. "Here's after them," says he.

In the mouth of day, the giant's daughter said that her father's breath was burning her back. "Put thy hand, quick," said she, "in the ear of the gray filly, and whatever thou findest in it, throw it behind thee."

"There is a twig of sloe tree," said he. "Throw it behind thee," said she.

No sooner did he that, than there were twenty miles of black thorn wood, so thick that scarce a weasel could go through it. The giant came headlong, and there he is fleecing his head and neck in the thorns.

"My own daughter's tricks are here as before," said the giant; "but if I had my own big axe and wood knife here, I would not be long making a way through this." He went home for the big axe and the wood knife, and sure he was not long on his journey, and he was the boy behind the big axe. He was not long making a way through the black thorn. "I will leave the axe and the wood knife here till I return," says he. "If thou leave them," said a Hoodie* that was in a tree, "we will steal them."

"You will do that same," says the giant, "but I will set them home." He returned and left them at the house. At the heat of day the giant's daughter felt her father's breath burning her back.

"Put thy finger in the filly's ear, and throw behind thee whatever thou findest in it." He got a splinter of gray stone, and in a twinkling there were twenty miles, by breadth and height, of great gray rock behind them. The giant came full pelt, but past the rock he could not go.

"The tricks of my own daughter are the hardest things that ever met me," says the giant; "but if I had my lever and my mighty mattock, I would not be long making my way through this rock also." There was no help for it, but to turn the chase for them; and he was the boy to split the stones. He was not long making a road through the rock. "I will leave

* The principal Gaelic vowels bear some resemblance to the cawing of a hoodie. They are all broad A.

D

the tools here, and I will return no more." "If thou leave them," says the hoodie, "we will steal them." "Do that if thou wilt; there is no time to go back." At the time of breaking the watch, the giant's daughter said that she was feeling her father's breath burning her back. "Look in the filly's ear, king's son, or else we are lost." He did so, and it was a bladder of water that was in her ear this time. He threw it behind him and there was a fresh-water loch, twenty miles in length and breadth, behind them.

The giant came on, but with the speed he had on him, he was in the middle of the loch, and he went under, and he rose no more.

On the next day the young companions were come in sight of his father's house. "Now," said she, "my father is drowned, and he won't trouble us any more; but before we go further," says she, "go thou to thy father's house, and tell that thou hast the like of me; but this is thy lot, let neither man nor creature kiss thee, for if thou dost thou wilt not remember that thou hast ever seen me." Every one he met was giving him welcome and luck, and he charged his father and mother not to kiss him; but as mishap was to be, an old greyhound was in and she knew him, and jumped up to his mouth, and after that he did not remember the giant's daughter.

She was sitting at the well's side as he left her, but the king's son was not coming. In the mouth of night she climbed up into a tree of oak that was beside the well, and she lay in the fork of the tree all that night. A shoemaker had a house near the well, and about mid-day on the morrow, the shoemaker asked his wife to go for a drink for him out of the well. When the shoemaker's wife reached the well, and when she saw the shadow of her that was in the tree, think-

ing of it that it was her own shadow—and she never
thought till now that she was so handsome—she gave
a cast to the dish that was in her hand, and it was
broken on the ground, and she took herself to the
house without vessel or water.

"Where is the water, wife?" said the shoemaker.
"Thou shambling, contemptible old carle, without
grace, I have stayed too long thy water and wood
thrall."* "I am thinking, wife, that thou hast turned
crazy. Go thou, daughter, quickly, and fetch a drink
for thy father." His daughter went, and in the same
way so it happened to her. She never thought till
now that she was so loveable, and she took herself
home. "Up with the drink," said her father. "Thou
home-spun† shoe carle, dost thou think that I am fit to
be thy thrall." The poor shoemaker thought that they
had taken a turn in their understandings, and he went
himself to the well. He saw the shadow of the maiden
in the well, and he looked up to the tree, and he sees
the finest woman he ever saw. "Thy seat is wavering,
but thy face is fair," said the shoemaker. "Come
down, for there is need of thee for a short while at my
house." The shoemaker understood that this was the
shadow that had driven his people mad. The shoemaker took her to his house, and he said that he had
but a poor bothy, but that she should get a share of all
that was in it. At the end of a day or two came a
leash of gentlemen lads to the shoemaker's house for
shoes to be made them, for the king had come home,
and he was going to marry. The glance the lads gave
they saw the giant's daughter, and if they saw her,
they never saw one so pretty as she. "'Tis thou hast
the pretty daughter here," said the lads to the shoemaker. "She is pretty, indeed," says the shoemaker,

* Tràill, a slave. † Peillag, felt, coarse cloth.

" but she is no daughter of mine." " St. Nail!" said one of them, " I would give a hundred pounds to marry her." The two others said the very same. The poor shoemaker said that he had nothing to do with her. " But," said they, " ask her to-night, and send us word to-morrow." When the gentles went away, she asked the shoemaker—" What's that they were saying about me?" The shoemaker told her. " Go thou after them," said she ; " I will marry one of them, and let him bring his purse with him." The shoemaker went after them, and he told that. The youth returned, and he gave the shoemaker a hundred pounds for tocher. They went to rest, and when she had laid down, she asked the lad for a drink of water from a tumbler that was on the board on the further side of the chamber. He went ; but out of that he could not come, as he held the vessel of water the length of the night. " Thou lad," said she, " why wilt thou not lie down?" but out of that he could not drag till the bright morrow's day was. The shoemaker came to the door of the chamber, and she asked him to take away that lubberly boy. This wooer went and betook himself to his home, but he did not tell the other two how it happened to him. Next came the second chap, and and in the same way, when she had gone to rest— " Look," she said, " if the latch is on the door." The latch laid hold of his hands, and out of that he could not come the length of the night, and out of that he did not come till the morrow's day was bright. He went, under shame and disgrace. No matter, he did not tell the other chap how it had happened, and on the third night he came. As it happened to the two others, so it happened to him. One foot stuck to the floor ; he could neither come nor go, but so he was the length of the night. On the morrow, he took his

soles out (of that), and he was not seen looking behind
him. "Now," said the girl to the shoemaker, "thine
is the sporran of gold; I have no need of it. It will
better thee, and I am no worse for thy kindness to me."
The shoemaker had the shoes ready, and on that very
day the king was to be married. The shoemaker was
going to the castle with the shoes of the young people,
and the girl said to the shoemaker, "I would like to
get a sight of the king's son before he marries."
"Come with me," says the shoemaker, "I am well
acquainted with the servants at the castle, and thou
shalt get a sight of the king's son and all the company."
And when the gentles saw the pretty woman that was
here they took her to the wedding-room, and they
filled for her a glass of wine. When she was going to
drink what is in it, a flame went up out of the glass,
and a golden pigeon and a silver pigeon sprung out of
it. They were flying about when three grains of barley
fell on the floor. The silver pigeon sprang, and he
eats that. Said the golden pigeon to him, "If thou
hadst mind when I cleared the byre, thou wouldst not
eat that without giving me a share." Again fell three
other grains of barley, and the silver pigeon sprang,
and he eats that, as before. "If thou hadst mind
when I thatched the byre, thou wouldst not eat that
without giving me my share," says the golden pigeon.
Three other grains fall, and the silver pigeon sprang,
and he eats that. "If thou hadst mind when I harried
the magpie's nest, thou wouldst not eat that without
giving me my share," says the golden pigeon; "I lost
my little finger bringing it down, and I want it still."
The king's son minded, and he knew who it was he
had got. He sprang where she was, and kissed her
from hand to mouth. And when the priest came they
married a second time. And there I left them.

This version of the Battle of the Birds was recited by John Mackenzie, April 1859, and written in Gaelic by Hector Urquhart. The reciter is a fisherman, and has resided for the last thirty-four years at Ceanmore, near Inverary, on the estate of the Duke of Argyll. He is a native of Lorn. He says he has known it from his youth, and he has been in the habit of repeating it to his friends on winter nights, as a pastime. *"He can read English and play the bagpipes, and has a memory like Oliver and Boyd's Almanac."* He got this and his other stories from his father and other old people in Lorn and elsewhere. He is about sixty years of age, and was employed, April 1859, in building dykes on the estate of Ardkinglas, where Hector Urquhart is gamekeeper. In reciting his stories he has all the manner of a practised narrator; people still frequent his house to hear his tales. I know the man, and I have heard him recite many. The Gaelic has some few north country words.

CATH NAN EUN.

Bha am ann uair, anns an robh na h' uile beathach 's eun a cruinneachadh gu cath. Thubhairt mac rìgh Cathair Shìomain, "Gu'n rachadh e a dh' fhaicinn a chath, agus gun d' thugadh e fios cinnteach dhachaidh do dh' athair an rìgh, co a bhiodh 'na rìgh air na beathaichean air a bhliadhna so." Bha 'n cath seachad mu 'n dràinig e, ach eadar aon-fhitheach mòr dubh agus nathair, agus bha aogas gu'm faigheadh an nathair buaidh air an fhitheach. 'Nuair a chunnaic mac an rìgh so, chuidich e 'm fitheach, agus le aon bhuille thugar an ceann do 'n nathair. 'Nuair a leig am fitheach anail, 'sa chunnaic e gu'n robh an nathair marbh, thubhairt e, "Air son do chaoimhneis dhòmhsa an diugh, bheir mise sealladh dhuit; thig a nios a nis air bun mo dhà sgéithe." Chaidh mac an rìgh suas air muin an fhithich agus mu 'n do stad e, thug e thairis e air seachd beanntaibh, seachd glinn, agus seachd monaidhean. "A nis," ars' am fitheach, "am bheil thu faicinn an tigh 'ud thàll; falbh a nis d'a 'ionnsuidh; 's i piuthar dhòmhsa a tha gabhail còmhnuidh ann agus théid mis 'an urras gu'r è do bheatha, agus ma dh' fhoighneachdas i dhìot, 'an robh thu aig Cath nan eun? abair thusa, 'gu'n robh'." "Agus ma dh' fheòraicheas i dhìot, 'am faca tu mo choltas-sa, abair thusa 'gu 'm faca, ach bi cinnteach gu'n coinnich thu mise moch am màireach anns an àite so." Fhuair mac an rìgh gabhail aige gu maith 's gu ro mhaith air an oidhche so, biadh dheth gach biadh, 's

deoch dheth gach deoch, uisge blàth d'a chasan 's leaba bhog d'a
leasan. Air an ath latha, thug am fitheach an sealladh ceudna dhà
thairis air seachd beanntaibh, seachd glinn, agus seachd monaidhean.
Chunnaic iad bothan fad' uatha ach ge b' fhad uatha, cha b' fhada 'ga
'ruigheachd. Fhuair e gabhail aig' air an oidhche so gu maith mar
an ceudna; pailteas biadh 's deoch, 's uisge blàth d'a chasan, 's leaba
bhog d'a leasan. Ansn treas maduinn an àit' an fhithich fhaicinn,
mar air na h-uairean roimhe, Co thug coinneamh dha, ach an t-ògan-
acha bu dhreachmhoire a chunnaic e riamh, agus pasgan aige na
làimh. Dh' fhoigneachd mac an rìgh do 'n òganach so, " Am fac e
fitheach mòr dubh?" Thubhairt an t-òganach ris, " Cha 'n 'f haic thu
'm fitheach tuillidh, Oir 's mise am fitheach a bha 'sin; bha mi air
mo chul fo gheasaibh agus 'se thusa a choinneachadh a dh' fhuasgail
mi, air son sin, tha thu a' faotainn a phasgain so." " Nis," ars' an
t-òganach, "pillidh tu air t'ais air a chois-cheum cheudna, agus
bithidh tu oidhche anns gach tigh mar a bha thu roimhe; ach am
bonn a tha agad ri dhèanamh, 'na fuasgail am pasgan sin a thug
mi dhuit, gus am bi thu anns an àite bu mhiannaiche leat a bhith
chòmhnuidh." Thug mac an rìgh a chùl air an òganach, agus thug
e aghaidh air tigh Athar, agus fhuair e aoidheachd aig peathraichean
an fhithich ceart mar a fhuair e 'dol air aghaidh. Nuair a bha e
dlùthachadh air tigh athar, bha e 'dol troimhe choille dhùmhail; air
leis gu 'n robh am pasgan a' fas trom, agus smaoinich e gu 'n sealladh e gu dé a bh' ann. 'Nuair a dh' fhuasgail e 'm pasgan, cha b'
ann gun iongantas a chur air fhéin. Ann am prioba na sùla, faicear
an aon àite bu bhrèagha a chunnaic e riamh caisteal mòr, agus lios,
anns an robh na h-uile seòrsa meas is luibhean mun cuairt air a'
chaisteal. Sheas e làn iongantais, agus aithreachais air son am pasgan fhuasgladh. Cha robh 'na chomas a chur air ais a rithist, agus
bu mhiann leis an t-àite bòidheach so a bhith air an lagan bhòidheach
uaine a bha fa chomhair tigh athar. Ach sùil do 'n d' thug e, faicear
famhair mòr, 's e gabhail d'a 'ionnsuidh. " 'S olc an t-àite anns an
do thog thu do thigh, a mhic an rìgh," ars' am famhair. " Seadh,
ach cha b' ann an so bu mhiannaiche leam e 'bhith, ge do thachair
e 'bhith ann gu tubaisteach," arsa mac an rìgh. " Ciod an duais a
bheireadh tu air son a chur air ais sa phasgan mar a bha e roimhe?"
"Ciod an duais a dh' iarradh tu?" arsa mac an rìgh. " Ma bheir
thu dhòmhs' a cheud mhac a bhitheas agad, 'nuair a bhitheas e seachd
bliadhna dh' aois," ars' am famhair. " Gheibh thu sin ma bhitheas
mac agam," thubhairt mac an rìgh. Ann am prioba na sùla chuir
am famhair gach lios is gàrradh is Caisteal 'sa phasgan mar a bha
iad roimhe. " Nis," ars' am famhair, " gabh thusa do rathad féin, 's

gabhaidh mise mo rathad féin, ach cuimhnich do ghealladh 's ged
nach cuimhnich thusa, cha di-chuimhnich mise." Thug mac an
rìgh an rathad air, 's an ceann beagan làithean ràinig e 'n t-àite bu
mhiannaiche leis; dh' fhuasgail e 'm pasgan, agus bha 'n t-àite
ceudna dìreach mar a bha e roimhe, agus a nuair a dh' fhosgail e
dorus a chaisteail, faicear an òigh bu dhreachmhoire air an d' thug e
sùil riamh. "Thig air t-aghaidh, a mhic an rìgh," ars' an nighean
bhòidheach, "tha gach ni an òrdugh air do shon, ma phòsas tu mise,
an nochd féin." 'S mis' an duine a bhitheas toileach," thubhairt
mac an rìgh; agus air an oidhche sin féin phòs iad. Ach an ceann
latha 's seachd bliadhna co 'm fear mòr a chithear a tighinn a dh'
ionnsuidh a chaisteail ach am famhair. Chuimhnich mac an rìgh a
ghealladh do 'n famhair, agus gus a so, cha d' innis e do 'n bhan-rìgh
a ghealladh. "Leig thus' eadar mise 's am famhair," ars' a bhan-
rìgh. "Cuir a mach do mhac," ars' am famhair; "cuimhnich do
ghealladh." "Gheibh thu sin," ars' an rìgh, " 'nuair a chuireas a
mhathair an òrdugh e air son a thurais." Sgeadaich a bhan-rìgh
mac a chòcaire agus thug i do 'n fhamhair air làimh e. Dh' fhalbh
am famhair leis, ach cha b' fhada a chaidh e, 'nuair a chuir e slatag
ann an làimh a ghille-bhig. Dh' fheòraich am famhair dheth, "Na
'm bitheadh an t-slatag sin aig t-athair, de 'dhèanadh e, leatha?"
"Na 'm biodh an t-slat so aig m' athair, ghabhadh e air na Coin 's
air na Cait na 'm biodh iad a dol a chòir biadh an rìgh," ars' an gille-
beag. " 'S tusa mac a chòcaire," ars' am famhair. Beirear air dha
chaol Cois' air, agus sgleogar e ris a chloich a bha ri' thaobh. Thill
am famhair air ais a dh' ionnsuidh a chaisteail ann am feirg is cuth-
ach, 's thubhairt e, "Mar cuireadh iad a mach dhàsan mac an rìgh, gu
'm b' e 'chlach a b' àirde a chlach a b' ìsle bhiodh do 'n chaisteal."
Thubhairt a bhan-rìgh ris an rìgh, "Feuchaidh sinn fathast e, tha
mac a bhuidealair an aon aois ri ar mac féin." Sgeadaich i mac a
bhuidealair, agus thugar do 'n fhamhair e air làimh. Cha deach
am famhair ach goirid, nuair a chuir e 'n t-slatag 'na làimh, "Na 'm
bitheadh an t-slat so aig t-athair," ars' am famhair, "dé a dhèanadh e leatha?" "Ghabhadh e air na Coin 's air na Cait 'nuair a
bhiodh iad a tighinn dlùth air botail 's air gloinneachan an rìgh."
" 'S tusa mac a bhuidealair," ars' am famhair, is spad e 'n t-eanchainn
as air an dòigh cheudna. Thill am famhair, ann am feirg is corruich
ro mhòr. Chrith an talamh fo 'bhonn, 's chrith an caisteal 's na bh'
ann. "MACH AN SO DO MHAC," ars' am famhair, "oir an nam prioba
na sùla 's e chlach is àirde, 'chlach is ìsle bhitheas do 'n aitreabh." 'S
e bh' ann gu m b' éiginn mac an rìgh thabhairt do 'n fhamhair. Thug
am famhair e d'a thigh féin, agus thog e mar mhac dha féin e.

Latha do na làithibh 's am famhair bho 'n bhaile, chuala an t-ògan-ach an ceòl bu bhinne a chual e riamh, ann an seòmar a bha 'm mullach tigh an fhamhair. Sùil do 'n d'thug e, chunnaic e an aghaidh bu bhrèagha a chunnaic e riamh. Smèid i air e thighinn ni bu dlùithe dhi, agus thubhairt i ris, " E' dh' fhalbh air an am so ach e bhith cinnteach e 'bhith anns an àite cheudna mu mharbh mheadhain-na h-oidhche so;" agus mar a gheall, choimhlion. Bha nighean an fhamhair ri' thaobh ann am prioba na sùla agus thubhairt i ris, "Am màireach gheibh thu do roghainn ri phosadh dheth mo dhà phiuth-ar; ach abair thusa nach gabh thu a h-aon dhiubh ach mise; tha m' athair air son gu 'm pòs mi mac rìgh na Cathair uaine, ach 's coma leam è." Air an latha màireach, thug am famhair a mach a thrinir nighean 's thubhairt e, "Nis a mhic rìgh na cathair shìomain, cha do chaill thu air a bhith leamsa cho fada : gheibh thu air son bean aon do 'n dithis is sine do m' nigheanaibh, agus bithidh cead agad dol dhachaidh leatha, an déigh na bainnse." "Ma bheir thu dhomh an té bheag bhòidheach so," arsa mac an rìgh, "gabhaidh mi air t-fhacal thu." Las fearg an fhamhair, agus thubhairt e, ma'm faigh thu sin, feumaidh tu na tri nitheanana a dh' iarras mis' ort a dhèan-amh." "Abair romhad," arsa mac an rìgh. Thug am famhair do 'n bhàthaich e. "Nis," ars' am famhair, "tha innear nan ceud damh an so, agus cha deach a chartadh o cheann seachd bliadhna. "Tha mise 'dol o 'n bhaile 'n diugh agus mar bi 'm bàthach so air a chart-adh mu 'n d'thig an oidhche cho ghlan 's gu'n ruith ubhall òir o cheann gu ceann, dith cha 'n e mhàin nach faigh thu mo nighean, ach 's e deoch dhe d'fhuil a chaisgeas mo phathadh a nochd." Toisichear air cartadh na bathaich, ach bu cheart cho maith teannadh ri taom-adh a chuain mhòir. 'N déigh mheadhoin-latha 's am fallus 'ga 'dhalladh thàinig nighean òg an fhamhair far an robh e 's thubh-airt i ris, "Tha thu 'ga'd' phianadh, a mhic an rìgh." "Tha mi 'n sin," arsa mac an rìgh. "Thig a nall," ars' ise, "agus leig do sgìos." " Ni mi sin," ars esan, "cha 'n 'eil ach am bàs a feitheamh orm co dhiu." Shuidh e sìos làimh rithe. Bha e cho sgìth, agus gu 'n do thuit e 'na chadal ri 'taobh. 'Nuair a dhùisg e, cha robh nighean an fhamhair ri fhaicinn; ach bha, bhathaich cho glan cairte 's gu 'n ruitheadh ubhall òir bho cheann gu ceann dhith. 'Steach thigear am famhair, 's thubhairt e, " Chairt thu 'm bathaich, a mhic an rìgh." " Chairt mi," ars' esan. " Chairt neach éiginn i," ars' am famhair. "Cha do chairt thus' i co dhiu," thubhairt mac an rìgh. "Seadh! Seadh!" ars' am famhair, bhon a' bha thu co tapaidh an diugh, gheibh thu gus an am so am màireach gu tubhadh a bhathaich so le clòimh eòin gun dà ite air an aon dath." Bha mac an rìgh air

a chois roi'n ghrein. Ghlac e a bhogha 's a bhalg-saighead a mharbhadh nan èun. Thug e 'm monadh air, ach ma thug, cha robh na h-
eòin cho furasda ri 'm faotainn. Bha e a ruith 'nan déigh, gus an
robh am fallus 'ga 'dhalladh. Mu mheadhon-la co 'thigeadh ach
nighean an fhamhair. "Tha thu ga'd' phianadh, a mhic an rìgh,"
ars' ise. "Tha mi," thubhairt esan, "cha do thuit ach an dà lon-
dubh so, agus iad air aon dath." "Thig a nall, 's leig do sgìos air a
chnocan bhòidheach so," arsa nighean an fhamhair. "'S mi tha toileach," thubhairt esan. Smaoinich e gun cobhaireadh i air air an
àm so cuideachd. Shuidh e sìos làimh rithe, 's cha b'fhad' a bha e 'n
sin gus an do thuit e 'na chadal; agus a nuair a dhùisg e, bha nighean an fhamhair air falbh. Smaoinich e tilleadh thun an tighe, 's
faicear am bathaich tùghte leis na h-itean. 'Nuair a thàinig am
famhair dhachaidh thubhairt e, "Thubh thu 'm bathaich, a mhic an
rìgh." "Thubh mi," ars' esan. "Thubh cuid-eiginn i," ars' am
famhair. "Cha do thubh thusa i," arsa mac an rìgh. "Seadh!
Seadh!" ars' am famhair. "'Nis," ars' am famhair, "tha craobh
ghiubhas ri taobh an loch ud shios agus tha nead pioghaid 'na
mullach." "Na h-uibhean a gheibh thu anns an nead, feumaidh iad
a bhi agamsa gu mo *cheud-lon, gaidh*; cha 'n fhàod a h-aon a bhith
sgàinte no briste, agus 's e còig a tha 'san nead." Moch 'sa mhaduinn, dh'fhalbh mac an rìgh far an robh a chraobh, 's cha robh sin
duilich amas oirre. Cha robh a leith-bhreac 'sa choill' air fad. Bho
'bonn gu ruig a ceud mheanglan, còig ceud troidh. Bha mac an rìgh
a dol ceithir thoimchioll air a chraoibh. Thàinig ise 'bha daonnan
a dèanamh furtachd dha: "Tha thu air call craiceann nan làmh 's
nan cas, a mhic an rìgh." "Ach tha," ars' esan, "cha luaithe shuas
na shìos mi." "Cha 'n à' fuireachd so," arsa nighean an fhamhair.
Shàth i' meur an déigh meur, gus an d' rinn i faradh do mhac an
rìgh gu dol suas do nead na pioghaid. 'Nuair a bha e aig an nead,
thubhairt ise, "Dèan cabhag a nuas leis na h-uibhean, oir tha anail
m' athar a' losgadh mo dhroma." Leis a chabhaig a bh' air-san, dh'
fhàg ise 'lùdag am mullach na craoibhe. "Nis," ars' ise, "théid
thu dhachaidh leis na h-uibhean gu luath, agus gheibh thu mise ri
phòsadh a nochd ma dh'aithnicheas tu mi; bithidh mis' agus mo
dha phiuthar air ar n-éideadh anns an aon trusgan, agus air ar
dèanamh coltach ri' chéile; Ach seall thus' ormsa 'nuair a their m'
athair 'falbh le d' mhnaoi, a mhic an rìgh; agus chi thu làimh gun
lùdag." Thug e na h-uibhean do'n fhamhair. "Seadh! Seadh!"
ars' am famhair, "bi' dèanamh deas chum do phòsadh." 'S ann an
sin a bha bhanais, 's b'e bhanais i, famhairean 's daoiné uaisle, 's
mac rìgh na Cathair uaine 'nam meadhon. Chaidh am pòsadh, 's

thòisich an dàmhsa, 's b'e sin an damhsa. Bha tigh an f hambair air
chrith bho 'mhullach gu 'bhonn. Ach thàinig àm dol a luidhe, 's
thubhairt am famhair, " Tha 'n t-àm dhuit dol a luidhe, a mhic rìgh
na cathair shìomain, thoir leat do bhean as am meadhon sin." Chuir
ise mach a làimh dheth 'n robh an lùdag agus rug e oirre air làimh.
" Dh' amais thu gu maith air an am so cuideachd, ach cha 'n'eil fios
nach coinnich sinn thu air dòigh eile," thubhairt am famhair. Ach
a luidhe chaidh iad. " A nis," thuirt ise; "cadal cha dèan thu, air
neo bàsaichidh tu; feumaidh sinn teicheadh gu luath, oir gun teagamh marbhaidh m' athair thu." A mach ghabh iad, agus air an loth
dhuinn a bha anns an stabull, chaidh iad. " Dèan socair beagan,"
ars' ise, "agus cluichidh mise cleas air an t-seann laoch." Leum i
stigh, agus gheàrr i ubhall 'na naoi earrannan, 's chuir i dà earrann
dhith aig ceann na leapa, agus dà earrann aig casan na leapa; dà
earrann aig an dorus-chadha, agus dà earann aig an dorus mhòr, agus
a h-aon air taobh a mach an tighe. Dhùisg am famhair, agus
ghlaodh e, " 'M bheil sibhse 'nur cadal." " Cha 'n 'eil fathast," ars'
an ubhall a bha aig ceann na leapa. An ceann ghreis ghlaodh e
rithist, " Cha 'n 'eil fathast," ars' an ubhall a bha aig casan na leapa.
Greis an déigh sin, ghlaodh e rithist, " Cha 'n 'eil fathast," thubhairt
an ubhal aig dorus a chadha. Ghlaodh am famhair a rithist, 's
f hreagair an ubhal a bha aig an dorus mhòr. " Tha sibh a' dol ni's
faide uam," ars' am famhair. " Cha 'n 'eil fathast," ars' an ubhal a
bha air taobh a mach an doruis. " Tha sibh a teichadh," ars' am
famhair. Leum am famhair air a chasan, agus gu ruig an leabaidh
chaidh e; ach bha i gu fuar, fàs, " Tha cuilbheartan mo nighean
féin a feuchainn rium," thubhairt am famhair. Air an tòir ghabh
e," Am beul an latha, thuirt nighean an f hamhair, " Gu 'n
robh anail a h-'athair a losgadh a droma." " Cuir do làmh gu
luath," ars' ise, "ann an cluais na loth dhuinn, agus ge be ni
gheibh thu innte tilg 'na d' dhéigh e." " Tha bior do sgitheach an
so," thubhairt esan. " Tilg as do dheigh e." Cha luaithe rinn e so,
na bha fichead mìle do sgitheach cho tiugh ann 's gum bu ghann do
neas dol troimhe. Thàinig am famhair 'na dhian 's sind e 'n coinncamh
a chinn 's amhach anns an sgitheach!! " Tha cuilbheartan mo nighean
féin an so mar an ceudna," thubhairt am famhair; "ach na 'm
biodh agamsa mo thuagh mhòr 's mo chorc choille an so, cha b'
f had' a bhithinn a dèanamh rathad troimhe so." Thill e dhachaidh air son na tuaidh mòire 's na corc choille, agus gun teagamh
cha robh e fad a' dèanamh rathad troi 'n sgitheach. " Fàgaidh
mi 'n tuadh 's a chorc choille 'n so, gus am till mi," ars' esan.
" MA DH' FHAGAS, thuirt feannag a bha ann an craobh," goididh

sinne iad." "Ni sibh sin fhéin," ars' am famhair, "ach cuiridh
mise dhachaidh iad." Thill e agus dh' fhàg e iad aig an tigh.
Ann an teas an latha mhothaich is anail a h'athar a losgadh a droma.
"Cuir do mheur ann an cluais na lotha, agus tilg na gheibb thu
innte as do dhéigh." Fhuair e sgealb do chlach ghlais 's thilg e as
a dhéigh i. Ann am prioba na sùla, bha fichead mìle do chreag
mhòr ghlas air leud 's air àirde as an déigh. Thàinig am famhar
'na dheann, ach seachad air a' chreag cha robh comas dha dol. "'Se
cuilbheartan mo nighinn féin rud as cruaidh' a thachair riamh rium,"
ars' am famhair. "Ach na 'm biodh agamsa mo gheamhlag 's
mo mhatag mhòr, cha b' fhada a bhithinn a dèanamh rathad roimh
'n chreig so cuideachd." B'fheudar tilleadh air an son, agus b'e
féin gille sgoltadh nan clach. Cha robh e fada a dèanamh rathad
troimh 'n chreag. "Fàgaidh mi an acfhuinn an so, 's cha thill
mi tuillidh." "MA DH' FHÀGAS," ars' an fheannag, "goididh sinn'
iad." "Tha sin 's a roghainn agad; cha 'n'eil tìom tilleadh ann."
Ann am bristeadh na faire thubhairt nighean an fhamhair, "gu'n
robh i mothachainn anail a h-athar a losgadh a droma." " Seall ann
an cluais na lotha, a mhic an rìgh, air neo tha sinn cailte." Rinn e
so, agus 's e aotroman làn uisge a bha 'na cluais air an am so.
"Tilg 'na d' dhéigh e," arsa nighean an fhamhair. Rinn e so, agus
bha loch uisge fichead mìle air fad 's air leud 'nan déigh. Thàinig
am famhair air aghaidh, ach leis an astar a bh' aige, bha e ann am
meadhoin an loch, agus chaidh e foidhe, 's cha d' éirich e ni's mò.
Air an ath latha, bha a chuideachd òg air tighinn am fradharc tigh
athar-san. "Nis," ars' ise, "tha m'athair bàite, 's cha chuir e
dragh tuillidh òirn; " Ach mu 'n d'théid sinn ni 's faide," ars' ise,
"rach thusa gu tigh t'athar, agus innis gu 'bheil mo leithid-sa
agad; ach am bonn a tha agad ri 'dhèanamh, na leig le duine na
crèutair do phògadh; oir ma ni thu sin, cha bhi cuimhn' agad gu
'faca tu riamh mi." Chuir gach neach mar a bha tachairt air fàilte
is furan air, 's thug e àithne d'a athair 's d'a mhàthair, gun esan a
phògadh; ach mar a bha 'n tubaist 'an dàn, bha sean mhial-chù do
ghalla 'steach 's dh' aithnich i e, 's leum i suas ri bheul, agus na
dhéigh sin dhi-chuimhnich e nighean an fhamhair. Bha ise 'na
suidhe aig taobh an tobair mar a dh' fhàg e i, ach cha robb mac an
rìgh a' tighinn. Ann am beul na h-oidhche, streap i suas ann an
craobh do dharach a bha ri taobh an tobair. Luidh i ann an
gobhall na craoìbhe fad na h'oidhche sin. Bha tigh aig greusaiche dlùth do 'n tobar, agus mu mheadhon là a' màireach, dh'
iarr an greusaich air a mhnaoi, i 'dhol airson deoch dha as an
tobar. 'Nuair a rainig bean a ghreusaiche an tobar, 's a chunnaic i

faileas na té a bha anns a chraoibh, air saoilsinn dh'ise gu 'm b'e
'faileas féin a bh' ann ('s cha do shaoil leatha gu so gu 'n robh i co
brèagha), thug i tilgeil do'n chuman a bha 'na làimh, 's bhrist i ris
an talamh e, 's thug i 'n tigh oirre gun chuinneag gun uisge!
"Cait' am bheil an t-uisge, a bhean," thubhairt an greusaiche.
"A bhodaich leibidich, shuaraich, gun mhaise, dh' fhan mi
tuilidh 's fada 'n am thràill uisge 's connaidh agad." "Tha mi
féin a smaoineachadh, a bhean, gu'n deach thu air bhoile ; falbh
thusa a nighean, gu luath 's faigh deoch do d' athair. Dh' fhalbh
a nighean, agus air an dòigh cheudna thachair dhi. Cha do
shaoil leatha gu so gu 'n robh i co tlachdmhor, 's thug i 'n tigh
oirre. "Nios an deoch," ars' a h-athair. "A pheallaig bhodaich
nam bròg, an saoil thu gu 'bheil mise gu bhi 'm thràill uisge agad."
Smaoinich an greusaiche bochd gu 'n d' thug iad car as am beachd, 's
dh' fhalbh e féin do 'n tobar. Chunnaic e faileas na gruagaiche san
tobar, 's dh'amhairc e suas do 'n chraoibh 's faicear am boirionnach bu
bhrèagha a chunnaic e riamh. "'S corrach do shuidheachan ach 's
maiseach do ghnùis," thubhairt an greusaiche. "Thig a nuas oir,
tha feum dhuit, car ùine ghearr 'nam thigh-sa." Thuig an greusaiche
gu'm b'e so am faileas a chuir a chuideachdsan air bhoile. Thug an
greusaich i gu thigh 's thubhairt e rithe, "nach robh aige-san ach
bothan bochd, ach gu 'm faigheadh i a cuid dhe na bh' ann." An
ceann latha na dhà 'na dhéigh so, tháinig triùir fhleasgach uasal gu
tigh a ghreusaiche, airson brògan a dhèanamh dhoibh, 's an rìgh air
tighinn dhachaidh, agus e 'dol a phòsadh. Ach sùil do 'n d' thug
na fleasgaich, chunnaic iad nighean an fhamhair, 's ma chunnaic,
cha 'n fhac iad riamh té co bòidheach rithe. "'S ann agad a tha 'n
nighean bhòidheach an so," thubhairt na fleasgaich ris a ghreusaiche.
"Ach cha 'n e mo nighean-sa th' ann." "Nàile!" arsa fear dhiubh,
"bheirinn féin ceud punnd air son a pòsadh." Thubhairt an dithis
eile a leithid cheudna. Thubhairt an greusaiche bochd, "nach robh
gnothuch aige-san ri a dhéanamh rithe." "Ach," ars' iadsan, "farraid
thusa dhith 'n nochd, agus leig fios thugainne 'màireach." Nuair
a dh' fhalbh na h'-uaislean, dh' fharraid i do'n ghreusaiche, "gu dé
sud a bha iad ag radh mu 'm dheibhinnse?" Dh' innis an greusaiche
dhith. "Falbh 'nan déigh," ars' ise, "pòsaidh mi fear aca a nochd
féin, 's thugadh e leis a sporan airgid." Dh' fhalbh an greusaiche
'nan déigh, 's dh' innis e 'n sin fein. Thill e'n t-òganach. Thug e ceud
punnd do 'n ghreusaiche, air-son tochar. "Chaidh i a luidhe, agus an
uair a bha aodach an òganaich dheth, dh' iarr i air deoch uisge as a
chòrn a bha air a bhòrd air taobh thall an t-seòmair; dh' fhalbh e,
ach as a' sin cha d' thigeadh e fad na h'-oidhche, is greim aig air an

t-soitheach uisge." Oglaich thu. Thubhairt ise, "cairson nach dig
thu a luidhe," ach as a' so cha diongadh e, gus an robh an latha geal
am màireach ann. Thàinig an greusaiche gu dorus an t-seòmair,
agus dh' iarr i air, "an slaodaire ballaich sin a thabhairt air
falbh." Dh' fhalbh an suiriche so, 's thug 'e 'n tigh air, ach cha
do dh' innis e mar dh' éirich dha do 'n dithis eile. Air an ath oidhche,
thàinig an darna fleasgach, agus air an doigh cheudna nuair a
chaidh i a luidhe, "Seall," thuirt ise, "am bheil an crann air an
dorus." Air a chrann ghabh a lamhan gréim, agus as a' sin cha d'
thigeadh e fad na h-oidhche, as a' so cha d' thigeadh e gu latha geal
am màireach. Dh' fhalbh e fo sprochd is nàire. Coma co dhiu, cha
d'innis e, mar thachair, do 'n fhleasgach eile, agus air an treas oidhche,
thàinig am fear eile, agus mar a thachair do 'n dithis eile thachair dha;
bha cas air an leabaidh 's cas eile air an urlar, cha d'thigeadh 's cha
rachadh e, ach, air an dòigh so bha e fad na h-oidhche. Am màireach
thug e 'bhuinn as, 's cha 'n fhacas e' scalltainn 'na dhéigh. "Nis,"
arsa 'n nighean ris a ghreusaiche, "'s leatsa an sporan òir, cha 'n'eil
feum agam-sa air, 's feàird thus' e, agus cha mhios'de mis' e, airson do
chaoimhneis dhomh." Bha na brògan ullamh aig a ghreusaiche,
agus air an latha sin féin, bha an rìgh gu pòsadh. Bha 'n greusaiche
dol do 'n chaisteal le brògan nan òganach, 's thubhairt an nighean
ris a ghreusaiche, "bu mhaith leam sealladh fhaicinn dhe mac an
rìgh, mu 'm pòsadh e." "Thig leamsa," ars' an greusaiche, "tha mi
mion eòlach air seirbheisich a' chaisteil, agus gheibh thu sealladh
air mac an rìgh 's na cuideachd uile." Agus a nuair a chunnaic na
h-uaislean am boireannach bòidheach a bha 'n so, thug iad i do
sheòmar na baiunse, agus liòn iad gloinne fìon dhi. 'Nuair a bha
i' dol a dh' òl na bha sa ghloinne, chaidh lasair suas aiste, agus
leum calman òir 's calman airgid as a' ghloinne. Bha iad ag
itealaich mu 'n cuairt, 'nuair a thuit tri ghràinnean eòrna air an
urlar. Leum an calman airgiod, agus ithear sud. Thubhairt an
calman òir ris, na'm biodh cuimhn' agad 'nuair a chairt mi 'm
bàthaich, CHA 'N 'ITHEADH TU SIUD GUN CHUID A THOIRT
DHOMHS'A. A rithist thuit tri gràinnean còrn' eile, 's leum an calman
airgiod agus ithear siud mar an ceudna. "Na'm bitheadh cuimhn'
agad 'nuair a thubh mi 'm bàthaich CHA 'N ITHEADH TU SIUD, GUN
MO CHUID A THOIRT DHOMHSA," ars' an calman òir. Tuitear tri
ghràinnean eile, s leum an calman airgiod, agus ithear siud cuideachd.
"Na 'm biodh cuimhn' agad 'nuair a chreach mi nead na pioghaid,
CHA 'N'ITHEADH TU SIUD GUN MO CHUID A THOIRT DHOMHSA," ars'
an calman òir. "Chaill mi 'n lùdag 'gad' thabhairt a nuas, agus
tha i dhìth orm fathast." Chuimhnich mac an rìgh, 's dh' aithnich

e co a bh' aige. Leum e far an robh i, 's phòg ei bho làimh gu i beul, agus a nuair a thàinig an sagairt, phòs iad an darna h-uair !! Agus dh' fhag mis' an sin iad.

HECTOR URQUHART.

2. There is another version of this tale current in Islay. It was taken down from the recitation of Ann Darroch by Hector Maclean. It is called the "Widow's Son." He goes to seek his fortune, and comes to a giant's house, where he engages himself as a servant for a peck of gold and a peck of silver. He is sent first to cleanse the seven byres that have never been cleansed for seven years. All he puts out at one door comes in at the other. The giant's daughter comes; he promises to marry her, and she says, "Gather, oh shovel, and put out, oh grape," and the tools work of themselves, and clear the byres. Next he has to thatch the byres with feathers, no quills to be upwards. He gets only one feather, and the giant's daughter takes three grains of barley, and throws them on the roof. The birds of the air gather, and thatch the byres in a minute. Next day he has to catch the steed that had never seen a blink of earth or air. The girl gives him a little rusty bridle, and the steed comes and puts her head into it. She makes six little cakes, which she places at the fire, the foot water, the door of the chamber, the side of the bed, and the kitchen door, and they mount the steed and ride off. The giant lies down and calls to his daughter. The cakes answer, till there are none left to reply. Then he rises, takes his clothes, his boots, and his sword of light; he makes seven miles at each step; he sees seven miles by the light of the sword—he follows; they hear him coming; the girl gives the widow's son a golden apple, and tells him to throw it at a mole on her father, where alone he is vulnerable; he fears that he will miss so small a mark, so she throws it herself, and the giant is dead in an instant.

They reach a big town. He is told to kiss nothing, or he will forget the girl and his promise. A big dog comes to meet him, and puts his paws on his shoulder and kisses him. He takes service with the king, and at last he is to be married to the king's daughter.

She takes service with a smith, disguised as a man, and

" comes on famously." The smith's daughter falls in love with her, and wants to marry her. She tells, at last, that she is a girl in search of her own lover. On a day of days the smith and his daughter and his servant are invited to the wedding of the widow's son with the king's daughter. They go, and the giant's daughter sets a golden cock and a silver hen on the board before the bridegroom. She takes a grain of barley from her pocket and throws it before them. The cock pecks the hen and eats the barley; and the hen says, "Gog, Gog, if thou hadst mind when I cleansed the seven byres for thee, thou wouldst not do that to me." She does this three times, and the birds remind him of what has been done; then he knows her, leaps over the board, catches her by the arm, leaves the king's daughter, and marries her.

3. There is another version current at Inverary, repeated to me by a stable boy who was then employed at the ferry of St. Katharines, and who repeated it in Gaelic while rowing the boat to Inverary. It began thus :—I will tell you a story about the wren. There was once a farmer who was seeking a servant, and the wren met him, and he said, "What art thou seeking for?" "I am seeking a servant," said the farmer. "Wilt thou take me?" said the wren. "Thee, thou poor little creature; what good wouldst thou do?" "Try thou me," said the wren, So he engaged him, and the first work he set him to was threshing in the barn. The wren threshed (what did he thresh with? —a flail to be sure), and he knocked off one grain. A mouse came out and she eats that. "I'll praise thee, and don't do that again," said the wren. He struck again, and he knocked off two grains. Out came the mouse and she eats that. So they arranged a contest that they might know which was strongest, and there was neither mouse nor rat on earth that did not gather, nor was there bird under heaven that did not come to the battle. The son of a gentleman heard of the fight, and he came also, but he slept before it was over, and when he awoke there was neither " mouse nor rat to be seen ; there was but one great black raven." The raven and the man agree to travel together, and they come to an inn. The gentleman goes in, but the raven is sent to the stable, because the porters and waiters object to the like of a

raven. Here he picks out all the horses' eyes, and in the
morning there is a disturbance. The gentleman pays and scolds,
and they go to another inn, where the raven is sent to the byre,
and picks out all the cows' eyes. Then they part. The raven
takes out a book, and gives it to his companion with a warning
not to open it till he gets home to his father's house. He breaks
the charge, looks, and finds himself in a giant's house. There he
takes service, and is sent to clean the byre. It had seven doors,
it had not been cleaned for seven years, and all that he put out
at one door came in at the other. Then came the giant's red-
haired daughter, and said, "If thou wilt marry me I will help
thee." He consents; and she sets all the grapes and forks
about the place to work of themselves, and the byre is cleansed.
Then the giant sets him to thatch the byre with feathers, and
every feather he put on the wind blew away. Then came the
giant's girl, and the promise was repeated; and she played a
whistle that she had, and he laid his head in her lap, and every
bird there was came, and they thatched the byre.

Then the giant sent him to the hill to fetch the gray horse
that was seven years old; and she told him that he would meet
two black dogs, and she gave him a cake of tallow and half a
cheese, and a tether; and she said that the dogs and the horse
would kill him unless he gave the dogs the food, and put the
tether on the horse. When the dogs ran at him, he put the
tallow in the mouth of one, and the cheese in the throat of the
other; and when the horse came down the hill to kill him with
his mouth open, he put the tether in his mouth and he followed
him quietly home. "Now," said she, "we will be off." So they
mounted and rode away, but first she took four apples, three she
placed about the house, which spoke as in the other tales, the
fourth she took with her. When the last of the apples had
spoken, the giant rose and followed. Then the girl felt her
father's breath on her back, and said, "Search in the horse's
ear." And he found a twig. "Throw it behind you," said she;
and he threw it, and it became the biggest wood that ever was.
The giant came, and returned for his "big axe and his little axe,"
and he hewed his way through; and the red-haired girl said
that she felt her father's breath. "Now," said she to the king's
son (here the narrator remembered that he was a prince instead

E

of a young farmer), " see in the filly's ear " (here he remembered that it was a filly). So he looked, and found a bit of stone, threw it, and it became a mountain. The giant came, looked for his big hammer and his little hammer, and smashed his way through the hill, and she felt his breath again. Then he sought in the ear, and found a (something) of water, and threw it, and it became a loch of fresh water. The giant came, and returned for his big scoop and his little scoop, and baled the water out, and he was after them again. Then she said, " My father is coming now, and he will kill us. Get off the filly, king's son," and he got off, and she gave him the apple, and she said, " Now put it under the filly's foot." And he did so ; and the filly put her foot on it, and it smashed to bits ; and the giant fell over dead, for his heart was in the apple. So they went on to his father's house, and she was made house-keeper, for they were not married ; then in a short time she became house-maid, then kitchen-maid, and then hen-wife ; and then the king was to be married (he had now become a king) ; and then first the porter, then the head waiter, and then some other servant, came and courted her. They promise to let her in to the wedding, and give her a fine dress each ; and each in turn is admitted into the hen-wife's room ; but the first goes to put the lid on the kettle, and is fast by the hands all night ; the second is, in like manner, fast to a window which he goes to shut ; and the feet of the third stick to the floor. Then she comes to the porter in her dirty dress. He drives her away, but he is at last obliged to give her a fine dress, and let her in. Then she comes to the head waiter who does the same. Then she comes to the servant, who does the same, but is forced to let her in to the wedding. Then she takes out a golden cock and a silver hen, which she had brought. She sets them on the floor, and they talk. " Dost thou remember how I cleansed byre ? Dost thou mind how I thatched the barn ? Dost thou remember how I saved thy life ?" And so on, till they repeat the whole story, reminding the king how she had been the house-keeper, house-maid, and hen-wife, and faithful throughout. And the king said, " Stop, I will marry thee." And when she said that, she showed the fine dresses that she had got from the porter, and the head waiter, etc., and they were married; and if they have not died since then, they are alive, merry, and rich.

4. The stable boy said that he had learned this from a very old man, now living near Lochgilphead, who could tell it much better than he could. A gentleman at the inn said that an old woman, now dead, used to tell something like this, and that her raven was the son of the king of Lochlin. The old woman lived near Dalmally, and her daughter is said to be there still, but I have been unable to find her out. On asking for her, and giving my reason, I was told by a waiter that "light had dawned in that district, and that ignorance was banished."

5. A very similar story is well known in South Uist, and a fragment of it is still told in Sutherland.

6. The Uist story told to me by Donald MacCraw as we walked along the road last September is called "Mother's Blessing." The lad, so called because he is so good, goes to seek his fortune. He plays cards, and wins from some gentles; then stakes seven years' service against so many thousands, and loses to a black dog who comes in with a looking-glass on every paw. He goes to serve the dog, and is shown a cave where there are a hundred stakes and ninety-nine heads on them. He is set to cleanse the byre, to catch the steed, and to rob the nest. The black dog's daughter helps. She throws out one spadeful, and the litter flies out, " seven spadefuls at each of seven doors for every one he throws out." She gives a rusty bridle for the steed. She strikes the sea with a rod, and makes a way to the island where the nest is, and gives her toes to make a ladder to climb up. He leaves one, and offers one of his own instead. She refuses, because " her father always washes her feet himself." They ride off on the horse—the dog and his company follow. A wood grows and a river flows from things found in the horse's ear, and the dog is defeated but not killed. She gives the lad a treasure which is found under a tuft of rushes. He goes home, speaks to his mother, and forgets all. He builds a palace, and is to be married to a lady, but she is so proud that she will have the widow's hut pulled down. Mother's Blessing will not, so the match is off, but after a time it is on again. The door opens, and in walks the black dog smoking a pipe. He goes to the priest and forbids the ceremony. The priest says, " Begone to thine own place down below." " It's many

a long day since *thou* art wanted there," says the dog. The
priest defies all fiends, and *will* marry the pair. The dog says,
" If I tell all I know thou wilt not." Then he whispers, and the
priest is silenced. Then he brings in a fine gentleman, and says
to the bride—" There is thy first lover ; marry him." And they
are married then and there. The dog brings in his own daughter ; Mother's Blessing marries her, and the dog danced at the
wedding with the priest. MacCraw said there was something left
out which his informant would not tell.

7. I have received yet another version of this tale, very well
written in Gaelic, from JOHN DEWAR, who, according to his own
account of himself, is now (October 1859) residing in Glendarnail,
and is about to proceed to Roseneath, where he used to get employment in making stobbs for the fences. He heads his story—
" Tales of the Gael in the Winter Nights," and promises to send
more. UIRSGEALN NAN GAEL S' NA OIDHCHENAN GEAMHRAIDH.
—His Gaelic spelling is rather phonetic—

He heard it from his mother, told nearly as the stable-boy
gave it ; and has heard it lately in Glen Darnail. He first heard
an abridgment four or five years before 1812 or 1813, when he
learned this from Mary MacCalum, a native of Glen Falloch, at
the head of Loch Lomond.

It begins with a quarrel between a mouse and a wren in a
barn about a grain of oats, which the mouse *will* eat. The wren
brings his twelve birds—the mouse her tribe. The wren says,
" Thou hast thy tribe with thee"—" As well as thyself," says the
mouse. The mouse sticks out her leg proudly, and the wren
breaks it with his flail. The creatures of the plain and of the air
all joined the quarrel, and there was a pitched battle on a set day.
They fought the battle in a field above a king's house; and the fight
was so fierce, that there were left but a raven and a snake. The
king's son looked out of a window, and saw the snake twined round
the raven's neck, and the raven holding the snake's throat in his
beak—GOB—and neither dared to let go. Both promised friend-
ship for help, and the king's son slew the serpent.—NATHAIR.

The raven lived for a year and a day in the palace, then took
the king's son hunting for the first time, and when he was tired,
carried him. "And he put his hands about the raven before his
wings, and he hopped with him over nine Bens, and nine Glens,

and nine Moors." They go to the three sisters, and the king's
son gets hospitality, because he comes from the land where the
birds set the battle, and brings news of the raven, who is yet
alive, and lived with him for a year and a day. Each day the
number of glens, and hills, and moors passed over, falls from nine
to six and three. The same thing is said by each of the three
sisters : " That is a year and a day for thee in this place, and a piece
in thy purse on the day when thou goest ;" but he keeps tryst, and
returns to the raven. On the third day came a mist, and the raven
was not to be found ; but when the king's son was nearly beat,
he looked over a rock, and saw FEAR LEADANACH BUIDHE BOIDH-
EACH AGUS CIR OIR ANSA N' DARNA LAIMH, AGUS CIR AIRGID SAN
LAIMH EILE, a beautiful yellow ringletted man, with a golden
comb in the one hand, and a silver comb in the other, who asked
if he would take him instead of the raven. He would not, " nor
half-a-dozen such." So the yellow ringletted man told him that he
was the FITHEACH CROM DUBH—the black humpy raven that was
laid under spells by a bad DRUIDH that knew how to put under
spells. He had been set free by coming to his father's house
with the king's son. Then he gave him a book, and told him to
go with the wind the way it might blow, and to look in the book
when he wished to see his father's house, but always from a hill
top.

The king's son soon got tired, and looked in the book at the
bottom of a glen, and saw his father's house at the bottom of a peat
hag, with all the doors and windows shut, and no way to get to it.

Then came a giant, who shewed him the way for the promise
of his first son. He shewed him his father's house on the top of
a hill, with each door and window open, and got the promise.
" And it was the giant who had cast DRUIDHEACHD upon him,
that he might see his father's house in the bottom of a peat hag."

" Long after that the old king died, and the son got the kingly
chair. He married ; he had a son ; and he was coming on to be
a brave lad, and they were dwelling happily in the castle. The
giant came to them, and he asked that the king's son should be
sent out to him there, and they were not very willing to do that ;
but the giant said, unless they sent him out, that the highest
stone of the castle would be the lowest presently ; and they
thought of arraying the cook's son bravely, and sending him out ;

and they did that. The giant went away with him, and he had a
rod in his hand, and when they were a little bit from the house,
the giant asked the cook's son—'What would thy father do with
this little rod if he had it?' 'I don't know myself,'said the cook's
son, 'unless he would beat the dogs away from the meat.' With
that the giant understood that he had not got the right one, and
he turned back with him, and he asked that the king's son should
be sent to him. Then they put brave clothes on the son of the
STIUARD, and they sent him out to the giant, but the giant was
not long till he did to him as he had done to the cook's son, and
he returned with him full of heavy wrath. He said to them, unless they sent out to him there the king's son, that the highest
stone in the castle would be the lowest presently, and that he
would kill all who were within; and then they were obliged to
send out the king's son himself, though it was very grievous;
and the giant went away with him. When they were gone a little
bit from the castle, the giant showed him the rod that was in his
hand and he said—'What would thy father do with this rod if
he were to have it?' And the king's son said—'My father has
a braver rod than that.' And the giant asked him—'Where will
thy father be when he has that brave (briagh) rod?' And the
king's son said—'He will be sitting in his kingly chair;' and
the giant understood that he had the right one. [*This passage is
translated entire, because, as I am told, there is a similar passage
in the Volsung tale*]. The giant took him home, and set him to
clean the byre that had not been cleansed for seven years; and in
case of failure, threatened SE'T FHUIL URAR ALUIN GHRINN A
BHITHIS AGUM A CHASGA M' IOTADH AGUS T' FHEOIL UR GHRINN MAR
MHILLISTAIN FHIACAL. It is thy fresh goodly beautiful blood I
will have quenching my thirst, and thy fresh, beautiful flesh as
sweetening of teeth;" and he went to bed.

The king's son failed of course; all that went out at one door
came in at another. Then came MARI RUADH, Auburn Mary,
the giant's daughter, and made him promise to marry her, and he
gave his hand and his promise. She made him set all the CAIBE
and shovels in order, waived her hand, and they worked alone, and
cleaned the byre. "She took an apple from her pocket—a golden
apple—and it would run from end to end, and would raise no stain
in any place, it was so clean."

The daughter "had been in sewing all day," when her father came home from hunting, and asked his housewife. Next came the thatching of the barn with "the feathers of all the birds the giant had ever killed, to be laid as close as ever they lay on the back of a heather hen or a black cock." The wind blew them away as fast as he put them on. The daughter came, and after a new promise, " CHATHUDH," she shook them as chaff (is shaken on hill tops now), with the wind, and the wind blew them straight to their own place. The giant came home from his hunting as usual, and asked—" Housewife, was Auburn Mary out at all to-day?" "No, she was within sewing." He went out, and brought in SRIAN BHRIAGH SHOILEIR DEARRSACH, a brave, clear, shiny bridle, and ordered the king's son to catch the FALAIRE, filly, on yonder hill, and tie her in the stable, or else, &c.

The fine bridle would not do. Then the daughter brought from the stable, SEAN SRIAN DUBH MEIRGACH, an old, black, rusty bridle that was behind one of the turf seats, and shook it, and the filly came and put her nose *into it*.

The giant had the usual talk, but gave no more orders, and his daughter told the king's son that he would kill him that night, but that she would save him if he would promise to marry her.

"She put a wooden bench in the bed of the king's son; two wooden benches in her own bed. She spat at the front of her own bed, and spat at the side of the giant's bed, and spat at the passage door, and she set two apples above the giant's bed, ready to fall on him when he should wake and set him asleep again." And they mounted and rode away, and set the filly " running with might."

The giant awoke, and shouted—"Rise, daughter, and bring me a drink of the blood of the king's son." " I will arise," said the spittle, in front of his bed ; and one of the apples fell and struck him between the two shoulders, and he slept. The second time it was—" Rise, wife ; " and the same thing happened. The third time he shouted—" Art thou rising to give me a drink of the blood of the king's son, Oh wife?" "Coming with it," said the spittle, " behind the door of the cabb."

Then he lay a while, and got up with an axe, and struck it into the bench in the bed of the king's son. [So did a giant to Jack the giant-killer, and so did Skrymir to Thorr in Gylfi's mocking. Edda (translated by G. W. Dasent, page 54.)] And when he saw what he had, he ran to his daughter's bed, and struck his axe into the two things which he found there. Then he ran into the stable, and then he ran after the fugitives. At the mouth of day, the daughter said—" I feel my father's breath burning me between the two shoulders;" and the king's son took a drop of water from the lilly's right ear, and threw it over his shoulder, and it became a lake which the giant could not cross. Then he said—This is a part of my own daughter's tricks; and he called out, FIRE FAIRE A MHARI RUADH AGUS NA THUG MISE DHUITSA DO DH' FHIOLUM AGUS DO IONNSACHADH N' E SO MAR A RINN THU ORM MA DHEIREADH. " Feere Faire, Auburn Mary, and all the learning and teaching I have given thee, is it thus thou hast done to me at last?" And, said she, CHAN EILE AGUD AIR ACH A BHI NAS GLIC A RITHISD. " Thou hast for it but to be wiser again." Then he said, if I had MO BHATA DUBH DIONACH FHEIN NACH FACA GAOTH NA GRIAN O CHEAN SEACHD BLIADHNA. My own tight black boat that saw neither wind nor rain since seven years' end. And his daughter said—" Thou hast for it but to go fetch her then."

Next time it was a little stone that was found in the left ear which became a great crag, and was broken through with the big hammer and the little hammer ORD MOR AGUS ORD BEAG, which broke and pounded a breach through the rock in an instant by themselves. The third time it was the seed of a tree which became a wood, and was cut through by the axes TUATHAN of the giant, which he set to work, and his wife brought up the black dogs.

The fourth time it was a very little tiny drop of water that was found in the left ear, which became a narrow loch, but so deep that the giant could not cross it. He had the usual talk with his daughter, and got the same reply; tried to drink the water, but failed, for a curious reason, then he thought he would leap it, but his foot slipped and he was drowned.

Then came the incident of the kiss and the old greyhound.

She went to the house of a sempstress, and engaged herself, and was a good workwoman. When the king's son was to be married to another, the cook sent one of his underlings to the well for water. She stood on a branch of a tree above the FUARAN cold spring, and when the maid saw her shadow in the well she thought she had grown golden herself, for there was " golden

weaving" on the dress of Auburn Mary. And she went back to
the cook and said: "Thou art the lad to send me to fetch thee
water, and I am a lump of gold." She sent another, with the
same result, so he went himself and saw Mary go to the house of
the sempstress. The cook told, and they asked about the stranger,
but no one knew anything about her, till the hen wife went to the
seamstress and found out "that she had come from a shore afar
off; that she never saw her like for sewing nor for shape, and
that if they had her at the wedding, she would make FEARTAN
miracles that would astonish them."

The hen wife told the queen, and she was engaged to help
to make the dresses. They were pleased with her, and asked her
to the wedding, and when there they asked her to show some of
her wonderful tricks.

"Then she got a pock, and showed that it was empty; and
she gave it a shake, and it grew thick, and she put in her hand
and took out a silver hen, and she set it on the ground, and it
rose and walked about the house. Then came the golden cock,
and the grain of corn, and the pecking, and the hen said—

> "Leig ma choir leam,
> Ma chuid do n' eorna.

Leave me my right, my share of the corn; and the cock pecked
her; and she stood out from him, and said—

Geog Geog Geōa.	Geog Geog Geōa.
A'n cuimhne leat an latha	Dost thou remember the day
Chuir mi m' bathach falamh	that I emptied the byre
Air do shon?	for thee?
'S an cuimhne leat an latha	Dost thou remember the day
A thubh mi n' Sabhal	that I thatched the barn
Air do shon?	for thee?
'S an cuimhne leat an latha	Dost thou remember the day
Ghlac mi n'fhailair	that I caught the filly
Air do shon?	for thee?
'S an cuimhne leat an latha	Dost thou remember the day
Bhàth mi m'athair	that I drowned my father
Air do shon?	for thee?

Then the king's son thought a little and he remembered
Auburn Mary, and all she had done for him, and he asked a voice

with her apart, and they had a little talk, and she told the king and the queen, and he found the "gin" kin good, and he turned his back on the other one, and he married Auburn Mary, and they made a wedding that lasted seven years; and the last day was no worse than the first day—

> S'ma bha na b'fhearr ann, bha,
> S'mar robh leig da

> And if there were better there were,
> And if not, let them be.

> The tale is ended.
> Tha crioch air 'n sgeul.

This version is probably the oldest. It is the most picturesque; it contains nearly all that is in the others, and it is full of the quaint expressions which characterize the telling of Gaelic tales. The quarrel is remarkably like a fable aimed at the greedy *castle* mouse and the sturdy *country* wren, a fable from the country side, for the birds beat the beasts of the plain, the raven beat the snake.

8. I have still another version, told by Roderick Mackenzie, sawyer, Gairloch, and written by Hector Urquhart. It is called, NIGHEAN DUBH GHEAL DEARG, The daughter of Black-white Red.

Three sons of the king of Erin were on a day playing shinny on a strand, and they saw birds whose like they had never seen, and one especially. Their father told them that this was MAC SAMHLADH NIGHINN DUBH GHEAL DEARG, and the eldest son said that he would never rest till he got the great beautiful bird for himself. Then his father sent him to the king of France (NA FRAINGE), and he struck palm on latch, and it was asked who it was, and he said that it was the son of Erin's king, going to seek the daughter of Black-white Red. He was entertained, and next day set off to the king of Spain (NA SPAINDE), and did the same; and thence he went to the king of Italy (NA 'HEADILT). He gave him an old man, BODACH, and a green boat, and they sailed (and here comes in a bit of the passage which is common to so many stories about hoisting the sails, etc., with one or two lines that I have found nowhere else, and here the three kings seem to replace the three old women, who are always appearing, for they know where the lad is going and help him on). The old man sailed the boat on shore, and up to the door of Black-white Red, a giant, who as usual said FIU FA FOAGRAICH, and threatened to make a shinny ball of his head, and eat him unless he performed the tasks set him. The giant's eldest daughter came and he knew her at once, and they played at cards all night. She gave him a tether to catch the little dun shaggy filly, which he would lose unless he put it on the first time.

Next he had to kill, TARBH MOR NA TANICH, the great bull of the cattle, (or perhaps of the earth, TAN). The daughter gave him her father's BOGHA SAIGHEAD, arrow bow, with which he pushed at the bull, and he followed him. He put the big black arrow in his forehead when he got to the house.

The third task was to cleanse the great byre of the seven stalls that had not been cleansed for seven years, or his head to be a football. The daughter came at night as usual and gave him BARA agus CROMAN, a barrow and a crook, and told him to say CAB CAB A CHROMAIN, CUIR AIR A BHARA A SHLUASAID, CUIR A MACH A BHARA, and the tools worked of themselves.

Then he had three more tasks set. The three daughters put three needles through three holes in a partition, he caught the one without " CHRO."(?) They put out three great pins, and he caught the one that had two " PHLOC " heads. Then they pushed out their little fingers, and he took the one with, CAB AS AN IONGA, a notch in the nail.

" Huh! huh!" said the giant, "thou hast her now, but to Erin thou goest not ; thou must stay with me." At last they got tired of the giant's way of living, and set off together and pushed out the barge (BIRLINN). The giant awoke and asked, what was that sound? One of the daughters answered, that it was a OIDCHE UAMHASACH LE TEIN-ADHAIR 'S TAIRNEANACH, a fearful night with heaven—fire and thunder. " It is well to be under the shelter of a rock," said the giant. The next scrape of the boat it was the same thing, and at the third the barge was out and under sail, but the giant was on foot, and he threw A CHEARTLEADH DHUBH, his black clue, and the boat sailed stern foremost. The giant sat down in the gravel to haul the boat, and the daughter shot an arrow, ANN AM BONN DUBH AN FHAMHAIR, into the giant's black sole, and there he lay.

Then they got to Erin. He went home first; she staid in the barge, till tired of waiting, she went to a smith's house where she staid with the smith and his mother.

One day the smith heard that the Ridir was going to be married, and told her. She sent him to the palace to tell the cook that the finest woman he ever saw was living with him, and would marry him if he would bring her a part of the wedding feast.

The cook came, and when he saw her, brought a back load of viands. Then they played the same trick to the butler, and he brought a back load of wine every day. Then she asked the smith to make her a golden cock, and a silver hen; and when he could not, she made them herself. Then she asked the butler if she could get a sight of the king's son and the bride, "and the butler was very much pleased that she had asked him, and not the cook, for he was much afraid that the cook was looking after her also." When the gentles saw her they asked her to the dancing room, and then came the cock and hen play, in which the hen said—A CHOILICH DHURDANICH DHUIBH, Thou black, murmuring cock, dost thou remember, etc. The prince remembers, marries the true girl, "and there I left them."

This version varies considerably from the others. It is very well told, and I much regret that space will not allow me to give it entire, the more so because the reciter has braved the prejudices of some of his neighbours who object to all fiction. I hope I have said enough to show that this story is worth preservation.

If stories be mythological this contains a serpent. NATHAIR, pronounced *Na-ir,* and a raven, FITHEACH, pronounced *Feeach,* who seem like transformed divinities, for they appear only to start the other characters, and then vanish into some undescribed kingdom. There is one passage (referred to) which resembles Norse mythology.

So far as I can make out, it seems to be best known near Cowal in Argyllshire, though it is known throughout the Highlands.

It would have been easy to construct one version from the eight here mentioned, but I have preferred to give the most complete, entire, and full abstracts of the rest. Many more versions can be got, and I shall be grateful to any one who will throw light on the story and its origin.

One of the tasks resembles one of those imposed on Hercules. It might have been taken from classical mythology if it stood alone, but Norwegian peasants and West Highlanders could not so twist the story of Hercules into the same shape.

All the Gaelic versions are clearly versions of the same story as the Master Maid, in Dasent's Norse Tales ; and there are other traits in other Norse stories, which resemble the Gaelic.

Of the forty-three heroes called Hercules, and mentioned in ancient lore, one, at least, is said to have made long voyages in the Atlantic beyond his own pillars. Another, or the same, was prevented from being present at the hunting of the Caledonian boar, having killed a man in " Calydo," which, by the way, is Gaelic for Black Forest. Another was an Indian, and this may be one of the same clan.

If stories be distorted history of real events, seen through a haze of centuries, then the giants in this tale may be the same people as the Gruagach and his brother in the last. They are here described as a wise learned race, given to magic arts, yellow or auburn haired. (RUADH) possessing horses, and knowing how to tame them—able to put the water between them and their pur-suers—able to sew better than the others—better looking—musical—possessing treasure and bright weapons—using king's sons of other races as slaves, and threatening to eat them. If the raven was one, they were given to combing their own golden ringlets with gold and silver combs and the giant maidens dressed the hair of their lovers who laid their heads in their laps, as I have often seen black haired Lapland ladies dress the hair of Lapland swains, and as ladies in popular tales of all lands always do. I will not venture to guess who this race may have been, but the race who contended with them would seem to have been dark complexioned. Nearly all the heroines of Gaelic songs are fair or yellow haired. Those are dark who now most admire yellow locks. A dark Southern once asked if a golden haired youth from the north had dyed his hair, for nothing natural could be so beautiful. Dark Celts and fair northmen certainly met and fought, and settled and intermarried, on the western isles and coasts, where this tale is current, but I am told that it has traits which are to be found in Eastern manuscripts, which were old long before the wars of the Northmen, of which we know, began. The task I have undertaken is to gather stories, not to account for them, but this much is sure, either Norway got this from Scotland or Scotland from Norway, when they were almost one country, or both got it from the same source. The Gaelic stories resemble each other about as much as they all resemble the Norse. The translation was published in 1859, and this story has been current in the islands at least for 40 years. I can remember to have heard part of it myself more than 20 years ago. I believe there is an Irish version, though I have not met with it in any book. I have traced the story amongst Irish labourers in London, who have told me that they used in their young days to sit about the fire whole winter nights, and tell about the fight between the raven and the snake; about the giants, Fin MacCoul and Conan Maol, "who had never a good word for any one," and similar tales. My informants were from Cork, their language, though difficult, could be made out from a knowledge of Gaelic only.

The bridle described seems to be the old Highland bridle which is still common. It has no bit, but two plates of wood or iron are placed at right angles to the horse's mouth, and are joined above and below by a rope, which is often made of horse-hair, heather, or twisted bent. The horse's nose goes INTO IT.

The ladder is also the Highland ladder still common in cottages. It consists of a long stick with pegs stuck *through* it.

There are many stories in Grimm's German collection which resemble the Battle of the Birds. They have incidents in common, arranged somewhat in the same order; but the German stories, taken together, have a character of their own, as the Gaelic versions have: and both differ from the Norwegian tale. Each new Gaelic version which comes to me (and I have received several since this was written), varies from the rest, but resembles them; and no single version is like any one of the German tales, though German, Norse, and Gaelic all hang together.

III.

THE TALE OF THE HOODIE.

From Ann MacGilvray, Islay.—April 1859.

THERE was ere now a farmer, and he had three daughters. They were waulking* clothes at a river. A hoodie † came round and he said to the eldest one, 'M-POS-U-MI, "Wilt thou wed me, farmer's daughter?" "I won't wed thee, thou ugly brute. An ugly brute is the hoodie," said she. He came to the second one on the morrow, and he said to her, "'M-POS-U-MI, wilt thou wed me?" "Not I, indeed," said she; "an ugly brute is the hoodie." The third day he said to the youngest, 'M-POS-U-MI, "Wilt thou wed me, farmer's daughter?" "I will wed thee," said she; "a pretty creature is the hoodie," and on the morrow they married.

The hoodie said to her, "Whether wouldst thou rather that I should be a hoodie by day, and a man at night; or be a hoodie at night, and a man by day?" "I would rather that thou wert a man by day, and a hoodie at night," says she. After this he was a splendid fellow by day, and a hoodie at night. A few days after they married he took her with him to his own house.

At the end of three quarters they had a son. In

---

* *Postadh.* A method of washing clothes practised in the Highlands—viz., by dancing on them barefoot in a tub of water.

† Hoodie—the Royston crow—a very common bird in the Highlands; a sly, familiar, knowing bird, which plays a great part in these stories. He is common in most parts of Europe.

the night there came the very finest music that ever
was heard about the house. Every man slept, and the
child was taken away. Her father came to the door in
the morning, and he asked how were all there. He
was very sorrowful that the child should be taken away,
for fear that he should be blamed for it himself.

At the end of three quarters again they had another
son. A watch was set on the house. The finest of music
came, as it came before, about the house; every man
slept, and the child was taken away. Her father came
to the door in the morning. He asked if every thing
was safe; but the child was taken away, and he did
not know what to do for sorrow.

Again, at the end of three quarters they had another
son. A watch was set on the house as usual. Music
came about the house as it came before; every one slept,
and the child was taken away. When they rose on the
morrow they went to another place of rest that they had,
himself and his wife, and his sister-in-law. He said to
them by the way, " See that you have not forgotten any
thing." The wife said, " I FORGOT MY COARSE COMB."
The coach in which they were fell a withered faggot,
and he went away as a hoodie.

Her two sisters returned home, and she followed after
him. When he would be on a hill top, she would follow
to try and catch him; and when she would reach the
top of a hill, he would be in the hollow on the other side.
When night came, and she was tired, she had no place
of rest or dwelling; she saw a little house of light far
from her, and though far from her she was not long
in reaching it.

When she reached the house she stood deserted at
the door. She saw a little laddie about the house,
and she yearned to him exceedingly. The housewife
told her to come up, that she knew her cheer and

travel. She laid down, and no sooner did the day come than she rose. She went out, and when she was out, she was going from hill to hill to try if she could see a hoodie. She saw a hoodie on a hill, and when she would get on the hill the hoodie would be in the hollow, when she would go to the hollow, the hoodie would be on another hill. When the night came she had no place of rest or dwelling. She saw a little house of light far from her, and if far from her she was not long reaching it. She went to the door. She saw a laddie on the floor to whom she yearned right much. The housewife laid her to rest. No earlier came the day than she took out as she used. She passed this day as the other days. When the night came she reached a house. The housewife told her to come up, that she knew her cheer and travel, that her man had but left the house a little while, that she should be clever, that this was the last night she would see him, and not to sleep, but to strive to seize him. She slept, he came where she was, and he let fall a ring on her right hand. Now when she awoke she tried to catch hold of him, and she caught a feather of his wing. He left the feather with her, and he went away. When she rose in the morning she did not know what she should do. The housewife said that he had gone over a hill of poison over which she could not go without horse-shoes on her hands and feet. She gave her man's clothes, and she told her to go to learn smithying till she should be able to make horse-shoes for herself.

She learned smithying so well that she made horse-shoes for her hands and feet. She went over the hill of poison. That same day after she had gone over the hill of poison, her man was to be married to the daughter of a great gentleman that was in the town.

There was a race in the town that day, and every

one was to be at the race but the stranger that had come over the poison hill. The cook came to her, and he said to her, Would she go in his place to make the wedding meal, and that he might get to the race.

She said she would go. She was always watching where the bridegroom would be sitting.

She let fall the ring and the feather in the broth that was before him. With the first spoon he took up the ring, with the next he took up the feather. When the minister came to the fore to make the marriage, he would not marry till he should find out who had made ready the meal. They brought up the cook of the gentleman, and he said that *this* was not the cook who made ready the meal.

They brought up now the one who had made ready the meal. He said, "That now was his married wife." The spells went off him. They turned back over the hill of poison, she throwing the horse-shoes behind her to him, as she went a little bit forward, and he following her. When they came back over the hill, they went to the three houses in which she had been. These were the houses of his sisters, and they took with them the three sons, and they came home to their own house, and they were happy.

———

Written down by Hector Maclean, schoolmaster at Bally-grant, in Islay, from the recitation of "Ann MacGilvray, a Cowal woman, married to a farmer at Kilmeny, one Angus Macgeachy from Campbelltown." Sent April 14, 1859.

The Gaelic of this tale is the plain everyday Gaelic of Islay and the west Highlands. Several words are variously spelt, but they are variously pronounced—falbh, folbh, tigh, taighe, taighean. There is one word, Tapaidh, which has no English equivalent; it is like *Tapper* in Swedish.

Bha tuathanach ann roimhe so; agus bha triùir nighean aige.
Bha cud a' postadh aig obhainn. Thàinig feannag mu'n cuairt 's
thuirt e ris an té bu shine, "Am pòs thu mise a nighean an tuathanaich." "Cha phòs mis' thu 'bheathaich ghrànnda : is grannda am
beathach an fheannag," ars' ise. Thàinig e thun na darna té an la 'r
na mhàireach, 's thuirt e rithe. "Am pòs thu mise." "Cha phòs
mi féin," ars' ise ; "'s grànnda am beathach an fheannag." An treas
la thuirt e ris an te b'òige. "Am pòs thu mise, a nighean an tuathanaich." "Pòsaidh," ars' ise ; "s bòidheach am beathach an fheannag." An la'r na mhàireach phòs èud. Thuirt an fheannag rithe.
'Cò 'ca is fheàrr leat mise a bhith am fheannag 'san latha 'sam dhuine
san oidhche, na bhith 'san oidhche am fheannag 's am dhuine 'san
latha?" "'S fhearr leam thu bhith a'd' dhuine 'san latha 's a'd' fheannag 'san oidhche," ars' ise. As a dhéigh so bha e na òganach ciatach
'san latha, 's na fheannag 's an oidhche. Am beagan làithean an déigh
dhaibh pòsadh thug e leis i 'ga 'thigh féin. Ann an ceann tri ràithean
bha mac aca. Anns an oidhche thàinig an aon cheòl timchiol an
taighe bu bhòidhche 'chualas riamh. Chaidil a h-uile duine, 's thugadh air folbh am pàisde. Thàinig a h-athair thun an doruisd sa mhadainn. Dh'fheòraich e dé mur a bha h-uile h-aon an siod ; 's bha
duilichinn mhòr air gun tugadh air folbh am pàisde, eagal agus gum
biodh coir' air a dhèanadh air féin air a shon. Ann an ceann tri
ràithhean a rithisd bha mac eile aca. Chuireadh faire air an tigh.
Thàinig ceòl ra bhòidheach mar a thàinig roimhid timchioll an
taighe ; chaidil a h-uile duine 's thugadh air folbh am pàisde. Thàini;
a h-athair thun an doruisd sa mhaiduinn dh'fheòraich e an robh
gach ni ceart ; ach bha 'm pàisde air a thoirt air folbh, 's cha robh
fhìos aige dé a dhèanadh e leis an duilichiun. Ann an ceann tri
ràithean a rithisd bha mac eile aca. Chaidh faire 'chur air an tigh
mar a b' àbhaist. Thàinig ceòl timchioll an taighe mar a thàini;
roimhid ; chaidil gach neach, 's thugadh am pàisde air folbh. Nur
a dh'éiridh iad an la 'r na mhàireach chaidh iad gu hàite tàmh eile
a bha aca, e feiu s a' bhean, 's a' phinthar chéile. Thuirt e riu air an
rathad. Feuch nach do dhichuimhnich sibh ni 'sam bith. Urs' a'
bhean, "Dhiochuimhnich mi mo chir gharbh." Thuit an carbad
anns an robh eud 'na chual chriònaich, s dh'fhalbh esan 'na fheann-
nag. Thill a dha phiuthair dhachaidh 's dh'fholbh ise 'na dhéigh-
san. Nur a bhiodh esan air mullach cnoic leanadh ise e feuch am
beireadh i air, 's nur a ruigeadh ise mullach a chnoic bhiodh esan

san lag an taobh eile. Nur a thàinig an oidhche 's i sgìth, cha robh
àite tàmh na fuireachd aice. Chunnaic i tigh beag soluisd fada
uaithe 's ma b' fhada uaithe cha b' fhada a bha ise 'ga ruìgheachd.
Nur a ràinig i an tigh sheas i gu dìblidh aig an dorusd. Chunnaic i balachan beag feadh an taighe, s theòigh i ris gu h-anabarrach.
Thuirt bean an taighe rithe tighinn a nìos, gu robh fios a seud 's a
siubhail aicese. Chaidh i laidhe, 's cha bu luaithe thàinig an latha
na dh' éiridh i. Chaidh i 'mach, 's nur a bha i 'mach bha i o chnoc
gu cnoc feuch am faiceadh i feannag. Chunnaic i feannag air cnoc,
's nur a rachadh ise air a' chnoc bhiodh an f heannag 'san lag nur
a rachadh i do'n lag bhiodh an f heannag air cnoc eile. Nur a
thàinig an oidhche cha robh àite taimh na fuireachd aice. Chunnaic i tigh beag soluisd fada uaithe 's ma b' f hada uaithe cha b' f hada
'bha ise 'g a ruigheachd. Chaidh i gus an dorusd. Chunnaic i balachan
air an urlar ris an do theòigh i gu ra mhòr. Chuir bean an taighe a
laidhe i. Cha bu mhoich' a thàinig an latha na ghabh i 'mach mar a
b'àbhaist. Chuir i seachad an latha so mar na làithean eile. Nur a
thàinig an oidhche ràinig i tigh. Thuirt bean an taighe rithe tighinn a nìos; gu 'robh fios a seud 's a siubhail aice-se; nach d' rinn
a fear ach an tigh f hàgail bho cheann tiota beag; i 'bhith tapaidh,
gum b' i siod an oidhche ma dheireadh dhi f haicinn, 's gun i 'chadal,
ach strì ri gréim a dhèanadh air. Chaidil ise, 's thàinig esan far an
robh i, 's lig e tuiteam do dh' f hàinn, air a làimh dheas. Nur a dhuisg
ise an so thug i làmh air breith air, 's rug i air ite d'a sgéith. Leig e
leatha an ite, 's dh' f halbh e. Nur a dh' éiridh i 'sa mhadainn cha
robh fios aice dé a dhèanadh i. Thuirt bean an taighe gu'n deach e
thairis air cnoc neamh air nach b'urrainn ise dol thairis gun chrùidh-
ean d'a làmhan agus d'a casan. Thug i dhi aodach fir 's thuirt i
rithe dol a dh' ionnsachadh na goibhneachd gus am biodh i com-
asach air crùidhean a dhèanadh dhì féin. Dh' ionnsaich i 'ghoibh-
neachd cho math 's gun d' rinn i crùidhean d'a làmhan agus da casan.
Dh 'f holbh i thairis air a chnoc neamh. An latha sin féin an déigh
dhi dol thairis air a chnoc neamh bha pòsadh ri bhith aig a fear ri
nighean duine uasail mhòir a bha 'sa bhaile. Bha rèis anns a bhaile
an latha sin, s bha h-uile h-aon ri bhith aig an réis ach an coigreach
a thàinig thairis air a' chnoc neamh. Thainig an còcaire a h-ionnsuidh, 's thuirt e rithe an rachadh i 'na àite a dhèanadh biadh na
bainnse. 's gu 'faigheadh e dol thun na réise. Thuirt i gu' rachadh.
Bha i furachail daonnan càite am biodh fear na bainnse 'na shuidhe.
Lig i tuiteam do 'n f hàinne agus do 'n ite 'sa bhrot a bha air a
bheulaobh. Leis a' chiad spàin thog e'm fàinne, s leis an ath spàin
thog e 'n ite. Nur a thàinig am ministir a làthair a dheanadh

a phòsaidh cha phòsadh esan gus am faigheadh e fios co a rinn
am biadh. Thug iad a' làthair còcaire an duine uasail, 's thuirt
esan nach b' e siod an còcaire a rinn am biadh. Thug iad an
làthair an so an t-aon a rinn am biadh. Thuirt esan gum b'e siod
a'bhean phòsda-san a nis. Dh' fholbh na geasan dheth. Thill iad
air an ais thairis air a' chnoc neamh ; ise a tilgeil nan crùidhean as a
déigh da 'ionnsuidhsan nur a thigeadh i treis air a h-aghaidh, 's
esan 'ga leantainn. Nur a thàinig eud air an ais thar a' chnoic,
chaidh iad thun nan tri taighean anns an robh ise. B'e sin tri taighean
a pheathraichean-san, thug iad leo an tri mic. Thàinig iad dhachaidh
g'an tigh féin, 's bha iad gu toilichte.

HECTOR MACLEAN.

2. I have a great many versions of this tale in Gaelic ; for
example, one from Cowal, written from memory by a labourer,
John Dewar. These are generally wilder and longer than the
version here given.

This has some resemblance to an infinity of other stories. For
example—Orpheus, Cupid and Psyche, Cinderella's Coach, The
Lassie and her Godmother (Norse tales), East o' the Sun and
West o' the Moon (ditto), The Master Maid (ditto), Katie
Wooden Cloak (ditto), The Iron Stove (Grimm), The Woodcut-
ter's Child (ditto), and a tale by the Countess d'Aulnoy, Prince
Cherie.

If this be history, it is the story of a wife taken from an inferior but civilized race. The farmer's daughter married to the
Flayer "FEANNAG," deserted by her husband for another in some
distant, mythical land, beyond far away mountains, and bringing
him back by steady, fearless, persevering fidelity and industry.

If it be mythology, the hoodie may be the raven again, and
a transformed divinity. If it relates to races, the superior race
again had horses—for there was to be a race in the town, and
every one was to be at it, but the stranger who came over the
hill ; and when they travelled it was in a coach, which was sufficiently wonderful to be magical, and here again the comb is
mixed up with the spells.

There is a stone at Dunrobin Castle, in Sutherland, on which
a comb is, carved with other curious devices, which have never
been explained. Within a few hundred yards in an old grave

composed of great slabs of stone, accidentally discovered on a
bank of gravel, a man's skeleton was found with teeth worn down,
though perfectly sound, exactly like those of an old horse.   It is
supposed that the man must have ground his teeth on dried peas
and beans—perhaps on meal, prepared in sandstone querns. Here,
at least, is the COMB near to the grave of the farmer.   The comb
which is so often found with querns in the old dwellings of some
pre-historic race of Britons ; the comb which is a civilized instru-
ment, and which in these stories is always a coveted object worth
great exertions, and often magical.

IV.

THE SEA-MAIDEN.

From John Mackenzie, fisherman, near Inverary.

THERE was ere now a poor old fisher, but on this year he was not getting much fish. On a day of days, and he fishing, there rose a sea-maiden at the side of his boat, and she asked him if he was getting fish. The old man answered, and he said that he was not. "What reward wouldst thou give me for sending plenty of fish to thee?", "Ach!" said the old man, "I have not much to spare." "Wilt thou give me the first son thou hast?" said she. "It is I that would give thee that, if I were to have a son; there was not, and there will not be a son of mine," said he, "I and my wife are grown so old." "Name all thou hast." "I have but an old mare of a horse, an old dog, myself, and my wife. There's for thee all the creatures of the great world that are mine." "Here, then, are three grains for thee that thou shalt give thy wife this very night, and three others to the dog, and these three to the mare, and these three likewise thou shalt plant behind thy house, and in their own time thy wife will have three sons, the mare three foals, and the dog three puppies, and there will grow three trees behind thy house, and the trees will be a sign, when one of the sons dies, one of the trees will wither. Now, take thyself home, and remember me when thy son is three years of age, and thou thyself wilt get plenty of fish after this." Everything happened as the sea-maiden said, and he himself was getting plenty of fish; but when the end of the three years was nearing, the old man was growing sorrowful, heavy hearted, while he failed each day as it came. On the namesake of the day, he went to fish as he used, but he did not take his son with him.

The sea-maiden rose at the side of the boat, and asked, "Didst thou bring thy son with thee hither to me?" "Och! I did not bring him. I forgot that this was the day." "Yes! yes! then," said the sea-maiden; "thou shalt get four other years of him, to try if it be easier for thee to part from him. Here thou hast his like age," and she lifted up a big bouncing baby. "Is thy son as fine as this one?" He went home full of glee and delight, for that he had got four other years of his son, and he kept on fishing and getting plenty of fish, but at the end of the next four years sorrow and woe struck him, and he took not a meal, and he did not a turn, and his wife could not think what was ailing him. This time he did not know what to do, but he set it before him, that he would not take his son with him this time either. He went to fish as at the former times, and the sea-maiden rose at the side of the boat, and she asked him, "Didst thou bring thy son hither to me?" "Och! I forgot him this time too," said the old man. "Go home then," said the sea-maiden, "and at the end of seven years after this, thou art sure to remember me, but then it will not be the easier for thee to part with him, but thou shalt get fish as thou used to do."

The old man went home full of joy; he had got seven other years of his son, and before seven years passed, the old man thought that he himself would be dead, and that he would see the sea-maiden no more.

But no matter, the end of those seven years was nearing also, and if it was, the old man was not without care and trouble. He had rest neither day nor night. The eldest son asked his father one day if any one were troubling him? The old man said that some one was, but that belonged neither to him nor to any one else. The lad said he *must* know what it was. His father told him at last how the matter was between him and the sea-maiden. "Let not that put you in any trouble," said the son; "I will not oppose you." "Thou shalt not; thou shalt not go, my son, though I should not get fish for ever." "If you will not let me go with you, go to the smithy, and let the smith make me a great strong sword, and I will go to the end of fortune." His father went to the smithy, and the smith made a doughty sword for him. His father came home with the sword. The lad grasped it and gave it a shake or two, and it went in a hundred splinters. He asked his father to go to the smithy and get him another sword, in which there should be twice as much weight; and so did his father, and so likewise it happened to the next sword—it broke in two halves. Back went the old man to the smithy; and the smith made a great sword, its like he never made before. "There's thy sword for thee," said the smith, "and the fist must be good that plays this blade." The old man gave the sword to his son, he gave it a shake or two. "This will do," said he; "it's high time now to travel on my way." On the next morning he put a saddle on the black horse that the mare had, and he put the world under his head,* and his black dog was by his side. When he went on a bit, he fell in with the carcass of a sheep beside the road. At the carrion were a great dog, a falcon, and an otter. He came down

* Took the world for his pillow.

off the horse, and he divided the carcass amongst the three. Three third shares to the dog, two third shares to the otter, and a third share to the falcon. "For this," said the dog, "if swiftness of foot or sharpness of tooth will give thee aid, mind me, and I will be at thy side." Said the otter, "If the swimming of foot on the ground of a pool will loose thee, mind me, and I will be at thy side." Said the falcon, "If hardship comes on thee, where swiftness of wing or crook of a claw will do good, mind me, and I will be at thy side." On this he went onward till he reached a king's house, and he took service to be a herd, and his wages were to be according to the milk of the cattle. He went away with the cattle, and the grazing was but bare. When lateness came (in the evening), and when he took (them) home they had not much milk, the place was so bare, and his meat and drink was but spare this night.

On the next day he went on further with them; and at last he came to a place exceedingly grassy, in a green glen, of which he never saw the like.

But about the time when he should go behind the cattle, for taking homewards, who is seen coming but a great giant, with his sword in his hand. "Hìu! Hàu!! Hogaraich!!!" says the giant. "It is long since my teeth were rusted seeking thy flesh. The cattle are mine; they are on my march; and a dead man art thou." "I said, not that," says the herd; "there is no knowing, but that may be easier to say than to do."

To grips they go—himself and the giant. He saw that he was far from his friend, and near his foe. He drew the great clean-sweeping sword, and he neared the giant; and in the play of the battle the black dog leaped on the giant's back. The herd drew back his sword, and the head was off the giant in a twinkling. He leaped on the black horse, and he went to look for the giant's house. He reached a door, and in the haste that the giant made he had left each gate and door open. In went the herd, and that's the place where there was magnificence and money in plenty, and dresses of each kind on the wardrobe with gold and silver, and each thing finer than the other. At the mouth of night he took himself to the king's house, but he took not a thing from the giant's house. And when the cattle were milked this night there *was* milk. He got good feeding this night, meat and drink without stint, and the king was hugely pleased that he had caught such a herd. He went on for a time in this way, but at last the glen grew bare of grass, and the grazing was not so good.

But he thought he would go a little further forward in on the giant's land ; and he sees a great park of grass. He returned for the cattle, and he puts them into the park.

They were but a short time grazing in the park when a great wild giant came full of rage and madness. " Hiu ! Haw !! Hoagraich !!!" said the giant. " It is a drink of thy blood that quenches my thirst this night." " There is no knowing," said the herd, " but that's easier to say than to do." And at each other went the men. *There* was the shaking of blades ! At length and at last it seemed as if the giant would get the victory over the herd. Then he called on his dog, and with one spring the black dog caught the giant by the neck, and swiftly the herd struck off his head.

He went home very tired this night, but it's a wonder if the king's cattle had not milk. The whole family were delighted that they had got such a herd.

He followed herding in this way for a time ; but

one night after he came home, instead of getting "all hail" and "good luck" from the dairymaid, all were at crying and woe.

He asked what cause of woe there was this night. The dairymaid said that a great beast with three heads was in the loch, and she was to get (some) one every year, and the lots had come this year on the king's daughter, "and in the middle of the day (to-morrow) she is to meet the uille Bheist at the upper end of the loch, but there is a great suitor yonder who is going to rescue her."

"What suitor is that?" said the herd. "Oh, he is a great General of arms," said the dairymaid, "and when he kills the beast, he will marry the king's daughter, for the king has said, that he who could save his daughter should get her to marry."

But on the morrow when the time was nearing, the king's daughter and this hero of arms went to give a meeting to the beast, and they reached the black corrie at the upper end of the loch. They were but a short time there when the beast stirred in the midst of the loch; but on the General's seeing this terror of a beast with three heads, he took fright, and he slunk away, and he hid himself. And the king's daughter was under fear and under trembling with no one at all to save her. At a glance, she sees a doughty handsome youth, riding a black horse, and coming where she was. He was marvellously arrayed, and full armed, and his black dog moving after him. "There is gloom on thy face, girl," said the youth. "What dost thou here?" "Oh! that's no matter," said the king's daughter. "It's not long I'll be here at all events." "I said not that," said he. "A worthy fled as likely as thou, and not long since," said she. "He is a worthy who stands the war," said the youth. He lay down beside her, and he said to her, if he should fall asleep, she should rouse him when she should see the beast making for shore. "What is rousing for thee?" said she. "Rousing for me is to put the gold ring on thy finger on my little finger." They were not long there when she saw the beast making for shore. She took a ring off her finger, and put it on the little finger of the lad. He awoke, and to meet the beast he went with his sword and his dog. But there was the spluttering and splashing between himself and the beast! The dog was doing all he might, and the king's daughter was palsied by fear of the noise of the beast. They would now be under, and now above. But at last he cut one of the heads off her. She gave one roar Raivic, and the son of earth Mactalla of the rocks (echo), called to her screech, and she drove the loch in spindrift from end to end, and in a twinkling she went out of sight. "Good luck and victory that were following thee, lad!" said the king's daughter. "I am safe for one night, but the beast will come again, and for ever, until the other two heads come off her." He caught the beast's head, and he drew a withy through it, and he told her to bring it with her there to-morrow. She went home with the head on her shoulder, and the herd betook himself to the cows, but she had not gone far when this great General saw her, and he said to her that he would kill her, if she would not say that 't was he took the head off the beast. "Oh!" says she, "'tis I will say it, Who else took the head off the beast but thou!'" They reached the king's house, and the head was on the General's shoulder. But here was rejoicing, that she should come home alive and whole, and this great captain with the beast's head full of blood in his hand. On the morrow they went away, and there was no question at all but that this hero would save the king's daughter.

They reached the same place, and they were not long there when the fearful uille Bheist stirred in the midst of the loch, and the hero slunk away as he did on yesterday, but it was not long after this when the man of the black horse came, with another dress on. No matter, she knew that it was the very same lad. "It is I am pleased to see thee," said she. "I am in hopes thou wilt handle thy great sword to-day as thou didst yesterday. Come up and take breath." But they were not long there when they saw the beast steaming in the midst of the loch.

The lad lay down at the side of the king's daughter, and he said to her, "If I sleep before the beast comes, rouse me." "What is rousing for thee?" "Rousing for me is to put the ear-ring that is in thine ear in mine." He had not well fallen asleep when the king's daughter cried, " rouse ! rouse !" but wake he would not ; but she took the ear-ring out of her ear, and she put it in the ear of the lad. At once he woke, and to meet the beast he went, but *there* was Tloopersteich and Tlaperstich rawceil s'tawceil, spluttering, splashing, raving and roaring on the beast ! They kept on thus for a long time, and about the mouth of night, he cut another head off the beast. He put it on the withy, and he leaped on the black horse, and he betook himself to the herding. The king's daughter went home with the heads. The General met her, and took the heads from her, and he said to her, that she must tell that it was he who took the head off the beast this time also. " Who else took the head off the beast but thou?" said she. They reached the king's house with the heads. Then there was joy and gladness. If the king was hopeful the first night, he was now sure that this great hero would save his daughter, and there was no question at all but that the other head would be off the beast on the morrow.

About the same time on the morrow, the two went away. The officer hid himself as he usually did. The king's daughter betook herself to the bank of the loch. The hero of the black horse came, and he lay at her side. She woke the lad, and put another ear-ring in his other ear ; and at the beast he went. But if rawceil and toiceil, roaring and raving were on the beast on the days that were passed, this day she was horrible. But no matter, he took the third head off the beast ; and if he did, it was not without a struggle. He drew it through the withy, and she went home with the heads. When they reached the king's house, all were full of smiles, and the General was to marry the king's daughter the next day. The wedding was going on, and every one about the castle longing till the priest should come. But when the priest came, she would marry but the one who could take the heads off the withy without cutting the withy. "Who should take the heads off the withy but the man that put the heads on?" said the king.

The General tried them, but he could not loose them ; and at last there was no one about the house but had tried to take the heads off the withy, but they could not. The king asked if there were any one else about the house that would try to take the heads off the withy? They said that the herd had not tried them yet. Word went for the herd ; and he was not long throwing them hither and thither. "But stop a bit, my lad," said the king's daughter, "the man that took the heads off the beast, he has my ring and my two ear-rings." The herd put his hand in his pocket, and he threw them on the board. "Thou art my man," said the king's daughter. The king was not so pleased when he saw that it was a herd who was to marry his daughter, but he ordered that he should be put in a better dress; but his daughter spoke, and she said that he had a dress as fine as any that ever was in his castle; and thus it happened. The herd put on the giant's golden dress, and they married that same night.

They were now married, and everything going on well. They were one day sauntering by the side of the loch, and there came a beast more wonderfully terrible than the other, and takes him away to the loch without fear, or asking. The king's daughter was now mournful, tearful, blind-sorrowful for her married man; she was always with her eye on the loch. An old smith met her, and she told how it had befallen her married mate. The smith advised her to spread everything that was finer than another in the very same place where the beast took away her man; and so she did. The beast put up her nose, and she said, "Fine is thy jewellery, king's daughter." "Finer than that is the jewel that thou tookest from me," said she. "Give me one sight of my man, and thou shalt get any one thing of all these thou seest." The beast brought him up. "Deliver him to me, and thou shalt get all thou seest," said she. The beast did as she said. She threw him alive and whole on the bank of the loch.

A short time after this, when they were walking at the side of the loch, the same beast took away the king's daughter. Sorrowful was each one that was in the town on this night. Her man was mournful, tearful, wandering down and up about the banks of the loch, by day and night. The old smith met him. The smith told him that there was no way of killing the uille Bheist but the one way, and this is it—"In the

island that is in the midst of the loch is Eillid Chais-
fhion—the white footed hind, of the slenderest legs,
and the swiftest step, and though she should be caught,
there would spring a hoodie out of her, and though
the hoodie should be caught, there would spring a trout
out of her, but there is an egg in the mouth of the
trout, and the soul of the beast is in the egg, and if
the egg breaks, the beast is dead.

Now, there was no way of getting to this island,
for the beast would sink each boat and raft that
would go on the loch. He thought he would try
to leap the strait with the black horse, and even so he
did. The black horse leaped the strait, and the black
dog with one bound after him. He saw the Eillid,
and he let the black dog after her, but when the black
dog would be on one side of the island, the Eillid
would be on the other side. "Oh! good were now
the great dog of the carcass of flesh here!" No sooner
spoke he the word than the generous dog was at his
side; and after the Eillid he took, and the worthies
were not long in bringing her to earth. But he no
sooner caught her than a hoodie sprang out of her.
"'Tis now, were good the falcon grey, of sharpest eye
and swiftest wing!" No sooner said he this than the
falcon was after the hoodie, and she was not long putting her to earth; and as the hoodie fell on the bank
of the loch, out of her jumps the trout. "Oh, that
thou wert by me now, oh otter!" No sooner said
than the otter was at his side, and out on the loch she
leaped, and brings the trout from the midst of the
loch; but no sooner was the otter on shore with the
trout than the egg came out from his mouth. He
sprang and he put his foot on it. 'Twas then the beast
let out a roar, and she said, "Break not the egg, and
thou gettest all thou askest." "Deliver to me my

G

wife ?" In the wink of an eye she was by his side.
When he got hold of her hand in both his hands he
let his foot (down) on the egg and the beast died.

The beast was dead now, and now was the sight to
be seen. She was horrible to look upon. The three
heads were off her doubtless, but if they were, there
were heads under and heads over head on her, and
eyes, and five hundred feet. But no matter, they left
her there, and they went home, and there was delight
and smiling in the king's house that night. And till
now he had not told the king how he killed the giants.
The king put great honour on him, and he was a great
man with the king.

Himself and his wife were walking one day, when
he noticed a little castle beside the loch in a wood ; he
asked his wife who was dwelling in it ? She said that
no one would be going near that castle, for that no one
had yet come back to tell the tale, who had gone there.

"The matter must not be so," said he ; "this very
night I will see who is dwelling in it." "Go not,
go not," said she ; "there never went man to this
castle that returned." "Be that as it pleases," says
he. He went ; he betakes himself to the castle.
When he reached the door, a little flattering crone met
him standing in the door. "All hail and good luck
to thee, fisher's son ; 'tis I myself am pleased to
see thee ; great is the honour for this kingdom, thy
like to be come into it—thy coming in is fame for
this little bothy ; go in first ; honour to the gentles ; go
on, and take breath." In he went, but as he was
going up, she drew the Slachdan druidhach on him, on
the back of his head, and at once—there he fell.

On this night there was woe in the king's castle,
and on the morrow there was a wail in the fisher's
house. The tree is seen withering, and the fisher's

middle son said that his brother was dead, and he made a vow and oath, that he would go, and that he would know where the corpse of his brother was lying. He put saddle on a black horse, and rode after his black dog; (for the three sons of the fisher had a black horse and a black dog), and without going hither or thither he followed on his brother's step till he reached the king's house.

This one was so like his elder brother, that the king's daughter thought it was her own man. He stayed in the castle. They told him how it befell his brother; and to the little castle of the crone, go he must—happen hard or soft as it might. To the castle he went; and just as befell the eldest brother, so in each way it befell the middle son, and with one blow of the Slachdan druidhach, the crone felled him stretched beside his brother.

On seeing the second tree withering, the fisher's youngest son said that now his two brothers were dead, and that he must know what death had come on them. On the black horse he went, and he followed the dog as his brothers did, and he hit the king's house before he stopped. 'T was the king who was pleased to see him; but to the black castle (for that was its name) they would not let him go. But to the castle he must go; and so he reached the castle.—"All hail and good luck to thyself, fisher's son : 't is I am pleased to see thee ; go in and take breath," said she (the crone). " In before me, thou crone : I don't like flattery out of doors ; go in and let' s hear thy speech." In went the crone, and when her back was to him he drew his sword and whips her head off; but the sword flew out of his hand. And swift the crone gripped her head with both hands, and puts it on her neck as it was before. The dog sprung on the crone, and she struck the generous dog with the club of magic; and there he lay. But this went not to make the youth more sluggish. To grips wth the crone he goes; he got a hold of the Slachdan druidhach, and with one blow on the top of the head, she was on earth in the wink of an eye. He went forward, up a little, and he sees his two brothers lying side by side. He gave a blow to each one with the Slachdan druidh-ach and on foot they were, and there was the spoil! Gold and silver, and each thing more precious than another, in the crone's castle. They came back to the king's house, and then there was rejoicing! The king was growing old. The eldest son of the fisherman was crowned king, and the pair of brothers stayed a day and a year in the king's house, and then the two went on their journey home, with the gold and silver of the crone, and each other grand thing which the king gave them; and if they have not died since then, they are alive to this very day.

Written, April 1850, by Hector Urquhart, from the dictation of John Mackenzie, fisherman, Kenmore, near Inverary, who says that he learned it from an old man in Lorn many years ago. He has lived for thirty-six years at Kenmore. He told the tale fluently at first, and then dictated it slowly.

The Gaelic is given as nearly as possible in the words used by Mackenzie, but he thinks his story rather shortened.

A MHAIGHDEAN MHARA.

Bha ann roimhe so, sean iasgair bochd, ach air a bhliadhna so, cha robh e faotainn a bheag do dh'iasg. Latha do na laithean 's e 'g-iasgach, dh' eirich maighdean-mhara ri taobh a bhàta, 's dh' fheòr-aich i dheth, An robh e faotainn a bheag do dh'iasg? Fhreagair an seann duine, 's thubhairt e nach robh. "De 'n duais a bheir-eadh tu dhòmhsa airson pailteas éisg a chuir thugad?" Ach ars' an

seann duine, "Cha 'n 'eil a bheag agamsa ri sheachnadh." "An
toir thu dhomh an cèud mhac a bhitheas agad?" ars' ise. "'S mise a
bheireadh sin dhuit na 'm biodh mac agam ; cha robh 's cha bhi mac
agamsa," ars' esan; "tha mi féin 's mo bhean air cinntinn co sean.
'Ainmich na bheil agad.' Cha 'n 'eil agamsa ach seann làir eich,
seana ghalla choin, mi féin 's mo bhean; sin agadsa na tha chreu-
tairean an t-saoghail mhòr agamsa." "So agad, mata, tri spilgeanan
a bheir thu do d' mhnaoi air an oidhche nochd, agus trì eile do 'n
ghalla, agus an tri so do 'n chapull, agus an tri so mar an ceudna,
cuiridh tu air cùl do thighe; agus 'nan am féin bithidh triùir mhac
aig do bhean, tri searraich aig an làir tri cuileanan aig a ghalla, agus
cinnidh tri chraobhan air cùl do thighe, agus bithidh na craobhan
'nan samhladh; 'nuair a bhasaicheas a h-aon do na mic seargaidh
té do na craobhan. Nis, thoir do thigh ort, agus coinnich mise dur
a bhitheas do mhac tri bliadhna 'dh' aois, 's gheibh thu féin pailteas
eisg an déigh so." Thachair na h-uile ni mar a thubhairt a mhaighdean-mhara ; agus bha e féin a faotainn pailteas éisg, ach a nuair a
bha ceann nan tri bliadhna a dlùthachadh bha an seann duine a fàs
cianail, trom-chridheach, 's e 'dol uaithe na h-uile latha mar bha
teachd. Air comhainm an latha, chaidh e' dh' iasgachd mar a
b'àbhaist, ach cha d'-thug e mhac leis.

Dh' éirich a mhaighdean-mhara ri taobh a bhàta, 's dh' fharraid
i, "an d'-thug thu leat do mhac thugam?" "Ach! cha d'-thug,
dhi-chuimhnich mi gu 'mi b'e so an latha." "Seadh! seadh! mata,"
ars' a mhaighdean-mhara, "gheibh thu cethir bliadhn' eile dheth:
faodaidh gur ann is usa dhuit dealachadh ris ;" so agad a chomh-
aoisc, 'si togail suas leanabh brèagha sultmhor, "am bheil do
mhac-sa cho brèagha ris?" Dh' fhalbh e dhachaidh làn sodain is
sòlais, a chionn gu 'n d' fhuair e ceithir bliadhn' eile d'a mhac; 's
bha e'g-iasgach 'sa' faotainn pailteas éisg. 'Ach an ceann na h-ath
cheithir bliadhna, bhuail mulad 's bròn e, 's cha ghabhadh e lòn 's
cha dèanadh e tùrn, 's cha robh a' bhean a tuigsinn dè a bha cur air.
Air an am so, cha robh fios aige de 'dhèanadh e, ach chuir e roimhe,
nach d'-thugadh e leis a mhac air an uair so nis mò. Dh'-fhalbh
e dh' iasgach mar air na h-uairean roimhe, 's dh'éirich a mhaighdean-mhara ri taobh a bhàta, 's dh' fheòraich i dheth, "An d' thug
thu thugam do mhac?" "Ach dhi-chuimhnuich mi e air an uair so
cuideachd, ars' an seann duine." "Falbh dhachaidh, mata," ars' a
mhaighdean-mhara, "agus an ceann seachd bliadhna na dheigh so,
tha thu cinnteach mis a choinneachadh; ach cha 'n ann an sin is usa
dhuit dealachadh ris ; ach gheibh thu iasg mar a b-àbhaist dhuit."

Chaidh an seann duine dhachaidh làn aoibhneis : fhuar e seachd

bliadhn' eile d'a mhac ! agus mu'n rachadh seachd bliadhna seachad,
bha 'n seann duine a smuaineachadh gu 'm biodh e féin marbh, agus
nach faiceadh e 'mbaighdean-mhara tuillidh.   Ach coma co dhiu, bha
ceann nan seachd bliadhna so a dlùthachadh cuideachd, agus ma 'bha
cha robh an seann duine gun chùram a's trioblaid.   Cha robh fois aige
a latha na dh' oidhche.   Dh' fheòraich am mac bu shine d'a athair,
aon latha, an robh ni air bith a' cuir dragh air?   Thubhairt an
seann duine, "gu'n robh, ach nach buineadh sin dhàsan, na
do neach air bith eile."   Thubhairt an t-òganach gu 'm feumadh
e fios fhaotainn air, 's dh'innis athair dha mu dheireadh mar
a bha chuis eadar e féin 'sa mhaighdean-mhara.   " Na cuireadh sin cùram 'sam bith oirbh," ars' am mac: "Cha téid,
mise na 'r n-aghaidh."   "Cha teid, cha teid, a mhic, ged nach
faighinn iasg a chaoidh."   "Mur leig sibh dhomh dol maille ribh,
rachaibh do'n cheàrdach, agus deanadh an gobha claidheamh mòr
làidir dhòmhsa, 's falbhaidh mi air ceann an fhortain."   Chaidh
athair do 'n cheardaich, 's rinn an gobha claidheamh foghainteach
dha.   Thàinig 'athair dhachaidh leis a chlaidheamh.   Rug an
t-òganach air 's thug e crathadh na dhà air, 's dh' fhalbh e 'na
cheud spealg.   Dh' iarr e air 'athair dol do'n cheàrdaich, agus
claidheamh eile fhaotainn deanta, anns am bitheadh a dhà uiread
do chudthrom; agus mar so rinn athair, agus air an dòigh cheudna
thachair do 'n chlaidheamh; bhrist e na dha leth.   Air ais chaidh
an seann duine do'n cheàrdaich, agus rinn an gobha claidheamh mòr ;
a leithid, cha 'd' rinn e riamh roimhe.   " So agad do chlaidheamh,"
ars' an gobha, " 's feumaidh an dorn a bhi maith a chluicheas an
lann so."   Thug an seann duine, an claidheamh d'a mhac; thug e
crathadh na dithis air; " Ni so feum," ars' am mac, " 's mithich a nis
triall air mo thuras," ars' esan.   Air maduinn an ath latha, chuir e
dìollaid air an each dubh a bha aig an làir, agus thug e 'n saoghal
fuidh' cheann 's an cùth dubh ri thaobh.   'N uair a chaidh e greis air,
aghaidh, thachair carcais caora ris aig taobh an rathaid.   Aig a
charcais bha madadh mòr, seabhag, agus dòbhran.   Theirin e bhàr
an eich, agus roinn e a' chlosach eadar an triùir.   Tri trianan do'n
mhadadh, da thrian do'n dòbhran, agus trian do'n t-seabhag.
" Airson so," ars' am madadh, " Ma ni luathas chas na géire fiacail,
cobhair dhuit, cuimhnich ormnsa, agus bithidh mi ri d' thaobh."
Thubhairt an dòbhran, " Ma ni snàmh coise air grund linne fuasgladh ort, cuimhnich ormsa agus bithidh mi ri 'd' thaobh."   Ars' an
t-seabhag, " Ma thig cruaidh chàs ort, far an deàn luathas itean na
crom ionga feum, cuimhnich ormsa, 's bithidh mi ri 'd' thaobh."
Ghabh e 'n so air aghaidh, gus an d'ràinig e tigh rìgh, 's ghabh e

muinntearas gu bhi 'na bhuachaille, agus 's ann a réir 's na bhitheadh do bhainne aig a chrodh a bhiodh a thuarasdal. Chaidh e
air falbh leis a chrodh, ach cha robh an t-ionaltradh ach lom.
'Nuair a thàinig an t-anmoch, 's a thug e dhachaidh iad, cha robh
'bheag do bhainn' aca, bha 'n t-àite co lom, 's cha robh 'bhiadh na
'dheoch ach suarrach air an oidhche so. Air an ath latha, ghabh e
air adhart ni b' fhaide leo, agus mu dheireadh thàinig e gu àite anabarrach fenrach, ann an gleann uaine nach fac e riamh a leithid.
Ach mu am dha dol mu chùl a chroidh gu 'n tabhairt dhachaidh, co
a chithear a' tighinn ach famhair mòr, 'sa chlaidheamh 'na làimh.
"Hiu! Hau! Hoagraich!" ars' am famhair, "'s fada bho 'n bha
meirg air m' fhiaclan ag iarraidh do chuid feola: 's leamsa 'n crodh,
tha iad air mo chrìch, agus is duine marbh thusa." "Cha dubhairt
mi sin," ars' am buachaille; "cha 'n 'eil fios nach usa sin a ràdh na
dhèanamh.
Ann am badaibh a' cheile gabhar e féin 's am famhair. Chunnaic
e gu 'n robh e fada bho a charaid 's dlu d'a nàmhaid. Tharruing e 'n claidheamh mòr nach fhagadh fuigheal beum, agus dhlùth-
aich e ris an fhamhair, agus ann am mireadh a chatha leum
an cù dubh air cùl an fhamhair, 's tharruing am buachaill' a chlaidheamh 's bha 'n ceann do 'n fhamhair ann am prioba na sùil. Leum
e air muin an eich dhuibh, agus chaidh e shealltainn airson tigh
an fhamhair. Ràinig e 'n dorus, agus leis a' chabhaig, a bha air
an fhamhair, dh' fhàg e gach geata 's gach dorus fosgailte. 'Steach
chaidh am buachaille, agus 'sann an sin a bha 'n greadhnachas,
òr 's airgiod ann am pailteas, 's trusgain dheth gach seòrsa air
am faitheam, le òr 's airgiod 's gach ni bu rìomhaiche na cheile.
Am beul na h-oidhche thug e caisteal an rìgh air, ach cha d' thug e,
dad air bith leis a tigh an fhamhair; agus a nuair a chaidh an crodh a
bhleoghan, 's ann an sin a bha 'm bainne. Fhuair e de bheatha
mhaith air an oidhche so, biadh 's deoch gun ghainne, agus bha an
rìgh anabarrach toilichte, gu 'n d' fhuair e greim air a leithid do
bhuachaille. Chaidh e air aghaidh air son ùine air an dòigh so, ach
mu dheireadh, dh' fhàs an gleann lom do dh' fheur, agus cha robh an
t-ionaltradh cho maith. Ach smaoinich e gun rachadh e air aghaidh
beagan ni b'fhaide a' stigh air còir an fhamhair, agus faicear pàirce
mhòr do dh' fheur. Thill e airson a chruidh agus cuirear a stigh do
'n phairce iad. Cha robh iad ach goirid ag ionaltradh 'sa phàirce, 'nuair
a thàinig famhair mòr, fiadhaich, lan fearg agus corruich. "Hèu!
hò! hoagraich!" ars' am famhair, "'se deoch do d' fhuil a chaisgeas
mo phathadh a nochd." "Cha 'n' eil fios," ars' am buachaille, "nach
fasa sin a ràdh na dheanamh." Ach na cheile ghabh na fir-'s ann

an sin a bha 'n crathadh lann. Mu dheireadh thall bha coltas air
gu'm faigheadh am famhair buaidh air a bhuachaille. 'N sin ghlaodh
e air a chù, agus le aon leum, rug an cù dubh air amhaich air an
fhamhair, 's ghrad bhuail am buachaille an ceann de.

Chaidh e dhachaidh glé sgìth air an oidhche so, ach nu'r thaing,
mar a' robh bainne aig crodh an righ ! 's bha 'n teaghlach air fad co
toilichte air son gun d' fhuair iad a' leithid so do bhuachaille. Lean
e air a bhuachailleachd air an dòigh so rè uine ; ach oidhche 's e air
tighinn dhachaidh, an àite do 'n bhanaraich furan, 's fàilte 'chur air,
's ann a bha iad air fad ri camha 's ri bròn. Dh' fhoighneachd e,
de 'n t-aobhar bròin a bha' so an nochd. Thubhairt a bhanarach, gu
'n robh beist mhòr le tri chinn 'san loch, agus gu 'n robh i ri aon
fhaotainn a h-uile bliadhna, agus gu 'n d' thàinig an crannchur am
bliadhna air nighean an rìgh, " 's mu mheadhon latha 'màireach, tha i
ri coinneachainn na huile-bhéist aig ceann shuas an loch ; ach tha
suiriche mòr an siud a tha 'dol g'a teàrnadh." " De 'n suiriche a
tha ann ?" thubhairt am buachaille. " O ! tha Seanalair mòr airm,"
thubhairt a' bhanarach, " agus a nuair a mharbhas e 'bhéist, pòsaidh
e nighean an rìgh ; oir thubhairt an rìgh 'ge b'è theàrnadh a nighean,
gu 'faigheadh e i ri phòsadh." Ach air an latha 'maireach,'nuair a bha
an t-am a dluthachainn, dh' fhalbh nighean an righ 's an gaisgeach airm
so gu coinneamh a thabhairt do 'n bheist, 's rainig iad an Coire dùbh
aig ceann shuas an loch. Cha robh iad ach goirid an sin 'nuair a
ghluais a bhéist ann am meadhon an loch ; ach air do'n t-Seanalair
an t-uamhas béiste so fhaicinn le tri chinn, ghabh e eagal, 's shèap
e air falbh 's dh' fhalaich e e féin, 's bha nighean an righ fo chrith
's fo eagal, gun neach ann a theàrnadh i. Sùil do 'n d' thug i, faicear
òganach foghainteach, dreachmhor a marcachd each dubh 's a' tighinn
far an robh i. Bha e air a sgeadachdhainn gu h-anabarrach 's fo làn
armachd 's an cù dubh a' siubhal 'na dhéigh. " Tha gruaim air do
ghnùis, a nighean," ars' an t-òganach ; " dé tha thu deanadh an so ?"
" O ! 's coma sin, thubhairt nighean an rìgh, cha 'n fhad'a bhitheas mi
ann co dhiu." " Cha dubhairt mi sin," ars' esan. " Theich laoch cho
coltach riutsa, 's cha 'n 'eil fada uaidhe," thubhairt ise. " 'Se laoch
a sheasas Cath," ars' an t-òganach. Shuidh e sìos làimh rithe 's
thubhairt e rithe, " Na 'n tuiteadh esan 'na chadal, i ga 'dhùsgadh
'n uair a chitheadh i 'bhéist a' deanamh air son tìr." " De 's dùsgadh
duit," thubhairt ise ? " 'S dusgadh dhomh am fàinne th' air do mheur
a chur air mo lughdag." Cha b' fhada bha iad an sin, 'n uair a
chunnaic i bhéist a dèanamh gu tìr. Thug i 'm fàinne bhàr a meur,
's chuir i air lughdag an òganaich e. Dhùisg e, agus an coinneamh
na béiste ghabh e, le 'chlaidheamh 's le chù ; ach 's ann an sin a bha

'n t-slupartaich 's an t-slapartaich eadar e féin 's a' bhéist ; 's bha 'n
cù dèanamh na b' urrainn e, 's bha nighean an rìgh air bhall-chrith
eagail le fuaim na béiste. Bhiodh iad uair fuidhe 's uair an uachdar,
ach ma dheireadh, gheàrr e fear do na cinn di ; thug i aon raibheic
aiste, 's ghoir mac-talla nan creag d'a sgrèuch, 's chuir i 'n loch 'na
lasair bho cheann gu ceann, agus ann am prioba na sùla, chaidh i as
an t-sealladh. " Piseach 's buaidh gu 'n robh ga 'd' leantainn, òganaich," arsa nighean an rìgh, "tha mise sàbhailt air son aon oidhche ;
ach thig a bheist a rithist, gu bràth gus an d' thig an dà cheann eile
dhi." Rug e air ceann na béiste, agus tharruing e gad roimhe 's
thubhairt e rithe, " I ga' thabhairt leatha 'm màireach an sud." Dh'
fhalbh i dhachaidh 's an ceann air a guallainn, 's thug am buachaille
na mairt air. Ach cha b' fhada bha i air a' rathad, 'n uair a choinnich an Seanalair mòr so i, agus thubhairt e rithe gu marbhadh e, i
mur canadh i gur esan a thug an ceann do 'n bhéist. " O! ars' ise,
's mi their! co eile 'thug an ceann do 'n bheist ach thu." Ràinig iad
tigh an rìgh 's an ceann air guallainn an t-Seanalair ; ach 's ann an
so a bha 'n t-aoibhneas, i 'thighinn dhachaidh beò slàn, agus ceann
na béiste làn fola aig a Chaiptean mhòr so 'na làimh. Air an latha
'màireach, dh'fhalbh iad, agus cha robh teagamh sam bith nach
teàrnadh an gaisgeach so nighean an rìgh. Ràinig iad an t-àite
ceudna, 's cha robh iad fad' an sin, 'n uair a ghluais an uile-bheist
oillteil ann am meadhon an loch, 's shèap an gaisgeach air falbh mar
a rinn e air an lath' dè. Ach cha b' fhad an déigh so, dur a thàinig
fear an eich dhuibh 's deis' eile air. Coma co dhiu, dh'aithnich i gur
e cheart òganach a bh' ann. " 'S mise tha toilichte d' fhaicinn" ars'
ise, "tha mi 'n dòchas gu làimhsich thu do chlaidheamh mòr an diugh
mar a rinn thu 'n dè ; thig a nìos 's leig t-anail." Ach cha b' fhada
bha iad an sin, 'n uair a chunnaic iad a bhéist a totail am meadhon an
loch. Luidh an t-òganach sìos ri taobh nighean an rìgh, 's thubhairt
e rithe, " Ma chaidleas mise mu 'n d'thig a bhéist, dùisg! mi." " De
as dùsgadh dhuit?" " 'S dùsgadh dhomh a chluais-fhail sin a tha
'na 'd' chluais, a chuir 'na mo thè féin." Cha mhath a chaidil e 'n uair
a ghlaodh nighean an rìgh, " Dùisg! dùisg! Ach dusgadb cha
dèanadh e ; ach thug i chluas-fhail as a cluais, agus chuir i 'n cluas
an òganaich e, 's air ball dhùisg e, 's an car na béiste chaidh e ; ach
's ann an sin a bha 'n t-slupartaich 's an t-slapartaich, raoiceil, 's
taoiceil air a bhéist. Lean iad mar so rè ùine fada, 's mu bheul na
h-oidhche, gheàrr e 'n ceann eile do 'n bhéist. Chuir e air à ghad e 's
leum e air muin an eich dhuibh, 's thug e 'bhuachailleachd air. Dh'
fhalbh nighean an rìgh dhachaidh leis na cinn : thachair an Seanalair rithe 's thug e uaipe na cinn, 's thubhairt e rithe, " Gu 'm feumadh

i 'chantainn gu 'm b' esan a thug an ceann do 'n bhéist air an uair so
cuideachd." "Co eile a thug an ceann do 'n bhéist ach thu ?" thuirt
ise. Ràinig iad tigh an rìgh leis na cinn, ach 's ann an sin a bha
'n t-aoibhneas 's an t-aighear. Ma bha an rìgh subhach an ceud
oidhche, bha e nis cinnteach gu 'n teàrnadh an gaisgeach mòr so a
nighean, 's cha robh teagamh sam bith nach bitheadh an ceann eile
do 'n bhéist air an latha màireach. Mu 'n am cheudna, dh' fhalbh
an dìthis air an latha 'màireach. Dh' fhalaich an t-oifigir e féin
mar a b-abhaist: thug nighean an rìgh bruaich an loch oirre, 's
thàinig gaisgeach an eich dhuibh, 's luidh e ri' taobh. Dhùisg i 'n t-
òlach 's chuir i cluas-fhail 'na chluais eile agus ann am bad na béiste
ghabh e. Ach ma bha raoiceil, is 'staoiceil air a bheist air na làithean a chaidh seachad, 's ann an diugh a bha 'n t-uamhas oirre. Ach
coma co dhiu, thug e 'n treas ceann do 'n bhéist, 's ma thug cha b'
ann gun spàirn. Tharruing e ro 'n ghad e, 's dh' fhalbh i dhachaidh
leis na cinn. 'N uair a ràinig iad tigh an rìgh, bha na h-uile làn
gàirdeachas, 's bha 'n Seanalair ri nighean an rìgh phòsadh air an
ath latha. Bha bhanais à dol air a h-aghaidh 's gach neach mu 'n
Chaisteal 's fadal air gus an d' thigeadh an sagairt. Ach a nuair a
thainig an sagairt, cha phòsadh i ach an neach a bheireadh na cinn
do 'n ghad gun an gad a ghearradh. "Co bheireadh na cinn do 'n
ghad, ach am fear a chuir na cinn air'," thubhairt an rìgh. Dh'
fheuch an Seanalair iad, ach cha b-urrainn e na cinn fhuasgladh;
's mu dheireadh, cha robh a h'aon mu 'n tigh nach d' fheuch ris' na
cinn a thoirt do 'n ghad, ach cha b-urrainn iad. Dh' fhoighneachd
an rìgh, "An robh neach air bith eile mu 'n tigh a dh' fheuchadh
ris na cinn a thoirt bhar a ghaid." Thubhairt iad, "Nach d' fheuch
am buachaille fathast iad." Chaidh fios air a' bhuachaille, 's cha
b' fhada bha esan a tilgeadh fear a null 's a nall diubh. "Ach
fan beagan òganaich," arsa nighean an rìgh: "am fear a thug na
cinn do 'n bhéist, tha 'm fainne agam sa aige, agus mo dhà chluais-
fhail." Chuir am buachaille 'làimh 'na phòca, 's thilg e air a bhòrd
iad. "S'-tusa mo dhuine-sa," arsa nighean an rìgh. Cha robh an rìgh
cho toilichte, 'n uair a chunnaic e gu 'm b'e 'bhuachaille a bha ri' nighean a phòsadh ; ach dh' òrduich e gu feum t' a chur ann an trusgan
ni b'fhearr. Ach labhair a nighean, 's thubhairt i, "Gun robh
trusgan aige cho rìomhach 'sa bha riamh 'na chaisteal ; agus mur so
thachair ; chuir am buachaille deis' òir an fhamhair air, agus phòs
iad air an oidhche sin féin.
   Bha iad a nis pòsda 's na h-uile ni dol air aghaidh gu maith. Bha
iad aon lath' a spaisdearachd mu thaobh àn locha, 's thàinig béist a
b-uamhasaiche na 'n te eile, 's thugar air falbh e gun athadh gun

fhoighneachd. Bha nighean an rìgh an so gu dubhach, dèurach,
dalla-bhròunach air son a fear-posda. Bha i daonnan 'sa sùil air
an loch. Thachair seana ghobha, rithe, 's dh' innis i dha mar
thachair da céile-pòsda. Chomhairlich an gobha dhi i 'sgaoileadh
gach nì bu bhreagha na chéile anns a cheart àite 'san 'd' thug
a bhéist air falbh a duine; agus mar so rinn i. Chuir a bhéist
suas a sròn, 's thubhairt i, "'S brèagh 'd' ailleas a nighean a rìghe."
"'S brèagha na sin an t-àilleagan a thug thu uam," thubhairt ise.
"Thoir dhomh aon sealladh do m' dhuine, 's gheibh thu aon ni do
na tha thu 'faicinn." Thug a' bhéist suas e. "Aisig dhomh e, 's
gheibh thu na tha thu 'faicinn," ars' ise. Rinn a' bhéist mar a
thubhairt i; thilg i beo slàn e air bruach an locha. Goirid 'na dheigh
sud, 's iad a sràidimeachd ri taobh an loch, thug a bhéist cheudna
air falbh nighean an rìgh. Bu bhrònach gach neach a bha 'sa
bhaile air an oidhche so. Bha a duine gu dubhach, deurach, a' siubhal
sìos agus suas mu bhruachan an locha a latha 's do dh' oidhche.
Thachair an seana ghobha ris. Dh' innis an gobha dha, Nach
robh dòigh air an uile-bheist a mharbhadh, ach aon dòigh, Agus 's e
sin. "Anns an eilean 'tha am meadhon an locha tha eilid chaisfhionn
as caoile cas 's as luaithe ceum, agus ge do rachadh beirsinn oirre,
leumadh feannag aisde, agus ged a rachadh beirsinn air an f heannag,
leumadh breac aisde; ach tha ubh am beul a bhric, agus tha anam
na béiste 'san ubh 's ma bhristeas an t-ubh, tha a' bhéist marbh."
Nis cha robh dòigh air faotainn do 'n eilean so, bho 'n chuireadh a
bhéist foidh gach bata 's gach ràth, a rachadh air an loch. Smaoinich e gu 'm feuchadh e 'n Caolas a leum leis an each dhubh,
agus mar so fhein rinn e. Leum an t-each dubh an Caolas, 's an
Cù dubh le aon leum as an déigh. Chunnaic e' n eilid, 's leig e 'n
cù dubh 'na déigh, ach an uair a bhiodh an cù air aon taobh do 'n
eilean bhiodh an eilid air an taobh eile. "O! bu mhath a nis
madadh mòr na closaiche feòla an so." Cha luaithe 'labhair e 'm
facal na bha 'm madadh còir ri' thaobh, agus an déigh na h-eilid
ghabh e 's cha b' f hada 'bha na laoich ga cuir ri talamh; ach cha bu
luaithe a rug e oirre, na leum feannag aisde; "'S ann a nis a bu
mhath an t-seobhag ghlas as geire suil 's is làidire sgiath." Cha
luaithe thubhairt e so, na bha 'n t-seobhag as déigh 'na feannaig, 's cha
b' f hada 'bha i ga cuir ri talamh; agus air tuiteam do 'n f heannaig air
bruach an locha, a mach aisde leumtar am breac. "O! nach robh thus'
agamsa a nis, a dhobhrain." Cha luaith' thubhairt na bha 'n dobhran
ri thaobh, agus a'mach air an loch leum i, 's thugar am breac a meadhon
an loch; Ach cha luaithe bha 'n dòran air tìr leis a bhreac na thainig
an t-ubh a mach as a bheul. Ghrad leum esan, 's chuir e 'chas air,

'S ann an sin a leig a bhéist raoic aisde, 's thubhairt i, "Na brist an t-ubh, 's gheibh thu na dh' iarras tu." "Aisig dhòmhsa mo bhean." Ann am prioba na sùla bha i ri 'thaobh. "Nuair a fhuair e greim air a laimh 'na dha' làimh, leig e chas air an ubh, 's bhàsaich a bhéist. Bha 'bheist marbh a nis, agus 'sann a nis a bha 'n sealladh ri fhaicinn. Bha i uamhasach ri sealltainn oirre, bha na tri chinn di gun teagamh, ach ma bha, bha ceann os-ceann cheann oirre, agus sùilean, 's cùig ceud cas. Coma co dhiu, dh' fhàg iad ann a 'sud i, 's chaidh iad dhachaidh. Bha sòlas is gàirdeachas ann an tigh an rìgh air an oidhche so, 's cha d' innis e do 'n rìgh gu so mar a mharbh e na famhairean. Chuir an rìgh urram mòr air, 's bha e 'na dhuine mòr aig an rìgh.

Bha e fein 's a' bhean a' sràidimeachd aon latha, 'n uair a thug e fainear caisteal beag ri taobh an loch, ann an coille. Dh' fharraid e do 'n mhnaoi. Co bha gabhail còmhnuidh ann? "Thubhairt i nach robh neach air bith a' dol a chòir a chaisteil ud, bho nach d'thainig neach air ais fathast a chaidh ann a dh' innseadh sgeùil." "Cha 'n fhaud a chùis a bhi mar sin," ars' esan; "a nochd féin chi mi, co' tha gabhail conhnuidh ann." "Cha d' theid, cha d' theid," thubhairt ise, "cha deach duine riamh do 'n chaisteal so a phill air ais." "Biodh sin 's a roghainn aige," ars' esan. Dh' fhalbh e, agus gabhar do 'n chaisteal 's nuair a ràinig e 'n dorus, thachair cailleach bheag, bhrosgulach ris 'na seasamh san dorus. 'Furan 's failte dhuit, a mhic an iasgair 's mi féin a tha toilichte t' fhaicinn; 's mòr an onair do 'n rìoghachd so do leithid a thighinn innte; 's urram do 'n bhothan bheag so thu thighinn a stigh; gabh a stigh air thoiseach, onair na h-uaisle, 's leig t' anail:" 's a steach ghabh e; ach a nuair a bha e air tì dol suas, tharruing i an slacan-druidheachd air an cùl a chinn, 's air ball thuit e 'n sin. "Air an oidhche so bha bròn ann an caisteal an rìgh agus air an latha màireach bha tuireadh ann an tigh an iasgair. Chunnacas a chraobh a seargadh 's thubhairt mac meadhonach an iasgair, "gu 'n robh a bhràthar marbh," 's thug e bòid is briathar gu falbhadh e s gu 'm biodh fios aige cait' an robh Corp a bhràthar na luidhe. Chuir e diollaid air each dubh, 's mharcaich e an déigh a' choin duibh (oir bha each dubh 's cù dubh aig triùir mhac an iasgair) agus gun dol a null na nall, lean e air ceum a bhràthair bu sine, gus an ràinig e tigh an rìgh. Bha e so co coltach ri 'bhràthair 's gu 'n d' shaoil le nighean an rìgh gu 'm be duine fein a bh' ann. Dh' fhan e 'n so 'sa chaisteal, 's dh' innis iad dha mar thachair d'a bhràthair, agus do chaisteal beag na cailliche dh' fheumadh e 'dol bog na cruaidh mar thachradh, 's do 'n, chaisteal chaidh e, agus ceart mar a thachair do 'n bhràthair bu sine, anns gach dòigh thachair do 'n mhac mheadhonach, 's le aon bhuille do 'n t-slacan dhruidheachd, leag a' chailleach e na shìneadh ri' taobh a bhràthar. Air faicinn an darna craobh a' seargadh do mhac òg an iasgair thubhairt e, "Gu 'n robh a nis a dhithis bhràithrean marbh, agus gu' feumadh fios a bhi aigesan de 'm bàs a thàinig orra. Air muin an eich dhuibh, ghabh e, 's lean e 'n cù mar a rinn a bhràthair, agus tigh au rìgh bhuail e mn 'n do stad e. 'Se 'n rìgh bha toil-ichte f haicinn, ach do 'n chaisteal dubh (oir 'se so ainm) cha leigadh iad e, ach do 'n chaisteal, dh' f heumadh e dol, 's mur sin ràinig e 'n caisteal. "Failte 's furan dhuit féin, a mhic an iasgair, 's mi tha toillichte t'f haicinn; gabh a steach 's leig t-anail," thuirt ise. " 'Stigh romham thu, a chailleach, 's coma leam sodal a muigh." " Rach a steach 's cluinneam do chòmhradh. A' steach, ghabh a chailleach, agus a nuair a bha cùl ris, tharruing e a chlaidheamh 's spadar a ceann dhi, ach leum an claidheamh as a làimh, 's ghrad rug à chailleach air a ceann le a da làimh, s cuirear air a h-amhaich e mar' bha e roimhe. Leum an cù air a chaillich, 's bhuail i m 'madadh Còir leis an t-slacan-dhruidheachd, 's luidh esan an sin, ach cha deach so air mhith-apadh do 'n òlach, 's an sàs sa chaillich gabhar e. Fhuair e gréim air an t-shlacan-dhruidheachd, agus le aon bhuille am mullach a cinn, bha i ri talamh ann am prioba na sùl. Chaidh e beagan air aghaidh suas, 's faicear a dha bhràthair na 'n luidhe taobh ri taobh. Thug e buille do gach fear dhiubh, leis an t-slacan dhruidheachd 's air an cois bha iad. Ach 's ann an so a bha 'n spuill òir 's airgid, 's gach ni bu luachmhoire na chèile ann an caisteal na cailliche. Thàinig iad air an ais do thigh an rìgh, 's ann an sin a bha 'n gàirdeachas. Bha 'n rìgh a fàs sean. agus chaidh mac bu shine an iasgair a chrùnadh 'na rìgh, 's dh' f han an dithis bhràithrean latha 's bliadhna ann an tigh an rìgh, 's dh' f halbh an dithis a nis dhachadh le òr 's airgiod na Cailliche, 's gach nì rìomhach eile 'thug an rìgh dhoibh ; 's mar do shuibhail iad uaidh sin, tha iad beo gus an latha 'n diugh.

HECTOR URQUHART.

2. Another version of this was told to me in South Uist, by JOHN MACPHIE, aged 79, in September 1859.

There was a poor old fisher in Skye, and his name was Duncan. He was out fishing, and the sea-maiden rose at the side of his boat, and said, " Duncan, thou art not getting fish." They had a long talk, and made a bargain ; plenty of fish for his first son. But he said, " I have none." Then the sea-maiden gave him something, and said, "Give this to thy wife, and this to thy mare, and this to thy dog, and they will have three sons, three foals, and three pups," and so they had, and the eldest son was Iain. When he was eighteen, he found his mother weeping, and learned that he belonged to the mermaid. "Oh," said he, "I will go where there is not a drop of salt water." So he mounted one of the horses and went away. He soon came to the carcass of an old horse, and at it a lion (leon), a wolf (matugally), and a falcon (sbowag). LEÒMHAN-MADAAH ALLUIDH SEABHAG or SEOBHAG.

The lion spoke, and *she* asked him to divide the carcass. He did so, and each thanked him, and said, "When thou art in need think of me, and I will be at thy side (*or thou wilt be a lion, a wolf, or a falcon, I am uncertain which he meant*), for we were here under spells till some one should divide this carcass for us."

He went on his way and became a king's herd. He went to a smith and bade him make him an iron staff. He made three. The two first bent, the third did well enough. He went a-herding, and found a fine grass park, and opened it and went in with the cattle. FUATH of the seven heads, and seven humps, and seven necks, came and took six by the tails and went away with them (*so Cacus dragged away cows by the tail*). "Stop," said the herd. The FUATH would not, so they came to grips. Then the fisher's son either thought of the lion, or became one, but at all events a lion seized the giant and put him to earth. "Thine is my lying down and rising up," said he. "What is thy ransom?" said the herd. The giant said, "I have a white filly that will go through the skies, and a white dress; take them." And the herd took off his heads.

When he went home they had to send for carpenters to make dishes for the milk, there was so much.

The next day was the same. There came a giant with the same number of heads, and took eight cows by their tails, and slung them on his back. The herd and the wolf (or as a wolf) beat him, and got a red filly that could fly through the air, and a red dress, and cut off the heads. And there were still more carpenters wanted, there was so much milk.

The third day came a still bigger giant and took nine cows, and the herd *as*, or *with* a falcon, beat him, and got a green filly that would go through the sky, and a green dress, and cut his heads off, and there was more milk than ever.

On the fourth day came the Carlin, the wife of the last giant, and mother of the other two, and the fisher's son went up into a tree. "Come down till I eat thee," said she. "Not I," said the herd. "Thou hast killed my husband and my two sons, come down till I eat thee." "Open thy mouth, then, till I jump down," said the herd. So the old Carlin opened her gab, and he thrust the iron staff down her throat, and it came out at a mole on her breast [*this is like the mole of the Gruagach in No.* 1], and she fell. Then he sprang on her, and spoke as before, and got a basin, and when he washed himself in it, he would be the most beautiful man that was ever seen on earth, and a fine silver comb, and it would make him the grandest man in the world; and he killed the Carlin and went home.

[*So far this agrees almost exactly with the next version, but there is a giant added here and a coarse comb left out*].

When the fisher's son came home, there was sorrow in the king's house, for the DRAYGAN was come from the sea. Every time he came there was some one to be eaten, and this time the lot had fallen on the king's daughter.

The herd said that he would go to fight the draygan, and the king said, "No: I cannot spare my herd." So the king's daughter had to go alone. [*The incident of the cowardly knight is here left out.*] Then the herd came through the air on the white filly, with the white dress of the Fuath. He tied the filly to the branch of a tree and went where the king's daughter was, and laid his head in her lap, and she dressed his hair, and he slept. When the draygan came she woke him, and after a severe battle he cut off one head, and the draygan said, "A hard fight to-morrow," and went away. The herd went off in the white filly, and in the evening asked about the battle, and heard his own story. Next day was the same with the red filly and the red dress, and the draygan said, "The last fight to-morrow," and he disappeared. On the third day she scratched a mark on his forehead when his head was in her lap: he killed the draygan, and when he asked about it all, there was great joy, for now the draygan was dead. Then the king's daughter had the whole kingdom gathered, and they took off their head clothes as they passed, but there was no mark. Then they bethought them of the dirty herd, and when he came he would not put off his head gear, but she made him, and saw the mark, and said, "Thou mightest have a better dress." He used his magic comb and basin, and put on a dress, and was the grandest in the company, and they married. It fell out that the king's daughter longed for dulse, and he went with her to the shore to seek it. The sea-maiden rose up and took him. She was sorrowful, and went to the soothsayer and learned what to do.

And she took her harp to the sea shore and sat and played, and the sea-maiden came up to listen, for sea-maidens are fonder of music than any other creatures, and when she saw the sea-maiden she stopped. The sea-maiden said, "Play on ;" but she said, "No, till I see my man again." So the sea-maiden put up his head. (*What do you mean? Out of her mouth to be sure. She had swallowed him.*) She played again, and stopped, and then the sea-maiden put him up to the waist. Then she played again and stopped, and the sea-maiden placed him on her palm. Then he thought of the falcon, and became one and flew on shore. But the sea-maiden took the wife.

Then he went to the soothsayer, and he said, "I know not what to do, but in a glen there is TARBH NIMH, a hurtful bull, and in the bull a ram, and in the ram a goose, and in the goose an egg, and there is the soul of the sea-maiden."

Then he called on his three creatures, and by their help got the goose, but the egg fell out in the loch.

Then the lion said *she* knew not what to do, and the wolf said the same. The falcon told of an otter in an island, and flew and seized her two cubs, and the otter dived for the egg to save her cubs. He got his wife, and dashed the egg on the stones, and the mermaid died. And they sent for the fisher and his sons, and the old mother and brothers got part of the kingdom, and they were all happy and lucky after that.

I asked if there was anything about one brother being taken for the other and the naked sword, and was told that the incident was in another story, as well as that of the withering of the three trees. These incidents were in the version of the stable boy; and as they are in Mackenzie's, they probably belong to the story as it was known in Argyllshire.

3. Another version of this was told in April 1859, by John MacGibbon, a lad who was rowing me across Loch Fyne, from St. Katharine's to Inverary; he said he had heard it from an old man living near Lochgilphead, who could tell many stories, and knew part of the history of the Feine.

The hero was the son of a widow, the youngest of ten; black-skinned and rough "carrach." He went to seek his fortune, and after adventures somewhat like those of the heroes in the other versions, he became like them a king's herd, and was in like manner beset by giants who claimed the pasture. Each fight was preceded by a long and curious parley across a ditch. The giants got larger each day, and last of all came the wife of one, and mother of the other two, who was worst of all.

He got spoil from each, which the conquered giant named as his ransom, and which, as usual, the herd took after killing his foe. From the mother he got a "golden comb, and when he combed his hair with the fine side, he was lovely, and when he combed it with the coarse side, he was hideous again," and a magic basin which made him beautiful when he washed in it. And he got wonderful arms, and dresses, and horses from the giants.

Then the king's daughter was to be given to a giant with three heads who came in a ship. When he leaped on shore, he buried himself to the waist, he was so heavy. The herd was asleep with his head in the lap of the princess, and dressed in the giant's spoil, combed with the fine gold comb, and washed in the magic basin, and beautiful, but nevertheless the princess dressed his hair.

He was awakened each day by biting a joint off his little finger—cutting a patch from the top of his head—and a notch from his ear. Each day he cut off a head, and the giant, when he leaped from the ship on the third day, only sunk to his ancles in the sand, for he had lost two heads.

The third head jumped on again as fast as it was cut off, but at last, by the advice of a hoodie, the cold steel of the sword was held on the neck till the marrow froze, and then the giant was killed, and the herd disappeared as usual.

A red-headed lad, who went to guard the princess, ran away and hid himself, and took the credit each day, but he could not

H

untie the knots with which the heads were bound together on a withy by the herd. Then when all the kingdom had been gathered, the herd was sent for, but he would not come, and he bound three parties of men who were sent to bring him by force.

At last he was entreated to come, and came, and was recognized by the marks, and then he combed his hair, and washed in the magic basin, and dressed in the giant's spoils, and he married the princess, and the Gille Ruadh was hanged.

Here the story ended, but so did the passage of the ferry.

4. I have another version written by Hector Maclean, from the dictation of a woman, B. Macaskill, in the small island of Berneray, Aug. 1859.—MAC A GHOBHA, The Smith's Son.

A smith takes the place of the old fisherman. The mermaid rises beside his boat, gets the promise of the son, and sends him fish. (*The three mysterious grains are omitted*). One son is born to the fisher, and the mermaid lets him remain till he is fourteen years of age.

BHA 'N GILLE 'N SO CHO MOR AN CEAUNN NAN CEITHIR BLIADHNA DIAG! CHA ROBH LEITHID RE FHAIGHIN CHO MOR 'S CHO GARBH 'S CHO FOGHAINTEACH RIS.

The lad was now *so* big at the end of the 14 years! His like was not to be found, so big, so rugged, so formidable as he.

Then he asked his father not to go in the wind of the shore or the sea, for fear the mermaid should catch him, and to make him a staff in which there should be nine stone weight of iron; and he went to seek his fortune. His father made him the staff, and he went, and whom should he meet but MADADH RUADH the fox, MADADH ALLUIDH the wolf, AGUS AN FHEANNAG, and the hoodie, AGUS OTHAISG ACA GA H'ITHEADH, and eating a year old sheep. He divided the sheep, and the creatures promised to help him, and he went on to a castle, where he got himself employed as a herd, and was sent to a park; "no man ever came alive out of it that ever went into it."

A big giant came and took away one of the cows, and then (SABAID) a fight began, and the herd was undermost, AGUS DE RINN AM BUACHAILL' ACH CUIMHNEACHADH AIR A MHADADH ALLUIDH AGUS GHRAD! BHA 'M BUACHAILL AN AIRD AGUS AM FUAMHAIR FODHA AGUS MHARBH E 'M FUAMHAIR, and what did the herd but remember the wolf, and swift! the herd was above and the giant below, and he killed the giant, and went home with the cattle, and his master said to the BANACHAGAN, " Oh, be good to the herd." (*The spoil, the dresses, and the horses are here all left out*). The second day it was the same, and he again thought of the wolf, and conquered after he was down.

The third day it was again the same. On the fourth day CAILLEACH MHOR a great carlin came. They fought, and he was undermost again, but thought of the wolf and was up. BAS AS DO CHIONN A CHAILLEACH ARS AM BUACHAILLE DE' T' EIRIG. ?*

" Death on thy top, Carlin," said the herd, "what 's thy value?" " That is not little," said the Carlin, " if thou gettest it. I have three TRUNCANNAN (*an English word with a Gaelic plural*) full of silver. There is a trunk under the foot-board, and two others in the upper end of the castle." " Though that be little, its my own," said he as he killed her.

On the morrow the king's daughter was to go to the great beast that was on the loch to be killed, and what should the herd do but draw the cattle that way, and he laid his head in her lap and slept, but first told the lady, when she saw the loch trembling, to take off a joint of his little finger. She did so. He awoke, thought of the fox, and took a head, a hump, and a neck off the beast, and he went away, and no one knew that he had been there at all. Next day was the same, but he had a patch cut from his head.

The third day she took off the point of his ear, he awoke, was again beaten by the beast, thought of the fox, and was uppermost, and killed the beast (S' BHA I NA LOCH UISGE N' UAIR A MHARBH E I) and she was a fresh water lake when he had killed her.

(*The cowardly general, or knight, or lad, or servant, is here left out.*) Then the king's daughter gave out that she would marry the man whose finger fitted the joint which she had cut off and kept in her pocket. Everybody came and cut off the points of their little fingers, but the herd staid away till it was found out by the

---

* EIRIG, a fine for bloodshed, a ransom. Fine anciently paid for the murder of any person. *Scottish Laws—Regiam Majestam:* (Armstrong dic.) *The Laws of the Brets and Scots,* in which every one was valued according to his degree (Innes's " Scotland in the Middle Ages").

dairymaids that he wanted the joint, and then he came and married the lady.

After they were married they went to walk by the shore, and the mermaid rose and took him away. "It is long since thou wert promised to me, and now I have thee perforce," said she. An old woman advised the lady to spread all her dresses on the beach, and she did so in the evening, and the mermaid came, and for the dresses gave back her companion, "and they went at each other's necks with joy and gladness."

In a fortnight the wife was taken away, "and sorrow was not sorrow till now—the lad lamenting his wife." He went to an old man, who said, "There is a pigeon which has laid in the top of a tree; if thou couldst find means to break the egg ANAIL, the breath of the mermaid is in it." SMAOINTICH E AIR AN FHEAN-NAIG 'S CHAIDH E NA FHEANNAIG 'S LEUM E GO BARR NA CRAOIBHE. He thought on the hoodie, and he became a hoodie (*went into his hoodie*), and he sprang to the top of the tree, and he got the egg, and he broke the egg, and his wife came to shore, and the mermaid was dead.

It is worth remarking the incidents which drop out of the story when told by women and by men. Here the horses and armour are forgotten, but the faithful lover is remembered. The sword is a stick, and the whole thing savours strongly of the every-day experience of the Western Isles, which has to do with fishing, and herding sheep and cattle. It is curious also to remark the variations in the incidents. The hero seems to acquire the qualities of the creatures, or be assisted by them.

5. I have another version from Barra, but it varies so much, and has so many new incidents, that I must give it entire, if at all, It most resembles MacGibbon's version. It is called AN 'T IASGAIR the fisher, and was told by Alexander MacNeill, fisherman.

6. I have a sixth version told by John Smith, labourer, living at Polchar in South Uist, who says he learned it about twenty years ago from Angus Macdonald, Balnish. It is called AN GILLE GLAS, the Grey lad. He is a widow's son, goes to seek his fortune, goes to a smith, and gets him to make an iron shinny (*that is a hockey club*), he becomes herd to a gentleman, herds cattle, and is beset by giants whom he kills with his iron club; he gathers the skirt of his grey cassock (*which looks like Odin*), he gets a copper

and a silver and a golden castle, servants (or slaves) of various colour and appearance, magic whistles, horses, and dresses, and rescues the daughter of the king of Greece. The part of the cowardly knight is played by a red headed cook. The language of this is curious, and the whole very wild. Unless given entire, it is spoilt.

In another story, also from Berneray, the incident of meeting three creatures again occurs.

There is a lion, a dove, and a rat. And the lion says :—

" What, lad, is thy notion of myself being in such a place as this ? "

" Well," said he, " I have no notion, but that it is not there the like of you ought to be ; but about the banks of rivers."

It is impossible not to share the astonishment of the lion, and but for the fact that the rat and the dove were as much surprised at their position as the lion, one would be led to suspect that Margaret MacKinnon, who told the story, felt that her lion was out of his element in Berneray. Still he is there, and it seems worth inquiring how he and the story got there and to other strange places.

1st. The story is clearly the same as Shortshanks in Dasent's Norse Tales, 1859. But it is manifest that it is not taken from that book, for it could not have become so widely spread in the islands, and so changed within the time.

2d. It resembles, in some particulars, the Two Brothers, the White Snake, the Nix of the Mill Pond, the Ball of Crystal, in Grimm ; and there are similar incidents in other German tales. These have long been published, but I never heard of a copy in the west, and many of my authorities cannot read. It is only necessary to compare any one of the Gaelic versions with any one German tale, or all together, to feel certain that Grimm's collection is not the source from which this story proceeded.

3d. A story in the latest edition of the Arabian Nights (Lane's, 1839), contains the incident of a genius, whose life was not in his body, but in a chest at the bottom of the Circumambient Ocean, but that book is expensive, and quite beyond the reach of peasants and fishermen in the west, and the rest of the story is different.

4th. There is something in Sanscrit about a fight for cattle between a herd and some giants, which has been compared with the classical story of Cacus.—(Mommsen's Roman History).

5th. I am told that there is an Irish "fenian" story which this resembles. I have not yet seen it, but it is said to be taken from a very old Irish MS. (Ossianic Society).

6th. It is clearly the same as the legend of St. George and the Dragon. It is like the classical story of Perseus and Andromeda, but Pegasus is multiplied by three, and like the story of Hercules and Hesione, but Hercules was to have six horses. On the whole, I cannot think that this is taken from any known story of any one people, but that it is the Gaelic version of some old myth. If it contains something which is distorted history, it seems to treat of a seafaring people who stole men and women, and gave them back for a ransom, of a wild race of "giants" who stole cattle and horses, and dresses, and used combs and basins, and had grass parks; and another people who had cattle, and wanted pasture, and went from the shore *in* on the giants' land.

If it be mythical, there is the egg which contains the life of the sea-monster, and to get which beast, bird, and fish, earth, air, and water, must be overcome. Fire may be indicated, for the word which I have translated SPINDRIFT LASAIR, generally means *flame*.

I am inclined to think that it is a very old tale, a mixture of mythology, history, and everyday life, which may once have been intended to convey the moral lesson, that small causes may produce great effects; that men may learn from brutes, Courage from the lion and the wolf, Craft from the fox, Activity from the falcon, and that the most despised object often becomes the greatest. The whole story grows out of a grain of seed. The giant's old mother is more terrible than the giants. The little flattering crone in the black castle more dangerous than the sea monster. The herd thought of the wolf when he fought the giants, but he thought of the fox when he slew the dragon. I can but say with the tale tellers, "dh, fhàg mise n' sin eud." "There I left them," for others to follow if they choose. I cannot say how the story got to the Highlands, and the lion into the mind of a woman in Berneray.

V.

CONALL CRA BHUIDHE.

From James Wilson, blind fiddler, Islay.

CONALL CRA BHUIDHE was a sturdy tenant in Eirinn: he had four sons. There was at that time a king over every fifth of Eirinn. It fell out for the children of the king that was near Conall, that they themselves and the children of Conall came to blows. The children of Conall got the upper hand, and they killed the king's big son. The king sent a message for Conall, and he said to him—"Oh, Conall! what made thy sons go to spring on my sons till my big son was killed by thy children? but I see that though I follow thee revengefully, I shall not be much the better for it, and I will now set a thing before thee, and if thou wilt do it, I will not follow thee with revenge. If thou thyself, and thy sons, will get for me the brown horse of the king of Lochlann, thou shalt get the souls of thy sons." "Why," said Conall, "should not I do the pleasure of the king, though there should be no souls of my sons in dread at all. Hard is the matter thou requirest of me, but I will lose my own life, and the life of my sons, or else I will do the pleasure of the king."

After these words Conall left the king, and he went home: when he got home he was under much trouble and perplexity. When he went to lie down he told his wife the thing the king had set before him. His wife took much sorrow that he was obliged to part from herself,

while she knew not if she should see him more. " Oh,
Conall," said she, " why didst not thou let the king do
his own pleasure to thy sons, rather than be going now,
while I know not if ever I shall see thee more?" When
he rose on the morrow, he set himself and his four sons
in order, and they took their journey towards Lochlann,
and they made no stop but (were) tearing ocean till
they reached it. When they reached Lochlann they did
not know what they should do. Said the old man to
his sons—" Stop ye, and we will seek out the house of
the king's miller."

When they went into the house of the king's
miller, the man asked them to stop there for the night.
Conall told the miller that his own children and the
children of the king had fallen out, and that his
children had killed the king's son, and there was
nothing that would please the king but that he should
get the brown horse of the king of Lochlann. " If thou
wilt do me a kindness, and wilt put me in a way to get
him, for certain I will pay thee for it." " The thing
is silly that thou art come to seek," said the miller ;
" for the king has laid his mind on him so greatly that
thou wilt not get him in any way unless thou steal
him ; but if thou thyself canst make out a way, I will
hide thy secret." " This, I am thinking," said Conall,
" since thou art working every day for the king, that
thou and thy gillies should put myself and my sons
into five sacks of bran." " The plan that came into
thy head is not bad," said the miller. The miller
spoke to his gillies, and he said to them to do this,
and they put them in five sacks. The king's gillies
came to seek the bran, and they took the five sacks
with them, and they emptied them before the horses.
The servants locked the door, and they went away.

When they rose to lay hand on the brown horse,

said Conall, " You shall not do that. It is hard to get
out of this ; let us make for ourselves five hiding holes,
so that if they perceive us we may go in hiding."
They made the holes, then they laid hands on the
horse. The horse was pretty well unbroken, and he
set to making a terrible noise through the stable.
The king perceived him. He heard the noise. " It
must be that that was my brown horse," said he to his
gillies ; " try what is wrong with him."

The servants went out, and when Conall and his
sons perceived them coming they went into the hiding
holes. The servants looked amongst the horses, and
they did not find anything wrong ; and they returned
and they told this to the king, and the king said to
them that if nothing was wrong that they should go to
their places of rest. When the gillies had time to be
gone, Conall and his sons laid the next hand on the
horse. If the noise was great that he made before, the
noise he made now was seven times greater. The king
sent a message for his gillies again, and said for certain
there was something troubling the brown horse. " Go
and look well about him." The servants went out, and
they went to their hiding holes. The servants rum-
maged well, and did not find a thing. They returned
and they told this. " That is marvellous for me," said
the king : " go you to lie down again, and if I perceive it again I will go out myself." When Conall
and his sons perceived that the gillies were gone, they
laid hands again on the horse, and one of them caught
him, and if the noise that the horse made on the two
former times was great, he made more this time.

" Be this from me," said the king ; " it must be
that some one is troubling my brown horse." He
sounded the bell hastily, and when his waiting man
came to him, he said to him to set the stable gillies on

foot that something was wrong with the horse. The
gillies came, and the king went with them. When
Conall and his sons perceived the following coming
they went to the hiding holes. The king was a wary
man, and he saw where the horses were making a
noise. " Be clever," said the king, " there are men
within the stable, and let us get them somehow."
The king followed the tracks of the men, and he found
them. Every man was acquainted with Conall, for he
was a valued tenant by the king of Eirinn, and when
the king brought them up out of the holes he said,
" Oh, Conall, art thou here?" " I am, O king, without question, and necessity made me come. I am
under thy pardon, and under thine honour, and under
thy grace." He told how it happened to him, and
that he had to get the brown horse for the king of
Eirinn, or that his son was to be put to death. " I
knew that I should not get him by asking, and I was
going to steal him." " Yes, Conall, it is well enough,
but come in," said the king. He desired his look-out
men to set a watch on the sons of Conall, and to give
them meat. And a double watch was set that night
on the sons of Conall. "Now, O Conall," said the
king, " wert thou ever in a harder place than to be
seeing thy lot of sons hanged to-morrow? But thou
didst set it to my goodness and to my grace, and that
it was necessity brought it on thee, and I must not
hang thee. Tell me any case in which thou wert as
hard as this, and if thou tellest that, thou shalt get the
soul of thy youngest son with thee." " I will tell a
case as hard in which I was," said Conall.

" I was a young lad, and my father had much
land, and he had parks of year-old cows, and one of
them had just calved, and my father told me to
bring her home. I took with me a laddie, and we

found the cow, and we took her with us. There fell a
shower of snow. We went in to herd's bothy, and we
took the cow and the calf in with us, and we were
letting the shower (pass) from us. What came in but
one cat and ten, and one great one-eyed fox-coloured
cat as head bard* over them. When they came in, in
very deed I myself had no liking for their company.
'Strike up with you,' said the head bard, 'why should
we be still? and sing a cronan to Conall Cra-Bhui.'
I was amazed that my name was known to the cats
themselves. When they had sung the cronan, said the
head bard, 'Now, O Conall, pay the reward of the
cronan that the cats have sung to thee.' 'Well, then,'
said I myself, 'I have no reward whatsoever for you,
unless you should go down and take that calf.' No
sooner said I the word than the two cats and ten
went down to attack the calf, and, in very deed, he
did not last them long. 'Play up with you, why
should you be silent? Make a cronan to Conall
Cra-Bhui,' said the head bard. Certainly I had no
liking at all for the cronan, but up came the one cat
and ten, and if they did not sing me a cronan then and
there! 'Pay them now their reward,' said the great
fox-coloured cat. 'I am tired myself of yourselves
and your rewards,' said I. 'I have no reward for you
unless you take that cow down there.' They betook
themselves to the cow, and indeed she did not stand
them out for long.

" ' Why will you be silent? Go up and sing a cronan to Conall Cra-Bhui,' said the head bard. And
surely, oh, king, I had no care for them or for their cronan, for I began to see that they were not good comrades. When they had sung me the cronan they betook
themselves down where the head bard was. ' Pay

* Or commander-in-chief.

now their reward,' said the head bard; and for sure, oh, king, I had no reward for them; and I said to them, 'I have no reward for you, unless you will take that laddie with you and make use of him.' When the boy heard this he took himself out, and the cats after him. And surely, oh, king, there was "striongan" and catterwauling between them. When they took themselves out, I took out at a turf window that was at the back of the house. I took myself off as hard as I might into the wood. I was swift enough and strong at that time; and when I felt the rustling 'toirm' of the cats after me I climbed into as high a tree as I saw in the place, and (one) that was close in the top; and I hid myself as well as I might. The cats began to search for me through the wood, and they were not finding me; and when they were tired, each one said to the other that they would turn back. 'But,' said the one-eyed fox-coloured cat that was commander-in-chief over them, 'you saw him not with your two eyes, and though I have but one eye, there's the rascal up in the top of the tree.' When he had said that, one of them went up in the tree, and as he was coming where I was, I drew a weapon that I had and I killed him. 'Be this from me!' said the one-eyed one—'I must not be losing my company thus; gather round the root of the tree and dig about it, and let down that extortioner to earth.' On this they gathered about her (the tree), and they dug about her root, and the first branching root that they cut, she gave a shiver to fall, and I myself gave a shout, and it was not to be wondered at. There was in the neighbourhood of the wood a priest, and he had ten men with him delving, and he said, 'There is a shout of extremity and I must not be without replying to it.' And the wisest of the men said, 'Let it alone till we hear it again.' The cats

began, and they began wildly, and they broke the
next root; and I myself gave the next shout, and in
very deed it was not weak.   'Certainly,' said the
priest, 'it is a man in extremity—let us move.' They
were setting themselves in order for moving. And the
cats arose on the tree, and they broke the third root,
and the tree fell on her elbow. I gave the third shout.
The stalwart men hasted, and when they saw how the
cats served the tree, they began at them with the spades ;
and they themselves and the cats began at each other,
till they were killed altogether—the men and the cats.
And surely, oh king, I did not move till I saw the last
one of them falling. I came home. And there's for
thee the hardest case in which I ever was ; and it
seems to me that tearing by the cats were harder than
hanging to-morrow by the king of Lochlann.

"Od! Conall," said the king, "thou art full of
words. Thou hast freed the soul of thy son with thy
tale ; and if thou tellest me a harder case than thy
three sons to be hanged to-morrow, thou wilt get thy
second youngest son with thee, and then thou wilt
have two sons." " Well then," said Conall, " on condition that thou dost that, I was in a harder case than
to be in thy power in prison to-night." " Let's hear,"
said the king.—" I was there," said Conall, " as a young
lad, and I went out hunting, and my father's land
was beside the sea, and it was rough with rocks, caves,
and geos.* When I was going on the top of the shore,
I saw as if there were a smoke coming up between two
rocks, and I began to look what might be the meaning
of the smoke coming up there. When I was looking,
what should I do but fall ; and the place was so full
of manure, that neither bone nor skin was broken. I
knew not how I should get out of this. I was not

* Rifts or chasms, where the sea enters.

looking before me, but I was looking over head the
way I came—and the day will never come that I could
get up there.   It was terrible for me to be there till I
should die.   I heard a great clattering 'tuarncileis'
coming, and what was there but a great giant and two
dozen of goats with him, and a buck at their head.
And when the giant had tied the goats, he came up
and he said to me, ' Hao O ! Conall, it's long since my
knife is rusting in my pouch waiting for thy tender
flesh.'   ' Och ! ' said I, ' it's not much thou wilt be
bettered by me, though thou should'st tear me asunder ;
I will make but one meal for thee.   But I see that
thou art one-eyed.   I am a good leech, and I will give
thee the sight of the other eye.'   The giant went and
he drew the great caldron on the site of the fire.   I myself was telling him how he should heat the water, so
that I should give its sight to the other eye.   I got
heather and I made a rubber of it, and I set him upright
in the caldron.   I began at the eye that was well, pretending to him that I would give its sight to the other
one, till I left them as bad as each other ; and surely
it was easier to spoil the one that was well than to
give sight to the other.

"When he 'saw' that he could not see a glimpse,
and when I myself said to him that I would get out in
spite of him, he gave that spring out of the water, and
he stood in the mouth of the cave, and he said that he
would have revenge for the sight of his eye.   I had
but to stay there crouched the length of the night,
holding in my breath in such a way that he might not
feel where I was.

"When he felt the birds calling in the morning, and
knew that the day was, he said—' Art thou sleeping ?
Awake and let out my lot of goats.'   I killed the buck.
He cried, ' I will not believe that thou art not killing

my buck.' 'I am not,' said I, 'but the ropes are so tight that I take long to loose them.' I let out one of the goats, and he was caressing her, and he said to her, 'There thou art thou shaggy, hairy white goat, and thou seest me, but I see thee not.' I was letting them out by the way of one and one, as I flayed the buck, and before the last one was out I had him flayed *bag wise*. Then I went and I put my legs in place of his legs, and my hands in place of his fore legs, and my head in place of his head, and the horns on top of my head, so that the brute might think that it was the buck. I went out. When I was going out the giant laid his hand on me, and he said, 'There thou art thou pretty buck; thou seest me, but I see thee not.' When I myself got out, and I saw the world about me, surely, oh, king! joy was on me. When I was out and had shaken the skin off me, I said to the brute, 'I am out now in spite of thee.' 'Aha!' said he, 'hast thou done this to me. Since thou wert so stalwart that thou hast got out, I will give thee a ring that I have here, and keep the ring, and it will do thee good.' 'I will not take the ring from thee,' said I, 'but throw it, and I will take it with me.' He threw the ring on the flat ground, I went myself and I lifted the ring, and I put it on my finger. When he said me then. 'Is the ring fitting thee?' I said to him, 'It is.' He said, 'Where art thou ring?' And the ring said, 'I am here.' The brute went and he betook himself towards where the ring was speaking, and now I saw that I was in a harder case than ever I was. I drew a dirk. I cut the finger off from me, and I threw it from me as far as I could out on the loch, and there was a great depth in the place. He shouted, 'Where art thou, ring?' And the ring said, 'I am here,' though it was on the ground of ocean. He gave a spring after the ring, and out he went in the sea.

And I was as pleased here when I saw him drowning, as though thou shouldst let my own life and the life of my two sons with me, and not lay any more trouble on me.

"When the giant was drowned I went in, and I took with me all he had of gold and silver, and I went home, and surely great joy was on my people when I arrived. And as a sign for thee, look thou, the finger is off me."

"Yes, indeed, Conall, thou art wordy and wise," said the king. "I see thy finger is off. Thou hast freed thy two sons, but tell me a case in which thou ever wert that is harder than to be looking on thy two sons being hanged to-morrow, and thou wilt get the soul of thy second eldest son with thee."

"Then went my father," said Conall, "and he got me a wife, and I was married. I went to hunt. I was going beside the sea, and I saw an island over in the midst of the loch, and I came there where a boat was with a rope before her and a rope behind her, and many precious things within her. I looked myself on the boat to see how I might get part of them. I put in the one foot, and the other foot was on the ground, and when I raised my head what was it but the boat over in the middle of the loch, and she never stopped till she reached the island. When I went out of the boat the boat returned where she was before. I did not know now what I should do. The place was without meat or clothing, without the appearance of a house on it. I raised out on the top of a hill. I came to a glen ; I saw in it, at the bottom of a chasm, a woman who had got a child, and the child was naked on her knee, and a knife in her hand. She would attempt to put the knife in the throat of the babe, and the babe would begin to laugh in her face, and she would begin to cry, and she would throw the knife behind her. I thought to myself that I was near my foe and far from my friends, and I called to the woman, 'What art thou doing here?' And she said to me, 'What brought thee here?' I told her myself word upon word how I came. 'Well then,' said she, 'it was so I came also.' She showed me to the place where I should come in where she was. I went in, and I said to her, 'What was in fault that thou wert putting the knife on the neck of the child.' 'It is that he must be cooked for the giant who is here, or else no more of my world will be before me.' I went up steps of stairs, and I saw a chamber full of stripped corpses. I took a lump out of the corpse that was whitest, and I tied a string to the child's foot, and a string to the lump, and I put the lump in his mouth, and when it went in his throat he would give a stretch to his leg, and he would take it out of his throat, but with the length of the thread he could not take it out of his mouth. I cast the child into a basket of down, and I asked her to cook the corpse for the giant in place of the child. 'How can I do that?' said she, 'when he has count of the corpses.' 'Do thou as I ask thee, and I will strip myself, and I will go amongst the corpses, and then he will have the same count,' said I. She did as I asked her. We put the corpse in the great caldron, but we could not put on the lid. When he was coming home I stripped myself, and I went amongst the corpses. He came home, and she served up the corpse on a great platter, and when he ate it he was complaining that he found it too tough for a child.

" 'I did as thou asked me,' said she. 'Thou hadst count of the corpses thyself, and go up now and count them.' He counted them and he had them. 'I see one of a white body there,' said he. I will lie

I

down a while and I will have him when I wake.
When he rose he went up and gripped me, and I
never was in such a case as when he was hauling me
down the stair with my head after me. He threw me
into the caldron, and he lifted the lid and he put the lid
into the caldron. And now I was sure I would scald
before I could get out of that. As fortune favoured
me, the brute slept beside the caldron. There I was
scalded by the bottom of the caldron. When she perceived that he was asleep, she set her mouth quietly to
the hole that was in the lid, and she said to me ' was I
alive.' I said I was. I put up my head, and the brute's
forefinger was so large, that my head went through easily.
Everything was coming easily with me till I began to
bring up my hips. I left the skin of my hips about
the mouth of the hole, and I came out. When I got
out of the caldron I knew not what to do ; and she
said to me that there was no weapon that would kill
him but his own weapon. I began to draw his spear,
and every breath that he would draw I would think I
would be down his throat, and when his breath came
out I was back again just as far. But with every ill
that befell me I got the spear loosed from him. Then
I was as one under a bundle of straw in a great wind,
for I could not manage the spear. And it was fearful to look on the brute, who had but one eye
in the midst of his face ; and it was not agreeable
for the like of me to attack him. I drew the dart as
best I could, and I set it in his eye. When he felt
this he gave his head a lift, and he struck the other end
of the dart on the top of the cave, and it went through
to the back of his head. And he fell cold dead where
he was ; and thou mayest be sure, oh king, that joy
was on me. I myself and the woman went out on
clear ground, and we passed the night there. I went

and got the boat with which I came, and she was no way lightened, and took the woman and the child over on dry land ; and I returned home."

The king's mother was putting on a fire at this time, and listening to Conall telling the tale about the child. "Is it thou," said she, "that wert there?" "Well then," said he, "'twas I." "Och! och!" said she, "'twas I that was there, and the king is the child whose life thou didst save ; and it is to thee that life thanks might be given." Then they took great joy.

The king said "Oh Conall, thou camest through great hardships. And now the brown horse is thine, and his sack full of the most precious things that are in my treasury."

They lay down that night, and if it was early that Conall rose, it was earlier than that that the queen was on foot making ready. He got the brown horse and his sack full of gold and silver and stones of great price, and then Conall and his four sons went away, and they returned home to the Erin realm of gladness. He left the gold and silver in the house, and he went with the horse to the king. They were good friends evermore. He returned home to his wife, and they set in order a feast ; and that was the feast, oh son and brother!

This story, told by a blind man, is a good instance of the way in which a popular tale adapts itself to the mind of everybody. The blinding of the giant and his subsequent address to his pet goat—"There thou art, thou shaggy, hairy, white goat : thou see'st me, but I see thee not"—comes from the heart of the narrator. It is the ornament which his mind hangs on the frame of the story.

"James Wilson learnt it from John MacLachlan, an old man at Kilsleven, upwards of forty years ago. The old man would be about eighty years of age at the time."

CRA BHUIDHE is probably a corruption of some proper name CRAG is a paw, a palm. BUIDHE, yellow.

CONALL CRA-BHUIDHE.

BHA Conall crà-bhuidhe na thuathanach foghainnteach ann an Eirinn. Bha ceathrar mhac aige. Bha anns an am sin rìgh air a h-uile còigeamh do dh' Eirinn. Thuit e mach do chlann an rìgh a bha fagus do Chonall gun deach iad féin agus clann Chonaill thar a' chéile. Fhuair clann Chonaill làmh an uachdar, 's mharbh iad mac mòr an rìgh. Chuir an rìgh fios air Conall 's thuirt e ris. "A Chonaill dé thug do d' mhicsa dol a leum air mo mhicsa gus an do mharbhadh mo mhac mòr le d' chloinnsa? Ach tha mi faiciun ged a leanuinn le dioghaltas thu nach mòr is f heàirde mi e, agus cuiridh mi nis ma d' choinneamh ni, agus ma ni thu e cha lean mi le dioghaltas thu. Ma gheobh thu féin agus do mhic dòmhsa each donn rìgh Lochlann gheobh thu anamanna do mhac." "Carson," arsa Conall, "nach déanainnsa toil an rìgh ged nach biodh anamanna mo mhac air a sgàth idir. 'S cruaidh an gnothach a tha thu 'g iarraidh orm, ach caillidh mi mo bheatha féin agus beatha mo mhac air neo ni mi toil an rìgh. An déigh nam briathran so dh' fhàg Conall an rìgh 's chaidh e dhachaidh. Nur a thàinig e dachaidh bha e fo mhòran trioblaid agus duibhthiamhas. Nur a chaidh e laidhe dh' innis e d'a bhean an ni chuir an rìgh ma choinneamh. Ghabh a' bhean mòran duilichinn gum b' éigin da dealachadh rìthe féin, 's gun fhios aice 'm faiceadh i tuillidh e." "A Chonaill," ars' ise, "carson nach do leig thu leis an rìgh a thoil féin a dhèanadh ri d' mhic, seach a bhi folbh a nis 's gun fhios'am am faic mi tuillidh thu."

Nur a dh' éiridh iad an la' r na mhàireach chuir e e féin 's a cheithir mic an òrdugh, 's ghabh iad an turas ma thuaiream Loch-lann, 's cha d' rinncadh stad leo ach a reubadh cuain gus an d' ràinig iad e. Nur a ràinig iad Lochlann cha robh fios aca de 'dhèanadh iad. Arsa 'n seann duine ra mhic, " Stadadh sibhse agus iarraidh sinn a mach tigh muilleir an rìgh." Nur a chaidh iad a stigh do thigh muilleir an rìgh chuir an duine iad a dh' fhantuinn anns an oiubche. Dh' innis Conall do 'n mhuilleir gun deach a chlann féin 's clann an rìgh thar a cheile 's gun do mharbh a chlannsan mac an rìgh 's nach robh ni sam bith a thoileachadh an rìgh ach e 'dh' fhaotainn each donn rìgh Lochlann. " Ma ni thusa rùn orm 's gun cuir thu air dòigh mi gum faigh mi e, gu diongalta pàighidh mi air a shon thu." Orsa Conall, " 'S amaideach an ni a thàinig thu 'dh' iarraidh," ars' am muillear, " chionn tha 'n rìgh air leagail inntinn air cho mòr 's nach fhaigh thu air dòigh sam bith e

mar an goid thu e; ach ma ni thu féin dòigh a mach ceilidh mise rùn
ort." "'S e tha mi smaointeachadh, ars' Conall o'n a tha thu 'g obair
h-uile latha do 'n rìgh, gun cuireadh thu féin 's do ghillean mi féin
's mo mhic ann an còig saic pruinn." "Cha dona 'n seòl a thàinig a
'd' cheann," orsa 'm muillear.

Bhruidhinn am muillear r'a ghillean, 's thuirt e riu so a dheànadh,
's chuir iad ann an còig saic iad. Thàinig gillean an rìgh a dh'
iarraidh a phruinn, 's thug iad leo na còig saic, 's dhoirt iad air
beulthaobh nan each iad. Ghlais na seirbheisich an dorusd, 's dh'
fholbh iad. Nur a dh' eirich iad a thoirt làmh air an each dhonn,
orsa Conall, "Cha dèan sibh sin, tha e doirbh faotainn as a' so;
deànamaid dhuinn féin còig tuill fhalaich, air alt 's ma mhòthachas
iad duinn gun d' theid sinn am falach." Rinn iad na tuill Thug
iad an sin làmh air an each. Bha 'n t-each gu math uaibhreach, 's
chaidh e gu stararaich fhuathasach feadh an stàbuill. Mhothaich
an rìgh dha; chual e 'n stararaich. "'S éigin gur h-e siod an
t-each donn agamsa," urs' e ra ghillean, "feuchaibh de tha ceàrr air."
Chaidh na seirbheisich a mach, 's nur a mhothaich Conall 's a mhic
daibh a tighinn chaidh iad 's na tuill fhalaich. Dh' amhairc na
seirbheisich feadh nan each, 's cha d' fhuair iad ni sam bith ceàrr.
Thill iad 's dh' innis iad so do 'n rìgh, 's thuirt an rìgh riu, mar an
robh stugh ceàrr iad a dhol d' an àite taimh. Nur a bha ùine aig
na gillean a bhith air folbh thug Conall 's a mhic an ath làmh air an
each. Ma bu mhòr an stararaich a rinn e roimhe, bu sheachd motha
an stararaich a rinn e nis. Chuir an rìgh fios air a ghillean a rìs 's
thuirt e gu cinnteach gun robh rudaigin a cur dragh air an each
dhonn. "Folbhaibh agus amhaircibh gu math timchioll air," ors'
esan. Chaidh na seirbheisich a mach, 's chaidh iadsan do na tuill
fhalaich. Rùraich na seirbheisich gu math, 's cha d' fhuair iad ni.
Thill iad 's dh' innis iad so. "Tha sin iongantach leamsa," ars' an
rìgh. "Theirigeadh sibse 'laidhe rithisd, 's ma mhòthachas mis' a
rithisd e théid mi féin a mach." Nur a mhothaich Conall 's a mhic
gun robh na gillean air folbh thug iad làmh a rithisd air an each, 's
rug fear ac' air, 's ma bu mhòr an stararaich a rinn an t-each an da
shiubhal roimhid, rinn e barrachd air an t-siubhal so. "Bhuam so,"
urs' an rìgh; "'s éigin gu 'bheil nitheigin a' cur dragh air an each
dhonn agamsa." Dh' fhuaim e 'n clag gu deifireach, 's nur a thàinig
a theachdaire da 'ionnsuidh thuirt e ris, gillean an stàbuill a chur air
ghluasad, gun robh rudaigin ceàrr air an each. Thàinig na gillean,
's dh' fholbh an rìgh leo. Nur a mhothaich Conall 's a mhic an tòir
a' tighinn chaidh iad do na tuill fhalaich. Bha 'n rìgh 'na dhuine
furachail, 's chunnaic e far an robh na bha toirt air na h-eich a bhi

a' dèanadh stararaich. " Bithibh tapaidh," urs' an rìgh, " Tha daoine a stigh 's an stàbull, 's faigheamaid iad air altaigin." Lean an rìgh faileachd nan daoine, 's fhuair e iad. Bha h-uile duine eòlach air Conall; chionn bha e 'na thuathanach measail aig rìgh Eireann. 'S nur a thug an rìgh nìos as na tuill iad thuirt e " U! Chonaill a' bheil thu 'n so!" " Tha rìgh mi 'n so gun chcist, 's thug an eigin orm tighinn ann tha mi fo d' mhathas agus fo d' onair agus fo d' ghras." Dh' innis e mar a thachair da, 's gun robh aige 'n t-each donn r'a fhaotainn do rìgh Eireann no 'mhac a bhi air a chur gu bàs. " Bha fhios'am nach fhaighinn e le iarraidh, 's bha mi 'dol g' a ghoid." " Seadh a Chonaill tha e glé mhath ach thig a stigh," ars an rìgh. Dh' iarr e air a luchd coimhead fàire chur air mic Chonaill, 's biadh a thoirt dhaibh; 's chuireadh faire dhùbailt' an oidhche sin air mic Chonaill. " Nis a Chonaill," ars' an rìgh, " An robh thu 'n àite riabh na bu chruaidhe na 'bhith 'faicinn do chuid mac 'gan crochadh am màireach; ach chuir thusa gum' mhathas agus gum' ghras e, 's gur e 'n èigin a thug ort e, 's cha 'n fhaod mi thusa a chrochadh. Innis domh càs 'sam bith 'san robh thu cho cruaidh ris a' so, 's ma dh' innseas thu sin gheobh thu anam do mhic is òige leat." " Innsidh mi càs cho cruaidh anns' an robh mi," orsa Conall.

" Bha mi ann am ghill' òg, 's bha mòran fearainn aig m' athair, 's bha pàircean bhiorach aige, 's bha te dhiu an deigh breith. Thuirt mo, mhathair rium a toirt dhachaidh. Dh' fholbh mi agus thug mi leam balachan, agus fhuair sinn a' bhò, 's thug sinn leinn i. Shìl fras shneachda, chaidh sinn a stigh do bhothag àiridh, 's thug sinn a bhò 's an laogh a stigh leinn, 's bha sinn a' leigeil dhinn na froise; dè' thàinig a stigh ach aona chat deug 's cat mor ruagh cam na cheannabhard orra. Nur a thàinig iad a stigh, gu dearbh, cha robh tlachd sam bith agam féin d'an cuideachd. " Suas sibh," ursa 'n ceannabhard, "carson a bhiodh sibh 'nar tàmh, agus seinnibh crònan do Chonall Crà-bhuidhe." Bha iongantas orm gum' b' aithne do na cait féin m' ainm. Nur a sheinn iad an crònan. urs' an ceannabhard. " Nis a Chonaill pàigh duais a' chrònain a sheinn na cait duit." "Mata, ursa mi fein "cha 'n 'eil duais agamsa dhuibh mar an d' théid sibh sios agus an laogh sin a ghabhail." Cha bu luaithe thuirt mi 'm facal na ghabh an da chat deug a sìos an dàil an laoigh, 's gu dearbh cha do sheas e fada dhaibh. " Suas sibh, carson a bhiodh sibh 'nar tosd seinnibh crònan do Chonall Crà-bhuidhe," ars an ceannard. Gu diongalta cha robh tlachd 'sam bith agam féin d'a'n crònan, ach a nios a ghabh an t-aon chat deug, 's mar an do sheinn iad dòmhsa crònan an sin agus an sin.

" Paigh a nis 'nan duais iad," ars an cat mor ruadh. Tha mi féin

sgith dhibh féin 's de 'r duais, arsa mise, cha 'n 'eil duais agamsa
dhuibh mar an gabh sibh am mart sin shios. Thug iad thun a
mhairt, 's gu dearbh cha do sheas i fada dhaibh. "Car-on a bhios
sibh 'nur tosd theirigibh suas agus seinnibh crònan do Chonall Cra-
bhuidhe," ars an ceannard. Gu cinnteach a rìgh cha robh amhuil
agam dhaibh féin no d' an crònan, chionn bha mi faicinn nach bu
chompanaich mhath iad. Nur a sheinn iad dòmhsa 'n crònan thug
iad a sìos orra far an robh an ceannard. "Pàidh a nis an duais,"
urs' an ceannabhard, "'S gu cinnteach a rìgh cha robh duais agamsa
dhaibh, 's thuirt mi riu," bha 'n 'eil duais agamsa dhuibh mar an
d' thoir sibh am balach sin leibh, 's feum a dhèanadh dheth. Nur
a chual am balach so thug e 'mach air, 's thug na cait as a dheigh ; 's
gu cinnteach a rìgh bha striongan eatorra. Nur a chaidh iad a
mach ghabh mise mach air uinneag sgroth a bha air taobh cùil an
tighe. Thug mi as cho cruaidh 's a dh' fhaodainn a stigh do 'n
choille. Bha mi gle luath, làidir 'san am sin. Agus nur a mhothaich
mi toirm nan cat a' m' dhéigh streap mi ann an craoibh cho àrd 's a
chunnaic mi 'san àite agus a bha dùmhail anns a bhàrr, 's dh'
fhalaich mi mi féin cho math 's a dh' fhaodainn. Thòisich na cait
air m'iarraidh feadh na coille, 's cha robh iad 'gam' fhaotainn, agus
nur a bha iad sgìth thuirt gach fear ra chéile gun tilleadh iad, ach
thuirt am cat cam, ruagh a bha 'na cheannabhard orra." Cha 'n
fhaca sibhs' e le 'ur da shùil, 's gun agams' ach an aon sùil. Siod an
slaightire shuas am bàrr na craoibhe ! Nur a thuirt e sin chaidh
fear dhiu suas 'sa chraoibh, 's nur a bha e tigh'n far an robh mi
tharruinn mi arm a bh' agam, agus mharbh mi e. "Bhuam so." urs'
am fear cam, "cha 'n fhaod mise 'bhi call mo chuideachd mur so.
Cruinnichibh ma bhun na craoibhe, agus cladhachaibh timchioll
urra, agus leagaibh au nuas an rògaire gu talamh." Chruinnich
iad an so timchioll urra, agus chladhaich iad ma 'bun, agus a chiad
fhreumh a gheàrr iad thug i uileann urra gu tuiteam, 's thug mi
féin glaodh asam 's cha b-ioghnadh e. Bha ann an iomall na coille
sagairt agus deich daoin' aig a ruamhar, 's thuirt e, "Tha 'n siod
glaodh sàraichte cha n 'fhaod mise gun a fhreagairt," Thuirt fear a
bu ghlice de na daoine. "Leigeamaid dà gus an cluinn sin a rithisd
e." Thòisich na cait's thòisich iad gu fiadhaich, 's bhrisd iad an ath
fhreumh, 's thug mi féin an ath ghlaodh asam, 's gu dearbh cha
robh e fann. "Gu cinnteach," ors' an sagairt, "'s duine 'na éigin a
th'ann gluaisemaid." Bha iad a' cuir an òrdugh gu gluasad, 's dh'
éiridh na cait air a chraoibh gus an do bhrisd iad an treas freumhach,
's thuit a chraobh air a h-uileann. Thug mi 'n treas glaodh asam.
Dheifirich na daoine foghainteach, 's nur a chunnaic iad an dìol a

bh' aig na cait air a chraoibh thòisich iad urra leis na spàdan, 's thòisich iad féin 's na cait air a cheile, gus an do mharbhadh gu léir, iad na daoin' agus na cait ; agus gu cinnteach a rìgh cha do charaich mise gus am faca mi 'n t-aon ma dheireadh a' tuiteam diu. Thàinig mi dachaidh, agus sin agad an cas an cruaidhe 'n robh mise riabh, 's air leam gum bu chruaidhe 'bhith gam' leòbadh aig na cait na bhith 'gam' chrochadh aig rìgh Lochlann a màireach.

"Od a Chonaill,"ars an rìgh, " 's briatharach thu, shaor thu anam do mhic le d' naigheachd, agus ma dh' innseas thu dhomh càs is cruaidhe na do thri mic a bhi 'gan crochadh a màireach gheobh thu do dharna mac is òige leat 's bidh an sin da mhac agad." " Mata," orsa Conall, air chùmhnant gun dèan thu sin, bha mi 'n cas à bu chruaidhe na 'bhi' agadsa 'nochd am prìosan. "Cluinneam e," urs' an righ. Bha mi 'n siod," orsa Conall, " am ghill' òg 's chaidh mi mach a shealgair-eachd, 's bha crìoch m' athar taobh na fairge, 's bha i garbh le creagan, uamhachan, agus geothachan. Nur a bha mi folbh aig bràigh a' chladaich chunnaic mi mar gum biodh toit a' tighinn a nìos cadar da chreag, 's thug mi làmh air amharc de bu chiall do'n toit a bhi tighinn a nìos an siod. Nur a bha mi 'g amharc dé rinn mi ach tuiteam sìos, 's bha 'n t-àite cho làn do leasachadh 's nach do bhrisdeadh cnàimh na craicionn. Cha robh fios 'am dé mur a gheobhainn a mach as an so. Cha robh mi 'g amharc romham ach bha mi 'g amharc as mo chionn an rathad a thàinig mi, 's cha d' thig an lath' a gheobhainn suas an sin. Bha e uamhasach leam a bhi 'n sin gus am bàsachainn. Chuala mi tuairneileis mhòr a' tighinn, 's de bha 'n sin ach famhair mòr, 's da dhusan gobhar leis, agus boc air an ceann, 's nur a cheangail am famhair na gobhair thainig e nìos 's thuirt e rium." " Haobh a Chonaill 's fhada mo chorc a' meirgeadh ann a' m' phòca a feitheamh air t-fheòil mhaoth." " Oh," arsa mise, "Cha mhor is fheàird thu mise ged a reubas thu mi as a' chéile, cha dean mi ach aon trath dhuit; ach tha mi faiciun gu 'bheil thu air aon sùil, 's léigh math mise 's bheir mi sealladh na sùil eile dhuit. Dh' fholbh am famhair 's tharrainn e 'n brothadair mor air làrach a ghealbhain, 's bha mi féin aig ionnsach-adh dha démur a theòigheadh e 'n t-uisge, chum gun d' thugainn a sealladh do'n t-sùil eile. Fhuair mi fraoch, 's rinn mi rubair dheth 's chuir mi 'na sheasamh anns a' bhrothadair e. Thòisich mi air an t-sùil a bha gu math, a' cur mar fhiachaibh air gun d' thugainn a sealladh do 'n te eile gus an d' fhàg mi cho dona r'a chèil 'iad; agus gu cinnteach b' fhasa 'n te bha gu math a mhilleadh, na 'sealladh a thoirt do 'n te eile. Nur a chunnaic e nach bu leur dha leus, 's a thuirt mi féin ris gum faighinn a mach gun taing dha, thug e 'n

lcum sin as au uisge 's sheas e ann am beul na h-uamha, 's thuirt e
gum biodh dioghladh aig airson scalladh a shuil. Cha robh agam
ach fantainn ann am pilleag an sin fad na h-oidhche, 'cumail m' anail
a stigh air dhòigh 's nach mòthchadh e càit' an robh mi. Nur a
mhothaich e na h-eòin a' gairm anns a mhaidinn, 's a dh' aithnich e
gun robh an lath' ann, thuirt e 'bheil thu 'd' chadal, dùisg agus leig a
mach mo chuid ghobhar. Mharbh mi 'm boc. Ghlaoidh esan," "Cha
chreid mi nach 'eil thu marbhadh mo bhuic." "Cha n' eil," orsa
mise ach tha na ròpaichean cho teann 's gun d' thoir mi fad' air am
fuasgladh." Leig mi mach te de na gobhair, 's bha e ga crìodachadh,
's thuirt e rithe. "Tha thus' an sin a ghobhar bhàn, riobagach,
ròineach, 's chi thusa mise, ach cha 'n fhaic mis' thusa. Bha mi
'gan cuir a mach a lìon té 's te 's a feannadh a bhuic 's ma'n robh 'n
te ma dheireadh dhiu 'mach bha feannadh builg agam air. Dh'
fholbh mi 'n so 's chuir mi mo chasan ann an àite 'chasan, deiridh 's
mo làmhan an àite 'chasan toisich, agus mo cheann an àite 'chinn, 's na
h-adhaircean air mullach mo chinn, air alt 's gun saoileadh a bhéisd
gur e 'm boc a bh' ann. Chaidh mi 'mach. Nur a bha mi 'dol a
mach chuir am famhair a làmh orm, 's thuirt e." "Tha thus' an sin a
bhuic bhòidhich, chi thusa mise ach cha 'n fhaic mis' thusa." Nur a
fhuair mi féin a mach, 's a chunnaic mi 'n saoghal ma 'n cuairt orm,
gu cinnteach a righ bha boch orm. Nur a bha mi mach, 's a chrath
mi dhiom an craicionn, thuirt mi ris a bhéisd. Tha mi mach a nis
gun taing duit. "Aha," urs' esan, "an d' rinn thu so orm; O 'n a bha thu
cho foghainteach 's gun d' fhuair thu mach, bheir mi dhuit fàinn' a
th' agam an so, 's gléidh am fàinne 's ni e feum dhuit." Cha ghabh
mi 'm fàinne uait, arsa mise, ach tilg e, 's bheir mi leam e. Thilg e
'm fàinn' air a bhlàr, chaidh mi fein 's thog mi 'm fàinne, 's chuir mi air
mo mheur e. Nur a thuirt e rinm an sin a' bheil am fàinne freagairt
duit, thuirt mi ris, tha. Urs' esan, Ca' 'bheil thu fhàinne; 's thuirt
am fàinne. "Tha mi 'n so." Dh' fholbh a' bhèisd 's thug e ionnsuidh air far an robh 'm fainne bruidhinn, agus chunnaic mi 'n so gun
robh mi 'n càs na bu chruaidhe na bha mi riabh. Tharruinn mi
biodag; ghearr mi dhìom a' mheur; 's thilg mi uam i cho fhada 's a
b' urrainn mi mach air an loch, 's bha dòimhneachd mhòr 's an
àite. Ghlaoidh esan Càit' a' bheil thu fhainne; 's thuirt am fàinne,
"Tha mi 'n so," ged a bha e 'n grunnd a chuain. Thug e leum as
déigh an fhàinne, 's a mach a ghabh e anns an fhairge 's bha mi
cho toilichte an so nur a chunnaic mi e 'ga bhàthadh, 's ged a leigeadh
thusa mo bheatha fein agus beatha mo mhac leam gun mìr dragh a
chuir orm. Nur a bhàthadh am famhair chaidh mi stigh 's thug mi
leam na bh' aige 'dh' òr 's do dh' airgiod, 's chaidh mi dhachaidh, 's gu

cinnteach bha toilinntinn mhòr air mo mhuinntir nur a ràinig mi 's mar chomharra dhuit fhaic thu 'mheur dhìom.

"Seadh a Chonaill 's briathrach seòlt' thu, ars an righ, tha mi faicinn do mheur dhìot. Shaor thu do dha mhac a nis ach innis domh càs is cruaidhe an robh thu riabh na bhi'g amharc air do dha mhac 'gan crochadh a màireach 's gheobh thu anam do dharna mic is sine leat."

"Dh' f holbh an siod m' athair," arsa Conal, "agus f huair e dhomh bean, 's bha mi air mo phòsadh. Dh' fholbh mi shealg. Bha mi folbh taobh na fairge 's chunnaic mi eilean thall am meadhon an loch, agus thainig mi far an robh bàta an sin, 's ropa roimpe 's ropa na deigh, 's mòran do nitheau luachmhor an taobh a stigh dhi. Dh' amhairc mi féin air a bhàta feuch dèmur a gheobhainn pàirt diu. Chuir mi stigh an darna cas 's bha 'chas eile air a ghrunnd, 's nur a thog mi mo cheann de ach a bha 'm bàta nunn am meadhon an loch, 's cha do stad i gus an d' ràinig i 'n t-eilean. Nur a chaidh mi mach as a bhàta thill am bàta far an robh i roimhid. Cha robh fiosam an so de' dhèanainn. Bha 'n t-àite gun bhiadh, gun aodach, gun choltas tighe air. Thog mi mach àir mullach cnoic. Thàinig mi gu gleann. Chunnaic mi ann an grunnd glomhais bean agus leanabh aice, 's an leanabh rùisgt' air a gluinean, agus sgian aice 'na làimh. Bheireadh i làmh air an sgian a chuir air muineal an lèinibh, 's thòiseachadh an leanabh air gàireachdaich na h-aodann, 's thòiseachadh ise air caoineadh, 's thilgeadh i 'n sgian air a h-ais. Smaointich mi féin gun robh mi fagus do m' naimhdean 's fad o m' chairdean, 's ghlaoidh mi ris a bhoireannach. "De' tha thu 'deanadh an so?" 'S thuirt i rium, "De thug thus' an so?" Dh' innis mi féin di facal air an f hacal mar a thàinig mi. "Mata," ors' ise, "'s ann mar sin a thàinig mise cuid-eachd." Sheòl i mi gus an àite 'n d' thiginn a stigh far an robh i. Chaidh mi stigh, 's thuirt mi rithe, De bu choireach thu bhi' cur na sgian air muineal a phàisde. "Tha gu 'feum mi e' bhi bruich airson an f hamhair a tha 'n so, air no cha bhi tuillidh do m' shaoghal romh-am." Chaidh mi suas ceumanna stàighreach, 's chunnaic mi seòmar làn do chuirp rùisgte. Thug mi plaìbean as a chorp a bu ghile, agus cheangail mi sreang ri cas a phaìsde 's sreang ris a phlaibean, 's chuir mi 'm plaibean 'na bheul, 's nur a bhiodh e' dol 'na mhuineal bheireadh e sìneadh air a chois, 's bheireadh e as a mhuineal, ach leis an fhad a bha 's an t-smàthainn cha b-urrainn e thoirt as a bheul. Thilg mi 'm pàisd' ann am baraille clòimhe, 's dh' iarr mi urra 'n corp a bhruich do 'n f hamhair an àite' phàisde. "Demur is urrainn mi sin a a dheanadh," ars' ise, 's gu bheil cunndas aig air na cuirp. Dèan thusa mar a tha mise 'g iarraidh ort, 's rùisgidh mise mi féin, 's theid mi' measg nan corp, 's bidh an cunndas aig an sin, ursa mise. Rinn i mar a dh' iarr mi urra. Chuir sin an corp anns a bhrothadair mhòr, ach chu h-urrainn duinn am brod a chur air. Nur a bha esan a tigh'n dachaidh rìusg mise mi fein 's chaidh mi measg nan corp. Thàinig esan dachaidh, 's chuir ise 'n corp air mias mhòr, 's nur a dh' ith e e bha e a' gearau gun robh e tuillidh is righinn leis do phàisde." " Rinn mise mar a dh' iarr thu," urs' ise, " Bha cunndas agad féin air na cuirp, 's theirig suas a nis agus cunnd iad." Chunnd e iad 's bha iad aige. " Tha mi 'faicinn fear corp geal an siod," urs' esan " 's théid mi 'laidhe treis, 's bidh e agam nur a dhùisgeas mi. Nur a dh' éiridh e chaidh e suas 's rug e orm, 's cha robh mi na leithid do chàs riamh, 's nur a bha e 'gam shlaodhadh sios an an staighir 's mo cheann as mo dhéigh. Thilg e anns a' choire mi. Thog e 'm brod, 's chuir e 'm brod anns a choire. Bha mi 'n so cinnteach gum bithinn sgàlte ma 'm faighinn as an siod. Mar bhuaidh fhortain dòmhsa chaidil a bhéisd taobh a choire. Bha mi 'n sin 'gam sgàladh le màs a' choire. Nur a mhothaich ise gun robh e 'na chadal chuir i 'beul gu réidh ris an toll a bha 'sa' bhrod, 's thuirt i rium an robh mi beò. Thuirt mi gun robh. Chuir mi suas mo cheann, 's bha corrag na beisde cho mòr 's gun deach mo cheann roimhe gu soirbh. Bha h-uile ni tigh 'n leam gu soirbh gus an do thòisich mi air toirt a nios mo chruachan. Dh' fhàg mi craicionn nan cruachan ma bheul an tuill, 's thàinig mi as. Nur a fhuair mi 'mach as a choire cha robh fhios 'am de' dhèanainn, 's thuirt ise rium nach robh arm sam bìth a mharbhadh e ach arm féin. Thòisich mi air tarruinn ua sleagh, 's a' h-uile tarruinn a bheireadh e air anail shaoilinn gum bithinn sìos 'na mhuineal, 's nur a chuireadh e 'mach anail bha mi cho fad a rithisd air m' ais. H-uile h-olc g' an d' fhuaireadh mi fhuair mi n t-sleagh fhuasgladh uaidh. Bha mi 'n sin mar gum bithinn fo ultach cònlaich ann an gaoith mhòr, 's nach h-urrainn mi 'n t-sleagh iomachar, 's b-oillteil a bhi 'g amharc air a bhèisd, 's gun ach aon sùil an clàr aodainn, 's cha b-aobhach do m' leithidsa dol 'na dhàil. Tharruinn mi 'n t-sleagh mar a b'fheàrr a b'urrainn mi, 's chuir mi 'na shùil i. Nur a mhothaich e so thug e togail air a cheann, 's bhuail e ceann eile na sleagh ri driom na h-uamha, 's chaidh i roimhe gu cùl a chinn, 's thuit e fuar, marbh far an robh e, 's gu cinnteach dhuitse a righ bha boch ormsa. Chaidh mi fein 's am boireannach a mach air fearann glan, 's chuir sin seachad an oidhche an sin. Dh' fholbh mi agus fhuair mi m bàta leis an d' thàinig mi, agus cha robh iodramanachd sam bith urra, 's thug mi 'bhean agus am pàisde nunn air talamh tioram, agus thill mi dhachaidh.

Bha mathair an rìgh a' cur air gealbhan san am, s a 'g éisdeachd

ri Conall aig innseadh an naigheachd ma 'n phàisde. " An tus'," urs'
ise, bha 'sin. " Mata, urs esan," 's mi. " Och! och!" ors' ise, "'s mise
'bha 'n sin, agus 's e 'n rìgh am pàisde d'an do shàbhail thu 'bheatha,
agus 's ann ort a dh' d'fhaodar buidheachas a bheatha thobhairt."
Ghabh iad an so toilinntinn mhòr. Urs' an rìgh, " A Chonaill
thàinig thu ro chàsan mòr, agus 's leat a nis an t-each donn, agus a
shachd do na nitheannan is luachmhoire 'th' ann a'm' òoumbas."
Chaidh iad a laidhe 'n oidhche, sin 's ma bu mhoch a dh' éiridh Conall
bu mhoiche na sin a bha bhanrigh air a cois a 'dheanadh deas.
Fhuair e an t-each donn, 's a shachd do dh' òr, 's do dh' airgiod, 's do
chlacha luachmhor, 's dh' fholbh an sin Conall 's a cheathrar mac, 's
thill iad dachaidh do rìoghachd aighearach Eirinn. Dh' fhàg e 'n
t-òr 's an t-airgiod aig an tigh, 's chaidh e leis an each thun an rìgh.
Chord a féin 's an rìgh, 's bha iad 'nan càirdean matha tuillidh.
Thill e dhachaidh thun a mhnatha s chuir iad an òrdugh cuìrm, 's bi
chuirm i a mhic 's a bhràthair.

VI.

THE TALE OF CONAL CROVI.

From Neill Gillies, fisherman, near Inverary.

THERE was a king over England once, and he had
three sons, and they went to France to get learning, and when they came back home they said to their
father that they would go to see what order was in the
kingdom since they went away; and that was the first
place to which they went, to the house of a man of the
king's tenants, by name Conal Crobhi.

Conal Crovi had every thing that was better than
another waiting for them; meat of each meat, and
draughts of each drink. When they were satisfied,
and the time came for them to lie down, the king's big
son said—

"This is the rule that we have since we came home
—The goodwife must wait on me, and the maid must
wait on my middle brother, and the guidman's
daughter on my young brother." But this did not
please Conal Crovi at all, and he said—"I won't
say much about the maid and the daughter, but I
am not willing to part from my wife, but I will go
out and ask themselves about this matter;" and out he
went, and he locked the door behind him, and he told
his gillie that the three best horses that were in the
stable were to be ready without delay; and he and
his wife went on one, his gillie and his daughter on

another, and his son and the maid on the third horse, and they went where the king was to tell the insult his set of sons had given them.

The king's watchful gillie was looking out whom he should see coming. He called out that he was seeing three double riders coming. Said the king, ha! hah! This is Conal Crovi coming, and he has my three sons under cess,* but if they are, I will not be. When Conal Crovi came the king would not give him a hearing. Then Conal Crovi said, when he got no answer, "I will make thy kingdom worse than it is," and he went away, and he began robbing and lifting spoil.

The king said that he would give any reward to any man that would make out the place where Conal Crovi was taking his dwelling.

The king's swift rider said, that if he could get a day and a year he would find out where he was. He took thus a day and a year seeking for him, but if he took it he saw no sight of Conal Crovi. On his way home he sat on a pretty yellow brow, and he saw a thin smoke in the midst of the tribute wood.

Conal Crovi had a watching gillie looking whom he should see coming. He went in and he said that he saw the likeness of the swift rider coming. "Ha, ha!" said Conal Crovi, "the poor man is sent away to exile as I went myself."

Conal Crovi had his hands spread waiting for him, and he got his choice of meat and drink, and warm water for his feet, and a soft bed for his limbs. He was but a short time lying when Conal Crovi cried, "Art thou asleep, swift rider?" "I am not," said he. At the end of a while again he cried, "Art thou asleep?" He said he was not. He cried again the third time, but there was no answer. Then Conal Crovi

* Cis, cess, tax, subjection.

cried, " On your soles ! all within, this is no crouching time. The following will be on us presently." The watch man of Conal Crovi was shouting that he was seeing the king's three sons coming, and a great company along with them. He had of arms but one black rusty sword. Conal Crovi began at them, and he did not leave a man alive there but the three king's sons, and he tied them and took them in, and he laid on them the binding of the three smalls, straitly and painfully, and he threw them into the peat corner, and he said to his wife to make meat speedily, that he was going to do a work whose like he never did before. " What is that, my man ?" said she. " Going to take the heads off the king's three sons." He brought up the big one and set his head on the block, and he raised the axe. " Don't, don't," said he, " and I will take thy part in right or unright for ever." Then he took the middle one, he set his head on the block and he raised the axe. " Don't, don't," said he, " and I will take with thee in right or unright for ever." Then he brought up the young one, and he did the very same to him. " Don't, don't," said he, " and I will take with thee in right or unright for ever. Then he went, himself and the king's three sons, where the king was.

The watching gillies of the king were looking out when they should see the company coming with the head of Conal Crovi. Then one called out that he was seeing the likeness of the king's three sons coming, and Conal Crovi before them.

" Ha, hah !" said the king, " Conal Crovi is coming, and he has my three sons under cess, but if they are I won't be." He would give no answer to Conal Crovi, but that he should be hanged on a gallows in the early morning of the morrow's day.

Now, the gallows was set up and Conal Crovi was

about to be hanged, but the king's big son cried, " I
will go in his place." The king's middle son cried, " I
will go in his place ;" and the king's young son cried,
" I will go in his place." Then the king took con-
tempt for his set of sons. Then said Conal Crovi,
" We will make a big ship, and we will go steal the
three black whitefaced stallions that the king of Eirinn
has, and we will make the kingdom of Sasunn as rich
as it ever was. When the ship was ready, her prow
went to sea and her stern to shore, and they hoisted
the chequered flapping sails against the tall tough
masts ; there was no mast unbent, nor sail untorn,
and the brown buckies of the strand were "glagid"ing
on her floor. They reached the " Paileas" of the King
of Eirinn. They went into the stable, but when Conal
Crovi would lay a hand on the black whitefaced stallions, the stallions would let out a screech. The King
of Eirinn cried, " Be out lads ; some one is troubling
the stallions." They went out and they tried down
and up, but they saw no man. There was an old
hogshead in the lower end of the stable, and Conal
Crovi and the king's three sons were hiding themselves in the hogshead. When they went out Conal
laid hands on the stallion and the stallion let out a
screech, and so they did three times, and at the third
turn, one of those who were in the party said, that
they did not look in the hogshead. Then they returned and they found the king's three sons and Conal
in it. They were taken in to the king, " Ha, ha,
thou hoary wretch," said the king, " many a mischief
thou didst before thou thoughtest to come and steal
my three black stallions."

The binding of the three smalls, straitly and painfully, was put on Conal Crovi, and he was thrown into the peat corner, and the king's three sons were

taken up a stair. When the men who were above had filled themselves full of meat and drink, it was then that the king thought of sending word down for Conal Crovi to tell a tale. 'T was no run for the king's big son, but a leap down to fetch him. Said the king, " Come up here, thou hoary wretch, and tell us a tale." " I will tell that," said he, "if I get the worth of its telling ; and it is not my own head nor the head of one of the company." " Thou wilt get that," said the king," " Tost ! hush ! over there, and let us hear the tale of Conal Crovi :"—

" As a young lad I was fishing on a day beside a river, and a great ship came past me. They said to me would I go as ' pilot' to go to Rome. I said that I would do it : and of every place as we reached it, they would ask was that Rome ? and I would say that it was not, and I did not know where in the great world Rome was.

" We came at last to an island that was there, we went on shore, and I went to take a walk about the island, and when I returned back the ship was gone. There I was, left by myself, and I did not know what to do. I was going past a house that was there, and I saw a woman crying. I asked what woe was on her ; she told me that the heiress of this island had died six weeks ago, and that they were waiting for a brother of hers who was away from the town, but that she was to be buried this day.

" They were gathering to the burying, and I was amongst them when they put her down in the grave ; they put a bag of gold under her head, and a bag of silver under her feet. I said to myself, that were better mine ; that it was of no use at all to her. When the night came I turned back to the grave.* When I

* The same word means cave and grave ; the grave is dug

K

had dug up the grave, and when I was coming up with the gold and the silver I caught hold of the stone that was on the mouth of the grave, the stone fell down and I was there along with the dead carlin. By thy hand, oh, King of Eirinn! and by my hand, though free, if I was not in a harder case along with the carlin than I am here under thy compassion, with a hope to get off."

"Ha! ha! Thou hoary wretch, thou camest out of that, but thou wilt not go out of this."

"Give me now the worth of my ursgeul," said Conal.

"What is that?" said the king.

"It is that the big son of the King of Sasunn, and the big daughter of the King of Eirinn, should be married to each other, and one of the black white-faced stallions a tocher for them."

"Thou shalt get that," said the king.

Conal Crovi was seized, the binding of the three smalls laid on him straitly and painfully, and he was thrown into the peat corner; and a wedding of twenty days and twenty nights was made for the young couple. When they were tired then of eating and drinking, the king said that it were better to send for the hoary wretch, and that he should tell them how he had got out of the grave.

'Twas no run, but a leap for the king's middle son to go to fetch him; he was sure he would get a marriage for himself as he had got for his brother. He went down and he brought him up.

Said the king, "Come up and tell to us how thou

because western graves are dug; but the stone falls on the mouth of the grave, probably because the story came from some country where graves were caves. There is an Italian story in which this incident occurs—Decameron of Boccacio.

gottest out of the grave." "I will tell that," said
Conal Crovi, "if I get the worth of telling it ; and it
is not my own head, nor the head of one that is in the
company." "Thou shalt get that," said the king.

"I was there till the day. The brother of the
heiress came home, and he must see a sight of his
sister ; and when they were digging the grave I cried
out, oh ! catch me by the hand ; and the man that
would not wait for his bow he would not wait for his
sword, as they called that the worst one was there ;
and I was as swift as one of themselves. Then I
was there about the island, not knowing what side I
should go. Then I came across three young lads, and
they were casting lots. I asked them what they were
doing thus. They said, 'what was my business what they
were doing?' 'Hud! hud!' said I myself, 'you will tell
me what you are doing.' Well, then, said they, a great
giant took away our sister. We are casting lots which
of us shall go down into this hole to seek her. I cast
lots with them, and there was but that the next lot
fell on myself to go down to seek her. They let me
down in a creel. There was the very prettiest woman
I ever saw, and she was winding golden thread off
a silver windle. Oh ! said she to myself, how didst
thou come here ? I came down here to seek thee ; thy
three brothers are waiting for thee at the mouth of the
hole, and you will send down the creel to-morrow to
fetch me. If I be living, 'tis well, and if I be not,
there's no help for it. I was but a short time there
when I heard thunder and noise coming with the
giant. I did not know where I should go to hide
myself ; but I saw a heap of gold and silver on the
other side of the giant's cave. I thought there was
no place whatsoever that was better for me to hide in
than amidst the gold. The giant came with a dead

carlin trailing to each of his shoe-ties. He looked down, and he looked up, and when he did not see her before him, he let out a great howl of crying, and he gave the carlins a little singe through the fire and he ate them. Then the giant did not know what would best keep wearying from him, but he thought that he would go and count his lot of gold and silver; then he was but a short time when he set his hand on my own head. 'Wretch!' said the giant, 'many a bad thing didst thou ever before thou thoughtest to come to take away the pretty woman that I had; I have no need of thee to-night, but 'tis thou shalt polish my teeth early to-morrow.' The brute was tired, and he slept after eating the carlins; I saw a great flesh stake beside the fire. I put the iron spit in the very middle of the fire till it was red. The giant was in his heavy sleep, and his mouth open, and he was snoring and blowing. I took the red spit out of the fire and I put it down in the giant's mouth; he took a sudden spring to the further side of the cave, and he struck the end of the spit against the wall, and it went right out through him. I caught the giant's big sword, and with one stroke I struck the head off him. On the morrow's day the creel came down to fetch myself; but I thought I would fill it with the gold and silver of the giant; and when it was in the midst of the hole, with the weight of the gold and silver, the tie broke. I fell down amidst stones, and bushes, and brambles; and by thy hand, oh, King of Eirinn! and by my hand, though free, I was in a harder case than I am to-night, under thy clemency, with the hope of getting out."

"Ah! thou hoary wretch, thou camest out of that, but thou wilt not go out of this," said the king.

"Give me now the worth of my ursgeul."

"What's that?" said the king.

"It is the middle son of the King of Sasunn, and the middle daughter of the King of Eirinn to be married to each other, and one of the black whitefaced stallions as tocher."

"That will happen," said the king.

Conal Crovi was caught, and bound with three slender ends, and tossed into the peat corner; and a wedding of twenty nights and twenty days was made for the young couple, there and then.

When they were tired of eating and drinking, the king said they had better bring Conal Crovi up, till he should tell how he got up out of the giant's cave. 'Twas no run, but a spring for the king's young son to go down to fetch him; he was sure he would get a "match" for him, as he got for the rest.

"Come up here, thou hoary wretch," said the king, "and tell us how thou gottest out of the giant's cave." "I will tell that if I get the worth of telling; and it is not my own head, nor the head of one in the company." "Thou wilt get that," said the king. "Tost! silence over there, and let us listen to the sgeulach of Conal Crovi," said the king.

"Well! I was there below wandering backwards and forwards; I was going past a house that was there, and I saw a woman there, and she had a child in one hand and a knife in the other hand, and she was lamenting and crying. I cried myself to her, 'Hold on thy hand, woman, what art thou going to do?' 'Oh!' said she, 'I am here with three giants, and they ordered my pretty babe to be dead, and cooked for them, when they should come home to dinner.' 'I see,' said I, 'three hanged men on a gallows yonder, and we will take down one of them; I will go up in the place of one of them, and thou wilt make him ready in place of thy babe.' And when the giants came home to dinner, one of them would say, 'This is the flesh of the babe;' and another would say, 'It is not.' One of them said that he would go to fetch a steak out of one of those who were on the gallows, and that he would see whether it was the flesh of the babe he was eating. I myself was the first that met them; and by thy hand, oh, King of Eirinn, and by my hand, were it free, if I was not in a somewhat harder case, when the steak was coming out of me, than I am to-night under thy mercy, with a hope to get out."

"Thou hoary wretch, thou camest out of that, but thou wilt not come out of this," said the king.

"Give me now the reward of my ursgeul?"

"Thou wilt get that," said the king.

"My reward is, the young son of the King of Sasunn, and the young daughter of the King of Eirinn, to be married, and one of the black stallions as tocher."

There was catching of Conal Crovi, and binding him with the three slender ends, straitly and painfully, and throwing him down into the peat corner; and there was a wedding made, twenty nights and twenty days, for the young pair. When they were tired eating and drinking, the king said that it were best to bring up that hoary wretch to tell how he came off the gallows. Then they brought myself up.

"Come up hither thou hoary wretch, and tell us how thou gottest off the gallows." "I will tell that," said I myself, "if I get a good reward." "Thou wilt get that," said the king.

"Well! when the giants took their dinner, they were tired and they fell asleep. When I saw this, I came down, and the woman gave me a great flaming sword of light that one of the giants had; and I was not long

throwing the heads off the giants. Then I myself, and
the woman were here, not knowing how we should get
up out of the giant's cave. We went to the farther end of
the cave, and then we followed a narrow road through a
rock, till we came to light, and to the giant's ' biorlinn '
of ships.* What should I think, but that I would
turn back and load the biorlinn with the gold and
silver of the giant; and just so I did. I went with
the biorlinn under sail till I reached an island that
I did not know. The ship, and the woman, and the
babe were taken from me, and I was left there to come
home as best I might. I got home once more to
Sasunn, though I am here to-night."

Then a woman, who was lying in the chamber,
cried out, "Oh, king, catch hold of this man; I was
the woman that was there, and thou wert the babe."
It was here that value was put on Conal Crovi; and
the king gave him the biorlinn full of the giant's
gold and silver, and he made the kingdom of Sasunn
as rich as it ever was before.

Told by Neill Gillies a fisherman at Inverary, about fifty-five
years old, who says that he has known the story, and has repeated it
for many years: he learned it from his parents. Written down by
HECTOR URQUHART.

SGEULACHD CHONAIL CHROBHIE.

BHA rìgh air Sasunn aon uair, agus bha triùir mhac aige, 's chaidh
iad do 'n Fhraing a dh' fhaotainn ionnsachadh, agus an uair a thill iad
dhachaidh, thuirt iad ri 'n athair gun rachadh iad a shealltainn de 'n
riaghailt a bha san rìoghachd o 'n a dh' fhalbh iad, agus b'e a cheud

* BIOR, a log; LINN a pool; LUINGEANACH, of ships; naval
barge; or LUNN, handle of an oar, oared barge.

àite do 'n deach iad do thigh fear do thuathanaich an rìgh do 'm b'ainn
Conal Cròbhi. Bha gach ni 'b 'fhearr na chéile aig Conal Cròbhi a
feitheamh orra, biadh dheth gach biadh, 's deoch dheth gach deoch.
'Nuair a bha iad subhach 'sa thàinig am dhoibh dol a luidhe, thuirt
mac mòr an rìgh, "'Se so an riaghailt a th' againne bho thàinig sinn
dhachaidh, gu 'm bi mise le bean an tighe nochd, agus mo bhràthair
meadhonach leis an t-searbhanta, 's mo bhràthair òg le nighean fir
an tighe." Ach cha do thaitinn so idir ri Conal Cròbhi, 's thubhairt
e, " Mu 'n nighean 's mu 'n t-searbhanta cha 'n abair mi mòran, ach cha
'n-'eil mi toilichte dealachadh ri m' bhean, ach théid mise mach agus
feòraichidh mi-dhiubh fhéin mu thimchioll na cùise so;" agus a
mach ghabh e, 's ghlais e 'n dorus na dhéigh 's dh' iarr e air a ghille
na tri eich a b' fheàrr a bha anns an stàbull a bhi deas gun dàil.
Chaidh e féin 's a' bhean air fear, 's a ghille 's a nighean air fear eile,
a mhac 's an searbhanta air an treas each, 's dh' fhalbh iad far an
robh an rìgh, a dh' innseadh am masladh a thug a chuid mac dhoibh.
Bha gille furachail an rìgh ag amharc a mach co a chitheadh e 'tighinn.
Ghlaodh e, " gun robh e 'faicinn triùir mharcaiche dùbailte a' tighinn."
Thuirt an rìgh, "ha! hath! so Conal Cròbhi a' tighinn, 's mo thriùir
mhac-sa fo chìs aige, ach ma tha iadsan, cha bhi mise." 'Nuair a thainig
Conal Cròbhi, cha d' thugadh an rìgh éisdeachd dha. Thuirt Conal
Cròbhi an sin, 'nuair nach d' fhuair e freagairt, " Ni mise do rìoghachd
na 's miosa na tha i," 's dh' fhalbh e 's dh' fhàg e e, 's thòisich e
air robaireachd, 's air togail chreach.

Thuirt an rìgh, gu 'n d' thugadh e duais air bith do dhuine a gheibh-
adh a mach an t-àite anns an robh Conal Cròbhi a' gabhail còmhnuidh.
Thuirt marcach gemeartach * an rìgh, "na 'm faigheadh esan latha 's
bliadhna, gu 'm faigheadh esan amach far an robh e." Thug e mar so
latha 's bliadhna 'ga 'iarraidh, ach ma thug, cha 'n fhac e scalladh do
Chonal Cròbhi. Air an rathad dhachaidh, shuidh e air maolan bòidheach buidhe 's chunnaic e caol smuid ann am meadhon na Coille ùbh-
laidh. Bha gille furachail aig Conal Cròbhi a' sealltainn co 'chitheadh
e 'tighinn. Chaidh e stigh, 's thuirt e gun robh e 'faicinn coslas a
mharcaich *ghemeartaich* a' tighinn. " Tha, tha, thuirt Conal Cròbhi,
tha 'n duine bochd air a chuir air falbh air fògradh mar chaidh mi
féin." Bha a làmhan sgaoilte aig Conal Cròbhi a' feitheamh air, 's
fhuair e rogha biadh 's deocha, 's burn blath d'a chasan, 's leaba bhog
d'a leasan. Cha robh e ach goirid 'na luidhe 'nuair a ghlaodh
Conal Cròbhi, "Am bheil thu 'd Chadal," a mharcaich' gheineartaich.

* Gemeartach, swift (*not in dictionaries*); probably from CEUM,
a pace.

" Cha n'eil," thuirt esan. 'N Ceann tacain a rithist, ghlaodh e, " 'm
bheil thu 'nad' chadal." Thuirt e, nach robh. Ghlaodh e 'rithist an
treas uair, ach cha robh freagradh ann. Ghlaodh Conal Cròbhi an
so, " Air bhur bonn na tha stigh ; cha 'n am crùban a th' ann, bithidh
an tòir oirnn an ceartair." Bha 'm fear faire aig Conal Cròbhi a
glaodhaich gun robh e 'faicinn triùir mhac an rìgh a' tighinn le
cuideachd mhòr maille riu." Cha robh do dh' airm aig' ach claidheamh meirgeach dubh. Thòisich Conal Cròbhi orra, 's cha d' fhàg
e duine beò, ach triùir mhac an rìgh. Cheangail e triùir mhac an rìgh
an sin 's thug e stigh iad. Chuir e ceangal nan tri chaoil orra gu daor
's gu docair, 's thilg e ann an cùil na mòn' iad, 's thuirt e ri 'bhean biadh
a dhèanamh gu luath, gu 'n robh e 'dol a dhèanamh obair nach d'
rinn e riamh roimhe a leithid. " Gu dé sin a dhuine," thuirt ise.
" Dol a thoirt nan ceann do thriùir mhac an rìgh." Thug e nìos am
fear mòr, 's chuir e 'cheann air an ealaig 's thog e 'n tuadh. " Na
dèan! na dèan," thuirt esan, " 's gabhaidh mi leat fhéin an còir 's an
eucoir gu bràth." Thug e nìos an sin am fear meadhonach ; chuir e
cheann air an ealaig, 's thog e 'n tuadh. " Na dèan! Na dèan! "
thuirt esan, " 's gabhaidh mi leat fhéin an còir 'san eucoir gu bràth."
Thug e nìos an sin am fear òg, 's rinn e 'leithid eile air. " Na dèan ! Na
dèan ! " thuirt esan, " 's gabhaidh mi leat an Còir 's an eucoir gu bràth."
Dh' fhalbh e fhéin an sin 's triùir mhac an rìgh far an robh an rìgh.
Bha gillean furachail an rìgh a' sealltainn a mach, cuin a chitheadh
iad a' tighinn a chuideachd le ceann Chonail Chròbhi. Ghlaodh fear
amach, gun robh e 'faicinn coslas triùir mhac an rìgh a' tighinn, 's
Conal Cròbhi air an toiseach. " Ha ! ha ! thuirt an rìgh," tha Conal
Cròbhi a' tighinn 's mo thriùir mhac aige fo Chìs, ach ma tha iadsan,
cha bhi mise. Cha d' thugadh e freagradh do Chonal Cròbhi, ach gu
'm bitheadh e air a chrochadh air Croich air Moch Maduinn an latha
Màireach. Nis chaidh a Chroich a chuir suas, 's bha Conal Cròbhi
gu bhi air a chrochadh ; ach ghlaodh mac mòr an rìgh, " Théid mise
na àite." Ghlaodh mac meadhonach an rìgh, " Théid mise 'na
àite." Ghlaodh mac òg an rìgh, " Théid mise 'na àite." Ghabh an
rìgh mìothlachd an so ri 'chuid mac. Thuirt Conal Cròbhi an sin,
" Ni sinn long mhòr agus théid sinn a ghoid na 'n tri òigeach bhlàra,
dhubha a tha aig rìgh Eirinn, 's ni sinn rìoghachd Shasuinn co
beartach sa bha i riamh.
    'Nuair a bha 'n long deas, chaidh a toiseach ri muir 's a
deireadh ri tìr, 's thog iad na siùil bhreaca, bhaidealach ri aghaidh
nan crann fada, fulannach, 's cha robh crann gun lùbadh na seòl
gun reubadh, 's bha faochagan ruadh a chladaich a glagadaich air
a h-urlar. Ràinig iad pàileas rìgh Eirinn ; Chaidh iad a stigh do 'n

stàbull, ach a nuair a chuireadh Conal Cròbhi a làmh air na h-òigeich
bhlàra, dhubha, leigeadh na h-oigeich sgreuch asda.   Ghlaodh righ
Eirinn, "Bithibh a mach, fhearaibh, tha Cuideiginn a cur dragh air
na h-òigeich."   Chaidh iad a mach, 's dh' fheuch iad shìos as shuas
ach cha n' fhac iad duine.   Bha seann togsaid an ceann shìos an
stàbuill, agus bha Conal Cròbhi 's triùir mhac an rìgh 'gam folach
fhéin 's an togsaid.   'Auair a chaidh iadsan a mach, chuir Conal a
làmh air an òigeach, ach leig an t-òigeach sgreuch as.   Rinn iad so
tri uairean, agus air an treas tromb, thuirt fear do na bha sa chuideachd, nach do sheall iad san togsaid.   Sheall iad an sin, 's fhuair
iad triùir mhac an rìgh agus Conal anns an togsaid.   Chaidh an
tabhairt a stigh a dh' ionnsaidh an rìgh.   "Ha! ha! a bhéist liath,"
thuirt an righ, "'s iomadh Cron a rinn thu, mu 'n do smaoinich thu
tighinn a ghoid nan òigeach dhubh agamsa."   Chaidh ceangal nan
tri chaoil gu daor 's gu docair a chur air Conal Cròbhi, 's thilgeadh an
cùil na moine e, 's chaidh triùir mhac an rìgh a thoirt an àird staidhir.
'Nuair a lìon na fir a bha gu h-àrd iad féin làn do bhiadh, 's do
dheoch, 's ann a smaoinich an rìgh fios a chur a nìos air Conal Cròbhi,
a dh' innseadh sgeulachd.   Cha bu ruith do mhac mòr an rìgh ach
leum sios, g'a iarraidh.   Thuirt an rìgh, "Thig a nìos an so, a bhéist
liath, 's innis dhuinn sgeulachd."   "Iunsidh mi sin," thuirt esan,
"ma gheibh mi fiach innseadh, 's cha 'n e mo cheann fhéin na ceann
aon do 'n chuideachd."   "Gheibh thu sin," thuirt an rìgh.   "Tosd!
thall an sin, 's 'éisdibh ri sgeulachd Chonail Chrobhi," thuirt an rìgh!
"'Nam' ghill' òg, bha mi 'g iasgach latha aig taobh aibhne, 's thàinig
long mhòr seachad orm; thuirt iad rium 'an gabhainn a' m' (philot)
gu dhol an Ròimh; thuirt mi gu 'n dèanainn e, agus na h-uil' àite,
do 'n ruigeamaid, dh' fheòraicheadh iad, am b'e siud an Ròimh? 's
theirinn-sa nach b'ì, 's cha robh fios agam, C'ait' air an t-saoghal mhòr
an robh an Ròimh.   Thàinig sinn mu dheireadh gu h-eilean a bha 'n
sin.   Chaidh sinn air tìr agus chaidh mise a ghabhail sràid feadh an
eilean, agus dur a thill mi air m' ais, bha 'n long air falbh.   Bha mi
'n sin air m' fhàgail leam fhéin, 's cha robh fios agam de a dhèanainn.
Bha mi 'dol seachad air tigh a bha 'n sin, 's chunnaic mi bean ri
caoineadh.   Dh' fheòraich mi dhi, de 'm bròn a bha orra?   Thuirt i
rium 'gu 'n do bhàsaich ban-oighre an eilean so bho cheann sèa
seachduinnean agus gu 'n robh iad a' feitheamh ri bràthair dhi 'bha
air falbh o'n bhaile, ach gu 'n robh i ri'tiòdhlacadh an latha so.   Bha
iad a' cruinneachadh gus an tiodhlacadh, 's bha mise 'nam measg,
's 'nuair a chuir iad sìos anns an uaigh i, chuir iad poc' oir 'fuidh
'ceann, 's poc' airgid fuidh casan.   Thuirt mise rium fhéin, gu 'm
b'fheàrr sud agam fhéin, nach robb e gu feum sam bith dh' ise.

'Nuair a thàinig an oidhche thill mi air m' ais gus an uaigh, 'nuair a chladhaich mi 'n uaigh, 's a bha mi tighinn a nìos leis an òr 's leis an airgiod, rug mi air a chlach a bha air beul na h-uaighe. Thuit a chlach a nuas, 's bha mise còmhladh ris a chailleach mharbh an sin. Air do làimhsa, a rìgh Eirinn, 's air mo làimh-sa, ge's saor e, mur robh mi ni bu chruaidh còmhladh ris a chaillich na tha mi 'n so fo t'iochd-sa, 's dùil ri dol as agam. "Ha! Ha! a bhéist liath, thàinig thu as an sin, ach cha téid thu as an so." "Thoir dhomh a nis fiach m' ursgeul," arsa Conal. "Gu de sin," thuirt an rìgh. 'Tha mac mòr rìgh shasuinn, agus nighean mhòr rìgh Eirinn a bhi air am pòsadh ri 'chéile, agus fear do na h-òigeich bhlàra, dhubha na thocharadh." "Gheibh thu sin, thuirt an rìgh." Chaidh beireachd air Conal Cròbhi, 's ceangal nan tri chaoil a chuir air gu daor 's gu dòcair, 's a thilgeil an cùil na moine, 's chaidh banais fichead oidhche 's fichead latha a dhèanamh do 'n chàraid òg. 'Nuair a bha iad sgith an sin ag itheadh 's ag òl, thuirt an rìgh, "gu 'm b'fheàrr fios a chuir air a bhéist liath, 's gu 'n innseadh é gu de mar f huair é as an uagh." Cha bu ruith ach leum le mac meadhonach an rìgh gu dol g'a iaraidh. Bha e cinnteach gu 'faigheadh e pòsadh dha f héin, mar f huair e d'a bhràthair. Chaidh e sìos 's thug e nìos e. Thuirt an rìgh, "Thig a nìos 's innis dhuinn ciounas a f huair thu as an uaigh." "Innsidh mi sin," thuirt Conal Crobhi, "ma gheibh mi fiach innseadh, 's cha 'n e mo cheann féin, na ceann h-aon a tha sa chuideachd." "Gheibh thu sin," thuirt an rìgh.

Bha mise an sin gus an latha. Thàinig bràthair na ban-oighre dhachaidh, 's dh' fheumadh e sealladh d'a phinthar f haicinn agus dar a bha iad a cladhach na h-uaighe, ghlaodh mise, O beir air làimh orm! 'S am fear nach fanadh ri 'bhogha cha 'n f hanadh ri 'chlaidheamh, 's iad a glaodhaich gu 'n robh am fear bu mhiosa an siud, 's bha mise cho luath ri h-aon aca f héin. Bha mi 'n sin air feadh an eilean gu 'n f hios dé 'n taobh a rachainn. Thàinig mi 'n sin tarsuinn air triùir ghillean òga, 's iad a cuir chrann.

Dh' fheòraich mi dhiubh, "Dè a bha iad a dèanamh mar siud." Thuirt iad "de mo ghnothuchsa de bha iad a dèanamh." "Hud! Hud!" arsa "mi f héin, innsidh sibh dhomh dé tha sibh a dèanamh." "Mata," thuirt iadsan, "thug fambair mòr air falbh ar piuthar 's tha sinn a cuir chrann feuch co againn a théid sìos do 'n toll so g'a h-iarraidh." Chuir mise crann leo 's cha robh ann ach gu'n d' thàinig an crann orm f héin gu dol sìos g' a h-iarraidh. Leig iad sìos mi ann an cliabh. Bha an sin an aon bhoirionnach bu bhòidhche a chunnaic mi riabh, 's i tochras snàth òir far eachan airgid. "O! thuirt," ise rium, f héin, "de mar thàinig thusa an so ?" " Thàinig mise a nuas gu d' iarraidh tha do thriùir bhràithrean a feitheamh ort aig beul an tuill, agus cuiridh sibh a nuas an cliabh am màireach gu m' iarraidh-sa." " Ma bhitheas mi beò 's maith, 's mar bi cha 'n 'eil atharrach air." Cha robh mi ach goirid an sin a nuair a chuala mi stairum 's stararaich a tighinn aig an fhamhair. Cha robh fios agam càite an rachainn am falach ; ach chunnaic mi dùn òir 's airgid an taobh thall uamh an fhamhair. Smaoinich mi nach robh àite air bhith a b' fheàrr dhomh dol am folach na 'measg an òir. Thàinig am famhair a stigh, 's cailleach mharbh slaodadh ris gach barrall bròig' aige. Sheall e shìos 's sheall e shuas, 's dar nach fac e is' air thoiseach air, leig e burrall mòr caoinidh as. Thug e dathadh air na cailleachan roimh 'n ghealbhan 's dh' ith e iad. Cha robh fhios aig an fhamhair an so de 'n rud a b' fheàrr a chumadh fhadal deth, ach smaointich e gu 'n rachadh e a chunntas a chuid oir a's airgid. Cha robh e ach goirid an sin 'nuair a chuir e làmh air mo cheann fhéin. " A Bhéist ! " thuirt am famhair, " 's ioma droch rud a rinn thu riamh mu 'n do smaoinich thu tighinn an so a thoirt air falbh a' bhoirinnaich bhòidheach a bh' agam-sa." " Cha 'n'eil feum agamsa ort an nochd, ach 's tu ghlanas m' fhiaclan moch am màireach. Bha a bhéist sgìth 's chaidil e 'n déigh na caillich itheadh. Chunnaic mi bior mòr feòla ri taobh a ghealbhain. Chuir mi 'n teis-meadhoin an teine am bior iaruinn, gus an robh e dearg. Bha 'm famhair 'na throm chadal, 's a bheul fosgailte, 's e 'rùchdail 's a séideil. Thug mi 'm bior dearg as an teine, 's chuir mi sìos am beul an fhamhair e. Thug e grad leum gu taobh thall na h-uaimh, 's bhuail e ceann a bhior ris a' bhalla 's chaidh e mach roi 'n cheann eile. Rug mi air claidheamh mòr an fhamhair, agus le aon bheum, chuir mi 'n ceann dheth. Air an latha màireach, thàinig an cliabh a nuas gu m' iarraidh fhéin. Ach smaoinich mi gu 'n lìonainn an cliabh do dh' òr 's do dh' airgiod an fhamhair, 's dar a bha e 'm meadhon an tuill, le cudthrom an òir 's an airgid, bhris an iris, thuit mi nuas a measg chlachan, 's phris, 's dhris, 's air do làimhsa, a rìgh Eirinn, 's air mo làimhs ge 'saor e, bha mi 'n càs bu chruaidhe na tha mi nochd fo t'iochdsa, 's dùil agam ri dol as." " Ah ! a bhéist liath, thàinig thu as an sin, ach chat éid thu as an so," ars' an rìgh. " Thoir dhomh a nis fiach m' ursgeul," arsa Conal. " De sin ? " thuirt an rìgh. " Tha mac meadhonach righ shasuinn 's nighean mheadhonach righ Eirinn a bhi air am pòsadh ri 'chéile 's fear do na h-òigeich bhlàra, dhubha mar thochradh." " Tachraidh sin," thuirt an righ. Chaidh beireachd air Conal Cròbhi 's a cheangal le tri chinn chaoil, sa thilgeadh an cuil na mòine, 's chaidh hanais fichead oidhche 's fichead latha a dhèanamh do 'n chàraid òig. An sin, 'nuair

a bha iad sgìth 'g itheadh 's ag òl, thuirt an rìgh, "gu 'm b'fheàrr
dhoibh Conal Cròbhi a thoirt a nìos gus an innseadh e cionnas a fhuair
e nìos a uamh an fhamhair." Cha bu ruith ach leum le mac òg an
rìgh dol sìos g' a iarraidh. Bha e cinnteach gu 'faigheadh e matcha
dha fhéin mar fhuair e do chàch. "Thig a nìos an so a bhéist liath,"
thuirt an rìgh, "'s innis duinn ciamar a fhuair thu a uaigh an
fhamhair." "Innsidh mi sin, ma gheibh mi fiach innseadh, 's cha 'n e
mo cheann fhein no ceann h-aon do na 'bheil sa chuideachd.'
"Gheibh thu sin," thuirt an rìgh. "Tosd! thall an sin, 's eisdeamaid
ri sgeulachd Chonail Chròbhi," thuirt an rìgh! (Well), bha mise gu
h-ìosal an sin, 's mi spaisdeireachd air m' ais 's air m' aghaidh. Bha
mi 'dol seachad air tigh a bha 'n sin 's chunnaic mi bean an sin, 's
leanabh aice san darna laimh, 's sgian aice san làimh eile, 's i
'caoinneadh. Ghlaodh mi fhéin rithe, "Cum air do làmh a bhean
de tha thu dol a dhèanamh mar sin?" "O!" thuirt ise, "tha mi aig
tri fàmhairean an so, agus dh' iarr iad orm, mo leanabh bòidheach
a bhi marbh 's air a bhruich air an cionn 'nuair a thigeadh iad
dhachaidh gu 'n dinneir. Chi mi," arsa mise, "triùir dhaoine crochta
air croich thall an siud, bheir sinn a nuas fear dhiubh, agus théid mise
suas na àite, 's deasaichidh tu esan an àite do leinibh." Agus a
nuair a thàinig na fàmhairean dhachaidh gu 'n dinneir, theireadh fear
dhiubh, "'S e so feòil an leinibh, 's theireadh fear eile," cha 'n e.
Thuirt fear dhiubh, gu 'n rachadh e a thoirt staoig a fear do na bha
air a chroich, agus gu 'faiceadh e co dhiu 's e feòil an leinibh a bha iad
ag itheadh. 'S mi fhéin a cheud fhear a thachair orra, 's air do
làimh, a rìgh Eirinn, 's air mo làimhsa, ge saor e, mur robh mi ann
an cruaidh-chàs ni bu mhò 'nuair a bha 'n staoig a tighinn asam, na
tha mi nochd fo t'iochdsa 's dùil ri dol as agam." "A bhéist liath,
thàinig thu as an sin, ach cha d' thig thu as an so,"ars' an rìgh. "Thoir
dhomh a nis dnais m' ursgeul." "Gheibh thu sin," ars' an rìgh.
"'S e mo dhuais, mac òg rìgh Shasuinn, 's nighean òg righ Eirinn a
bhi posda, 's fear do na h-òigeich dhubha mar thochradh. Chaidh
beireachd air Conal Cròbhi, 'sa cheangal le cinn nan tri chaoile gu
daor 's gu docair, 's a thilgeadh sìos an cùil na mòine, 's chaidh banais
fichead latha 's fichead oidhche a dhèanamh do 'n chàraid òig. 'Nuair
a bha iad sgìth 'g itheadh 's a g' òl, thuirt an rìgh, "gu b'fheàrr a bhéist
liath ad a thoirt a nìos, a dh' innseadh de mar thàinig e bhàrr na
croiche." Thug iad an so a nìos mi fhéin. "Thig a nìos, a bhéist
liath an so, 's innis dhuinn de mar fhuair thu bharr na Croiche."
"Innsidh mi sin," arsa mi fhéin, "ma gheibh mi duais mhaith."
"Gheibh thu sin," thuirt an rìgh. (Well) a nuair a ghabh na
fàmhairean an dinneir bha iad sgìth, 's thuit iad 'nan cadal.

'Nuair a chunnaic mise so, thàinig mi nuas 's thug a' bhean dhomh claidheamh mòr, lasrach soluis a bha aig fear do na famhairean, 's cha robh mi fada a tilgeadh nan ceann do na famhairean. Bha mi fhéin 's am boirionnach an so gun fhios againn cionnas a gheibheamaid a nìos a' uamh an fhamhair. Dh' fhalbh sinn gu ceann shìos na h-uaimh 's lean sinn an sin rathad cumhang roi chreag gus an d' thàinig sinn gu solus 's gu bior-linn luingeanach an fhamhair. Smuainich mi fhéin gum pillinn air m' ais agus gu 'n luchd-aichinn a bhior-linn le òr 's le airgiod an fhamhair, agus mar so fhéin rinn mi. Dh' fhalbh mi leis a bhior-linn fo shèol gus an d' thàinig mi gu h-eilean nach b' aithne dhomh. Chaidh an long, 's am boirionach, 's an leanabh a thoirt uam, 's fagar mise an sin gu tighin dhachaidh mar a b'fheàrr a dh' fhaodainn. Fhuair mi dhachaidh aon uair eile do Shasunn, ged tha mi 'n so a nochd. Ghlaodh boirionnach a bha na luidhe san t-seomar, " O a rìgh, beiribh air an duine so." " Bu mhise am boirionach a bha 'n sin, 's bu tusa an leanabh." 'S ann an so a bha 'm meas air Conal Cròbhi, 's thug an rìgh dha a bhior-linn làn òir 's airgid an fhamhair 's rinn e rioghachd Shasuinn cho beartach 's a bha i riamh.

This story was told to me at Inverary, April 25, 1859, by Gillies. It was told with the air of a man telling a serious story, and anxious to tell it correctly. The narrative was inter-larded with explanations of the words used, and the incidents described. Those who sat about the fire argued points in the story. These were John MacKenzie, fisherman; John Mac-Donald, travelling tinker; John Clerk, our host, formerly miller to the Duke of Argyle; and some others, whose names I have forgotten. The story is very correctly written. I took notes at the time, and they agree with the Gaelic as written by Hector Urquhart, from the dictation of Gillies.

THE TALE OF CONNAL.

From Kenneth MacLennan, Pool Ewe.

THERE was a king over Eirinn once, who was named
King Cruachan, and he had a son who was called
Connal MacRigh Cruachan. The mother of Connal
died, and his father married another woman. She was
for finishing Connal, so that the kingdom might belong
to her own posterity. He had a foster mother, and it
was in the house of his foster mother that he made his
home. He and his eldest brother were right fond of
each other; and the mother was vexed because Connal
was so fond of her big son. There was a bishop in
the place, and he died; and he desired that his gold
and silver should be placed along with him in the
grave. Connal was at the bishop's burying, and he
saw a great bag of gold being placed at the bishop's
head, and a bag of silver at his feet, in the grave.
Connal said to his five foster brothers, that they
would go in search of the bishop's gold; and when
they reached the grave, Connal asked them which they
would rather; go down into the grave, or hold up the
flagstone. They said that they would hold up the
flag. Connal went down; and whatever the squealing
was that they heard, they let go the flag and they took
to their soles home. Here he was, in the grave on

top of the bishop. When the five of foster brothers reached the house, their mother was somewhat more sorrowful for Connal than she would have been for the five. At the end of seven mornings, there went a company of young lads to take the gold out of the bishop's grave, and when they reached the grave they threw the flag to the side of the further wall ; Connal stirred below, and when he stirred they went, and they left each arm and dress they had. Connal arose, and he took with him the gold, and arms and dress, and he reached his foster mother with them. They were all merry and lighthearted as long as the gold and silver lasted.

There was a great giant near the place, who had a great deal of gold and silver in the foot of a rock ; and he was promising a bag of gold to any being that would go down in a creel. Many were lost in this way ; when the giant would let them down, and they would fill the creel, the giant would not let down the creel more till they died in the hole.

On a day of days, Connal met with the giant, and he promised him a bag of gold, for that he should go down in the hole to fill a creel with the gold. Connal went down, and the giant was letting him down with a rope ; Connal filled the giant's creel with the gold, but the giant did not let down the creel to fetch Connal, and Connal was in the cave amongst the dead men and the gold.

When it beat the giant to get another man who would go down in the hole, he sent his own son down into the hole, and the sword of light in his lap, so that he might see before him.

When the young giant reached the ground of the cave, and when Connal saw him he caught the sword of light, and he took off the head of the young giant.

Then Connal put gold in the bottom of the creel, and he put gold over him ; and then he hid in the midst of the creel, and he gave a pull at the rope. The giant drew the creel, and when he did not see his son, he threw the creel over the top of his head. Connal leaped out of the creel, and the black back of the giant's head (being) towards him, he laid a swift hand on the sword of light, and he took the head off the giant. Then he betook himself to his foster mother's house with the creel of gold and the giant's sword of light.

After this, he went one day to hunt on Sliamh na leirge. He was going forwards till he went into a great cave. He saw, at the upper part of the cave, a fine fair woman, who was thrusting the flesh stake at a big lump of a baby ; and every thrust she would give the spit, the babe would give a laugh, and she would begin to weep. Connal spoke, and he said,— " Woman, what ails thee at the child without reason ?" " Oh, said she, " since thou art an able man thyself, kill the baby and set it on this stake, till I roast it for the giant." He caught hold of the baby, and he put a plaid that he had on about the babe, and he hid the baby at the side of the cave.

Then were a great many dead bodies at the side of the cave, and he set one of them on the stake, and the woman was roasting it.

Then was heard under ground trembling and thunder coming, and he would rather that he was out. Here he sprang in the place of the corpse that was at the fire, in the very midst of the bodies. The giant came, and he asked, " Was the roast ready ?" He began to eat, and he said, " Fiu fau hoagrich ; it's no wonder that thy own flesh is tough ; it is tough on thy brat."

When the giant had eaten that one, he went to count

the bodies ; and the way he had of counting them was, to catch hold of them by the two smalls of the leg, and to to toss them past the top of his head ; and he counted them back and forwards thus three or four times ; and as he found Connal somewhat heavier, and that he was soft and fat, he took that slice out of him from the back of his head to his groin. He roasted this at the fire, and he ate it, and then he fell asleep. Connal winked to the woman to set the flesh stake in the fire. She did this, and when the spit grew white after it was red, he thrust the spit through the giant's heart, and the giant was dead.

Then Connal went and he set the woman on her path homewards, and then he went home himself. His stepmother sent him and her own son to steal the whitefaced horse from the King of Italy, " Eadailt ;" and they went together to steal the whitefaced horse, and every time they would lay hand on him, the whitefaced horse would let out an *ialt* (neigh ?). A "company" came out, and they were caught. The binding of the three smalls was laid on them straitly and painfully. "Thou big red man," said the king, "wert thou ever in so hard a case as that?" "A little tightening for me, and a loosening for my comrade, and I will tell thee that," said Connal.

The Queen of the Eadailt was beholding Connal. Then Connal said :—

" Seven morns so sadly mine,
    As I dwelt on the bishop's top,
    That visit was longest for me,
    Though I was the strongest myself.
    At the end of the seventh morn
    An opening grave was seen,
    And I would be up before
    The one that was soonest down.

They thought I was a dead man,
As I rose from the mould of earth;
At the first of the harsh bursting
They left their arms and their dresses.
I gave the leap of the nimble one,
As I was naked and bare.
'T was sad for me, a vagabond,
To enjoy the bishop's gold."

"Tighten well, and right well," said the king;
"it was not in one good place that he ever was; great
is the ill he has done." Then he was tightened somewhat tighter, and somewhat tighter; and the king
said, "Thou great red man, wert thou ever in a harder
case than that?" "Tighten myself, and let a little
slack with this one beside me, and I will tell thee
that."

They did that. "I was," said he,

"Nine morns in the cave of gold;
My meat was the body of bones,
Sinews of feet and hands.
At the end of the ninth morn
A descending creel was seen;
Then I caught hold on the creel,
And laid gold above and below;
I made my hiding within the creel;
I took with me the glaive of light,
The luckiest turn that I did."

They gave him the next tightening, and the king
asked him, "Wert thou ever in case, or extremity,
as hard as that?" "A little tightening for myself,
and a slack for my comrade, and I will tell thee that."

They did this.

"On a day on Sliabh na leirge,
As I went into a cave,
I saw a smooth, fair, mother-eyed wife,
Thrusting the stake for the flesh

At a young unreasoning child. 'Then,' said I,
'What causes thy grief, oh wife,
At that unreasoning child?'
'Though he's tender and comely,' said she,
'Set this baby at the fire.'
Then I caught hold on the boy,
And wrapped my 'maundal' around;
Then I brought up the great big corpse
That was up in the front of the heap;
Then I heard, Turstar, Tarstar, and Turaraich,
The very earth mingling together;
But when it was his to be fallen
Into the soundest of sleep,
There fell, by myself, the forest fiend;
I drew back the stake of the roast,
And I thrust it into his maw."

There was the Queen, and she was listening to each thing that Connal suffered and said; and when she heard this, she sprang and cut each binding that was on Connal and on his comrade; and she said, "I am the woman that was there;" and to the king, "thou art the son that was yonder."

Connal married the king's daughter, and together they rode the whitefaced horse home; and there I left them.

From HECTOR URQUHART, June 27, 1859. Recited by KENNETH MACLENNAN of Turnaig, Pool Ewe, Ross-shire, aged 70, who learned it from an old man when he was a boy.

SGEULACHD CHONAILL.

BHA righ air Eirinn aon uair da 'm b-ainm righ Cruachan, 's bha mac aige, ris an abradh iad Conall, mac rìgh Cruachan. Chaochail mathair Chonaill, agus phòs athair bean eile. Bha i air son cu'r as

do Chonall, chum 's gu'm biodh an rioghachd aig a sliochd féin.
Bha muime chìche aige-san, agus 's ann an tigh a mhuime bha e
'dèanamh a dhachaidh. Bha e féin 's a bhràthair bu shine ro
mheasail aig a' chéile, agus bha mhàthair gamhlasach air son gu robh
Conall cho measail aig a mac mòr. Bha Easbuig anns an àite, agus
chaochail e, agus dh' iarr e 'n t-òr 's an t-airgiod aige, a chuir cuide ris
anns an uaigh. Bha Conall aig tiodhlacadh an Easbuig, agus chunnaic e pòc mòr òir a dol aig ceann an Easbuig, agus pòc airgid aig a
chasan 's an uaigh. Thubhairt Conall ri chuignear chomh-dhaltan,
"gu 'rachadh iad air thòir òr an Easbuig," agus nur a ràinig iad an
uaigh, dh' fheòraich Conall dhiubh-san. "Co b' fhearr leo dol sìos
do 'n uaigh na 'n leac a chumail suas?" Thuirt iadsan gu cumadh
iad an leac suas. Chaidh Conall sìos, agus ge b' e sgiamhail a chual'
iadsan, leig iad as an leac, agus thug iad na buinn asda dhachaidh.
Bha e 'n so 's an uaigh air muin an Easbuig. 'Nuair a ràinig na
cuignear bhràithrean altrum an tigh, bha 'm màthair ni bu bhrònaiche
airson Chonaill na bhitheadh i airson a Chùigear. An ceann seachd
tràithean, dh' fhalbh Cuideachd do ghillean òga a thoirt an òir a
uaigh an easbuig' agus nur a ràinig iad an uaigh, thilg iad an leac ri
taobh a bhalla thall Ghluais Conall sìos, agus nur a ghluais, dh'
fhalbh iadsan: dh' fhàg iad gach arm 's aodach 'bha aca; dh'eirich
Conall, 's thug e leis gach òr, 's gach arm, 's gach aodach, 's ràinig e
mhuime chiche leis. Bha iad uile gu subhach, sòlasach, cho fad, 's a
mhair an t-òr 's an t-airgiod. Bha famhair mòr dlùth do'n àite, aig
an robh mòran òir 's airgid ann an Cois Creige, agus bha e 'gealltainn
poc òir do neach sam bith a rachadh sìos ann an cliabh. Bha mòran
air an call mar so. Nur a leigeadh am famhair sìos iad, 's a lìonadh
iad an Cliabh, cha chuireadh am famhair sìos an cliabh tuillidh, gus
am bàsaicheadh iadsan 'san toll. Latha do na làithean, thachair
Conall ris an fhamhair, agus gheall e poc òir dha airson a dhol sìos
do 'n toll a lìonadh cliabh do'n òr. Chaidh Conall sìos, agus
bha 'm famhair 'ga leigeil sìos le ròp. Lìon Conal cliabh an
fhamhair do 'n òr, ach cha do leig am famhair sìos an cliabh air
thoir Chonaill, 's bha Conall 'san uaigh measg nan daoine marbha, 's
an òir. 'Nuair a dh' fhairslich air an fhamhair duine tuillidh
fhaotainn a rachadh sìos do 'n toll, chuir e 'mhac féin sìos do 'n
toll 's an claidheamh soluis air uchd, chum 's gu 'faiceadh e roimhe.
Nur a ràinig am famhair òg grund na h-uaimh, 'sa chunnaic Conall
e, rug e air a chlaidheamh sholuis, agus thug e 'n ceann do 'n fhamhair òg. Chuir Conall an so òr ann am màs a' chleibh, agus chuir
e òr os a cheann: rinn e 'n so fhalach am meadhon a' chléibh: thug
e tarruing air an ròp; tharruing am famhair an cliabh, agus dur nach

fac e 'mhac 'sa chliabh, thilg e 'n cliabh thar mullach a chinn. Leum
Conall as a' chliabh, 's dubh chùl cinn an f hamhair ris: thug e grad
làmh air a' chlaidheamh sholuis, agus thug e 'n ceann do 'n f hamhair.
Thug e 'n so tigh a mhuime chìch' air, leis a chliabh òir, 's claidheamh soluis an f hamhair. 'Na dhéigh so, chaidh e latha a shealg do
shliabh na leirge. Bha e gabhail air adhart, gus an deach e stigh,
do dh' uaimh mhòr. Chunnaic e 'n uachdar na h-uaimh bean bhàn,
bhrèagha 's i putadh bior na feola ri ultach mòr do leanabh, 's na h-
uile putadh a bha ise 'toirt do 'n bhior, dhèanadh an leanabh gàire,
's thòisicheadh ise air caoineadh. Labhair Conall, 's thubhairt e,
" De fàth do bhròin, a bhean, ris an òganach gun chiall." " O !" os
ise, " bho 'n is duine tapaidh thu f héin, marbh an leanabh, 's cuir air a
bhior so e, gus an ròist mi e do 'n f hamhair." Rug e air an leanabh,
's chuir e 'n cleòc a bha air mu 'n leanabh, 's dh' f holuich e 'n leanabh
am taobh na h-uaimh. Bha mòran do chuirp mharbh' an taobh na
h-uaimh, 's chuir e fear dhiubh air a' bhior, 's bha 'm boirionnach 'ga
ròstadh. Chualas fo 'n talamh, crith 's toirm a' tighinn, 's b' f hèarr
leis gun robh e 'muigh: leum e 'n so an àite 'chuirp a bha ris an teine,
an teis-meadhon nan Corp. Thàinig am famhair 's dh' f heòraich e,
" 'n robh ròsta bruich." Thòisich e air itheadh, 's thubhairt e, " fiu
fou! hoagrich! cha 'n ioghnadh feòil righinn a bhi ort f héin, 's
righinn air d'isean i." Dur a dh' ith am famhair am fear ud, dh
f halbh e chunntadh nan corp, agus se 'n dòigh chunntais a bh' aig
orra, beireachd air dhà chaol cois' orra, agus 'gan tillgeadh seachad
thar mullach a chinn, agus chunnt e air ais 's air adhart iad mar so
tri no ceithir do dh' uairean; agus bho m a f huair e Conall ni bu
truime, 'se bog reamhar, thug e 'n stiall ud as bho chùl a chinn gu
mhanachan. Ròist e so ris an teine, 's dh'ith e i. Thuit e 'n sin 'na
chadal. Smèid Conal air a bhoirionnach, bior na feòla chuir 'san teine.
Rinn i so, agus dur a dh' f hàs am bior geal an déigh bhi dearg,
shàth e 'm bior troi' chridhe an f hamhair, 's bha 'm famhair marbh.
Dh' f halbh Conall an so, 's chuir e 'bhean air a slighe dhachaidh.
Chaidh e 'n so dhachaidh e f héin. Chuir a mhuime air falbh e sa'
mac f héin a ghoid a Bhlàr-aghan bho rìgh na h-Eadailt, agus dh'
halbh iad a ghoid a bhlàr-aghan le chéile, agus na h-uile uair, a
chuireadh iad an làimh air a bhlàr-aghan, leigeadh am blàr-aghan
(ialt) as. Thàinig cuideachd a mach 's chaidh an glacadh. Chaidh
ceangal nan tri chaoil a chuir orra gu daor 's gu daingean. " Fhir
mhòr ruaidh," ars' an rìgh, 'n robh thu 'n càs riamh cho cruaidh
an sin ?" " Teannachadh beag dhomh f héin, agus lasachadh do m'
chompanach 's innsidh mi sin," arsa Conall. Bha banrigh na h-
Eadailte 'ga f haicinn. Thubhairt Conall an sin.

" Seachd tràth gu bronach dhomh,
'S mi chomhnuidh air muin an easbuig.
'Sann leamsa 'b' fhad' a' chéilidh sin,
Ged 'sann leam féin bu treise.
An ceann na seachdamh tràth,
Chunnacas uaigh 'ga fosgladh,
'S ge b'e bo luaithe bhiodh a nuas aca,
'S mise a bhiodh suas air thoiseach.
Shaoil leosan gu 'm bu mharbhan mi,
Bho 'n uir thalmhaidh 's mi 'g éiridh,
Ann an toiseach a gharbh-bhristidh,
Dh' fhag iad an airm 's an eudach,
Thug mise leum an Uisleagan,
'Smi ruisgte, nochdta,
Bu bhochd dhomhsa 's mi 'm fhògarrach,
Bhi maitheadh òr do 'n Easbuig."

" Teannaichibh e gu maith 's gu ro mhaith," ars' an rìgh. "cha b'
ann an aon àite maith a bha e riamh, 's mòr an t-olc a rinn e." Chaidh
an sin a theannachadh ni bu teinne, 's ni bu teinne, 's thubhairt an
rìgh, " Fhir mhòir ruaidh, 'n robh thu 'n càs riamh bu chruaidh na
sin." " Teannaich mi féin, 's leig lasachadh do 'n 'fhear so laimh
rium, 's innsidh mi 'n sin." Rinn iad so. Bha mise os esan.

" Naoi tràtha ann an uaimh an òir,
'Se bu bhiadh domh a' cholainn chnàmh,
Feithean chas agus làmh.
An ceann an naoidheadh tràth,
Chunnacas cliabh a' tighinn a mhàn;
Rug mi 'n sin air a' chliabh,
'S chuir mi òr fotham 's òr tharam,
'S rinn mi m' fholach ann sa 'chliabh,
'S thug mi leam an claidheamh soluis
Tùrn is sona rinn mi riamh."

Thug iad an ath theannachadh dha, s' dh' fhoighneachd an rìgh
dheth, " An robh thu 'n càs na h-eiginn riamh cho chruaidh 'sin ?'
" Teannachadh beag dhomh féin, 's lasachadh do m' chompanach,
's innsidh mi 'n sin." Rinn iad so.

" Latha air sliabh na leirge dhomh
'S mi dol a steach do dh' uamh,
Chunnaic mi bean mhìn, bhan, mhathair-shuileach
'Si putadh bior na feòla
Ri òganach, 'se gun chiall.

Thubhairt mise an sin,
De fath do bhròin, a bhean,
Ris an òganach 'snach eil ceillidh,
' Oir a mhin oir a mhaise,' ars' ise
' Cuir an leanabh so ri teallach '
Rug mi 'n sin air a mhacan
'S shuain mi mo mhanndal uime
'S thug mi nios an rod mòr colainn
A bha shuas an tùs na tuime
Chnala mi 'n sin, turtar, tartur, agus turaraich
Fior thalamh dol am measg a cheile
Ach air bhith dhàsan tuiteam
Anns an t-suain chadail
'S an do thuit fuathan na coille
Thug mi tarruing air bior an ròstaidh
'S sheòl mi sud ri còrr a ghoile."

Bha a' bhanrigh faicinn 's ag éisdeachd gach ni bha Conall a'
fulang 's ag radh, agus dur a chual i so, leum i 's gheàrr i gach
ceangal a bha air Conall 's air a chompanach, agus thubhairt i, " 'S
mise 'm boirionnach a bha 'n sin, agus ris an righ 's tusa a mac a bha
'n sind." Phòs Conall nighean an righ, 's mharcaich iad le chéile am
blàradhan dachaidh. 'S dh fhag mise ann a sin iad.

Recited by Kenneth MacLennan, Turnaig, Pool Ewe, Ross-shire.
Written by Hector Urquhart, June 27, 1859.

4. Another story, which seems to be a fragment of this tale made
reasonable, forms part of a collection very well written in the
Gaelic of Gearrloch, Ross-shire, from the telling of old men, by
Mr. Thomas Cameron, schoolmaster, at the request of Osgood H.
MacKenzie, Esq., July 1859.

ALEXANDER MACDONALD, INVERASDALE, tells how Uisdean
Mor MacIlle Phadraig, a local hero, famous for slaying
"Fuahthan" (bogles), in a winter that was very cold, on a day
of hailing and snowing (sowing and winnowing) was taking the
way of "A BHRAIGHE MHOIR" (the great top), and was determined to reach as far as Lochbhraoin. Coming through a place
called Lead leacbacacban mu Thuath (na Fuath ?), he fell in with
a woman, and he soon fell in with a new-born child. No house
was near, so he killed his horse, put the mother and child inside, and left them in the snow. He went for help, and when

he came back he found them warm and well. He took care of them till the woman could do for herself, and the child grew to be an able lad. He was named "MacMhuirich a curach an Eich," which name has stuck to his race to this day.

After this Uisdean came to poverty. On a cold winter's night of hailing and snowing, he was going on a street in Dun Edin (Edinburgh), a woman put her head out of a window and cried, "It is cold this night on Leathad leacachan mu Thuath." "It is," said he. When she heard his Gaelic, she thought she was not far wrong, and asked him in. "What is the hardest 'Cath' that ever befel thee?" said the woman. He repeated the story, and ended with,—"And though I am this night in Dun Edin, many is the hard fight that I have wrestled with." "I am the woman that was there, and this is the child," said she; and she offered him shelter for the rest of his days.

Surely these are Connal, the robber; and the king and his mother; and the king's horse put to a new use, transferred to the Cowgate from Eirinn and Lochlann, and the forests of Germany; brought down from the days of Sindbad, or of Ulysses, or from the fifteenth century, from the age of romance to the nineteenth century and to prose.

5. I have another version of this story, called AN GADAICHE DUBH, The Black Robber, told by Alexander MacNeill, fisherman in Barra, and written by Hector MacLean in August 1859. It varies much from the others. The outline is nearly the same, but the pictures are different. I hope to find room for it.

The story resembles—

1st. The Robber and his Sons, referred to in Grimm's third volume, as taken from a MS. of the fifteenth century. An old robber desires to become an honest man, but his three sons follow their profession, and try to steal the queen's horse. They are caught, and the old robber tells three stories of his own adventures to rescue them.

In the first, he is caught by a giant and about to be eaten, but escapes by putting out the giant's eyes with "destructive ingredients." He gets out of a cave by putting on the skin of a sheep. He puts on a gold ring which the giant gave him, which forces him to call out "here I am." He bites off his own finger, and so escapes.

Next—In a wilderness, haunted by strange creatures, he finds a woman about to kill her child as a dinner for some wild men. He makes her cook a hanged thief instead; hangs himself on a tree in place of the cooked thief, and has a slice cut from his side.

Lastly, the giants, frightened by a clap of thunder, run away; he returns to a civilized country, and the queen, as a reward for his stories, liberates the three sons.

2d. Part of this is manifestly the same as the Adventures of Ulysses in the Cave of the Cyclop.—(Odyssey, book ix.) .

3d. And the adventure of Sindbad with the giants and dwarfs, on his third voyage (Arabian Nights). The Cat adventure, in the Islay version, may be compared with Sindbad's meeting with the serpents and with the elephants. And

4th. With a Highland story, of some laird of Rasa, whose boat was upset by a company of cats, headed by one large black cat; supposed to be a troop of witches headed by their master.

6. The incident of being buried in a treasure cave with the dead, is common to the Arabian Nights. *See* Sindbad's Fourth Voyage, and Alladdin; and also,

7. To the Deccameron, second day, novel 5; where a man, after a number of adventures, is lowered into a well by two thieves. He is hauled up with a wheel and a rope by the watch, who are frightened and run away, leaving their arms.

The three meet once more; go to the cathedral, and raise up a marble slab laid over the grave of an archbishop. When "Andreuccio" has gone in and robbed the grave, they send him back for a ring, and drop the slab. The priests come on the same errand as the thieves; he frightens them, gets out with the ring, and returns to Perugia from Naples—" having laid out his money on a ring, whereas the intent of his journey was to have bought horses."

In all these, Greek, Italian, Arabic, German, and Gaelic, there is a general resemblance, but nothing more.

I have given three versions of the same story together, as an illustration of the manner in which popular tales actually exist; and as specimens of language. The men who told the story live as far apart as is possible in the Highlands. I heard one of them tell it; each has his own way of telling the incidents; and each gives something peculiar to himself, or to his locality, which the others leave out. Ewan MacLachlan, in discussing the MSS. in the Advocate's Library in 1812, referring to Dean Mac-Greggor's MS., written about 1526, says:—" MacDougall is compared to MacRuslainn, the Polyphemus of our winter tales." It would seem, then, that this story has been long known, and it is now widely spread in the Highlands.

The manners and customs of the king and his tenant are very highland, so far as they can be referred to the present day. Probably they are equally true pictures of bygone days. The king's sons probably visited their vassals, and got into all manner of scrapes. The vassals in all probability resented insults, and rebelled, and took to the wild woods and became outlaws. So the mill was probably the resort of idlers and the place for news, as it still is. The king, in all likelihood, lived very near his own stable, for there are no ruins of palaces; and it seems to have been the part of a brave man to submit without flinching, to have his wrists and ankles tied to the small of his back, and be "tight-ened" and tortured; and then to recite his deeds as an Indian brave might do.

It seems, too, that " Lochlann," now Scandinavia, was once within easy sail of England and Ireland ; and that the King of Lochlann knew the tenants of the neighbouring king. From the history of the Isle of Man, it appears that there really was a king called " Crovan," who is also mentioned by Warsaae (page 287) as the Norwegian Godred Crovan who conquered Man, A.D., 1077. And in this, the stories are probably true recollections of manners and events, so far as they go. When it comes to giants, the story is just as likely to be true in the same sense. There probably was a race of big man-eating savages somewhere on the road from east to west, if not all along the route ; for all popular tales agree in representing giants and wild men as living in caves, hoarding wealth, eating men, and enslaving women.

In these stories the caves are described from nature. When Conal walks along the top of the high shore, "rough with caves and geos," and falls into a cave which has an opening below, he does that which is not only possible but probable. I know many caves on the west coast, where a giant might have walked in with his goats from a level sandy beach, near a deep sea, and some where a man might fall into the further end through a hole in a level green sward, and land safely; many are full of all that belongs to a sheep-fold, or a shelter used by goats and cattle, and by the men who take care of them.

I know one where a whole whisky distillery existed not very long ago; I first landed in it from a boat to pick up a wild pigeon; I afterwards scrambled into it from the shore; and I have looked down into it from smooth green turf, through a hole in the roof, into which there flowed a little stream of water. An active man might drop into the far end on a heap of fallen earth.

And here again comes the notion, that the so-called giants had swords so bright, that they shone in the dark like torches, and that they owned riches hid underground in holes.

Perhaps we may believe the whole as very nearly true. It may be that there really were such people, and that they were miners and shepherds; when those who now tell stories about them, were wandering huntsmen armed with stone weapons.

The third version is remarkable as an instance of the way in which poems of greater merit used to be commonly, and still are occasionally recited. "Cuchullin" was partly told, partly recited, by an old man near Lochawe, within the memory of a clergyman who told me the fact. I heard Patrick Smith, in South Uist, and other men, so recite stories in alternate prose and verse, in 1859; and it appears that the Edda was so composed. Poems of the same nature as "the poems of Ossian," if not the poems themselves, were so recited by an old man in Bowmore more than sixty years ago, when my friend Mr. John Crawford, late Governor of Singapore, and a well-known linguist, was a school boy, who spoke little but Gaelic; and when it was as rare to find a man amongst the peasantry in Islay who could speak English, as it is now remarkable to find one who cannot.

VIII.

MURCHAG A 'S MIONACHAG.

From Ann Darroch, James Wilson, Hector MacLean, Islay,
and many others in other parts of the Highlands.

MOORACHUG and Meenachug went to gather
fruit, and as Moorachug would gather Meenachug
would eat. Moorachug went to seek a rod to lay on
Meenachaig, and she eating his share of fruit.

"What's thy news to-day, oh Voorachai?" said
the rod. "'T is my own news, that I am seeking a rod
to lay on Meenachug, and she eating my share of fruit."

"Thou wilt not get me until thou gettest an axe that
will reap me." He reached the axe. "What's thy
news to-day, oh Voorachai?" "'T is my own news
that I am seeking an axe to reap rod—rod to lay on
Meenachug—and she eating my share of fruit."

"Thou wilt not get me until thou gettest a stone to
smooth me." He reached a stone. "What's thy
news to-day, oh Voorachai?" said the stone. "'T is my
own news that I am seeking stone to smooth axe—axe
to reap rod—rod to lay on Meenachaig—and she eating
my share of fruit."

"Thou wilt not get me," said the stone, "till thou
gettest water will wet me." He reached the water.
"What's thy news to-day, oh Voorachai?" said the
water. "'T is my own news that I am seeking—water
to stone—stone to smooth axe—axe to reap rod—rod

to lay on Meenachaig—and she eating my share of fruit."

"Thou wilt not get me," said the water, "till thou gettest a deer to swim me." He reached the deer. "What's thy news to-day, oh Voorachai?" said the deer. "'Tis my own news, that I am seeking—deer to swim water—water to stone—stone to smooth axe—axe to reap rod—rod to lay on Meenachaig—and she eating my share of fruit."

"Thou wilt not get me," said the deer, "until thou gettest a dog to run me." He reached the dog. "What's thy news to-day, oh Voorachai?" said the dog. "'Tis my own news that I am seeking—dog to run deer—deer to swim water—water to stone—stone to smooth axe—axe to reap rod—rod to lay on Meenachaig—and she eating my share of fruit."

"Thou wilt not get me," said the dog, "till thou gettest butter to be rubbed to my feet." He reached the butter. "What's thy news to-day, oh Voorachai?" said the butter. "'Tis my own news, that I am seeking—butter to feet of dog—dog to run deer—deer to swim water— water to stone—stone to smooth axe—axe to reap rod—rod to lay on Meenachaig—and she eating my share of fruit."

"Thou wilt not get me," said the butter, "till thou gettest a mouse will scrape me." He reached the mouse. "What's thy news to-day, oh Voorachai?" said the mouse. "'Tis my own news, that I am seeking—mouse to scrape butter—butter to feet of dog—dog to run deer—deer to swim water—water to stone—stone to smooth axe—axe to reap rod—rod to lay on Meenachaig—and she eating my share of fruit."

"Thou wilt not get me," said the mouse, "till thou gettest a cat to hunt me." He reached the cat. "What's thy news to-day, oh Voorachai?" said the cat. "'Tis my own news, that I am seeking—cat to hunt mouse—mouse to scrape butter—butter to feet of dog—dog to run deer—deer to swim water—water to stone—stone to smooth axe—axe to reap rod—rod to lay on Meenachaig—and she eating my share of fruit."

"Thou wilt not get me," said the cat, "until thou gettest milk for me." He reached the cow. "What's thy news to-day, oh! Voorachai?" said the cow. "'Tis my own news, that I am seeking—milk for the cat—cat to hunt mouse—mouse to scrape butter—butter to feet of dog—dog to run deer—deer to swim water—water to stone—stone to smooth axe—axe to reap rod—rod to lay on Meenachaig—and she eating my share of fruit."

"Thou wilt not get milk from me till thou gettest a whisp from the barn gillie." He reached the barn gillie. "What's thy news to-day, oh Voorachai?" said the barn gillie. "'Tis my own news, that I am seeking—a whisp for the cow—a cow will shed milk for the cat—cat to hunt mouse—mouse to scrape butter —butter to feet of dog—dog to run deer—deer to swim water—water to stone—stone to smooth axe—axe to reap rod—rod to lay on Meenachaig—and she eating my share of fruit."

"Thou wilt not get a whisp from me," said the barn gillie, "till thou gettest a bonnach for me from the kneading wife." He reached the kneading wife. "What's thy news to-day, oh Voorachai?" said the kneading wife. "'Tis my own news, that I am seeking—bonnach to the barn gillie—whisp to the cow from the barn gillie—milk from the cow to the cat— cat will hunt mouse—mouse will scrape butter—butter to feet of dog—dog to run deer—deer to swim water —water to stone— stone to smooth axe—axe to reap rod—rod to lay on Meenachaig—and she eating my share of fruit."

"Thou wilt not get bonnach from me till thou bringest in water will knead it."

"How will I bring in the water?"   "There is no vessel but that sowen's sieve."

Moorachug took with him the sowen's sieve.   He reached the water, and every drop he would put in the sowen's sieve it would go through.   A hoodie came over his head, and she cried, "Gawr-rag, gawr-rag, little silly, little silly."   "Thou art right, oh hoodie," said Moorachug.   "Crèah rooah s' còinneach, crèah rooah s' còinneach," said the hoodie.

Moorachug set crèah rooah s' còinneach brown clay and moss to it, and he brought in the water to the kneading wife—and he got bonnach from the kneading wife to barn gillie—whisp from the barn gillie to the cow—milk from the cow to the cat—cat to hunt mouse—mouse to scrape butter—butter to feet of dog—dog to run deer—deer to swim water—water to stone—stone to smooth axe—axe to reap rod—rod to lay on Meenachaig—and she eating his share of fruit.   And when Moorachug returned Meenachag had just BURST.

This is the best known of all Gaelic tales.   It is the infant ladder to learning a chain of cause and effect, and fully as sensible as any of its kind.   It used to be commonly taught to children of five or six years of age, and repeated by school boys, and it is still remembered by grown-up people in all parts of the Highlands.   There are few variations.   In one version the crow was a little bird; in another a gull was introduced, which advised the use of sand to stuff the riddle.

The tale has sixteen steps, four of which contain double ideas.   The English house that Jack built has eleven.   The Scotch old woman with the silver penny has twelve.   The Norsk cock and hen a-nutting twelve, ten of which are double.   The German story in Grimm has five or six, all single ideas.   All these are different. In Uist the actors are Biorachan mor agus Bior-chan Beag; in Sutherland, Morachan agus Mionachan.

The speech of the Hoodie is always a very close imitation of his note. In another version she says, " CUIR CRIADH RIGHIN RUADH RIS—Put tough red clay to it;" and the gull said, " CUIR POLL BOG RIS—Put soft mud to it;" which is rather the speech of some other bird. There are several rare words in this; for example, " Gadhar," a dog.

MURCHADH A'S MIONACHAG.

DH 'fholbh Murchadh a's Mionachag a bhuain sugh, 's mar a bhuaineadh Murchadh dh' itheadh Mionachag. Dh 'fholbh Murchadh a dh' iarraidh slat a a ghabhail air Mionachaig 's i 'g itheadh a chuid sugh—" De do naigheachd an diugh a Mhurchaidh?" urs' an t-slat. " 'Se mo naigheachd féin gu 'bheil mi 'g iarraidh Slat a ghabhail air Mionachag 's i 'g itheadh mo chuid sugh." " Cha 'n fhaigh thu mise gus am faigh," " thu tuagh a bhuaineas mi." Ràinig e 'n tuagh. " De do naigheachd an diugh a Mhurchaidh?" Se mo naigheachd féin gu 'bheil mi 'g iarraidh Tuagh a bhuaineas slat Slat a ghabhail air Mionachaig 's i 'g itheadh mo chuid sugh— " Cha 'n fhaigh thu mise gus am fhaigh thu clach a liobhas mi." " Ràinig e 'chlach. Dé do naigheachd an diugh a Mhurchaidh?" urs' a' chlach. " 'Se mo naigheachd féin gu 'bheil mi 'g iarraidh Clach a liobhadh tuagh—Tuagh a bhuain slat—Slat a ghabhail air Mionachaig 's i 'g itheadh mo chuid sugh." " Cha n fhaigh thu mis'," urs' a' chlach, " gus am faigh thu uisge a fhliuchas mi." Ràinig e 'n t-uisge—" De do naigheachd an diugh a Mhurchaidh?" urs' an t-uisge. 'S e mo naigheachd féin gu bheil mi 'g iarraidh Uisge ma chloich—Clach a liobhadh tuagh—Tuagh a bhuain slat—Slat a ghabhail air Mionach-aig 's i 'g itheadh mo chuid sugh. Cha 'n fhaigh thu mis', urs' an t-uisge, gus am faigh thu fiadh a shnàmhas mi." Ràinig e 'm fiadh. " Dé do naigheachd an diugh a Mhurchaidh?" urs' am fiadh. " 'Se mo naigheachd féin gu 'bheil mi 'g iarraidh Fiadh a shnàmh uisg'. Uisge ma chloich. Clach a liobhadh tuagh. Tuagh a bhuain slat. Slat a ghabhail air Mionachaig 's i 'g itheadh mo chuid sugh." " Cha 'n fhaigh thu mis'," urs' am fiadh, " gus am faigh thu gadhar a ruith-eas mi." Ràinig e 'n gadhar. " De do naigheachd an diugh a Mhurch-

M

aidh?" urs' an gadhar. "'S e mo naigheachd féin gu 'bheil mi 'g iarraidh Gadhar a ruith fiadh. Fiadh a shnàmh uisg'. Uisge ma chloich. Clach a liobhadh tuagh. Tuagh a bhuain slat. Slat a ghabhail air Mionachaig 's i 'g itheadh mo chuid sugh." "Cha 'n fhaigh thu mis," urs' an gadhar, "gus am faigh thu im a rubar ri m' chasan." Ràinig e 'n t-im. "De do naigheachd an diugh a Mhurchaidh?" urs' an t-im. "'Se mo naigheachd féin gu 'bheil mi 'g iarraidh Im chasa gadhair. Gadhar a ruith fiadh. Fiadh a shnàmh uisg'. Uisge ma chloich. Clach a liobhadh tuagh. Tuagh a bhuain slat. Slat a ghabhail air Mionachaig 's i 'g itheadh mo chuid sugh." "Cha 'n fhaigh thu mis'," urs' an t-im, "gus am faigh thu luch a sgrìobas mi." "Ràinig e 'n luch. "De do naigheachd an diugh a Mhurchaidh?" urs' an luch. "Se mo naigheachd féin gu bheil mi 'g iarraidh. Luch a sgriobadh im. Im chasa gadhair. Gadhar a ruith fiadh. Fiadh a shnàmh uisg'. Uisge ma cloich. Clach a liobhadh tuagh. Tuagh a bhuain slat. Slat a ghabhail air Mionachaig 's i 'g itheadh mo chuid sugh." "Cha 'n fhaigh thu mis'," urs' an luch, "gus am faigh thu cat a shealgas mi." Ràinig e 'n cat. "De do naigheachd an diugh a Mhurchaidh?" urs' an cat. "'Se mo naigheachd féin gu 'bheil mi 'g iarraidh Cat a shealg luch. Luch a sgrìobadh im. Im chasa gadhair. Gadhar a ruith fiadh. Fiadh a shnàmh uisg'. Uisge ma chloich. Clach a liobhadh tuagh. Tuagh a bhuain slat. Slat a ghabhail air Mionachaig 's i 'g itheadh mo chuid sugh." "Cha 'n fhaigh thu mis'," urs' an cat, "gus am faigh thu bainne dhomb." Ràinig e 'Bhò. "De do naigheachd an diugh a Mhurchaidh?" urs' a' bhò. "'Se mo naigheachd féin gu' bheil mi 'g iarraidh Bainne do 'n chat. Cat a shealg luch. Luch a sgrìobadh im. Im chasa gadhar. Gadhar a ruith fiadh. Fiadh a shnàmh uisg'." Uisge ma chloich. Clach a liobhadh tuagh. Tuagh a bhuain slat. Slat a ghabhail air Mionachaig 's i 'g itheadh mo chuid sugh. "Cha 'n fhaigh thu bainne uamsa, gus am faigh thu sop o 'n ghille shabhaill. Ràinig e 'n gille sabhaill. "Dé do naigheachd an diugh a Mhurchaidh?" urs' an gille sabhaill. "'Se mo naigheachd féin gu 'bheil mi 'g iarraidh. Sop a gheobh bò. Bo bhligheadh bainne do 'n chat. Cat a shealg luch. Luch a sgrìobadh im. Im chasa gadhar. Gadhar a ruith fiadh. Fiadh a shnàmh uisg'. Uisge ma chloich. Clach a liobhadh tuagh. Tuagh a bhuain slat. Slat a ghabhail air Mionachaig 's i 'g itheadh mo chuid sugh. "Cha 'n fhaigh thu sop uamsa," urs' an gille sabhaill, "gus am faigh thu Bonnach dhomb o 'n Bhean fhuinne." Ràinig e 'bhean fhuinne. "De do naigheachd an diuch a Mhurchaidh?" urs' a' bhean fhuinne. "'Se mo naigheachd féin gu 'bheil mi' g iarraidh Bonnach do 'n ghille shabhaill. Sop do 'n Bho o 'n Ghille shabhaill. Bainn' o 'n Bho do 'n chat. Cat a shealgas luch. Luch a sgrìobas im. Im chasa gadhair. Gadhar a ruith fiadh. Fiadh a shnàmh uisg'. Uisge ma chloich. Clach a hobhadh tuagh. Tuagh a bhuain slat. Slat a ghabhail air Mionachaig 's i 'g itheadh mo chuid sugh. "Cha 'n fhaigh thu bonnach uamsa mar an d' thoir thu stigh uisg' a dh' fhainneas e." Dé mar a' bheir mi stigh an t-Uisge?" "Cha 'n 'eil soitheach ann ach an Criathar Cabhrach sin." Thug Murchadh leis an Criathar Cabhrach, 's ràinig e n t-uisge, 's a h-uile deur a chuireadh e 's a' Chriathar Chabhrach rachadh e roimhe. Thàinig Feannag as a chionn 's ghlaoidh i "Gòrrag, gòrrag." "Tha thu ceart fheannag," ursa Murchadh. "Crèadh ruagh 's còinneach, crèadh ruagh 's còinneach." Chuir Murchadh crèadh ruagh 's còinneach ris, 's thug e 'stigh an t-Uisge, 's fhuair e Bonnach o 'n Bhean fuinne do 'n Ghille shabhaill. Sop o 'n Ghille shabhaill do 'n Bhò. Bainn' o 'n Bhò do 'n chat. Cat a shealg luch. Luch a sgrìobadh im. Im chasa gadhair. Gadhar a ruith fiadh. Fiadh a shnàmh uisg'. Uisge ma chloich. Clach a hobhadh tuagh. Tuagh a bhuain slat. Slat a ghabhail air Mionachaig 's i 'g itheadh a chuid sugh. 'S nur a thill Murchadh bha Mionachag an déigh SGAINEADH !!

IX.

THE BROWN BEAR OF THE GREEN GLEN.

From John MacDonald, Travelling Tinker.

THERE was a king in Erin once, who had a leash of sons. John was the name of the youngest one, and it was said that he was not wise enough; and this good worldly king lost the sight of his eyes, and the strength of his feet. The two eldest brothers said that they would go seek three bottles of the water of the green Isle that was about the heaps of the deep.* And so it was that these two brothers went away. Now the fool said that he would not believe but that he himself would go also. And the first big town he reached in his father's kingdom, there he sees his two brothers there, the blackguards! "Oh! my boys," says the young one, "is it thus you are?" "With swiftness of foot," said they, "take thyself home, or we will have thy life." "Don't be afraid, lads. It is nothing to me to stay with you." Now John went away on his journey till he came to a great desert of a wood. "Hoo, hoo!" says John to himself, "It is not canny for me to walk this wood alone." The night was coming now, and growing pretty dark. John ties the cripple white horse that was under him to the root of a tree, and he went up in the top himself. He was but a very short time in the top, when he saw a bear

* "Eilean uaine a bha 'n iomal torra domhain.

coming with a fiery cinder in his mouth. " Come down, son of the king of Erin," says he. " Indeed, I won't come. I am thinking I am safer where I am." " But if thou wilt not come down, I will go up," said the bear. " Art thou, too, taking me for a fool ? " says John. " A shaggy, shambling creature like thee, climbing a tree ! " " But if thou wilt not come down I will go up," says the bear, as he fell out of hand to climbing the tree. " Lord ! thou canst do that same ? " said John ; " keep back from the root of the tree, then. and I will go down to talk to thee." And when the son of Erin's king drew down, they came to chatting. The bear asked him if he was hungry. " Weel ! by your leave," said John, " I am a little at this very same time." The bear took that wonderful watchful turn and he catches a roebuck. " Now, son of Erin's king," says the bear, " whether wouldst thou like thy share of the buck boiled or raw ? " " The sort of meat I used to get would be kind of plotted boiled," says John ; and thus it fell out. John got his share roasted. " Now," said the bear, " lie down between my paws, and thou hast no cause to fear cold or hunger till morning." Early in the morning the Maon (bear) asked, " Art thou asleep, son of Erin's king ? " " I am not very heavily," said he. " It is time for thee to be on thy soles then. Thy journey is long — two hundred miles ; but art thou a good horseman, John ? " " There are worse than me at times," said he. " Thou hadst best get on top of me, then." He did this, and at the first leap John was to earth.

" Foil ! foil ! " says John. " What ! thou art not bad at the trade thyself. Thou hadst best come back till we try thee again." And with nails and teeth he fastened on the Mathon, till they reached the end of the two hundred miles and a giant's house. " Now,

John," said the Mathon, "thou shalt go to pass the
night in this giant's house;" thou wilt find him
pretty grumpy, but say thou that it was the brown
bear of the green glen that set thee here for a night's
share, and don't thou be afraid that thou wilt not get
share and comfort." And he left the bear to go to the
giant's house. "Son of Ireland's King," says the
giant, "thy coming was in the prophecy; but if I did
not get thy father, I have got his son. I don't know
whether I will put thee in the earth with my feet, or
in the sky with my breath." "Thou wilt do neither
of either," said John, "for it is the brown bear of the
green glen that set me here." Come in, son of Erin's
king," said he, "and thou shalt be well taken to this
night." And as he said, it was true. John got meat
and drink without stint. But to make a long tale
short, the bear took John day after day to the third
giant. "Now," says the bear, "I have not much acquaintance with this giant, but thou wilt not be long in
his house when thou must wrestle with him. And if he
is too hard on thy back, say thou, 'If I had the brown
bear of the green glen here, that was thy master.'"
As soon as John went in—Ai! ai!! or ee! ee!!" says
the giant, "If I did not get thy father, I have got his
son;" and to grips they go. They would make the
boggy bog of the rocky rock. In the hardest place
they would sink to the knee; in the softest, up to the
thighs; and they would bring wells of spring water
from the face of every rock. The giant gave John a
sore wrench or two. "Foil! foil!!" says he. "If I
had here the brown bear of the green glen, thy leap
would not be so hearty." And no sooner spoke he the
word than the worthy bear was at his side. "Yes! yes!"
says the giant, "son of Erin's king, now I know
thy matter better than thou dost thyself." So it was

that the giant ordered his shepherd to bring home the best wether he had in the hill, and to throw his carcass before the great door. "Now, John," says the giant, "an eagle will come and she will settle on the carcass of this wether, and there is a wart on the ear of this eagle which thou must cut off her with this sword, but a drop of blood thou must not draw." The eagle came, but she was not long eating when John drew close to her, and with one stroke he cut the wart off her without drawing one drop of blood. (*"Och! is not that a fearful lie?"*) "Now," said the eagle, "come on the root of my two wings, for I know thy matter better than thou dost thyself." He did this; and they were now on sea, and now on land, and now on the wing, till they reached the Green Isle. "Now, John," says she, "be quick, and fill thy three bottles; remember that the black dogs are away just now." (*"What dogs?"* *"Black dogs; dost thou not know that they always had black dogs chasing the Gregorach!"*) When he filled the bottles with the water out of the well, he sees a little house beside him. John said to himself that he would go in, and that he would see what was in it. And the first chamber he opened, he saw a full bottle. (*"And what was in it?"* *"What should be in it but whisky."*) He filled a glass out of it, and he drank it; and when he was going, he gave a glance, and the bottle was as full as it was before. "I will have this bottle along with the bottles of water," says he.

Then he went into another chamber, and he saw a loaf; he took a slice out of it, but the loaf was as whole as it was before. "Ye gods! I won't leave thee," says John. He went on thus till he came to another chamber. He saw a great cheese; he took a slice off the cheese, but it was as whole as ever. "I

will have this along with the rest," says he. Then he
went to another chamber, and he saw laid there the
very prettiest little jewel of a woman he ever saw.
"It were a great pity not to kiss thy lips, my love,"
says John.

Soon after, John jumped on top of the eagle, and she
took him on the self same steps till they reached the
house of the big giant, and they were paying rent to
the giant, and there was the sight of tenants and giants
and meat and drink. "Well! John," says the giant,
"didst thou see such drink as this in thy father's house
in Erin?" "Pooh," says John, "Hoo! my hero;
thou other man, I have a drink that *is* unlike it."
He gave the giant a glass out of the bottle, but the
bottle was as full as it was before. "Well!" said the
giant, "I will give thee myself two hundred notes, a
bridle and a saddle for the bottle." "It is a bargain,
then," says John, "but that the first sweetheart I ever
had must get it if she comes the way." "She will get
that," says the giant; but, to make the long story short,
he left each loaf and cheese with the two other giants,
with the same covenant that the first sweetheart he
ever had should get them if she came the way.

Now John reached his father's big town in Erin,
and he sees his two brothers as he left them—the
"blackguardan!" "You had best come with me, lads,"
says he, "and you will get a dress of cloth, and a horse
and a saddle and bridle each." And so they did;
but when they were near to their father's house, the
brothers thought that they had better kill him, and so
it was that they set on him. And when they thought
he was dead, they threw him behind a dike; and they
took from him the three bottles of water, and they
went home. John was not too long here, when his
father's smith came the way with a cart load of rusty

iron. John called out, "Whoever the Christian is that
is there, oh! that he should help him." The smith
caught him, and he threw John amongst the iron;
and because the iron was so rusty, it went into each
wound and sore that John had; and so it was, that
John became rough skinned and bald. Here we will
leave John, and we will go back to the pretty little
jewel that John left in the Green Isle. She became
pale and heavy; and at the end of three quarters, she
had a fine lad son. "Oh! in all the great world," says
she, "how did I find this?" "Foil! foil!" says the hen-
wife, "don't let that set thee thinking. Here's for
thee a bird, and as soon as he sees the father of thy
son, he will hop on the top of his head." The
Green Isle was gathered from end to end, and the
people were put in at the back door and out at the
front door; but the bird did not stir, and the babe's
father was not found. Now here, she said she would
go through the world altogether till she should find the
father of the babe. Then she came to the house of
the big giant and sees the bottle. "Ai! ai!!" said
she, "who gave thee this bottle?" Said the giant, "It
was young John, son of Erin's king, that left it."
"Well, then, the bottle is mine," said she. But to
make the long story short, she came to the house of
each giant, and she took with her each bottle, and each
loaf, and each cheese, till at length and at last she came
to the house of the king of Erin. Then the five-fifths
of Erin were gathered, and the bridge of nobles of the
people; they were put in at the back door and out at
the front door, but the bird did not stir. Then she
asked if there was one other or any one else at all in
Erin, that had not been here. "I have a bald rough-
skinned gillie in the smithy," said the smith, "but,"——
"Rough on or off, send him here," says she. No sooner

did the bird see the head of the bald rough-skinned gillie, than he took a flight and settles on the bald top of the rough-skinned lad. She caught him and kisse him. Thou art the father of my babe."

"But, John," says the great king of Erin, "It is thou that gottest the bottles of water for me." "Indeed, 't was I," says John. "Weel, then, what art thou willing to do to thy two brothers?" "The very thing they wished to do to me, do for them;" and that same was done. John married the daughter of the king of the Green Isle, and they made a great rich wedding that lasted seven days and seven years, and thou couldst but hear leeg, leeg, and beeg, beeg, solid sound and peg drawing. Gold a-crushing from the soles of their feet to the tips of their fingers, the length of seven years and seven days.

SGEULACHD AIR MATH-GHAMHAINN DONN A GHLINN UAINNE.

Bha rìgh air Eirinn aon uair, aig an robh triùir mhac, 's b' ainm don fhear a b' òige Iain, 's bha e air a radh nach robh e glic na leòir, agus chaill an rìgh saoghalta so sealladh a shùilean, 's lùgh nan cas. Thubhairt an da bhràthair bu shine gun rachadh iadsan air tòir tri botuil usige do'n eilean uaine a bha 'n iomall torra domhain, agus 'se bh' ann gun d' fhalbh an da bhràthair so. Thubhairt an t-amadan nach creideadh e fèin nach falbhadh e cuideachd, agus a cheud bhaile-mòr do 'n d' thàing e ann an rìoghachd athar, faicear a dha bhràthair an sin 'nam blaigeartan! "O a bhalacha!" ars' am fear òg, "an ann mar so a tha sibhse." "Air luathas do chas," ars' iadsan, "thoir an tigh ort air neo bithidh do bheatha againn." "Na bitheadh eagal oirbh rombam cha 'n fhiach leamsa fanachd maille ribh." D'fhalbh Iain an so air a thurus, gus an d' thàinig e gu fàsach mòr do choille. Hu! Huth! ars' Iain ris fèin, "Cha 'neil e cneasda dhòmhsa a' choille so a choiseachd leam fhéin." Bha 'n oidhche a' tighinn a nis, 's i

fàs gu math dorcha. Ceangailear Iain an t-each bacach, bàn a bha
foidhe ri bun craoibhe 's chaidh e féin suas 'na bàrr. Cha robh e
ach goirid 'na bàrr gus am fac e math-ghamhainn a' tighinn 's eibh-
leag theine na bheul. " Thig a nuas, a mhic rìgh Eirinn," ars' esan.
" Gu dearbh, cha d' thig, tha mi smaointeachadh gu' bheil mi nis
tèaruinte far am bheil mi." " Ach mur d' thig thusa nuas théid mise
suas," arsa 'm math-ghamhainn. "'M bheil thusa 'gam ghabhail 'nam
amadan cuideachd," thuirt Jain. Creutair robagach, liobarta coltach
riutsa a streapadh chraobh. " Ach mur d' thig thusa nuas, théid mise
suas," ars' am math-ghamhainn 's e 'toirt a ghrad làimh air streapadh
na craoibhe. "'S dia ni thu sin fhéin," thuirt Iain. " Fan air t' ais fo
bhun na craoibhe mata, 's théid mi sìos a bhruidhinn rint." Agus dur a
theirinn mac rìgh Eirinn a nuas, thàinig iad gu cracaireachd. Dh'
fheòrich a' mhath-ghamhainn dheth, 'an robh an t-acras air ? " Uill
le 'r cead," ars' Iain, " tha beagan orm dheth 'sa cheart am so fein."
Thug am math-ghamhainn an sgrìob uallach, aighearach 'ud, 's
beirear air boc earba. " A nis, a mhic rìgh Eirinn," arsa am math-
ghamhainn, " Co 's feàrr leat do chuid do 'n bhoc bruich na amh."
" An seòrsa bìdh a b' àbhairt dhòmhsa fhaotainn, bhitheadh seòrsa
plotadh bruich air," ars' Iain. Agus 'sann a so mar thachair.
Fhuair Iain a chuid fhéin ròiste. " A nis," arsa 'm math-ghamhainn,
" luidh sìos eadar mo spògan-sa, 's cha 'n eagal fuachd no acrais dhuit gu
madainn." Moch 'sa mhadainn, dh' fhoighneachd am math-ghamhainn,
" Am bheil thu 'd chadal, a mhic rìgh Eirinn." " Cha 'n 'eil anabarrach trom," thuirt esan. Tha 'n t-àm dhuit a bhi air do bhuinn
mata, tha 'n t-astar fada, da cheud mìle ; ach am bheil thu 'nad
'mharcaiche math, Iain ? " Tha na 's miosa na mi air amannan,"
thuirt esan. "'S feàrr dhuit tighinn air mo mhuinn mata." Rinn e
so, agus air a cheud leum, bha Iain ri talamh. " Fòil! Fòil!" ars'
Iain, dè 'cha 'n 'eil thu fhein dona air a cheaird! 'S feàrr dhuit
tighinn air t-ais gus am feuch sinn a rithist thu ; 's leiongan 's fiaclan
ghreimich e ris a mha'ghan, gus an d' ràinig iad ceann an dà cheud
mìle, 's tigh famhair. " Nis Iain," arsa 'm ma'ghan, " théid thu chuir
seachad na h-oidhche ann an tigh an fhamhair so." Gheibh thu e gu
maith gnò, ach abair thusa gur e mathghamhainn donn a' ghlinn
uaine, a chuir thusa an so air son cuid oidhche, agus na biodh eagal
ort nach fòaigh thu cuid 'us comhnadh. 'S dh 'fhàg am mathghamhainn e 'dol gu tigh an fhamhair. "A mhic rìgh Eirinn," ars' 'am famh
air, bha 'san targradh thu bhi tighinn, ach mar d' fhuair mi t' athair,
fhuair mi 'mhac ; cha 'n 'eil fios agam co dhiu chuireas mi 'san talamh
thu le m' chasan, no 'san adhar le m'anail." " Cha deàn thu aon chuid
do 'n da chuid," thuirt Iain. " Oir se mathghamhainn donn a' ghlinn
uaine a chuir mise 'n so." " Thig a stigh, a mhic rìgh Eirinn,"

thuirt esan, "'s gheibh thu gabhail agad gu maith a nochd ;" agus
mar thubhairt b 'fhìor. Fhuair Iain biadh 's deoch gun ghainne ; ach
gus an sgeulachd fada a dheànamh goirid, thug am mathghamhainn
Iain latha an déigh latha gus an treas famhair. "'A nis," ars' am
mathghamhainn, " cha 'n 'eil mòran eòlais agamsa air an fhamhair so,
ach cha bhi thu fada 'na thigh dar a dh' fheumas tu dol a ghleachd
ris, agus ma bhitheas e tuillidh 's cruaidh air do shon, abair thusa na
'm biodh agamsa ma'ghan donn a ghlinn uaine, b'e sin do maighstir."   Co luath 'sa chaidh Iain a stigh, Ai! Ai! ars' am famhair
mòr, mar d'fhuair mi t' athair, fhuair mi 'mhac, agus 'sa chéile ghabh
iad ; 's dhèanadh iad a bhogan don chreagan—an t-aite bu chruaidhe,
rachadh iad foidh gu'n glùinean, san t-àite bu bhuige gu 'n sléisdean,
's bheireadh iad fuaranan fìor uisge a h-aodann gach creagain. Thug
am famhair fàsgadh goirt na dithis do'dh' Iain. " Fòil! Fòil!," thuirt
esan, na'm biodh agamsa an so mathghamhainn donn a' ghlinn
uaine, cha bhiodh do leum co sunndach ;" agus cha luaith a labhair
e 'm facal na bha am ma'ghan còir ri 'thaobh. " Seadh! Seadh! ars'
am famhair, a mhic righ Eirinn, tha fios agam a nis air do ghnothach n' is feàrr na tha agad fhéin." 'Se bh' ann gun d-òrduich am
famhair do 'n chìobair aige am molt a b' fheàrr a bha 'sa' bheinn a
thoirt dhachaidh, agus a' chlosach a thilgeadh ma choinneamh an
doruis mhòir.   " A nis, Iain, ars' am famhair, thig iolaire, agus
luidhidh i air closach a mhuilt so, agus tha foinneamh air cluais na
h-iolaire so, a dh' fheumas tusa a ghearradh dhi le aon bheum leis a'
chlaidheamh so, ach deur fola cha 'n 'fheud thu tharruinn." Thàinig
an iolaire, 's cha robh i fada 'g itheadh dar a theann Iain rithe, 's le
aon bheum gheàrr e 'm foinneamh dhi gun aon deur fola a tharruinn.
" Anis arsa 'n iolaire, thig air bun mo dha sgéithe, bho 'n a tha fios
agam air do ghnothuch n' is feàrr na th' agad féin." Rinn e so, agus
bha iad uair air muir, 's uair air talamh, 's uair air an sgiathan, gus an
d' ràinig iad an t-Eilean uaine.   " Nis Iain, ars' ise, bi calamh, 's
lìon do bhotuil ; cuimhnich gu bheil na coin dhubha air falbh an
ceartair." Nuair a lìon e na botuil do 'n uisge as an tobar, faicear
tigh beag làimh ris.   Thuirt Iain ris féin gu'n rachadh e stigh, s gu
'm faiceadh e dé bh' ann, agus a cheud seòmar a dh' fhosgail e,
chunnaic e botull làn do dh-uisge beatha, lìon e gloinne as, 's dh' òl
e 'san uair a dh' òl, thug e sùil, 's bha 'm botull cho làn sa bha e
roimhe. " Bithidh 'm botull so agam còmhla ris na botuil uisge," ars'
esan. Chaidh e 'n sin a stigh do sheomar eile, 's chunnaic e builionn ;
thug e sliseag as, ach bha 'm builionn cho slàn sa bha e roimhe.
" S' Dia cha 'n fhàg mi thus'," ars' Iain. Chaidh e air aghaidh mar
so gus an d' ràinig eseò mar eile ; chunnaic e mulachag mhòr chàise,
thug e sliseag do 'n mhulachaig, ach bha i cho slàn sa bha i roimhe.

"Bithidh so agam còmhla ri càch," ars' esan. Chaidh e 'n so gu
seòmar eile, 's faicear 'na luidhe an sin an t-aon àilleagan boirrionn-
aich bu bhòidche a chunnaic e riamh. "Bu mhòr am beud gun
phòg beòil a thoirt dhuit, a ghaoil," ars' Iain. Beagan 'na dheigh so,
leum Iain air muin na h-iolaire 's thug i e air a chas cheum cheudna,
gus an d-ràinig iad tigh an fhamhair mhòir, 's bha iad a pàidheadh a
mhàil do 'n famhair, agus 's ann an sin a bha 'n sealladh air tuathanaich, 's famhairean, 's biadh, 's deoch. "Wél, Iain," ars' am famhair,
"am fac thu 'leithid so do dheoch ann an tigh t' athar an Eirinn."
"Puth! ars' Iain, hu! a laochain, a dhuine eile, tha deoch agamsa
nach ionann." Thug e gloinne do 'n fhamhair as a bhotul, ach bha
'm botul cho làn 'sa bha e roimhe. "Mata, ars' am famhair, bheir mi
fhéin da chèud nott dhuit air son a' bhotuil, srian, agus dìollaid."
"'S bargain e mata," ars' Iain, "ach gu 'feum an ceud leannan a bha
agamsa fhaotainn ma thig i 'n rathad." "Gheibh i sin," ars' am
famhair, "ach gus an sgeulachd fada a dhèanamh goirid, dh' fhàg e
gach builionn 's gach mulachag aig an da fhamhair eile, air a'
chumhnant cheudna gu' faigheadh an ceud leannan bha aige-san iad
na 'n d' thigeadh i 'n rathad. Ràinig Iain an so baile mòr athar ann
an Eirinn, 's faicear a dha bhràthair mar dh' fhàg e iad 'nam blaigeartan. "'S feàrr dhuibh tighinn dhachaidh leamsa, illean," ars' esan,
's gheibh sibh deis' eudaich, 's each, 's dìollaid. 's srian am fear; agus
mur so rinn iad; ach dar a bha iad dlùth do thigh an athair, smaoinich a bhràithrean gum b' fheàrr dhoibh a mharbhadh, agus 's e bh' ann
gun do thòisich iad air, 's dar a shaoil leo e bhi marbh, thilg iad e air
cùl gàrraidh, 's thug iad uaidh na tri botuil uisge, 's dh' fhalbh iad
dhachaidh. Cha robh Iain ro fhada an so, nuair a thàinig an gobha
aig athair an rathad le làn cairt do dh' iarunn meirgeach. Ghlaodh
Iain a mach co air bith an crìosduidh tha 'n sin, O! e dheanamh
cobhair dhàsan. Rug an gobha air, 's thilg e Iain am measg an
iaruinn, agus leis cho meirgeach 'sa bha 'n t-iarrunn, chaidh e
ann's gach lot 's creuchd a bh' air Iain, agus 's e bh' ann,
gun do chinn Iain maol, carrach. Fàgaidh sinn Iain an so, agus
tillidh sinn ris an àilleagan bhòidheach a dh' fhàg Iain 'san eilean
uaine. Chinn i 'n so trom, torrach, breac, ballach, 'san ceann tri ràithean, bha mac brèagh gille aice. "O air an t-saoghail mhòr," ars'
ise, "cia mar a fhuair mise so?" "Foil! Foil!" ars' a' chailleach
chearc, "na cuireadh sin smaointeach ort; so dhuit eun, agus co luath
sa chi e athair do mhic, leumaidh e air mullach a chinn. Chaidh an
t-eilean uaine a chruinneachadh bho cheann gu ceann, 's an sluagh
a chur a stigh air an dorus chùil 's amach air an dorus bheòil, ach
cha do ghluais an t-eun, 's cha d' fhuaireadh athair an leinibh. Thubhairt i 'n so "gu falbhadh i feadh an t-saoghail gu leir, gus am faigheadh

i athair a leinibh. Thainig i 'n so gu tigh an fhamhair mhòir," agus
faicear am botul. "Ai! Ai! deir ise, co thug dhuit am botul so?"
Thuirt am famhair, "'se lain òg mac rìgh Eirinn a dh' fhàg e."
" Mata 's leamsa am botul," thuirt ise, ach gu an sgeulachd fad' a
dheànamh goirid, thàinig i gu tigh gach famhair, 's thug i leatha
gach botul 's gach builionn 's gach mulachag chàise : Gus ma dheireadh thall, thàinig i gu tigh rìgh Eirinn. Chaidh 'n so cuig cuig-
eamh na h-Eirinn a chruinneachadh 's drochaid cheudan na maith.
Chaidh an cur a stigh air an dorus chùil, 's a mach air an dorus bheòil,
ach cha do ghluais an t-eun. "Dh' fheòraich i 'n so, an robh a h-aon
na h-aon idir eile ann an Eirinn nach robb 'n so?" "Tha gille maol,
carrach anns a' cheàrdach agamsa," thuirt an gobha ach ; " "Car air
na dheth, cuir an so e, deir ise ; 's cha bo luaithe a chunnaic an t-eun
ceann a ghille mhaoil charraich na 'thug e iteag 's luidhear air maol
mhullaich a' ghille charrich. Rug i air 's phòg i e." " 'S tusa athair mo
leinibh." "Ach Iain," arsa rìgh mòr Eirinn," 's tusa a fhuair na botuil
uisge dhòmhsa." "Ach gu dearbh 's mi." ars' Iain. " Will, mata, dè
tha thu toileach a dhèanamh ri 'd' dhithis bhraithrean ?" "A cheart
rud a bha iadsan toileach a dhèanamh ormsa, cur as doibh ; " agus 's
e sin fein a rinneadh. Phòs Iain 's nighean rìgh an Eilean Uaine, 's
rinn iad banais mhòr ghreadhnach a mhair seachd lathan 's seachd
bliadhna 's cha chluinneadh tu ach lig, lig, 's big, big, fuaim tail
's tarruing pinne, òr 'ga phronnadh bho bhonn an coise gu barr am
meòir fad sheachd bliadhna 's sheachd lathan.

Written from the recitation of JOHN MACDONALD, travelling
tinker. He wanders all over the Highlands, and lives in a tent
with his family. He can neither read nor write. He repeats
some of his stories by heart fluently, and almost in the same
words. I have followed his recitation as closely as possible, but
it was exceedingly difficult to keep him stationary for any length
of time. HECTOR URQUHART.

The tinker's comments I got from the transcriber. John
himself is a character ; he is about fifty years of age ; his father,
an old soldier, is alive and about eighty ; and there are numerous
younger branches ; and they were all encamped under the root of
a tree in a quarry close to Inverary, at Easter 1859.

The father tells many stories, but his memory is failing. The
son told me several, and I have a good many of them written
down. They both recite ; they do not simply tell the story, but
act it with changing voice and gesture, as if they took an interest

in it, and entered into the spirit and fun of the tale.   They belong
to the race of "Cairds," and are as much nomads as the gipsies
are.

The father, to use the son's expression, "never saw a school."
He served in the 42d in his youth.   One son makes horn spoons,
and does not know a single story; the other is a sporting character, a famous fisherman, who knows all the lochs and rivers in
the Highlands, makes flies, and earns money in summer by teaching
Southerns to fish.   His ambition is to become an underkeeper.

This bear story is like a great many others which I have got
elsewhere in the Highlands, but I have none told exactly in the
same way.   It should be much longer, but the wandering spirit
of the man would not let him rest to dictate his story.   They had
to move to an outhouse and let him roam about amongst the
shavings, and swing his arms, before this much was got out of him.

I have found the same restlessness amongst wanderers elsewhere.   I could never get Lapps to sit still for ten minutes when
I tried to draw them; and the air of a house seemed to oppress
them.   I have hitherto failed in catching an English tinker,
whom I let slip one day in London, and to whom I promised good
pay if he would come and dictate a story which he had told me.
There is a similar wandering population in Norway and Sweden.
They own boats and carts, and pretend to magic arts; and are
feared and detested by householders as wizards and thieves.   It
is said that these Norwegian wanderers hold a meeting on a hill
near Christiania, once a year, and barter and sell, and exchange
whatever they may have acquired in their travels.   I have heard
a great deal about them from peasants.   I have seen them, but
very seldom in Norway.   I once met a party in the gloaming on
a Swedish road, and a little girl, who was following and driving a
gentleman in a posting-cart, when she met them, flogged her
horse and galloped for dear life.

There is a similar race in Spain, and though they are not all
gipsies, they are classed with them.   The history of these wanderers would be curious if it could be learned.   Borrow's Bible in
Spain gives some insight, but there is still much to be known
about them.   "London Labour and the Poor," and reports on
"Ragged Schools," treat of similar people.

This story may be compared with Grimm's Water of Life.

X.

THE THREE SOLDIERS.

From James MacLachlan, servant, Islay.

THERE was before a regiment in Dublin in
Erin, and it was going a long journey. There
was a sergeant, a corporal, and a single soldier, who
had sweethearts in the town. They went to see them
on the day that they were to go, and they stayed too
long, and the regiment left them; they followed it,
and they were going and going till the night came on
them. They saw a light a long way from them; and
if it was a long way from them, it was not long they
were in reaching it. They went in, the floor was
ready swept, and a fire on it, and no one in; they
sat at the fire toasting themselves; they were not long
there when the single soldier rose, to whom was the
name of John, to look what was in the chamber, because there was a light in it. There was there a board
covered with every sort of meat, and a lighted candle
on it; he went up, he began to eat, and the rest began to hinder him, for that he had no business with it.
When they saw that he did not stop, they went up
and they began themselves. There were three beds in
the chamber, and one of them went to lie in each bed;
they had not laid long when three great red girls
came in, and one of them stretched herself near each
one of the beds; and when they saw the time fitting

in the morning, they rose and went away. When the girls rose, it could not be known that a bit had ever come off the board. They sat and they took their meat. The sergeant said that they had better follow the regiment; and John said that they should not follow it; as long as he could get meat and rest that he would not go. When dinner time came they sat and they took their dinner. The sergeant said they had better go; and John said that they should not go. When supper time came they sat and they took their supper; after supping they went to lie down, each one to his own bed. The girls came this night too, and went to lie down as before. In the morning when they saw the time fitting, they rose and they went away. When the lads rose the board was covered, and it could not be known that a bit had ever come off it. They sat and they took their meat; and when they took their meat, the sergeant said that they *would* go at all events. John said that they should not go. They took their dinner and their supper as they used; they went to lie down; the girls came and they lay down after them. In the morning the eldest gave the sergeant a purse, and every time he would unloose it, it would be full of gold and silver.

She said to the middle one, " What wilt thou give to thine ?" " I will give him a towel, and every time he spreads it it will be full of every sort of meat." She gave the towel to the corporal; and she said to the youngest, " What wilt thou give to thine own ?" " I will give him a whistle, and every time he plays it he will be in the very middle of the regiment." She gave him the whistle; they left their blessing with them, and they went away. " I wont let it rest here," said John; " I will know who they are before I go further forward." He followed them, and he

N

saw them going down a glen ; and when he was about to be down, they came to meet him, crying. " What is the matter with you ? " says he. " Much is the matter with us," said they, " that we are under charms, till we find three lads who will spend three nights with us without putting a question to us ; and if thou hadst stayed without following us we were free." Is there any way that you can get free but that ? " said he. " There is," said they. "There is a tree at the end of the house, and if you come at the end of a day and year and pluck up the tree, we were free." John turned back where the rest were, and he told them how it happened to him ; and they gave this advice to each other that they should return back to Dublin again, because it was not worth their while to follow the regiment. They returned back to Dublin.

That night John said,—" I had better go to see the king's daughter to-night." "Thou had'st better stay in the house," said the rest, "than go there." " I will go there, at all events," says he. He went, and he reached the king's house ; he struck at the door, one of the gentlewomen asked him what he wanted ; and he said that he wished to be speaking to the king's daughter. The king's daughter came where he was, and she asked what business he had with her. " I will give thee a whistle," said he, " and when thou playest it thou wilt be in the middle of such a regiment." When she got the whistle she drove him down stairs, and she shut the door on him. " How went it with thee ? " said they. " She wheedled the whistle from me," said he. He did not stop till he had beguiled a loan of the purse from the sergeant. " I had better," said he, " go to see the king's daughter again." He went away and he reached the house; he saw the king's daughter; she wheedled the purse from him, and drove him down stairs as she did before; and he turned back. He did not stop till he beguiled a loan of the towel from the corporal. He went again where the king's daughter was. "What wilt thou give me this journey?" said she. "A towel, and when it is opened it will be full of every sort of meat." "Let me see it," said she. "We will spread it out," said he. He spread it out, and there was a corner that would not lie right. He said to her to stand on the corner; she stood on it; he stood himself on another corner, and he wished to be in the uttermost isle of the deep; and himself and the king's daughter, and the towel, were in it in five minutes. There was the very prettiest island that man ever saw, and nothing in it but trees and fruits. There they were, going through the island backwards and forwards, and sleep came on him. They came to a pretty little hollow, and he laid his head in her lap; and he took a death grip of her apron, in order that she should not get away without his perceiving her. When he slept she loosed the apron; she left him there; she took the towel with her; she stood on it; she wished herself to be in her father's house, and she was in it. When he awoke he had nothing to get, he had nothing to see but trees and birds; he was then keeping himself alive with the fruits of the island, and hit upon apples; and when he would eat one sort of them they would put a deer's head on him; and when he would eat another sort of them, they would put it off him.

One day he gathered a great many of the apples, and he put the one sort in the one end of the pock, and the other sort in the other end. He saw a vessel going past, he waved to her; a boat came to shore, and they took him on board. The captain took him down to meat, and he left the pock above. The sailors opened the pock to see what was in it; when they saw that apples were in it, they began to eat them. They ate the sort that would put deers' horns on them, and they began fighting till they were like to break the vessel. When the captain heard the row, he came up; and when he saw them, he said, "Thou bad man, what hast thou done to my men now?" "What," said John, "made thy men so impudent that they would go and look into any man's pock?" "What wilt thou give me," said John, "if I leave them as they were before?" The skipper took fright, and he said that he would give him the vessel and cargo at the first port they reached. Here he opened the pock, and he gave them the other sort, and the horns fell off them. It was a cargo of gold was on the ship, and it was to Dublin she was going. When they arrived the captain said to him to be taking care of the vessel and cargo, that he was done with it. "Be patient," said John, "till we see how it goes with us at the end of a few days." He went away on the morrow to sell the apples about the town with nothing on but torn clothes. He went up through the town, and he came opposite the king's house, and he saw the king's daughter with her head out of the window. She asked that a pound of the apples should be sent up to her. He said she should try how they would agree with her first. He threw up an apple to her of the sort that would put a deer's head on her; when she ate the apple there came a deer's head and horns on her. The king sent forth word, that if any man whatsoever could be found, who would heal his daughter, that he should get a peck of gold, and a peck of silver, and herself to marry. She was thus many days, and

no man coming that could do any good at all. John
came to the door with the torn clothes, asking to get
in ; and when they saw his like, they would not let
him in ; but she had a little brother who saw them
keeping him out, and he told it to his father ; and his
father said, " Though it were the beggar of the green!"
Word went after him that he should return, and he
returned. The king said to him, " Could he heal his
daughter ?" and he said " that he would try it." They
took him up to the chamber where she was. He sat,
and he took a book out of his pocket, with nothing in
it, pretending that he was reading it. " Didst thou,"
said he, " wheedle a whistle from a poor soldier; when
he would play it, it would take him to the middle of
the regiment ?" " I wheedled," said she. " If that
is not found," said he, " I cannot heal thee." " It is,"
says she. They brought the whistle to him. When
he got the whistle he gave her a piece of apple, and
one of the horns fell off her. " I can't," said he, " do
more to-day, but I will come here to-morrow. Then
he went out, and his old comrades met him. The
trade they had was to be slaking lime and drawing
water for stone masons. He knew them, but they did
not know him ; he noticed nothing at all, but he gave
them ten shillings, and he said to them, " Drink the
health of the man who gave them." He left them
there, and he returned to the ship. On the morrow
he went where the king's daughter was ; he took out
the book, and he said to her, " Didst thou wheedle a
purse from a poor soldier, that would be full of gold
and silver every time it was opened ?" " I wheedled,"
said she. " If that is not found," said he, " I cannot
heal thee." " It is," said she ; and they gave him the
purse. When he got the purse he gave her a piece of
the apple, and another horn fell off her. " I can do

no more to-day," said he, " but I will come the next
night."   He went where his old comrades were, and
he gave them other ten shillings, and he said to them,
" To drink the health of the man who gave them."
Then he returned to the vessel.   The captain said to
him, " Was he going to take charge of the vessel
now ?"   Said he, " Catch patience till the end of a
day or two, till we see how it goes with us."   He returned the next night to see the king's daughter.   He
gave a pull at the book as he used to do,—" Didst
thou wheedle," said he, " a towel from a poor soldier,
that would be full of every kind of meat every time it
was undone ?"   " I wheedled," said she.   " If that
towel is not to be found, I cannot cure thee," says he.
" It is," says she.   They gave it to him ; as quick as
he got it, he gave her a whole apple ; and when she
ate it she was as she was before.   Here he got a peck
of gold and a peck of silver ; and they said to him
that he would get herself to marry.   " I will come
to-morrow," said he.   He went the way of his old
comrades this time too ; he gave them ten shillings,
and he said to them, " To drink the health of the man
who gave them."   Said they, " It would be pleasing
to us to know what kind friend is giving us the like of
this every night."   " Have you mind," said he, " when
we were in such a place, and that we promised to the
three girls that we would go there again a year from
the time."   Then they knew him.   " That time has
gone past long ago," said they.   " It is not gone,"
said he ; " next night is the night."   He returned
where the captain was ; he said to him that himself
and his cargo might be off ; that he would not be
troubling him ; that he had enough.   On the morrow
he went past the king's house, and the king's daughter
said to him, " Art thou going to marry me to-day ?"

"No, nor to-morrow," said he. He returned where the rest were, and he began to set them in order for going where they promised. He gave the purse to the sergeant, the towel to the corporal, and the whistle he kept himself. He bought three horses, and they went riding with great haste to the place to which they had promised to go. When they reached the house they caught the tree, and it came with them at the first pull. The three girls came so white and smiling where they were, and they were free from the spells. Every man of them took his own with him; they came back to Dublin, and they married.

URSGEUL.

Bha roimhe so réiseamaid ann am Baileclíath an Eírínn, 's bha i 'folbh air turas fada. Bha séirdsean, corporal, agus saighdear sìngilte aig an robh leannain anns a' bhaile. Chaidh iad a'm faicinn an latha bha iad ri folbh, 's dh' fhan iad tuillidh is fada, 's dh' fhàg an réiseamaid iad. Lean iad i 's bha iad a' folbh 's a' folbh gus an d' thàinig an oidhche orra. Chunnaic iad solus fada uatha, 's ma b' fhada uatha cha b' fhada bha iadsan 'ga ruigheachd. Chaidh iad a stigh. Bha 'n t-urlar réidh, sguabte, 's gealbhan air, 's gun duine stigh. Shuidh iad aig a' ghealbhan 'gan garadh. Cha b' fhada 'bha iad mur sin nur a dh' éiridh an saighdear singilte, d' am b' ainm Iain, a dh' amharc de 'bha 'san t-seombar, a thaobh gun robh solus ann. Bha 'n sin bord air a chùirneachadh leis a' h-uile seòrsa bìdh, 's coinneal laist' air. Chaidh e suas; thòisich e air itheadh; 's thòisich càch air a bhacail, o nach robh gnothach aige ris. Nur a chunnaic iad nach do stad e, chaidh iad suas, 's thòisich iad féin. Bha tri leap-aichean anns an t-seombar, 's chaidh fear dhiu 'laidhe anns gach leaba.

Cha b' fhada a bha iad 'nan laidhe nur a thàinig tri nigheanan mòra 'ruagha stigh, 's shìn té aca i féin aig beulthaobh gach té de na leapaichean, 's nur a chunnaic iad an t-am iomchuidh anns a' mhaidinn dh' éiridh iad, agus dh' fholbh iad.

Nur a dh' éiridh na saighdearan cha 'n aithnichte gun d' thàinig mìr bhàr a' bhùird riamh. Shuidh iad, 's ghabh iad am biadh. Thuirt an seirdsean gum b' fheàrra dhaibh an réiseamaid a leantainn, 's thuirt Iain nach leanadh. Fhad 'sa gheibheadh e bhiadh 'na thàmh nach folbhadh e. Nur a thàinig an t-am dinnearach, shuidh iad 's ghabh iad an dinneir. Thuirt an séirdsean gum b' fheàrra dhaibh folbh, 's thuirt Iain nach folbhadh. Nur a thàinig am sioparach, shuidh iad 's ghabh iad an siopair. An déigh an sioparach chaidh iad a laidhe, gach fear d'a leaba féin.

Thàinig na nigheanan an oidhche so cuideachd, s chaidh té 'laidhe anns a' h-uile leaba dhiu. Anns a' mhaidinn, nur a chunnaic iad an t-am iomchuidh, dh' éiridh iad 's dh' fholbh iad.

Nur a dh' éiridh na gillean bha 'm bòrd cùirnichte, 's cha n aithnichte gun d' thàinig mìr riamh dheth. Shuidh iad 's ghabh iad am biadh, 's nur a ghabh iad am biadh thuirt an seirdsean gum folbhadh iad codbiu. Thuirt Iain nach folbhadh. Ghabh iad an dinneir 's an siopair mur a b' àbhaist. Chaidh iad a laidhe.

Thàinig na nigheanan 's laidh iad as an déigh. Anns a' mhaidinn thug an té 'bu shine sporan do 'n t-seirdsean, 's a' h-uile h-uair a dh' fhosgladh i e bhiodh e làn òir is airgid. Urs' i ris an té mheadhonaich, " De 'bheir thusa do t' fhear fein?" " Bheir mise dha tuthailt, 's a' h uile h-uair a sgaoileas e i bidh i làn de na h-uile seòrsa bidh." Thug i 'n tuthailt do 'n chorporal, 's thuirt i ris an té b' òige, " Dé 'bheir thusa do t' fhear fein?" " Bheir mi dha fìdeag, 's a' h-uile h-uair a sheinneas e i bidh e 'n teis meadhoin na réiseamaid." Thug i dha an fhìdeag. Dh' fhàg iad beannachd aca 's dh' fholbh iad.

" Cha leig mi leis an so e," urs' Iain, " bidh fhios 'am co iad ma 'n d' théid mi na 's faide air m' aghaidh." Lean e iad, 's chunnaic e iad a' dol sìos le gleann, 's nur a bha e thun a bhi shìos thàinig iad 'na choinneamh, 's iad a' caoineadh. " De th' oirbh?" urs' esan. " 'S mòr a th' oirnn," urs' iadsan ; " tha sinn fo gheasan gus am faigh sinn tri gillean a laidheas leinn tri oidchean gun cheisd a chur oirnn, 's nam fanadh thusa gun ar leantainn bha sinn ma sgaoil." " Am bheil dòigh sam bith air am faigh sibh ma sgaoil," urs' esan, " ach sin ? " " Tha," urs' iadsan; " tha craobh aig ceann an tighe, 's na'n d' thigeadh sibh, an ceann la is bliadhna, 's a' chraobh sin a spìonadh bha sinne ma sgaoil."

" Thill Iain air ais far an robh càch; dh' innis e dhaibh mar a thachair dha; s chuir iad an comhairle r'a chéile gun tilleadh iad air an ais do Bhailecliath a rithisd, chionn nach b' fhiach dhaibh an réiseamaid a leantainn. Thill iad do Bhailecliath air an ais. An oidhche sin urs' Iain, " 'S fheàrra dhomh dol a dh' amharc nighean an rìgh nochd." "'S fheàrra dhuit fantainn aig an tigh," arsa càch, "na dol ann." " Théid mi ann codhin," urs' esan.

Dh' fholbh e 's rainig e tigh an rìgh. Bhuail e aig an dorus. Dh' fheòraidh h-aon de na mnnathan uaisle de 'bha dhìth air, 's thuirt e gun robh toil aige 'bhi 'bruidhinn ri nighean an rìgh. Thàinig nighean an rìgh far an robh e, 's dh' fheòraich i dé 'n gnothuch a bh' aige rithe. " Bheir mi dhuit fìdeag," urs' esan, " 's nur a sheinneas thu i bidh thu ann am meadhon a leithid so do reiseamaid." Nur a fhuair ise an fhìdeag bhreab i leis an staighir e, 's dhùinn i 'n dorus air. " Démur chaidh dhuit ?" urs' iadsan. " Mheall i 'n fhìdeag uam," urs' esan. Cha do stad e gus an do mheall e coingheall de 'n sporan o 'n t-séirdsean. " 'S fheàrra dhomh," urs' esan, " dol a dh' fhaicinn nighean an rìgh 'rithisd."

Dh' fholbh e 's ràinig e 'n tigh. Chunnaic e nighean an rìgh ; mheall i 'n sporan uaidhe ; bhreab i leis an staighir e mar a rinn i roimhid ; 's thill e air ais. Cha do stad e gus an do mheall e coingheall de 'n tuthailt o 'n chorporal.

Chaidh e 'rithisd far an robh nighean an rìgh. " De 'bheir thu dhomh air an t-siubhal so ?" urs' ise. " Tuthailt, 's nur a dh' fhosg-lar i bidh i làn de na h-uile seòrsa bìdh." " Leig fhaicinn domh i," urs' ise. " Sgaoilidh sin a mach i," urs' esan. Sgaoil e mach i, 's bha oisean di nach laidheadh gu ceart. Thuirt e rithe seasamh air an oisean. Sheas i air. Sheas e féin air oisean eile, 's ghuidh e bhi ann an eilean iomallach na doimhne. 'S bha e féin, is nighean an rìgh, 's an tuthailt ann ann an còig mionaidean. Bha 'sin an aon eilean a bu bhòidhche a chunnaic duine riamh, 's gun ni ann ach craobhan is measan. Bha iad an sin a' folbh feadh an eilean air an ais 's air an aghaidh, 's thàinig an cadal airsan. Thàinig iad gu lagan bòidheach, 's chuir esan a cheann 'na h-uchdse, 's rinn e gréim bàis air a h-apran, air alt 's nach fhaigheadh i air folbh gun e mhòth-chuinn di. Nur a chaidil esan dh' fhuasgail ise an t-apran ; dh' fhàg i 'n sin e ; thug è leatha an tuthailt ; sheas i urra ; ghuidh i bhi 'n tigh a h-athar ; 's bha i ann.

Nur a dhùisg esan cha robh ni ri fhaotainn aige, 's cha robh ni ri fhaicinn aige, ach craobhan is eunlaith. Bha e 'n sin a' tighinn beò air measan an eilean, 's dh' amais ubhlan air, 's nur a dh' itheadh e aon seòrsa dhiu chuireadh iad ceann féidh air, 's nur a dh' itheadh e seòrsa eile dhiu chuireadh iad deth e. Aon latha chruinnich e mòran de na h-ubhlan, s chuir e 'n darna seòrsa ann an aon cheann do 'n phoca, 's an seòrsa éile anns a' cheann eile. Chunnaic e soitheach a' dol seachad ; chrath e rithe ; thàinig bàta gu tìr ; 's thug iad air bòrd e. Thug an caibhtinn sìos e gu biadh, 's dh' fhàg e 'm poca gu h-ard. Dh' fhosgaill na seòladairean am poca a dh' amharc de 'bh' ann. Nur a chunnaic iad gur h-ubhlan a bh'ann thòisich iad air an itheadh. Dh' ith iad an seòrsa 'chuireadh adhaircean féidh orra. Chinn adhaircean féidh orra, 's thòisich iad air leum air a chéile gus an robh iad a' brath an soitheach a bhrisdeadh. Nur a chuala an caibhtim an starum thàinig e nìos, s nur a chunnaic e iad thuirt e, " 'Dhroch dhuine dé tha thu an déigh a dhèanadh air mo dhaoine nis ? " " De," urs' Iain, " a chuir do dhaoine-sa cho mìomhail 's gun rachadh iad a dh' fhaicinn de bhiodh ann am poca duine sam bith ? De bheir thu dhomh," urs' Iain, " ma dh' fhàgas mi iad mur a bha iad roimhid ?" Ghabh an sgiobair eagal, 's thuirt e gun d' thugadh e dha an saitheach agus an luchd aig a' chiad phort a ruigeadh iad. Dh' fhosgail e 'n so am poca, 's thug e dhaibh an seòrs' eile, s thuit na h-adhaircean diu. 'S e luchd òir a' bh' air an t-soitheach, agus 's ann a Bhailecliath a bha i 'dol. Nur a ràinig iad thuirt an caibhtinn ris, e 'bhi 'gabhail cùram de 'n t-soitheach 's de 'n luchd, gun robh esan réidh is i, " Dèan faighidinn," urs' Iain, " gus am faic sinn démur a théid duinn ann an ceann beagan làithean.

Dh' fholbh e 'n la 'r na mhàireach a reic nan ubhlan feadh a' bhaile, 's gun air ach aodach srachdte. Chaidh e suas feadh a' bhaile, 's thàinig e ma choinneamh tigh an rìgh, 's chunnaic e nighean an rìgh 's a ceann a mach air uinneig. Dh' iarr i punnd de na h-ubhlan a chur suas a 'h-ionnsuidh. Thuirt esan i dh' fheachainn démur a chòrdadh iad rithe an toiseach. Thilg e 'suas ubhal urra de 'n t-seòrsa 'chuireadh ceann féidh urra. Nur a dh' ith i 'n ubhal thàinig ceann féidh is cabair urra. Chuir an rìgh fios a mach nam faighte duine sam bith a léighseadh a nighean gum faigheadh e peic òir is peic airgid, 's i féin r'a pòsadh. Bha i mur sin mòran làithean, 's gun duine 'tighinn a bha dèanadh math sam bith. Thàinig Iain gus an dorusd leis an aodach shrachdte 'g iarraidh a stigh, 's nur a chunnaic iad a choslas cha leigeadh iad a stigh e, ach bha bràthair beag aicise a chunnaic iad 'ga chumail a mach 's dh' innis e d'a athair e, 's thuirt a h-athair ged a b' e bleidire an lòin a bhiodh ann a leigeil a stigh. Chaidh fios as a dhéigh a 'thilleadh, agus thill e. Thuirt an rìgh ris an léighseadh e 'nighean, 's thuirt e gum feuchadh e ris. Thug iad suas e do 'n t-seombar fa an robh i. Shuidh e, 's thug e 'mach leobhar a a phòca s gun ni sam bith ann, a' leigeil air gun robh e 'ga 'leubhadh. " An do mheall thusa," urs' esan, " fìdeag o shaighdear bochd, nur a sheinneadh e i 'bheireadh e gu meadhon a réiseamaid." " Mheall," urs' ise. " Mar a' bheil sin air faotainn," urs' esan, " cha 'n urrainn mise do leigheas." " Tha," urs' ise. Thug iad a' ionnsuidh an fhìdeag. Nur a fhuair e 'n fhideag thug e dhi pìosa de dh' ubhal, s thuit fear de na cabair dhi "Cha 'n urrainn mi," urs' esan, "tuillidh a dhèanadh an diugh, ach thig mi 'm màireach."

Dh' fholbh e 'n sin a mach, 's thachair a sheana chompanaich air, 's e cheaird a bh' aca 'bhi buacadh aoil, 's a' tarruinn uisge do chlachairean. Dh' aithnich esan iadsan, ach cha d' aithnich iadsan esan. Cha do leig e rud sam bith air, ach thug e dhaibh deich tasd-ain, 's thuirt e riu, "òlaibh deoch slàinte an fhir a thug dhuibh e."

Dhealaich e 'n sin riu, 's thill e gus an t-soitheach. An la 'r na mhàireach chaidh e far an robh nighean an rìgh. Thug e mach an leabhar, 's thuirt e rithe, "An do mheall thusa sporan o shaighdear bochd a bhiodh làn òir is airgid h-uile h-uair a dh' fhosgailt' e?" "Mheall," ars' ise. "Mar a' bheil sin air faotainn," urs' esan, "cha 'n urrainn mise do leigheas." "Tha," urs' ise, "'s thug iad dha 'an sporan. Nur a fhuair e e thug e dhi pìosa do 'n ubhal, 's thuit cabar eile dhi. Cha 'n urrainn mi tuillidh a dhèanadh an diugh,' urs' esan, "ach thig mi 'n ath oidhche."

Chaidh e far an robh 'sheana chompanaich, 's thug e dhaibh deich tasdain eile, 's thuirt e riu deoch slàinte an fhir a thug dhaibh e òl. Thill e 'n sin thun an t-soithich. Thuirt an caibhtinn ris an robh e 'dol a ghabhail cùram do 'n t-soitheach a nis. Thuirt esan, "Glac faighidinn gu ceann latha na dha gus am faic sinn dèmur a théid duinn." Thill e an ath oidhche a dh' fhaicinn nighean an rìgh. Thug e tarruinn air a leabhar mar a b' àbhaist dha. "An do mheall thusa," urs' esan, "tuthailt o shaighdear bochd a bhiodh làn de na h-uile seòrsa bìdh a' h-uile h-uair a dh' fhosgailt i?" "Mheall," urs' ise. "Mar a' bheil an tuthailt sin air faotainn cha 'n urrainn mise do leigheas," urs' esan. "Tha," urs' ise. Thug iad dha i. Cho luath 's a fhuair esan i thug e ubhal shlàn dhi, 's nur a dh' ith i i bha i mar a bha i roimhid. Fhuair e 'n sin peic òir is peic airgid, 's thuirt iad ris gum faigheadh e i féin ri 'pòsadh. "Thig mi 'm màir-each," urs' esan.

Ghabh e rathad a sheana chompanach air an t-siubhal so cuid-eachd; thug e deich tasdain daibh; 's thuirt e riu deoch slàinte an fhir a thug dhaibh e òl. Urs' iadsan, "Bu mhail leinn fios a bhi againn co an caraid caoimhneil a tha 'toirt duinn a' leithid so a' h-uile h-oidhche?" "Am bheil cuimhn' agaibh," urs' esan, "nur a bha sinn 'na leithid so do dù' àite, 's a gheall sin do na tri nigheanan gun rachamaid ann bliadhna o 'n am sin a rithisd?" Dh' aithnich iad an sin e. "Chaidh an ùine sin seachad o chionn fada," urs' iadsan. "Cha deachaidh," urs' esan; "'s i an ath oidhche an oidhche." Thill e far an robh an caibhtinn, 's thuirt e ris gum faodadh e féin 's a luchd a bhi folbh, nach biodh esan a' cur dragh air, gun robh na leòir aige.

An la 'r na mhàireach chaidh e seachad tigh an rìgh, s thuirt nighean an righ ris, " Am bheil thu dol am' phòsadh an diugh?" "Cha 'n' eil na 'mhàireach," urs' esan. Thill e far an robh càch, 's thòisich e air cur an òrdugh air son dol far an do gheall iad. Thug e 'n sporan do 'n séirdsean, an tuthailt do 'n chorporal, 's ghléidh e féin an fhìdeag. Cheannaich e tri eich, 's dh' fholbh iad air mharcachd ann an cabhaig mhòir do 'n aite an do gheall iad dol. Nur a ràinig iad an tigh rug iad air a chraoibh, 's thainig i leo air a' chiad spìonadh. Thàinig na tri nigheanan gu geal, gàireachdach far an robh iad, 's bha iad saor o na geasan. Thug a' h-uile fear dhiu leis a thè féin, 's thàinig iad air an ais do Bhaileecliath, 's phòs iad.

Got this tale from a young lad of the name of James M'Lachlin, who is at present in my own employment. I have had the preceding tale from him also. He has had them from an old woman that lives somewhere up the way of Portaskaig, who, he says, can repeat several more, and to whom I intend immediately to apply.

May 27, 1860.—After speaking to the old woman MacKerrol, I find that, from age and loss of memory, she is unable now to tell any of the tales she was wont to repeat.

HECTOR MACLEAN.

Another version of this has been sent by Mr. Osgood Mackenzie from Gairloch. It was recited by HECTOR MACKENZIE at Dibaig, who learned it some years ago from KENNETH MACKENZIE at Dibaig; and it was written by ANGUS MACRAE at Dibaig. This Dibaig version tells how—

1. There was a soldier, by name Coinneach Buidhe, Kenneth the Yellow, in the army of old, and he belonged to Alba. He deserted, and his master sent a " corpaileir" after him ; but the corporal deserted too ; and so did a third. They went on till they reached the " yearly wood," in America. After a time, they saw on a certain night, a light which led them to a large house ; they found meat and drink, and all that they could desire. They saw no one for a year and a day, except three maidens, who

never spoke, but called in at odd times; and as they did not speak, the soldiers were silent.

At the end of the year the maidens spoke, and praised them for their politeness, explained that they were under spells, and for their kindness, gave to the first a cup that would be ever full, and a lamp of light; to the second, a table-cover on which meat was ever; and to the third, a bed in which there would ever be rest for them at any time they chose; and besides, the "TIADH-LAICEAN" would make any one who had them get anything he wished. They reached a certain king, whose only daughter pretended to be fond of Kenneth the Yellow, and wheedled him till he gave her the TIADHLAICEAN, when she ordered him to be put in an island in the ocean. When there alone he grew hungry, and ate "abhlan," and a wood like thatch grew through his head, and there remained till he ate "ABHLAN" of another kind, when the wood vanished. He got off in a ship with "ABHLAN" of each sort, and reached the big town of the king where he had been before, where he set up a booth. On a certain day a fair lad came in to sell ABHLAN, and through him the other kind were sold to the king's daughter, and a wood grew on her head. Kenneth the Yellow got back the TIADHLAICEAN, and found his two companions AGUS BHA IAD UILE TUILLEADH ANN AM MEAS AGUS SOIRBHEACHADH GUS A CHRIOCH. And they were all after in worship and prosperousness till the end.

This is manifestly the same story shortened, and made reasonable. It is very well written, and spelt according to rule.

3. I have another version of this told by Hector Boyd, fisherman, Castle Bay, Barra, who says he learned it from John Mac-Neill, who has left the island; and from Neill MacKinnon, Ruagh Lias. In this the three soldiers are English, Scotch, and Irish. The two last desert; and the first, a sergeant, is sent after them. They persuade him to desert also, and they come to a castle. The Irishman acts the part of John in the Islay version; and the first night they eat and go to sleep, and find dresses when they wake. In the morning they get up and put on their dresses; and the board was set over with meat and with drink, and they took their TRATH MADAIN, breakfast. They went

to take a walk without. The Englishman had a gun, and he
saw three swans swimming on a loch, and he began to put a
charge in his gun. The swans perceived him, and they cried to
him, and they were sure he was going to shoot at them. They
came on shore and became three women. " How are these
dresses pleasing you?" said they. " The like will be yours every
day in the year, and your meat as good as you got ; but that you
should neither think or order one of us to be with you in lying
down or rising up." And so they remained for a year in the
castle. One night the Irishman thought of the swans, and in the
morning they had nothing but their old dresses.

They went to the loch ; the swans came on shore, became
women, and gave a purse that would always be full of gold and
jewels, to the Englishman ; a knife to the Scotchman, and whenever it was opened he would be wherever he wished ; and to the
Irishman a horn, and when he blew in the small end there would
be a thousand soldiers before him ; and when he blew in the big
end none of them would be seen.

They go to a big town, and build a house on a green hill with
money from the purse ; and when the house was built, one about
went to the town to buy meat. The Irishman fell in love
with the king's daughter, and was cheated out of his magic horn ;
borrowed the purse, and lost that ; and then, by the help of the
knife, transported himself and the king's daughter to an island
which could hardly be seen in the far ocean. And there they
were, and there they stayed for seventeen days, eating fruits.
One day he slept with his head on her knee, and she looked at her
hands and saw how long the nails had grown ; so she put her hand
in his pocket and took out the knife to pare them. " Oh," said she,
" that I were where the nails grew on me," and she was in her
father's house. Then he found red apples and grey apples ; and
no sooner had he eaten some of the red apples than his head was
down, and his heels were up, from the weight of the deer's horns
that grew on his head. Then he bethought him that one of the
grey apples might heal him ; and he stretched himself out with
his head downwards, and kicked down one of the apples with his
feet, and ate it, and the horns fell off him. Then he made bas-
kets, and filled them with the apples ; climbed a tree, saw a
ship, tore his shirt and waved it on a stick, and was seen.

The skipper was under an oath that he would never leave a man in extremity. They came on shore for him, and were terrified at his beard, thinking that he was the evil spirit. When he got on board, a razor was got, and (as the narrator said) SHEUDH-AIG E he was shaved. The ship sailed straight to the king's house. The lady looked out of a window. He sold her a red apple for a guinea. She ate it, the horns grew, and there were not alive those who could take her from that. They thought of saws, and they sent for doctors; and he came, and then there is a scene in which he pretends to read a divining book, and tries saws on the horns, and frightens the lady and recovers the lost gifts. Then he went to his friends, and they went to the swans; and the spells went off them, and they married them.

The story is very well told, especially the last scene; but it is too like the Islay version to make it worth translating at full length.

4. I have another story, from a Ross-shire man, now in Glasgow, which begins in the same manner, but the incidents are very different.

This story has a counterpart in German, Der Krautesel; and it has a very long pedigree in Grimm's third volume. It seems to be very widely spread, and very old, and to belong to many languages; many versions are given. In one a soldier, one of three, eats apples in a forest, and his nose grows right through the forest, and sixty miles beyond it; and the king's daughter's nose is made to grow, exactly as horns are made to grow on the princess in the Highlands; and she is forced to give up the things which she had got from the soldiers; and which are a purse, a mantle, and a horn of magic power.

In another version, it is a young huntsman who changes a witch and her daughter into donkeys, by giving them magic cabbages, which had previously transformed him.

The swans in the third version seem to belong to Sanscrit, as well as to Norse and other languages. In "Comparative Mythology," by Max Muller, Oxford Essays, 1856, a story is given from the Brâhmana of the Yagurveda, in which this passage occurs—"Then he bewailed his vanished love in bitter grief; and went near Kurukshetra. There is a lake there called Anyatah-

plaksha, full of lotus flowers ; and while the king walked along
its border, the fairies were playing there in the water in the
shape of birds ; and Urvasi discovered him, and said, ' That is
the man with whom I dwelt so long.' Then her friends said, ' Let
us appear to him,' " etc., etc.

The rest of the Eastern story has many Western counterparts,
such as "Peter Wilkins and the Flying Ladies," and a story which
I have from Islay. The incident of birds which turn out to be
enchanted women, occurs in a great many other Gaelic stories ;
and is in Mr. Peter Buchan's "Green Sleeves" (see introduction); and, as I am told, in the Edda.

BAILECLIATH is Dublin, and takes its Gaelic name from a
legend. The name should be Baile ath Cliath, the town of
Wattle Ford ; either from wattled boats, or a bridge of hurdles ;
and as it appears, there was a weaver, or tailor, residing at Ath
Cliath, Wattle Ford, who got his living by making creels or
hurdles, CLIATHAN, for crossing the river. There was a fluent,
gabby old man, who was a friend of his ; and from his having
such a tongue, the maker of the creels advised him to become a
beggar, as he was sure to succeed. He began, and got plenty of
money. He wore a cap or currachd, and all the coin he got he
buried under a stone, at the end of the wattle bridge. The bridge
maker died ; the beggar got ill and kept his cap on, and never
took it off; and when he was dying he asked his wife to bury
him in it ; and he was buried with his cap on. The widow's son
found out about the buried treasure, and dug it up ; but the beggar's ghost so tormented the boy, that he had to go to the minister, who advised them to build a bridge with the money ; so they
built DROCHAID ATH CLIATH, and there it is to this very day.

I do not know which of the Dublin bridges is meant, but the
story was got from a woman at Kilmeny in Islay, and this is a
mere outline of it. It is known as the story of the red-haired
beggar, Am Bochd Ruagh.

Bailecliath is a great place in Gaelic songs.

The story of the Three Soldiers is one of which I remember
to have heard a part in my childhood. I perfectly remember con-
triving with a companion how we would have given the cruel
princess bits of different kinds of apples, mixed together, so as to
make the horns grow, and fall off time about ; but I cannot re

member who told me the story. The version I have given is the most complete, but the language of the Barra version is better.

There are one or two inconsistencies. They travel on the towel which had the commissariat, and do not use the locomotive whistle at all. But there are touches of nature. The mason's labourers thought the time had passed, but the adventurer did not find time so long; and he alone remembered the day.

THE STORY OF THE WHITE PET.

From Mrs. MacTavish, widow of the late minister of Kildalton, Islay.

THERE was a farmer before now who had a White Pet (sheep), and when Christmas was drawing near, he thought that he would kill the White Pet. The White Pet heard that, and he thought he would run away ; and that is what he did.

He had not gone far when a bull met him. Said the bull to him, " All hail ! White Pet, where art thou going ?" " I," said the White Pet, " am going to seek my fortune ; they were going to kill me for Christmas, and I thought I had better run away." " It is better for me," said the bull, " to go with thee, for they were going to do the very same with me."

" I am willing," said the White Pet ; " the larger the party the better the fun."

They went forward till they fell in with a dog.

" All hail ! White Pet," said the dog. " All hail ! thou dog." " Where art thou going ?" said the dog.

" I am running away, for I heard that they were threatening to kill me for Christmas."

" They were going to do the very same to me," said the dog, " and I will go with you." " Come, then," said the White Pet.

They went then, till a cat joined them. " All hail ! White Pet," said the cat. " All hail ! oh cat."

"Where art thou going?" said the cat. "I am going to seek my fortune," said the White Pet, "because they were going to kill me at Christmas."

"They were talking about killing me too," said the cat, "and I had better go with you."

"Come on then," said the White Pet.

Then they went forward till a cock met them. "All hail! White Pet," said the cock." "All hail to thyself! oh cock," said the White Pet. "Where," said the cock, "art thou going?" "I," said the White Pet, "am going (away), for they were threatening my death at Christmas."

"They were going to kill me at the very same time," said the cock, "and I will go with you."

"Come, then," said the White Pet.

They went forward till they fell in with a goose. "All hail! White Pet," said the goose. "All hail to thyself! oh goose," said the White Pet. "Where art thou going?" said the goose.

"I," said the White Pet, "am running away because they were going to kill me at Christmas."

"They were going to do that to me too," said the goose, "and I will go with you."

The party went forward till the night was drawing on them, and they saw a little light far away; and though far off, they were not long getting there. When they reached the house, they said to each other that they would look in at the window to see who was in the house, and they saw thieves counting money; and the White Pet said, "Let every one of us call his own call. I will call my own call; and let the bull call his own call; let the dog call his own call; and the cat her own call; and the cock his own call; and the goose his own call." With that they gave out one shout—GAIRE!

When the thieves heard the shouting that was without, they thought the mischief was there; and they fled out, and they went to a wood that was near them. When the White Pet and his company saw that the house was empty, they went in and they got the money that the thieves had been counting, and they divided it amongst themselves; and then they thought that they would settle to rest. Said the White Pet, "Where wilt thou sleep to-night, oh bull?" "I will sleep," said the bull, "behind the door where I used" (to be). "Where wilt thou sleep thyself, White Pet?" "I will sleep," said the White Pet, "in the middle of the floor where I used" (to be). "Where wilt thou sleep, oh dog?" said the White Pet. "I will sleep beside the fire where I used" (to be), said the dog. "Where wilt thou sleep, oh cat?" "I will sleep," said the cat, "in the candle press, where I like to be." "Where wilt thou sleep, oh cock?" said the White Pet. "I," said the cock, "will sleep on the rafters where I used" (to be). "Where wilt thou sleep, oh goose?" "I will sleep," said the goose, "on the midden, where I was accustomed to be."

They were not long settled to rest, when one of the thieves returned to look in to see if he could perceive if any one at all was in the house. All things were still, and he went on forward to the candle press for a candle, that he might kindle to make him a light; but when he put his hand in the box the cat thrust her claws into his hand, but he took a candle with him, and he tried to light it. Then the dog got up, and he stuck his tail into a pot of water that was beside the fire; he shook his tail and put out the candle. Then the thief thought that the mischief was in the house, and he fled; but when he was passing the White Pet, he gave him a blow; before he got

past the bull, he gave him a kick ; and the cock began to crow ; and when he went out, the goose began
to belabour him with his wings about the shanks.

He went to the wood where his comrades were, as
fast as was in his legs. They asked him how it had
gone with him. " It went," said he, " but middling ;
when I went to the candle press, there was a man in
it who thrust ten knives into my hand ; and when I
went to the fireside to light the candle, there was a
big black man lying there, who was sprinkling water
on it to put it out ; and when I tried to go out, there
was a big man in the middle of the floor, who gave me
a shove ; and another man behind the door who pushed
me out ; and there was a little brat on the loft calling
out CUIR-A-NEES-AN-SHAW-AY-S-FONI-MI-HAYN-DA—Send
him up here and I'll do for him ; and there was a
GREE-AS-ICH-E, shoemaker, out on the midden, be-
labouring me about the shanks with his apron."

When the thieves heard that, they did not return
to seek their lot of money ; and the White Pet and
his comrades got it to themselves ; and it kept them
peaceably as long as they lived.

SGEULACHD A PHEATA BHAIN.

BHA Tuathanach ann roimhe so aig an robh Peata bàn ; agus 'n
uair a bha an Nollaig a' teannadh air smuaintich e gu 'marbhabh e
'm Peata bàn. Chuala am Peata bàn sin agus smuaintich e gun
teichadh e, agus 'se sin a rinn e. Cha deachaidh e fada 'n uair a thachair Tarbh air. Thubhairt 'n tarbh ris, " Fàilte dhuitse a' pheata bhàin ;
c ite am bheil thusa a' dol ? " " Tha mi," ars' am peata ban. " a' falbh
a dh' iarridh an fhortain, bha iad a' dol a m' mharbhadh a dh' ionnsuidh
na Nollaig agus smuaintich mi gum b' fheàrr domh teicheadh." " S'
feàrr dommhsa ars' 'n Tarbh falbh leat : oir bha iad a' dol a dhianadh a
leithid eile ormsa." " Tha mi toileach," ars' 'm Peata bàn ; mar is mò
a' chuideachd 'sann is fheàrr 'n làn-aidhir." Ghabh iad air 'n aghaidh
gus an do thachair Cù orra. " Fàilte dhuit a Pheata bhàin," ars' 'n

Cu, "Fàilte dhuit fhé' 'choin." "Càite 'm bheil thu a' dol?" ars' m Cu. "Tha mi aig teicheadh bho 'n a chuala mi gun robh iad a' brath mo mharbhadh air son na Nollaig." Bha iad a' dol a dhianadh a leithid cheùdna ormsa," ars' an Cu, "agus falbhaidh mi leibh." "Thig," mata ars' am peata bàn? Dh' fhalbh iad an sin gus an do chomhlaich Cat iad? "Fàilte dhuit a pheata bhàin ars' 'n cat. Fàilte dhuit fhé' a Chàit." "Càite am bheil thu a' dol?" ars' an Cat. "Tha mi a' dol a dh' iarridh an fhortain," ars' am Peata Ban, "a chionn gu'n robh iad a' dol am' mharbhadh air 'n Nollaig." "Bha iad aig iomradh air mise mharbhadh cuideachd," ars n Cat, "agus 's féarr dhomh falbh leibh, Thugainn mata?" ars' 'm peata bàn. Ghabh iad an sin air an aghaidh gus an do choinnich Coileach iad. "Fàilte dhuit a pheata bhàin," ars' an Coileach. "Fàilte dhuit fhé'," ars' am Peata Bàn. "Càite," ars' an Coileach, "am bheil thu a dol?" "Tha mi," ars' am peata bàn, "a' falbh' o 'n a bha iad a mòidheadh mo mharbhadh aig an Nollaig." "Bha iad a' dol am' mharbhadh-sa aig an am cheudna," ars' an Coileach, "agus theid mi leibh." "Thig mata," ars' am Peata Bàn. Ghabh iad air an aghaidh gus an do thachair giadh orra. "Fàilte dhuit a pheata bhàin," ars' an gèadh. "Fàilte dhuit fhé' a gheoidh," ars' am Peata Bàn. "Càite am bheil thu a dol?" ars' an gèadh. "Tha mise," ars' am peata ban, "a' teichadh, a chionn gu 'n robh iad a dol am' mharbhadh aig an Nollaig." "Bha iad a dol a' dhèanadh sin ormsa cuideachd," ars' an Gèadh, "agus falbhaidh mi leibh." Ghabh a' chuideachd air an aghaidh gus an robh an oidhche 'teannadh orra, agus 'chunnaic iad solus beag fada bhuatha s ge b' fhada bhuatha cha bh' fhada 'ga ruigheachd. An uair a ràinig iad an tigh, thubhairt iad ri 'cheile gun amhairceadh iad a stigh air an uinneag a dh' fhaicinn co a bha anns an tigh; agus chunnaic iad meairlich a' cunntas airgid; agus thubhairt am Peata Bàn. "Glaoidhidh na uile aon aguinn a ghlaodh féin; glaiodhidh mise mo ghlaoidh féin; agus glaoidhidh an Tarbh a ghlaodh fein; glaoidhidh an Cù a ghlaodh fein; agus an Cat a glaodh fein; agus an Coileach a ghlaodh fein; agus an gèadh a ghlaodh fein." Leis sin thug iad aon ghàir asda. An uair a chuala na meairlich a' ghàir a bha muidh shaoil iad gun robh an donas ann, agus theich iad amach, agus dh' falbh iad do choille a bha dlùth daibh. An uair a chunnaic am Peata Bàn agus a chuideachd gun robh n tigh falamh 'chaidh iad a stigh, agus fhuair iad an t-airgid a bha aig na meairlich 'ga chunntas, agus roinn iad eatorra fein e. An sin smuaintich iad gun gabhadh iad mu thàmh. Thubhairt am Peata Bàn, "Càite an caidil thus' an nochd a Thairbh." "Caidlidh mise," ars' an tarbh, "cùl an doruis far an àbhaist domh."

"Caite an caidil thu fein a pheata bhàin?" " Caidlidh mise," ars' am Peata Bàn am meadhan an ùlair far an àbhaist domh." "Caite an caidil thus' a choin?" ars' am Peata Bàn. "Caidlidh mise taobh an teine far an àbhaist dommh," ars' an Cù, "Caite an caidil thus' a chait?" "Caidlidh mis'," ars' an Cat, "ann am preass nan Coinnlean far an toil leam a bhith." "Caite an caidil thus' a choilich?" ars' am Peata Bàn. "Coidlidh mise," ars' an Coileach, "air an spàrr far an àbhaist domh." "Caite an Caidil thus a gheòidh?" "Caidlidh mise," ars' an gèadh air an dùnan far an robh mi cleachte ri bhith."

Cha robh iad fada air gabhail mu thamh an uair a thill fear do na meairlich a dh' amharc a stigh feuch am mòicheadh e an robh aon sa' bith 'san tigh. Bha na uile sàmhach agus dhealluith e air aghaidh gu preass nan coinnlean airson coinneal a lasadh e dheanadh soluis da, ach an uair a chuir e làmh 'sa bhocsa shàbh 'n cat mean na laimh, ach thug e leis a' choinneal agus dh' fheuch e ri 'lasadh. An sin dh' eirich an cù agus chuir e earball ann am poit uisge bha aig taobh an teine; chrath e earball agus chuir e as a choinneal. Shaoil am Meairleach an sin gu robh an donus 'san tigh agus theich e; ach an uair a bha e dol seachad air a' pheata bhàn thug e buille dha; mun d' fhuar e seachad air an tarbh thug e breab dha; agus thòisich an coileach air glaoidhich; agus an uair a chaidh e mach thòisich an gèadh air a ghreadadh le 'sgiathan mu na luirgnean. Chaidh e don Choillidh far an robh a chompanich co luath 'sa bha 'na chasan dh' fheòraich iad dheth cia mar chaidh dha. "Cha deachaidh," ars' esan, " ach meadhonach an uair a chaidh mi gu preass nan coinnlean bha fear ann a shàth deich sgeanan ann a' m' laimh, agus an uair a chaidh mi gu taobh an teine a lasadh na coinneal bha fear mor, dubh 'na luidhe ann a bha spreadadh uisge urra 'ga cuir as, agus an uair a thug mi làmh air do' amach bha fear mor am meadhan an urlair a thug utag domh, agus fear eil' aig cùl an doruis a phut amach mi, agus bha ablach beag air an fharadh aig glaoidhich amach, "*cuir an nios an so e 's foghnaidh mi fhein dha agus* bha *Griasaich* amach air an dùnan 'gam ghreadadh mu na casan le apran. A nuair a chual na meairlich sin cha do phill iad a dh' iarridh an cuid airgid, agus t-fhuair am peata bàn agus a chompanaich dhaibh fein e, agus chum e socair iad am feadh 'sa bha iad beo.

Mrs. MacTavish got this story from a young girl in her service, November 1859, who learned it in Oa, a district of Islay, last year, when she was employed in herding cattle.

It is a version of the same tale as Grimm's "Bremer Stadt Musikanten," which appears to have been long known in Germany in various shapes.

The crowing of the cock is imitated in Gaelic and in German. The Gaelic is closer. "Bringt mir den Schelm her" is not so close to "kikeriki" as the Gaelic words—which I have tried to spell phonetically—are to the note of a cock. There is a bull in the Gaelic tale, instead of an ass; and a sheep and a goose, in addition to the dog, cat, and cock, which are common to both. There are six creatures in the one tale, commonly found about the Highland cottage, which is well described; four in the other, common about German cottages. My own opinion is, that the tale is common to both languages and old, but it might have been borrowed from a book so well known in England as Grimm's Stories are. It is worth remark, that the dog and the cat were to die at Christmas, as well as the sheep and bull, who might reasonably fear to be eaten anywhere, and who have been sacrificed everywhere; the goose, who is always a Christmas dish in the Highlands; and the cock, who should die last of his family, because the toughest. The dog was once sacrificed to Hecate on the 30th of every month; and there was a dog divinity in Egypt. Cats drew the car of Freya, a Norse divinity; they were the companions of Scotch witches, and did wondrous feats in the Highlands. See "Grant Stewart's Highland Superstitions. To roast a cat alive on a spit was a method of raising the fiend and gaining treasure, tried, as it is asserted, not very long ago. I myself remember to have heard, with horror, of a cruel boy, who roasted his mother's cat in an iron pot on a Sunday, while the rest were at church, though it was not said why he did it. A cock has been a sacrifice and sacred amongst many nations; for instance, a cock and a ram's head were emblems of Æsculapius. The crowing of a cock is a terror to all supernatural, unholy beings, according to popular mythology everywhere. When the mother, in these stories, sends her children into the world to seek their fortune, she bakes a cake, and kills a cock. A fowl, as I am informed by a minister in one of the Orkneys, is still, or was lately, buried alive by nurses as a cure for certain childish ailments. In short, the dog, the cat, and the cock may possibly have had good reason to fear death at a religious festival, if this part of their history came from the East with the Celts. The goose also has been sacred time out of mind. Bernacle geese are supposed to be hatched from a seashell. The goose was the great cackler who laid the egg of the

world, according to Egyptian inscriptions on coffins. He was
the emblem of Seb; he is sacred at the present day in Ceylon.
He was sacred in Greece and at Rome; and the Britons would
not eat his flesh in the days of Cæsar. Perhaps the custom of
eating a goose at Christmas, which, to the best of my knowledge,
is peculiar to the Scotch Highlands, may be a custom begun by
the first British Christians to mark their conversion, and carried
on ever since. Much will be found on this subject in " Rawlinson's Herodotus," p. 122, etc.; in " Mills and Wilson's History
of British India;" and in books on Ceylon. At all events, this
Gaelic story is well known in Islay, for MacLean writes that he
has often heard it, and all the creatures mentioned in it have had
to do with mythology at some period somewhere.

I suspect that it is one of the class given in "Contes et Apologues Indiens" (Paris, 1860), a class which includes such well
known stories as " *The Goose with the golden Eggs*," as a man
who cut down a tree to get at the fruit (No. 45); " *The Belly
and the Members*," as a quarrel between the head and tail of a
serpent (No. 40), a story which somewhat resembles that which
is quoted in the introduction, as " *MacLeod's Fool*," " Le Sage
et le Fou" (No. 18); "The two Geese that carried a Tortoise"
(No. 14); " Le Jeune Brâmane qui c' est sali le Doight " (No. 64),
which is a schoolboy story in Scotland in another shape; " The
Ass in the Lion's Skin" (No. 59); "Les Choses impossibles et les
Reliques du Bouddha" (No. 110), which has a parallel in Gaelic,
in broad Scotch, and in Norse. The Gaelic poet describes im-
possibilities, such as a shell-fish bringing heather from the hill,
and the climax is a certain great laird dressed in homespun.
The Scotch rhyme came to me from a little boy of five years old,
and is called " The Mantle Joe." It begins " 'Twas on a Monday Mornin' when the Cat crew Day :" There are " Twenty-four
Weavers riding on a Paddock ;" "A Hare and a Haddie racin'
owre the Lea," and such like; and it ends, " Frae Beginning to
the End it's a' big Lees." The Norse song was written out for
me by an officer on board a steamer, and includes " Two Squirrels
taming a Bear," and other such events; and the Sanscrit,
which Chinese and French savants have translated, names
similar absurd events which might sooner happen than the dis-
covery of the reliques of Buddha. In short, European stories are to
be traced in the east, and this White Pet may be one of the kind.

XII.

THE DAUGHTER OF THE SKIES.

From James MacLauchlan, servant, Islay.

THERE was there before now a farmer, and he had a leash of daughters, and much cattle and sheep. He went on a day to see them, and none of them were to be found; and he took the length of the day to search for them. He saw, in the lateness, coming home, a little doggy running about a park.

The doggy came where he was—"What wilt thou give me," said he, "if I get thy lot of cattle and sheep for thee?" "I don't know myself, thou ugly thing; what wilt thou be asking, and I will give it to thee of anything I have?" "Wilt thou give me," said the doggy, "thy big daughter to marry?" "I will give her to thee," said he, "if she will take thee herself."

They went home, himself and the doggy. Her father said to the eldest daughter, "Would she take him?" and she said she would not. He said to the second one, "Would she marry him?" and she said, "she would not marry him, though the cattle should not be got for ever." He said to the youngest one, "Would she marry him?" and she said, "that she would marry him." They married, and her sisters were mocking her because she had married him.

He took her with him home to his own place.

When he came to his own dwelling-place, he grew into a splendid man. They were together a great time, and she said she had better go see her father. He said to her to take care that she should not stay till she should have children, for then she expected one. She said she would not stay. He gave her a steed, and he told her as soon as she reached the house, to take the bridle from her head and let her away; and when she wished to come home, that she had but to shake the bridle, and that the steed would come, and that she would put her head into it.

She did as he asked her; she was not long at her father's house when she fell ill, and a child was born. That night men were together at the fire to watch. There came the very prettiest music that ever was heard about the town; and every one within slept but she. He came in and he took the child from her. He took himself out, and he went away. The music stopped, and each one awoke; and there was no knowing to what side the child had gone

She did not tell anything, but so soon as she rose she took with her the bridle, and she shook it, and the steed came, and she put her head into it. She took herself off riding, and the steed took to going home; and the swift March wind that would be before her, she would catch; and the swift March wind that would be after her, could not catch her.

She arrived. "Thou are come," said he. "I came," said she. He noticed nothing to her; and no more did she notice anything to him. Near to the end of three quarters again she said, "I had better go see my father." He said to her on this journey as he had said before. She took with her the steed, and she went away; and when she arrived she took the bridle from the steed's head, and she set her home.

That very night a child was born. He came as he did before, with music; every one slept, and he took with him the child. When the music stopped they all awoke. Her father was before her face, saying to her that she must tell what was the reason of the matter. She would not tell anything. When she grew well, and when she rose, she took with her the bridle, she shook it, and the steed came and put her head into it. She took herself away home. When she arrived he said, "Thou art come." "I came," said she. He noticed nothing to her; no more did she notice anything to him. Again at the end of three quarters, she said, "I had better go to see my father." "Do," said he, "but take care thou dost not as thou didst on the other two journeys." "I will not," said she. He gave her the steed and she went away. She reached her father's house, and that very night a child was born. The music came as was usual, and the child was taken away. Then her father was before her face; and he was going to kill her, if she would not tell what was happening to the children; or what sort of man she had. With the fright he gave her, she told it to him. When she grew well she took the bridle with her to a hill that was opposite to her, and she began shaking the bridle, to try if the steed would come, or if she would put her head into it; and though she were shaking still, the steed would not come. When she saw that she was not coming, she went out on foot. When she arrived, no one was within but the crone that was his mother. "Thou art without a houseman to-day," said the crone; "and if thou art quick thou wilt catch him yet." She went away, and she was going till the night came on her. She saw then a light a long way from her; and if it was a long way from her, she was not long in reach-

ing it.   When she went in, the floor was ready
swept before her, and the housewife spinning up in
the end of the house.   "Come up," said the housewife, "I know of thy cheer and travel.   Thou art
going to try if thou canst catch thy man ; he is going
to marry the daughter of the King of the Skies."   "He
is !" said she.   The housewife rose ; she made meat
for her ; she set on water to wash her feet, and she
laid her down.   If the day came quickly, it was
quicker than that that the housewife rose, and that
she made meat for her.   She set her on foot then for
going ; and she gave her shears that would cut alone ;
and she said to her, "Thou wilt be in the house of
my middle sister to-night."   She was going, and
going, till the night came on her.   She saw a light a
long way from her ; and if it was a long way from
her, she was not long in reaching it.   When she
went in the house was ready swept, a fire on the
middle of the floor, and the housewife spinning at the
end of the fire.   "Come up," said the housewife, "I
know thy cheer and travel."   She made meat for her,
she set on water, she washed her feet, and she laid her
down.   No sooner came the day than the housewife
set her on foot, and made meat for her.   She said she
had better go ; and she gave her a needle would sew
by itself.   "Thou wilt be in the house of my youngest
sister to-night," said she.   She was going, and going,
till the end of day and the mouth of lateness.   She
saw a light a long way from her ; and if it was a long
way from her, she was not long in reaching it.   She
went in, the house was swept, and the housewife
spinning at the end of the fire.   "Come up," said she,
"I know of thy cheer and travel."   She made meat
for her, she set on water, she washed her feet, and she
laid her down.   If the day came quickly, it was

quicker than that that the housewife rose ; she set her
on foot, and she made her meat ; she gave her a clue
of thread, and the thread would go into the needle by
itself ; and as the shears would cut, and the needle
sew, the thread would keep up with them.   " Thou
wilt be in the town to-night."   She reached the town
about evening, and she went into the house of the
king's hen wife, to lay down her weariness, and she
was warming herself at the fire.   She said to the
crone to give her work, that she would rather be
working than be still.   "No man is doing a turn in
this town to-day," says the hen wife ; " the king's
daughter has a wedding."   " Ud !" said she to the
crone, " give me cloth to sew, or a shirt that will keep
my hand going."   She gave her shirts to make ; she
took the shears from her pocket, and she set it to
work ; she set the needle to work after after it ; as the
shears would cut, the needle would sew, and the thread
would go into the needle by itself.   One of the king's
servant maids came in ; she was looking at her, and it
caused her great wonder how she made the shears and
the needle work by themselves.   She went home and
she told the king's daughter, that one was in the house
of the hen wife, and that she had shears and a needle
that could work of themselves.   " If there is," said
the king's daughter, " go thou over in the morning,
and say to her, ' what will she take for the shears.'"   In
the morning she went over, and she said to her that
the king's daughter was asking what would she take
for the shears.   " Nothing I asked," said she, " but
leave to lie where she lay last night."   " Go thou
over," said the king's daughter, " and say to her that
she will get that."   She gave the shears to the king's
daughter.   When they were going to lie down, the
king's daughter gave him a sleep drink, so that he

might not wake. He did not wake the length of the
night ; and no sooner came the day, than the king's
daughter came where she was, and set her on foot
and put her out. On the morrow she was working
with the needle, and cutting with other shears.
The king's daughter sent the maid servant over, and
she asked "what would she take for the needle ?" She
said she would not take anything, but leave to lie
where she lay last night. The maid servant told this
to the king's daughter. "She will get that," said the
king's daughter. The maid servant told that she
would get that, and she got the needle. When they
were going to lie down, the king's daughter gave him
a sleep drink, and he did not wake that night. The
eldest son he had was lying in a bed beside them ; and
he was hearing her speaking to him through the night,
and saying to him that she was mother of his three
children. His father and he himself were taking a
walk out, and he told his father what he was hearing. This day the king's daughter sent the servant
maid to ask what she would take for the clue ; and
she said she would ask but leave to lie where she lay
last night. "She will get that," said the king's
daughter. This night when he got the sleep drink, he
emptied it, and he did not drink it at all. Through
the night she said to him that he was the father of her
three sons ; and he said that he was. In the morning, when the king's daughter came down, he said to
her to go up, that she was his wife who was with him.
When they rose they went away to go home. They
came home ; the spells went off him, they planted together and I left them, and they left me.

Bha 'siod ann roimhe so tuathanach, 's bha triùir nigheanan aige, 's
mòran cruidh is chaorach. Dh' fholbh e la' a'm faicinn 's cha robh
gin r'a fhaotainn dhiu, 's thug e fad an latha 'gan iarraidh. Chunnaic
e, anns an anamoch a' tighinn dachaidh, cuilean beag a' ruith feadh
pàirce. Thàinig an cuilean far an robh e, " De bheir thu dhòmhs',"
urs' esan, " ma gheobh mi do chuid cruidh is caorach dhuit?" " Cha
'n 'eil fhios 'am féin a ruid ghrannda. " De bhios thu 'g iarraidh?
's bheir mise dhuit e de ni sam bith a th' agam." " An d' thoir thu
dhomh," urs' an cuilean, " do nighean mhòr r'a pòsadh." " Bheir
mise dhuit i," urs' esan, " ma ghabhas i féin thu." Chaidh iad
dhachaidh, e féin 's an cuilean. Dh' fhoighneachd a h-athair d'a nighean
bu shine an gabhadh i e, 's thuirt i nach gabhadh. Thuirt e ris an
darna té am pòsadh ise e, 's thuirt i nach pòsadh, ged nach faighte an
crodh gu bràth. Thuirt e ris an té 'b òige am pòsadh ise e, 's thuirt
i gum pòsadh. Phòs iad, 's bha 'peathraichean a' magadh urra
airson gun do phòs i e. Thug e leis dhachaidh i d'a àite féin. Nur a
thàinig e g'a àite còmhnuidh féin dh' fhàs e 'na dhuine ciatach. Bha
iad còmhla ùine mhòr, 's thuirt ise gnm b' fheàrra dhi dol a dh'
amharc a h-athar. Thuirt esan rithe i thoirt an aire nach fhanadh i
gus am biodh clann aice. Bha i torrach 'san am. Thuirt i nach
fanadh. Thug e dhi steud, 's thuirt e rithe, cho luath 's a ruigeadh i
'n tigh an t-srian a thoirt a a ceann, 's a leigeil air folbh, 's nur a
bhiodh toil aice tighinn dachaidh nach robh aic' ach an t-srian a
chrathadh, 's gun d' thigeadh an steud 's gun cuireadh i 'ceann innte.
Rinn i mar a dh' iarr e urra. Cha robh i fad' an tigh a h-athar nur a
dh' fhàs i gu bochd 'sa chaidh a h-asaid. An oidhche sin bha daoine
cruinn aig a' ghealbhan 'ga 'faire. Thàinig an aona cheòl a bu bhinne
chualas riamh feadh a' bhaile, 's chaidil a' h-uile duine stigh ach ise.
Thàinig esan a stigh 's thug e uaithe am pàisde. Ghabh e 'mach 's
dh' fholbh e. Stad an ceòl, 's dhùisg gach duine, 's cha robh fios de 'n
taobh a chaidh am pàisde. Cha d' innis i ni sam bith, ach cho luath
's a dh' 'éiridh i thug i leatha an t-srian, 's chrath i i, 's thàinig an
steud, 's chuir i 'ceann innte. Ghabh i air mharcachd urra, 's ghabh
an steud air folbh dhachaidh; bheireadh ise air a ghaoith luath mhàrt
a bh' air thoiseach orra, 's cha bheiseadh a ghaoth luath mhàrt a bha
na déigh orra. Ràinig i.

" Thàinig thu," urs' esan. " Thàinig," urs' ise. Cha do leig e
rud sam bith air rithe, 's cha mhotha leig ise rud sam bith orra risan.
Dlùth air ceann tri ràithean a rithisd thuirt ise, " 'S fheàrra dhomh

dol a dh' amharc m' athar." Thuirt e rithe air an t-siubhal so mar
a thuirt e roimhid. Thug i leatha an steud 's dh' fholbh i. Nur a
ràinig i thug i n t-srian a ceann na steud, 's leig i dhachaidh i, 's an
oidhche sin féin chaidh a h-asaid. Thàinig esan mar a rinn e roimhid
le ceòl. Chaidil a' h-uile duine, 's thug e leis am pàisde. Nur a stad
an ceòl dhùisg iad air fad. Bha 'h-athair air a h-aodann ag ràdh
rithe gum feumadh i innseadh de bu chiall de 'n ghnothach. Cha 'n
innseadh ise ni sam bith. Nur a dh' fhàs i gu math, 's a dh' éiridh i,
thug i leatha an t-srian, chrath i i, 's thàinig an steud, 's chuir i
ceann innte. Ghabh i air folbh dhachaidh. Nur a ràinig i thuirt
esan. "Thàinig thu." "Thàinig," urs' ise. Cha do leig e rud sam
bith air rithe, 's cha mhotha 'leig ise urra risan. An ceann tri
ràithean a rithisd thuirt i, " 'S fheàrra dhomh dol a dh' amharc m'
athar." "Dèan," urs' esan, "ach thoir an aire nach dèan thu mar a
rinn thu an da shiubhal roimhid." "Cha dèan," urs' ise. Thug e
dhi an steud, 's dh' fholbh i. Ràinig i tigh a h-athar, 's dh' asaid-
eadh i 'n oidhche sin féin. Thàinig an ceòl mar a b' àbhaist, 's
thugadh am pàisd' air folbh. Bha 'h-athair air a h-aodann an sin, 's
e 'dol a 'marbhadh mar an innseadh i dé 'bha tachairt do na pàisdean,
no dé 'n seòrsa duine a bh' aice. Leis an eagal a chuir e urra
dh' innis i dha e. Nur a dh' fhàs i gu math, thug i leatha an
t-srian gu cnoc a bha ma 'coinneamh, 's thòisich i air crathadh na
sréine feuch an d' thigeadh an steud, na'n cuireadh i 'ceann innte, 's
ged a bhiodh i 'crathadh fhathasd cha d' thigeadh an steud. Nur a
chunnaic i nach robh i 'tighinn ghabh i mach 'na cois. Nur a ràinig
i cha robh duine stigh ach a' chailleach a bu mhàthair dha. "Tha
thusa gun fhear tighe an diugh," urs' a' chailleach, " 's ma bhios thu
tapaidh beiridh thu air fhathasd."

Ghabh i air folbh, 's bha i 'folbh gus an d' thàinig an oidhche orra.
Chunnaic i 'n sin solus fada uaithe, 's ma b' fhada uaithe cha b' fhada
bha ise 'ga 'ruigheachd. Nur a chaidh i stigh bha urlar réidh sguabte
roimhpe, 's bean an tighe 'snìomh shuas an ceann an tighe. "Thig a
nìos," ursa bean an tighe, "tha fios do sheud 's do shiubhail agamsa."
Tha thu folbh feuch am beir thu air t-fhear. Tha e 'folbh a phòsadh
nighean rìgh nan speur." "Tha!" urs' ise. Dh' éiridh bean an
tighe; rinn i biadh dhi; chuir i air uisge 'ghlanadh a cas; 's chuir i
'laidhe i. Ma bu luath a thàinig an latha bu luaithe na sin a dh'
éiridh bean an tighe 'sa rinn i biadh dhi. Chuir i air a cois i 'n sin
airson folbh, 's thug i dhi siosar a ghearradh leis féin, 's thuirt i rithe.
"Bidh thu ann an tigh mo phiuthar mheadhonachsa nochd." Bha i
'folbh 's a' folbh gus an d' thàinig an oidhche urra. Chunnaic i solus
fada uaithe, 's ma b' fhada uaithe cha b' fhada bha ise 'ga ruigheachd.

Nur a chaidh i stigh bha 'n tigh réidh, sguabte; gealbhan air meadh
on an urlair, 's bean an tighe 'suìomh an ceann a' ghealbhain.
"Thig a nìos," ursa bean an tighe, "tha fios do sheud 's do shiubhail
agamsa." Rinn i biadh dhi; chuir i air uisge; ghlan i 'casan 's
chuir i laidhe i. Cha bu luaithe a thàinig an latha na 'chuir
bean an tighe air a cois i, 's a rinn i biadh dhi. Thuirt i rithe
gum b' fheàrra dhi folbh, 's thug i dhi snàthad a dh' fhuaigheadh
leatha féin. "Bidh thu ann an tigh mo pheathar is òige a nochd,"
urs' ise.

Bha i folbh 's a' folbh gu deireadh latha 's beul anamoich. Chunnaic i solus fada uaithe, 's ma b' fhada uaithe cha b' fhada bha ise 'ga
ruigheachd. Chaidh i stigh. Bha 'n tigh sguabte, 's bean an tighe
'snìomh os ceann a' ghealbhain. "Thig a nìos," urs' ise, "tha fios do
sheud 's do shiubhail agamsa." Rinn i biadh dhi; "chuir i air uisge;
ghlan i 'casan, 's chuir i laidhe i. Ma bu luath a thàinig an latha,
bu luaithe na sin a dh' éiridh bean an tighe; chuir i air a cois i, 's
rinn i biadh dhi. Thug i dhi ceairsle shnàth, 's rachadh an snàth-
ainn anns an t-snàthad leis féin, 's mur a ghearradh an siosar, 's mur
a dh' fhuaigheadh an t-snàthad, chnmadh a cheairsle snàth ruitha.
"Bidh thu anns a' bhaile nochd."

Ràinig i 'm baile ma fheasgar 's chaidh i stigh do thigh chailleach
chearc an rìgh. Shuidh i 'leigeil a sgìos; bha i ga garadh aig a'
ghealbhan; thuirt i ris a' chaillich obair a' thoirt dhi, gum b' fheàrr
leatha 'bhi 'g obair na bhi 'na tàmh. "Cha 'n 'eil duine dèanadh
turn 'sa' bhaile so n diugh," ursa a' chailleach; "tha pòsadh aig nighean an rìgh." "Ud!" urs' ise ris a' chaillich, "thoir dhomh aodach r'a
fhuaghal, na léine 'chumas mo làmh air folbh." Thug i dhi léintean
r'a dhèanadh. Thug i mach siosar a a pòca; chuir i dh' obair e;
chuir i 'n t-snàthad a dh' obair as a dhéigh. Mar a ghearradh an siosar
dh' fhuaigheadh an t-snàthad, 's rachadh an snàth anns an t-snàthaid
leis féin. Thàinig té do shearbhantan an rìgh stigh; bha i 'g amharc
urra; 's bha e cur ioghnadas mòr urra démur a bha i 'toirt air an t-siosar
's air an t-snàthad oibreachadh leotha féin. Chaidh i dhachaidh, 's dh'
innis i do nighean an rìgh gun robh té ann an tigh chailleach nan
cearc, 's gun robh siosar agus snàthad aice a dh' oibreachadh leotha
féin. "Ma tha," ursa nighean an rìgh, "theirig thusa nunn anns a'
mhaidinn, 's abair rithe de 'ghabhas i air an t-siosar." Anns a'
mhaidinn chaidh i 'nunn, 's thuirt i rithe gun robh nighean an rìgh
a' foighneachd dé ghabhadh i air an t-siosar. "Cha 'n iarr mi," urs'
ise, "ach cead laidhe far an do laidh i féin anràir." "Theirig thusa
nunn," ursa nighean an rìgh, "'s abair rithe gum faigh i sin."
Thug i 'n siosar do nighean an rìgh.

Nur a bha iad a' dol a laidhe thug nighean an righ deoch chadail dàsan, air alt 's nach dùisgeadh e. Cha do dhùisg e fad na h-oidhche, 's cha bu luaithe a thàinig an latha na thàinig nighean an rìgh far an robh ise, 'sa chuir i air a cois i. An la 'r na mhàireach bha i 'g obair leis an t-snàthaid, 's a' gearradh le siosar eile. Chuir nighean an rìgh an searbhanta nunn a dh' fhoighneachd dé 'ghabhadh i air an t-snàthaid. Thuirt i nach gabhadh ni sam bith ach cead laidhe far an do laidh i rair. Dh' innis an searbhanta so do nighean an rìgh. " Gheobh i sin," ursa nighean an rìgh. Dh' innis an searbhanta gum faigheadh i siod, 's fhuair i 'n t-snàthad. Nur a bha iad a' dol a laidhe thug nighean an rìgh deoch chadail da, 's cha do dhùisg e 'n oidhche sin. Bha 'm mac a bu shine bh' aige ann an leaba làmh riutha, 's bha e 'ga 'cluinntinn a' bruidhinn ris feadh na h-oidhche, 's ag ràdh ris gum b'i màthair a thriùir chloinn' i. Bha athair 's e féin a' gabhail sràid a mach, 's dh' innis e d'a athair dé 'bha e 'cluinntinn. An latha so chuir nighean an rìgh an searbhanta a dh' fheòraich de 'ghabhadh i air a' cheairsle, 's thuirt i rithe nach iarradh i ach cead laidhe far an do laidh i 'n rair. " Gheobh i sin," ursa nighean an rìgh. An oidhche so nur a fhuair e 'n deoch chadail thaom e i, 's cha d' òl e idir i. Feadh na h-oidhche thuirt ise ris gum b' e athair a triùir mac, 's thuirt esan gum b' e.

Anns a mhaidinn, nur a thàinig nighean an rìgh nuas, thuirt e rithe i 'dhol suas, gum bi 'bhean a bha leis. Nur a dh' eiridh iad dh' fholbh iad airson dol dachaidh. Thàinig iad dachaidh ; dh' fholbh na geasan deth. Chuir iad còmbla 's dhealaich mise riutha, 's dheal- aich iadsan riumsa.

This is but another version of No. III., " The Hoodie ;" but it has certain magic gifts which I have not found in any other Gaelic story ; and the *little dog* who goes to the skies, and is abont to marry the daughter of the king, and is transformed into a man at home, may turn out to be a Celtic divinity. When so little is known of Celtic mythology, anything may be of use. The raven, the crow, and the serpent, have appeared as transformed beings of superior power. Now, the little dog appears, and there are mystic dogs elsewhere in Gaelic stories, and in other Celtic countries. In the Isle of Man is the well-known " Modey dhu," black dog which used to haunt Peel Castle, and frightened a sol- dier to death.

In a cnrious book, written to prove Gaelic to be the original language (History of the Celtic Language, by L. MacLean, 1840), there is a great deal of speculation as to the Farnese Globe ; and the dog-star in particular is supposed to have been worshipped by the Druids.   Without entering into such a wide field, it is worth notice that " Anubis," the dog-star, was son of Osiris and Nephthys, had the nature of a dog, and was represented with the head of one.   He was a celestial double deity, and watched the tropics.   The servant lad who told this story ; and the old woman, Mac Kerrol, from whom he learned it, are not likely persons to have heard of Anubis, or the Farnese Globe ; so anything got from them may be taken at its value, whatever that may be.   The opinion that Celts came from the East by way of Phœnicia, has been held by many, and some one may wish to follow the trail of the little dog ; so I give his history as it came to me, rather than fuse it into one story with the Hoodie, as I was at first tempted to do before the plan of this work was decided on.

The beginning of this tale is the Gaelic " Once upon a time."

Bha   siod   ann   roimhe so.

Was yonder in it ere   this.

TRIUR is a collective noun of number for three, and answers to *leash ;* or to *pair, brace, dozen*, for two; twelve.

STEUD is clearly the same word as steed.   It is commonly used in these stories, and 1 have never heard it used in conversation.   It is feminine, like FALAIRE, the other word commonly used for a horse in stories and poetry ; and hardly ever in ordinary speech.

Many words are derived from steud, and I do not think that it is imported.

XIII.

THE GIRL AND THE DEAD MAN.

From Ann Darroch, Islay.

THERE was before now a poor woman, and she had a leash of daughters. Said the eldest one of them to her mother, "I had better go myself and seek for fortune." "I had better," said her mother, "bake a bannock for thee." When the bannock was ready, her mother said to her, "Whether wouldst thou like best the bit and my blessing, or the big bit and my curse ?" "I would rather," said she, "the big bit and thy curse." She went away, and when the night was wreathing round her, she sat at the foot of a wall to eat the bannock. There gathered the sreath chuilean-ach and her twelve puppies, and the little birds of the air about her, for a part of the bannock. "Wilt thou give us a part of the bannock," said they. "I won't give it, you ugly brutes ; I have not much for myself." "My curse will be thine, and the curse of my twelve birds ; and thy mother's curse is thy worst of all." She rose and she went away, and she had not half enough with the bit of the bannock. She saw a little house a long way from her ; and if a long way from her, she was not long reaching it. She struck in the door. "Who's there ?" "A good maid seeking a master." "We want that," said they, and she got in. She had now a peck of gold and a peck of silver to get; and she was to be awake every night to watch a dead man, brother of the housewife, who was under spells. She had besides, of nuts as she broke, of needles as she lost, of thimbles as she pierced, of thread as she used, of candles as she burned, a bed of green silk over her, a bed of green silk under her, sleeping by day and watching by night. The first night when she was watching she fell asleep; the mistress came in, she struck the magic club on her, she fell down dead, and she threw her out at the back of the midden.

Said the middle one to her mother, "I had better go seek fortune and follow my sister." Her mother baked her a bannock; and she chose the big half and her mother's curse, as her elder sister did, and it happened to her as it happened to her sister.

Said the youngest one to her mother, "I had better myself go to seek fortune too, and follow my sisters." "I had better bake a bannock," said her mother. "Whether wouldst thou rather the little bit and my blessing, or the big bit and my curse?" "I would rather the little bit and your blessing." She went, and the night was wreathing round her, and she sat at the foot of a wall to eat the bannock. There gathered the sreath chuileanach and the twelve puppies, and the little birds of the air about her. "Wilt thou give us some of that?" "I will give, you pretty creatures, if you will keep me company." She gave them some of the bannock; they ate and they had plenty, and she had enough. They clapped their wings about her till she was snug with the warmth. She went, she saw a little house a long way from her; and if it was a long way from her, she was not long reaching it. She struck in the door. "Who's there ?" "A good maid seeking a master." "We have need of that." The wages she had were a peck of gold and a peck of silver; of nuts as she broke, of needles as she lost, of thimbles as she pierced, of thread as she used, of candles as she burned, a bed of the green silk over her, and a bed of the green silk under her. She sat to watch the dead man, and she was sewing; on the middle of night he rose up, and screwed up a grin. "If thou dost not lie down properly, I will give thee the one leathering with a stick." He lay down. At the end of a while, he rose on one elbow, and screwed up a grin; and the third time he rose and screwed up a grin. When he rose the third time, she struck him a lounder of the stick; the stick stuck to the dead man, and the hand stuck to the stick; and out they were. They went forward till they were going through a wood; when it was low for her it was high for him; and when it was high for him it was low for her. The nuts were knocking their eyes out, and the sloes taking their ears off, till they got through the wood. After going through the wood they returned home. She got a peck of gold and a peck of silver, and the vessel of cordial. She rubbed the vessel of cordial to her two sisters, and brought them alive. They returned home; they left me sitting here, and if they were well, 'tis well; and if they were not, let them be.

AN NIGHINN AGUS AN DUINE MARBH.

Bha bean bhochd ann roimhe so, 's bha triùir nighean aice. Thuirt an té bu shine dhiu r'a màthair, "'S fheàrra dhomh fhéin dol a dh' iarraidh an fhortain." "'S fheàrra dhòmhs," ursa a màthair, "bonn- ach a dheasachadh dhuit." Nur a bha 'm bonnach réidh thuirt a mathair rithe, cò'ca 's fheàrr leat a' bhlaidh bheag 's mo bheannachd na 'bhlaidh mhor 's mo mhollachd." "'S fheàrr leam," urs' ise, "a' bhlaidh mhòr 's do mhollachd." Dh' fholbh i. Nur a bha 'n oidhche 'casadh urra shuidh i 'chois gàrraidh a dh' itheadh a' bhonnaich. Nur a shuidh i 'dh' itheadh a' bhonnaich chruinnich an t-sreath chuileanach, 's a da chuilean deug, 's eòin bheag an athar timchioll urra airson pàirt de 'n bhonnach. "An d' thoir thu dhuinne pàirt de 'n bhonnach," urs' iadsan. "Cha d' thobhair a bheathaichean grànnda; cha mhòr a th' agam dhomh féin. "Biodh mo mhollachds' agadsa, 's mollachd mo dha eun deug, 's e mollachd do mhàthar is measa dhuit air fad."

Dh' éiridh i 's dh' fholbh i, 's cha robh leith a leoir 's a' bhlaidh bhonnaich. Chunnaic i tigh beag fada uaithe, 's ma b' fhada uaithe cha b' fhada bha ise 'ga ruigheachd. Bhuail i 'san dorusd. "Co tha siod?" "Searbhanta math aig iarraidh maighstir." "Tha sin a dhìth oirnne," urs' iadsan, s' fhuair i 'stigh. Bha peic òir is peic airgid aice r'a fhaotainn, 's i ri aithreachach a' h-uile h-oidhch' a' faire duine marbh, bràthair do bhean an tighe 'bha fo gheasan Bha aice cuideachd de chnuthan mar a bhrisdeadh i ; de shnàthadan mar a chailleadh i ; 's do mheurain mar a tholladh i ; de shnàth mar a chosdadh i ; de choinnlean mar a loisgeadh i ; leaba do n t-sìod' uaine thairte ; leaba de 'n t-sioda uaine fòiche ; codal 'san latha, 's aith- reachadh 'san oidhche.

A' chiad oidhche, nur a bha i 'faire, thuit i 'na cadal. Thàinig a banamhaighstir a stigh ; bhuail i 'n slachdan draoidheachd urra ; thuit i sìos marbh ; 's thilg i mach cùl an dùnain i.

Thuirt an té mheadhonach r'a màthair, "'S fhearra domh dol a dh' iarraidh an fhortain, 's mo phuithar a leantainn." Dheasaich a màthair bonnach, 's roighnich ise an leith mhòr is mollachd a màthar, mar a rinn a piuthar a bu shine. Thachair dhi mar a thachair d'a piuthar.

Thuirt an té b' òige r'a màthair, "'S fheàrra dhomh féin dol a dh' iarraidh an fhortain cuideachd, 's mo pheathraichean a leantainn." "'S fheàrra dhòmhsa bonnach a dheasachadh," urs' a màthair. "Cò'ca 's fheàrr leat a' bhlaidh bheag 's mo bheannachd, na 'bhlaidh mhòr 's mo mhollachd, "'S fheàrr leam a bhlaidh bheag 's bhur beann- achd." Dh' fholbh i. Bha 'n oidhche 'casadh urra, 's shuidh i 'chois gàrraidh a dh' itheadh a bhonnaich. Chruinnich an t-sreath chuil- eanach, 's an da chuilean deug, 's eòin bheag an athair timchioll urra. "An d' thobhair thu dhuinne rud dheth sin ?" "Bheithir a bheath- aichean bòidheach, ma ni sibh comaith rium féin. Thug i dhaibh rud de 'n bhonnach ; dh' ith iad e ; 's bha na leoir acasan 's na leòir aice féin. Chlap iad an sgiathan timchioll urra, 's bha i 'na falas leis a' bhlàthas

Dh' fholbh i. Chunnaic i tigh beag fada uaithe, 's ma b' fhada uaithe cha b' fhada 'bha ise 'ga 'ruigheachd. Bhuail i 'san dorus. "Co siod?" "Searbhanta math aig iarraidh maighstir." "Tha sin a dhìth òirnne." Se 'n tuarasdal a bh' aice peic òir is peic airgid; de chnuthan mar a bhrisdeadh i; de shnàthadan mar a chailleadh i; de mheurain mar a tholladh i; de shnàth mar a chosdadh i; de choinnlean mar a loisgeadh i; leaba de n t-sìod' uaine thairte, 's leaba de 'n t-sìod uaine fòiche.

Shuidh i 'faire an duine mhairbh, 's bha i fuaghal. Air a' mheadhon oidhche dh' éiridh esan, 's chas e braoisg air. "Mar an laidh thu sìos mar a th' agad bheir mise aon straoileadh dhuit de bhata." Laidh e sìos. Ann ceann tacan beag a rithi-d dh' éiridh e air a leith-nilinn, 's chas e braoisg air, 's an treas uair dh' éiridh e 's chas e braoisg air!!" Nur a dh' éiridh e 'n treas uair bhuail i straoileadh de 'n bhat' air. Lean am bata ris an duine mharbh; lean an lamh ris a' bhata! 's a mach a bha iad. Ghabh iad air an aghaidh gus an robh iad a' dol romh choille. Mar a b' iseal dise e b' àrd dhàsan e, 's mar a b' àrd dhàsan e b' iseal dise e. Bha na cnuthan a' toirt nan sùl asda, 's na h-àirnean a' toirt nan cluas dhiutha, gus an d' fhuair iad romh 'n choille. An déigh dol romh 'n choille thill iad dachaidh. Fhuair i peic òir is peic airgid, 'sam ballan ìocshlaint. Rub i 'm ballan ìocshlaint r'a da phiuthar, 's thug i beò iad. Thill iad dhachaidh. Dh' fhàg iad mise a'm 'shuidhe so, 's ma bha iad gu math 's math, 's mar an robh leigear dhaibh.

This story has some relation to "The man who travelled to learn what fear was;" but I know nothing quite like it in Gaelic, or in any other language. Ann Darroch, who told it to Hector MacLean in May 1859, learned it from an old woman, Margaret Conal, of whom MacLean writes—

"I have some recollection of her myself; she was wont to repeat numerous 'ursgeuln' (tales). Her favourite resorts were the kilns, where the people were kiln-drying their corn; and where she was frequently rewarded, for amusing them in this manner, by supplies of meal. She was paralytic; her head shook like an aspen leaf, and whenever she repeated anything that was very exciting, her head shook more rapidly; which impressed children with great awe."

Some of the phrases are evidently remembered, and said by heart; the maid's wages, for instance; and the creatures that came to the wandering daughters. The vessel of Balsam occurs often in Gaelic stories, and I cannot make out what it really means. BALLAN IOCSHLAINT, teat, of ichor, of health, seems to be the meaning of the words.

In former days the kilns were not always used for drying corn. It is related that one of the first excisemen who went to the West, found and caught a large party of men kiln-drying malt. He made a seizure of course, and was not a little surprised when he was seized himself, and his arms tied fast behind him. His eyes were bound also; and then he was led to the kiln and set down near the fire; and they gave him the malt to smell and taste; and then they told him it was to be used in making whisky; and then they gave him a drop, and then a dram, till the gauger was so drunk that they left him there, and departed with their malt kiln-dried and ground.

This I have heard told of the very place which Margaret Conal used to haunt, and of a time when she might have been a little girl; I cannot vouch for the truth of my story, but the kiln and the men about it may be seen now; and such scenes may well account for the preservation of wild stories. A child would not easily forget a story learned amongst a lot of rough farmers, seated at night round a blazing fire, listening to an old crone with palsied head and hands; and accordingly, I have repeatedly heard that the mill, and the kiln, were the places where my informants learned their tales.

There is a word in this tale which the narrator, the translator, the transcriber, the dictionary, and the " old men," have failed to explain.

SREATH CHUILEANACH means some kind of bird, and she has twelve " puppies," DA CHUILEAN DEUG. The narrator maintains that the words are right as she heard them.

THE KING WHO WISHED TO MARRY HIS DAUGHTER.

From Ann Darroch, Islay.

THERE was a king before now, and he married, and he had but one daughter. When his wife departed, he would marry none but one whom her clothes would fit. His daughter one day tried her mother's dress on, and she came and she let her father see how it fitted her. It was fitting her well. When her father saw her he would marry no woman but her. She went, crying where her muime was ; and her foster mother said to her, " What was the matter with her ?" She said, " That her father was insisting that he would marry her." Her muime told her to say to him, " That she would not marry him till he should get her a gown of the swan's down." He went, and at the end of a day and a year he came, and the gown with him. She went again to take the counsel of her muime. " Say to him," said her muime, " that thou wilt not marry him till he gets thee a gown of the moorland canach." She said this to him. He went, and at the end of a day and year he returned, and a gown of the moorland canach with him. " Say now to him," said her muime, " that thou wilt not marry him till he brings thee a gown of silk that will stand on the ground with gold

and silver." At the end of a day and year he returned
with the gown. "Say to him now," said her muime,
"that thou wilt not marry him till he brings thee a
golden shoe, and a silver shoe." He got her a golden
shoe and a silver shoe. "Say to him now," said her
muime, "that thou wilt not marry him unless he
brings thee a kist that will lock without and within,
and for which it is all the same to be on sea or on
land." When she got the kist, she folded the best of
her mother's clothes, and of her own clothes in it.
Then she went herself into the kist, and she asked her
father to put it out on the sea to try how it would
swim. Her father put it out; when it was put out,
it was going, and going, till it went out of sight.

It went on shore on the other side; and a herd
came where it was, intending to break it, in hopes that
there were findings in the chest. When he was going
to break it she called out, "Do not so;" but say to
thy father to come here, and he will get that which
will better him for life." His father came, and he took
her with him to his own house. It was with a king
that he was herd, and the king's house was near him.
"If I could get," said she, "leave to go to service to
this great house yonder." "They want none," said
the herd, "unless they want one under the hand of
the cook." The herd went to speak for her, and she
went as a servant maid under the hand of the cook.
When the rest were going to the sermon; and when
they asked her if she was going to it, she said that she
was not; that she had a little bread to bake, and that
she could not go to it. When they went away, she
took herself to the herd's house, and she put on a
gown of the down of the swan. She went to the sermon, and she sat opposite the king's son. The king's
son took love for her. She went a while before the

sermon skailed, she reached the herd's house, she
changed her clothes, and she was in before them.
When the rest came home, it was talking about the
gentlewoman that was at the sermon they were.

The next Sunday they said to her, "Was she
going to the sermon;" and she said, "That she was
not, that she had a little bread to bake." When they
went away, she reached the herd's house, and she put
on a gown of the moorland canach; and she went to
the sermon. The king's son was seated where she was
the Sunday before, and she sat opposite to him. She
came out before them, and she changed, and she was
at the house before them; and when the rest came
home, it was talking about the great gentlewoman
that was at the sermon they were. The third Sunday,
they said to her, "Was she going to the sermon;" and
she said, "That she was not, that she had a little
bread to bake." When they went away, she reached
the herd's house; she put on the gown that would
stand on the ground with gold and silver, and the
golden shoe and the silver shoe, and she went to
the sermon. The king's son was seated where she was
the Sunday before, and she sat where he was. A
watch was set on the doors this Sunday. She arose,
she saw a cranny, and she jumped out at the cranny;
but they kept hold of one of the shoes.

The king's son said, "Whomsoever that shoe
would fit, she it was that he would marry."

Many were trying the shoe on, and taking off their
toes and heels to try if it would fit them; but there
were none whom the shoe would fit. There was a
little bird in the top of a tree, always saying as every
one was trying on the shoe, "Beeg beeg ha nan doot
a heeg ach don tjay veeg a ha fo laiv a hawchkare."
"Wee wee, it comes not on thee; but on the wee one

under the hand of the cook." When he could get none whom the shoe would fit, the king's son lay down, and his mother went to the kitchen to talk over the matter. "Wont you let me see the shoe?" said she; "I will not do it any harm at all events." "Thou! thou ugly dirty thing, that it should fit thee." She went down, and she told this to her son. "Is it not known," said he, "that it wont fit her at all events? and can't you give it her to please her?" As soon as the shoe went on the floor, the shoe jumped on her foot. "What will you give me," said she, "to let you see the other one?" She reached the herd's house, and she put on the shoes, and the dress that would stand on the floor with gold and silver. When she returned, there was but to send word for a minister, and she herself and the king's son married.

URSGEUL.

Bha 'siod rìgh ann roimhe so, 's phòs e, 's cha robh aige ach an aon nighean. Nur a shiubhail a' bhean cha phòsadh e gin ach te 'fhreagradh a h-aodach dhi. Dh' fheuch a nighean latha aodach a màthar urra, 's thàinig i 's leig i fhaicinn d'a h-athair mar a fhreagradh e dhi. Bha e 'freagairt e dhi. Bha e 'freagairt dhi gu math. Nur a chunnaic a h-athair i, cha phòsadh e bean ach i. Chaidh i 'caoineadh far an robh a muime, 's thuirt a muime rithe dè bh' urra. Thuirt i gun robh a h-athair a' cur roimhe gum pòsadh e i. Thuirt a muime rithe 'ràdh ris nach pòsadh e i gus am faigheadh e dhi guthann de chlòimhe na h-eala.

Dh' fholbh e 's an ceann la is bliadhna thàinig e, 's an guthann leis. Chaidh i 'rithisd a ghabhail comhairl' a muime. "Abair ris," urs' a muime, "nach pòs thu e gus am faigh e dhuit guthann de chanach an t-sléibhe. Thuirt i so ris. Dh' fholbh e, 's an ceann la is bliadhna thill e 's guthann de chanach an t-sléibhe leis. "Abair ris a nis," urs' a muime, "nach pòs thu e gus an d' thoir e 't' ionnsuidh guthann siod' a sheasas air an làr le h-òr 's le airgiod. An ceann la is bliadhna thill e leis a ghuthann. "Abair ris a nis," urs' a muime, "nach pòs

thu e gus an a thoir e 't 'ionnsuidh bròg òir is bròg airgid." Fhuair
e dhi bròg òir is bròg airgid. "Abair ris a nis," ursa a muime,
"nach pòs thu e mar an d' thoir e 't' ionnsuidh cisde a ghlaiseas
a mach 's a stigh, 's is coingeis leatha bhi air muir na air tìr.

Nur a fhuair e chisde phaisg i chuid a b' fheàrr de dh' aodach a
màthar 's d'a h-aodach féin innte. Chaidh i féin an sin a stigh 's a'
chisde, 's dh' iarr i air a h-athair a cur a mach air an fhairge feuch
démur a shnàmhadh i. Chuir a h-athair a mach i. Nur a chaidh a
chisd' a mach, bha i folbh 's a' folbh gus an deach i as an t-sealladh.
Chaidh i air tìr air an taobh eile, 's thàinig buachaille far an robh i
airson a brisdeadh, an dùil gun robh feudail anns a' chisde. Nur a
bha e 'dol a 'brisdeadh ghlaoidh ise, "Na dèan ach abair ri t' athair
tighinn an so, 's gheobh e na 's fheàird e r'a bheò. Thàinig 'athair
's thug e leis g'a thigh féin i. 'S ann aig righ bha 'm buachaille, 's
bha tigh an righ dlùth air. "Nam faighinn," urs' ise, "dol air
fasdadh do 'n tigh mhòr so thall." "Cha 'n eil gin a dhìth orr'," urs'
am buachaille, "mar am bheil té dhìth orra fo làimh a' chòcaire."
Chaidh am buachaille 's bhruidhin e air a son, 's chaidh i 'na searbhanta
fo làimh a' chòcaire.

Nur a bha càch a' dol do 'n t-searmoin, 's a dh' fheòraidh iad dhise
an robh i dol ann, thuirt i nach robh gun robh beagan arain aice r'a
dheasachadh, 's nach b' urrainn i dol ann. Nur a dh' fholbh iadsan
thug i urra tigh a' bhuachaille, 's chuir i urra guthann de chlòimhe na
h-eala. Chaidh i do 'n t-searmoin, 's shuidh i ma choinneamh mac an
rìgh. Ghabh mac an rìgh gaol urra. Dh' fholbh ise tacan ma'n do
sgaoil an t-searmoin; ràinig i tigh a' bhuachaille; dh' atharraich i
h-aodach; 's bha i stigh rompa. Nur a thàinig càch dhachaidh 's ann
aig iomradh air a' bhean uasal mhòr a bha 's an t-searmoin a bha
iad. An ath dhòmhnach thuirt iad rithe, an robh i dol do 'n t-searmoin, 's thuirt i nach robh, gun robh beagan arain aice r'a dheasachadh. Nur a dh' fholbh iadsan ràinig i tigh a' bhuachaille, 's chuir i
urra guthann de chanach an t-sléibhe, 's chaidh i do 'n t-searmoin.
Bha mac an rìgh 'na shuidhe far an robh ise an dòmhnach roimhid,
's shuidh ise ma choinneamh. Thàinig i mach air thoiseach orra;
dh' atharraich i, 's bha i aig an tigh rompa; 's nur a thàinig
càch dhachaidh 's ann aig iomradh air a' bhean uasal mhòr a bha 'san
t-searmoin a bha iad. An treas dòmhnach thuirt iad rithe an robh
i dol do 'n t-searmoin, 's thuirt i nach robh 'gun robh beagan arain
aice r'a dheasachadh. Nur a dh' fholbh iadsan ràinig i tigh a bhuachaille; chuir i urra an guthann a sheasadh air an làr le b-òr 's le
h' airgiod; 's a' bhròg òir 's a' bhròg airgid; 's chaidh i 'n t-searmoin.
Bha mac an rìgh 'na shuidhe for an robh ise an dòmhnach roimhid

's shuidh ise far an robh esan. Chaidh faire 'chur air na dorsan an dòmhnach so. Dh' éiridh ise. Chunnaic i fruchag, s' leum i mach air an fhruchaig, ach ghléidh iad gréim air té de na brògan. Thuirt mac an rìgh té sam bith d'am freagradh a' bhròg gur h' i 'phòsadh esan. Bha mòran a feuchainn na bròig orra, 's a' toirt dhiu nan ladharan agus nan sàiltean feuch am freagradh i dhaibh, ach cha robh gin d'an robh a' bhrog a' freagairt. Bha eun beag am bàr craoibhe, 's e daonnan ag ràdh, h-uile té bha feuchainn na bròig urra. "Big, big, cha 'n ann duit a thig, ach do 'n te bhig a tha fo làimh a' chòcaire." Nur nach robh iad a' faotainn gin d'am freagradh a' bhròg laidh mac an rìgh, 's chaidh a' mhàthair do 'n chidsin a dh' iomradh air a' ghnothach. "Nach leig sibh fhaicinn dòmhs' a' bhròg," urs' ise; "cha dèan mi coire urra co dhiu." "Thusa a ruid ghrannda, shalaich! gum freagradh i dhuitse!" Chaidh i sìos 's dh' innis i so d'a mac. "Nach 'eil fhios," urs' esan, "nach freagair i dhi co dhiu, 's nach fhaod sibh a toirt dhi a 'toileachadh." Cho luath 's a chaidh a' bhròg air an urlar, leum a' bhròg air a cois. "De 'bheir sibh dhòmhs'," urs' ise, "'s an te eile 'leigeil fhaicinn duibh." Rainig i tigh a bhuachaille, 's chuir urra na brògan, 's an trusgan a sheasadh air an làr le òr 's le airgiod. Nur a thill i cha robh ach fios a chur air ministir, 's phòs i féin is mac an rìgh.

Ann Darroch got this tale from Margaret Connel.

The chest meant by the narrator of this version is clearly the kist, which every well provided highland lass takes to service. Such kists, and such lassies seated on them, may be seen in every highland steam-boat; and still finer kists may be seen in every cottage in Norway, where wood is more plentiful, and kists are on a larger scale. The contents of all are alike; the clothes of generations. The mother's Sunday dresses, and the grandmother's, with some fine shawl, or cap, or bonnet, or something hideous, modern, and fashionable, more prized by far than the picturesque old plaid, or bright red cloak of Scotch women, or the endless Norse costumes, which are going out of fashion in the same way. The little bird's note is imitated, and I have tried to spell the speech in English.

2d. I heard a version of this in the island of South Uist, in September 1859, from my companion MacCraw, who got it from a girl then in the inn at the Sound of Benbecula,

Mohag a chota Bhain, Margery White Coats. A king had four
daughters, and his wife died, and he said he would marry any
one whom his dead wife's clothes would fit. One day the
daughters tried, and the youngest only could wear them. The
king saw them from a window, and wished to marry her, and
she went for advice to her mother's brother. He advised her to
promise to marry the king if he would bring her a gown of birds'
down, and a gown of the colours of the sky, woven with silver;
and when he got that, a gown of the colours of the stars, woven
with gold, and glass shoes. When he had got them, she escaped
with all her clothes, by the help of her uncle, on a filly, with a
magic bridle, she on one side, and her chest of clothes on the
other. She rode to a king's palace, hid the chest in a hill under
a bush of rushes, turned the filly loose, and went to the palace
with nothing on but a white petticoat and a shift. She took
service with the cook, and grew dirty and ugly, and slept on a
bench by the kitchen fire, and her work was to blow under the
great caldron all day long. One day the king's son came home,
and was to hold a feast; she went to the queen and asked leave
to go, and was refused because she was so dirty. The queen had
a basin of water in her hand, and threw it at her, and it broke.
She went to the hill, took out the dress of down and silver, and
shook her magic bridle; the filly came, and she mounted, and
rode to the feast. "The king's son took her by the hand, and
took her up as high as any there, and set her on his own lap;
and when the feast was over, there was no reel that he danced
but he gave it to her." He asked her whence she came, and she
said, from the kingdom of Broken Basins; and the prince said
that he had never heard of that land, though he had travelled far.
She escaped and returned to the cook, and all were talking about
the beautiful lady. She asked about her, and was told not to
talk about what she did not understand, "a dirty little wretch
like her." Then the prince had another feast; and she asked
leave again, and the queen refused, and threw a candlestick at
her, and it broke, and she did as before. She put on another
dress and went; the king's son had eight men on each side of
the door to catch her. The same scene went on, and she said
she came from the country of Candlesticks—"Tir nan Coil-
learan," and escaped, leaving a glass shoe. Then the king's son

fell sick (of course), and would only marry the woman whom the shoe would fit; and all the ladies came and cut off their toes and heels, but in vain. Then he asked if there was none other. Then a small creature put his head in at the door and said, "If thou didst but know, she whom thou seekest is under the cook." Then he got the history of the basin and candlestick from his mother. The shoe was tried and fitted, and he was to marry Morag. All were in despair, and abused her; but she went out to her chest, shook the magic bridle, and arrayed herself, and came back on the filly, with a "powney" behind with the chest. Then all there that had despised her fell on their knees, and she was married to the prince. "And I did not get a bit there at the wedding," said the girl.

This was told as we walked along the road, and is but a short outline of what was told me, written from notes made in the evening. The man said that the girl told it with a great deal of the queer old language, which he could not remember.

The girl and her chest on the same horse may be seen in the Highlands. The girl, in her white coats and short gown, may be seen blowing the fire in highland inns, the queen's likeness might be found; and the feast is a highland ball; the filly and the magic bridle are common in other stories; the incidents of the basin and candlestick have an equivalent in Norse; and I got them from a woman at the Sound of Barra afterwards, in another story. This shows what may be lost by dignified travelling. While the man was enjoying himself in the kitchen, the employer was smoking in solitary dignity, up stairs in his bed-room, writing a journal, and utterly unconscious that the game he pursued was so near.

I have other versions of this tale from other sources, and may find room for them hereafter.

The beginning is clearly the same as the French story of "Peau d'Ane," and the end of it is the same as the Norse "Katie Wooden Cloak;" that is the same as Mr. Peter Buchan's "Rashen Coatie" (MSS. collection); and that again has something of "The Sharp Grey Sheep" in Gaelic; and that has to do with half a dozen stories in Grimm; and this is like "Cinderella," and like a Scotch story, quoted in a review of Chambers' Nursery Rhymes in Tait's Edinburgh Magazine.

In fifteen volumes which I explored one fine day, to see if Tait could account for highland stories, I found few popular tales ; and of these taken from the German, which I did find, I have found none in the west, so far as I can remember. Tait's stories are polished, but in some of the original poetry legends can be traced.

"Finette Cendron," in the collection of the Contesse d' Aulnoy, belongs to the same class ; and the story exists in Stra- parola, a book which is now very little known, and which de- serves to be forgotten, but which contains useful information nevertheless. Those who hold that popular tales are derived from books, will look on Straparola's story as the original. It was printed at Venice in Italian in 1567, that is 293 years ago. Those who hold that popular tales are preserved in all countries, and in all languages alike, will hold that the Italian, German, French, Norse, English, and Gaelic, are all versions of the same story, and that it is as old as the common stock from which all these races sprang.

After working for a year, and weighing all the evidence that has come in my way, I have come to agree with those who hold that popular tales are generally pure traditions ; but in order that others may judge, I give the following short outline of the story in Straparola. Favola iv.

Tebaldo, prince of Salerno, promises to his dying wife, that he will only marry another, if he can find one whom a certain ring will fit. After a time the promise becomes known, and it is noised abroad that the prince wishes to marry again. Ladies come ; but the ring is too small for one, too large for another, and fits no one. One day, Doralice, the daughter of Tebaldo, tries on her mother's ring, and shows her father that it fits, and then the same strange unnatural wish to marry his daughter seizes the Prince of Salerno that seizes the fathers in the French and Gaelic stories, and caused the Cenci tragedy ; but the French and Gaelic stories have something about dresses, which the Italian has not.

Doralice goes to her old nurse for advice, and hides herself in a wardrobe which none could open from without but the nurse, who puts in a supply of a certain liquor of which a spoonful, however small, would keep a person alive for a long time. The wardrobe is described, and it is such a one as would be found in an Italian palace. The father, having missed the daughter, cannot abide the sight of the wardrobe, orders it to be carried to the piazza by servants, and it is sold to a Genoese merchant. He carries it over sea in a ship to Britannia, and there sells it to the king " Genese."

Here let me remark that the form of the popular tale was exactly the same as it is now, nearly three hundred years ago. The scene is laid somewhere, a long way off; the names are those which the narrator happens to know, misapplied; the ornaments are those about him; and the incidents, within a certain range, are preserved entire. The story is an old play, with new scenery, and decorations in every country, and with fresh actors in every age.

King Genese of England comes on board the ship, and is taken with the beauty of the wardrobe, buys it, and has it taken to his own chamber. The hidden lady comes out when she is left alone, adorns the chamber, sweeps it and keeps it neat, and at last she is discovered, and the king marries her.

And here the Italian story goes off on quite a different road. It does as popular tales seem to do everywhere else. No sooner has a seeming origin been discovered for one bit, than the whole changes into something else. It is as if some convulsion were to overturn the Vatican, and break the statues once more, and some future antiquary were to try to fit the heads, legs, and arms to the proper bodies. The head of Apollo would not do for the Torso Farnese, but it might seem to fit some strapping Venus, and her arms might go on to some Apollino ; and so, when only a few fragments of popular tales are known, it is perfectly hopeless to try to restore them. If all the fragments of all the statues in the Vatican were gathered together, then there might be some hope of mending them ; but some are strongly suspected not to wear their own heads even now. If all the fragments of all the popular tales in the world were gathered, something might be reconstructed ; but, unless each collector is content to bring his gatherings without alteration, the restorer will have hard work.

But to return to Straparola. The king marries the beautiful lady who keeps his room so tidy in so mysterious a manner, and they have two sons. The wicked Tebaldo, wandering over the world in disguise, arrives in Britain, knows his daughter, obtains access to the palace, murders the two children, and leaves a bloody knife in the Queen's possession. An astrologer is consulted, tells that the knife will be found, and it is found in the Queen's keeping; and she is to die. The astrologer, who knows everything, goes off to the old nurse, who comes at once to England, and tells the king all that has happened. Tebaldo is caught, and torn to pieces by four horses, and his flesh given to rabid dogs.

So end the wicked in many Gaelic tales. " He was torn between horses, burned amongst fires, and his ashes let fly with the wind," is the end of one.

The French story, "Peau d' Ane," is in "les Contes des Fées de Charles Perrault," the wicked father was sent for "Robes," "Couleur du temps," "Couleur du soleil," "Couleur de la Lune," and got them; and then for a donkey's skin, in which the lady disguised herself. But then the French story goes off on another road, for the donkey was precious and magical, and pieces of gold were found in his stall; and he belongs to another class of stories, which have Gaelic relations. (Perrault died 1703).

And so popular tales are woven together in a network which seems to pervade the world, and to be fastened to everything in it. Tradition, books, history, and mythology, hang together; no sooner has the net been freed from one snag, and a mesh gained, than another mesh is discovered; and so, unless many hands combine, the net and the contents will never be brought to shore.

XV.

THE POOR BROTHER AND THE RICH.

From Flora MacIntyre, Islay.

THERE was a poor brother and a rich brother before now. The work that the poor one had, was
to be at drains ; he hired a gillie, and they had
nothing with their mealtime but to take it without
sauce. " Hadn't we better," said the gillie, " steal a cow
of thy brother's lot ?" They went and they did this.

The rich brother was taking a notion that it was
they who stole his cow ; and he did not know in what
way he could contrive to find out if it were they who
stole her. He went and he put his mother-in-law in
a kist, and he came to seek room for the kist in his
brother's house ; he put bread and cheese with the
crone in the kist ; and there was a hole in it, in
order that she might find out everything. The gillie
found out that the crone was in the kist ; he wetted
sacks and threw them on top of the kist; the
water was streaming out of the sacks on the crone,
and she was not hearing a word. He went, in the
night, where the crone was, and he said to her, " Was
she hearing ?" " I am not," said she. " Art thou
eating a few ?" " I am not." " Give me a piece of
the cheese, and I will cut it for thee." He cut the
cheese, and he stuffed it into her throat till she was
choked. The kist was taken home, and the dead crone
in it. They buried the crone, and they laid out but
little on her.

In the night, said the poor man's gillie to his master, "Is it not lamentable that such and such linen should go with the crone to the cell,* while the children are so much in want of shirts?" He went, and he took a spade with him, and he reached the church-yard. He dug the grave, and he took the crone from the coffin; he took off her the tais dress, he threw her on his back, and he came to the house of the rich brother; he went in with her, and he placed her seated at the fireside, and the tongs between her two feet. When the maid servant rose in the morning, she fell in a faint when she saw the crone before her. The rich brother thrashed his wife because of her mother saying, "that she was about to bring him to bare ruin." He went to the house of his poor brother and told that the crone had come home. "Ah ha!" said the gillie, "because thou didst not spend enough on her living, thou wilt spend it on her dead; I saw the like of this before; thou must lay out a good deal on her."

They bought a good lot of things for the funeral, and they left the one half of it in the house of the poor brother and they buried the crone again. "Is it not lamentable," said the poor brother's gillie to his master, "that such a lot of linen should go on the crone, while thou art so much in want of a shirt thyself?" He went to the cell that night again, he raised the crone, he took off her the tais clothes, and he took her with him on his back; he went into the house of the rich brother, as was usual, and he set the crone standing at the end of the dresser, with her claw full of seeds from the dish of sowens, as if she were eating it. When the man of the house saw her back in the morning, he thrashed his wife soundly, because of her

* " KILL," cell a small church; hence applied to church-yards.

mother. He went then to the house of his poor brother, and he told that the crone had come home again. "Aha!" said the gillie, "because thou didst not spend money on her living, thou wilt spend it on her dead; I saw the like of this before." "Go thou, then, and lay out a good deal on her, for I am tired of her," said the man. He bought a good lot for the crone's funeral, and he took the one half to his master's house. They buried the crone. In the night, said the gillie to his master, "Is it not lamentable that such linen should go with the crone to the cell, while I myself am in such want of a shirt." He took himself to the cell, he raised the crone, he took off her the tais dress, he put her on top of him, and he reached the rich brother's house. He did not get in this journey, so he went with her to the stable, and he tied her on top of a year-old colt. When they rose in the morning, they were well pleased when they did not see the crone before them. He was going from home; he went out to the stable, and he took the mare with him; but he never perceived that the crone was on top of the year-old. When he went away on top of the mare, after him went the year-old with the crone clattering on top of him. He turned back when he saw the crone, and he was like to kill his wife this time. He went to his brother's house and he told that the crone had come back again.

"As thou didst not spend money on her living," said the gillie, "thou must spend it on her dead."

"Go and lay out as thou wilt on her," said he to the gillie, "but keep her away."

He went this time and he bought a good lot for the crone's funeral, and he invited every one in the place. They buried the crone again; and the poor brother was as wealthy as the other, by reason of the funerals.

URSGEUL.

BHA bràthair bochd agus bràthair beairteach ann roimhe so. 'Se 'n obair a bh' aig an fhear bhochd a bhi dèanadh dhraintan. Dh' fhasdaidh e gille, 's cha robh mìr aca le am biadh ach 'ga 'ghabhail tur. "Nach fheàrra dhuinn," urs' an gille; "bò de chuid do bhràthar a ghoid." Dh' fholbh iad agus rinn iad so. Bha 'm bràthair beairteach a' gabhail amharuis gur h-iad a ghoid a' bhò, 's cha robh fhios aige dè 'n dòigh a dhèanadh e air faotainn a mach an iad a ghoid i.

Dh' fholbh e 's chuir e 'mhàthair chéile ann an cisde, 's thàinig e dh' iarraidh rum de 'n chisde ann an tigh a bhràthar. Chuir e aran is càise leis a' chaillich anns a' chisde, 's bha toll urra, air alt gu' mòchadh ise do na h-uile gnothuch. Mhothaich an gille gun robh a' chailleach anns a' chisde. Fhliuch e saic, is thilg e air muinn na cisd' iad. Bha 'n t-uisge 'sruthadh as na saic air a' chaillich, 's cha robh i 'cluinntinn smid. Chaidh e anns an oidhche far an robh a' chailleach, 's thuirt e rithe an robh i cluinntinn. "Cha 'n 'eil," urs' ise. "Am bheil thu 'g itheadh a' bheag?" "Cha 'n 'eil." "Thoir dhòmhsa pìosa de 'n chàise 's gearraidh mi dhuit e." Gheàrr e 'n càise, 's dhinn e 'na muineal e gus an do thachd e i. Chaidh a' chisde 'thoirt dachaidh, 's a' chailleach marbh innte. Thìolaic iad a' chailleach, 's cha d' rinn iad ach cosdas beag urra. Anns an oidhche thuirt gille an fhir bhochd r'a mhaighstir, "Nach déisneach a leithid siod de dh' anart a dhol leis a' chaillich do 'n chill, 's cho feumail 's a tha na pàisdean air léintean."

Dh' fholbh e 's thug e leis spàd; ràinig e 'n clagh; chladhaich e 'n uaigh; thug e 'chailleach as a chiste-luidh; thug e dhi an t-ais-aodach; thilg e air a mhuinn i; 's thàinig e gu tigh a' bhràthair bheairteach. Chaidh e stigh leatha, 's chuir e i 'na suidhe aig a' ghealbhan, 's an clotha eadar a da chois. Nur a dh' éiridh an searbhanta anns a' mhaidinn thuit i ann am paiseanadh, nur a chunnaic i 'chailleach roimpe. Ghabh am bràthair bearteach air a' bhean airson a màthar ag ràdh gun robh i brath a sgrios. Chaidh e gu tigh a' bhràthair bhochd, 's dh' innis e gun d' thàinig a' chailleach dhachaidh. "A ha!" urs' an gille, "O nach do chosd thu r'a beò e cosdaidh thu r'a marbh e! Chunnaic mise leithid so roimhid. Feumaidh tu cosdas math a dheanadh urra."

Cheannaich iad cuid mhath de ghnothuichean airson an tòrraidh, 's dh' fhàg iad an darna leith dheth ann an tigh a' bhrathair bhochd. Thìolaic iad a' chailleach a rithisd. "Nach déisneach," ursa gille

'bhrathair bhochd r'a mhaighstir, " a leithid siod do dh' anart a dhol
air a' chaillich, 's cho feumail 's a tha thu féin air léine."

Chaidh e do 'n chill an oidhche sin a rithisd.   Thog e 'chailleach,
's thug e dhith an t-ais-aodach, 's thug e leis air a' mhuinn i. Chaidh e
stigh do thigh a' bhràthair bheairtich mar a b' àbhaist, 's chuir e
'chailleach 'na seasamh aig ceann an dresseir, 's a cròg làn do chàith
as an t-soitheach chabhrach, mar gum biodh i 'ga itheadh.   Nur a
chunnaic fear an tighe air a h-ais i anns a mhaidinn, ghabh e air a'
bhean gu h-iomlan airson a màthar.   Chaidh e 'n sin do thigh a'
bhrathar bhochd, 's dh' innis e gun d' thàinig a' chailleach dhachaidh a rithisd. " A ha !" urs' an gille, " O nach do chosd thu r'a
beò e, cosdaidh thu r'a marbh e." Chunnaic mise 'leithid so roimhid,
" Folbh thusa mata 's dean cosdas math urra chionn tha mise sgìth
dhi."

Cheannaich e cuid mhath thun tòrradh na caillich, 's thug e 'n
darna leith thun tigh a' mhaighstir. Thìolaic iad a' chailleach. Anns
an oidhche urs' an gille r'a mhaighstir, " Nach déisneach a' leithid
siod do dh' anart a dhol leis a' chaillich do 'n chill, 's mi féin cho
feumail air léine."   Thug e 'chill air; thog e chailleach; thug e dhi
an t-ais-aodach; chuir e air a mhuinn i; 's ràinig e tigh a' bhràthar
bheairteach. Cha d' fhuair e stigh air an t-siubhal so.   Chaidh e
leatha do 'n stàbull, 's cheangail e i air muinn bliadhnach eich. Nur
a dh' éiridh iad 's a' mhaidinn bha iad gu toilichte, nur nach fhac iad
a' chailleach romhpa.   Bha esan a' dol o 'n tigh. Chaidh e mach do
'n stàbull, 's thug e leis an capull, ach cha do mhothaich e gun robh
'chailleach air muinn a bhliadhnaich; nur a dh' fholbh esan air
muinn a chapuill, as a dheigh a bha 'm bliadhnach, 's a' chailleach a'
glaigeileis air a mhuinn. Thill e air ais nur a chunnaic e chailleach,
's theab e bhean a mharbhadh air an uair so.   Chaidh e do thigh a'
bhràthar, 's dh' innis e gun d' thainig a' chailleach dhachaidh a rithisd.   " O nach do chosd thu r'a beò e," ars' an gille, " feumaidh
tu 'chosd r'a marbh."   " Theirig agus dean do rogha cosdus rithe,"
ars' esan ris a' ghille, " ach cum air folbh i." Chaidh e air an t-
siubhail so agus cheannaich cuid mhath airson tòrradh na caillich
's chuir e gach duine bha 'san àite. Thìolaic iad a' chailleach a rithisd,
's bha 'm bràthair bochd cho beairteach ris an fhear eile air tàilleabh
nan tòrradh.

One James MacQueen, who lived at Tirneagan, near Kilmeny, but who is not living now, gave this to one Flora Mac-
Intyre, at Kilmeny, who told it to Hector MacLean.—May 1859.

This story is not like any other that I know. It is one of a kind which is common, in which mortals alone play a part. Some are humorous, and some free. One such has been versified by Allan Ramsay, page 520, vol. 2 ; and is nearly the same as Tom Totherhouse, the Norse tale.

The expensive funeral was once truly highland ; and the invitation to all the world characteristic. It used to be told of one such funeral party, that they dropped the coffin out of a cart on the way over a strand, and never found it out till they got to the churchyard. They returned and finished the funeral, but went home afterwards very drunk; the sons shouting " Horo ! it's the carlin's wedding." The funeral dinner was within my memory, and still may be, a solemn feast. Such toasts as " Comfort to the distressed," and " The memory of the deceased," were drank in solemn silence ; and the whole matter was conducted with gravity and decorum, but with profuse and necessary hospitality, for the funeral guests had often to travel great distances, and the coffin had to be carried many miles. No Highlander, if his friends can help it, is buried anywhere but at home ; coffins may be seen on board the steamers, conveying to the outer islands the bodies of those who have died on the main land. It is a poetic wish to be buried amongst friends, and one that is in full force in the Highlands to this day. The curse of Scotland may occasionally intrude even on such solemn occasions ; but a funeral is almost always decorously conducted. In some places, as I am told, a piper may still be seen at the head of the funeral procession, playing a dirge. There is no want of reverence, but death is treated as an ordinary event. I have seen a man's tombstone, with a blank for the date, standing at the end of his house, while he was quite well.

It was lately said of a man who went home to die, " He took his own body home ;" and so he did.

There is something mythological about the old woman who will not rest, because enough has not been laid out on her funeral. It may be some remnant of a notion of purgatory ; but I suspect it is something heathen.

Romans had to pay their passage, perhaps Celts had to do so likewise.

THE KING OF LOCHLIN'S THREE DAUGHTERS.

From Neill Gillies, fisherman, near Inverary.

THERE was a king over Lochlin, once upon a time, who had a leash of daughters ; they went out (on) a day to take a walk ; and there came three giants, and they took with them the daughters of the king, and there was no knowing where they had gone. Then the king sent word for the sheanachy, and he asked him if he knew where his lot of daughters had gone. The sheanachy said to the king that three giants had taken them with them, and they were in the earth down below by them, and there was no way to get them but by making a ship that would sail on sea and land ; and so it was that the king set out an order, any one who would build a ship that would sail on sea and on land, that he should get the king's big daughter to marry. There was a widow there who had a leash of sons ; and the eldest said to his mother on a day that was there, "Cook for me a bannock, and roast a cock ; I am going away to cut wood, and to build a ship that will go to seek the daughters of the king." His mother said to him, "Which is better with thee, the big bannock with my cursing, or a little bannock with my blessing ?" "Give me a big bannock, it will be small enough before I build a ship." He got a bannock and he went away. He arrived where there was a great wood and a river, and there he sat at the side of the river to take the bannock. A great Uruisg came out of the river, and she asked a part of the bannock. He said that he would not give her a morsel, that it was little enough for himself. He began cutting the wood, and every tree he cut would be on foot again ; and so he was till the night came.

When the night came, he went home mournful, tearful, blind sorrowful. His mother asked, "How went it with thee to-day, son ?" He said "That it went but black ill ; every tree I would cut would be on foot again." A day or two after this the middle brother said that he himself would go ; and he asked his mother to cook him a cake and roast him a cock ; and in the very way as happened to his eldest brother, so it happened to him. The mother said the very same thing to the young one ; and *he* took the little bannock. The Uruisg came, and she asked a part of the cake and the cock. He said to her, "That she should get that." When the Uruisg had eaten her own share of the cake and of the cock, she said to him "That she knew what had brought him there as well as he himself, but he was to go home ; but to be sure to meet her there at the end of a day and year ; and that the ship would be ready at the end.

It was thus it happened : At the end of a day and a year the widow's young son went, and he found that the Uruisg had the ship floating on the river, fully equipped. He went away then with the ship, and a leash of gentlemen, as great as were in the kingdom, that were to marry the daughters of the king. They were but a short time sailing when they saw a man drinking a river that was there. He asked him, "What art thou doing there?" "I am drinking up this river." "Thou hadst better come with me, and I will give thee meat and wages, and better work than that." "I will do that," said he. They had not gone far forward, when they saw a man eating a stot in a park. "What art thou doing there?" said he. "I am here going to eat all the stots in this park." "Thou hadst better go with me, and thou wilt get work, and wages better than raw flesh." "I will do that," said he. They went but a short distance when they saw another man with his ear to the earth. "What art thou doing there?" said he. "I am here hearing the grass coming through earth." "Go with me, and thou wilt get meat, and better wages than to be there with thy ear to the earth." They were thus sailing back and forwards, when the man who was listening said, "That this was the place in which were the king's daughters and the giants." The widow's son, and the three that had fallen in with them, were let down in a creel in a great hole that was there. They reached the house of the big giant. "Ha! ha!" said he, the giant, "I know well what thou art seeking here. Thou art seeking the king's daughter, but thou wilt not get that, unless thou hast a man that will drink as much water as I." He set the man who was drinking the river to hold drinking against the giant; and before he was half satisfied the giant burst. Then they went where the second giant was. "Ho, hoth! ha, hath!" said the giant, "I know well what sent thee here; thou art seeking the king's daughter; but thou shalt not get her, if thou hast not a man who will eat as much flesh as I." He set the man who was eating the stot to hold the eating of flesh against the giant; but before he was half satisfied the giant burst.

Then he went where the third giant was. "Haio!" said the giant, "I know what set thee here; but thou wilt not get the king's daughter, by any means, unless thou stayest a day and a year by me a sgalag" (slave, servant). "I will do that," said he; and he sent up in the basket, first the three men, and then the king's daughters. The three great men were waiting at the mouth of the hole till they should come up, and they went with them where the king was; and they told the king that they themselves had done all the daring deeds that there were.

When the end of a day and year had come, he said to the giant, "That he was going." The giant said, "That he had an eagle that would set him up to the top of the hole." The giant set the eagle away with him, and five stots and ten for a meal for her; but the eagle went not half way up through the hole when she had eaten the stots, and she returned back again.

Then the giant said to him, "Thou must remain by me another day and year, and then I will send thee away." When the end of this year came he sent the eagle away with him, and ten stots and twenty. They went this time well further on than they went before, but she ate the stots and she turned back. "Thou must," said the giant, "stay by me another year, and then I will send thee away." The end of this year came, and the giant sent them away, and three score of stots for the eagle's meat; and when they were at the mouth of the hole the stots were expended, and she was going to turn back; but he took a steak out of his own thigh, and he gave this to the eagle, and with one spring she was on the surface of the earth.

At the time of parting the eagle gave him a whistle, and she said to him, "Any hard lot that comes on thee, whistle and I will be at thy side." He did not allow his foot to stop, or empty a puddle out of his shoe, till he reached the king's big town. He went where there was a smith who was in the town, and he asked the smith if he was in want of a gillie to blow the bellows. The smith said that he was. He was but a short time by the smith, when the king's big daughter sent word for the smith. "I am hearing," said she, " that thou art the best smith in the town ; but if thou dost not make for me a golden crown, like the golden crown that I had when I was by the giant, the head shall be taken off thee." The smith came home sorrowfully, lamentably ; and his wife asked him his news from the king's house. "There is but poor news," said the smith ; "the king's daughter is asking that a golden crown shall be made for her, like the crown that she had when she was under the earth by the giant ; but what do I know what likeness was on the crown that the giant had." The bellows-blowing gillie said, " Let not that set thee thinking ; get thou for me enough of gold, and I will not be long making the crown." The smith got of gold as he asked, with the king's order. The gillie went in to the smithy, and he shut the door ; and he began to splinter the gold asunder, and to throw it out of the window. Each one that came the way was gathering the gold, that the bellows lad was hurling out. Here, then, he blew the whistle, and in the twinkling of an eye the eagle came. "Go," said he to the eagle, "and bring here the golden crown that is above the big giant's door." The eagle went, and she was not long on the way, and the crown (was) with her. He gave the crown to the smith. The smith went so merrily, cheerily with the crown where the king's daughter was. "Well then," said she, "if I did not know that it could not be done, I would not believe that this is

not the crown I had when I was with the big giant."
The king's middle daughter said to the smith, "Thou
wilt loose the head if thou dost not make for me a
silver crown, like the one I had when I was by the
giant." The smith took himself home in misery ; but
his wife went to meet him, expecting great news and
flattery ; but so it was, that the gillie said that he
would make a silver crown if he could get enough of
silver. The smith got plenty of silver with the king's
order. The gillie went, and he did as he did before. He
whistled ; the eagle came. "Go," said he, "and bring
hither here to me, the silver crown that the king's
middle daughter had when she was by the giant."

The eagle went, and she was not long on the
journey with the silver crown. The smith went
merrily, cheerily, with the silver crown to the king's
daughter. "Well, then," said she, "it is marvellously like the crown I had when I was by the giant."
The king's young daughter said to the smith that
he should make a copper crown for her, like the copper crown she had when she was by the giant. The
smith now was taking courage, and he went home
much more pleasantly this turn. The gillie began to
splinter the copper, and to throw it out of each door
and window ; and now they were from each end of
the town gathering the copper, as they were gathering
the silver and gold. He blew the whistle, and the
eagle was at his side. "Go back," said he, "and bring
here hither to me the copper crown that the king's
young daughter had when she was by the giant." The
eagle went, and she was not long going and coming.
He gave the crown to the smith. The smith went
merrily, cheerily, and he gave it to the king's young
daughter. "Well, then !" said she, "I would not
believe that this was not the very crown that I had

R

when I was by the giant underground, if there were a way of getting it." Here the king said to the smith, that he must tell him where he had learned crown making, "for I did not know that the like of thee was in the kingdom." "Well, then," said the smith, "with your leave, oh king, it was not I who made the crowns, but the gillie I have blowing the bellows." "I must see thy gillie," said the king, "till he makes a crown for myself."

The king ordered four horses in a coach, and that they should go to seek the smith's gillie; and when the coach came to the smithy, the smith's gillie was smutty and dirty, blowing the bellows. The horse gillies came, and they asked for the man who was going to look on the king. The smith said, "That was he yonder, blowing the bellows." "Oov! oov!" said they; and they (set) to catch him, and throw him head foremost into the coach, as if they had a dog.

They went not far on their journey when he blew the whistle. The eagle was at his side. "If ever thou didst good for me, take me out of this, and fill it full of stones," said he. The eagle did this. The king was out waiting on the coach; and when the king opened the door of the coach, he was like to be dead with the stones bouncing on top of him. There was catching of the horse gillies, and hanging them for giving such an affront to the king.

Here the king sent other gillies with a coach; and when they reached the smithy, "Oov! oov!" said they. "Is this the black thing the king sent us to seek? They caught him, and they cast him into the coach as if they had a turf peat. But they went not far on their way when he blew the whistle, and the eagle was at his side; and he said to her, "Take me out of this, and fill it with every dirt thou canst get." When the coach reached the king's palace, the king went to open the door. Each dirt and rubbish fell about the king's head. Then the king was in a great rage, and he ordered the horse gillies to be hanged immediately. Here the king sent his own confidential servant away; and when he reached the smithy, he caught the black bellows-blowing gillie by the hand. "The king," said he, "sent me to seek thee." "Thou hadst better clean a little of the coal off thy face." The gillie did this; he cleaned himself well, and right well; and the king's servant caught him by the hand, and he put him into the coach. They were but a short time going, when he blew the whistle. The eagle came; and he asked her to bring the gold and silver dress that was by the big giant here without delay, and the eagle was not long going and coming with the dress. He arrayed himself with the giant's dress. And when they came to the king's palace, the king came, and he opened the door of the coach, and there was the very finest man the king ever saw. The king took him in, and he told the king how it happened to him from first to last. The three great men who were going to marry the king's daughters were hanged, and the king's big daughter was given him to marry; and they made them a wedding the length of twenty nights and twenty days; and I left them dancing, and I know not but that they are cutting capers on the floor till the day of to-day.

———

SGEULACHD AIR NIGHEANAN RIGH LOCHLAINN.

BHA rìgh air Lochlainn aon uair aig an robh triuir nigheanan. Chaidh iad a mach latha ghabhail sràid, agus thàinig trì famhairean, 's thug iad leo nigheanan an rìgh, 's cha robh fios c'àite an deach iad.

Chuir an rìgh fios an sin air an t-seanachaidh aige, 's dh' fheòraich e dheth, "An robh fios aige c'àite an deach a chuid nigheanan?" Thuirt an seanachaidh ris an rìgh gu 'n d-thug tri famhairean leo iad, agus gun robh iad anns an talamh gu h-ìosal aca, 's nach robh dòigh air am faotuinn, ach le long a dhèanamh a sheòladh air muir 's air tìr." Agus 'se bha'nn gun do chuir an rìgh òrdugh a mach, "Co air bith a thogadh long a sheòladh air muir 's air tìr, gu' faigheadh e nighean mhòr an rìgh ri phòsadh." Bha bantrach an sin aig an robh triù'r mhac, agus thubhairt am fear 'bu shine ri 'mhàthair latha bha 'n sin, "Bruich dhòmhsa bonnach 's ròist coileach; tha mi falbh a ghearradh coille 's a thogail long, a théid a dh' iarraidh nigheanan an rìgh." Thuirt a mhàthair ris, "Cò'ca s' feàrr leat am bonnach mòr le m' mhallachd na 'm bonnach beag le m' bheannachd." "Thoir dhòmhsa 'm bonnach mòr; bithidh e beag na leòir mu 'n tog mi long." Fhuair e 'm bonnach 's dh' fhalbh e. Ràinig e far an robh coille mhòr agus abhuinn. Shuidh e an sin ri taobh na h-abhunn a ghabhail a' bhonnaich. Thàinig ùruisg mhòr a mach as an abhuinn, agus dh'iarr i pàirt do 'n bhonnach. Thubhairt esan nach d' thugadh e mìr dhi, gun robh e beag na leòir dha féin. Thòisich e air gearradh na coille, 's na h-uile craobh a ghearradh e, bhiodh i air a bonn a rithist; 's bha e mur sin gus an d' thàinig an oidhche. Nuair a thàinig an oidhche, chaidh e dhachaidh dubhach, deurach, dalla-bhrònach. D' fhoighnichd a mhàthair dheth. "De mar a chaidh dhuit an diugh, a mhic." Thubhairt esan, nach deach ach gu dubh dona "Na h-uile craobh a ghearrainn, bhiodh i air a bonn a rithist." Latha na dhà an déigh so, thubhairt am bràthair meadhonach, "gu' falbhadh e fhéin, 's dh' iarr e air a mhàthair, bonnach a bhruich s' coileach a ròstadh; agus air a' cheart dòigh mar thachair d'a bhràthair a bu shine, thachair dhàsan. Thubhairt a mhàthair a' cheart ni ris an fhear òg, agus ghabh e 'm bonnach beag. Thàinig an ùruisg, s' dh'iarr i pàirt do 'n bhonnach s' do 'n choileach. Thubhairt e rithe, "Gu 'm faigheadh i sin." Nuair a dh'ith an ùruisg a cuid fhéin do 'n bhonnach 's do 'n choileach, thubhairt i ris, "Gun robh fios aice-se dé 'thug an sud e co maith ris fhéin, ach esan a dhol dachaidh, ach a bhi cinnteach ise a choinneachainn an sud an ceann latha 's bliadhna, agus gu 'm bitheadh an long deas air a cheann." 'Sann mar so a thachair. An ceann latha 's bliadhna dh' fhalbh mac òg na bantraich, agus fhuair e 'n long air snàmh air an abhuinn fuidh làn uidheam aig an ùruisg. Dh' fhalbh e an sin leis an luing, agus triùir dhaoine uaisle cho mòr 'sa bha 'san rìoghachd, a bha gu nigheanan an rìgh a phòsadh. Cha robh iad ach goirid a seòladh an uair a chunnaic iad fear ag òl suas abhuinn a bha 'sin

Dh' fheòraich iad dheth, " De 'tha thu deànamh an sin? " " Tha ag òl suas na h-aibhne so." " 'S feàrr dhuit falbh leam fhéin, 's bheir mi dhuit biadh, 's tuarasdal, 's obair a's feàrr na sin." " Ni mi sin," ars' esan. Cha deachaidh iad fad air an aghaidh gus am fac iad fear eile ag itheadh dhamh aun am pàirc. " De 'tha thu deanamh an sin?" Thubhairt esan, " Tha mi 'n so a' dol a dh' itheadh na tha dhaimh anns a' phàirc so." " 'S feàrr dhuit falbh leam fhéin, 's gheibh thu obair 's tuarasdal a's feàrr na feòil àmh." " Ni mi sin," thubhairt esan. Cha deach iad ach goirid dar * a chunnaic iad fear eile 'sa' chluas ris an talamh. " De tha thu deànamh an sin?" Thubhairt esan, " Tha mi an so a' cluintinn an fheòir a' tighinn troi 'n talamh." " Falbh leam fhéin 's gheibh thu biadh 's tuarasdal a's feàrr na bhi 'n sin, 's do chluas ris an talamh." Bha iad mur so a' seòladh air an ais s' air an aghaidh nuair a thubhairt am fear a bha' g eisteachd, " Gu 'm be sud an t-àite anns an robh nigheanan an rìgh agus na famhairean." Chaidh mac na bantraich agus an triùir a thachair orra a leigeil sìos ann an cliabh, ann an toll mòr a bha 'n sin. Ràinig iad tigh an fhamhair mhòir. " Ha! ha!" thuirt esan, " tha fios agam gu maith de 'tha thu 'g iarraidh an so; tha thu 'g iarraidh nighean an rìgh, ach cha 'n fhaigh thu sin mar 'eil fear agad a dh' òlas uiread uisge riumsa." Chuir esan am fear a bha ag òl na h-aibhne a chumail òl ris an fhamhair, 's mun robh esan leith bhuidheach, sgàin am famhair. Chaidh iad an sin far an robh an darna famhair. " Ho! Hoth! Ha! Hath!" thubbairt am famhair, " tha fios agamsa gu maith, de chuir an so thu; tha thu 'g iarraidh nighean an rìgh, ach cha 'n fhaigh thu i mar 'eil fear agad a dh' itheas uiread feòla riumsa." Chuir esan am fear a bha 'g' itheadh nan damh a chumail itheadh feòla ris an fhamhair so: ach mun robh esan leith bhuidheach; sgàin am famhair. Chaidh iad an sin far an robh an treas famhair. " Haio!" ars' am famhair, " tha fios agamsa de chuir an so thu, ach cha 'n fhaigh thu nighean an rìgh, idir mar fan thu agamsa latha, 's bliadhna ann a'd' sgalaig." " Ni mi sin," thubbairt esan. Chuir e suas ann an cliabh an toiseach na tri daoine, agus an sin nigheanan an righ. Bha 'n triùir dhaoine mòra aig beul an tuill a' feitheamh gus an d' thigeadh iad a nìos, agus dh' fhalbh iad leo far an robh an rìgh, 's dh' innis iad do 'n rìgh gu 'm b' iad féin a rinn gach uile thapachd a bha ann.

" Nuair a thàinig ceann latha 's bliadhna," thubbairt esan ris am famhair, " guu robh e 'falbh." Thubhairt am famhair, " Gun robh fiolaire aige-san a chuireadh suas e gu mullach an tuill." Chuir am

famhair an iolaire air falbh leis, agus cùig daimh dheug air son lòn
dhi ; ach cha deach na iolaire leith suas troi 'n toll, nuair a dh'ith i na
daimh, agus thill i air a h-ais a rithist. Thubhairt am famhair ris an
sin, "Feumaidh tu fantainn agamsa latha 's bliadhna eile, agus
cuiridh mi 'n sin air falbh thu." Nuair a thàinig ceann na bliadhna
so, chuir e air falbh an iolaire leis, agus deich daimh fhichead. Chaidh
iad air an am so gu maith ni b' fhaide air an aghaidh, na chaidh iad
roimh, ach dh'ith i na daimh, 's thill i air a h-ais. "Feuma tu,"
ars' am famhair, "fantainn agamsa bliadhna eile, agus an sin cuiridh
mi air falbh thu." Thàinig ceann na bliadhna so, agus chuir am
famhair air folbh iad, agus tri-fichead damh air son biadh do 'n iolaire.
An uair a bha iad aig beul àrd an tuill, theirig na daimh, 's bha i 'dol
a thilleadh ; ach thug esan staoig as a leis fhéin, 's thug e so do 'n
iolaire, agus le aon leum bha i air uachdar talamh. An am deal-
achaidh thug an iolaire dha feadag agus thubhairt i ris, "cruaidh-
chàs sam bith a thig ort, leig fead agus bithidh mise ri d' thaobh."
  Cha do leig esan stad d'a chois na lodan as a bhròig gus an d'
ràinig e baile mòr an rìgh. Chaidh e far an robh gobhainn a bha
'sa' bhaile, 's dh' fheòraich e do 'n ghobha, "An robh gille a dhìth
air, airson seideadh a' bhuilg ?" Thubhairt an gobha "Gu'n robh."
Cha robh e ach goirid aig a' ghobha, nuair a chuir nighean mhòr an
rìgh fios air a' ghobha. "Tha mi 'cluintinn," ars' ise, "gur tusa gobhainn a's feàrr 'sa' bhaile ; ach mur dèan thu dhòmhsa crùn òir coltach ris a' chrùn òir a bh' agam nuair a bha mi aig an fhamhair, théid
an ceann a thoirt dhìot." Thàinig an gobha dhachaidh gu dubhach
brònach, 's dh' fhoighneachd a bhean deth, dé a naigheachd a tigh
an rìgh ? "Cha 'n 'eil ach naigheachd bochd," thuirt an gobha
"Tha 'nighean ag iarraidh crùn òir a dhèanamh dhi coltach ris a
chrùn a bha aice an uair a bha i fo 'n talamh aig an fhamhair ;
ach gu de 'fios a tha agamsa de 'n coslas a bha air a' chrùn
a bha aig an fhamhair." Thubhairt gille séididh a' bhuilg,
"Na cuireadh sin smaontinn ort. Faigh thusa dhòmhsa nis gu leòir
do dh' òr, 's cha bhi mise fada a' dèanamh a chrùin." Fhuair an gobha
na dh' iarr e dh' òr le òrdugh an rìgh. Chaidh an gille stigh do 'n
cheàrdaich, 's dhùin e 'n 'dorus, agus thòisich e air spealgadh an òir
as a' chéile, 'sa thilgeadh a mach air an uinneig. Bha gach neach a
thigeadh an rathad a' tional an òir a bha gille a' bhuilg, a' smùideadh a
mach. Shéid e 'n so an fheadag, agus ann am prioba na sùil, thàinig
an iolaire. "Falbh," thubhairt esan ris an iolaire, "agus thoir an so an
crùn òir a tha fos ceann an doruis aig an fhamhair mhòr." Dh' fhalbh
an iolaire, 's cha b' fhada bha i air a turus, 'san crùn aice. Thug e 'n
crùn do 'n ghobhainn. Dh' fhalbh an gobhainn gu subhach, sunnd-

ach leis a' chrùn far an robh nighean an rìgh. "Mata," thubhairt
ise, "mur b'e gum bheil fios agam nach gabhadh e deànamh, cha
chreidinn nach e so an crùn a bha agam an uair a bha mi leis an
fhamhair mhòr." Thubhairt nighean mheadhonach an rìgh ris a'
ghobhainn, "Caillidh tu 'n ceann mar dèan thu crùn airgid dhòmhsa
coltach ris an fhear a bh' agam an uair a bha mi aig an fhamhair."
Thug an gobha an tigh air fo sprochd, ach chaidh a bhean 'na
choinneamh an dùil ri naigheachd mhòr 's brosguil; ach 'se bh' ann
gun d' thubhairt an gille, "gun deànadh esan crùn airgid, na 'm
faighadh e na leòir do dh' airgiod." Fhuair an gobha ni's leòir do
dh' airgiod le òrdugh an rìgh. Chaidh an gille 's rinn e mar a rinn
e roimhe. Leig e fead; thainig an iolaire. "Falbh," thubhairt
esan, "agus thoir thugam-sa an so an crùn airgid a bha aig nighean
mheadhonach an rìgh an uair a bha i aig an fhamhair." D' fhalbh
an iolaire, 's cha b' fhada bha i air a turus leis a' chrùn airgid.
Dh' fhalbh an gobhainn gu subhach, sunndach leis a' chrùn airgid
gu nighean an rìgh. "Mata," thubhairt ise, "tha e anabarrach
coltach ris a' chrùn a bh' agam dar a bha mi aig an fhamhair."
Thubhairt nighean òg an rìgh ris a' ghobha, "E a dheànamh crùn
copair dh' ise, coltach ris a chrùn chopair a bha aice, nuair a bha i
aig an fhamhair." Bha 'n gobha an so a' gabhail misnich, 's chaidh
e dhachaidh mòran ni bu toilichte air an trò so. Thòisich an gille
air spealgadh a' chopair, 's air a thilgeadh a mach air gach dorus 's
uinneag. Bha iad an so as gach ceann do 'n bhaile a' tionail a' chopair mar a bha iad a' tionail an òir 's an airgid.
Shéid e 'n fheadag, 's bha 'n iolaire ri 'thaobh. "Rach air
t' ais," thubhairt esan, "agus thoir an so thugamsa an crùn copair a bha aig nighean òg an rìgh an uair a bha i aig an fhamhair."
Dh' fhalbh an iolaire, 's cha robh i fada 'dol 'sa' tighinn. Thug e 'n
crùn do 'n ghobhainn; dh' fhalbh an gobhainn gu subhach, sunndach, 's thug e do nighean òg an rìgh e. "Mata," thubhairt ise, "cha
chreidinn nach b'e so an dearbh chrùn a bha agam an uair a bha mi
aig an fhamhair fo 'n talamh, na'm biodh dòigh air fhaotainn."
Thubhairt an rìgh an so ris a' ghobhainn, "Gu' feumadh e innseadh
dhàsan, càite an d' ionnsaich e deànamh nan crùn, rir cha robh fios
agam gun robh do leithid 'san rìoghachd." "Mata," thubhairt an
gobha, "le 'r cead, a rìgh, cha mhise a rinn na crùin, ach an gille
'tha agam a' séideadh a' bhuilg." "Feumaidh mi do ghill' fhaicinn,"
thubhairt an rìgh, "gus an dèan e crùn dhomh fhéin." Dh' òrdaich
an rìgh ceithir eich ann an (coacha), 's iad a dhol a dh' iarraidh gille
a' ghobha. An uair a thàinig an (coacha) a dh' ionnsaidh na ceàrdach,
bha gille a' ghobha gu dubh, salach a' séideadh a' bhuilg. Thàinig na

gillean each, 's dh' fheòraich iad air son an duine a bha 'dol a shealltainn an rìgh. Thubhairt an gobha gu'm b'e sud e thall a' sèid-
eadh a' bhuilg. " Ubh ! Ubh !" thuirt iadsan, 's iad a beireachd air,
's 'ga thilgeadh an comhair a chinn a stigh don (choacha), mar gum
bitheadh cù aca. Cha deach' iad fada air an turus dar a shèid esan
an fheadag. Bha 'n iolaire ri 'thaobh. " Ma rinn thu feum riamh
dhomh, thoir mise a mach as so, agus lìon e làn chlach," thubhairt
esan. Rinn an iolaire so. Bha 'n rìgh a mach a feitheadh a chòidse,
agus an uair a dh' fhosgail an rìgh dorus a' chòidse, theab e bhi
marbh leis na clachan a' dòrtadh air a mhuin. Chaidh beireachd air
na gillean each, 'san crochadh airson a leithid do thàmailt a thabhairt
do 'n rìgh. Chuir an rìgh an so air falbh gillean le còidse, agus
an uair a ràinig iad a' cheàrdach, " Ubh ! Ubh !" thuirt iadsan, " n'e
so an rud dubh a chuir an rìgh sinn a dh' iarraidh." Rug iad air, 's
thilg iad a stigh do 'n chòids' e, mar gum bitheadh fòid mòine aca.
Ach cha deach iad fada air an slighe, nuair a shèid esan an fheadag,
's bha 'n iolaire ri 'thaobh, 's thubhairt e rithe, " Thoir mise as
a' so, agus lìon e do ghach salachar a gheibh thu." Nuair a ràinig
an còidse pàileis an rìgh, chaidh an rìgh 'dh' fhosgladh an doruis.
Thuit gach salachar 's gach baggaist mu cheann an rìgh. Bha fearg
ro mhòr air an rìgh, 's dh' òrdaich e na gillean each a bhi air an
crochadh air ball. Chuir an rìgh a' ghille cinnteach fhèin air falbh,
agus an uair a ràinig e a' cheàrdach, rug e air làimh air gille dubh
sèididh a' bhuilg. " Chuir an rìgh," thuirt esan, " mise gu d'
iarraidh s 'feàrr dhuit beagan do 'n ghual a ghlanadh dheth t' aodann."
Rinn an gille so, ghlan e fèin gu maith 's gu ro mhaith, 's rug gille
an rìgh air làimh air, 's chuir e stigh do 'n chòids' e. Cha robh iad
ach goirid air falbh, dar a shèid e 'n fheadag. Thàinig an iolaire, 's
dh' iarr esan oirre an deise òir 's airgid a bha aig an fhamhair mhòr a
thoirt an sud gun dàil ; 's cha robh an iolaire fada 'dol 'sa' tighinn
leis an deise. Sgeadaich esan e fèin le deise an fhamhair, 's an uair
a thàinig iad gu pàileas an rìgh, thàinig an rìgh, 's dh' fhosgail e dorus
a chòidse 's bha 'n sin an aon duine bu bhrèagha a chunnaic an rìgh
riamh. Thug an rìgh stigh e, 's dh' innis e do 'n rìgh mar a dh'
èirich dha fo thùs gu deireadh. Chaidh an triùir dhaoine mòra bha
'dol a phòsadh nigheanan an rìgh a chrochadh, 's nighean mhòr an
rìgh thabhairt dhàsan ri phòsadh ; 's rinn iad banais dhoibh fad
fichead oidhche 's fichead latha, 's dh' fhàg mise a' dannsa iad, 's cha
'n'eil fios agamsa nach 'eil iad a' cuir nan car air an urlar gus an
latha 'n diugh.

This story was written, May 1859, by Hector Urquhart, game-keeper, from the dictation of Neill Gillies, a fisherman and builder of stone dykes, who lives near Inverary.   He is now about fifty-five, and says he learned the story from his father, who used to tell it when he was about sixteen or seventeen.

It has something of many other Gaelic tales.   In particular, one called " Bolgum More," in which there are more gifted men. It has some resemblance to Fortunio ; and the part which goes on under ground resembles part of many other popular tales.   The Three Giants, with their gold, silver, and copper crowns, are like the Gnomes of the Mine.   Similar Giants, ruling over metals, and living in castles made of gold, silver, and copper, are mentioned in a story from South Uist, which resembles the Sea Maiden.

As a whole, No. 16 is unlike anything I know, but nearly every incident has a parallel woven in with something else, and it most resembles Grimm's Golden Goose.

The Enchanted Ship, which could sail on sea and land, belongs to Norse tales and to Norse mythology.   The gods had such a ship.

The Eagle is peculiarly eastern : he is but a genius in another shape ; the underground treasures are also eastern ; and it is worth remark, that two of the daughters are not provided for at all.   The three gentlemen were hanged, and the smith's servant married the eldest princess with the golden crown, so the two youngest remain spinsters.   It is suggested by the author of Norse Tales, that similar incidents may show the change from Eastern to Western manners.   There would be no hitch, if it were lawful to marry the three ladies in this story ; and in the Norse story of Shortshanks, it is suggested that the second brother is added, to make all things proper.   In No. 22, a man marries a round dozen.

The clothes of these giants fit the lad, so they were but under-ground men.

There is the usual moral.   The least becomes the greatest ; but there is a dash of character in the pride of the smith's lad, who will not come till he is taken by the hand by the king's own confidential servant.   And this is characteristic of the race.   A Celt can be led anywhere, but he will not be driven.   The king, who opens his own coach door, is somewhat like a farmer. The coach and four is but the grandest of the vehicles seen in the neighbour-hood—one of which was compared by a friend of mine, to "a packing box upon wheels, lined with an old blanket." In the mouth of a city narrator, it would have been a lord mayor's coach, and it probably was a palanquin at some time.

This story may be compared with "The Big Bird Dan," Norse Tales, No. 55. Gifted men are to be found in "The Master Maid," No. 11. Such men are also in German, "How six tra-velled through the World;" and, according to the notes in the third volume of Grimm, the story is widely spread, and common to Italian.

XVII.

MAOL A CHLIOBAIN.

From Ann MacGilvray, Islay.

THERE was a widow ere now, and she had three daughters ; and they said to her that they would go to seek their fortune. She baked three bannocks. She said to the big one, "Whether dost thou like best the half and my blessing, or the big half and my curse ?" "I like best," said she, "the big half and thy curse." She said to the middle one, "Whether dost thou like best the big half and my curse, or the little half and my blessing ?" "I like best," said she, "the big half and thy curse." She said to the little one, "Whether dost thou like best the big half and my curse, or the little half and my blessing ?" "I like best the half and thy blessing." This pleased her mother, and she gave her the two other halves also. They went away, but the two eldest did not want the youngest to be with them, and they tied her to a rock of stone. They went on ; but her mother's blessing came and freed her. And when they looked behind them, whom did they see but her with the rock on top of her. They let her alone a turn of a while, till they reached a peat stack, and they tied her to the peat stack. They went on a bit (but her mother's blessing came and freed her), and they looked behind them, and whom did they see but her coming, and the peat stack on top of her. They let her alone a turn of a while, till they reached a tree, and they tied her to the tree. They went on a bit (but her mother's blessing came and freed her), and when they looked behind them, whom did they see but her, and the tree on top of her.

They saw it was no good to be at her; they loosed her, and let her (come) with them. They were going till night came on them. They saw a light a long way from them; and though a long way from them, it was not long that they were in reaching it. They went in. What was this but a giant's house! They asked to stop the night. They got that, and they were put to bed with the three daughters of the giant. (The giant came home, and he said, " The smell of the foreign girls is within.") There were twists of amber knobs about the necks of the giant's daughters, and strings of horse hair about their necks. They all slept, but Maol a Chliobain did not sleep. Through the night a thirst came on the giant. He called to his bald, rough-skinned gillie to bring him water. The bald, rough-skinned gillie said that there was not a drop within. " Kill," said he, " one of the strange girls, and bring to me her blood." " How will I know them ? " said the bald, rough-skinned gillie. " There are twists of knobs of amber about the necks of my daughters, and twists of horse hair about the necks of the rest."

Maol a Chliobain heard the giant, and as quick as she could she put the strings of horse hair that were about her own neck and about the necks of her sisters about the necks of the giant's daughters; and the knobs that were about the necks of the giant's daughters about her own neck and about the necks of her sisters;

and she laid down *so* quietly. The bald, rough-skinned gillie came, and he killed one of the daughters of the giant, and he took the blood to him. He asked for MORE to be brought him. He killed the next. He asked for MORE; and he killed the third one.

Maol a Chliobain awoke her sisters, and she took them with her on top of her, and she took to going. (She took with her a golden cloth that was on the bed, and it called out.)

The giant perceived her, and he followed her. The sparks of fire that she was putting out of the stones with her heels, they were striking the giant on the chin; and the sparks of fire that the giant was bringing out of the stones with the points of his feet, they were striking Maol a Chliobain in the back of the head. It is this was their going till they reached a river. (She plucked a hair out of her head and made a bridge of it, and she run over the river, and the giant could not follow her.) Maol a Chliobain leaped the river, but the river the giant could not leap.

"Thou art over there, Maol a Chliobain." "I am, though it is hard for thee." "Thou killedst my three bald brown daughters." "I killed them, though it is hard for thee." "And when wilt thou come again?" "I will come when my business brings me."

They went on forward till they reached the house of a farmer. The farmer had three sons. They told how it happened to them. Said the farmer to Maol a Chliobain, "I will give my eldest son to thy eldest sister, and get for me the fine comb of gold, and the coarse comb of silver that the giant has." "It will cost thee no more," said Maol a Chliobain.

She went away; she reached the house of the giant; she got in unknown; she took with her the combs, and out she went. The giant perceived her, and after her he was till they reached the river. She leaped the river, but the river the giant could not leap. "Thou art over there, Maol a Chliobain." "I am, though it is hard for thee." "Thou killedst my three bald brown daughters." "I killed them, though it is hard for thee." "Thou stolest my fine comb of gold, and my coarse comb of silver." "I stole them, though it is hard for thee." "When wilt thou come again?" "I will come when my business brings me."

She gave the combs to the farmer, and her big sister and the farmer's big son married. "I will give my middle son to thy middle sister, and get me the giant's glave of light." "It will cost thee no more," said Maol a Chliobain. She went away, and she reached the giant's house; she went up to the top of a tree that was above the giant's well. In the night came the bald rough-skinned gillie with the sword of light to fetch water. When he bent to raise the water, Maol a Chliobain came down and she pushed him down in the well, and she drowned him, and she took with her the glave of light.

The giant followed her till she reached the river; she leaped the river, and the giant could not follow her. "Thou art over there, Maol a Chliobain." "I am, if it is hard for thee." "Thou killedst my three bald brown daughters." "I killed, though it is hard for thee." "Thou stolest my fine comb of gold, and my coarse comb of silver." "I stole, though it is hard for thee." "Thou killedst my bald rough-skinned gillie." "I killed, though it is hard for thee." "Thou stolest my glave of light." "I stole, though it is hard for thee." "When wilt thou come again?" "I will come when my business brings me." She reached the house of the farmer with the glave of light; and her middle sister and the middle son of the farmer married. " I will give thyself my youngest son," said the farmer, "and bring me a buck that the giant has." " It will cost thee no more," said Maol a Chliobain. She went away, and she reached the house of the giant ; but when she had hold of the buck, the giant caught her. " What," said the giant, " wouldst thou do to me ; if I had done as much harm to thee as thou hast done to me, I would make thee burst thyself with milk porridge ; I would then put thee in a pock ; I would hang thee to the roof-tree ; I would set fire under thee ; and I would set on thee with clubs till thou shouldst fall as a faggot of withered sticks on the floor." The giant made milk porridge, and he made her drink it. She put the milk porridge about her mouth and face, and she laid over as if she were dead. The giant put her in a pock, and he hung her to the roof-tree ; and he went away, himself and his men, to get wood to the forest. The giant's mother was within. When the giant was gone, Maol a Chliobain began—" 'Tis I am in the light ! 'Tis I am in the city of gold !" " Wilt thou let me in ?" said the carlin. " I will not let thee in." At last she let down the pock. She put in the carlin, cat, and calf, and cream-dish. She took with her the buck and she went away. When the giant came with his men, himself and his men began at the bag with the clubs. The carlin was calling, " 'Tis myself that's in it." " I know that thyself is in it," would the giant say, as he laid on to the pock. The pock came down as a faggot of sticks, and what was in it but his mother. When the giant saw how it was, he took after Maol a Chliobain ; he followed her till she reached the river. Maol a Chliobain leaped the river, and the giant could not leap it. " Thou art over there, Maol a Chliobain." " I am, though it is hard for thee."

"Thou killedst my three bald brown daughters."   "I killed, though it is hard for thee."   "Thou stolest my golden comb, and my silver comb."   "I stole, though it is hard for thee."   "Thou killedst my bald rough-skinned gillie."   "I killed, though it is hard for thee."   "Thou stolest my glave of light."   "I stole, though it is hard for thee."   "Thou killedst my mother."   "I killed, though it is hard for thee."   "Thou stolest my buck."   "I stole, though it is hard for thee."   "When wilt thou come again?"   "I will come when my business brings me."   "If thou wert over here, and I yonder," said the giant, "what wouldst thou do to follow me?"   "I would stick myself down, and I would drink till I should dry the river."   The giant stuck himself down, and he drank till he burst.   Maol a Chliobain and the farmer's youngest son married.

MAOL A CHLIOBAIN.

Bha bainnteach ann roimhe so, 's bha tri nigheanan aice, 's thuirt iad rithe gun rachadh iad a dh' iarraidh an fhortain.   Dheasaich i tri bonnaich.   Thuirt i ris an té mhòir, "Cò'ca 's fheàrr leat, an leith bheag 's mo bheannachd, na'n leith mhòr 's mo mhollachd?"   "'S fheàrr leam," urs' ise, "an leith mhòr 's do mhollachd."   Thuirt i ris an te mheadhonaich, "Cò'ca is fheàrr leat an leith mhòr 's mo mhollachd na'n leith bheag 's mo bheannachd?"   "'S fheàrr leam," urs' ise, "an leith mhòr 's do mhollachd."   Thuirt i ris an tè bhig, "Cò'ca is fheàrr leat an leith mhòr 's mo mhollochd n'an leith bheag 's mo bheannachd?"   'S fheàrr leam an leith bheag 's do bheannachd.   Chòrd so r'a màthair, 's thug i dhi an da leith eile cuideachd.

Dh' fholbh iad, ach cha robh toil aig an dithisd a bu shine an té b' òige 'bhi leò, 's cheangail iad i ri carra cloiche.   Ghabh eud air an aghaidh, 's nur a dh' amhairc iad as an déigh, co a chunnaic iad ach ise, 's a' chreag air a muin.   Leig iad leatha car treis gus an d' ràinig

iad cruach mhònadh, 's cheangail iad i ris a' chruaich mhònadh.
Ghabh iad air au aghaidh treis, 's dh' amhairc iad 'nan déigh, 's co a
chunnaic iad ach ise a' tighinn, 's a' chruach mhònadh air a muin.
Leig iad leatha car tacan gus an d' ràinig iad craobh, 's cheangail iad
ris a' chraobh i. Ghabh iad air an aghaidh treis, 's nur a dh' amhairc
iad 'nan déigh, co a chunnaic iad ach ise a' tighinn, 's a' chraobh air
a muin. Chunnaic iad nach robh math a bhith rithe. Dh' fhuasgail iad i, 's lig iad leo i. Bha iad a' folbh gus an d' thàinig an
oidhche'orra. Chunnaic iad solus fada uatha, 's ma b'fhada uatha cha
b'fhada a bha iadsan 'ga 'ruigheachd. Chaidh iad a stigh. Dé a bha
'so ach tigh famhair. Dh' iarr iad fuireachd 'san oidhche. Fhuair iad
sin, 's chuireadh a laidhe iad le tri nigheanan an fhamhair.
Bha caran de chneapan òmbair ma mhuinealan nigheanan an
fhamhair, agus sreanganan gaoisid ma'm muineilsan. Chaidil iad
air fad, ach cha do chaidil Maol a' chliobain. Feadh na h-oidhche
thàinig paghadh air an fhamhair. Ghlaoidh e r'a ghille maol carrach
uisge thoirt a 'ionnsuidh. Thuirt an gille maol, carrach, nach robh
deur a stigh. " Marbh," urs' esan, " te de na nigheanan coimheach, 's
thoir a m' ionnsuidh a fuil." " Demur a dh' aithneachas mi eatorra ?"
urs' an gille maol, carrach. "Tha caran de chneapan ma mhuinealan mo nigheanansa, 's caran gaoisid ma mhuineil chàich." Chuala
Maol a' chliobain am famhair, 's cho clis 's a b'urrainn i, chuir i na
sreangannan gaoisid a bha ma 'muineal féin 's ma mhuineail a peathraichean ma mhuineil nigheanan an fhamhair, agus na cneapan a
bha ma mhuineil nigheanan an fhamhair ma 'muineal féin, 's ma
mhuineil a peathraichean, 's laidh i sìos gu sàmhach. Thàinig an gille
maol carrach, 's mharbh e té de nigheanan an fhamhair, 's thug e'n
fhuil a 'ionnsuidh. Dh' iarr e tuillidh a thoirt a 'ionnsuidh. Mharbh
e an ath té. Dh' iarr e tuillidh, 's mharbh e 'n treas te. Dhùisg
Maol a' chliobain a peathraichean, 's thug i leath' air a muin iad, 's
ghabh i air folbh. Mhothaich am famhair di, 's lean e i.
Na spreadan teine a bha ise cur as na clachan le a sàiltean, bha
iad a' bualadh an fhamhair 'san smigead ; 's na spreadan teine a bha
'm famhair a' toirt as na clachan le barraibh a chas, bha iad a'
bualadh Mhaol a' chliobain an cùl a' chinn. " 'Se so a bu dual daibh
gus an d'ràinig iad obhainn. Leum Maol a chliobain an obhainn, s
cha b'urrainn am famhair an obhainn a leum." " Tha thu thall a
Mhaol a chliobain." "Tha ma 's oil leat e." " Mharbh thu mo tri
nigheanan maola, ruagha." "Mharbh ma 's oil leat e." "'S cuin a
thig thu 'rithisd ?" " Thig nur* bheir mo ghnothach mi."

_____

* NUR, from *an trath*, or *an uair*, the time.

S

Ghabh iad air an aghaidh gus an d' ràinig iad tigh tuathanaich. Bha aig an tuathanach tri mic. Db' innis iad mar a thachair dhaibh. Urs' an tuathanach ri Maol a chliobain, "Bheir mi mo mhac is sine do 'd' phiuthar is sine, 's faigh dhomh cìr mhìn òir 's cìr gharbh airgid a tha aig an fhamhair." "Cha chosd e tuillidh dhuit," ursa Maol a chliobain. Dh' fholbh i, 's ràinig i tigh an fhamhair. Fhuair i stigh gun fhios. Thug i leatha na cìrean, 's ghabh i 'mach. Mhothaich am famhair di; is as a déigh a bha e gus an d' ràinig e 'n obhainn. Leum ise an obhainn, 's cha b'urrainn am famhair an obhainn a leum. "Tha thu thall a Mhaol a chliobain." "Tha ma's oil leat e." "Mharbh thu mo thri nigheanan maola, ruagha." "Mharbh ma's oil leat e. Ghoid thu mo chìr mhìn òir 's mo chir gharbh airgid." "Ghoid ma's oil leat e." "Cuin a thig thu 'rithisd?" "Thig nur bheir mo ghnothach mi."

Thug i na cìrean thun an tuathanaich, 's phòs a piuthar mhòr 's mac mòr an tuathanaich.

"Bheir mi mo mhac meadhonach do d' phiuthar mheadhonach, 's faigh dhomh claidheamh soluis an fhamhair." "Cha chosd e tuillidh dhuit," ursa Maol a chliobain. Ghabh i air folbh, 's ràinig i tigh an fhamhair. Chaidh i 'suas ann am bàrr craoibh' a bha as cionn tobar an fhamhair. Anns an oidhche thàinig an gille maol, carrach, 's an claidheamh soluis leis, a dh' iarraidh uisge. Nur a chrom e 'thogail an uisge thàinig Maol a chliobain a nuas, 's phut i sìos 'san tobar e, 's bhàth i e, 's thug i leatha an claidheamh soluisd. Lean am famhair i gus an d' ràinig i an obhainn. Leum i an obhainn, 's cha b'urrainn am famhair a leantainn. "Tha thu thall a Mhaol a chliobain." "Tha ma's oil leat e." "Mharbh thu mo thri nigheanan maola, ruagha." "Mharbh ma's oil leat e." "Ghoid tha mo chìr mhìn òir 's mo chìr gharbh airgid." "Ghoid ma's oil leat e." "Mharbh tha mo ghille maol, carrach." "Mharbh ma's oil leat e." "Ghoid tha mo chlaidheamh soluis." "Ghoid ma's oil leat e." "Cuin a thig thu 'rithisd." "Thig nur bheir mo ghnothach mi." Ràinig i tigh an tuathanaich leis a' chlaidheamh sholuis, 's phòs a piuthar mheadhonach, 's mac meadhonach an tuathanaich.

"Bheir mi dhuit féin mo mhac is òige," urs' an tuathanach, 's thoir am' ionnsuidh, "Boc a tha aig an fhamhair." "Cha chosd e tuillidh dhuit," ursa Maol a' chliobain. Dh' fholbh i 's ràinig i tigh an fhamhair, ach nur a bha gréim aic' air a' bhoc rug am famhair urra. "De," urs' am famhair, "a dheànadh thus' ormsa na'n deànainn uibhir coir' ort 's a rinn thus' ormsa." "Bheirinn ort gu 'sgàineadh thu thu féin le brochan bainne; chuirinn an sin ann am poc' thu; chrochainn thu ri driom an tighe; chuirinn teine fodhad; 's ghabhainn

duit le cabair gus an tuiteadh thu 'd' chual chrìonaich air an urlar.
Rinn am famhair brochan bainne, 's thugr ure' òl. Chuir ise am brochan bainne ma' beul 's ma h-aodam, 's luidh i seachad mar gum biodh
i marbh. Chuir am famhair am poc' i, 's chroch e i ri drìom an tighe,
's dh' fholbh e féin 's a dhaoine a dh' iarraidh fiodh do 'n choille. Bha
màthair an fhamhair a stigh. Theireidh Maol a' chliobain nur a dh'
fholbh am famhair, " 'S mise a tha ann 'san t-sòlas 's mise a tha ann
'sa' chathair òir." "An leig thu mis' ann," urs' a' chailleach. "Cha
leig gu dearbh." Ma dheireadh leig i 'nuas am poca ; chuir i stigh a'
chailleach, is cat, is laogh, is soitheach uachdair; thug i leatha am
boc ; 's dh' fholbh i. Nur a thàinig am famhair thòisich e féin 's a
dhaoine air a' phoca leis na cabair. Bha 'chailleach a' glaodhach,
" 'S mi féin a th' ann." " Tha fios agam gur tu féin a th' ann,"
theireadh am famhair, 's e 'g éiridh air a' phoca. Thàinig am poca
'nuas 'na chual chrìonaich, 's dé 'bha ann ach a mhàthair. Nur a
chunnaic am famhair mur a bha, thug e as déigh Mhaol a' chliobain.
Lean e i gus an d ràinig i 'n obhainn. Leum Maol a' chliobain an
obhainn, s cha b'urrainn am famhair a leum. " Tha thu thall a
Mhaol a chliobain." " Tha ma 's oil leat e." " Mharbh thu mo thri
nigheanan maola, ruagha." " Mharbh ma 's oil leat e." " Ghoid thu
mo chìr mhin òir 's mo chìr gharbh airgid." " Ghoid ma 's oil leat e."
" Mharbh thu mo ghille maol, carrach." " Mharbh ma 's oil leat e."
" Ghoid thu mo chlaidheamh soluisd." " Ghoid ma 's oil leat e."
" Mharbh thu mo mhàthair." " Mharbh ma 's oil leat e." " Ghoid
thu mo bhoc." " Ghoid ma 's oil leat e." " Cuin a thig thu rithisd."
" Thig nur bheir mo ghnothach mi." " Na'm biodh thusa bhos 's mise
thall," ursa am famhair, " de 'dheànadh thu airson mo leantainn?"
" 'Stopainn mi féin, 's dh' òlainn gus an traoighinn an obhainn." Stop
am famhair e féin, 's dh' òl e gus an do sgàinn e. Phòs Maol a chliobain mac òg an tuathanaich.

This story came to me from four sources. First, the one
which I have translated, into which several passages are introduced (in brackets) from the other versions. This was written
down by Hector MacLean.

2d. A version got by the same collector from Flora Macintyre, in Islay ; received June 16, 1859. In this the whole of the
first part is omitted; it begins at the giant's house. The incidents are then nearly the same till she runs away, when she
leaps the river with her sisters under her arms. The farmer or
king is omitted. She returns, is caught by the giant, tied to a

peat-stack, and a rock, which she takes away, and she makes the giant kill; the three cropped red girls: and she kills the cropped rough-skinned gillie: she steals the white glave of light, a fine comb of gold, and a coarse comb of silver. She makes the giant kill his mother, and his dog and cat entic d into a sack; at last she sets the giant to swill the river; he bursts, and she goes home with the spoil. The bit about the sack is worth quoting. She put the crone in the pock, and a cat, and a dog, and a cream-dish with her. When the giant and his men came, they began laying on the pock. The crone cried out, " It's myself thou hast;" and the giant said, " I know, thou she rogue, that it's thou." When they would strike a stroke on the dog, he would give out a SGOL; when they would strike a stroke on the cat, he would give out a MIOG; and when they would strike a stroke on the cream-dish, it would give out a STEALL (a spurt). I have,

3rd. A version very prettily told, at Easter 1859, by a young girl, nursemaid to Mr. Robertson, Chamberlain of Argyll, at Inverary. It was nearly the same as the version translated, but had several phrases well worth preservation, some of which will be found in brackets; such as, " but her mother's blessing came and freed her." The heroine also stole a golden cover off the bed, which called out; and a golden cock and a silver hen, which also called out. The end of the giant was thus: At the end of the last scolding match, the giant said, " If thou wert here, and I yonder, what wouldst thou do?" " I would follow thee over the bridge," said she. So Maol a chliobain stood on the bridge, and she reached out a stick to him, and he went down into the river, and she let go the stick, and he was drowned. " And what became of Maol a chliobain? did she marry the farmer's youngest son? " Oh, no; she did not marry at all. There was something about a key hid under a stone, and a great deal more which I cannot remember. My father did not like my mother to be telling us such stories, but she knows plenty more,"—and the lassie departed in great perturbation from the parlour.

The 4th version was got by John Dewar from John Crawfort, herring-fisher, Lochlonghead, Arrochar, and was received on the 2d of February 1860. Dewar's version is longer than any, but it came too late. It also contains some curious phrases

which the others have not got, some queer old Gaelic words, and
some new adventures. The heroine was not only the youngest,
but "maol carrach" into the bargain, and the rest called her
Maol a Mhoibean; but when they went on their travels she chose
the little cake and the blessing. The others tied her to a tree,
and a cairn of stones, which she dragged away. Then they
let her loose, and she followed them till they came to a burn.
" Then the eldest sister stooped to drink a draught from the burn,
and there came a small creature, named Bloinigain, and he
dabbled and dirtied the burn, and they went on. The next
burn they came to the two eldest sisters stooped, one on each
side of the burn, to drink a draught ; but Bloinigain came and he
dabbled and dirtied the burn ; and when they had gone on
another small distance, they reached another burn ; and the
youngest sister, whom the rest used to call Maol a Mhoibean,
was bent down drinking a draught from the burn, and Bloinigain
came and stood at the side of the burn till she had drank her
draught, and the other two came ; but when they stooped to
drink their draught, Bloinigain dabbled the burn, and they went
on ; and when they came to another burn, the two eldest were
almost parched with thirst. Maol a Mhoibean kept Bloinigain
back till the others got a drink ; and then she tossed Bloinigain
heels over head, CAR A MHUILTEAN, into a pool, and he followed
them no more."

This Bloinigain plays a great part in another story, sent by
Dewar ; and his name may perhaps mean " fatty;" BLONAG, fat,
suet, lard ; BLOINIGEAN-GARAIDH, is spinnage.

The next adventure is almost the very same. The giant's
three red-haired polled daughters had PAIDIREANAN of gold about
their necks (which word *may* be derived from *pater*, and a name
for a rosary), and the others had only strings.

When they fled they came to a great EAS, cataract, and " there
was no way of getting over it, unless they could walk on two
hairs that were as a bridge across the cataract ; and their name
was DROCHAID AN DA ROINEAG, the two-hair bridge ; and Maol
a Mhoibean ran over the eas on the two hairs ; but her sisters
could not walk on the two hairs, and Maol a Mhoibean had to
turn back and carry her sisters, one after one, over the eas on the
two-hair bridge." The giant could not cross, and they scolded

each other across the river as in the other stories.   The giant shouted, " Art thou yonder, Maol a Mhoibean ?" and she said " AIR MO NODAIG THA ;" and when she had told her deeds, she said, "I will come and go as my business brings me ;" and the three sisters went on and took service with the king.

This two-hair bridge over the fall may possibly be a double rainbow ; many a time have I sat and watched such a bridge over a fall ; and the idea that the rainbow was the bridge of spirits, is old enough.

> "Still seem as to my childhood's sight
> A midway station given,
> For happy spirits to alight
> Betwixt the earth and heaven."

The Norse gods rode over the bridge, Bif-raust, from earth to heaven ; and their bridge was the rainbow which the giants could not cross.   There is also a bridge, as fine as a hair, over which the Moslem pass to Paradise ; and those who are not helped, fall off and are lost.

The sisters took service ; one was engaged to sew, the other to mind the house, and the youngest said she was good at running errands ; so at the end of a day and year she was sent for the giant's CABHRAN full of gold, and CABHRAN full of silver ; and when she got there the giant was asleep on a chest in which the treasure was.

"Then Maol a Mhoibean thought a while, in what way she should get the giant put off the chest ; but she was not long till she thought on a way ; and she got a long broad bench that was within, and she set the bench at the side of the chest where the giant was laid ; she went out where the burn was, and she took two cold stones from the burn, and she went in where the giant was, and she would put one of the stones in under the clothes, and touch the giant's skin at the end of each little while with the stone ; and the giant would lay himself back from her, till bit by bit the giant went back off the chest on to the bench ; and then Maol a Mhoibean opened the chest, and took with her the cabhran of gold, and the cabhran of silver."   The rest of the adventure is nearly the same as in the other versions ; and the eldest sister married the king's eldest son.

The next was the Claidheamh Geal Soluis, white glave of light.

She got in and sat on a rafter on a bag of salt; and as the giant's wife made the porridge, she threw in salt. Then the giant and his son sat and supped, and as they ate they talked of how they would catch Maol, and what they would do to her when they had her; and after supper they went to bed." Then the giant got very thirsty, and he called to his son to get him a drink; and in the time that the giant's son was seeking a CUMAN (cup), Maol a Mhoibean took with her the fill of her SGUIRD (skirt) of salt, and she stood at the outside of the door; and the giant's son said to him "that there was no water within;" and the giant said "That the spring was not far off, and that he should bring in water from the well;" and when the giant's son opened the door, Maol a Mhoibean began to throw salt in his face; and he said to the giant, "That the night was dark, and that it was sowing and winnowing hailstones (GUN ROBH AN OIDHCHE DORCHA AGUS CUR S' CABHADH CLACH-A-MEALLAIN AN); and the giant said, "Take with thee my white glave of light, and thou wilt see a great distance before thee, and a long way behind thee."

When the young giant came out, it was a fine night; and he went to the well with the bright sword, and laid it down beside him; while he stooped to take up the water, Maol followed him, and picked up the sword, and SGUIDS I A'N CEANN, she whisked the head off the giant's son. Then came the flight and pursuit, and escape, and scolding match, and the second son of the king married the second sister.

The next adventure was the theft of Boc CLUIGEANACH, the belled buck. She went over the bridge and into the goats' house, and the goats began at BEUCHDAICH, roaring; and the giant said, "Maol a Mhoibean is amongst the goats;" and he went out and caught her; and he said, "What wouldst thou do to me if thou shouldst find me amongst thy goats, as I found thee?" And she said, "It is (this) that I would kill the best buck that I might have, and I would take out the paunch, and I would put thee in the paunch, and I would hang thee up till I should go to the wood; and I would get clubs of elder, and then I would come home, AGUS SHLAC-AINN GU BAS THU, and I would belabour thee to death." "And that is what I will do thee," said the giant.

Then comes the bit which is common to several other stories, in various shapes ; and which is part of a story in Straparola.

When she was hung up in the goat's paunch, and the giant gone for his elder-wood clubs, Maol a Mhoibean began to say to the giant's wife, " Oh ! it's I that am getting the brave sight ! Oh ! it's I that am getting the brave sight !" as she swayed herself backwards and forwards ; and the giant's wife would say to her, " Wilt thou let me in a little while ?" and Maol a Mhoibean would say (I will) *not let* (thee in) CHA LEIGH, and so on till the wife was enticed into the paunch, and then Maol took the belled buck and went away with him. " AGUS AN UAIR A' B AIRD ISE D' ISLE EASAN, S' AN NUAIR A D' AIRD ASAN B' ISLE ISE ;" and the time she was highest he was lowest, and the time he was highest she was lowest, till they reached the two-hair bridge. The giant came home and belaboured his wife to death, and every blow he struck, the wife would say, " IS MI FHEIN A THA ANN, O S MI FHEIN A THA ANN—It is myself that is in it : Oh ! it is myself that is in it ;" and the giant would say, " I know it is thyself that is in it."

[And in this the giant is like the water-horse in another story, and like the cyclop in the Odyssey, and like all other giants throughout mythology. He was a great, strong, blundering fool, and his family were as stupid as himself.]

Maol married the king's third son, and the king said, " There is one other thing yet of what the giant has that I want, and that is, A SGIATH BHALLABHREAC AGUS A BHOGH S A DH'ORLACH— his lumpy bumby shield, and his bow and his quiver, or in poetical language, his variegated bossy shield, and his bow and quiver —and I will give thee the kingdom if thou wilt get me them." This is a good instance of what may happen in translating Gaelic into English, one language into another, which is far removed from it, both in construction and meaning. BHALABHREAC applies to almost anything that is round or spotted. The root of the epithet is BALL, which, in oblique cases, becomes BHALL, vall, and means a spot, a dot, and many other things. It is the same as the English word ball. A shield was round, and covered with knobs ; a city wall was round, and it was the shield of the town ; an egg was round, and the shell was the shield or the wall of the egg ; a skull is round, and the shield of the brain, and a head is

still called a knob in English slang; a toad-stool is round,—and so this word ball has given rise to a succession of words, which at first sight appear to have nothing to do with each other, and the phrase *might* be translated speckled wings. The epithet is applied to clouds and to many things in Gaelic poetry, and has been translated in many ways, according to the taste of each translator. Those who felt the beauty of the passages used the words which they found applicable. Those who do not, may, if they choose, search out words which express their feeling; and so a poem which stands on its own merit, in its own language, is at the mercy of every translator; and those who work at Gaelic with dictionaries for guides, may well be puzzled with the multitude of meanings assigned to words.

So Maol went, and the giant's dog barked at her, and the giant came out and caught her, and said he would cut her head off; and she said she would have done worse to him; and "What was that?" "Put him in sack and roast him;" so he said he would do that, and put her in, and went for wood. She got her hand out, untied the string, and put in the dog and cat, and fled with the arms, and the giant roasted his own dog and cat, AGUS BHA AM MADADII AN 'S AN SGALAILLE AGUS AN CATE AN 'S AN SGIADHUIL—and the dog was in, and the squalling; and the cat (was) in, and the squealling, and the giant would say, "FEUCH RUIT A NIS—Try thyself now." When he found out the trick, he pursued, and when they got to the bridge, his hand was on her back, and he missed his step and fell into the EAS, and there he lay. And the king's son and Maol a Mhoibean were made heirs in the kingdom, and if they wanted any more of the giant's goods, they got it without the danger of being caught by the giant.

The Gaelic given in Dewar's version is spelt as it came, and is somewhat Phonetic. The writer knows his own language well, but has had very little practice in writing it. As he spells in some degree by ear, his phonetics have their value, as they have in his English letter given in the introduction.

5. A gentleman at the inn at Inverary remembered to have heard a similar story "long ago about a witch that would be running in and out of a window on a bridge of a single hair."

6. "Kate ill Pratts" is referred to in a review of Chambers'

Nursery Rhymes, at page 117, vol. 10; 1853—Tait's Edinburgh
Magazine. The story is mentioned as told in Perthshire, and
seems to be of the same kind; with a bit of Cinderella, as known
in the west, with the advice of the hoodie in Murchadh and
Mionachag put in the mouth of a little bird—

> " Stuff wi' fog, and clem wi' clay,
> And then ye 'll carry the water away."

These sounds are not imitations of any bird's note, and the
Gaelic sounds are; so I am inclined to think the Gaelic older
than the low country version.

The story is well known as Little Thumb. It is much the
same as Boots and the Troll, Norse Tales, p. 247. It is somewhat like part of Jack and the Bean-stalk. Part of it is like Big
Peter and Little Peter, Norse Tales, p. 395; and that is like some
German Stories, and like a story in Straparola. The opening is
like that of a great many Gaelic Stories, and is common to one
or two in Grimm.

There is something in a story from Polynesia, which I have
read, in which a hero goes to the sky on a ladder made of a plant,
and brings thence precious gifts, much as Jack did by the help
of his bean-stalk. In short, this story belongs to that class which
is common to all the world, but it has its own distinctive character in the Highlands; for the four versions which I have, resemble
each other much more than they do any other of which I know
anything.

FABLES.

1. From J. MacLeod, fisherman on the Laxford, Sutherland.

ONE day the fox succeeded in catching a fine fat goose asleep by the side of a loch, he held her by the wing, and making a joke of her cackling, hissing and fears, he said,—

"Now, if you had me in your mouth as I have you, tell me what you would do ?"

"Why," said the goose, "that is an easy question. I would fold my hands, shut my eyes, say a grace, and then eat you."

"Just what I mean to do," said Rory, and folding his hands, and looking very demure, he said a pious grace with his eyes shut.

But while he did this the goose had spread her wings, and she was now half way over the loch ; so the fox was left to lick his lips for supper.

"I will make a rule of this," he said in disgust, "never in all my life to say a grace again till after I feel the meat warm in my belly."   C. D.

The wild goose in the Highlands has her true character; she is one of the most wary and sagacious of birds, and a Gaelic proverb says :—

Sealgair thu mar a mharbhas thu Gèadh a's Corr' a's Crotach.

Sportsman thou, when killest thou goose, and heron, and curlew ?

Rory is a corruption of a Gaelic proper name, which means, one whose hair is of the colour of the fox "Ruadh." The fox is called by various descriptive and other names. BALGAIR, he with the "BALG," bag or quiver, from which the shape of the quiver may be surmised to have resembled the foxes' brush. MADADH RUADH, the red-brown dog. GILLE MARTUINN, the servant of Martin, or perhaps the Martinmas lad, but the true Gaelic, according to my instructor, a Lorn man, is SIONNACH, pronounced *Shunach*, which is surely the same as the Sanscrit SVAN, dog. SUNUH SHUNI, dog-bitch.

2. From John Campbell, piper; and many other sources lately.

The fox is much troubled by fleas, and this is the way in which he gets rid of them. He hunts about till he finds a lock of wool, and then he takes it to the river, and holds it in his mouth, and so puts the end of his brush into the water, and down he goes slowly. The fleas run away from the water, and at last they all run over the fox's nose into the wool, and then the fox dips his nose under and lets the wool go off with the stream.

This is told as a fact. The place where an "old grey fellow" was seen performing this feat, was mentioned by one of my informants. The fox was seen in the sea near the Caithness hills.

3. " Tha biadh a's ceol n seo," as the fox said when he ate the pipe bag.

This saying I have known from my childhood, and the story attached to it is that the fox being hungry one day, found a bag-pipe, and proceeded to eat the bag, which is generally, or was till lately, made of hide. There was still a remnant of breath in the bag, and when the fox bit it the drone gave a groan, when the fox surprised but not frightened said :—

" Here is meat and music !"

4. From D. M. and J. MacLeod, Laxford, Sutherland.

One day the fox chanced to see a fine cock and fat hen, off which he much wished to dine, but at his approach they both jumped up into a tree. He did not lose heart, but soon began to make talk with them, inviting them at last to go a little way with him. "There was no danger," he said, "nor fears of his hurting them, for there was peace between men and beasts, and among all animals." At last after much parleying the cock said to the hen, "My dear, do you not see a couple of hounds coming across the field?"

"Yes," said the hen, "and they will soon be here."

"If that is the case, it is time I should be off," said the sly fox, "for I am afraid these stupid hounds may not have heard of the peace."

And with that he took to his heels and never drew breath till he reached his den. C. D.

This fable is very well known, and is probably derived from Æsop, though the narrator did not know the fact. I give it because the authority cannot be impeached, and because equally well-known fables are found in old Chinese books, and are supposed to be common property. This *may* be pure tradition, though I suspect it to be derived indirectly from some book. I myself lately told the fable of the Monkey and the Cats, in Gaelic, to a high-lander who was going to law; and it is impossible to be sure of the pedigree of such well-known fables.

The next two are of the same kind, and were new to me when they arrived.

5. THE FOX AND THE FOX-HUNTER.

Once upon a time a Tod-hunter had been very anxious to catch our friend the fox, and had stopped all the earths in cold weather. One evening he fell asleep in his hut; and when he opened his eyes he saw the fox sitting very demurely at the side of the fire. It had entered by the hole under the door provided for the convenience of the dog, the cat, the pig, and the hen.

"Oh! ho!" said the Tod-hunter, "now I have you." And he went and sat down at the hole to prevent Reynard's escape.

"Oh! ho!" said the fox, "I will soon make that stupid fellow get up." So he found the man's shoes, and putting them into the fire, wondered if that would make the enemy move.

"I shan't get up for that, my fine gentleman," cried the Tod-hunter.

Stockings followed the shoes, coat and trousers shared the same fate, but still the man sat over the hole. At last the fox having set the bed and bedding on fire, put a light to the straw on which his jailor lay, and it blazed up to the ceiling.

"No! that I cannot stand," shouted the man, jumping up; and the fox taking advantage of the smoke and confusion, made good his exit.

Note by the Collector.—This is the beginning of Reineke Fuchs in the Erse. I cannot get any one to write them down in Gaelic, which very few people can *write*. Most of the tales are got from my guide, the gamekeeper; but I have got them from many others.   C. D.

Having told this story to a man whom I met near Oban, as a bait, I was told the following in return.—J. F. C.

6. "The fox is very wise indeed. I don't know whether it is true or not, but an old fellow told me that he had seen him go to a loch where there were wild ducks, and take a bunch of heather in his mouth, then go into the water, and swim down with the wind till he got into the middle of the ducks, and then he let go the heather and killed two of them."

7. THE FOX AND THE WRENS.

A fox had noticed for some days, a family of wrens, off which he wished to dine. He might have been satisfied with one, but he was determined to have the whole lot,—father and eighteen sons,—and all so like that he could not tell one from the other, or the father from the children.

"It is no use to kill one son," he said to himself, "because the old cock will take warning and fly away with the seventeen. I wish I knew which is the old gentleman."

He set his wits to work to find out, and one day seeing them all threshing in a barn, he sat down to watch them; still he could not be sure.

"Now I have it," he said; "well done the old man's stroke! He hits true," he cried.

"Oh!" replied the one he suspected of being the head of the family, "If you had seen my grandfather's strokes, you might have said that."

The sly fox pounced on the cock, ate him up in a trice, and then soon caught and disposed of the eighteen sons, all flying in terror about the barn.

C. D.

This is new to me, but there is something like it in the Battle of the Birds, where the wren is a farmer threshing in a barn. Why the wren should wield the flail does not appear, but I suppose there was some good reason for it " once upon a time."

J. F. C.

8. From John Dewar, Inveraray, August 27, 1860.

A fox one day met a cock and they began talking.

"How many tricks canst thou do?" said the fox.

"Well," said the cock, "I could do three; how many canst thou do thyself?"

"I could do three score and thirteen," said the fox.

"What tricks canst thou do?" said the cock.

"Well," said the fox, "my grandfather used to shut one eye and give a great shout."

" I could do that myself," said the cock.

" Do it," said the fox. And the cock shut one eye and crowed as loud as ever he could, but he shut the eye that was next the fox, and the fox gripped him by the neck and ran away with him. But the wife to whom the cock belonged saw him and cried out, " Let go the cock; he's mine."

Say thou " S'E MO CHOILEACH FHEIN A TH' ANN" (it is my own cock), said the cock to the fox.

Then the fox opened his mouth to say as the cock did, and he dropped the cock, and he sprung up on the top of a house, and shut one eye and gave a loud crow; and that's all there is of that sgeulachd.

I find that this is well-known in the west.

9. HOW THE WOLF LOST HIS TAIL.

One day the wolf and the fox were out together, and they stole a dish of crowdie. Now the wolf was the biggest beast of the two, and he had a long tail like a greyhound, and great teeth.

The fox was afraid of him, and did not dare to say a word when the wolf ate the most of the crowdie, and left only a little at the bottom of the dish for him, but he determined to punish him for it; so the next night when they were out together the fox said :

" I smell a very nice cheese, and (pointing to the moonshine on the ice) there it is too."

" And how will you get it ?" said the wolf.

" Well, stop you here till I see if the farmer is asleep, and if you keep your tail on it, nobody will see you or know that it is there. Keep it steady. I may be some time coming back."

So the wolf lay down and laid his tail on the moonshine in the ice, and kept it for an hour till it was fast. Then the fox, who had been watching him, ran in to the farmer and said : " The wolf is there ; he will eat up the children,—the wolf ! the wolf !"

Then the farmer and his wife came out with sticks to kill the wolf, but the wolf ran off leaving his tail behind him, and that's why the wolf is stumpy tailed to this day, though the fox has a long brush.

C. D.

This is manifestly the same as the Norse story,—" Why the bear is stumpy tailed ?" and it errs in ascribing a stumpy tail to the wolf. There was not time for the " Norse Tales " to become known to the people who told the story, so perhaps this may be a Norse tradition transferred from the bear to the wolf. There is another wolf story in Sutherland, which was told to me by the Duke of Sutherland's head forester in 1848. It was told in Gaelic by a fine old highlander, who is now dead. His sons have succeeded him, and will probably remember this story which I quote from recollection.

J. F. C.

10. HOW THE LAST WOLF WAS KILLED IN SUTHERLAND.

There was once a time when there were wolves in Sutherland, and a woman that was living in a little town lost one of her children. Well, they went all about the hills looking for the lad, but they could not find him for three days. Well, at the end of that time they gave up, but there was a young lad coming home late through a big cairn of stones, and he heard the crying of a child, and a kind of a noise, and he went up to the cairn, and what should he see, in a hole under a big stone, but the boy and two young wolves with him.

Well he was frightened that the old wolf would come, so he went home to the town, and got two others with him, and in the morning they went back to the cairn and they found the hole.

Well, then, one of the lads stopped outside to

T

watch, and the other two went in, and they began to kill the young wolves, and they were squealing, and the old one heard them, and she came running to the place, and slipped between the legs of the lad who was watching, and got her head into the hole, but he held her by the tail.

"What," said the lad who was inside "is keeping the light from us."

MA BHRISTEAS BUN FIONN BITHIIDH FIOS AGAD.

"If the root of Fionn (or if the hairy root) breaks, thou wilt know," said the man outside.

Well, he held on, and the lads that were inside killed the wolf and the young ones, and they took the boy home to his mother, and his family were alive in the time of my grandfather, and they say they were never like other people.

This is manifestly the same as the story of Romulus and Remus, but it appears on very strong evidence that wolves really carry off and suckle children in Oude now, and that these children grow up to be half savages. It is either a fact in natural history, or a tradition, believed to be a fact in Sutherland and in Oude. I have heard the same story told in the Highlands of a wild boar, but the boar's tail would be but a slippery hold.   J. F. C.

According to Innes (Scotland in the Middle Ages, Pp. 125), in 1283, there was an allowance for one hunter of wolves at Stirling; and there were wild boars fed at the King's expense in 1263, in Forfarshire. There are plenty of wolves now in Scandinavia, and in Brittany, and wild boars in Germany, and elsewhere in Europe. The Gaelic names for wolf are MADADH, ALLUIDH, commonly used; FAOL CHU, ALLA MHADADH, all of which are composed of an epithet, and a word which now means dog. Dic. etc. MAC TIRE, Earth's Son; FAOL, Armstrong.

A Boar is TORC, CULLACH, FIADH CHULLACH.

The Fox appears as a talking creature in several stories. So does the Bear in No. IX., and the Wolf and Falcon, No. IV. The Dog appears in No. XII.; the Sheep, Cat, Cock, Goose, Dog, and Bull, in No. XI; the Frog in No. XXXIII; the Cat and the Mouse in No. XLIX. The Rat and the Lion, and the Dove, appear in a story to which I have referred in No. IV. Other creatures, also, not mentioned in stories, are gifted with speech, but their speech is generally but a translation of their notes into Gaelic.

11. Bi Glic, Bi Glic, *Bee Gleechk,* be wise, say the Oyster-catchers, when a stranger comes near their haunts.

12. Gòrach, Gòrach, *Gawrach,* "silly," says the Hoodie, as he sits on a hillock by the way side and bows at the passengers.

13. Here is another bit of crow language,—a conversation with a frog. When it is repeated in Gaelic it can be made absurdly like the notes of the creatures.

"Ghille criosda mhic Dhughail cuir a nios do mhàg.

Ghille criosda mhic Dhughail cuir a nios do mhàg."

Christ's servant, son of Dugald, put up thy paw.

"Tha eagal orm, tha eagal orm, tha eagal orm."

I fear.

"Gheibh thu còta gorm a's léine. Gheibh thu còta gorm a's leine."

Thou shalt have a blue coat and a shirt.

Then the frog put up his hand and the hoodie took him to a hillock and began to eat him, saying,

"Bian dona lom! 's bu dona riabh thu."

Bad bare meat and bad wert thou ever.

"Caite bheil do ghealladh math a nis?" said the frog, "where is thy good promise now?"

"Sann ag ol a bha sinn an latha sin. Sann ag ol a bha sinn an latha sin."

It is drinking we were on that day.

"Tol ort a ruid ghrannda gur beag feola tha air do chramhan."

"Tol ort!" said the hoodie.

A hole in thee, ugly thing! how little flesh is on thy bones.

Why the frog is called Gilchrist MacDugald, unless the story was made to fit some real event, I do not know. The story used to be told by an old Islay man, Donald Macintyre, to Hector MacLean; and I remember to have heard part of it in my childhood.

The Hoodie has appeared in many places already, and he and his family, the Crows, have been soothsayers time out of mind, and in many lands. A more mischievous, knowing bird does not exist, or one that better deserves his character for wisdom.

The old fable of the bird which dropped a tortoise on a stone, is enacted every day by Hoodies. Any one who will take the trouble to watch, may see hoodies on the shores of the Western Isles, at low tide, flying up into the air and dropping down again.

It will be found that they are trying to drop large stranded muscles and other shells, on the stones on the beach; and if left to their own devices, they will go on till they succeed in cracking the shell, and extracting the inhabitant.

Keepers who trap them most successfully, do it by beating them at their own weapons. They put a bait into a pool of water, and make a show of hiding it, and set the trap on a knoll at some distance. The Hoodie makes a gradual approach, reconnoitering the ground as he advances, and settling on the knolls which command a view, perhaps repeating his song of silly, silly, till he settles on the trap, and next morning his head is on the kennel door with the mortal remains of other offenders.

I suspect that the Hoodie was made a soothsayer because of his natural wisdom.

14. The Grouse Cock and his wife are always disputing and may be heard on any fine evening or early morning quarrelling and scolding about the stock of food.

This is what the hen says,—
" Faic thusa 'n la ud 's 'n la ud eile."
And the cock, with his deeper voice, replies,—
" Faic thusa 'n cnoc ud 's 'n cnoc ud eile."
See thou younder day, and yon other day.
See thou younder hill, and yon other hill.

Of all the stories I have gathered and heard, this is all
I have about the Grouse. It is remarkable; for if these stories
were home-made, and in modern times, they would surely treat of
the only bird whose births, deaths, and marriages are chronicled
in the newspapers,—and which is peculiar to the British Isles.

15. The Eagle and the Wren once tried who could
fly highest, and the victor was to be king of the birds.
So the Wren flew straight up, and the Eagle flew in
great circles, and when the Wren was tired he settled
on the Eagle's back.
When the Eagle was tired he stopped and
" C' aite bheil thu dhreolain ?" urs' an iolair.
" Tha mise n so os do ceann," urs' n' dreolan.
" Where art thou, Wren?" said the Eagle.
" I am here above thee," said the Wren.
And so the Wren won the match.

This was told me in my childhood, I think, by the Rev. Mr.
MacTavish. There is a much better version of the story in
Grimm's "King Wren," in which the notes of many creatures are
made into German; but this describes the flight of eagle and
wren correctly enough. I lately, Sept. 1860, heard it in Skye.

16. Tha Fios Fithich agud. Thou hast ravens'
knowledge, is commonly said to children who are
unusually knowing about things of which they have no
ostensible means of gaining knowledge.

Odin had two ravens who names meant Mind and Memory,
which told him everything that passed in the world.

17. Nead air Bride.   Ubh air Inid eun air caisg mar am bi sin aig an Fhitheach bithidh am bas.

Nest at Candlemas, egg at inid, bird at Pash.
If that hath not the Raven, death he hath.

This is rather a bit of popular natural history than anything else, but it shews that the raven is at least as important a personage amongst Celts as the grouse is amongst Saxons.

18. S' bigead thu siod, ars an dreolan 'n ur thunn e, gob ans an Fhairige.

Thou'rt lessened by that, said the Wren, when he dipped his beak in the sea.

There are a great number of similar stories current in the islands, but it is very hard to persuade any one that such trifles can be of any value.   I have lately heard of a number of stories of the kind.   For example—

19. John Mackinnon, stable-boy at Broadford, in Skye, tells that "a man was one day walking along the road with a creel of herrings on his back, and two foxes saw him, and the one, who was the biggest, said to the other, 'Stop thou here, and follow the man, and I will run round and pretend that I am dead.'   So he ran round, and stretched himself on the road.   The man came on, and when he saw the fox, he was well pleased to find so fine a beast, and he picked him up, and threw him into the creel, and he walked on.   But the fox threw the herrings out of the creel, and the other followed and picked them up; and when the creel was empty, the big fox leaped out and ran away, and that is how they got the herrings.   Well, they went on together till they came to a smith's house, and there was a horse tied at the door, and he had a golden shoe, and there was a name on it.

" ' I will go and read what is written on that shoe,'

said the big fox, and he went; but the horse lifted his foot, and struck a kick on him, and drove his brains out.

" 'Ghill' ghill' ars an siunnach beag cha sgolair mi s' cha 'n ail leam a bhi.'

" 'Lad, Lad,' said the little fox, 'no scholar me. nor wish I to be;"' and, of course, he got the herrings, though my informant did not say so.

20. A boy, Alexander Mackenzie, who walked with me from Carbost, in Skye, told that a bee seillean met a mouse and said,

" Teann a nall 'us gun deanamaid tigh."

" Come over till we make a house."

" I will not," said Luchag, the mousie.

> Fear dha 'n dug thusa do mhil shamraidh
> Deanadh e tigh gheamhraidh dhuit
> Tha tigh agamsa fo thalamh
> Nach ruig air gallian na gaoith
> Bith tusa an ad iscan pheallach
> A ruidh air barradh nan craobh.

He to whom thou gavest thy summer honey,
Let him make a winter house for thee ;
I have a little house under the ground,
That can reach neither cold nor breeze,
Thou wilt be a ragged creature,
Running on the tops of the trees.

21. The same boy told that there was a mouse in the hill, and a mouse in a farm.

" It were well," said the hill mouse, "to be in the farm where one might get things."

Said the farm mouse, " S' fhearr an t-sith." Better is peace.

22. The following is not strictly speaking a fable, but it is a sort of moral tale, and may be classed with fables. It seems to inculcate a lesson of self-reliance and self-help. I wrote it in English from the Gaelic repetition of John Mackenzie at Inverary in 1859, and made him repeat it in 1860, when I made up several omissions. Other versions have come to me from other sources, and the tale seems to be well known in the Highlands. If it is in any book, I have not been able to find it. Mackenzie says he learned it from a native of Uist, and I have a very well written version of it, told by Macintyre in Benbecula, to Mr. Torrie. It is called the "Provost of London," and begins with the family history of the hero of the tale. A great lady fell in love with a poor Highland lad, and he was ashamed of the love she had taken for him, and went away to an uncle who was a colonel, and who got him made a major. The lady took to black melancholy, and he was sent for, and they married. He went to the wars, bought a small estate, was killed, and his brother-in-law brought up his son. Then comes the dream, the journey for three years in Scotland, Ireland, and England ; the meeting with "one of the people of Cambridge," and the rest of the incidents nearly as they were told to me by Mackenzie, but in different words.

BAILLIE LUNNAIN.

Told by John Mackenzie, at Inverary, to J. F. C.   August 1859
and 1860.

THERE were at some time of the world two brothers
in one farm, and they were very great friends, and
they had each a son : and one of the brothers died,
and he left his brother guardian. When the lad was
near to be grown up, he was keeping the farm for his
mother almost as well as his father could have done.
One night he saw a dream in his sleep, the most beautiful lady that there was in the world, and he dreamed
of her three times, and he resolved to marry her and
no other woman in the world ; and he would not stay
in the farm, and he grew pale, and his father's brother
could not think what ailed him ; and he was always
asking him what was wrong with him. " Well, never
mind," one day he said, " brother of my father, I have
seen a dream, the most beautiful woman that there is
in the world, and I will marry no other but she ; and
I will now go out and search for her over the whole
world till I find her."

Said the uncle, " Son of my brother, I have a
hundred pounds ; I will give them to thee, and go :
and when that is spent come back to me, and I will
give thee another hundred."

So the lad took the hundred pounds, and he went

to France, and then he went to Spain, and all over the world, but he could not find the lady he had seen in his sleep. At last he came to London, and he had spent all his money, and his clothes were worn, and he did not know what he should do for a night's lodging.

Well, as he was wandering about the streets, whom should he see but a quiet-looking respectable old woman ; and he spoke to her ; and, from less to more, he told her all that had happened to him ; and she was well pleased to see a countryman, and she said,

"I, too, am a Highland woman, though I am in this town." And she took him to a small house that she had, and she gave him meat and clothes.

And she said, "Go out now and take a walk ; maybe thou mayest see here in one day what thou mightest not see in a year."

On the next day he was out taking a walk about the town, and he saw a woman at a window, and he knew her at once, for she was the lady he had seen in his sleep, and he went back to the old woman.

"How went it with thee this day, Gael?" said she.

"It went well," said he.

"Oh, I have seen the lady I saw in my sleep," said he. And he told her all about it.

Then the old woman asked about the house and the street ; and when she knew—"Thou hast seen her," said she. "That is all thou wilt see of her. That is the daughter of the Bailie of London ; but I am her foster mother, and I would be right glad if she would marry a countryman of my own. Now, do thou go out on the morrow, and I will give thee fine highland clothes, and thou wilt find the lady walking in such a street ; herself and three maidens of company will go out together ; and do thou tread on her gown ; and when she turns round to see what is the matter, do thou speak to her."

Well, the lad did this. He went out and he found the lady, and he set his foot on her dress, and the gown rent from the band; and when she turned round he said, "I am asking you much grace—it was an accident."

"It was not your fault; it was the fault of the dressmaker that made the dress so long," said she.

And she looked at him; and when she saw how handsome he was, she said, "Will you be so kind as to come home with me to my father's house and take something?"

So the lad went and sat down, and before she asked him anything she set down wine before him and said, "Quicker is a drink than a tale."

When he had taken that, he began and he told her all that happened, and how he had seen her in his sleep, and when, and she was well pleased.

"And I saw thee in my sleep on the same night," said she.

He went away that day, and the old woman that he was lodging with asked him how he had got on, and he told her everything that had happened; and she went to the Bailie's daughter, and told her all the good she could think of about the young lad; and after that he was often at the Bailie's house; and at last the daughter said she would marry him. "But I fear that will not do," said she. "Go home for a year, and when thou comest back I will contrive to marry thee," said she, "for it is the law of this country that no one must be married unless the Bailie himself gives her by the hand to her bridegroom," said she; and she left blessing with him.

Well, the lad went away as the girl said, and he

was putting everything in order at home; and he told his father's brother all that had happened to him; but when the year was nearly out he set off for London again, and he had the second hundred with him, and some good oat-meal cakes.

On the road, whom should he meet but a Sassanach gentleman who was going the same road, and they began to talk.

"Where art thou going?" said the Saxon.

"Well, I am going to London," said he

"When I was there last I set a net* in a street, and I am going to see if it is as I left it. If it is well I will take it with me; if not, I will leave it."

"Well," said the other, "that is but a silly thing. How can lintseed be as thou hast left it? It must be grown up and trodden down by ducks and geese, and eaten by hens long ago. I am going to London, too; but I am going to marry the Bailie's daughter."

Well, they walked on together, and at long last the Saxon began to get hungry, and he had no food with him, and there was no house near; and he said to the other, "Wilt thou give me some of thy food?"

"Well," said the Gael, "I have but poor food— oaten bread; I will give you some if you will take it; but if I were a gentleman like you I would never travel without my own mother."

"How can I travel with my mother?" said the Saxon. "She is dead and buried long ago, and rotting in the earth; if not, why should I take her with me?"

And he took the oat cake and ate it, and they went on their way.

They had not gone far when a heavy shower came

* To set a net and to sow lint are expressed by the same words.

on, and the Gael had a rough plaid about him, but the Saxon had none ; and he said to the other,

"Wilt thou lend me thy plaid ?"

"I will lend you a part of it," said the Gael ; " but if I were a gentleman like you, I would never travel without my house, and I would not be indebted to any one for favours."

"Thou art a fool," said the Saxon ; " my house is four storeys high. How could any man carry a house that is four storeys high about with him ?"

But he wrapped the end of the Highlander's plaid about his shoulders, and they went on.

Well, they had not gone far till they came to a small river, and the water was deep after the rain, and there was no bridge, for in those days bridges were not so plentiful as they are now ; and the Saxon would not wet his feet, so he said to the Highlander,

"Wilt thou carry me over ?"

"Well," said the Gael, "I don't mind if I do ; but if I were a gentleman like you, I would never travel without my own bridge, and I would not be in any man's debt for favours."

"Thou art a silly fellow," said the Saxon. "How can any man travel about with a bridge that is made of stone and lime. Thou art but a 'burraidh,' and weighs as much as a house ?"

But he got on the back of his fellow-traveller nevertheless, and they travelled on till they got to London. Then the Saxon went to the house of the Baillie, and the other went to the little house of his old countrywoman, who was the foster-mother of the Bailie's daughter.

Well, the Saxon gentleman began to tell the Bailie all that had happened to him by the way ; and he said—

"I met with a Gael by the way, and he was a perfect fool—the greatest booby that man ever saw. He told me that he had sown lint here a year ago in a street, and that he was coming to fetch it, if he should find it as he left it, but that if he did not, he would leave it ; and how should he find that after a year ? He told me I should never travel without my mother, and my house, and my bridge ; and how could a man travel with all these things ? But though he was nothing but a fool, he was a good-natured fellow, for he gave me some of his food, and lent me a bit of his plaid, and he carried me over a river."

"I know not but he was as wise as the man that was speaking to him," said the Bailie ; for he was a wise man. "I'll tell you what he meant," said he.

"Well, I will shew that he was a fool as great as ever was seen," said the Saxon.

"He has left a girl in this town," said the Bailie, "and he is come to see if she is in the same mind as she was when he left her ; if so, he will take her with him, if not, he will leave her ; he has set a net," said he. "Your mother nourished you, and a gentleman like you should have his own nourishment with him. He meant that you should not be dependent on him. It was the booby that was with him," said the Bailie. "A gentleman like you should have his own shelter, and your house is your shelter when your are at home. A bridge is made for crossing a river, and a man should always be able to do that without help ; and the man was right, and he was no fool, but a smart lad, and I should like to see him," said the Bailie ; "and I would go to fetch him if I knew where he was," said he. According to another version, the house and bridge meant a coach and a saddle-horse.

Well, the next day the Bailie went to the house

where the lad was, and he asked him to come home to his dinner ; and the lad came, and he told the Bailie that he had understood all that had been said.

"Now," said he, "as it is the law that no man may be married here unless the Bailie gives him the bride by the hand, will you be so kind as to give me the girl that I have come to marry, if she is in the same mind ? I will have everything ready."

And the Bailie said, "I will do that, my smart lad, to-morrow, or whenever thou dost choose. I would go farther than that for such a smart boy," said he.

"Well, I will be ready at such a house to-morrow," said the lad ; and he went away to the foster-mother's house.

When the morrow came, the Bailie's daughter disguised herself, and she went to the house of her foster-mother, and the Gael had got a churchman there ; and the Bailie came in, and he took his own daughter by the hand ; but she would not give her hand to the lad.

"Give thy hand, girl," said the Bailie. "It is an honour for thee to marry such a smart lad." And he gave her to him, and they were married according to law.

Then the Bailie went home, and he was to give his daughter by the hand to the Saxon gentleman that day ; but the daughter was not to be found ; and he was a widower, and she was keeping the house for him, and they could not find her anywhere.

"Well," said the Bailie, "I will lay a wager that Gael has got her, after all." And the Gael came in with the daughter, and he told them everything just as it had happened, from the beginning to the end, and how he had plenty in his own country.

And the Bailie said, " Well, since I myself have given thee my daughter by the hand, it is a marriage, and I am glad that she has got a smart lad like thee for a husband."

And they made a wedding that lasted a year and a day, and they lived happily ever after, and if they have not died since then they are alive yet.

THE SLIM SWARTHY CHAMPION.

From James Wilson. blind fiddler, Islay, 1859.

THERE was a poor man dwelling in Ard na n
Uamha, and a son was born to him, and he gave
him school and learning till he was fourteen years of
age. When he was fourteen years of age, he said to
his father,

"Father, it is time for me to be doing for myself.
if thou wouldst give me a fishing-rod and a basket."

The poor man found every chance till he got a
fishing-rod and a basket for him. When he got the
fishing-rod and the basket, he went round about Loch
Aird na n Uamha, and took down (by) Loch Thorabais ; and after he had fished Loch Thorabais closely.
he came to Loch Phort an Eillean ;* and after he had
fished Loch Phort an Eillean before him, he took out
by Loch Allalaidh. He stayed the night in Aird
Eileastraidh, and every trout he had left with a poor
woman that was there.

On the morrow he thought that he would rise out,
and that he would betake himself to Eirinn. He
came to the garden of Aird Inneasdail, and he plucked
with him sixteen apples, and then he came to Mull of
Otha.† He threw an apple out into the sea, and

* The lake in which is the island where the Lords of the Isles
had their dwelling.

† The nearest point to Ireland.

he gave a step on it: he threw the next one, and he gave a step on it: he threw thus one after one, until he came to the sixteenth, and the sixteenth took him on shore in Eirinn.

When he was on shore he shook his ears, and he thought that it was in no sorry place he would stay.

> " He moved as sea heaps from sea heaps,
> And as playballs from playballs—
> As a furious winter wind—
> So swiftly, sprucely, cheerily,
> Right proudly,
> Through glens and high-tops,
> And no stop made he
> Until he came
> To city and court of O'Domhnuill.
> He gave a cheery, light leap
> O'er top and turret
> Of court and city
> Of O'Domhnuill."*

O'Domhnuill took much anger and rage that such an unseemly ill stripling should come into his court, while he had a doorkeeper for his town.

"I will not believe," said the Champion, but "that thou art taking anger and rage, O'Domhnuill."

"Well, then, I am," said O'Domhnuill, "if I did but know at whom I should let it out."

"My good man," said the Champion, "coming in was no easier for me than going out again would be."

"Thou goest not out," said O'Domhnuill, "until thou tellest me from whence thou camest."

> " I came from hurry-skurry,
> From the end of endless spring,

---

* The only authority for writing this as poetry is the rhythm and alliteration of the original.

From the loved swanny glen—
A night in Islay and a night in Man,
A night on cold watching cairns.
On the face of a mountain
In the Scotch king's town
Was I born.
A soiled, sorry Champion am I,
Though I happened upon this town."

"What," said O'Domhnuill, "canst thou do, oh Champion? Surely, with all the distance thou hast travelled, thou canst do something."

"I was once," said he, "that I could play a harp."

"Well, then," said O'Domhnuill, "it is I myself that have got the best harpers in the five-fifths of Eirinn, or in the bridge of the first of the people, such as—Ruairidh O'Cridheagan, Tormaid O'Giollagan, and Thaog O'Chuthag."

"Let's hear them playing," said the Champion.

"They could play tunes and "CIRT" and "ORGAIN,"
Trampling things, tightened strings,
Warriors, heroes, and ghosts on their feet,
Ghosts and spectres, illness and fever,
They'd set in sound lasting sleep
The whole great world,
With the sweetness of the calming tunes
That the harpers could play."

The music did not please the Champion. He caught the harps, and he crushed them under his feet, and he set them on the fire, and made himself a warming, and a sound warming at them.

O'Domhnuill took much lofty rage that a man had come into his court who should do the like of this to the harps.

"My good man, I will not believe that thou art not taking anger," said the Champion.

" Well, then, I am, if I did but know at whom I should let it out."

" Back, my good man; it was no easier for me to break thy harps than to make them whole again," said the Champion.

" I will give anything to have them made whole again," said O'Domhnuill.

" For two times five marks I will make thy harps as good as they were before," said the Champion.

" Thou shalt get that," said O'Domhnuill.

O'Domhnuill gave him the marks, and he seized on the fill of his two palms of the ashes, and he made a harp for Ruairidh O'Cridheagan; and one for Tormaid O'Giollagan; and one for Thaog O'Chuthag; and a great choral harp for himself.

" Let's hear thy music," said O'Domhnuill.

" Thou shalt hear that, my good man," said the Champion.

The Champion began to play, and och! but he was the boy behind the harp.

> " He could play tunes, and UIRT and ORGAIN
> Trampling things, tightened strings,
> Warriors, heroes, and ghosts on their feet,
> Ghosts and souls, and sickness and fever,
> That would set in sound lasting sleep
> The whole great world
> With the sweetness of the calming tunes
> That the champion could play."

" Thou art melodious, oh Champion!" said O'Domhnuill.

When the harpers heard the Champion playing, they betook themselves to another chamber, and though he had followed on, still they had not come to the fore.

O'Domhnuill went away, and he sent a bidding to meat to the Champion.

"Tell the good man that he will not have that much to gloom on me when I go at mid-day to-morrow," said the Champion.

O'Domhnuill took much proud rage that such a man should come into his court, and that he would not take meat from him. He sent up a fringed shirt, and a storm mantle.

"Where is this going?" said the Champion.

"To thee, oh Champion," said they.

"Say you to the good man that he will not have so much as that to gloom on me when I go at mid-day to-morrow," said the Champion.

O'Domhnuill took much anger and rage that such a man had come into his court and would not either take meat or dress from him. He sent up five hundred Galloglachs to watch the Champion, so that O'Domhnuill might not be affronted by his going out by any way but by the door.

"Where are you going?" said the Champion.

"To watch thee, Champion, so that thou shouldst not go to affront O'Domhnuill, and not to let thee out but as thou shouldst," said they.

"Lie down there," said the Champion, "and I will let you know when I am going."

They took his advice, and they lay down beside him, and when the dawn broke, the Champion went into his garments.

"Where are my watchers, for I am going?" said the Champion.

"If thou shouldst stir," said the great Galloglach, "I would make a sharp sour shrinking for thee with this plough-board in my hand."

The Champion leaped on the point of his pins, and

he went over top and turret of court and city of
O'Domhnuill.

The Galloglach threw the plough-board that was in
his hand, and he slew four and twenty persons of the
very people of O'Domhnuill.

Whom should the Champion meet, but the tracking lad of O'Domhnuill, and he said to him—

" Here's for thee a little sour grey weed, and go in
and rub it to the mouths of those whom it killed and
bring them alive again, and earn for thyself twenty
calving cows, and look behind thee when thou partest
from me, whom thou shalt see coming."

When the tracking lad did this he saw no being
coming, but he saw the Champion thirteen miles on
the other side of Luimineach (Limerick).

> " He moved as sea-heaps o' sea-heaps,
>   And as playballs o' playballs,
>   As a furious winter wind—
>   So swiftly, sprucely, cheerily,
>   Right proudly,
>   Through glens and high tops,
>   And he made no stop
>   Until he reached
>   MacSeathain,* the Southern Earl."

He struck in the door. Said MacSeathain, the
southern Earl, " Who's that in the door ?"

" I am Duradan o' Duradan Dust of Dust," said
the champion.

"Let in Dust of Dust," said MacSeathain, the
southern Earl ; " no being must be in my door without getting in."

They let him in.

" What couldst thou do, Duradan o' Duradan ?"
said the southern Earl.

* Seathain is supposed to be John, therefore Johnson.

"I was on a time, and I could play a juggle," said he.

"Well, then, it is I myself that have the best juggler in the five-fifths of Eirinn, or the bridge of the first of the people, as is Taog Bratach Mac a Cheallaich, rascally Taog, the son of Concealment."

They got up the juggler.

"What," said the southern Earl, "is the trick that thou canst do, Dust of Dust?"

"Well, I was on a time that I could bob my ear off my cheek," said he.

The Champion went and he takes the ear off the cheek.

Said rascally Taog, the son of Concealment, "I could do that myself."

He went and he took down his ear, and up he could not bring it! but the Champion put up his own ear as it was before.

The Earl took much anger and rage that the ear should be off his juggler.

"For five merks twice over," said the Champion, "I would set the ear as it was before."

He got the five merks twice over, and he put the ear on the juggler as it was before.

"I see," said the Earl, "that the juggling of this night is with thee."

Rascally Taog went away; and though they should have staid there the length of the night, he would not have come near them.

Then the Champion went and he set a great ladder up against the moon, and in one place of it he put a hound and a hare, and in another place of it he put a carl and a girl. A while after that he opened first where he had put the hound and the hare, and the hound was eating the hare; he struck him a stroke of the edge of his palm, and cast his head off. Then he opened again where were the carl and the girl, and the carl was kissing the girl. He struck him a stroke of the edge of his palm, and he cast his head off.

"I would not for much," said the Earl, "that a hound and a carl should be killed at my court."

"Give five merks twice over for each one of them, and I will put the heads on them," said the Champion.

"Thou shalt get that," said the southern Earl.

He got the five merks twice over, and he put the head on the hound and the carl as they were before; and though they should be alive till now, the hound would not have touched a hare, nor the carl a girl, for fear their heads should be taken off.

On the morrow, after their meat in the morning, he went hunting with the Earl. When they were amongst the wood, they heard a loud voice in a knoll (or a bush).

"Be this from me," said Dust of Dust, "I must go to see the foot of the carl MacCeochd. He went out—

"And moved as sea-heaps o' sea-heaps,
And as playballs o' playballs;
As a furious winter wind—
So swiftly, sprucely, cheerily,
Right proudly,
Through glens and high tops,
And no stop made he
Until he reached
The house of the Carl MacCeochd."

He struck at the door. "Who's that?" said the carl MacCeochd.

"I," said he, "am the leech's lad."

"Well," said the carl, "many a bad black leech is coming, and they are not doing a bit of good to me."

"Give word to the carl that unless he will not let me in, I will be going," said the Champion.

"Let in the leech's lad; perhaps he is the one in whom is my help," said the carl MacCeochd.

They let him in.

"Rise up, carl MacCeochd, thou art free from thy sores," said the Champion.

Carl MacCeochd arose up, and there was not a man in Eirinn swifter or stronger than he.

"Lie down, carl MacCeochd, thou art full of sores," said the Champion.

The carl MacCeochd lay down, and he was worse than he ever was.

"Thou didst ill," said the carl MacCeochd, "to heal me and spoil me again."

"Thou man here," said the Champion, "I was but shewing thee that I could heal thee."

"I have," said the carl MacCeochd, "but the one daughter in the world, and thou shalt get her and half of all I have, and all my share when I go way, and heal my leg."

"It shall not be so, but send word for every leech that thou hast had, that I might get talking with them," said the leech's lad.

They sent word by running lads through the five-fifths of Eirinn for the leeches that were waiting on the carl, and they came, all thinking that they would get pay, and when they came riding to the house of the carl, the Champion went out and he said to them,

"What made you spoil the leg of the carl Mac-Ceochd, and set himself thus?"

"Well then," said they, "if we were to raise the worth of our drugs, without coming to the worth of our trouble, we would not leave him the worth of his shoe in the world.

Said the leech's lad, " I will lay you a wager, and that is the full of my cap of gold, to be set at the end of yonder dale, and that there are none in Eirinn that will be at it sooner than the carl MacCeochd."

He set the cap full of gold at the end of the dale, and the leeches laid the wager that that could never be.

He went in where the carl MacCeochd was, and he said to him,

" Arise, Carl MacCeochd, thou art whole of sores, I have laid a wager on thee."

The carl got up whole and healthy, and he went out, and he was at three springs at the cap of gold, and he left the leeches far behind.

Then the leeches only asked that they might get their lives. Promise of that they got not, (but) the leech's lad got in order.

He snatched his holly in his fist, and he seized the grey hand plane that was on the after side of his haunch, and he took under them, over them, through and amongst them ; and left no man to tell a tale, or earn bad tidings, that he did not kill.*

When the carl was healed he sent word for the nobles and for the great gentles of Eirinn to the wedding of his daughter and the Champion, and they were gathering out of each quarter.

" What company is there ?" said the leeches' lad.

" There is the company of thine own wedding, and they are gathering from each half and each side," said the carl MacCeochd.

" Be this from me !" said he ; " O'Conachar the Shelly (or of Sligo) has a year's service against me," and he put a year's delay on the wedding.

* This seems like mock heroics, an imitation of such tales as the Knight of the Red Shield and Murachadh MacBrian.

"Out he went as Voorveel o Voorveel
And as Veerevuil o Veerevuill,
As a furious winter wind,
So swiftly, sprucely, cheerily,
Right proudly,
Through glens and high tops,
And no stop did he make
Till he struck in the door
Of Conachar of Sligo."

" Who's that?" said O'Conachar of Sligo.

" I," said he, " Goodherd."

" Let in Goodherd," said O'Conachar of Sligo, for great is my need of him here."

They let him in.

" What couldst thou do here?" said O'Conachar.

" I am hearing," said he, to O'Conachar of Sligo, " that the chase is upon thee. If thou wilt keep out the chase, I will keep in the spoil," said Goodherd.

" What wages wilt thou take?" said O'Conachar of Sligo.

" The wages I will take is that thou shouldst not make half cups with me till the end of a day and year," said Goodherd.

O'Conachar made this covenant with him, and the herdsman went to herd.

The chase broke in on O'Conachar of Sligo, and they betook themselves to where the herdsman was, to lift the spoil. When the herdsman saw that they had broken in, he took the holly in his fist, and seized the grey hand-plane that was on the after side of his haunch, and left no man to tell a tale, or earn bad tidings, that he did not kill. He went into a herd's bothy, and he (was) hot, and he saw O'Conachar Sligheach just done drinking a boyne of milk and water.

"Witness, gods and men, that thou hast broken thy promise," said Goodherd.

"That fill is no better than another fill," said O'Conachar Sligheach.

"That selfsame fill thou didst promise to me," said Goodherd.

He took anger at O'Conachar Sligheach, and he went away, and he reached the house of the carl MacCeochd. The daughter of the carl made him a drink of green apples and warm milk, and he was choked.

And I left them, and they gave me butter on a cinder, porridge kail in a creel, and paper shoes; and they sent me away with a big gun bullet, on a road of glass, till they left me sitting here within.

AN CEATHAIRNEACH CAOL, RIABHACH.

Bha duine bochd a bha ann an Aird na h-Uamha a chòmhnuidh. agus rugadh mac dha, 's thug e sgoil a's ionnsachadh dha gus an robh e ceithir bliadhna deug a dh' aois thuirt e r'a athair, "Athair, 's mithidh dhomhsa 'bhith deànadh air mo shon fhèin; na'n d thugadh thu dhomh slat-iasgaidh as basgaid;" Fhuair an duine bochd a' h-uile cothrom gus an d' fhuair e slat-iasgaidh as basgaid da.

Nur a fhuair e'n t slat-iasgaidh 's a bhasgaid chaidh e ma'n cuairt Loch Aird na h-Uamha, 's ghabh e 'nuas Loch Thòrabais, 's an deigh dha Loch Thòrabais a chliabairt thàinig e gu Loch Phort an Eilean, 's an deigh dha Loch Phort an Eilean iasgach roimhe ghabh e 'mach Loch Allalaidh. Dh' fhan e 'san oidhche 'n Aird Eileastraidh, 's a' h-uile breac a bh' aige dh' fhàg e aig boireannach bochd a bha 'n sin eud.

An la'r na mhàireach smaointich e gu'n togadh e' mach agus gun d' thugadh e Eirinn air. Thàinig e gu gàrradh Aird Inneasdail agus spìon e leis sè ubhla deug, 's thàinig e'n sin gu Maol na h-Otha. Thilg e ubhal a mach 's an fhairge 's thug e ceum urra. Thilg e 'n ath tè agus thug e ceum eil' urra. Thilg e, mur seo, tè an deigh te, gus an d' thàinig e gus an t-seathamh tè deug, 's thug an t-seatho té deug air tir an Eirinn e.

Nur a bha e air tir chrath e chluasan, as smaointich e nach b' ann
an àite suarrach a dh' fhanadh e.

> Ghluais e mar mhuir-mhill o mhuir-mhill,
> 'S mar mhire-bhuill o mhire-bhuill;
> Mar ghaoith ghailbheach gheamhraidh,
> Gu sitheach, sothach, sauntach,
> Sàr-mheamnach,
> Tr̀d ghleanntan as ard-mhullach;
> 'S cha d' rinneadh stad leis
> Gus an d' thàinig e
> Gu cuirt Agus cathair O Domhnuill.
> Thug e leum sunndach soilleir
> Thar bàrr agus baideil
> Cùirt agus cathair
> O Domhnuill.

Ghabh O Dòmhnuill mòran feirg agus corruich a leithid de shru-
tha, dhona, ao-dhealbach a thighinn a stigh d' a chùirt, agus dorsair
a bhith aige fèin r'a bhaile.

"Cha chreid mi fèin," ars' an ceathairneach, "nach 'eil thu 'gabhail feirg agus corruich O Domhnuill?"

"Mata tha," ors' O Domhnuill, "na'm biodh fios agam co ris a
liginn a mach e?"

"A dhuine mhath," ors' an Ceathairneach, "cha b' fhasa dhomhsa
tighinn a stigh na dol e mach a rìs."

"Cha d' theid thu 'mach," ors' O Domhnuill, "gus an innis thu
dhomhsa co as a thàinig thu."

> Thàinig mi o ghriobhaill o ghrabhaill,
> O bhun an tobair dhùlinn,
> O ghleann àluinn ealaich;
> Oidhch' an Ile 's oidhch' am Manainn;
> Oidhch' air charna fuara faire;
> An aodann monaidh
> Am baile righ Alba
> Rugadh mi;
> Ceàrnach suarrach, salach mi,
> Gad thàrladh air a' bhaile seo mi.

"Dé," urs' O Domhnuill, "a cheathairnich a dhèanadh thusa? 's
cinnteach, 's na 'shiubhail thu 'dh' astar gu'n deanadh thu rudaigin."

"Bha mi uair," urs' esan, "agus sheinninn cruit."

"Mata," urs' O Domhnuill, "'s ann agam fèin a tha na cruitearan a 's fheàrr ann an còig chòigeamh na h-Eireann, na'n Drochaid-cheudan na Mith; mar a tha Ruairidh O Cridheagan, Tormaid O Giollogan, agus Taog O Chuthag."

"Cluinneam a' seinn eud," urs' an Ceathairneach. Thòisich na clàrsairean.

> Sheinneadh eud puirt, agus uirt, agus orgain,
> Nitheanna tearmad, teudan tairteil;
> Curaidhean, laoich, as aoig air an casan;
> Aoig, as àinn, as galair, as fiabhrais;
> Chuireadh eud 'nan sìon sioram suain
> An saoghal mòr gu léir,
> Le binnead nam port shìogaidh
> A sheinneadh na clàrsairean.

Cha do chòrd an ceòl ris a' Cheathairneach. Rug e air na clàrs-aichean, 's phrann e fo a chasan eud, 's chuir e air teinidh eud, 's rinn e gharadh, 's a chruaidh-gharadh riu.

Ghabh O Domhnuill mòran àrdain gun d' thànaig duine 'stigh do 'n chuirt aige 'dhèanadh a leithid seo air na clàrsaichean.

"Cha chreid mi fhéin a dhuine mhath nach 'eil thu 'gabhail corr-nich," ars' an Ceathairneach.

"Mata tha, nam biodh fhios'am co ris a liginn a mach e."

"Air 'ur n-ais a dhuine mhath! Cha b' fhasa dhomhsa do chlàrsaichean a bhrisdeadh na'n slànachadh a rìs!" ars' an Ceath-airneach.

"Bheir mi ni sam bith seachad airson an slànachadh a rìs," ars' O Domhnuill.

"Air chòig mhairg da uair ni mise do chlàrsaichean cho math 'sa bha eud roimhid," urs' an Ceathairneach.

"Gheibh thu sin," ars' O Domhnuill.

Thug O Domhnuill na mairg da agus rug e air làn a dha bhoise do 'n luaith, 's rinn e clàrsach do Ruairidh O Cridheagan, 's té do Thormaid O Giollagan, 's té do Thaog O Chuthag agus clàrs-ach mhòr, choirealach da fhé.

"Cluinneam do cheòl," ars' O Domhnuill.

"Cluinnidh tu sin a dhuine mhath," urs' an Ceathairneach.

Thòisich an Ceathairneach air seinn, as, och! b' e 'm balach air chùl na clàrsaich e!

> Sheinneadh e puirt, agus uirt, agus orgain,
> Nitheanna tearmad; teudan tairteil;
> Curaidhean, laoich, as aoig air an casan;
> Aoig, as àinn, as galair, as fiabhrais.

'S gun cuirte 'nan sìon sioram suain,
An saoghal mòr gu léir,
Le binnead a' phuirt shìogaidh,
A sheinneadh an Ceathairneach.

" 'S binn thus' a Cheathairnich," ars' O Domhnuill.

Nur a chuala na clàrsairean an Ceathairneach a' seinn thùg eud seombar 'eil' orra, 's gad a leanadh e fhathasd cha d' thigeadh eud an làthair.

Dh' fhalbh O Domhnuill 's chuir e còmhnainn bhìdh thun a Ceathairnich.

"Abraibh ris an duine mhath nach bi 'n uibhir sin aige r'a mhùigheadh ormsa nur a dh' fhuolbhas mi air a' mheadhon lath' am máireach," urs' an Ceathairneach.

Ghabh O Domhnuill moran àrdain a leithid de dhuine 'thighinn a staigh d'a chùirt, 's naeh gabhadh e biadh uaidh. Chuir e nìos léin' air ialtan 's madal donnain. "Cà' 'bheil seo a' dol?" urs' an Ceathairneach. "A t' ionnsuidh-sa, 'Cheathairneach," urs' eudsan. "Abraibh-se ris an duine mhath nach bi 'n uibhir sin aige r'a mhùigheadh ormsa nur a dh' fholbhas mi air a' mheadhan lath' an la'r na mhàireach," urs' an Ceathairheach. Ghabh O Domhnuill mòran feirg agus cormich, a leithid de dhuine 'thighinn a staigh d'a chùirt, 's nach gabhadh, e aona-chuid, biadh na aodach uaidh. Chuir e 'nìos còig ciad galloglach a dh' fhaire 'Cheathairnich, air alt 's nach biodh masladh air a thoirt do dh' O Domhnuill le e 'dhol a mach, rathad sam bith, ach air an dorus."

"Cà' 'bheil sibhse 'dol?" ars' an Ceathairneach.

"A t' fhaire-sa 'Cheathairnich, air alt 's nach fhalbh thu, 'thoirt masladh do dh' O Domhnuill, gun do ligeil a mach ach mar is còir duit," urs' eudsan.

"Laidhibh sios ann an sin," ars' an Ceathairneach, " 's nur a bhios mise 'g imeachd bheir mi fios duibh."

Ghabh eud a chomhairle, 's laidh eud sìos làmh ris, 's nur a bhrisd am fàire chaidh an Ceathairnich 'na éideadh.

"Càite 'bheil mo luchd faire-sa, tha mi 'g imeachd," ars' na Ceathairneach.

"Na 'n carachadh thu," urs' an gall-oglach mòr, "dhèanainn crupan geur, goirt dhiot leis a' bhòrd-urchair so a'm' làimh."

Leum an Ceathairneach air barraibh a phuthag 's chaidh e thar barr agus baideil cùirt agus cathair O Domhnuill. Thilg an galloglach am bòrd-urchair a bha 'na laimh, 's mharbh e ceithir pearsanna fichead de dh' fhìor-mhuinntir O Domhnuill.

Co 'choinnich an Ceathairneach ach gille-leantainn O Domhnuill, 's thuirt e ris, " Seo dhuit luigh bheag, bhiorach, ghlas, 's theirig a staigh, 's rub ri bilean na feadhnach a mharbhadh i, 's thoir beò cud, 's coisinn duit fhéin fichead mart laoigh, 's amhairc as do dhéigh, nur a dhealachas tu riumsa, co 'chi thu teachd."

Nur a rinn an gille-leantainn seo cha 'n fhac e neach a' teachd ; ach chunnaic e 'n Ceathairneach tri mìle deug an taobh thall de Luimineach.

Ghluais e mar mhuir-mhill o mhuir-mhill,
'S mar mhire-bhuill o mhire-bhuill ;
Mar ghaoith ghailbheach gheamhraidh,
Gu sitheach, sothach, sanntach,
Sàr-mheamnach,
Trìd ghleanntan as ard-mhullach ;
'S cha d' rinneadh stad leis,
Gus an d' ràinig e
Mac Seathain, an t-Iarl deas.

Bhuail e anns an dornsd. Thuirt MacSeathain an t-Iarl Deas ris, " Co siod 'san dornsd ?"

" Tha mise, Dùradan O Dùradan," urs' an Ceathairneach.

Thuirt MacSeathan, an t-Iarl Deas, " Ligibh a staigh Dùradan O Dùradan ; cha 'n fhaod neach a bhith a'm' dhornsd-sa 'bualadh gun faotainn a staigh."

Lig eud a staigh e " Dé 'dhèanadh thusa' Dhuradain O Dùradan?" ars' an t-Iarl Deas.

" Bha mi uair 's dhèanainn cleas," ars' esan.

" Mata 's ann agam fhéin a tha 'n aona chleasaiche 's fheàrr ann an còig chòigeamh na h-Eireann, na 'n Drochaid cheudan nam Mìth, mar a tha Taog pratach Mac a Cheallaich."

Fhuair eud a nìos an cleasaiche. " Dé," ursa 'n t-Iarl Deas, " an cleas a dhèanadh thusa, Dhuradain O Dùradan.

Mata bha mi uair 's bhogainn a' chluas bhàr mo leithcheinn," ars' esan.

Dh' fholbh an Ceathairneach 's thugar a' chluas bhàr a leithcheinn.

Orsa Taog pratach a' Cheallaich, " Dhèanainn fhéin sin."

Dh' fholbh e 's thug e 'nuas a chluas, 's a suas cha d' thugadh e i ! ach chuir an Ceathairneach a suas a chluas fhéin mar a bha roimhid !

Ghabh an t-Iarla mòran feirg agus corruich a' chluas a bhith d'a chleasaiche.

" Air chòig mhairg da uair," ars' an Ceathairneach, " chuirinn-sa 'chluas mar a bha i roimhid."

Fhuair e na còig mhairg da uair, 's chuir e 'chluas air' a chleasaiche mar a bha i roimhid.

" Tha mi 'faicinn," ars' an t-Iarla, " gur leat fhéin cleasachd na h-oidhche 'nochd."

Dh' fholbh Taog pratach, 's gad a dh' fhanadh eud an sin fad na h-oidhche, cha d' thigeadh e a 'n còir.

Dh' fholbh an Ceathairneach an sin, 's chuir e dreumaire mòr suas ris a' ghealaich ; 's chuir e ann an aon àite dheth cù agus gearraidh ; 's chuir e ann an àite eile dheth bodach agus caile. Treis as a dhéigh seo dh' fhosgail e, 'n toiseach, far an do chuir e 'n cù agus an gearradh ; 's bha 'n cù 'g itheadh a' ghearraidh. Bhuail e buille de dh' oir a bhois' oir a' chù, 's thilg e 'n ceann deth. Dh' fhosgail e rithisd far an robh am bodach 's a' chaile ; 's bha 'm bodach a' pògadh na caile. Bhuail e buille de dh' oir a bhois' air 's thilg e 'n ceann deth.

" Cha bu gheamha leam," ars' an t-Iarl, " air mòran, cù agus bodach a bhith air am marbhadh ann a' m' chùirt."

" Thoir còig mhairg da uair airson gach aon diu 's cuiridh mise na cinn orra 'rìs," urs' an Ceathairneach.

" Gheibh thu sin," ars' an t-Iarl Deas.

Fhuair e na còig mhairg da uair, 's chuir e 'n ceann air a' chù 's air a' bhodach mar a bha eud roimhid ; 's gad a bhiodh eud beò gus an seo, cha d' thugadh an cù làmh air gearraidh, na 'm bodach air caile, air eagal gun tug-te na cinn din.

An la 'r na mhàireach, an déigh am bidh, anns a' mhaidinn, chaidh e 'shealgaireachd leis an Iarla. Nur a bha eud feadh na coille chual eud coireal ann an tom.

" Bhuam seo," ursa Dùradan O Dùradan ! feumaidh mi dol a dh' amharc cas a' Bhodaich 'Ic Ceochd.

> Ghabh e 'mach,
> 'S ghluais e mar mhuir-mhill o mhur-mhill,
> 'S mar mhire-bhuill o mhire-bhuill ;
> Mar ghaoith ghailbheach gheamhraidh,
> Gu sitheach, sothach, sanntach,
> Sàr-mheamnach,
> Trìd ghleanntan as ard-mhullach ;
> Agus stad cha d' rinneadh leis,
> Gus an d' ràinig e,
> Taigh a' Bhodaich 'Ic Ceochd.

Bhuail e anns an dorusd. "Co siod ?" urs' am Bodach Mac Ceochd.
" Mis?" urs' esan, "Gill' an Leigh."

"Mata," urs' am bodach, "'s iomadh léigh dugh, dona 'tighinn,
's cha 'n 'eil cud a' dèanadh mir feum domhsa."

"Thugaibh fios do 'n bhodach, mar an lig e 'staigh mi, gu'm bi
mi 'g imeacnd," ars' an Ceathairneach.

"Ligibh a staigh Gill' an Léigh, cha lughaide gur h-ann ann a-
tha mo chobhair," ars' am Bodach Mac Ceochd.

Lig eud a staigh e.

"Eirich suas a Bhodaich 'Ic Ceochd, tha thu saor o chreuchdan,"
urs' an Ceathairneach.

Dh' éiridh am Bodach Mac Ceochd suas, 's cha robh duin' an
Eirinn a bu luaithe 's a bu làidireacha na e !

"Laidh sìos a Bhodaich 'Ic Ceochd tha thu làn chreuchdan,"
ars' an Ceathairneach. Laidh am Bodach Mac Ceochd sìos, 's bha e
na bu mhiosa na bha e riabh !

"'S olc a rinn thu," urs' am Bodach Mac Ceochd, "mo leigheas
agus mo mhilleadh a rìs."

"A dhuine seo," ursa Gill' an Léigh; "cha robh mi ach a'ligeil
fhaicinn duit gum b'urrainn mi do leigheas !"

"Cha 'n 'eil agam," urs' am Bodach Mac Ceochd, "ach an aon
nighean rìs an t-saoghal, 's geobh thu i, 's leith 's na th'agam, 's mo
chuid air fad nur a shiubhlas mi, agus leighis mo chas."

"Cha'n e sin mar a bhitheas, ach cuir fios air a' h-uile léigh a
bh'agad, 's gum fàighinn-sa 'bhith bruidhinn riutha," arsa Gill' an
Léigh !

Chuir eud fios le gillean-ruith, feadh chòig chàigeamh na h-
Eireann, airson nan lighichean a bha 'feitheamh air a' bhodaich; 's
thàinig eud air fad, a saoilsinn gu'faigheadh eud pàigheadh. Agus
nur a thàinig eud, a' marcachd gu taigh a' Bhodaich, chaidh an
Ceathcùrneach a mach 's thuirt e riu.

"Dé 'thug dhuibhse cas a' Bhodaich 'Ic Ceochd a mhilleadh, 's e
fhéin a chur fo ainbheach mur seo?"

"Mata," urs' eudsan, "na'n togamaide luach ar cungan, gun
tighinn air luach ar saoithreach, cha 'n fhàgamaid luach a bhròg aige
ris an t-saoghal."

Ursa Gill' an Leigh ! "Cuiridh mi geall ruibh; agus 's e sin
làn mo churraichd do dh' òr a chur aig ceann na dalach ud shuas,
's nach 'eil giu an Eirinn a bhios aige na 's luaithe na'm Bodach
Mac Ceochd !"

Chuir e'n currachd làn òir aig ceann na dalach; 's chuir na
leighean geall ris nach b'urrainn siod a bhith.

Chaidh e 'staigh far an robh 'm Bodach Mac Ceochd, 's thuirt e ris. "Eirich a Bhodaich 'Ic Ceochd, tha thu slàn O chreuchdan! Chuir mi geall as do leith." Dh' eiridh am Bodach Mac Ceochd gu slàn, fallan, s' chaidh e mach, 's bha e thri Ceumannan aig a' churr-achd òir, 's dh' fhàg e fad' air deireadh na leighean.

Cha d' iarr na leighean an seo ach na 'm faigheadh eud am beatha leo! Gealladh air a' siod cha d' fhuair eud! Chaidh gill' an leigh air dòigh!

Spàrr e 'chuilionn 'na dhorn, as ghlac e'n làmh-lochdair liath a bh' air taobh piar a thòine, 's thug e fòcha 's tharta, 's frìd as rompa; 's cha d' fhàg e fear innseadh sgeoil na chosnadh tuarasdail nach do mharbh e!

Nur a bha 'm bodach leighiste chuir e fios air maithibh 's air mòr-uaislean na h-Eireann thun banais a nighinn 's a' Cheathairnich, 's bha eud a' cruinneachadh as gach ceàrn.

"De 'chuideachd a tha 'n siod?" arsa Gill' an Leigh! "Tha 'n siod cuideachd na bàinns' agad fhein, 's eud a cruinneachadh as gach leith agus as gach taobh," urs' am Bodach Mac Ceochd. "Bhuam seo," ars' esan, "tha fasdadh bliadhn' aig O Conachar an Sligeach orm;" 's chuir e dàil bliadhna 's a' phòsadh.

> Ghabh e 'mach mar mhuir-mhill o mhuir-mhill,
> 'S mar mhirc-bhuill o mhire-bhuill;
> Mar ghaoith ghailbheach gheamhraidh;
> Gu sitheach, sothach, sanntach,
> Sàr-mheamnach,
> Trìd ghleanntan as ard-mhullach;
> 'S cha d' rinneadh stad leis,
> Gus an do bhuail e ann an dornsd
> O Conachar Sligeach.

"Co siod?" urs' O Conachar Sligeach. "Mis'," urs' esan, "Buachaille Math." "Ligibh a staigh Buach-aille Math," ars' O Conachar Sligeach;" chionn tha feum mòr agams' air anns an am seo."

Lig eud a staigh e.

"Dé 'dheanadh thusa 'Bhuachaill?" ors' O Conachar Sligeach.

"Tha mi 'cluinntinn," ors' e ri O Conachar Sligeach, "gu 'bheil an toir ort." "Tha," urs' O Conachar Sligeach. "Ma chumas tusa mach an tòir; cumaidh mise staigh a' chreach?" arsa Buachaille Math! "Dé 'n tuarasdal a ghabhas tu?" ars' O Conachar Sligeach.

"Se 'n tuarasdal a ghabhas mi, nach dèan thu leath-chomaith orm gu ceann lath' as bliadhna," arsa Buachaille Math!

Rinn O Conachar Sligeach an cùmhnanta seo ris. Chaidh am buachaille 'bhuachailleachd.

Bhrisd an tòir a staigh air O Conachar Sligeach, 's thug eud orra far an robh 'm buachaill' a thogail na creiche. Nur a chunnaic am buachaille gun do bhrisd eud a staigh, ghabh e 'chuilionn 'na dhorn, as ghlac e 'n lamh-lochdair liath a bh' air taobh piar a thòine; 's cha d' fhag e fear innseadh sgeoil na 'chosnadh tuarasdail an sin nach do mharbh e! Chaidh e staigh do bhothag àirich, agus e teith, 's chunnaic e O Conachar Sligeach an déigh miodar bùirn agus bainne 'chriochanachadh d'a òl.

"Fhiannis air dia 's air daoine gu 'n do bhrisd thu do ghealladh!" arsa Buachaille Math!

"Cha 'n fheàrr an làn 'ud na làn eile," ars' O Conachar Sligeach.

"An làn 'ud fhéin gheall thu dhomhsa," arsa Buachaille Math!

Ghabh e corrnich ri O Conachar Sligeach, 's dh' fholbh e 's ràinig e taigh a' Bhodaich 'Ic Ceochd. Rinn nighean a' bhodaich deoch dha de òh' ubhlan réim 's de bhainne blàth, 's thachdadh e.

'S dhealaich mise rin; 's thug eud dhomh im air eibhleig, 's brochan-càil an créileig, 's bròga pàipeir, 's chuir eud air folbh mi le peileir gunna-mhòir 'air rathad-mòr gloine gus an d' fhàg eud a'm' shuidhe 'staigh an seo mi.

SECOND VERSION.

THE HISTORY OF THE CEABHARNACH.

From John Campbell, Strath Gearloch, Ross-shire.

ON the day when O'DONULL came out to hold right and justice, he saw a young chap coming. His two shoulders were through his old SUAINAICHE (sleeping coat?) his two ears through his old AIDE hat, his two squat kick-er-ing tatter-y-shoes full of cold roadway-ish water, three feet of his sword sideways on the side of his haunch, after the scabbard had ended.

He blest with easy true-wise maiden's words.

O'Donull blest him in the like of his own words.

O'Donull asked him what was his art?

"I could do harping," said the Ceabharnach.

"There are twelve men with me," said O'Donull, "and we will go to look on them."

"I am willing to do that," said the Ceabharnach.

When they went in O'Donull asked them to begin. "Hast thou ever heard music, oh Ceabharnach, finer than that?"

"I came past by the Isle of Cold, and I did not hear a screech in it, that was more hideous than that."

"Wouldst thou play a harp thyself, Ceabharnach?" said O'Donull.

"Here is her player, and who should not play!"

"Give him a harp," said O'Donull.

"Well canst thou play a harp," said O'Donull.

"It is not as thou pleasest but as I please myself, since I am at work."

The music of the Ceabharnach put every harper O'Donull had asleep.

"I will be taking fare thee well," said the Ceabharnach to O'Donull.

"Thou wilt not do that to me," said O'Donull, "thou must awaken my men."

"I am going to take a turn through Eirinn," said the Ceabharnach, "if I come the way they will see, and if I come not they will be thus with thee."

He left him, and he met with one herding. "Thy master's harpers are asleep, and they will not wake till they are awakened. Go thou and awaken them, and thou wilt get what will make a rich man of thee?"

"How shall I do that?" said the herd.

"Take a tuft of that grass and dip it in water, and shake it on them, and thou wilt awaken them."

He left the man and he reached SEATHAN MOR MAC

AN LASRLE, great Seathan the son of the Earl, thirteen miles on the western side of Lumraig.

He saw a young chap coming, his two shoulders were through his old coat, his two ears through his old hat, his shoes full of cold roadway-ish water, three feet of his sword sideways on the side of his haunch after the scabbard was ended.

He asked him what was his trade? He said that he could do juggling.

"I have jugglers myself, we will go to look on them."

"I am willing enough," said the Ceabharnach.

"Shew thy juggling," said the great Seathan, "till we see it."

He put three straws on the back of his fist and he blew them off it.

"If I should get half five marks," said one of the king's lads, "I would make better juggling than that."

"I will give thee that," said the Ceabharnach.

He put three straws on the back of his fist and the fist went along with the straws.

"Thou art sore, and thou wilt be sore," said his master; "my blessing on the hand that gave it to thee."

"I will do other juggles for thee," said the Ceabharnach.

He caught a hold of his own ear, and he gave a pull at it.

"If I could get half five marks," said another of the king's lads, "I would make a better juggle than that."

"I will give thee that," said the Ceabharnach.

He gave a pull at the ear and the head came away with the ear.

"I am going away," said the Ceabharnach.

"Thou wilt not leave my set of men so."

"I am for taking a turn through Eirinn.   If I

come the way I will see them, and if I come not they will be so along with thee."

He went away, and he met with a man threshing in a barn. He asked him if his work could keep him up.

" It was no more than it could do."

" I," said the Ceabharnach, "will make thee a free man for thy life. There are two of thy master's lads, one with his fist off, and one with his head off. Go there and put them on again, and thy master will make thee a free man for life."

" With what shall I bring them alive ?"

" Take a tuft of grass, hold it in water, shake it on them, and thou wilt heal them."

He went away and he came to FEAR CHUIGEAMH MUGHA,* a nasty man that could not bear a man to go the way of his house, to look at him when he was taking his food. There were twelve men with axes at the outer gate, and twelve men of swords on the inner gate ; a porter at the great door.

They saw a young chap coming, his two shoulders through his old coat, his two ears through his old hat, his two squat kick-ering tatter-y shoes full of cold roadway-ish water.

He asked their license in to see Fear Chuigeamh Mugha.

One of them raised his axe to drive his head off, but so it was that he struck it on his own comrade.

They arose on each other till they killed each other ; and he came to the men of the sword, one raised his sword to strike off his head, but he cut the head off his comrade with it, and they all fell to slaying each other.

He reached the porter ; he caught him by the small of the legs, and he struck his head on the door.

* The man of Munster, Cuige mumhe.

He reached the great man as he sat at his dinner; he stood at the end of the board.

"Oh evil man," said the king, "great was thy loss before thou camest here," as he rose to catch hold of his sword to strike his head off. His hand stuck to the sword, and his seat stuck to the chair, and he could not rise; no more could his wife leave her own place. When he had done all he wished he went away, and he met a poor man that was travelling the world.

"If thou wilt take my advice," said the Ceabharnach, "I will make a lucky man of thee as long as thou art alive."

"How wilt thou do that?" said the man.

"The king and the queen are fast in their chairs; go thou and loose them, and the king will make a great man of thee."

"How shall I loose them?"

"Shake water on them and they will arise."

He went out of that, and he reached Rob Mac-Sheoic Mhic Lagain with a pain in his foot for seven years.

He struck palm to bar. The porter asked "Who was there?"

He said there was a leech.

"Many a leech has come," said the porter. "There is not a spike on the town without a leech's head but one, and may be it is for thy head that one is."

"It might not be," said the Ceabharnach. "Let me in."

"What is putting upon thee, Rob?" said the Ceabharnach.

"My foot is taking to me these seven years. She has beat the leech and leeches."

"Arise and stretch out thy foot with the stitch," said the Ceabharnach;" and let's try if thou canst catch the twelve leeches, or if the twelve leeches will catch thee."

He arose, no man could catch him ; and he himself could catch every other one.

"I have but one begotten, a champion of a girl, and I will give her to thee and half my realm."

" Be she good or bad," said the Ceabharnach, " let her be mine or thine."

An order was made for a wedding for the Ceabharnach ; but when they had got the wedding in order, he was swifter out of the town than a year-old hare. He came to TAOG O-CEALLAIDH, who was going to raise the spoil of CAILLICHE BUIDHNICHE.

A young chap was seen coming, his two shoulders through his old coat, his two ears through his old hat, his two squat kick-ering tatter-y shoes full of cold roadway-ish water, three feet of his sword sideways on the side of his haunch after the scabbard was ended.

" What's this that puts on thee ?" said the Ceabharnach. " Hast thou need of men ?"

" Thou wilt not make a man for me," said O-Ceallaidh.

"Shall I not get a man's share if I do a man's share ?"

" What's thy name ?" said Taog.

" There is on me (the name of) Ceabharnach Saothrach Suarach Siubhail—the servile sorry strolling kern."

" What art thou seeking for thy service ?"

" I am but asking that thou shouldst not forget my drink."

" Whence camest thou ?"

" From many a place ; but I am an Albanach."

They went to raise the raid of the carlin. They raised the spoil, but they saw the following coming.

" Be stretching out," said great Taog to the Ceabh-arnach, "Thou wilt not make thy legs at least. Whether wouldst thou rather turn the chase or drive the spoil with thy set of men ?"

" I would not turn the chase, but if the chase would turn, we would drive the spoil at least."

The Ceabharnach cut a sharp, hard whistle, and the drove lay down on the road.

He turned to meet them. He caught each one of the slenderest legs, and the biggest head, and he left them stretched legs on head. He returned after the spoil.

" Thyself and thy lot of men can hardly drive the spoil."

" The spoil will never get up," said Taog.

He cut a whistle : the drove got up, and he drove it home.

It happened that the great man forgot to give the first drink to the Ceabharnach.

" Mine is the half of the spoil," said the Ceabharn-ach.

" That is more than much for thee," said the king.

" Many a time was I," said the Ceabharnach, "and Murcha MacBrian hewing shields and splitting blades ; his was the half of the spoil, and mine was the other half."

" If thou art a comrade of that man, thou shalt have half the spoil," said Taog.

But he went away, and he left themselves and the spoil.

" Health be with thee, oh Ceabharnach. Arise not for ever."

EACHDRAIDH A' CHEABHARNAICH.

An latha 'n d' thàinig O Domhnuill a mach a chumail còir agus ceartais, chunnaic e òglach a' tighinn. Bha 'dha ghuallainn trìd a sheann suanaiche; a dha chluais trìd a sheann aide; a dha bhròig cheigeanach, bhreabanach, riobanach, làn a dh' uisge fuar ròdanach; tri troidhean dhe'n chlaidheamh air an taobh siar dhe 'thoin, an deigh dh'an scabard teireachduinn. Bheannaich e le briathraibh farasda, fìor-ghlic, mìne, maighdeana. Bheannaich O Domhnuill, dha air homain a bhriathraibh féin. Dh' fheòràich O Domhnuill deth ciod bu nòs da. "Dhèanainn clàrsaireachd," ars' an Ceabharnach. "Tha da fhear dheug agam fhéin," ars' O Domhnuill, "'s theid sinn a shealtainn orra." "Tha mi toileach sin a dheanamh," ars' an Ceabharnach.

An uair a chaidh iad a steach dh' iarr O Domhnuill orra tòiseachadh, 's thoisich iad. "An cual thu ceòl riamh, a Cheabharnaich a 's brèagha na sin?" ars' O Domhnuill. "Thàinig mi seachad air Ifrinn; 's cha chuala mi sgread innte 's gràinnde na sin!" ars' an Ceabharnach.

"An seinneadh tu féin cruit, a Cheabharnaich," ars' O Domhnuill.

"So a sheinneadair!—agus Cò nach seinneadair!! ars' an Ceabharnach!

"Thugaibh cruit dha," ars' O Domhnuill.

"Is math a sheinneas tusa cruit!" ars' O Domhnuill.

"Cha'n ann mar thogras tusa, ach mar a thogras mi féin; oir is mi 'tha 'g obair," ars' esan.

Chuir ceòl a Cheabharnaich na-h-uile clàrsair a bh' aig O Domhnuill 'na chadal.

"Bithidh mis' a' gabhail slàn leat," ars an Ceabharnach ri O Domhnull.

"Cha dèan thu sin ormsa," ars' O Domhnuill: "feumaidh tu mo dhaoine 'dhùsgadh."

"Tha mi 'd l a thoirt sgrìob feadh Eirinn," ars' an Ceabharnach; "ma thig mi 'n rathad chli iad, agus mur d' thig biodh iad mar sin agad féin."

Dh' fhàg se e agus thachair e air fear a buachailleachd.

"Tha clàrsairean do mhaighstir 'nan cadal," ars' an Ceabharnach ris a' bhuachaille," agus cha dùisg iad gus an dùisgear iad. Falbh thus' agus dùisg iad, 's gheibh thu na ni duine beartach dhìot"

"Cionnus a ni mi sin?" thuirt am buachaille.

"Gabh bad de'n fheur sin, agus tum ann an uisg' e, agus crath
orr' e, 's dùisgidh tu iad," ars' an Ceabharnach.   Dh'fhàg e'n duine,
's ràinig e s Seathan mòr Mac an Iarla, tri mìle deug an taobh siar
de Lunıraig.

Chunnaic e òglach a' tighinn.   Bha 'dha ghualainn trìol a sheann
suanaiche, a dha chluais trìol a sheann aide, a dha bhròig làn a dh'
uisge fuar, ròdanach, tri troidhean dhe 'n chlaidheamb air an taobh
siar dhe thòin, an déigh dh'an scabard teireachdainn.

Dh' fheoraich e dheth ciod bu nòs dha.   Tbuirt e gu'n dèanadh
e cleasachd.

"Tha cleasaichean agam fein; theid sinn a dh' amharc orra."

"Tha mi glé dheònach," ars' an Ceabharnach.

"Nochd do chleasachd," ars' an Seathan mòr," ach am faic sinn e.
Chuir e tri stràbhan air cùl a dhuirn agus shéid e dheth iad.

"Na 'm faighinn-sa," orsa fear de ghillean an rìgh," leith chùig
mhairg, dhèanainn cleasachd a b' fhearr na sin.

"Bheir mise sin duit," ars' an Ceabharnach.

Chuir e tri stràibhean air cùl a dhùirn, agus dh' fhalbh an dorn
maille ris na stràibhean.

"Tha thu goirt, agus bidh tu goirt," ars' a mhaighstir."   Mo
bheannachd air an làimh a thug dhuit e."

"Ni mi cleasachd eile dhuit," ars' an Ceabharnach.

Rug e air a' chluais aige féin, agus thug e tarruinn oirre.

"Na 'm faighinn-sa leith chùig mheirg," arsa fear e' de ghillean'
an rìgh, "dhèannain cleasachd a b' fheàrr na sin.

"Bheir mise sin duit," ars' an Ceabharnach.

Thug e tarruinn air a chluais, 's thàinig an ceann leis a chluais.

"Tha mi 'falbh," ars' an Ceabharnach.

"Cha 'n fhàg thu mo chuid daoine-sa agam mar sin."

"Tha mi 'dol a thoirt sgrìob feadh Eirinn; ma thig mi 'n rathad
chi mi iad, agus mar d' thig biodh iad mar sin agad féin," ars' an
Ceabharnach.

Dh' fhalbh e agus thachair e air duine 'bualadh ann an sabhal,
agus dh' fheòraich e dheth am b' urrainn 'obair a chumail suas.

"Cha mhòr nach b' uilear dhomh e," ars' am fear bualaidh.

"Ni mis'," ars an Ceabharnach, "duine saor dhìot ri d' bheò.
Tha dithis de ghillean do mhaighstir, 's fear 's an dorn dheth, agus
fear eile 's an cean deth; falbh thus' agus cuir orr' iad, 's ni do
mhaighstir duine saoibhir dhìot ri d' bheò."

"Co leis a bheir mi beò iad?" ars' am fear a bha 'bualadh.

"Gabh bad fodair; tum ann an uisg 'e, crath orr' e, agus ni thu
'n leigheas," ars' an Ceabharnach.

Dh' fhalbh e, agus thainig e gu fear chùigeamh Mhumha, duine mosach nach fuilingeadh do dhuine 'dhol rathad a thaighe; gu h-àraid an uair a bhiodh e 'gabhail a bhìdhe. Bha dha dheug a luchd thuadhan air a' gheata 'muigh; a dha dheug a luchd chlàidhean air a' gheata 'staigh; dorsair air an dorus mhòr.

Chunnaic iad òglach a' tighinn; a dha ghualainn trìd a sheann suanaiche; a dha chluais trid a sheann aide; a dha bhròig cheigean-ach, bhreabanach, riobanach, làn a dh' uisge fuar, rodanach.

Dh' iarr e 'chead orra 'staigh a dh' fhaicinn Fear Chuigeamh Mhumha. Thog fear dhiu a thuadh gus an ceann a chur dheth, ach 's ann a bhuail e air a chompanach i. Dh' éirich iad air a chéile, gus an do mharbh iad a chéile. Thàinig e gu luchd nan clàidhean. Thog fear a chlaidhe gus an ceann a chur dheth, ach ghearr e 'n ceann d'a chompanach, agus dh' eirich iad uile 'mharbhadh a chéile. Ràinig e 'n dorsair. Rug e air chaol chasan air agus bhuail e cheann ris an dorus. Ràinig e 'n Duine mòr, agus e 'na shuidhe aig a dhìthit. Sheas e aig ceann a' bhùird.

"O'Dhroch Dhuine!" ars' an rìgh, "bu mhòr do chall mu 'n d' thàinig thu 'n so!" agus e 'g éiridh 's a' breith air a' chlaidhe, gus a' cheann a thoirt deth. Lean a làmh ris a chlaidhe, agus lean a mhàs ris a' chaithir, agus cha b' urrainn a bhean a h-àite féin fhàgail.

An uair a rinn e na h-uile ni 'bu mhiann leis dh' fhalbh e, agus thachair e air duine bochd a bha 'falbh an t-saoghail. "Ma ghabhas tu mo chomhairle-sa," ars' an Ceabharnach ris an duine bhochd, "ni mi duine sona dhìot fhad 's is beò thu."

"Cionnus a ni thu sin?" ars' an duine bochd.

"Tha 'n rìgh agus a' bhan-righ le 'm màsan ceangailte ri 'n caith-richean; falbh thus' agus fuasgail iad, agus ni 'n rìgh duine mòr dhìot," ars' an Ceabharnach.

"Cionnus a dh' fhuasglas mis' iad?" ars' an duien bochd.

"Crath uisg' orra agus eirìdh iad," ars' an Ceabharnach.

"Dh' fhalbh e as a' sin, agus ràinig e Rob Mac Shcoic Mhic a' Lagain, agus e fuidh eucail 'na chois fad sheachd bliadhna. Bhuail' e bas ri crann. Dh' fheòraich an dorsair co 'bh' ann. Thuirt esan gu 'robh leighiche.

"'S iomadh leighiche 'thàinig," ars' an dorsair; "cha 'n eil ceann stob 's a' bhaile gun cheann leighich' ach an t-aon; agus, dh' fhaododh e 'bhith gur h-ann airson do chinn-sa 'tha 'm fear sinn."

"Cha 'n fhaodadh," ars' an Ceabharnach; "leig a stigh mi."

"Ciod a tha 'cur ort a Rob?" ars' an Ceabharnach.

"Tha, mo chas a' gabhail rium o cheann sheachd bliadhna. Dh'

fhairtlich i air leigh agus leighichean," arsa Rob Mac Sheoic 'Ic a'
Lagain.

"Sin do chas uait," ars' an Ceabharnach, "dh' fheuchainn am
beir thu air an da leigh dheug, no 'm beir an da leigh dheug ort."

Dh' eirich e. Cha bheireadh duine sam bith airsan, agus bheireadh e fein air na h-uile fear eile!

"Cha 'n eil agam ach aon-ghin buadhach nighinn," orsa Rob,
"agus bheir mi dhuit i, agus leith mo rioghachd."

"Math no olc i," ars' an Ceabharnach, "bidh agamsa no agad
fein."

Chaidh àrd a chur air banais do 'n Cheabharnach; ach 'nuair a
bha iad an deign a' bhanais ullachadh, bu luaith' e as a' bhaile na
geàrr-bhliadhnach. Thàinig e gu Taog mòr O Ceallaidh, agus e
'dol a thogail creach na bailliche Buidhniche.

> Chunncas òglach a' tighinn,
> A dha ghualainn trìd a sheann suanaiche;
> A dha chluais trìd a sheann aide;
> A dha bhròig cheigeanach, bhreabanach, riobauach,
> Làn a dh' uisge fuar, rodanach;
> Tri troidhean dhe 'n chlaidheamh
> Air an taobh siar d'a dheireadh.
> An déigh do 'n truaill teireachdainn.

"Ciod so 'tha 'cur ort?" ars' an Ceabharnach ri Taog mor O
Ceallaidh, 'Am bheil feum dhaoin' ort?"

"Cha dèan thusa duine dhomh," ars' O Ceallaide.

"Nach faigh mi cuid fir ma ni mi cuid fir?" ars' an Ceabharnach.

"C' ainm a th' ort?" arsa Taog.

"Tha Ceabharnach saothrach, suarach siubhail orm," ars' esan.

"Ciod a tha thu 'g iarraidh airson do sheirbhis?" arsa Taog.

"Cha 'n 'eil ach gun thu 'dhèanamh dearmad dibh' orm," ars' an
Ceabharnach.

"Co as a thàinig thu?" arsa Taog.

"A iomadh àit', ach is Albannach mi," ars' esan.

Dh' fholbh iad a thogail creach na cailliche. Thog iad a' chreach,
ach chunnaic iad an tòir a' tighinn.

"Bi 'sìneadh as," arsa Taog mòr ris a' Cheabharnach. "Cha
dean thusa do chasan co-dhiu. Co 'is fèarr leat an tòir a philleadh
na 'chreach iomain le d' chuid daoine."

"Cha phillear an toir ach na 'm pilleadh an toir dh' iom-
aineamaid a' chreach co-dhiu."

Gheàrr an Ceabbarnach fead chaòl, chruaidh, 's luidh a chreach air an rathad-mhor. Phill e 'n coinneamh na toir.

Rug e air na h-uile fear a bu chaoile cas agus a bu mho ceann, 's dh' fhàg e iad 'nan sineadh cas air cheann. Phill e 'n déidh na creiche.

" Is dona 'dh' iomaineas tu féin agus do chuid daoine chreach," ars' an Ceabbarnach.

" Cha 'n éirich a' chreach gu bràth," arsa Taog.

Ghearr e fead, 's dh' éirich a' chreach, 's dh' iomain e dhach-aidh iad.

Thachair gu 'n do dhearmaid an Duine mor an dibh a thoirt air tùs do 'n Cheabharnach.

" Is leamsa leith na creiche," ars' an Ceabharnach.

" Tha 'n sin tuilleadh a's cus duit " ars' an rìgh.

" Is minig a bha mis'," ars' an Ceabbarnach, " agus Murchadh MacBrian a' gearradh sgiath 's a' sgoltadh lann ; bu leis-san leith eile," ars' an Ceabharnach.

" Ma 's companach thu do 'n duine sin gheibh thu leith na creiche," arsa Taog.

Ach dh' fhalbh e, 's dh' fhàg e iad féin agus a' chreach.

Slàn leat a' Cheabharnaich ; na eirich gu bràth.

3. A third version of this curious tale was told to me in South Uist, by MacPhie. It was very like the version told by James Wilson, blind fiddler in Islay.

It is evidently a composition fallen to bits, and mended with prose, and it is equally clear that it points to Ireland, though the hero was made a Scotchman by the three old men.

As a picture of bygone manners, this is curious, and I know nothing at all like it in any collection of popular tales.

I believe it to be some bardic recitation half-forgotten. It is said that in the mouth of one reciter in Islay, the story used to last for four hours.

I lately (September 1860) heard MacPhie repeat his version in part. It was a mixture of the two versions here given, and a fifth, Irish grandee, was added.

XVIId.

THE TALE OF THE SHIFTY LAD,
THE WIDOW'S SON.

From John Dewar, Arrochar, June 1860.

THERE was at some time or other before now a
widow, and she had one son. She gave him good
schooling, and she was wishful that he should choose
a trade for himself; but he said he would not go to
learn any art, but that he would be a thief.

His mother said to him, "If that is the art that
thou art going to choose for thine ownself, thine end is
to be hanged at the bridge of Baile Cliath,* in Eirinn.

But it was no matter, he would not go to any art,
but to be a thief; and his mother was always making
a prophecy to him that the end of him would be,
hanging at the Bridge of Baile Cliath, in Eirinn.

On a day of the days, the widow was going to the
church to hear the sermon, and was asking the Shifty
Lad, her son, to go with her, and that he should give
over his bad courses; but he would not go with her;
but he said to her, "The first art of which thou hear-
est mention, after thou hast come out from the sermon,
is the art to which I will go afterwards."

She went to the church full of good courage,
hoping that she would hear some good thing.

* Dublin.

He went away, and he went to a tuft of wood that was near to the church ; and he went in hiding in a place where he could see his mother when she should come out of the church; and as soon as she came out he shouted, " Thievery ! thievery ! thievery !" She looked about, but she could not make out whence the voice was coming, and she went home. He ran by the way of the short cut, and he was at the house before her, and he was seated within beside the fire when she came home. He asked her what tale she had got ; and she said that she had not got any tale at all, but that " thievery, thievery, thievery, was the first speech she heard when she came out of the church."

He said "That was the art that he would have."

And she said, as she was accustomed to say, " Thine ending is to be hanged at the bridge of Baile Claith, in Eirinn."

On the next day, his mother herself thought, that as nothing at all would do for her son but that he should be a thief, that she would try to find him a good aid-to-learning ; and she went to the gadaiche dubh of Aachaloinne, the black gallows bird of Aachaloinne, a very cunning thief who was in that place ; and though they had knowledge that he was given to stealing, they were not finding any way for catching him. The widow asked the Black Rogue if he would take her son to teach him roguery. The Black Rogue said, " If he were a clever lad that he would take him, and if there were a way of making a thief of him that he could do it ; and a covenant was made between the Black Rogue and the Shifty Lad

When the Shifty Lad, the widow's son, was making ready for going to the Black Rogue, his mother was giving him counsel, and she said to him, " It is against my will that thou art going to thievery ; and I

Y

was telling thee, that the end of thee is to be hanged at the bridge of Baile Cliath, Eirinn;" but the Shifty Lad went home to the Black Rogue.

The Black Rogue was giving the Shifty Lad every knowledge he might for doing thievery; he used to tell him about the cunning things that he must do, to get a chance to steal a thing; and when the Black Rogue thought that the Shifty Lad was good enough at learning to be taken out with him, he used to take him out with him to do stealing; and on a day of these days the Black Rogue said to his lad,

"We are long enough thus, we must go and do something. There is a rich tenant near to us, and he has much money in his chest. It was he who bought all that there was of cattle to be sold in the country, and he took them to the fair, and he sold them; he has got the money in his chest, and this is the time to be at him, before the people are paid for their lot of cattle; and unless we go to seek the money at this very hour, when it is gathered together,* we shall not get the same chance again."

The Shifty Lad was as willing as himself; they went away to the house, they got in at the coming on of the night, and they went up upon the loft,† and they went in hiding up there; and it was the night of SAMHAIN, Halloween; and there assembled many people within to keep the Savain hearty as they used to do. They sat together, and they were singing songs, and at fun burning the nuts;‡ and at merry-making.

The Shifty Lad was wearying that the company

* Bound to each other.
† The loft meant, is the space in the roof of a cottage which is above the rafters, and is used as a kind of store.
‡ See Dewar's note at the Gaelic for his account of this.

was not scattering; he got up and he went down to
the byre, and he loosed the bands off the necks of the
cattle, and he returned and he went up upon the loft
again. The cattle began goring each other in the byre,
and roaring. All that were in the room ran to keep
the cattle from each other till they could be tied again :
and in the time while they were doing this, the Shifty
Lad went down to the room and he stole the nuts with
him, and he went up upon the loft again, and he lay
down at the back of the Black Rogue.

There was a great leathern hide at the back of the
Black Rogue, and the Shifty Lad had a needle and
thread, and he sewed the skirt of the Black Rogue's
coat to the leathern hide that was at his back ; and
when the people of the house came back to the dwelling room again, their nuts were away ; and they were
seeking their nuts ; and they thought that it was some
one who had come in to play them a trick that had
taken away their nuts, and they sat down at the side
of the fire quietly and silently.

Said the Shifty Lad to the Black Rogue, " I will
crack a nut."

" Thou shalt not crack (one)," said the Black
Rogue ; " they will hear thee, and we shall be
caught."

Said the Shifty Lad, " I never yet was a Savain
night without cracking a nut," and he cracked one.

Those who were seated in the dwelling-room heard
him, and they said,

" There is some one up on the loft cracking our
nuts, we will go and catch them."

When the Black Rogue heard that, he sprang off
the loft and he ran out, and the hide dragging at the
tail of his coat. Every one of them shouted that there
was the Black Rogue stealing the hide with him. The

Black Rogue fled, and the people of the house after
him ; and he was a great distance from the house before he got the hide torn from him, and (was able) to
leave them. But in the time that the people of the
house were running after the Black Rogue, the Shifty
Lad came down off the loft ; he went up about the
house, he hit upon the chest where the gold and the
silver was ; he opened the chest, and he took out of it
the bags in which the gold and silver was, that was in
the chest ; and he took with him a load of the bread
and of the butter, and of the cheese, and of everything
that was better than another which he found within ;
and he was gone before the people of the house came
back from chasing the Black Rogue.

When the Black Rogue reached his home, and he
had nothing, his wife said to him, " How hast thou
failed this journey ? "

Then the Black Rogue told his own tale ; and he
was in great fury at the Shifty Lad, and swearing that
he would serve him out when he got a chance at him.

At the end of a little while after that, the Shifty
Lad came in with a load upon him.

Said the wife of the Black Rogue, " But, I fancy
that thou art the better thief ! "

The Black Rogue said not a word till the Shifty
Lad shewed the bags that he had full of gold and silver ; then, said the Black Rogue, " But it is thou that
wert the smart lad ! "

They made two halves of the gold and silver, and
the Black Rogue got the one half, and the Shifty Lad
the other half. When the Black Rogue's wife saw the
share that came to them, she said, " Thou thyself art
the worthy thief ! " and she had more respect for him
after that, than she had for the Black Rogue himself.

At the end of a few weeks after that, a wedding

was to be in the neighbourhood; and it was the custom of the country, when any who were well off were
asked, that they should send some gift or other to the
people of the wedding. There was a rich tenant, and
he was asked; and he desired his herd to go to the
mountain moor and bring home a wether for the people
of the wedding. The herd went up the mountain and
he got the wether, and he was going home with it :
and he had it on his back when he was going past the
house of the Black Rogue.

Said the Shifty Lad to his master, "What wager
wilt thou lay that I do not steal the wether from the
back of that man yet, before he reaches the house."

Said the Black Rogue, "I will lay thee a wager of
a hundred marks that thou canst not ; how shouldst
thou steal the thing that is on his back !"

"Howsoever I do it, I will try it," said the Shifty Lad.

"Well, then, if thou dost it," said the Black
Rogue, "I will give thee a hundred marks."

"It is a bargain," said the Shifty Lad ; and with
that he went away after the herd.

The herd had to go through a wood, and the Shifty
Lad took the ground that was hidden from him until
he got before him ; and he put some dirt in his shoe,
and he set his shoe on the road before the herd, and
he himself went in hiding ; and when the herd came
forward, and he saw the shoe, he said, "But thou art
dirty, and though thou art, if thy fellow were there I
would clean thee ;" and he went past.

The Shifty Lad lifted the shoe, and he ran round
about and he was before the herd, and he put his other
shoe on the road before him. When the herd came
forward and saw the other shoe on the road before
him, he said to himself, "But there is the fellow of the
dirty shoe."

He set the wether on the ground, and he said to himself, "I will return back now, and I will get the dirty shoe, and I will clean it, and I shall have two good shoes for my trouble; and he ran swiftly back again.

The Shifty Lad ran swiftly, and he stole with him the wether, and he took with him the two shoes; and he went home to his master, and he got a hundred marks from his master.

The herd went home and he told his own master himself how it had befallen him. His master scolded the herd; and the next day he sent him again up the mountain to seek a kid, instead of the wether he had lost.

The herd went away to the hill and he got hold of a kid, and he tied it; he put it on his back, and he went away to go home with it. The Shifty Lad saw him, and he went to the wood, and he was there before the herd; and he went in hiding, and he began at bleating like the wether. The herd thought that it was the wether that was in it; and he put the kid off him, and he left it at the side of the road, and he went to seek the wether. At the time when the herd was seeking the wether, the Shifty Lad went and he stole the kid with him, and he went home with it to the Black Rogue.

When the herd went back to where he had left the kid, the kid was gone, the kid was not in it; he sought the kid, and when he could not find the kid, he went home and he told his master how it had befallen him; and his master scolded him, but there was no help for it.

On the next day the tenant asked his herd to go up the mountain and bring home a stot; to be sure that he did not lose it. The herd went up the mountain, and he got a good fat stot, and he was driving it home. The Shifty Lad saw him, and he said to the Black Rogue,

"Tugain, come along, and we will go and try to steal the stot from the herd when he is going through the wood with it."

The Black Rogue and the Shifty Lad went away to the wood before the herd ; and when the herd was going through the wood with the stot, the Black Rogue was in the one place baa-ing, and the shifty lad in another bleating like a goat. The herd heard them, and he thought that he would get the wether and the kid again. He tied the stot to a tree, and went all about the wood seeking the wether and the kid, and he sought them till he was tired. While he was seeking the wether and the kid, the Shifty Lad went, and he stole with him the stot, and he took it home with him to the house of the Black Rogue. The Black Rogue went home after him, and they killed the stot, and they put it in hiding, and the Black Rogue's wife had good puddings for them that night. When the herd came back to the tree where he had left the stot tied, the stot was not there. He knew that the stot had been stolen. He went home and he told his master how it had happened, and his master scolded him, but there was no help for it.

On the next day his master asked the herd to go up the mountain and to bring home a wether, and not let it come off his back at all till he should come home, whatever he might see or hear. The herd went away, and he went up the mountain and he got the wether, and he succeeded in taking that wether home.

The Black Rogue and the Shifty Lad went on stealing till they had got much money, and they thought that they had better buy a drove (of cattle) and go to the fair with it to sell, and that people would think that it was at drovering they had made the money that they had got. The two went, and they bought a great drove of cattle, and they went to a fair that was far on the way from them. They sold the drove, and they got the money for them, and they went away to go home. When they were on the way, they saw a gallows on the top of a hill, and the Shifty Lad said to the Black Rogue, " Come up till we see the gallows ; some say that the gallows is the end for the theives at all events."

They went up where the gallows was, and they were looking all about it. Said the Shifty Lad, " Might we not try what kind of death is in the gallows, that we may know what is before us, if we should be caught at roguery. I will try it myself first."

The Shifty Lad put the cord about his own neck, and he said to the Black Rogue, " Here, draw me up, and when I am tired above, I will shake my legs, and then do thou let me down.

The Black Rogue drew the cord, and he raised the Shifty Lad aloft off the earth, and at the end of a little blink the Shifty Lad shook his legs, and the Black Rogue let him down.

The Shifty Lad took the cord off his neck, and he he said to the Black Rogue, " Thou thyself hast not ever tried anything that is so funny as hanging. If thou wouldst try once, thou wouldst have no more fear for hanging. I was shaking my legs for delight, and thou wouldst shake thy legs for delight too if thou wert aloft."

Said the Black Rogue, " I will try it too, so that I may know what it is like."

" Do," said the Shifty Lad ; " and when thou art tired above, whistle and I will let thee down."

The Black Rogue put the cord about his neck, and the Shifty Lad drew him up aloft ; and when the Shifty Lad found that the Black Rogue was aloft

6

THE TALE OF THE SHIFTY LAD.

against the gallows, he said to him, " Now, when thou
wantest to come down, whistle, and if thou art well
pleased where thou art, shake thy legs."

When the Black Rogue was a little blink above,
he began to shake his legs and to kick ; and the Shifty
Lad would say, "Oh ! art thou not funny ! art thou
not funny ! art thou not funny ! When it seems to
thee that thou art long enough above whistle."

But the Black Rogue has not whistled yet. The
Shifty Lad tied the cord to the lower end of the tree
of the gallows till the Black Rogue was dead ; then he
went where he was, and he took the money out of his
pouch, and he said to him, " Now, since thou hast no
longer any use for this money, I will take care of it
for thee." And he went away, and he left the Black
Rogue hanging there. Then he went home where was
the house of the Black Rogue, and his wife asked
where was his master ?

The Shifty Lad said, " I left him where he was,
upraised above the earth."

The wife of the Black Rogue asked and asked him
about her man, till at last he told her, but he said to
her, that he would marry her himself. When she
heard that, she cried that the Shifty Lad had killed
his master, and he was nothing but a thief. When
the Shifty Lad heard that he fled. The chase was set
after him ; but he found means to go in hiding in a
cave, and the chase went past him. He was in the
cave all night, and the next day he went another way,
and he found means to fly to Eirinn.

He reached the house of a wright, and he cried at
the door, " Let me in."

" Who art thou ?" said the wright.

" I am a good wright, if thou hast need of such,"
said the Shifty Lad.

The wright opened the door, and he let in the Shifty Lad, and the Shifty Lad began to work at carpentering along with the wright.

When the Shifty Lad was a day or two in their house, he gave a glance thither and a glance hither about the house, and he said, " O choin ! what a poor house you have, and the king's store-house so near you."

" What of that," said the wright.

" It is," said the Shifty Lad, " that you might get plenty from the king's store-house if you yourselves were smart enough."

The wright and his wife would say, " They would put us in prison if we should begin at the like of that."

The Shifty Lad was always saying that they ought to break into the king's store-house, and they would find plenty in it ; but the wright would not go with him ; but the Shifty Lad took with him some of the tools of the wright, and he went himself and he broke into the king's store-house, and he took with him a load of the butter and of the cheese of the king, and he took it to the house of the wright. The things pleased the wife of the wright well, and she was willing that her own husband should go there the next night. The wright himself went with his lad the next night, and they got into the storehouse of the king, and they took with them great loads of each thing that pleased them best of all that was within in the king's storehouse.

But the king's people missed the butter and the cheese and the other things that had been taken out of the storehouse, and they told the king how it had happened.

The king took the counsel of the Seanagal about the best way of catching the thieves and the counsel

that the Scanagal gave them was that they should set
a hogshead of soft pitch under the hole where they were
coming in.   That was done, and the next night the
Shifty Lad and his master went to break into the king's
storehouse.

The Shifty Lad put his master in before him, and
the master went down into the soft pitch to his very
middle, and he could not get out again.   The Shifty
Lad went down, and he put a foot on each of his master's shoulders, and he put out two loads of the king's
butter and of the cheese at the hole ; and at the
last time, when he was coming out, he swept the head
off his master, and he took the head with him, and he
left the trunk in the hogshead of pitch, and he went
home with the butter and with the cheese, and he took
home the head, and he buried it in the garden.

When the king's people went into the storehouse,
they found a body without a head in the hogshead of
pitch ; but they could not make out who it was.   They
tried if they could find any one at all that could know
him by the clothes, but his clothes were covered with
pitch so that they could not make him out.   The king
asked the counsel of the Seanagal about it ; and the
counsel that the Scanagal gave was, that they should
set the trunk aloft on the points of the spears of the
soldiers, to be carried from town to town, to see if they
could find any one at all that would take sorrow for it ;
or to try if they could hear any one that would make
a painful cry when they should see it ; or if they
should not see (one crying) one that should seem about
to make a painful cry when the soldiers should be going past with it.   The body was taken out of the hogshead of pitch, and set on the points of the spears ; and
the soldiers were bearing it aloft on the points of their
long wooden spears, and they were going from town to

town with it; and when they were going past the house
of the wright, the wright's wife made a tortured scream,
and swift the Shifty Lad cut himself with the adze;
and he kept saying to the wright's wife, "The cut is
not so bad as thou thinkest."

The commander-in-chief, and his lot of soldiers,
came in and they asked,

"What ailed the housewife?"

Said the Shifty Lad, "It is that I have just cut
my foot with the adze, and she is afraid of blood;" and
he would say to the wife of the wright, "Do not be so
much afraid; it will heal sooner than thou thinkest."

The soldiers thought that the Shifty Lad was the
wright, and that the wife whom they had was the wife
of the Shifty Lad; and they went out, and they went
from town to town; but they found no one besides,
but the wife of the wright herself that made cry or
scream when they were coming past her.

They took the body home to the king's house;
and the king took another counsel from his Scanagal,
and that was to hang the body to a tree in an open
place, and soldiers to watch it that none should take it
away, and the soldiers to be looking if any should
come the way that should take pity or grief for it.

The Shifty Lad came past them, and he saw them;
he went and he got a horse, and he put a keg of whisky
on each side of the horse in a sack, and he went past
the soldiers with it, as though he were hiding from them.
The soldiers thought that it was so, that he had taken
something away from them, or that he had something
which he ought not to have; and some of them ran after
him and they caught the old horse and the whisky; but
the Shifty Lad fled, and he left the old horse and the
whisky with them. The soldiers took the horse and
the kegs of whisky back to where the body was hang-

ing against the mast. They looked what was in the
kegs ; and when they understood that it was whisky
that was in them, they got a drinking cup, and they
began drinking until at last every one of them was
drunk, and they lay and they slept. When the Shifty
Lad saw that, that the soldiers were laid down and
asleep and drunk, he returned and he took the body
off the mast. He set it crosswise on the horse's back,
and he took it home ; then he went and he buried
the body in the garden where the head was.

When the soldiers awoke out of their sleep, the
body was stolen away ; they had for it but to go and
tell it to the king. Then the king took the counsel of
the Seanagal ; and the Seanagal said to them, all that
were in his presence, that his counsel to them was, to
take out a great black pig that was there, and that
they should go with her from town to town ; and when
they should come to any place where the body was
buried, that she would root it up. They went and
they got the black pig, and they were going from farm
to farm with her, trying if they could find out where
the body was buried. They went from house to house
with her till at last they came to the house where the
Shifty Lad and the wright's widow were dwelling.
When they arrived they let the pig loose about the
grounds. The Shifty Lad said that he himself was sure
that thirst and hunger was on them ; that they had
better go into the house and that they would get meat
and drink ; and that they should let their weariness
from off them, in the time when the pig should be
seeking about his place.

They went in, and the Shifty Lad asked the
wright's widow that she should set meat and drink before the men. The widow of the wright set meat and
drink on the board, and she set it before them ; and

in the time while they were eating their meat, the Shifty Lad went out to see after the pig; and the pig had just hit upon the body in the garden; and the Shifty Lad went and he got a great knife and he cut the head off her, and he buried herself and her head beside the body of the wright in the garden.

When those who had the care of the pig came out, the pig was not to be seen. They asked the Shifty Lad if he had seen her; he said that he had seen (her), that her head was up and she was looking up-wards, and going two or three steps now and again; and they went with great haste to the side where the Shifty Lad said that the pig had gone.

When the Shifty Lad found that they had gone out of sight, he set everything in such a way that they should not hit upon the pig. They on whom the care of the pig was laid went and they sought her every way that it was likely she might be. Then when they could not find her, they had for it but to go to the king's house and tell how it had happened.

Then the counsel of the Scanagal was taken again; and the counsel that the Scanagal gave them was, that they should set their soldiers out about the country at free quarters; and at whatsoever place they should get pig's flesh, or in whatsoever place they should see pig's flesh, unless those people could shew how they had got the pig's flesh that they might have, that those were the people who killed the pig, and that had done every evil that had been done.

The counsel of the Scanagal was taken, and the soldiers sent out to free quarters about the country; and there was a band of them in the house of the wright's widow where the Shifty Lad was. The wright's widow gave their supper to the soldiers, and some of the pig's flesh was made ready for them; and the soldiers were eating the pig's flesh, and praising it exceedingly. The Shifty Lad understood what was the matter, but he did not let on. The soldiers were set to lie out in the barn ; and when they were asleep the Shifty Lad went out and he killed them. Then he went as fast as he could from house to house, where the soldiers were at free quarters, and he set the rumour afloat* amongst the people of the houses, that the soldiers had been sent out about the country to rise in the night and kill the people in their beds ; and he found (means) to make the people of the country believe him, so that the people of each house killed all the soldiers that were asleep in their barns ; and when the soldiers did not come home at the time they should, some went to see what had happened to them ; and when they arrived, it was so that they found the soldiers dead in the barns where they had been asleep ; and the people of each house denied that they knew how the soldiers had been put to death, or who had done it.

The people who were at the ransacking for the soldiers, went to the king's house, and they told how it had happened ; then the king sent word for the Seanagal to get counsel from him ; the Seanagal came, and the king told how it had happened, and the king asked counsel from him. This is the counsel that the Seanagal gave the king, that he should make a feast and a ball, and invite the people of the country ; and if the man who did the evil should be there, that he was the man who would be the boldest who would be there, and that he would ask the king's daughter herself to dance with him. The people were asked to the feast and the dance ; and amongst the rest the Shifty Lad was asked. The people came to the feast, and amongst

* Cuir e a ceil.

the rest came the Shifty Lad. When the feast was past, the dance began; and the Shifty Lad went and he asked the king's daughter to dance with him; and the Seanagal had a vial full of black stuff, and the Seanagal put a black dot of the stuff that was in the vial on the Shifty Lad. But it seemed to the king's daughter that her hair was not well enough in order, and she went to a side chamber to put it right; and the Shifty Lad went in with her; and when she looked in the glass, he also looked in it, and he saw the black dot that the Seanagal had put upon him. When they had danced till the tune of music was finished, the Shifty Lad went and he got a chance to steal the vial of the Seanagal from him unknown to him, and he put two black dots on the Seanagal, and one black dot on twenty other men besides, and he put the vial back again where he found it.

Between that and the end of another while, the Shifty Lad came again and he asked the king's daughter to dance. The king's daughter had a vial also, and she put a black dot on the face of the Shifty Lad; but the Shifty Lad got the vial whipped out of her pocket, unknown to her; and since there were two black dots on him, he put two dots on twenty other men in the company, and four black dots on the Seanagal. Then when the dancing was over, some were sent to see who was the man on whom were the two black dots. When they looked amongst the people, they found twenty men on whom there were two black dots, and there were four black dots on the Seanagal; and the Shifty Lad found (means) to go swiftly where the king's daughter was, and to slip the vial back again into her pocket. The Seanagal looked and he had his black vial; the king's daughter looked and she had her own vial; then the Seanagal and the king took

counsel ; and the last counsel that they made was that
the king should come to the company, and say, that
the man who had done every trick that had been done,
must be exceedingly clever ; if he would come forward
and give himself up, that he should get the king's
daughter to marry, and the one half of the kingdom
while the king was alive, and the whole of the kingdom after the king's death.   And every one of those
who had the two black dots on their faces came
and they said that it was they who had done every
cleverness that had been done.   Then the king and
his high council went to try how the matter should
be settled ; and the matter which they settled was,
that all the men who had the two black dots on
their faces should be put together in a chamber, and
they were to get a child, and the king's daughter was
to give an apple to the child, and the child was to be
put in where the men with the two black dots on their
faces were seated ; and to whatsoever one the child
should give the apple, that was the one who was to
get the king's daughter.

That was done, and when the child went into the
chamber in which the men were, the Shifty Lad had
a shaving and a drone (sliseag us dranndan), and the
child went and gave him the apple.   Then the shaving and the drone were taken from the Shifty Lad,
and he was seated in another place, and the apple
was given to the child again ; and he was taken out
of the chamber, and sent in again to see to whom
he would give the apple ; and since the Shifty Lad
had the shaving and the drone before, the child went
where he was again, and he gave him the apple.
Then the Shifty Lad got the king's daughter to marry.

And shortly after that the king's daughter and the
Shifty Lad were taking a walk to Baile Cliabh ; and

z

when they were going over the bridge of Baile Cliabh,
the Shifty Lad asked the king's daughter what was
the name of that place; and the king's daughter told
him that it was the bridge of Baile Cliabh, in Eirinn;
and the Shifty Lad said—

"Well then, many is the time that my mother
said to me, that my end would be to be hanged at the
bridge of Baile Cliabh, in Eirinn; and she made me
that prophecy many a time when I might play her a
trick."

And the king's daughter said, "Well then, if
thou thyself shouldst choose to hang over the little
side (wall) of the bridge, I will hold thee aloft a little
space with my pocket napkin."

And they were at talk and fun about it; but at
last it seemed to the Shifty Lad that he would do it for
sport, and the king's daughter took out her pocket
napkin, and the Shifty Lad went over the bridge, and
he hung by the pocket napkin of the king's daughter, as she let it over the little side (wall) of the
bridge, and they were laughing to each other.

But the king's daughter heard a cry, "The king's
castle is going on fire!" and she started, and she
lost her hold of the napkin; and the Shifty Lad fell
down, and his head struck against a stone, and the
brain went out of him; and there was in the cry but
the sport of children; and the king's daughter was
obliged to go home a widow.

SGEULACHD A GHILLE CHARAICH MAC NA BANTRACH.

Bha uair eigeinn ann roimh so Bantrach, agus bha aona mhac aic.
Thug i d à sgoil mhath, agùs bha i bos gu 'n taghadh e ceaird air a
shon fein, ach thubhairt esan, nach rachadh e a dh' ionnsaidh ealdhain air bith, ach gn 'm bitheadh e na mhearlach.

Thubhairt a mhathair ris, " Ma is è sin an caldhain a tha thu a dol a thaghadh dhuit fein, is e is deireadh dhuit, a bhi air do chrochadh aig drochaid Bhaile-cliabh an Eirinn." Ach bu choma cò dhuibh, cha rachadh esan gu ealdhain air bith, ach gu a bhith ann na mhearlach. Agus bhitheadh a mhathair daonnan a deanamh faisinneachd d à, gu 'm e bu deireadh dhàsan a bhith air a chrochadh aig drochaid Bhaile-cliabh an Eirinn. Latha do na laitheanan bha a Bhantrach a dol do 'n eaglais, a dh eisdeachd searmoin, agus bha i ag iarraidh air a' ghille-charrach a mac e a dhol leatha, 's e a thoirt thairis do a dhroch stiùireanan, ach cha rachadh e leatha, ach thuirt e rithe. " Is e a chiad ealdhain air an cluinn thusa iomradh, an deigh dhuit tighinn a mach o 'n t-searmoin, an caldhaid gu 's an teid mise a rithis."

Dh fhalbh ise do 'n eaglais, 's i làn misnich au dùil gu 'n cluinneadh i rud-eiginn math. Dh fhalbh casan 's chaidh e do bhad coille, a bha dlùth do 'n eaglais, 's chaidh e 'm fallach ann an àite far am faiceadh e a mhathair, a nuair a thigeadh i a mach as an eaglais. Agus cho luath is a thainig i a mach, ghlaodh esan; "Mèirle, mèirle, mèirle." Sheall ise ma'n cuairt, ach cha b' urrainn di aithneachadh cia as a bha 'n guth a tighinn, 's dh fhalbh i dachaidh. Ruith esan rathad ath-ghiorra, 's bha e aig an tigh air thoiseach oirre, 's bha e na shuidh e a stigh taobh an teine tra a thainig i dachaidh. Dh fharraid e di, cia-dé an sgeul a fhuair i? Thubhairt ise, nach d-fhuair i sgeul air bith, ach gu 'm b'e mèirle, mèirle, mèirle, a' chiad chainnt a chual' i tra thainig i a mach as an eaglais. Thubhairt esan, gu 'm b'e sin an ealdhainn a bhitheadh aigeasan, s thubhairt ise mar a b' àbhaist di a ghradh. " Is e is deireadh dhuit a bhith air do chrochadh aig drochaid Bhaile-cliabh an Eirinn." An ath latha smuaintich a mhathair, fhun nach deanadh nì air bith tuille gnothach le a mac, ach e a bhith ann na mhèirlach, gu 'm feuchadh i ri oide-ionnsaich math fhaotuinn dà. Agus chaidh i a dh ionnsaidh gadaiche dubh Achalòine, meirleach anbharra seolta, a bha ann 'san àite sin. Agus ged a bha fios aca gu 'n robh e ri goid, cha robh iad a faotuinn doigh air bith air beireachd air. Dh' fharraid a' bhantrach do 'n ghadaiche dhubh an gabhadh e an gille-carrach a mac gus a ghadachd ionnsachadh dha. Thubhairt an gadaiche dubh, ma bha e 'na ghille tapaidh gu 'n gabhadh, agus ma bha doigh air mèirleach a dheanamh dheth, gu 'n deanadh esan e, agus chaidh cumhnant a dheanamh eadar an gadaiche dubh, a 's an gille-carrach. Tra bha an gille-carrach mac na bantraich a deanamh deis gu dol chun a' ghaduiche dhuibh, bha a mhathair a toirt chomhairlean air, agus tbuirt i ris. " Is ann au aghaidh mo thoil-sa a tha thu a' dol thun na mèirle, agus tha mi ag innse dhuit, gur è is deireadh dhuit a bhith air do chrochadh aig drochaid Bhaile-cliabh an Eirinn." Ach Chaidh an gille carrach dachaidh thun a' ghadaiche dhuibh.

Bha an gadaiche dubh a tabhairt na h-uile foghlum a dh fhaodadh e do 'n ghille-charrach air mèirle a dheanamh. Bhitheadh e ag innse dha ma 'n t-seoltachd a dh' fheumadh e a dheanamh, gus an coram fhaotuinn air rud a ghoid. Agus tra bha leis a' ghadaiche dhubh, gu 'n robh an gille-carrach glé mhath air fhoghlum, gu e a bhith air a thoirt a mach leis, bhitheadh e ga thoirt a mach leis gu goid a dheanamh. Agus latha do na laithean sin thubhairt an gad-uiche dubh, ri a ghille.

"Tha sinn gle fhada mar so, is fheudar duinn dol a dheanamh rudaiginn; tha tuathanach beartach dlùth dhuinn, agus tha mòran airgid aige 'na chiste, is e a cheannaich na bha do chrodh ri reic ann 'san duthaich, agus thug e chun na faidhir iad, 's chreic e iad, tha an t-airgiod aige 'na chiste, agus 'se so an t-am gu bhith aige, ma'n teid na daoine a phaidh air son an cuid cruidh, s mar teid sinn a dh iarr-aidh an airgiod an ceart-uair, tra a tha e cruinn ri cheile, cha 'n fhaigh sinn an coram ciadaiun a rithis."

Bha an gille-carrach cho toileach ris fein. Dh fhalbh iad chun an taigh 'us fhuair iad a stigh aig tighinn na h-oidhche, agus chaidh iad an aird air an fharadh, 's chaidh iad am fallach gu h-àrd ann an sin. Agus is è oidhche shamhuadh a bha 'nn, agus chruinnich mòran do fheadhainn a stigh a ghleidheadh na samhuinn gu cridheil mar a b' abhaist doibh. Shuidh iad comhla, agus bha iad a seinn oran, a 's ri aighear, agus a' losgadh nan cnò,* agus ri abhachd.

Bha an gille-carrach a gabhail fadail nach robh a chuideachd a sgaoileadh, dh'eirich e 's chaidh e sios do'n bhàthaich, 's dh fhuasgail e

---

* One of the amusements which highland. people used to enter-tain themselves with, is what they call burning nuts on hallow-eve, the last night of October. A party of young people would collect to-gether in one house for to make merry; one of their amusements was, they would propose a marriage between some lad and lass, and they would name a nut for each of them. The two nuts would be placed beside each other in the fire. If the two nuts burned together, and blazed over each other, that was called a good omen; it was a sign that the party for whom the nuts was named were to be married yet, and live happy together; but if either of the nuts puffed, or flew away, that was a sign that the person for whom that nut was named was proud, and would not accept of the other party.

na naisg far amhaichean a chruidh, 's thill e 's chaidh e air an fharadh a rithis. Thòisich an crodh air purradh a cheile ann 'sa bhàthaich, 's air raoiceadh, ruidh na bha ann sa chearnadh, a chumail a' chruidh o 'cheile gus an rachadh an ceangal a rithis. An tiom a bha iadsan a deanamh sin, chaidh an gille-carrach sios do 'n chearnadh, 's ghoid e leis na cno 'n, 's chaidh e an àird air an fharadh a rithisd, agus luidh e air cùlamh a ghadaiche dhuibh.

Bha seiche mhòr leathraich aig cùlamh a ghadaiche dhuibh, 's bha suathad agus snathainn aig a ghille-charrach agus dh fhuaigh e iomall còta a ghadaiche dhuibh, ris an t-seiche leathraich a bha aig a chùlamh, agus tra thainig muinntir an taighe air an ais do 'n chearnadh a rithisd, bha na cno 'n aca air falbh, agus bha iad ag iarraidh nan cno 'n, agus shaoil iad gu 'm b'e cuid-eiginn a thainig a stigh a dheanamh chleas orra, a thug air falbh na cno 'n, agus shuidh iad aig taobh an teine gu sàmhach tosdach.

Thubhairt an gille-carrach ris a ghadaiche dhubh, "Cnacaidh mi cno."

"Cha chnac, thuirt an gadaiche-dubh, cluinnidh iad thu 's theid beireachd oirnn."

"Thubhairt an gille-carrach, cha robh mi-fein riamh roimh oidh-che shamhnadh gu 'n chnò a chnacadh." Agus chnachd e te.

Chuala an fheadhainn a bha 'nan suidhe 's a chearnadh e, 's thubh-airt iad, "Tha cuid-eiginn gu h-ard air an fharadh, a cnacadh nan cnò 'n again, theid sinn agus beiridh sìnn orra."

Tra chuala an gadaiche dubh sin, leum e far an fharaidh, 's ruith e a mach, 's an t-seiche an slaodadh ris. Theich an gadaiche-dubh 's muinntir an taighe as a dheigh, 's bha e astar mor o'n tigh ma'n d' fhuair e an t-seiche a reubadh deth agus a fàgail. Ach an tiom a bha muinntir an taighe a ruith a ghadaiche-dhuibh, thainig an gille-carr-ach a nuas far an fharaidh, chaidh e air feadh an taighe, dh' amais e air a chiste far an robh an t-òr 's an t-airgiod aig an tuathanach ga ghleidheadh dh fhosgail e a chiste, 's thug e a mach aiste na buílg ann 'san robh an t-airgiod a bha innte, agus thug e innte, agus thug e leis eallach do 'n aran 's do'n ìm 's do'n chàise, a's dona h-uile nì a b' fhearr na cheile a fhuair e a stigh. Agus bha esan air falbh, ma'n d' thainig muinntir an taighe air an ais o bhith a ruith a ghadaiche dhuibh.

Nuair a rainig an gadaiche-dubh dachaidh, 's nach robh nì air bith aige, thubhairt a bhean ris, "cia-mar a chaidh fairsleachadh ort air an turus so ?"

An sin dh innis an gadaiche-dubh a sgeul fein, agus bha fearg mor air ris a ghille-charrach, 'se a boideachadh, gu 'n deanadh e dioltas tra gheibheadh e coram air. Aig ceann uine ghoirid na dheigh sin thainig an gille-carrach a stigh. agus callach air. Thubhairt bean a ghadaiche dhuibh, "Ach tha duil agam gur tusa meirleach is fhearr."

Cha dubhairt an gadaiche-dubh diog, gus gu'n do leig an gille-carrach fhaicinn na builg a bha aige làn do òr s do airgiod, an sin thubhairt an gadaiche-dubh "Ach bu tu an gille tapaidh!"

Rinn iad dà leth air an òr, 's air an airgiod, 's fhuair an gadaiche dubh an darna leth, agus an gille carrach an leth eile. Tra a chunnaic bean a ghadaiche dhuibh an roinn a thainig oirre thubhairt i, "Is tu fein am meirleach fiachail, "s bha tuille meas aic air na dheigh sin na bha aic air a ghadaiche dhubh e fein."

Aig ceann beagan sheachdainnean na dheigh sin, bha banais gu bhith ann sa coimhearnachd agus b' è fasan na duthcha, tra rachadh feadhainn a bhitheadh saoibhir a chuireadh, gu'n cuireadh iad tabhartas a thaobhaiginn a dh ionnsaidh muinntir na bainse. Bha tuathanach beartach ann a chaidh a chuireadh, agus dh' iarr e air a bhuachaille aige e a dhol ris a mhonadh, 's e a thoirt dachaidh molt air son muinntir na bainse. Chaidh am buachaille ris a mhonadh, 's fhuair e am molt 's bha e a dol dachaidh leis, 's e aige air a dhruim, a nuair a bha e a dol seachad air tigh a ghadaiche dhuibh. Thubhairt an gille carrach, ri a mhaighstir "Cia-dé an geall a chuireas tu nach goid mi am molt far druim an fhir sin, ma 'n ruig e an tigh fhathasd?" Thubhairt an gadaiche dubh, "Cuiridh mi geall ciad marg nach urrainn duit, ciamar a ghoideadh tu an rud a tha air a dhruim !"

"Cia air bhith mar a nì mi e feuchaidh mi ris," orsa an gille-carrach.

"Ma ta ma nì thu a, thuirt an gadaiche dubh, bheir mise dhuit ciad marg." "Is bargain e," orsa an gille carrach, a's le sin dh fhalbh e an deigh a bhuachaille. Bha aig a bhuachaille ri dol troimh choille, agus ghabh an gille carrach falacha-talmhainte air, gus gu'n d' fhuair e air thoiseach air, agus shalaich e 'na bhròig, 's chuir e a bhròg air an rathad air thoiseach air a bhuachaille, 's chaidh e fein am fallach. An uair a thainig am buachaille air aghaidh, a's a chunnaic e a bhròg thubhairt e, "Ach tha thu salach 's ged do thà, na 'm bitheadh do leth-bhreac ann ghlanainn thu," 's chaidh e seachad.

Thog an gille carrach a' bhròg, 's ruidh e ma 'n cuairt, 's bha e air thoiseach air a' bhuachaille, 's chuir e bhròg eile air an ratbad air thoiseach air. Thubhairt e ris fhein, "ach tha ann an sin leth bhreac na bròig e salache."

Chuir e am molt air làr, agus thubhairt e ris-fein, "Tillidh mi an nis 's gheibh mi a bhrog shalach, 's glanaidh mi i, 's bithidh dà bhroig mhath agam air son mo shaoireach," 's ruith e gu luath air ais. Ruith au gille-carrach gu luath 's ghoid e leis am molt, 's thug e leis an an da bhroig, 's chaidh e dachaidh chun a mhaighistir, s fhuair e a chiad marg o a mhaighistir.

Chaidh am buachaille dachaidh, 's dh' innis e do a mhaighistir fein mar a thachair dà. Throid a mhaighistir ris a bhuachaille. An ath latha chuir an tuathanach a rithis ris a mhonadh e a dh-iarraidh eirionnach an àite a mhuilt a chaill e. Dh fhalbh am buachaille ris a mhonadh, 's fhuair e greim air eirionnach, cheangail se e, chuir e air a dhruim e, 's dh-fhalbh e gu dol dachaidh leis. Chunnaic an gille-carrach e, 's chaidh e do'n choille, 's bha e an sin air thoiseach air a bhuachaille, 's chaidh e am falach, 's thòisich e air mèilich coltach ris a' mholt. Shaoil am buachaille gu 'm b'e am molt a bha ann, 's chuir e deth an t-eirionnach, 's dh fhàg se aig taobh an rathaid e, 's chaidh e a dh iarraidh a mhuilt. An tiom a bha am buachaille ag iarraidh a' mhoilt' chaidh an gille carrach 's ghoid e leis an t-eir-ionnach, 's dh fhàg se aig taobh an rathaid e, 's chaidh e dachaidh leis chun a, ghadaiche dhuibh. Tra chaidh am buachaille air ais far an d fhàg e an t-eirionnach, bha an t-eirionnach air falbh, cha robh an t-eirionnach ann, dh iarr e air son an eirionnach ann. Dh iarr e air son an eirionnach, 's a nnair nach b'urrainn d'a an t-eirionnach fhaot-uinn, chaidh e dachaidh 's dh innis e do a mhaighistir mar a dh eirich d' à, agus throid a mhaighistir ris, ach cha robh comas air. An ath latha dh iarr an tuathanach air a bhuachaille aige, e a dhol ris a mhonadh, agus e a thoirt dachaidh damh, e a bhith cinnteach nach cailleadh se a. Chaidh am buachaille ris a mhonadh, 's fhuair e damh math reamhar, 's bha e ga iomain dachaidh. Chunnaic an gille-carrach e, s' thubhairt e ris a' ghadaiche dhubh, "Tingainn, 's theid sinn a dh fheuchainn ris an damh a ghoid o'n bhuachaille, tra a bhitheas e a dol troimh an choille leis."

Dh' fhalbh an gadaiche dubh as an gille-carrach do 'n choille air thoiseach air a bhuachaille. Agus tra bha am buachaille a dol troimh an choille leis an damh, bha an gadaiche dubh an aon àite, s è a mèailich, 's an gille-carrach an àite eile, s è a migeartaich coltach ri gabhar. Chuala am buachaille iad, 's shaoil e gu 'm faigheadh e am molt, agus an t-eirionnach a rithisd. Cheangail e an damh ri craoibh, 's chaidh e air feadh na coille, ag iarraidh a' mhuilt agus an eirrionn-aich. S dh iarr e iad gus gu 'n robh e sgìth. An tiomsa bha esan ag iarraidh a mhuilt 's an eirionnaich, chaidh an gille-carach 's ghoid e leis an damh 's thug e leis dachaidh e chun tigh a ghaduiche dhuibh. Chaidh an gaduiche dubh dachaidh as a dheigh, 's mharbh iad an damh, 's chuir iad am fallach e, 's bha maragan math aig bean a ghad-uiche dhuibh an oidhche sin. Tra thainig am buachaille air ais thun

na craoibh, far an d' fhàg e an damh ceangailte, cha robh an damh
ann. Dh' aithnich e gu 'n deach an damh a ghoid, chaidh e dachaidh
's db innis e do a mhaighistir mar a thachair, agus throid a mhaighistir ris, ach cha robh comas air.

An ath latha dh' iarr a mhaighistir air a bhuachaille aige e a
dhol ris a mhonadh, 's e a thoirt dachaidh molt, 's gu 'n e ga leigidh far
a dhruim idir, gus gu 'n tigeadh e dachaidh, cia air bith a chitheadh
na a chluinneadh e. Dh' fhalbh am buachaille, 's chaidh e ris a
mhonadh, 's fhuair e am molt, 's chaidh aige air a mholt sin a thoirt
dachaidh.

Chabh an gadaiche-dubh 's an gille-carrach air an aghaidh ri goid
gus gu 'n robh moran airgid aca, agus smuaintich iad gu 'm b' fhearr
doibh dròbh a cheannach, 's dol chun faidhir leo gu'n creic, agus gu 'n
saoileadh feadhainn gu'm b'ann air an dròbh aireachd a rinn iad an
t-airgiod. Chaidh an dithis agus cheannaich iad drobh mor cruidh.
Agus chaidh iad a dh' ionnsaidh faidhir a bha fad air astar leo.
Chreic iad an dròbh, 's fhuair iad an t-airgiod air an son, 's dh'
fhalbh iad gu dol dachaidh. Tra a bha iad air an rathad, chunnaic
iad croich air mullach cnoic agus thubhairt an gille-carach ris a'
ghadaiche dhubh, "Tiugainn an àird is gu 'm faic sin a' chroich, tha
feadhainn ag ràdh, gur h-i a' chroich is deireadh do na mèirlich co-
dhiubh."

Chaidh iad an àird far an robh a' chroich, 's bha iad a' sealltuinn ma
'n-cuairt oirre. Thubhairt an gille-carach, "Nach fhaodamaid fheuchainn cia-dé an seòrsa bàis a tha ann sa' chròchadh, gu m bì fios
againn cia-dé a tha ann 'sa chròchadh, gu 'm bì fios againn cia-dé a
a tha romhainn ma bheirear oirnn ri gadachd; feuchaidh mi-fein an
toiseach e."

Chuir an gille-carach an còrd ma amhaich fein, 's thubhairt e ris
a' ghadaiche-dhubh. "So tarruing an àird mi, 's tra bhitheas mi sgìth
gu h-àrd crathaidh mi mo chas 'n, 's an sin leig thusa a nuas mi."

Tharruing an gaduiche-dubh an còrd, 's thog e an gille-carach an
àird far an talmhainte, agus aig ceann seal beag chrath an gille
carach a chas'n, 's leig an gaduiche-dubh a nuas e.

Chuir an gille carach an còrd far amhaich, 's thubhairt e ris a'
ghadaiche-dhubh, "Cha d' fheuch thu-fhein nì riamh, a tha cho eibh-
inn ris a' chrochadh, na 'm feuchadh tu aon uair e cha bhitheadh eagal
ort romh 'n chrochadh tuille, bha mise a crathaidh mo chasan leis an
oibhinneas 's chrathadh tusa do chasan leis an aoibhneas cuideachd
na m bithedh tu gu h-ard."

Thuirt an gaduiche dubh, "Feuchaidh mise e cuideachd, 's gu 'm
bith fios agam co ris a's coltach e."

"Dean," orsa gille-carach, "'s tra a bhitheas tu sgìth gu h-ard, dean fead 's leigidh mise an nuas thu."

Chuir an gadaiche-dubh an còrd ma amhaich, 's tharruing an gille-carach an àird e, 's tra fhuair an gille-carach gu 'n robh an gaduiche-dubh gu h-ard ris a' chroich, thuirt e ris. "An nis tra bhitheas tu ag iarraidh a nuas dean fead, 's ma tha thu toilichte far am bheil thu, crath do chas 'n."

Tra a bha an gadaiche dubh seal beag gu h-àrd, thòisich e air crath-adh a chasan, 's air breabadh, 's theireadh an gille-carach, " O ! nach aighearach thu, nach aighearach thu. O, nach aighearach thu, tra bhithis leat gu 'm bheil thu glé fhada gu h-àrd dean fead."

Ach cha do rinn an gaduiche-dubh fead fhathast; cheangail an gille-carach an còrd ri iochdar crann na croiche, gus gu 'n robh an gaduiche-dubh marbh. An sin, chaidh an gille-carach far an robh e, 's thug e as a phòc an t-airgiod, 's thubhairt se ris, 'An nis fhun nach eil feum agadsa air an airgiod so na is faide, gabhaidh mise cùram deth air do shon." 'S dh' fhalbh e 's dh' fhag e an gaduiche-dubh, a crochadh ann an sin. An sin chaidh e dachaidh far an robh tigh a ghaduiche dhuibh. S dh' fharraid bean a ghaduiche-duibh deth, c'aite an robh a mhaighistir? Thuirt an gille-carach, "Dh' fhàg mise e far an robh e air àrdachadh os-ceann an talaimh." Dh fharraid, agus dh' fharraid bean a' ghaduiche deth ma dhéidhinn a fir, gus ma dheireadh gu 'n d' innis e d' i, ach thuirt e rithe gu 'm pòsadh e-fhein i. Tra chuala ise sin ghlaodh i gu 'n do mharbh an gille-carach a mhaighistir is nach robh ann ach meàrlach. Tra chuala an gille-carach sin theich e. Chaidh an toir a chuir air' a dheigh, ach fhuair esan dol am falach ann an uaimh, 's chaidh an tòir seachad air. Bha e 'san uaimh fad na h-oidhche, agus an ath latha chaidh se rathad eile, 's fhuair e teicleadh do dh' Eirinn.

Rainig e tigh saoir, 's ghlaodh se aig an dorus, "Leigibh a stigh mi."

"Co thusa?" orsa an saor.

"Thà saor math, ma tha a leithid a dùith ort," orsa an gille carach.

Dh fhosgail an saor an dorus 's leig e a stigh an gille-carach, 'n s thòisich an gille-carach air obair air an t-saorsaineachd comhla ris an t-saor.

Tra a bha an gille-carach latha na dhà anns an tigh aca, thug e sealladh a null, 's sealladh an nall air feadh an taighe 's thubhairt e, "O chòin is bochd an tigh agaibh a's tigh-taisg an righ cho dluth oirbh."

"Cia-dé dheth sin?" orsa an saor.

"Thà," arsa an gille carach, "gu 'm faodadh sibh am pailteas fhaotuinn as tigh stòir an righ na 'm bitheadh sibh fein glé thapaidh."

Theireadh an saor 's a bhean, " Chuireadh iad ann priosan sinn na 'n tòisicheadh sinn air a leithid sinn."

Bha an gille-carach daonnan ag radh gu 'm bu chòir dòibh dol a bhristeadh a stigh do thigh-taisg an righ, 's gu 'm faigheadh iad am pailteas ann, ach cha rachadh an saor leis. Ach thug an gille-carach leis pairt do dh' acfhuinn an t-saoir, a's chaidh e fhein is bhrisd e a stigh do thigh-taisg an righ, 's thug e leis ealach do 'n im 's do 'n chàise aig an righ, 's thug e do thigh an t-saoir e. Thaitinn na gnothaichen gu math ri bean an t-saoir, 's bha i toileach gu 'n rachadh am fear aic' e fhein ann an ath oidhche. Chaidh an saor e-fhein le a ghille an ath oidhche, 's fhuair iad a stigh do thigh-taisg an righ, 's thug iad leo eallachan mòra dò gach nì a b' fhearr a thaitinn riu do na bha stigh ann an tigh taisg an righ. Ach dh' ionndrainn muinntir an righ an t-im 's an càise, 's na rudan eile a chaidh a thoirt as an tigh-thaisg, 's dh innis iad do 'n righ mar a thachair.

Ghabh an righ comhairle an t-seanaghail ma 'n doigh a b' fhearr gu beireachd air na mèirleich. Agus is è a chomhairle a thug an seanghall orra, iad a chuir togsaid làn do phic bhog fo'n toll far an robh iad a' tighinn a stigh. Chaidh sin a dheanamh. Agus an ath oidhche chaidh an gille-carach 's a mhaighistir a bhrisdeadh a stigh do thigh-taisg an righ. Chuir an gille-carrach a mhaighistir a stigh air thoiseach air. Agus chaidh am maighistir sios anns a' phic bhog gu a theis-meadhoin, 's cha n fhaigheadh e as a rithisd. Chaidh an gille caràch sios, 's chuir e cas air gach gualann aig a mhaighistir, 's chuir e a mach dà eallach do 'n im 's do 'n chàise aig un righ air an toll, 's an uair ma dheireadh tra a bha e a tighinn a mach sgiull e an ceann far a mhaighistir, 's thug e leis an ceann, 's dh fhàg e a cholunn anns an togsaid phic. A's chaidh e dachaich leis an im 's leis a' chàise, agus thug e dachaidh an ceann, agus dh' adhlaic e anns a ghàrradh e.

Tra a chaidh muinntir an righ a stigh do 'n tigh-thaisg fhuair iad colunn gu 'n cheann anns an togsaid phic. Ach cha b' urrainn doibh aithneachadh cò é. Dh' fheuch iad am faigheadh iad h-aon air bith a dh aithneachadh air aodach e, ach bha aodach comhdaichte le pic, air doigh is nach b' urrainn doibh aithneachadh. Dh fharraid an righ comhairle an t-sheanghal ma dheidhinn. Agus ise a chomhairle a thug an seanaghall orra iad a chuir na coluinn an aird air bharr shleaghan, 's na saighdearan gu a giullan o bhaile gu baile, a sheall am faiceadh iad h-aon air bith a ghabhadh truadhas deth, na a dh' fheuchainn an cluinneadh iad a h-aon air bith a dheanamh glaodh

gointe tra chitheadh iad é, na ged nach faiceadh, gu m bitheadh iad
ealamh gu glaodh gointe a dheanamh, tra bhitheadh na saighdearan a
dol seachad leis. Chaidh a choluinn a thoirt as an Togsaid phic, 's a
cuir air bharr nan sleaghan, 's bha na saighdearan g'a ghiùlan an
aird air bharr nan sleaghan fada crannach aca, 's iad a dol o bhaile gu
baile leis. Agus tra bha iad a dol seach tigh an t-saoir, rinn bean
an t-saoir sgreuch ghointe, agus ghradghearr an gille-carach e-fein
leis an tàl, 's theireadh e ri bean an t-saoir, " Cha 'n 'eil an gearradh
cho dona is a tha thu a smuainteachadh."

Thainig an ceannard 's cuid do na saighdearan a stigh agus dh'
fharraid iad, " Cia dé a dh aithrich bean an taighe." Thubhairt an
gille-carach, " Thà gu 'm bheil mise air gearradh mo choise leis an
tàl, agus tha eagal aice romh fhuil." Agus theiridh e ri bean an t-
saoir, " Na bitheadh na h-uibhir eagail ort, leigheisidh e na is luaith
na tha thu a smaointeachadh."

Shaoil na saighdearan gu 'm b'e an gille-carach an saor, agus gu
'm e a bhean a bha aig an t-saor bean a ghille-charaich, agus dh'
fhabh iad a mach, 's chaidh iad o bhaile gu balle, ach cha d' fhuair iad
a h-aon tuille, ach banntrach an t-saoir i fhein a rinn glaodh na
sgreuch tra a bha iad a tighinn seachad orra.

Thug iad a cholunn dachaidh chun tigh an righ. Agus ghabh an
righ comhairle eile on t-seanaghall aige, 's b' e in a cholunn a chrochadh ri crann ann an àite follaiseach, agus saighdearan a chuir a thabhairt aire air nach tugadh gin air falbh e, as na saighdeairean gu a
bhith a shealltinn, an tigeadh feadhainn air bith an rathad a ghabhadh truaigheas na doilghios deth.

Thainig an gille-carach seachad orra, agus chunnaic se iad, chaidh
e agus fhuair e each, agus chuir e buideal uisge-bheatha, air gach taobh
do 'n each, ann an sachd, 's chaidh e seach na saighdearan leis, 's e
mar gu 'm bitheadh e a' fuireachd am falach orra. Shaoil na saighdearan gu 'm b' ann a thug se rudaiginn air falbh orra, na gu 'n robh
rudaiginn aige nach bu chòir d'a a bhith aige, agus ruith cuid dinbh
air a dheigh, 's bheir iad air an t-seann each s air an uisge-bheatha,
ach theich an gille-carach, 's dh fhàg e an seann each 's an t uisge-
beatha aca.

Thug na saighdearan an t-each 's na buideail uisge-bheath' air
ais far an robh a' cholunn an crochadh ris a' chrann. Sheall iad cia-
dé a bha anns na buideail, 's tra thuig iad gur ae uisge-beatha a
bha ann fhuair iad còrn, 's thisich iad air òl, gus ma dheireadh, gu
'n robh na h-uile h-aon diubh air mhisg, 's luidh 's chaodil iad. Tra
chunnaic an gille-carach gu 'n robh na saighdeairean, 'nan luidh 's nan
cadal air a mhisg, thill e 's thug e a nuas a' cholunn fàr a' chroinn,

chuir e crosgach air druim an eich e 's thug e dachaidh e, chaidh e an
sin agus dh' adhlaic e a' cholunn anns a ghàradh far an robh an
ceann.

Tra a dhùisg na saighdearan as an cadal, bha a cholunn air a goid
air falbh. Cha robh aca air ach dol 's ìnnse do 'n righ. An sin ghabh
an righ comhairle an t-seanaghal. Agus thubhairt an seanaghal
riutha, na bha anns an làthair, Gu 'm b'-e a chomhairle doibh, iad a
thoirt a mach muc mhòr dhubh a bha an siod, 's iad a dh' fhalbh
leatha o-bhaile gu baile, agus tra thigeadh iad thun an àite far am
bitheadh a' cholunn adhlaicte, gu m buraicheadh i an àird è. Chaidh
iad 's fhuair iada mhuc dhubh, 's bha iad a dol o bhaile gu baile
leatha, a dh' feuchainn am faigheadh i am mach caite an robh a' cholunn
air a h-adhlac. Chaidh iad o' thigh gu tigh leatha, gus ma dhèireadh
gu'n d' thainig iad gus an tigh far an robh an gille-carach agus banntrach an t-saoir a chomhnuich. A nuair a rainig iad, leig iad a
mhuc mapsgaoil air feadh an talmhuinn. Thubhairt an gille-carach
riutha, gu 'n robh e-fein cinnteach, gu 'm bitheadh paghadh 's acras
orra, gu 'm b' fhearr doibh dol a stigh do 'n tigh, 's gu'm faigheadh iad
biadh 's deoch, 's iad a leigeil an sgìtheas dhiubh, an tiom a bhitheadh
a mhuc ag iarraidh ma thimchioll an àite aige-san. Chaidh iadsan a
stigth, 's dh iarr an gille carach air bantrach an t-saoir i a chur biadh
's deoch air beulamh nan daoine. Chuir bantrach an t-saoir biadh 's
deoch air bòrd, 's chuir i air am beulamh e, 's an tiom a bha iadsan
ag itheadh am biadh, chaidh an gille carach a mach a shealltuinn an
deigh na muice, 's bha a mhuc air amas air a choluinn anns a ghàrradh,
's chaidh an gille-carach agus fhuair e sgian mhòr, agus ghearr e an
ceann di. Agus dh adhlaic e i-fein a 's a ceann, lamh-ris a choluinn
aig an t-saor anns a ghàrradh. Tra a thainig an fheadhainn air an
robh cùram na muic' a mach, cha robh a mhuc ri fhaicinn. Dh fharraid
iad do 'n ghille-charach am faca e i. Thubhairt esan gu 'm faca, gu
'n robh a ceann an àird agus i ag amharc suas, agus a dol da na tri
a cheumannan an dràsda is a rithisd. Agus dh fhalbh iadsan le cabhaig mbòir, an taobh a thubhairt an gille-carach a chaidh a' mhuc.
Tra fhuair an gille-carach gu 'n deach iadsan as an t-sealladh, chuir e
gach nì air doigh nach amaiseadh iadsan air a mhuic. Chaidh an
fheadhainn air an robh curam na muic e agus dh iarr iad i na h-uile
rathad anns am bu coltach i a bhith. An sin tra nach b' urrainn
doibh a faotuinn, cha robh aca air ach dol gu tigh an righ, agus
ìnnse mar a thachair.

An sin chaidh comhairle an t-seanaghail a ghabhail a rithisd.
Agus is e a' chomhairle a thug an seanaghal orra, iad a chuir nan
saighdeirean a mach air feadh na duthcha air cheithearnan, agus cia

aite air bith am faigheadh iad muic-fheoil, na cia aite air bith am faiceadh iad muic-fheoil ; mar b'-urrainn da n fheadhinn sin, a leigeadh
fhaicinn cia mar a fhuair iad a mhuic-fheoil a bhitheadh aca, gu 'm
b' iad sin an fheadhainn a mharbh a mhuc 's a rinn na h-uile cron a
chaidh a dheanamh. Chaidh comhairle an t-seanaghail a ghabhail 's
na saighdearan a chuir a mach air cheithearnan air feadh na duthcha,
's bha buidheann diubh ann an tigh banntrach an t-saoir far an robh
an gille-carach. Thug banntrach an t-saoir, an t-suipeair do na
saighdearan, 's bha cuid do 'n mhuic-fheoil air a deanamh deàs doibh,
agus bha na saighdearan ag itheadh na muicfheoil, agus ga shàr mholadh.
Thuig an gille-carach cia-dé a bha air an aire, ach cha do leig e
air. Chaidh na saighdearan a chuir a luidh a mach anns an t-sabhal,
agus tra bha iad 'nan cadal, chaidh an gille-carach a mach agus
mharbh se iad. An sin chaidh e cho luath as a b' urrainn da o thigh
gu tigh far an robh na saighdeirean air cheithearnan, agus chuir e an
céill do mhuinntir nan taighean, gu 'm b' ann a chaidh na saighdearan,
a chuir a mach air feagh na duthcha, gu iad a dh'eiridh air feadh na
h-oidhche, agus an sluagh a mharbhadh anns na leapaichean aca,
agus fhuair e a thoirt air muinntir na duthcha chreidsinn, gun do
mharbh muinntir gach tighe, na bha do shaighdeirean 'nan cadal anns
na sabhailean aca. Agus an uair nach d' thainig na saighdeirean
dachaidh aig an tiom bu chòir doibh, chaidh feadhainn a shealltuinn
cia-dé a thainig riutha. Agus tra rainig iadsan is ann a fhuair iad
na saighdeirean marbh anns na saibhlean, far an robh iad 'nan cadal.
Agus dh aicheidh muinntir gach tighe, gu 'n robh fios aca cia mar a
chaidh na saighdeirean a chuir gu bàs, na cò a rinn e.

Chaidh na daoine a bha ris an rannsachadh air son nan saighdeirean gu tigh an righ, agus dh' innis iad mar a thachair. An sin
chuir an righ fios air an t-seanaghal, a dh' fhaotuinn comhairle
uaidh. Thainig an seanaghal, agus dhinnis an righ dhà mar a
thachair, agus dh' iarr an righ comhairle air. Agus is e a chomhairle a thug an seanaghal air an righ, e a dheanamh cuirm agus iob-
dannsa (a bàll) 's e chuireadh sluagh na duthcha, agus nam bitheadh
am fear a rinn an cron an sin, gu 'm b'e am e fear bu dana a bhithidh
an sin, agus gun iarradh e nighean an righ fein a dhannsa leis.
Chaidh an sluagh iarraidh a chum na cuirm, 's an dannsaidh. Agus
a measg chaich chaidh an gille carach iarraidh. Thainig an sluagh
a chum na cuirm, agus a measg chaich thainig an gille carach. Tra
a bha a' chuirm seachad thòisich an dannsa, agus chaidh an gille-
carach is dh' iarr e nighean an righ gu dannsa leis, agus bha searrag
làn do rud dubh aig an t-seanaghal, agus chuir an seanaghal ball
dubh de'n rud a bha anns an t-searrag air a ghille-charach, ach bha

le nighean an righ nach robh a falt glé mhath ann an òrdugh, 's
chaidh i do sheòmar taobhaidh gus a chuir ceart, agus chaidh an
gille-carach a stigh leatha, 's tra sheall ise anns a ghloine sheall easan
cuideachd ann, 's chunnaic e ann ball dubh a chuir an seanaghal air.
Tra dhainns iad gus an robh am port ciuil seachad chaidh an gille
carach agus fhuair e cothrom air an t-searag aig an t-seanaghall-
ghoid uaidh gu n fhios d'a, agus chuir esan da bhall dubh air an t
sheanaghal, agus aon a bhall dubh air fichead fear eile g'a thuile, 's
chuir e an t shearag air ais a rithis far an d' fhuair se a.   Eadar sin
's ceann a ghreis, thainig an gille-carach a rithis 's dh iarr e nighean
an righ gu dannsa.   Bha searag aig nighean an righ cuideachd, 's
chuir i ball dubh air aodann a ghille-charaich ach fhuair an gille-
carach an t-searag a thiulpa as a poca gu 'n fhios di, agus fun a bha
dà bhall aire-san, chuir e da bhall air fichead fear eile anns a chuideachd, agus ceithir buill dhubh air an t seanaghal.   An sin tra a
bha an dannsa seachad, chaidh feadhainn a chuir a dh fhaicin cò e
am fear air an robh an dà bhall dhubh.   Tra sheall iadsan air feadh
an t sluaigh fhuair iad fichead fear, air an robh da bhall dhubh,
agus bha ceithir buill dhubh air an t seanaghal, 's fhuair an gille-
carach caladh far an robh nighean an righ, agus an t-searag a
thiulpa na poca a rithis, sheall an seanaghal agus bha searagan
diubh aige, sheall nighean an righ 's bha a searaig fein aicse, an sin
ghabh an seanaghal a's an righ combairle, agus is e a chomhairle
sinn a rinn iad, an Righ a thighinn do 'n chuideachd, agus e agh-
radh gu 'm b' anabharra tapaidh a dh fheumadh am fear a rinn na
h-uile cleas a chaidh a dheanamh a bhith, na n tigeadh e air aghaidh
s e fein a thoirt suas, gu 'm faighidh e nighean an righ ri phòsadh
agus dàrna leth na rioghachd an neo is a bhithidh an an righ beò,
agus an t iomalain do n rioghchd an deigh bàs an righ. Agus thainig
na h-uile gin do n fheadhainn aig an robh an da bhall dhubh air an
aodann, agus thubhairt iad gu'm b' iadsan a rinn na h-uile tapadh a
chaidh a dheanamh.   An sin chaidh an righ 's an àrd chomhairle, a
dh fheuchainn cia-mar a ghabhadh a chuis socrachadh, agus is è a
chuse a shocruich iad, na h-uile fear aig an robh an da bhall dubh
air an aodann, a chuir comhla ann an seomar, agus bha iad gu pàisde
fhaotuinn, agus bha nighean an righ gus ubhall a thoirt do n phàisde
agus bha am pàisde gus a chuir a stigh far an robh na fir aig an robh
na buill dhubh air an aodann, nan suidh, agus ge b-è h-aon air bith do
'n tugadh am pàisde an t-ubhall, b-e sin an t-aon a bha gus nighean
an righ fhaotuinn.
   Chaidh sin a dheanamh, agus tra chaidh am pàisde a chuir a stigh
do 'n t seomar anns an robh na fir, bha liseag s draunndan aig a

ghille-charrach 's chaidh am paisde 's thug se an t-ubhall d'a. Chaidh an sin an t-sliseag 's au dranndan, a thoirt o 'n gille-charach agus a chuir na shuidh ann an àite eile, agus chaidh au t-ubhall a thoirt do 'n phàisde a rithis, agus a thoirt a mach as am t-seomar, 's a chuir a stigh a rithis a sheall cò dh'à a bheiridh e an t-ubhall, agus fun a bha an t sliseag 's an dranndan aig a ghille-charach a roimh, chaidh am pàisde far an robh e a rithis, s thug se dh à an t-ubhall. Au sin fhuair an gille-carach nighean an righ ri phòsadh.

Agus goirid na dheigh sin bha nighean an righ, 's an gille-carach, a ghabhail sràide do Bhaile-cliabh, agus a nuair a bha iad a dol thairis air drochaid Bhaile-chiabh, dh' fharraid an gille carach de nighean an righ, cia ainm a bha air an aite sin, Agus dh innis, nighean an righ gun robh drochaidh Baile-cliabh ann an Eirinn, Agus thubhairt an gille-carach.

" Ma ta is tric a thubhairt mo mhathair riumsa gu am bu e bu deireadh dhomh a bhith air mo chrochadh aig drochaid Bhaile-cliabh an Eirinn, 's rinn i an fhàisineachd sin domh iomadh uair, tra bhithinn a deanin phrat oirre."

Agus thubhairt nighean an righ, Mata mo shanntaich tu fein cro-chadh thairis air taobhann an drochaid, cumaidh mise an àird thu tacan beag le mo napaigean poca."

Agus bha iad ri caiunt 's ri aighear ma deidhinn, ach ma-dheireadh bha leis a ghille-charach gu 'n deanadh se a, air s on abhachd, agus thug nighean an righ a mach a neapaigeau poca, agus chaidh an gille-carach thair an drochaid, agus chroch e ri neapaigean poca nighean an righ, 's i ga leigeadh fhein thairis air taobhan na droch-aid, 's iad a gairichdeich ri cheile.

Ach chuala nighean an righ eubh, "Tha caisteal an righ a dol ri-theine," agus chlisg i, agus chaill i a greim air an neapaigean agus thuit an gille-carach sios, agus bhuail a cheann ri cloich, 's chaidh an eanchainn as, 's cha robh anns an eubh ach falrasg claoine 's b' eiginn do nighean an righ dol dachaidh na banntraich.

From Kate Macfarlane, in or near the year 1810; A. Campbell, Roseneath, 1860; and J. M'Nair, Clachaig, 1860.

Some incidents in this story I have known as long as I can remember. They used to be told me as a child by John Camp-bell, piper. Some of them were told me in 1859 by John Mac-kenzie at Inverary, who said they were part of a long story of which he could not repeat the rest. Others are alluded to in the Sutherland collection as known in that county. The

version given came to me with the pedigree given above, and
is unaltered, except in orthography and punctuation here and
there.

It may be compared with a very great many stories in many
languages, but I know none exactly like it, (See note on No. 40,
page 263, vol. ii.)

Some of the incidents are very like part of the story of Rampsintus (Rawlinson's Herodotus, vol. ii. p. 191), which were told
to Herodotus more than two thousand years ago by priests in
Egypt, and the most natural conclusion to arrive at is, that these
incidents have been spread amongst the people by those members
of their families who study the classics at the Scotch universities,
and who might well repeat what they had learned over a winter
fire in their father's cottages, as their share of a night's entertainment.

But the incidents in this story, which resemble the classical
tale, are associated with a great many other incidents which are
not in Herodotus. Some of these have a resemblance to incidents
in the Norse story of "The Master Thief;" and, according to Mr.
Dasent's Introduction, these have a resemblance to Sanscrit
stories, which are not within my reading. They have a relation
to Italian stories in Straparola, and, according to a note in
Rawlinson's Herodotus, the story of Rampsintus "has been
repeated in the Pecorone of Ser Giovanni, a Florentine of the
fourteenth century, who substitutes a Doge of Venice for the
king."

I am told that the barrel of pitch and the marks on the men
are introduced into an old German story; but there are several
incidents such as that of the pig which was to discover the dead
body as pigs now do truffles, and the apple which as usual is mystical, which so far as I know are in Gaelic only.

On the whole, then, there seems to me nothing for it but to
admit this to be the Gaelic version of a popular tale, traditionally
preserved for ages, altering as times roll on, and suiting itself to
the manners of the narrators and of the time.

To suppose it to be derived from books is to suppose that
these books have all been read at some time so widely in
Scotland as to have become known to the labouring population who speak Gaelic, and so long ago as to have been for-

gotten by the instructed, who speak English and study foreign languages.

Either this is a traditional popular tale, or learning must have been much more widely spread in the west at some former period than it is at present.

My own opinion is that the tale is traditional, but there is room enough for speculation. On the 25th and 27th of August, I heard parts of the story told by Dewar, and MacNair, and John Mackenzie. Hector Urquhart told me that his father used to tell it in Ross-shire when he was a child. In his version, the storehouse was a treasury full of gold and silver, and the entrance a loose stone in the wall; the man was caught in "CEP," a gin for catching foxes. The pig was a hungry boar, and the lad killed him with an arrow. Even John the tinker, who was present, knew the story, though not well enough to repeat it. It is manifestly widely spread in the Highlands.

The Gaelic is somewhat peculiar, and there are some errors in it which have not been corrected.

END OF VOL. I.

www.ingramcontent.com/pod-product-compliance
Lightning Source LLC
Chambersburg PA
CBHW031348290326
41932CB00044B/363